THE INVESTOR'S ENCYCLOPEDIA

THE
Investor's
ENCYCLOPEDIA

BY CHET CURRIER
BUSINESS NEWS, ASSOCIATED PRESS

A GROLIER COMPANY

FRANKLIN WATTS, INC.
NEW YORK ■ TORONTO ■ 1985

REFERENCE

This publication contains the author's opinion on the subject. It must be noted that neither the publisher nor the author is engaged in rendering investment, legal, tax, accounting, or similar professional services. While investment, legal, tax, and accounting issues in this book have been checked with sources believed to be reliable, some material may be affected by changes in the laws or in the interpretations of such laws since the manuscript for this book was completed. Therefore, the accuracy and completeness of such information and the opinions based thereon are not and cannot be guaranteed. In addition, state or local tax laws or procedural rules may have a material impact on the recommendations made by the author, and the strategies outlined in this book may not necessarily be suitable in every case. If legal, accounting, tax, investment, or other expert advice is required, one should obtain the services of a competent practitioner. The publisher and author hereby specifically disclaim any personal liability for loss or risk incurred as a consequence of the advice or information presented in this book.

Library of Congress Cataloging in Publication Data

Currier, Chet.
   The investor's encyclopedia, a systematic review of
77 types of investments from annuities to zero coupon
bonds.

   Includes index.
   1. Investments—Handbooks, manuals, etc.   I. Associated
Press.   II. Title.
HG4527.C87   1985   332.6'78   84-25624
ISBN O-531-09586-X

ACKNOWLEDGMENTS

So many people and organizations contributed information and encouragement in the writing of this book that it would be impossible to acknowledge them all here. Some invaluable sources were obliged to help anonymously. They all have the author's deepest appreciation.

Special thanks are owed to William Clark at Merrill Lynch, Pierce, Fenner & Smith; James Grinder and Sharon Gamsin at the New York Stock Exchange; Robert Shabazian at the American Stock Exchange; Arthur Samansky at the Federal Reserve Bank of New York; Fritz Elmendorf at the American Bankers Association; Thomas O'Hara at the National Association of Investors Corporation; Howard Cosgrove at the Credit Union National Association; Allan Lyons at Value Line Inc.; Norman Fosback at the Institute for Econometric Research; Jeffrey Fried; Frank Sainz; John Currier; Kelly Dolgon; Editors William Newton, Dan Perkes and Kent Kilpatrick; and Financial Editor Michael Millican and the staff of the Business News Department at The Associated Press.

Awards of merit for patience and understanding are due Carol, Craig and Dana Currier.

ABOUT THE AUTHOR

Chet Currier has been writing about business and investment subjects for more than 15 years. Since 1974, he has covered Wall Street for The Associated Press, which distributes his daily and weekly reports on the stock market and investing to thousands of newspapers and radio and television stations around the world. In 1979, he began writing On the Money, a weekly column on personal finance, for the AP.

He is the author of a previous book, "Careers in the '80s," published by The Associated Press. When not attempting to solve the riddles of the financial markets, he enjoys constructing crossword puzzles, which have been published in The New York Times, Games magazine, and in "The Associated Press Sunday Crossword Puzzle Book," volumes I and II.

He lives in Connecticut with his wife and two children.

CONTENTS

HOW TO USE THIS BOOK

Managing money, in large amounts or small, has always been a challenging task. But the job has grown much more complex in the last few years as the choices available to investors have multiplied at a rapid rate. People who once dealt only with passbook savings accounts, stocks, bonds and a few other alternatives now are confronted with money market mutual funds, financial futures, stock-index options, zero-coupon bonds, adjustable-rate securities, several new types of life insurance, and many other vehicles that did not exist, or were largely unknown to the public, just five or 10 years ago.

The investment revolution occurred in part because inflation and unprecedented fluctuations in interest rates changed the financial landscape in the 1970s and early 1980s. It was spurred on by deregulation of the financial-services industry, with the breaking down of barriers that had existed for decades dividing banking, securities brokerage, the insurance industry and other distinct segments of the money business.

The proliferation of new investment products, in the view of some observers, poses new potential risks and problems for the financial system. Indeed, some Wall Street firms have complained that it has occurred so quickly that even their professional representatives have been unable to keep up with it properly.

But many new breed investments wouldn't have flourished if they didn't meet the new needs and demands of people with money to manage. Along with the confusion it may create, the modern menu of investment choices can present many opportunities to investors who have the necessary knowledge to select wisely from it.

This book is designed to help provide the reader with that knowledge. It can only serve as a starting point on the road to that goal. But if it fulfills that function effectively, it will have met the author's most ambitious goals.

Whether the subject you are interested in is annuities, zero-coupon bonds or something in between, a separate chapter of this book attempts to explain what the investment in question is, how it works (or is supposed to work), and what special opportunities and pitfalls it may involve. Each entry is organized under eight headings:

DESCRIPTION

Before you invest in anything, you should have an understanding not only of what the vehicle represents, but why the proposition is available to the public, and what characteristics have made it a popular or, in some cases, not so popular type of investment. The most popular investments, by the way, are not always the best ones.

In some chapters, such as those on bonds and stocks, this section may cover ground that is already familiar to many investors. However, there can be many misconceptions about even the most well-known investments. In the case of many newer, more exotic vehicles, a description is the obvious and necessary starting point.

HOW AND WHERE TO GET
INFORMATION AND INVEST

Sources of investment information can be just about endless. Indeed, an inquisitive mind is regarded as one of the prime attributes for success in managing money. In this section of each entry, an effort has been made to direct you to some of the most likely sources of information, and to the places where you can most readily buy or sell the investment involved.

Whatever information you receive should, of course, always be considered in the light of the motives of the source of that information. It is a fact of life that much of the best information available on investments comes from people and institutions that have a financial stake in how you act on that information. A broker, quite naturally, wants to sell you stocks or bonds or some other product. A life insurance agent wants to sell you life insurance.

With most investments, buying and selling is done through an agent such as a dealer or a broker. Many experienced investors say the selection of a broker or dealer with whom you are compatible and on whose counsel and competence you can rely is a key step toward investment success.

COSTS OF BUYING,
OWNING AND SELLING

Most, but not all, investments involve some incidental expense when you buy and sell them. Sometimes these are clearly stated and known beforehand; in many other cases, they are built into the purchase or sales price in ways that tend to obscure them. Frequently, investments also carry with them continuing costs of ownership—for example, upkeep on developed real estate—that can be variable or not completely understood beforehand.

It is possible to pay too much attention to costs when they are small in relation to the overall size of the investment being made and the goal being pursued. But it is also possible to pay too little attention to them before a commitment is made.

This section of each entry includes, if it applies, a discussion of the minimum amount you are likely to need to get started in a given investment market. You will also find frequent references to *opportunity costs.* These are not out-of-pocket costs, but opportunities you must forego in a given type of investment. For example, when you buy tangible assets like gold or collectibles, your money normally brings you no interest or dividends, which it could obtain if it were invested elsewhere.

Much recognition has been given lately to the *time value* of money. If your cash reserves are sewn into your mattress or buried in your back yard, they are safe from declining securities prices, bank failures and a good many other perils. But they are not at work earning any return, and their purchasing power can be drastically eaten away by inflation.

CAPITAL GAINS
POTENTIAL

Capital gains are profits that result from selling something at a higher price than you paid for it. They are subject to tax rules that can differ significantly from those covering ordinary income like wages, salaries and interest received. The differences are especially favorable for long-term capital gains.

The Tax Reform Act of 1984 set the holding period to qualify for long-term status at six months and one day, for assets acquired after

June 22, 1984. It had previously been a year and a day. When you sell a long-term holding at a profit, 60 percent of the gain is excluded from taxes. The remainder is subject to tax at rates of up to 50 percent. So the net effect is to put a maximum tax rate of 20 percent on long-term gains.

Beyond their special tax aspects, capital gains are normally sought by investors with goals for the future, rather than present financial needs. Accordingly, this section of each entry may also include a discussion of how well the investment involved is generally suited for pursuing long-term growth. But it also usually contains an assessment of whether the investment affords a chance to seek short-term, or speculative, profits.

INCOME POTENTIAL

Income from investments normally comes in the form of periodic payments of dividends or interest. The money is generally called a dividend when the investment you hold—for example, shares of common stock—represents a part ownership, or equity position, in the entity that issued the security. It is classified as interest if the investment represents a loan.

High-income investments normally appeal most to people who want or need the greatest possible return on their assets to meet their current living costs. Retirees make up a large proportion of this group. Since people in these circumstances usually are eager to minimize risk, this section includes an assessment of the safety and reliability of the investment involved.

RISKS AND DRAWBACKS

All investments carry some degree of risk, ranging from negligible to limitless. In an uncertain world, risk is difficult to evaluate with absolute precision. But it is always sensible to examine closely the prospective risk that goes with any given investment before you put your money into it.

Low-risk or high-risk, no single investment is perfectly suited to all people in all circumstances. For each advantage a given vehicle affords, there is usually some other possible benefit the investor must be willing to give up. Some investments that were mainstays of financial planning years ago have lost a lot of their luster as the economy has changed. Drawbacks of this type are discussed in this section of each entry.

LIQUIDITY

Liquidity refers to the ease with which can you expect to move your money in and out of an investment on short notice, under favorable circumstances. With the rapid changes and fluctuations the economy and the investment markets have undergone in recent years, many investors have placed an increasing emphasis on liquidity.

Of course, if you have a long-term goal such as the financing of a child's college education, and can readily afford to set aside money now toward that goal, liquidity may not rank high on your list of concerns. People willing to commit money for long periods can often receive enhanced returns on their money in exchange for that commitment.

TAX ADVANTAGES
AND DISADVANTAGES

An old axiom among financial experts holds that tax considerations should be secondary in most investment decisions. But as American investors collectively have moved into higher and higher tax brackets, the question of how an investment is treated for tax purposes has become more and more important in their planning. The category of investments designed as *tax shelters*—discussed in one chapter of this book—has experienced explosive growth.

This final section of each entry in this book is designed to help you evaluate an investment for its potential after-tax results. It also, where appropriate, discusses the eligibility and suitability (or the lack thereof) of each given investment vehicle for individual retirement accounts, Keogh plans and similar tax-favored savings and investment programs.

Readers are urged to bear in mind that the U.S. tax system, as it applies to investments, has been significantly changed several times in recent years, and may undergo further revisions in the future. At the time of this writing, several proposals were pending in Congress to overhaul the system completely. Whenever you are contemplating an investment that has significant tax consequences, you should be sure you are up to date on current tax rules and court rulings.

Following the main text of this book are several appendices providing specific information on the performance in 1984 of a variety of investments, as well as tables designed to help you keep track of the securities markets through the reports that are published in daily newspapers and the financial press, or disseminated through computer systems.

A few words now about what this book is not: Like most other reference books, it is not designed to be read in sequence, front to back. In saying this, the author does not wish to discourage anyone from reading every word between these covers. But since each entry in the text that follows is intended to stand alone, frequent repetition of key points could not be avoided.

It is hard to imagine a single investor who would have use for all 77 of the vehicles described in the chapters that follow. As an aid in seeking out those that most closely correspond to your particular needs and goals, a series of indexes has been included listing the chapters that are likely to be of most interest to people with specific objectives.

In practice, many successful investors concentrate on just one or a few specialties, developing as much expertise as possible in their chosen areas. Still, some exploratory reading on a subject like banker's acceptances or convertible securities might, for some readers, provide an introduction to alternatives they have not previously considered.

Some of the chapters, such as those on stocks, bonds, mutual funds, options and real estate, are divided into several entries. When the reader has an interest in one of the individual types of investments covered in these entries—for example, Stock-Index Options—it may be helpful to read first the introductory section of the chapter—in the case of the example, Options.

This book is also not meant as an exercise in scholarship. Where it seemed relevant, some historical discussion of investments and institutions like stock exchanges has been included. However, the primary goal of this book is to provide a practical and convenient refer-

ence for understanding and evaluating the various types of investments. So discussions of historical and theoretical matters have been
kept to a minimum.

Encyclopedia or not, this book could not possibly embrace every
conceivable type of investment you could make. Farming, operating a
small business, breeding horses, making a loan to a friend, or any
other in an endless list of endeavors and activities can be considered
investments. The contents of this book are, of necessity, limited to the
recognized tools available for managing money, and for attempting to
make it grow and to protect it from the erosive effects of inflation.

Lastly, this book, unlike many on investment subjects, is not written
from a point of view about the future of the United States economy or
the world political situation. After studying such matters at length, and
noting the difficulty others have encountered in trying to divine the
future, the author confesses that he does not know whether the stock
market, the price of gold, the inflation rate, or the total return available
on convertible subordinated debentures will rise or fall during any
given period in the future. Accordingly, the pages that follow are
intended to provide information, not investment advice or recommendations of any kind.

All that having been said, experience and observation do strongly
suggest that informed investing and money management are well
worth the effort. Wisely put to use, money can work very hard and very
productively for its owners.

INDEX FOR BASIC SAVINGS PLAN

If your primary interest lies in STARTING AND BUILDING A BASIC SAVINGS PLAN, the following sections of this book may be of special interest:

INDEX FOR MAXIMUM SAFETY OF YOUR INVESTMENTS

If your primary interest lies in MAXIMUM SAFETY OF YOUR IN-VESTMENTS, the following sections of this book may be of special interest:

INDEX FOR CURRENT INCOME FROM YOUR ASSETS

If your primary interest lies in CURRENT INCOME FROM YOUR ASSETS, the following sections of this book may be of special interest:

INDEX FOR SAVING AND INVESTING FOR RETIREMENT

If your primary interest lies in SAVING AND INVESTING FOR RE-
TIREMENT, the following sections of this book may be of special
interest:

INDEX FOR PROTECTING YOUR ASSETS FROM INFLATION

If your primary interest lies in SEEKING PROTECTION OF YOUR ASSETS FROM INFLATION, the following sections of this book may be of special interest:

INDEX FOR HIGHLY LIQUID INVESTMENTS

If your primary interest lies in HIGHLY LIQUID INVESTMENTS, the following sections of this book may be of special interest:

INDEX FOR SHORT-TERM GAINS

If your primary interest lies in SPECULATING OR INVESTING FOR SHORT-TERM GAINS, the following sections of this book may be of special interest:

INDEX FOR INVESTING FOR LONG-TERM GROWTH

If your primary interest lies in INVESTING FOR LONG-TERM GROWTH, the following sections of this book may be of special interest:

INDEX FOR TAX-ADVANTAGED INVESTMENTS

If your primary interest lies in TAX-ADVANTAGED INVESTMENTS, the following sections of this book may be of special interest:

ANNUITIES

DESCRIPTION

The original idea of an annuity was pretty simple. An investor paid a lump sum to an insurance company, which in turn agreed to make specified regular payments back to the investor over the rest of his or her life. It made no difference whether the investor died a month after the contract was signed, or 40 years later. The payments would continue until death, and no longer.

The concept had appeal to many people in the later years of their lives, particulary those of limited means and those who had no heirs or institutions to whom they wished to leave an estate. It solved the retiree's problem of deciding what to spend, and what to conserve, each year from his or her accumulated savings. With an annuity, there was no chance the money would run out before death, and the retirees could make spending decisions without constantly having to consider this fearful prospect.

For its part, the insurance company could enter into such a contract confident of its ability to keep its part of the bargain, assuming that it was sound financially and had a large number of annuity customers. It knew, from actuarial tables, the statistical likelihood of how long those customers would live.

Since there are many potential annuity customers with varying financial needs and desires, and since there are many insurance companies competing for those people's business, it was inevitable that many variations on the basic annuity would evolve. Today, shopping for annuities is a bit like shopping for a car. They come in many sizes and models, with a great number of options. And the wise buyer does a lot of comparison shopping and asks a lot of questions before making a decision.

HOW AND WHERE TO GET
INFORMATION AND INVEST

Annuities are issued only by insurance companies, but they are marketed by a wide variety of institutions. You can probably find information, and arrange a deal, at a securities brokerage firm or your local bank, as well as from specialized insurance salespeople.

COSTS OF BUYING,
OWNING AND SELLING

The actual and potential costs of investing in annuities can be complicated, and are an important question to bear in mind as you shop for
one. Traditionally, annuities, like many life insurance policies, were
sold with large front-end sales charges built into the purchase price.
Today, more and more annuities are available at no sales charge. But
they may carry annual fees, charges and tax penalties for early withdrawal, and other costs. You should be aware of, and understand, all
the cost provisions of an annuity before you invest.

Annuity sponsors normally set a minimum investment. In the case
of deferred annuities (explained below), which permit you to accumulate money over time before you start receiving payments, this minimum is typically in the $1,000 to $5,000 range.

CAPITAL GAINS
POTENTIAL

In their simplest form, annuities involve no oppportunity for capital
gains. If you plunk down a lump sum on retirement and begin receiving payments immediately, of course, you are looking for income,'not
capital gains. But the modern deferred annuity does offer the attraction of growth in your assets before you start making withdrawals. If it
is a variable annuity, you may even choose to have your money
invested in securities that will produce capital gains.

A deferred annuity , as the name implies, is one that does not start
paying you money until some time—perhaps many years—after you
buy it. It may call for a single premium investment at the time you strike
a deal, or it may allow for many contributions after the initial investment is made.

Either way, the money in your account earns more money, which
compounds until you withdraw it. What's more, the tax rules generally
provide that the income is exempt from current taxes. This greatly
accelerates the compounding process.

If you are willing to take on some extra risk during the accumulation
period, you can invest in a variable annuity. In this kind of annuity, you
can choose to have the premiums you pay in, and the money those
premiums earn, invested in any one of several mutual funds, some of

which may seek capital gains as an objective. Whatever course you choose to follow, the object is naturally to build up the largest possible nest egg in your account before you start collecting annuity payments from it.

INCOME POTENTIAL

The standard purpose of investing in annuities, no matter how you go about it, is to obtain maximum income from a certain date—such as when you retire—that is assured for the rest of your life. Many modern annuities offer considerable flexibility of choice in how you collect this income.

In fact, they may also let you select from among several options beyond the basic payments to you as an individual until your death. You may choose an arrangement, for example, that provides for continuing payments to your spouse if you die first. As a general rule, you pay a price for these extras in the form of lower regular payments to you.

When you buy a deferred annuity, it is essential to know exactly what return the insurance company promises to pay on your investment in all the years until you begin receiving payments. Often, these contracts set a competitive rate for the first year or few years, but do not specify an exact rate after that. It makes sense to tally up the minimum return called for in the contract, through the entire time you expect to be accumulating money, and calculate what actual annual rate that works out to. Then you can compare it to other alternative investments and evaluate its chances of protecting you from inflation.

RISKS AND DRAWBACKS

The nemesis of the traditional fixed annuity, and anyone who invests in it, is inflation. If you bought such an annuity in 1970, and were still alive and collecting on it in 1980, you might well have been very distressed. The purchasing power of a fixed income over that period declined drastically.

That is the principal reason why more flexible annuity products were developed. Buyers of deferred annuities have at least the hope of some protection from inflation, in the form of higher interest rates on the money invested during periods of high inflation.

But anyone considering annuities should still carefully consider inflation risk, as it applies during both the period of accumulating money and the period in which you expect to collect the proceeds. Futhermore, in considering annuities, it is wise to view them as part investment, part insurance. The insurance element is the guarantee that your income will not run out before you die. For this guarantee, you must pay a price. The premiums you and other annuity investors pay and whatever investment income they earn must cover not only the money paid back to those investors, but also the annuity issuer's costs of operations.

An annuity investment with a reputable, well-managed issuer is presumed to be very safe. But it does not offer the absolute security available in, say, government-guaranteed Treasury bonds. In the early 1980s, one major issuer of annuities filed for protection under the federal bankruptcy law. Large brokerage firms that had sold many of this company's annuities to their customers subsequently said they would cover any losses suffered by investors. But the incident remained a cautionary one. Since security is by definition a central concern for anyone investing in annuities, you should be very confident of the strength and integrity of whatever institution you buy one from.

One further point to consider about annuities: They normally deplete assets you might otherwise leave in your estate after your death. This fundamental characteristic of them should be weighed against any legacies you wish to provide for. Obviously, this is a matter of your own personal preferences and circumstances.

LIQUIDITY

Annuities are long-term propositions. In modern deferred annuities, there are generally provisions for early withdrawals, but they may provide for special charges or penalties. In a deferred-annuity account in which money is compounded on a tax-deferred basis, you may also incur a penalty tax.

When you are considering a given annuity, all the conditions covering early withdrawal should be throroughly understood before you invest. Even if the provisions are quite generous, you should not invest money in an annuity that you reasonably expect you might need for other purposes in the near future.

TAX ADVANTAGES
AND DISADVANTAGES

Annuities have some appealing tax features. Earnings from money invested in a deferred annuity are not subject to current income tax— a fact that adds dramatically to the power of compounding as the investment grows.

When you receive payments from an annuity, part of the money is not subject to tax, since it is a return of your original investment. In this respect, annuities differ significantly from other tax-deferred savings programs such as individual retirement accounts. All distributions from IRAs are taxed as current income.

Annuities are marketed for use in IRAs, Keogh plans and other similar tax-favored savings accounts. Before you buy an annuity for your IRA, however, you might consider that annuities already have significant tax advantages of their own. Putting them in an IRA may nullify some of those advantages, or at least make them redundant. It may be most sensible to use annuities, if they appeal to you, as a separate supplement to an IRA and any other financial planning for retirement.

BANKER'S ACCEPTANCES

DESCRIPTION

Banker's acceptances are a common form of short-term, high-yielding and relatively safe investment. But most individual investors are only dimly aware of their existence, if they have heard of them at all. One reason for the obscurity of acceptances is that it takes some study to grasp how they are created and what they represent. Another is the general impression—which is not completely accurate—that banker's acceptances are the exclusive preserve of professional investors and financial institutions, dealing in millions of dollars per transaction.

Actually, individual investors may be able to obtain acceptances in relatively small amounts. Whether they might find it desirable to do so depends on prevailing credit conditions and their own circumstances and inclinations. If you invest in money market mutual funds, chances are you are or have been an indirect owner of bankers' acceptances. Many money funds include them in their portfolios.

A banker's acceptance is typically created when a bank acts as a middleman in a sale of goods, usually in foreign trade. Suppose, for example, that an exporter in a foreign country agrees to sell a given amount of some commodity to an importer in the United States. They have no problem agreeing on the price. But the exporter wants to get paid immediately, and the importer does not want to pay until he or she has received the goods and can process and resell them.

In simplest terms, a bank resolves this situation by "accepting" a document representing the financial part of the transaction—in fact, it may actually stamp the word "accepted" along with its name and the date on the document. The bank can then hold the document to maturity (normally 30 to 90 days) or it can sell it to an investor. It frequently chooses the latter course.

When an investor buys the acceptance, the money he or she puts up goes to pay the exporter. When the importer later pays up, the money is then directed to the investor. Obviously, the bank and investor don't volunteer their services for free in this whole arrangement. The bank collects fees, and the investor receives, at maturity, an amount greater than he or she put up at the outset. The difference is considered to be the equivalent of interest received on a loan.

HOW AND WHERE TO GET
INFORMATION AND INVEST

Once you have an understanding of banker's acceptances and have decided you are interested in them, you can start making inquiries at individual banks. Do they offer acceptances to individual investors? In what denominations? If they are available, what is the prevailing interest rate?

Your best chances for attractive deals may lie with a bank that actively engages in the acceptance business, and at which you are already an established and valued customer. Information about bankers' acceptances and money market mutual funds that invest in them is available directly from the funds, in their prospectuses and other literature.

COSTS OF BUYING,
OWNING AND SELLING

If you invest with a bank that issues acceptances, you may incur only modest or no fees, especially if you already do a lot of business with that bank. If, conversely, you invest with a bank that must obtain an acceptance for you from some other bank, you can expect to pay a fee that at least covers the costs of the transaction. In any case where a fee is imposed, it should be included in your calculations of the return you expect to get on your investment.

Since money market mutual funds are almost always no load funds, the only cost normally associated with investing in these funds is the annual management fees collected by the fund's sponsor from the fund's assets.

CAPITAL GAINS
POTENTIAL

Investors in banker's acceptances receive a greater sum at maturity than they pay at the time of purchase. However, this profit counts not as capital gains, but as interest. Large dealer firms trade acceptances in the credit markets in hopes of realizing profits. This is not a feasible endeavor for most individuals, even wealthy ones.

INCOME POTENTIAL

Especially in periods when short-term interest rates are high, bankers' acceptances can offer attractive income prospects. Of course, if you are investing in small amounts, you probably will not be able to command the kind of yield that a multimillion-dollar buyer can get. At any time when you are considering banker's acceptances, it makes sense to compare what they have to offer with the return available in other competing investments like Treasury bills, bank certificates of deposit, and even money market funds themselves.

Rates on banker's acceptances can change rapidly, and they are short-term investments. Therefore, they are unsuitable for people who want to "lock in" an assured level of return on their money for long periods of time. When it comes time three, six, or nine months from now to reinvest the proceeds of a banker's acceptance you buy today, the choices available to you will be determined by the unpredictable conditions then prevailing in the credit markets.

RISKS AND
DRAWBACKS

Banker's acceptances are considered highly safe because they have two entities standing behind them. Both the issuing bank and the original buyer in the transaction that gave rise to the acceptance—the importer, in the example above—have obligated themselves to make good on them.

However, investors considering banker's acceptances should always bear in mind that these vehicles are not deposits, and therefore are not covered by federal deposit insurance. Neither do they have government backing, as Treasury bills do. For these reasons, returns available on bankers' acceptances should logically be somewhat higher than those available on, say, Treasury bills. They normally are.

Whether out of mere inertia or informed consideration, many individual investors don't take the trouble to invest directly in vehicles like banker's acceptances. If they want money market returns, they turn instead to something like a money market mutual fund. In addition to convenience, money funds offer a diversified portfolio that tends to dissipate risk, and their shareholders do not have to take the trouble to monitor the credit markets regularly and make frequent investment decisions. Nevertheless, it is sensible for people entrusting their savings to money fund managers to have at least a basic understanding of how bankers' acceptances work, and to be aware that direct investment in bankers' acceptances may be an alternative open to them.

LIQUIDITY

There is an active secondary market in which dealers buy and sell bankers' acceptances, but it is not set up to accommodate small investors. If you want or need to sell an acceptance before it matures, your only reasonable option may be to ask the issuing bank to buy it back from you. The bank's response to your request may depend on your standing with it as a customer. Even if it is willing to do so, the bank may expect you to accept a price concession.

Of course, liquidity questions like these are relatively unimportant with an investment that has only a few months of life. If you want absolute day-to-day liquidity, you can choose a money market fund that invests in bankers' acceptances and other short-term vehicles, rather than buying acceptances directly yourself.

TAX ADVANTAGES
AND DISADVANTAGES

The money you earn investing in bankers' acceptances is taxable interest. In the past, it has been said that acceptances were popular with some investors because some transactions in them "tended not to get reported" to the Internal Revenue Service.

This book, naturally, does not advocate any illegal non-reporting of taxable income on anyone's tax return. In any event, "forgetting" to list any source of income like a banker's acceptance on a tax return may be a riskier proposition in the future than it was in the past, given the recent tightening of reporting requirements by the IRS.

Bankers' acceptances may have a place in an individual retirement account, Keogh plan or other tax-favored savings program, providing that it can be arranged for the custodian of the plan to acquire them under favorable circumstances. Perhaps more simply, you can invest IRA or Keogh money in a money market mutual fund that in turn holds bankers' acceptances in its portfolio.

BONDS

DESCRIPTION

The basic idea of a bond is simple. It is a security that represents a loan by the bond buyer to the bond issuer, be it the U.S. government, an agency of that government, a state, local or foreign government, or a private business. As in most other types of loans, the issuer (borrower) agrees to make periodic payments of interest to the buyer (lender) as long as it has the use of the borrowed money, and to pay back the principal amount at an agreed-upon maturity date.

It may take just a few minutes to grasp those fundamentals. But you can spend years gaining an understanding of the many possible forms and uses of bonds in the modern world, of the broad range of investment stategies in which they can be employed, and of the potential risks and rewards involved in those stategies.

Would-be investors in bonds first need to be aware of how they differ from another major class of investments, stocks. A share of stock represents part ownership in an enterprise. A bond, by contrast, is merely a financial contract between two separate parties. It represents a claim on the assets of the issuer only in the event that the issuer is unable to live up to its part of the bargain. Should default occur, however, that claim comes ahead of stockholders' interests. This is why bonds are referred to as *senior* securities.

The umbrella term *bond* actually may be used to describe many specific types of securities, ranging in maturities from one year to about 30 years from the date of issue. Bonds with lives of 10 years or less are usually called notes. Bonds that are not secured by a mortgage on specified assets of the issuer, but rather only on a good-faith promise to pay, are known as debentures.

In the not-too-distant past, most bonds were *bearer* bonds, printed certificates presumed to be owned by whomever had physical possession of them. Bearer bonds typically have a series of coupons attached to them, which the owner clips off one by one and presents to the issuer or a bank to collect his or her interest payments. Today, more and more bonds are registered in the name of the owner in records kept by the issuer or a custodian. Interest payments on registered bonds are typically made automatically by the issuer on the scheduled date.

Almost all bonds are negotiable—that is, one investor can sell them to another at any time. There is a large secondary market for bonds, on stock exchanges and in the over-the-counter market, in which they are traded much like stocks.

In the past, the bond market rarely drew much attention from the public, despite its size. It didn't fluctuate much, and any ups and downs that did take place weren't of great concern to investors anyway. They had no intention of selling their bonds before maturity, and the price they expected to receive at maturity was fixed and known.

Today the standard legal structure of bonds is the same as it always was. But the economic and financial circumstances that influence them has changed drastically, and so has the bond market. Large and sometimes rapid changes in inflation and interest rates have subjected bond prices to once-unthinkable ups and downs. Studies have found them to be more volatile, in some recent periods, than stocks. Because of the influence it can exert on general interest rate trends, the bond market as an entity has become a powerful economic and political force.

The modern era has brought innovation, as well as upheaval, to the bond market. On the menu available to bond investors today may be found such exotic items as Yankee bonds (dollar-denominated issues sold in this country by foreign governments); bonds backed by pools of home mortgages; and floating-rate bonds or notes, securities on which the interest payments are adjusted regularly to reflect prevailing interest rates. More new variations on the bond theme will doubtless appear in the future.

HOW AND WHERE TO GET
INFORMATION AND INVEST

Bonds may be bought and sold through brokers, banks, or dealers that specialize in a given segment of the market, such as municipal bonds. These organizations can provide you with abundant information about bonds. Generally, these firms have a strong desire to persuade you to place an order with them, and the information they provide you with should be considered in that light.

There are many mutual funds, unit trusts and closed-end funds that invest in bonds of all types. Information about these funds and trusts is available from brokers or the organizations that sponsor them.

General-interest newspapers, financial publications and invest-ment advisory services report regularly on developments of interest to bond investors. Some specialized publications, news services and advisory services devote all their attention to bonds.

Several companies, among them Moody's Investors Service Inc. and Standard & Poor's Corp., evaluate the quality and safety of indi-vidual bond issues and assign them letter ratings from triple-A (top quality) to D (in default). These can be used as guidelines in selecting a bond that most closely conforms to the degree of risk you want to take in quest of the highest possible return on your investment.

COSTS OF BUYING,
OWNING AND SELLING

Whenever you buy bonds, or sell them before maturity, the broker or dealer handling the transaction collects a fee. Sometimes this is ex-plicitly charged to you as a commission. Often, it is charged to you implicitly, with the broker or dealer building it into the price you pay or receive. When bonds are offered to investors for the first time, the brokers or other institutions that act as underwriters in the offerings collect their fees from the issuer.

This variety of methods can confuse investors. But no matter how fees are collected, they amount to an integral factor in the price you pay to buy and the proceeds you realize when you sell. So in shopping for a bond to buy, for example, you can deal with the question of costs by comparing the yields available to you on comparable bonds after all costs are taken into account.

Small investors are traditionally at a disadvantage in the bond mar-ket. A *round lot* (the standard minimum trading unit) for many types of bonds is $100,000. In any transaction smaller than that amount, in-vestors normally get less attractive prices than those available to big investors. Even if you have $100,000 to work with, you may not be in a good position to diversify your money among several bonds. Because of these circumstances, many financial advisers say small investors interested in bonds may be better off choosing among pooled bond investments such as mutual funds, unit trusts or closed-end funds. The minimum amount required to invest in these vehicles ranges from a few hundred to a few thousand dollars.

This recommendation need not be taken as a blanket rule, however. Especially if you are a good customer of a given broker or dealer, you may be able to find good deals now and then among small lots of bonds that the firm has in its inventory and wishes to dispose of. Furthermore, if you make a relatively small direct investment in a bond with a firm intention of holding it to maturity, you need not worry about having to accept any price concession when you cash in your investment.

CAPITAL GAINS
POTENTIAL

In theory, you invest in stocks if your primary goal is capital gains, and in bonds for the highest possible current income. Bondholders have no ownership interest in the issuer, and thus no way to benefit from the issuer's future earnings growth. In practice, however, capital gains and losses have become a fact of life in the modern bond market, since bond prices constantly change to adjust to current levels of interest rates (prices rise when rates decline and fall when rates rise).

You can experience capital gains or losses against your wishes, if you want or need to sell a bond before maturity. Though short-term trading in bonds in quest of capital gains is an impracticable venture for most individual investors, there are ways to buy bonds in hopes of realizing long-term profits. For instance, you can speculate in *junk bonds,* which are discussed in a separate section of this chapter.

For really fast action, you can buy bonds on margin, using money borrowed from a broker to finance a large part of the purchase price. This practice isn't considered suitable, however, for anyone without a large amount of capital and a willingness to put it at great risk. An investor contemplating such a stategy can consider alternative ways of speculating on interest-rate changes, such as options and futures.

INCOME POTENTIAL

In the old days, most everyone bought bonds for income. Lots of investors still do. A bond issuer is committed to making regular interest payments, normally every six months. If you buy the right bond at the right time, you can "lock in" an attractive return on your money for long periods of time.

These days, however, buying bonds of even top-quality issuers involves a gamble. What looks like a very high interest rate today may seem paltry just a few months or a few years from now. Interest-rate risk, as well as credit risk, is a factor to consider before investing in bonds, particularly if you are a conservative investor seeking maximum income with a high degree of safety.

RISKS AND
DRAWBACKS

As the foregoing discussion emphasizes, bonds involve a variety of risks that require careful evaluation. The issuer can default. Or the price of even a top-quality bond can be ravaged by inflation and rising interest rates. Beyond these possibilities, bonds have some other inherent risks and drawbacks.

One question to take into account before buying a bond is the possibility that you will be required to sell it back to the issuer before maturity, either because it has been selected to go into a *sinking fund* (a method some bond issuers use to amass funds over time to pay off a bond issue at maturity), or because the entire issue has been *called* by the issuer. All sinking fund and call provisions should be understood before you invest in any given bond.

Furthermore, most bonds, unlike stocks, offer no hope of future increases in their payouts. With a straight bond, the interest rate is fixed for the life of the security. As inflation progresses, the purchasing power of this fixed payout will decline.

Though it is possible to invest in bonds for capital gains, they are still generally not considered good vehicles for investors looking for long-term growth. If an issuer prospers, bondholders don't stand to gain any special benefit because they have no ownership interest.

Inflation is a paramount concern for bond investors. A long-term commitment to a bond or bonds today is, in effect, a bet that inflation will be much less virulent in the future than it has been in the recent past.

LIQUIDITY

Huge amounts of bonds are traded every day. But the secondary market in which this activity takes place is set up to accommodate large players, such as institutions, professional investors and the wealthiest individuals. Small investors cannot generally participate on favorable terms. Thus, though bonds do have some liquidity, they are generally regarded as a long-term proposition.

Accordingly, they are not a logical place to put money you might need for other purposes before maturity. Investors who want to put such money to work earning interest can find many alternatives in short-term money market vehicles.

TAX ADVANTAGES
AND DISADVANTAGES

The tax treatment of bond interest varies widely among different types of bonds. Treasury bond interest is subject to federal, but not state and local, taxes. Municipal bond interest is exempt from federal taxes, and may or may not be subject to state and local taxes, depending on whether you live in the state or locality of the issuer. Corporate bond interest is subject to both federal and state and local tax as ordinary income.

Given these differences, it is important to assess the relative merits of bond investments available to you on the basis of the after-tax return you can expect from them. As your tax bracket changes, so will the comparative appeal to you of each type of bond investment.

The 1984 tax law made a significant change in the rules covering profits realized on bonds bought at a "discount"—that is, a price below their face value. On most "market discount" bonds, except for municipals, a certain amount of that profit is taxed as though it were interest paid, rather than a capital gain. The change, however, applies only to bonds issued after July 18, 1984, the date the law was enacted.

Bond investments in their many forms, with the notable exception of municipal bonds, may be appropriate for an individual retirement account, Keogh plan or other tax-favored savings program.

CORPORATE BONDS

DESCRIPTION

Thousands of corporations raise capital in the United States by selling bonds. The two basic classes of these securities are mortgage bonds, which have the backing of a lien on some specified assets of the issuer, such as its production facilities, and debentures, backed by the issuer's *full faith and credit* but no specific assets. In theory a bond may be a better credit risk than a debenture. But in practice, debentures of top-quality companies can and often do merit top credit standing.

Most buyers and owners of corporate bonds are conservative investors, concerned primarily with high income and safety. They generally choose among bonds in the top four categories assigned by the principal rating agencies AAA, AA, A and BBB in the case of Standard Poor's Corp.; Aaa, Aa, A, and Baa in the case of Moody's Investors Service Inc. Bonds with lower ratings, often called *junk bonds,* are discussed in a separate section of this chapter.

The attraction of high-rated corporate bonds is that they usually offer higher yields than comparable government bonds, at what most investment professionals regard as only a small increase in risk. For all corporate bonds, there is some chance, however slight, that the issuer will run into circumstances that prevent it from making timely payments of interest and principal. No matter how strong a company's business and financial status may be, it cannot offer the degree of assurance against credit risk that the federal government can. Nevertheless, a top-rated corporate bond is considered a very safe credit risk.

All that having been said, modern times have been unkind to corporate bonds. Inflation and volatile interest rates have subjected them to increased fluctuations in price. Furthermore, inflation has pushed Americans into higher and higher tax brackets, so that corporate bonds—whose interest payments are subject to federal, state and local income tax—have been faced with increased competition for investors' money from municipal bonds—whose interest payments are exempt from federal income tax, and in some circumstances, state and local income tax as well.

There are many subgroups within the broad category of corporate bonds. For purposes of evaluating them as credit risks, analysts distinguish industrial bonds from bonds issued by electric utilities, tele-phone companies, financial institutions and finance companies. Spe-cialized types of corporate bonds include equipment trust certificates issued by transportation companies, in which actual transportation equipment such as rail cars serves as security for the loan.

Many issues of corporate bonds have a single maturity date, with a *sinking fund* provision that allows for some of the issue to be retired each year. Convertible debentures (see the separate chapter of this book on convertible securities) are popular with many companies. In the last decade, some issuers have sold floating-rate notes.

HOW AND WHERE TO GET
INFORMATION AND INVEST

Keeping track of the full range of the corporate bond market is a more difficult assignment for the non-professional investor than, say, moni-toring stocks or mutual funds. But tables of price and other trading information on corporate bonds listed on the New York and American stock exchanges are published by many newspapers. A good broker should be able to supply you with examples of available issues.

Picking a corporate bond to buy is very different from choosing a common stock. With a bond, your chief concern is the issuer's ability to pay its debts in the future, rather than such matters as potential earnings growth. You might have no interest in a "stodgy" company's stock, but at the same time find its bonds very appealing.

COSTS OF BUYING,
OWNING AND SELLING

When you buy corporate bonds at the time of their original sale to the public, you may incur no out-of-pocket commission cost, since the selling brokers normally collect their fee from the issuer. If you buy existing corporate bonds, or sell them before maturity, you can expect to pay a commission, which may be smaller on a percentage basis than what a broker would charge for a stock transaction.

However, if you are operating with small amounts of capital, you may encounter an effective cost in the form of a price concession from a dealer or broker. To buy bonds directly, investment experts say you normally should have at least $5,000 to invest. If you have any intention of trying to trade corporate bonds successfully, you will probably need much more than that.

To invest relatively small amounts—say $1,000 or more—in corporate bonds, and to gain an interest in a diversified portfolio as a cushion against credit risk, you can consider a mutual fund, unit trust, or other managed pool of money that invests in corporate bonds. These typically involve fees that lower the net return on your investment somewhat. But the convenience, liquidity and professional management that comes with them may be worth that cost.

CAPITAL GAINS POTENTIAL

Traditionally, corporate bonds were bought by investors with no thought of capital gains. But in times of volatile interest rates, bond prices fluctuate widely. So today's corporate bond investors can realize capital gains or losses whether they want to or not.

There are some ways to use even top-grade corporate bonds for speculative purposes. You can buy them on margin, using credit from your broker. Much or all of the interest you receive will go to paying interest costs of your margin loan—indeed, in some cases it may not cover all your margin costs. But because margin gives you leverage, you may seek to realize large profits from even a moderate increase in the price of your bonds if interest rates fall.

Some corporate bond issues are sold with warrants to buy the issuer's common stock, additional bonds or some other security. These warrants, which usually become separate, saleable securities after the completion of the bond offering, can appreciate significantly in value if the price of their underlying security rises. A separate chapter of this book is devoted to warrants.

INCOME POTENTIAL

Particularly if you have the skill or luck to buy a good corporate bond at a time when interest rates are at or near a peak, you can "lock in" attractive interest yields for long periods of time with these securities. Battered as they have been by inflation, corporate bonds still play a prominent role in income investing in this country. However, if you have a substantial amount of money to invest, you probably are also in a high tax bracket. In that case, you should consider whether you can achieve a better after-tax return in municipal bonds rather than corporates.

Logic suggests that yields on corporate bonds would naturally tend to settle at levels where their after-tax return was competitive with yields available on municipal bonds of comparable credit standing. But some major participants in the corporate bond market are institutions like pension funds that are not subject to current taxes. This is a point to bear in mind when you are considering making a taxable investment in corporate bonds.

RISKS AND DRAWBACKS

Top-rated corporate bonds have a time-honored position in the pantheon of American investments as a safe place to seek generous income. But in their traditional form they offer no protection from inflation. Unlike stocks, they hold out no hope of higher income in the future.

Corporate bonds, like stocks, are now subject to significant price volatility. But their long-term growth potential is much more limited than that of a well-chosen stock. Corporate bonds need a return to a more stable economy to regain some of their lost stature for individual investors.

A direct investment in corporate bonds may not provide any convenient way to compound interest. Furthermore, buyers of corporate bonds normally have no way of knowing what return they will be able to earn when they seek to reinvest future dividends received. One or both of these drawbacks may be avoided by looking to a bond mutual fund that allows for automatic dividend reinvestment, or a zero-coupon bond (see the chapter on zero-coupon investments) that provides a known return in advance on all your money.

LIQUIDITY

There are many, many corporate bonds to choose from, and an active secondary market in which these bonds are bought and sold. But most of this trading is done in very large amounts. Normally, individual investors of relatively moderate means are best off viewing these securities as long-term commitments, unsuitable for money they might need for other purposes before a given bond's maturity date.

TAX ADVANTAGES
AND DISADVANTAGES

Among the major categories of bonds, corporate issues have the least attractive tax characteristics. The interest they pay is taxable at the federal, state and local levels. Their pre-tax yield may only partially compensate you for this disadvantage.

But when an investor is operating free of current tax liabilities, yields available on corporate bonds may appear alluring at any given time. For this reason, they are a candidate for an individual retirement account, Keogh plan or other tax-deferred savings program.

JUNK BONDS

DESCRIPTION

Almost all investment precepts stress the search for quality and value. The idea of using your hard-earned savings to buy something labeled as *junk* might seem absurd on its face. Indeed, fans of junk bonds often prefer to call them by some more euphemistic name—say, high-yielding bonds, or speculative bonds. But however they are described, some venturesome investors regard junk bonds as one of the most intriguing areas of the markets. These investors may even make a specialty of studying junk bonds and buying them, with the hope of earning a combination of fat interest yields and handsome capital gains.

It is important at the start to have a precise idea of what constitutes a junk bond. They are debt securities that sell at relatively low prices, and-or significantly higher yields than top-grade bonds, because their issuers have problems of one kind or another. Those problems are regarded by bond investors and credit-rating agencies as significant enough to raise questions about whether the interest and principal on them will be paid in the future.

One of those agencies, Standard & Poor's Corp., says bonds to which it assigns ratings of BB, B, CCC, and CC "are regarded, on balance, as predominantly speculative with respect to capacity to pay interest and repay principal in accordance with the terms of the obligation. BB indicates the lowest degree of speculation and CC the highest degree of speculation. While such bonds will likely have some quality and protective characteristics, these are outweighed by large uncertainties or major risk exposures to adverse conditions."

Deeper down in the pile are C-rated bonds, on which no interest is being paid, and those with D ratings, which are in default and in arrears on payment of interest and-or principal. All these categories are candidates for junk-bond investing, depending on the size of investors' appetites for prospective rewards and their concomitant tolerance for risk. Junk bonds are very different from, and should not be confused with, deep-discount bonds—debt securities of solid issuers that are selling well below their face value simply because interest rates in general have risen since the time they were issued.

HOW AND WHERE TO GET
INFORMATION AND INVEST

Most brokerage firms and bond dealers can supply you with information on junk bonds, and take your orders to buy and sell them. Selection of which junk bond or bonds to buy is obviously much more important than if you are choosing among gilt-edged bonds with triple-A ratings. Thus, it is helpful to get well-reasoned recommendations of given junk bonds from a knowledgeable adviser, or develop expertise on your own in analyzing whether a company with junk bonds outstanding is likely to surmount its problems or sink deeper into its quagmire of difficulties. Some mutual funds and other professionally selected pools of money concentrate on junk bonds.

COSTS OF BUYING,
OWNING AND SELLING

Brokers and dealers handling junk bonds typically charge standard commissions or *spreads*—differences between their buying and selling prices—when you buy and sell. Depending on how severe the bond issuer's troubles are, a buyer of a junk bond must be prepared to face the possibility that interest and principal payments due may not be forthcoming.

CAPITAL GAINS
POTENTIAL

More than many other bonds, junk bonds offer the hope of capital gains. That is because the price at which you buy them presumably already reflects all the known and anticipated problems the issuer faces. If the issuer's fortunes improve, or even if they do not turn out to be as bad as investors generally expected, the bond-trading community may come to view a junk bond in a more favorable light, and thus bid up its price. An improving state of affairs at the company may also sooner or later prompt rating agencies to raise their appraisal of the bond, enabling it to sell at higher prices.

The inevitable other side of the coin is the possibility, or even the likelihood, that the issuer's circumstances will continue to deteriorate, causing the bond's price to fall even further. In the extreme, the issuer could fall into hopeless bankruptcy, leaving you with little or nothing.

In these respects, it can be seen that a junk bond behaves in some ways like a speculative stock. However, junk-bond owners retain one edge on holders of the issuer's common shares—their claim on the company's assets comes ahead of that of the stockholders in case of bankruptcy liquidation.

INCOME POTENTIAL

Junk-bond buyers also hope to profit from their investments by realizing greater income than a higher-rated debt security offers. To the degree that the present or future health of an issuer is in question, bond-market forces normally set a junk bond's price at a level that produces a high yield from interest payments.

Naturally, there is a gamble involved here. If timely payments of interest were certain, the market theoretically wouldn't let the bond sell at such a high-yielding level. And should payments on the debt represented by the bond stop for any reason, suddenly there is no income for the bond owner at all. Thus, while junk bonds can pay off handsomely in income, they are a dubious proposition for people who rely on a steady stream of income from their investments, with an emphasis on safety of their principal.

RISKS AND
DRAWBACKS

As the above discussions emphasize, investing in junk bonds is a risky endeavor. The degree of risk involved with any given bond can be measured in two ways: by the letter assessment the bond rating agencies assign to the security, and by its yield in comparison with yields offered by top-grade securities with similar terms, maturities and other characteristics. The lower the bond rating, the greater the risk as assessed by professional credit analysts. The greater the yield disparity, the greater the risk as assessed by participants in the market itself.

One tactic you can use to reduce risk in junk-bond investing is to diversify the money you have available into bonds of several different issuers. That way, if some of the investments do not work out, your losses on them may be more than offset by profits from your successful choices. If you do not have the capital to do this on your own, you can search out a mutual fund or other pooled investment that owns a diversified portfolio of junk bonds.

Junk bonds, furthermore, are not immune to interest-rate risk. At their depressed prices, most owners of a junk bond may be more concerned with events taking place affecting the issuer than with the general levels of interest rates. But if prices of all long-term debt securities make a sustained move in either direction, they will probably pull a junk bond's price along with them. As should be clear from all of the foregoing, money invested in junk bonds should be money you can afford to lose.

LIQUIDITY

Since conservative investing institutions and individuals tend to shy away from junk bonds, the market for them cannot be expected to enjoy as much consistent liquidity as the markets for top-grade interest-bearing securities. But speculative interest in junk bonds is often great enough to enable you to find one that can be traded relatively easily at a time of your choosing. This applies, however, only as long as the issuer's situation doesn't get too hopeless. Once a case gets into bankruptcy court, you may have only two choices: to sell at a very depressed price, or to wait years to find out whether you will get anything of value at all in return for your investment.

Of course, speculation in junk bonds often goes on even at the bankruptcy level. That is when some especially aggressive investors like to buy, in the hope that a resolution of the situation will someday bring handsome rewards.

Timing is almost always a major uncertainty when you invest in securities of troubled issuers. Junk bond buyers often must be prepared to wait for long periods to learn whether their hopes will be rewarded. Therefore, junk bonds are not a logical place to pursue short-term financial goals, or to put money you may need for other purposes in the near future.

TAX ADVANTAGES
AND DISADVANTAGES

Profits and losses realized on junk bonds are taxed at capital gains rates, long-term or short-term, depending on the length of time between purchase and sale. Interest received is subject to the normal tax treatment of interest. If you speculate in the depressed bonds of a troubled municipality or other issuer of tax-free bonds, whatever you receive that is designated as interest will be exempt from federal income tax.

An aggressive investor might choose to put, say, shares of a junk-bond mutual fund in an individual retirement account, Keogh plan or other tax-favored savings plan. More conservative investors would probably be better off looking elsewhere for IRA and Keogh investments.

MUNICIPAL BONDS

DESCRIPTION

Municipal bonds—the general term used to describe interest-bearing securities issued by state and local government entities—occupy a special place in the investment spectrum because the interest they pay is exempt from federal income tax. In the past they were considered primarily a vehicle for banks and wealthy individuals. But as inflation has pushed more and more Americans into high tax brackets, they have come to appeal to a wide range of investors.

The municipal-bond market is huge, with tens of thousands of issuing entities and hundreds of thousands of individual issues. It operates through a network of full-service financial firms and specialized municipal-bond dealers across the country who maintain contact through telephone and electronic linkups. Any individual investor operating with a relatively modest amount of capital is a small frog in this very big pond. But as a group, individual investors are an important factor in the market.

Municipals come in two basic categories—general obligation and revenue bonds. General obligation issues are backed by the full financial power of the issuer, including its ability to set and collect taxes. Revenue bonds, by contrast, are typically backed only by the income expected from a given source for which the bond issue provides capital—for example, a toll highway or sewer system. General obligation bonds are generally thought of as the better credit risk of the two types, all other things being equal.

A municipal bond used to finance low-income housing may have the backing of a federal government agency. A municipal bond issue or managed municipal bond portfolio, such as a unit trust, may be covered by private insurance on timely payment of interest and principal. However, as a general rule, no municipal bond is quite as safe as a U.S. Treasury security that carries a blanket pledge of the federal government.

The presence of credit risk in municipal bonds was emphasized in investors' minds by the financial problems of New York City in the mid-1970s and the Washington Public Power Supply System (whose acronym led to the nickname *Whoops* in the early 1980s). Still, as a class, municipals are generally ranked just a bit below U.S. government securities, and a bit above corporate bonds, as safe investments.

HOW AND WHERE TO GET
INFORMATION AND INVEST

Unless you are a full-time professional equipped with elaborate facilities, you probably cannot hope to monitor all that occurs in the municipal bond markets on your own. But many specialized municipal-bond dealers and financial-services firms market municipal bonds aggressively, and stand ready to provide you with a wide array of information on municipal bonds and available issues. There are numerous mutual funds and unit trusts investing in municipal bonds to choose among.

COSTS OF BUYING,
OWNING AND SELLING

In some cases, you may pay a commission when you buy or sell a municipal bond, say, if you conduct the transaction through a financial institution that is not normally an active participant in the market. But normally, brokers and dealers collect their fees on municipal fund sales and purchases in the form of a spread between their buying and selling prices. Thus, it can be difficult to know your precise costs when you invest in municipals.

This does not deter many investors, however. They seek to mitigate the difficulty of comparing transaction costs charged by one dealer or another by shopping around for the best yield available on comparable issues, after all transaction costs.

Depending on whom you ask, the minimum investment with which you should seek to make an attractive direct purchase of municipal bonds is $5,000, $10,000, $25,000 or even higher. Just about everyone agrees that you will need $100,000 or more if you want a diversified portfolio of bonds or expect to sell the bonds you are buying before maturity at attractive rates.

With relatively small amounts to invest, many advisers say investors are better off shopping among municipal-bond unit trusts and mutual funds. An exception to this general rule may arise, however, if you establish a good working relationship with a broker or dealer who can find you *odd lots,* small tag ends of bond issues, that are priced at attractive yields to get them out of a bond firm's inventory.

CAPITAL GAINS
POTENTIAL

Like all fixed-income securities, municipal bonds are subject to price fluctuations in periods of volatile interest rates. For investors seeking tax-free income, this means that municipals pose the risk of capital losses, and also the chance of capital gains that they may not particularly want. Long-term capital gains are taxed at relatively low rates, but they are taxed.

Professional dealers regularly realize gains and losses on municipal bonds in the course of doing business. But most individual investors lack the time, the resources and the expertise to buy and sell municipal bonds in the hope of realizing trading profits.

INCOME POTENTIAL

The primary appeal of municipal bonds for most individual investors is generous after-tax income. Whether they are a desirable way for you to pursue that goal depends on your individual tax bracket and prevailing market conditions.

Assume, for the sake of illustration, that you are faced with the choice of a municipal bond, exempt from federal income taxation of interest, yielding 8 percent, and a taxable corporate bond of the same credit standing yielding 12 percent. If you are in the 50 percent tax bracket, the municipal bond has the evident edge, since the corporate issue would leave you with only a 6 percent return after taxes. But if you are in, say, the 28 percent tax bracket, you would come out slightly ahead with the corporate bond.

The emotional appeal of *tax-free* income can cause some investors to buy municipals in haste without considering the alternatives. Most securities firms will readily provide you with a table that makes this arithmetical exercise a simple task.

RISKS AND
DRAWBACKS

Many people are first drawn to municipal securities when they realize with a shock how much of their interest from a bank or savings institution is being drained off by taxes. When they see advertising that shows "how much better off" they would be in municipals, they are quick to respond.

However, municipal bonds are not strictly comparable with vehicles like bank certificates of deposit. There is the matter of federal deposit insurance on the bank account, for one thing. Even if you opt for a municipal security that has backing from a federal agency, or some other insurance or guarantee that looks ironclad, there is market risk to be considered. Prices of municipal bonds change constantly as interest rates rise and fall.

The temptation of tax-free income can also attract investors who might be better off seeking long-term growth of their capital in stocks, say, or real estate. However, for people who want or need high current after-tax income, who are in relatively high tax brackets and who understand municipal bonds, the allure of their tax advantage can be very real and compelling.

LIQUIDITY

It is axiomatic that investors should buy municipal securities with the intention of holding them to maturity, unless they are dealing in very large amounts. The secondary market in municipals is big and active, but most dealers prefer to handle orders only in large amounts. So if you should want to sell, say, $10,000 in bonds that have several years of life remaining, you may have to accept a significant price concession to reach a deal.

However, you can cope with this liquidity obstacle in several ways. First of all, the amount of municipals available at any given time is usually large, in maturities ranging from a few weeks to many years. So you can generally choose a maturity at the time you buy that pretty well fits your circumstances.

If you are very unsure about when you might want or need your principal back, you can choose a mutual fund that offers the constant opportunity to redeem any or all of your investment on short notice. Or you might select a municipal bond with a *put* feature that gives you the right, under certain specified conditions, to cash it in.

The reverse of a *put* privilege in some municipal bonds, as in other types of bonds, is a *call* provision. This spells out conditions under which the issuer can call in a given bond issue early, at its discretion. No bond, municipal or otherwise, should be bought without a thorough understanding of any and all circumstances in which you might be required to redeem your investment early.

TAX ADVANTAGES
AND DISADVANTAGES

The tax appeal of municipal bonds seems straightforward indeed—investors who own them need pay no federal income tax on the interest they receive. But that interest may be subject to state and local income tax, unless you pick a bond of the city or state in which you live. Sellers of municipal bonds and bond fund and trusts heavily promote "double" or "triple-tax-free" products in places where state and local, as well as federal, income taxes are substantial.

Investors in municipal bonds need to manage their activities carefully if they also are engaged in borrowing money. The government has imposed rules to prevent people from taking out loans, with tax-deductible interest, to buy tax-exempt bonds. Even if this is not your intended purpose, an ill-timed loan you take out may be construed by the tax authorities to be a violation of this rule.

Municipal bonds, with their own separate tax advantages, are unsuitable for use in tax-favored savings programs such as individual retirement accounts and Keogh plans.

FLOATING-RATE AND PUT BONDS

DESCRIPTION

When volatile interest rates brought instability to the bond market in the 1970s and early 1980s, some bond issuers and their advisers on Wall Street responded by devising new types of bonds designed to float more comfortably in choppy financial waters. The first was the floating-rate note or bond, whose interest payments are regularly adjusted to conform with prevailing interest-rate trends. For example, Citicorp, the New York-based bank holding company, has an issue of floating-rate notes due to mature in the year 2010. As with most other bonds, interest payments on these notes are made just twice a year. But the rate to be paid is adjusted monthly. Other issuers may change the rate more or less often.

A second alternative that gained increasing acceptance in the 1980s was a bond with a *put* provision—a contractual clause that gives owners the right to sell the bond back to the issuer, at a specified time or times, before maturity at face value. The put privilege is intended to keep the bond's price from straying very far from face value, regardless of the ups and downs of interest rates.

Both types of securities, because of their special structures, take on some characteristics of short-term money market securities, despite their relatively long lives. They may be less vulnerable to price fluctuations than straight bonds. For this benefit, however, you must normally pay a price in the form of lower yields than would be available from a fixed-rate bond. Furthermore, these yields are unpredictable.

Floating-rate and put bonds have been sold by various types of issuers, including corporations and state and local governments. Another variation on this theme is a put unit trust, with a portfolio of municipal bonds bought from financial institutions that agree to buy them back at any time during the life of the trust.

HOW AND WHERE TO GET
INFORMATION AND INVEST

Any good broker will most likely be able to provide you with information on floating-rate and put bonds, and can handle your orders to buy or sell them. Some floating-rate issues of large bank holding companies are listed and traded on stock exchanges. Others are bought and sold by dealers in the over-the-counter bond markets. Some investment firms package and sell securities of this type in the form of unit trusts.

Issuers normally advise their investors and the public when they change the interest rate on a floating-rate bond. If you do not regularly follow such developments in the bond market, a broker should be able to bring you up to date on current prices and interest rates.

COSTS OF BUYING, OWNING AND SELLING

If you buy a floating-rate or put bond in the secondary market, or sell it before maturity, you can expect to pay the standard commission on bond transactions. Buying a newly issued floating-rate or put bond, and cashing it in at maturity, normally involves little or no out-of-pocket cost to investors. Before investing in a put bond, you may wish to determine what, if any, charges would be incurred should you exercise your put privilege. If you invest through a unit trust, you may be charged a sales commission of perhaps 3 percent to 4 percent.

CAPITAL GAINS POTENTIAL

These securities are designed for investors who want stability of principal, rather than the possibility of capital gains or losses. But while floating-rate or put bonds may be cushioned against market risk, they are not always immune to it. Thus you may, inadvertently, realize a capital gain or loss from an investment in a floating-rate or put bond. However, these vehicles are not a logical place to seek long-term growth through price appreciation, or short-term trading profits.

INCOME POTENTIAL

Floating-rate and put bonds are set up to provide a relatively long-term investment that can compete, to a certain degree at least, with short-term securities like Treasury bills and commercial paper. Indeed, the interest payments made on floating-rate bonds are typically calculated from a formula based on some specified open-market interest rate or rates.

Because they are long-term commitments involving some long-term risk, floating-rate and put bonds generally must carry yields at least slightly higher than returns available on, say, Treasury bills, in order to attract investors. These yields, however, tend to be well below what investors can get on straight long-term securities. That lower interest outlay is what makes the concept of floating-rate and put bonds attractive to issuers.

With floating-rate bonds, you cannot "lock in" a given interest rate for a long period of time. With put bonds, you can lock in a given rate, but it is unlikely to be competitive with yields available on other fixed bonds.

RISKS AND
DRAWBACKS

Floating-rate and put bonds represent a kind of compromise between long- and short-term interest-bearing investments. As with any other hybrid type of security, they bear some careful study. To an active, aggressive investor, they might have limited appeal. If you think interest rates are going to rise, such an investor might say, you are best off putting your money in ordinary money market investments. If you think interest rates are going to fall, you are best off buying fixed-rate bonds whose prices will benefit most from such a drop.

As was stated above, floating-rate and put bonds may minimize market risk, but they don't necessarily eliminate it. Floating-rate issues usually have preset floor and ceiling levels beyond which their rates cannot be adjusted. If prevailing rates surpass the ceiling point, a given floating-rate issue will tend to start acting more like a fixed-rate bond, and its price will decline. Similarly, a put bond whose put privilege doesn't become effective until a date, say, five years away, will probably not have the kind of flexibility in the eyes of investors that a Treasury bill would.

Though in some ways they may behave like short-term investments, floating-rate and put bonds retain some of the important characteristics, and drawbacks, of ordinary fixed-rate securities. They represent long-term commitments of your money, and require a long-term evaluation as credit risks—i.e., the extent of danger that the issuer might not be able to make timely payments of interest and principal. Though they are designed to provide a measure of price stability, they are still subject to constant evaluation by the markets themselves. If a given issue or these securities as a group should decline in popularity with investors, the going price may reflect that by declining as well.

Put bonds also generally have call provisions, spelling out circumstances under which the issuer can require investors to cash them in before maturity. These can adversely affect their prices and yields from the investor's point of view, and merit thorough understanding and evaluation before you invest.

LIQUIDITY

The liquidity of various floating-rate and put bonds varies from specific security to security. For example, a put bond whose put privilege becomes effective in the very near future may be a highly liquid place to put your money. A unit trust made up of floating-rate bonds may be redeemable at any time through the trust's sponsor.

However, investors should always bear in mind that these are relatively long-term securities, and cannot as a class match the liquidity of something like a money market mutual fund. Their liquidity in the future may vary with their general popularity. The short history of these investments suggests that they are most popular when interest rates are high and volatile, and less popular when rates are low.

TAX ADVANTAGES
AND DISADVANTAGES

Interest paid on these securities is subject to the standard tax rules for bonds. In the case of municipal floating-rate and put bonds, it is exempt from federal income tax. In the case of corporate issues, it is taxable. Any gains or losses realized when you sell or cash in your investment come under the standard capital-gains tax rules.

A taxable floating-rate or put issue is eligible for use in an individual retirement account, Keogh plan or other tax-favored savings program, if you find these securities an appealing way to minimize the time you spend worrying about the ups and downs of interest rates.

CERTIFICATES OF DEPOSIT

DESCRIPTION

Certificates of deposit issued by banks and savings institutions play a major role in the American financial system. They come in many forms and sizes, with maturities ranging from a few days or weeks to several years. There are "jumbo" CDs in which institutions and professional investors may routinely invest millions of dollars at a crack. And there are time deposit CDs, sometimes called savings certificates, which small investors may buy for as little as a few hundred dollars. No matter how it is structured, a CD is fundamentally a simple proposition—a loan of money by the buyer to a bank or savings institution for a specified period of time, in return for interest on that money.

The dividing line that separates big from small CDs is $100,000—the maximum amount of federal deposit insurance on principal and interest allowed for any single account with any single institution. If you invest more than $100,000 in a CD, you take some degree of credit risk—the chance that the issuer will fail, or for some other reason be unable to make timely payments of principal and interest.

If you buy a small CD, by contrast, there is theoretically no credit risk, assuming that the federal deposit insurance agencies can fulfill their promise to cover any losses in any situation. Financial experts may debate this assumption philosophically, but in practice it seems safe to take it as a given. If events ever reach the point that federal government insurance can't withstand them, just about all types of financial investments would probably suffer greatly in the resulting collapse of confidence.

HOW AND WHERE TO GET
INFORMATION AND INVEST

With bank deregulation, finding the best possible deal in a CD is no longer a simple matter of inquiring at your local bank or savings institution. Depository institutions are free to offer whatever interest rates they choose on CDs, and to set other terms such as minimum deposits and methods of compounding interest at their own discretion. So at least a reasonable amount of shopping around is in order.

In the mid-1980s, many securities brokerage firms got into the CD act. The brokerage houses bought packages of CDs from depository institutions that were seeking additional ways to attract deposits, and then resold them to individual investors. Since the brokers could easily shop the nationwide market, they were often able to find CDs with very attractive yields. Furthermore, they could make a continuous market in these CDs, thus permitting investors to cash them in before maturity without incurring the standard penalty for early withdrawal.

At this writing, however, federal regulators were moving toward curbing or eliminating brokered CDs. They argued that the practice allowed weak or poorly managed banks in effect to abuse the federal deposit insurance program, putting more strain on that program than it was designed to take.

COSTS OF BUYING, OWNING AND SELLING

There are normally no commissions or other fees involved in buying or cashing in CDs at maturity. But you can incur a substantial cost if you want to take money out of a time-deposit savings certificate before it reaches maturity. The rules state that, in cases involving certificates of one year or less, the minimum penalty that must be charged is 31 days' interest. For longer maturities, it is three months' interest. Individual institutions can set higher penalties if they choose.

Whatever the specified penalty, it applies even if you have not owned the CD long enough to earn sufficient interest to cover it. For example, suppose you bought a six-month CD a week ago, and now find that you have a pressing need for the money. If you make an early withdrawal, you will have to give up the week's interest you earned, plus enough of the money you originally invested to cover 24 more days' worth of interest.

CAPITAL GAINS POTENTIAL

Specialized dealers and other financial institutions trade large CDs routinely in the money markets, realizing profits and losses as they do. Because of the huge amounts they deal in and the sophistication of their operations, it is not a practical proposition for individual investors to seek to participate in this market. Otherwise, CDs offer no hope for capital gains. But they can be used as a means of seeking long-term growth through compounding of interest.

INCOME POTENTIAL

CDs are a primary money-management tool for savers and investors who want maximum income and safety from their assets. Small CDs once were relatively inflexible, available only in a few maturities under strict regulations. But since many banking rules have been lifted, that problem has largely disappeared.

Some depository institutions offer *designer CDs*—certificates in any maturity you wish, from three months to, say, 10 years. If you want to put an odd amount like $4,675.22 in a CD for 177 days, the institution will simply consult its current formula for the interest rates it will pay and quote you a rate on the deal you want. Alternatively, you can tell an institution that operates this way how much money you want to have by a given future date, and the institution will compute how much you need to invest now to achieve that result.

Not all banks and savings institutions offer this virtually unlimited flexibility. But any good one should at least have a wide array of choices available. When you are shopping for a CD, designer or otherwise, it makes sense to inquire at several institutions. After making certain that all of these are covered by federal deposit insurance— most, but not all, depository institutions are—you may find that they quote rates in a variety of ways (simple interest, for instance, or with compounding presumed). The most pertinent question to ask at this point is the actual yield you will receive over the life of the CD.

In periods of volatile interest rates, timing is of the essence in buying CDs. Ideally, you should have your money in a money market deposit account, money market mutual fund, or very short-term CD in periods when interest rates are rising. Just as rates hit their peak, you shift your money into a long-term CD, "locking in" a high return while yields on short-term investments begin to drop.

If this kind of thing were easy to do, many, many people would live in mansions and own yachts. Predicting interest-rate changes is a challenge that has defied the most knowledgeable and respected experts. You may count yourself fortunate and astute if you are even moderately successful in timing your investments in CDs.

RISKS AND
DRAWBACKS

CDs may offer attractive returns on your money. In amounts of less than $100,000, insured CDs are exceedingly safe. If you are a conscientious saver, you can build up a nice nest egg over time investing in CDs. But they do not offer the kind of growth, under favorable tax circumstances, that you can seek in investments like stocks or real estate. The degree of protection from inflation you get with a CD is limited at best.

Furthermore, an ill-timed purchase of a CD can be a very disappointing investment, especially if you go with a long-term one. Suppose, for example, that you put your entire savings of $25,000 in a five-year CD at an interest rate of 9 percent. Within a few months, interest rates rise substantially. CDs are now available at 12 percent, but your money is locked up.

In extreme cases like this, especially when you have held an old CD for a while, it may pay to consider making an early withdrawal, incurring the penalty, and investing what remains in a new CD. Before you buy a CD, you may wish to inquire whether the institution with which you are dealing would permit you to take such a step in the future.

LIQUIDITY

As the foregoing discussion indicates, CDs, particularly long-term ones, present a liquidity problem. If you want or need money in a CD before it matures, you face the early-withdrawal penalty. In addition, a depository institution may refuse to allow the withdrawal—especially in cases where no emergency or hardship is involved.

Some people seek to improve the liquidity of their CD investments by spreading their money among several maturities. For example, you could put one sixth of your savings in a six-month CD every month for six months, reinvesting in new six-month CDs as each one matures. That way, you would have regular access to some of your capital. Before you embark on such a plan, it makes sense to assess how much more you can earn on your money in that way than you could by simply sticking with a liquid short-term money market investment.

TAX ADVANTAGES
AND DISADVANTAGES

CDs are popular vehicles for individual retirement accounts, Keogh plans and other tax-favored savings programs. Beyond that, their virtues are few from a tax viewpoint. All interest earned on CDs is taxable as ordinary income for the year in which it is paid. If taxable investors reinvest their interest, seeking the benefits of compounding, they still must face that tax obligation.

There is one consolation of sorts for people who must pay early-withdrawal penalties to get their money out of a CD. The penalty is tax-deductible.

CENTRAL ASSETS ACCOUNTS

DESCRIPTION

In the late 1970s, the investment firm of Merrill Lynch, Pierce, Fenner & Smith, introduced a multi-purpose money mangement and investment vehicle known as the Cash Management Account. It was designed to attract investors interested in consolidating their stock and bond trading, money market investing and borrowing in a single account, covered by one monthly statement.

Attract them it did. Within a few years, Merrill Lynch had more than 1 million CMA customers, and many other brokerage firms, as well as a few mutual fund compaines and a growing number of banks and savings institutions, were offering similar accounts under various names. They came to be known generically as central assets accounts.

The financial institutions had their own reasons for liking these accounts. They enabled them to build a solid customer base, and provided a ready source of information on which of their customers were prime candidates for each of the financial services they provided.

No two central assets accounts are exactly alike. But all typically offer stock and bond brokerage service—full service, discount, or both—a credit or debit card, ready access to credit through checkwriting, and an automatic *sweep* of any idle funds into an interest-bearing money market account. Some make available such extras as investment and tax planning services.

Their great popularity is eloquent testimony to the appeal of central assets accounts. Before opening such an account, however, investors should consider whether the benefits to be gained will be worth the cost in fees. People who have trouble managing their use of credit should proceed especially carefully, because these accounts may make it extremely easy to borrow as well as to save and invest.

HOW AND WHERE TO GET
INFORMATION AND INVEST

Institutions that offer central assets accounts typically have abundant information about them ready to provide at the slightest sign of interest on your part. It makes sense to study the literature from several institutions before deciding to proceed. In particular, it is necessary to consider what features of a central assets account you are likely to use most, and whether these features seem to be strong points in a given institution's account.

Close attention should be given to the sample monthly statement in the literature (if it is not included, ask for one). Does it give you a clear picture of what you are getting? A key element in central assets accounts is the quality of service the sponsoring institution provides. If the promotional material for them and the sample monthly statement don't seem well designed, you may well have reason to question the kind of service you can expect after an account is opened.

COSTS OF BUYING,
OWNING AND SELLING

Most sponsors of central assets accounts charge an annual fee to cover their administrative costs in processing information for the accounts. Most are in the $40 to $125 range, while some providing extensive planning and consultation service are much higher. In addition, your activities will still incur all the other standard costs. If you buy or sell securities, you will pay a brokerage commission. If you borrow money, you will be charged interest. It is important to determine how any individual institution sets its rates on these transactions, and whether they would differ significantly from what you would pay if you managed your finances some other way.

A minimum initial investment is normally required to open a central assets account. It may be set at $5,000, $10,000 or $100,000, or somewhere in between. For this opening ante, some institutions will accept marketable securities as well as cash. Once the account is open, most institutions don't require that your account always meet the initial-balance standard.

CAPITAL GAINS
POTENTIAL

Operating through a central assets account won't cause an overnight improvement in your skill as an investor, or magically transform your broker into a stock-picking wizard. But it may lighten your paperwork load in pursuing your capital-gains goals, and help you go about your mission better organized than you were before.

INCOME POTENTIAL ·

One of the primary attractions of central-assets accounts is the automatic investment of any surplus, idle funds in a money market investment that keeps the money at work earning interest. Details of this *sweep* arrangement can vary significantly from institution to institution. But in most cases, this feature can materially improve the income you receive on all the money at your disposal. At least part of any added income realized, of course, will be consumed by the annual fee charged for maintaining the account.

RISKS AND
DRAWBACKS

Investments made through central-assets accounts carry all the standard risks. The money market aspect of the account may be extremely safe—in fact, it may be covered by federal deposit insurance up to $100,000 per account. It is important to understand, however, that insurance in no way applies to money you put at risk in, say, stocks.

A central assets account also may give you access to sources of credit you are not used to dealing with. Using your new plastic card or checkbook, for instance, you may find it all too convenient to borrow instantly for consumer purchases from your life's savings. People who know they have problems with this sort of temptation might well approach central assets accounts warily.

On the other hand, a central assets account can in some cases give you access to benefits—for example, free checking, if it is offered—you might not have previously been able to obtain. Managed successfully, it could enhance your credit standing and encourage you to explore investment opportunities you had not previously considered.

LIQUIDITY

Central assets accounts, by their very nature, are highly liquid. The cornerstone on which they are based, a money market mutual fund or money market deposit account, affords instant liquidity. In addition, they can facilitate the use of your money to best advantage by providing a convenient means of tapping any and all of your assets when an opportunity arises.

However, you must still weigh individually the prospective liquidity of investments you choose to make through a central assets account, and the safeguards it offers—e.g., federal deposit insurance and-or membership in the Securities Investor Protection Corp.

TAX ADVANTAGES
AND DISADVANTAGES

A central assets account confers no special tax status on your money-management activities. Gains and losses realized, dividends received, and interest earned and paid, are all subject to their usual tax treatment. Many central assets accounts offer investors choices to reduce their taxes—for instance, the option of using a short-term tax-free money fund in place of a taxable money fund or money market deposit account.

The use of a central assets account, moreover, may be helpful in tax planning by providing you with a running picture of the taxable income and losses you have realized at any point in a given year. It may pay to investigate beforehand how much help a sponsor of a central assets account is likely to be in this regard by inquiring, for example, whether the institution returns checks written on the account, or makes other adequate provisions for tax-record keeping.

CLOSED-END FUNDS

DESCRIPTION

Closed-end funds, formally called publicly traded investment companies, are a close but relatively little-known relative of the more common mutual funds. They are companies organized to pool their shareholders' money and invest in a portfolio of stocks, bonds or both. Unlike mutual funds, however, closed-end funds do not continuously offer new shares to investors, nor do they stand ready to redeem shares for cash at any time of a shareholder's choosing. Instead, their shares are bought and sold on stock exchanges or in the over-the-counter market.

Some closed-end funds invest in a wide range of securities. Others confine themselves to specialties like bonds, or securities of a single country (examples: the Japan Fund, the Mexico Fund, and ASA Ltd., which concentrates on South African gold-mining stocks). Another variation on the same theme is the dual purpose closed-end fund, which issues two classes of stock. One entitles the holder to all the dividend and interest income produced by the fund's portfolio; the other gives the holder a claim on all capital gains attained.

An intriguing feature of closed-end funds is that the prices of their shares, as determined in the open market, tend to fluctuate either above (at a *premium*) or below (at a *discount*) the net asset values of their portfolios. Some followers of the industry advocate trading strategies aimed at taking advantage of these fluctuations.

HOW AND WHERE TO GET
INFORMATION AND INVEST

A typical stockbroker may not aggressively push closed-end funds, but any good one should be able to provide you with information on them if you ask for it. In fact, there are some brokers who make a specialty of following the funds and buying and selling them for clients. Large investment advisory services such as the Value Line Investment Survey also publish information on them. A trade group, the Association of Publicly Traded Investment Funds, has headquarters at 201 N. Charles St., Baltimore, Md. 21201.

Brokers handle buy and sell orders for closed-end fund shares just as they do for any other listed or over-the-counter stocks. Many financial and general-interest newspapers publish daily or weekly tables of closed-end fund net asset values and the current discounts or premiums at which they are trading.

COSTS OF BUYING,
OWNING AND SELLING

Brokers charge commissions to buy and sell closed-end funds, just as they do with other stocks. Investors who rely on their own research to make decisions about closed-end fund investments can seek to minimize commission costs by dealing with a discount broker.

As with a mutual fund, the return a closed-end fund can produce is reduced by the management fee charged by the fund's sponsor, which is paid periodically out of the fund's assets. It is recommended that investors considering buying shares in a closed-end fund familiarize themselves beforehand with all fees collected by the sponsor.

CAPITAL GAINS
POTENTIAL

The capital gains potential of closed-end funds naturally varies with their stated objectives. Aggressive stock funds typically emphasize capital appreciation as a goal, while a bond fund organized primarily to provide income may give such gains a low priority. However, because the value of an investment in a closed-end fund is determined by the open market from day to day, all of these funds have at least some capital gains potential and the attendant risk of capital losses. This potential can be enhanced by changes in a fund's share price from a large discount as compared with net asset value to a smaller discount, or even a premium.

Some brokers and investment advisers recommend a strategy of buying closed-end funds in periods when their discounts are large by historical standards, and selling them when they trade at small discounts or premiums. In the bear markets of the 1970s, closed-end stock funds typically traded at large discounts. After the bull market that began in 1982, many rose to premiums.

In addition, a special set of circumstances can occasionally arise that creates a capital gain for closed-end fund investors. This occurs when a decision is made, either by fund management or outside shareholders with the necessary voting strength, to liquidate a fund selling at a discount, or alternatively to convert it to open-ended (i.e., mutual fund) status. Example: When a closed-end fund selling for $15, with a net asset value of $18, is converted into a mutual fund, stockholders can redeem their shares directly through the fund at the net asset value of $18.

INCOME POTENTIAL
Closed-end funds specializing in bonds tend to offer yields comparable with those available in bond mutual funds and directly in bonds themselves. Students of closed-end bond funds watch them closely, however, for any occasion in which a widening discount in the fund's price pushes its yield above prevailing levels on alternative investments.

RISKS AND
DRAWBACKS
As with any investment company, the basic risk with a closed-end fund is that its portfolio of securities will perform poorly. Unlike mutual funds, however, closed-end funds present a second layer of risk— even if they invest well, market conditions may be such that the price of their stock falls, say, from a premium to a discount. This can happen in any period when investor enthusiasm for closed-end funds declines. Even if a fund is bought at a discount from its net asset value, there is no assurance that the discount will not be even wider when you want to sell.

Some funds may invest in securities that they cannot easily sell, for one reason or another. For instance, they may hold an interest in a company whose stock is not publicly traded. Share prices of such funds may be especially volatile. Before investing in a closed-end fund, it is important to be sure you understand its investment goals and philosophy, and determine that they are consistent with your own aims.

LIQUIDITY

The larger closed-end funds traded actively on stock exchanges or in the over-the-counter market enjoy the liquidity that those popular marketplaces provide. Under normal conditions, they can be bought and sold as easily as any other stock with an active market. This liquidity, however, is presumed rather than assured for any given time in the future. It could be reduced in periods when markets are depressed.

Smaller funds with less active markets are likely to be less liquid. When you sell any significant amount of their shares, it is possible that you may have to accept a price well below the last reported trade.

TAX ADVANTAGES
AND DISADVANTAGES

Closed-end funds carry the same prospective tax advantages and disadvantages as other common stocks. If shares of a fund are held for more than six months, they qualify for long-term federal tax treatment, with a maximum tax rate of 20 percent on any gains realized. Some states and localities also impose taxes on capital gains.

Short-term capital gains on any shares sold within six months of purchase are subject to federal income tax at ordinary-income rates of up to 50 percent. So are dividends and interest earned and paid out by the funds. Some states and localities impose taxes on these sources of income as well.

Closed-end funds may be a candidate for individual retirement plans, Keogh plans and other tax-favored savings programs, particularly if you have a self-directed plan with a brokerage firm.

COLLECTIBLES

DESCRIPTION

In the late 1970s, when inflation was running at a fever pitch in the U.S. economy, *collectibles* became the rage of the investment world. Prices of these tangible objects—ranging from art works, antiques, gems and numismatic coins to baseball cards and old model trains—rose at rates that protected their owners from the ravages of inflation, and often brought them handsome after-inflation profits as well. Almost anything seemed to qualify as a collectible, as long as it had some aesthetic or cultural appeal and scarcity value.

When inflation subsided in the early 1980s, the collectibles craze cooled noticeably. Many of their owners discovered, if they already didn't know, that promises of big profits stretching out into the infinite future were exaggerated. It is possible to pay too high a price for anything, no matter how rare or beautiful it may be. All that having been said, collectible investments still have a large and loyal fan club. Collecting for enjoyment and the hope of profit has a long history, and doubtless a long future as well.

Most experts say the key to success in collectibles is to pick a field that particularly interests you and specialize in it, developing as much expertise as possible. As with any type of investment, the value of a collectible is the highest price any available buyer is willing to pay for it at any given moment. But with rare or aesthetic objects, there is no daily table in the newspaper, as there is with financial investments like stocks, to keep you readily informed of what that price might be.

Markets for most collectibles operate through loose networks of dealers and sophisticated investors adept at spotting both bargains to acquire, and uninformed buyers to whom they can sell at high prices. To participate successfully, you need enough information and experience to match wits with them and at least hold your own.

Expertise is also necessary because, in the case of almost every collectible, there is the possibility of being sold an outright fake. Or you could be fooled by an item that has been altered, cleaned or repaired in a way that gives it an impressive appearance to the uninformed eye, but greatly diminishes its value among knowledgeable investors. If you are just starting out in a given collectibles field, it is very helpful to have the advice and counsel of a dealer or other expert whom you know well and trust.

HOW AND WHERE TO GET
INFORMATION AND INVEST

Collectibles can be found almost anywhere—at stores and shops that specialize in them, at auctions and in catalogs, but also unexpectedly at flea markets or, in the classic dream, covered with dust but otherwise unblemished in your grandmother's attic. Sources of information on collectibles are just as diverse—dealers and fellow collectors, specialized publications such as magazines or newsletters.

As in most investment markets, the most valuable information is often that which is known to the fewest people. Many serious collectors develop their own private networks of sources, including dealers who know the collector's interests, tastes and approximate investment budget. The hope of doing repeat business with a valued customer provides an incentive to consistently fair, reasonable and honest practices on the part of a dealer.

COSTS OF BUYING,
OWNING AND SELLING

Cost is a very important consideration in collectibles. For the beginner in particular, you must often buy at retail prices and sell at wholesale when your source is a dealer. Dealers, like any other business people, need to cover their costs of operating and want to make a profit. In addition, commercial sales of collectibles are frequently subject to sales tax.

The costs don't usually stop with the purchase, either. Depending on the type of item involved, you may have to spend a good deal of money on a regular basis to keep it in optimum condition and protect it from the ravages of time, heat, cold, moisture and natural deterioration. If and whenever you need an appraisal, you will probably have to pay a fee for it.

Any object of value must be safeguarded, and thus may incur storage costs (e.g., for a safe deposit box). Because of the possibility of fire damage or theft, you may well need insurance. It should never be assumed that a standard home or renter's policy automatically covers some special item of value that you acquire.

There is, furthermore, an opportunity cost that goes with owning non-financial assets. When you invest in them, you must forego the dividends and interest your money could earn if it were in stocks, bonds or a bank.

CAPITAL GAINS
POTENTIAL

The two primary forces that drive the collectibles markets are the psychic rewards of collecting and the hope of long-term capital gains. The right investment at the right time in the right item in the right field can bring you plentiful amounts of both. But it must always be borne in mind that collectibles markets can be very fickle. At the time you buy, say, a two-tone sedan built in 1954, autos from that era may be considered fascinating examples of Americana, rare treasures of a unique period. At the time you want to sell, it is just possible that autos from the 1950s may be considered used cars.

Past evidence has shown that some collectibles markets are less prone to faddishness than others. These tend to be ones at the top end of the price spectrum, where you must compete with other investors possessed of great knowledge and sophistication and armed with large capital resources. Because of the way most collectibles markets work, it is generally difficult at best to try to turn a short-term profit in them, unless you are very sure of what you are doing and know where the prospective buyers and sellers are.

INCOME POTENTIAL

Collectibles are unsuitable, in general, for money from which you want or need to earn current income. Because of the costs involved, in fact, they most often wind up as a drain on your cash flow, when you buy them and as long as you own them. This does not mean that if you invest primarily for income, you automatically ought to sell a precious family heirloom and put the proceeds in bonds. The psychic and emotional value of a collectible item can be just as important as, or indeed much more important than, its financial value.

RISKS AND DRAWBACKS

Most of the varied, and substantial, risks and drawbacks of investing in collectibles have been mentioned above. There is the possibility that almost any item you buy could fall out of vogue, rot, rust, wrinkle, burn up in a fire, or even prove to be a forgery. Your dog could chew a hole in it, a thief could make off with it, or time could turn its silvery surface to a permanantly grotesque green. Years after you buy it, when you hope to cash in your profits, the economy could be mired in a recession, depression or panic in which nobody has a nickel to spend on collectibles.

Balancing these perils to at least some extent, however, is the special enjoyment you can get from collectibles while you own them—the admiring looks of friends and neighbors at the newest print on your wall, the joy of completing a set from diverse sources, the aesthetic delight that collecting adds to your life. Since there are intangible as well as tangible rewards to be obtained from investing in collectibles, each would-be participant in the game must compute his or her own risk-and-reward equation.

LIQUIDITY

Liquidity can be a chancy proposition with most collectibles. Some-thing that can probably only be sold through consignment to a dealer or auction house is not likely to be a well-advised place in which to put money you might need at a moment's notice. Liquidity varies greatly in degree from one type of collectible to another.

This problem can be neutralized, or nearly so, if you are in touch with a fellow collector or dealer of the most reliable sort who gives you a standing offer to buy an item or items from you at any time of your choosing. Some dealers in collectibles sell with a promise to buy back whenever you might wish. They may even specify a mimimum price. In cases like this, it pays to consider before buying whether the firm is still likely to be operating, in the same place and the same healthy financial condition, years from now when you want to take it up on that promise.

TAX ADVANTAGES
AND DISADVANTAGES

Because collecting can be considered either a hobby or a for-profit investment endeavor, tax considerations can be tricky in collectibles. If your prime purpose is profit, it is necessary to know and follow the sometimes arcane tax rules that determine whether your costs and any losses you suffer can be deducted on your tax returns. Whether it's the fun or the financial aspects that attract you, profits realized on sales of collectibles are taxable at capital gains rates.

Direct investments in collectibles are not permitted in tax-favored savings programs such as individual retirement accounts and Keogh plans, since they are regarded as "sterile" investments that don't do much to create jobs and promote growth in the economy. This rule has brought protests from some collectibles fanciers, but most investment advisers agree that collectibles aren't very well suited for IRAs and Keoghs anyway.

COMMERCIAL PAPER

DESCRIPTION

When an industrial corporation, finance company, bank holding company or state or local government wants to borrow money conveniently for a short period of time, it may sell commercial paper—a form of IOU. It may be backed by a bank line of credit or some other assurance, but is not secured by any assets of the issuer.

Commercial paper is issued in maturities ranging from a few days to nine months, commonly on a *discount* basis. In this kind of arrangement (which is also used with Treasury bills and some other money market investments), investors pay less than the face amount when they buy, and receive the face amount at maturity, with the difference constituting the interest they receive.

Like some other money market instruments, commercial paper is considered a vehicle primarily suited for professional investors and institutions. Indeed, the Securities and Exchange Commission, which does not require that commercial paper be registered with the SEC as long as issuers follow specified guidelines, has declared that paper should be sold only to "sophisticated" investors. Paper is most often bought and sold in six- or seven-figure amounts that put it beyond the practical reach of small investors.

But if you as an individual meet the standard of sophistication, and are convinced that commercial paper fits your money management needs, you may find direct sellers of paper willing to accommodate you in amounts as small as $25,000. Example: General Motors Acceptance Corp., the financial arm of the giant automobile manufacturer.

Even if you aren't sophisticated, you may well be an indirect investor in commercial paper if you own shares of a money market mutual fund. Many funds put some of their assets in commercial paper; some put all of them into it.

With the growth of money funds as a major participant in the commercial paper market, there has been relatively little incentive for brokers and other financial-services firms to develop other ways to market paper to individual investors. Even if your finances qualify you for direct investment in commercial paper, a money fund may be a preferable alternative because of the convenience, liquidity and diversification it offers. Diversification is an especially noteworthy attribute, because there is credit risk, ranging from slight to considerable, with any individual issue of commercial paper.

HOW AND WHERE TO GET
INFORMATION AND INVEST

When you read financial publications and the business sections of the general interest press, you seldom see advertisements promoting the availability of commercial paper issues and the returns they offer. There is a good reason for this: Government regulators discourage it. If you want to buy paper from direct issuers, therefore, you most likely will have to seek them out on your own. Friends or your local library may be of help.

You may also consult a banker, broker or other financial services firm. However, such organizations may understandably not be eager to go to a lot of trouble digging up information for you about direct investments in paper on which they stand to collect no fee. Some newspapers and financial publications do regularly publish information about current interest rates on commercial paper in their money market tables. These rates are for the large-denomination institutional market, however, and you should not take them as representative of what is available to individual investors dealing in comparatively small amounts. Information about money funds that invest in commercial paper is readily available from the funds.

COSTS OF BUYING,
OWNING AND SELLING

A purchase of commercial paper from a direct issuer normally involves no costs other than telephone bills or postage. If, on the other hand, you buy through a banker or broker, you can expect to pay a commission or other transaction fee. This will effectively reduce the return you can expect on your investment. Since most money market funds are *no load,* investing in them usually involves no out-of-pocket costs on your part. However, sponsors of these funds collect annual management fees from the funds' assets, which also effectively reduce the yield you can realize.

CAPITAL GAINS POTENTIAL

Though you may buy commercial paper at a lower price (a *discount*) than you receive at maturity, the difference is considered interest, not a capital gain. It is impractical at best for individual investors to buy and sell commercial paper before maturity. For that reason, paper offers no reasonable prospect for capital gains. It is not intended for that purpose.

INCOME POTENTIAL

In times of high short-term interest rates, commercial paper may offer attractive income prospects. When you are evaluating paper from this point of view, it makes sense to compare the returns it offers with other, competing vehicles like Treasury bills, bank and savings institution accounts and money market funds.

If you do not have both the capital to diversify your commercial paper holdings and the time to monitor the money markets closely, you may find paper less attractive than, say, a bank savings certificate or government security. That goes particularly for investors who seek reliable long-term income, with absolute safety of principal, from their investments.

RISKS AND DRAWBACKS

Investing in commercial paper involves some credit risk, because these IOUs are neither insured by any government agency nor secured by any assets of the issuer. The historical default rate on paper has been very low. But that fact wasn't much consolation to the holders of $82 million in Penn Central commercial paper when that company (since revived as a completely different entity) defaulted in 1970.

Today a large amount of the commercial paper outstanding carries ratings assigned to it by one or more of the firms that specialize in evaluating credit risk. With low-rated or unrated paper, it makes sense to proceed warily unless you have some special knowledge or assurance of the reliability of the issuer.

Investment advisers say that ultra-cautious investors in money funds may prefer funds that invest only in government securities, or that limit their paper holdings to a certain percentage of their portfolios. In any case, it makes sense to check a fund's prospectus before investing to see what methods it employs for evaluating and limiting credit risk in its commercial paper investments.

As with other short-term interest-bearing investments, rates on commercial paper can be volatile. When you invest for, say, six months, there is no way of knowing for sure what kinds of returns will be available when you want to reinvest the proceeds after maturity.

Buying commercial paper directly has its greatest appeal for activist investors with a lot of time to devote to the subject. It typically involves making frequent decisions about maturities and other factors. If you are busy with other matters, such as a nonfinancial career, it might be preferable to do your money market investing in a money fund or money market deposit account at a bank or savings institution. On the other hand, if you are a full-time investor in a situation that permits you to invest directly in paper under favorable circumstances, you may well pride yourself on the returns you attain without having to pay someone else (i.e., a mutual fund manager) in the process.

LIQUIDITY

Commercial paper is generally considered a highly liquid investment, in the sense that it never involves tying up your funds for extended periods of time. However, it should be noted that there is no secondary market for paper—no established place where an investor can readily sell it to someone else before maturity. If you find yourself in pressing need, an issuer may agree to buy it back from you beforehand. But the issuer is unlikely to be eager to do this very often or for reasons that it considers frivolous.

Thus, it is obviously important whenever you invest directly in commercial paper to select a maturity that fits your circumstances. Achieving this objective should be a relatively simple assignment, since a broad selection of maturities is normally available. Another way to forestall any liquidity problems is to invest in a money fund, rather than directly in paper. Money fund shares normally can be redeemed at will by such simple means as writing a check or telephoning the fund.

TAX ADVANTAGES
AND DISADVANTAGES

Interest earned on commercial paper is subject to federal income tax as ordinary income, as well as any state and local taxes levied on interest where you live. So are the dividends money funds pay out from their earnings on commercial paper investments. An exception to this general rule is paper issued by state and local governments which, like other municipal securities, is exempt from federal taxation on interest income. In practice, municipal paper is often treated as a member of the municipal bond class, rather than as a form of commercial paper.

Taxable commercial paper may have a place in an individual retirement account, Keogh plan or other tax-favored savings plan if it can be arranged for the trustee to invest in paper under favorable circumstances. One obvious way to make this arrangement is to put your IRA or Keogh money in a money market fund that has commercial paper in its portfolio.

COMMON STOCKS

DESCRIPTION

No form of American investment gets more attention and generates more emotion than common stocks. Politicians, pundits and just plain ordinary people watch the ups and downs of the stock market with varying degrees of enthusiasm, concern, and puzzlement. Indeed, the market is widely regarded as a sort of running public opinion poll on the state of the economy and the general mood of the country.

Yet for all the publicity they get, the function of stocks and the stock market can be misunderstood. All businesses have owners, of course. If a business is incorporated, the owner or owners are stockholders. If that business goes public, it extends the right of part ownership to anyone who has the money to buy its common shares. The shares are continuously traded in the *secondary market*—which operates at the New York Stock Exchange, the American Stock Exchange, several regional exchanges around the country, and in the *over-the-counter market,* a network of dealers overseen by the National Association of Securities Dealers.

This market has room for just about every kind of investor willing to take the risks involved in part ownership of a business that may or may not thrive in the future. Some people try to trade stocks actively, "playing the market." Others buy stocks of companies with promising prospects, holding them in hopes of long-term gains. Still others invest conservatively, buying stocks for the dividend income they produce, and hoping that future dividend increases will help them keep pace with inflation.

Countless strategies, formulas, philosophies and techniques have been developed over the years for trying to profit from investing in stocks. Using them, some people have been highly successful—although the dream of getting rich in the stock market can be a very elusive goal. Others, confronted with setback after setback, close out their brokerage accounts and vow "never again."

After many bull markets (periods of rising stock prices) and bear markets (including the infamous Great Crash of 1929), however, the stock market retains an enduring appeal. Once you have provided yourself or your family with a home, a savings reserve invested in a safe place, adequate life insurance if appropriate, and enough income to keep food on the table, many investment advisers say it makes sense to consider stocks as a means of making your money grow. You can choose, if you have the requisite time, expertise and temperament, to invest in stocks directly yourself. You can operate on the advice of a broker you trust. Or you can turn to some professional investment firm, like a mutual fund, bank trust department or private money manager.

HOW AND WHERE TO GET
INFORMATION AND INVEST

There is enough raw information (facts, rules, statistics) and quasi-information (books, market letters, gossip with friends, and so forth) available to devote a lifetime of study to stocks. With financial deregulation, more and more organizations stand ready and eager to inundate you with this information.

The law requires all public companies to disclose a great deal of information about themselves and their operations. Serious investors learn the art of reading annual reports, proxy statements, prospectuses and other disclosure documents to glean as much information as possible about companies in which they have invested or might consider investing.

Most large general interest newspapers carry daily accounts of the market's doings, the latest readings of the averages and indexes that are used to measure overall market trends, and tables of the previous day's trading results for many individual stocks. Many books and periodicals devote their attention entirely to matters of interest to stock market investors. Among the best-known general business and financial publications are Barron's, Business Week, Forbes, Fortune, Money and the Wall Street Journal. Investors with an active interest in a given industry also may subscribe to trade publications covering that industry.

When you decide that you are ready to buy or sell, you have a variety of choices. If, say, you own some stock you want to sell, and your next-door neighbor wants to buy it, you are perfectly free to conduct the transaction at your kitchen table, at any mutually agreed upon price (making sure you follow the correct administrative procedures).

Since this circumstance seldom arises, you normally buy and sell through a stockbroker. If you want a great deal of advice and-or other ancillary services, you may prefer a full-service broker. If you make your own decisions, you may instead turn to a discount broker (see the chapter on discount brokerage services).

COSTS OF BUYING, OWNING AND SELLING

There are ways to buy stock "free," or even at what amounts to a discount. If you purchase shares that are being offered to the public for the first time, you are normally charged no commission—although there is an effective cost to you, since the company in which you are buying a part interest pays the selling brokers a fee for their services. If you participate in a company's dividend reinvestment plan, you may be able to buy stock without commissions or other fees, and even possibly at a below-market price.

Stock of the company for which you work may be available through several attractive arrangements. Under *incentive compensation* plans, for example, some employees receive stock options that give them the right to buy shares at a set price. Many companies now operate employee stock ownership plans, or ESOPs, which permit their workers to buy stock through payroll withholding or some other arrangement.

This kind of deal can have many advantages. Frequently, companies with ESOPs contribute a proportional amount of extra money when participants buy shares. And as an employee at any level in the company hierarchy, you may be in a good position to evaluate the merits of your employer as an investment proposition.

With all these alternatives, the most common way stocks are bought and sold remains through a broker. Whenever you deal with a broker, the precise cost you pay can be hard to measure. Beyond the stated commission, there may be a cost calculated into the price you pay or receive, based on a dealer's spread or markup or markdown from the price he or she paid for it. Whether the stated commission is low or high, you also may incur an effective cost if the brokerage firm does a poor job of execution—that is, obtaining or selling the stock for you at the most advantageous price possible.

CAPITAL GAINS POTENTIAL

The quest for capital gains is the primary source of energy that drives the stock market. Just about every investor dreams of finding the next IBM or Xerox—buying stock in a company that is still young and undiscovered, and then watching its value soar as the company grows to prosperity, gains a wide following on Wall Street, and becomes a standard holding in the portfolios of investing institutions like pension funds.

These future stars in the market firmament are hard to spot, of course. Even if you happen on one, you may have to wait years to have your hopes validated. And of course, the higher you aim, the greater the risk of loss you must usually take.

You can choose to play it conservative in the stock market, picking only stocks that historically have not fluctuated much in value, and that pay a dividend large enough to cushion your capital from any modest decline in prices. But all common stocks expose you to the likelihood of some degree of capital gain or loss. With changes in business and economic conditions, today's conservative stock can become tomorrow's high-risk issue.

INCOME POTENTIAL

Many investors venture into the stock market with income as their primary objective. They may buy stocks in stable, mature industries that produce yields approaching or even exceeding what is available in competing fixed-income alternatives. Most stocks, except those of companies in trouble or of enterprises that are in the early, fast-growth stages of their existence, pay at least a token dividend. And if a given company is in reasonably good financial condition, there is always the chance and hope that the dividend will be increased in the future.

But income-conscious investors should always bear in mind that owners of stocks receive no absolute assurance of future dividend income. When they sell bonds, companies promise to pay a stated amount of interest, and sometimes pledge some of their assets as collateral to back up that promise. When they sell preferred stock, they make a lesser commitment. When they sell common stock, they normally make no legal commitment at all.

In practice, most companies do not reduce or eliminate their dividends unless they have little other choice. Their directors have no wish to alienate the investing public. But if they deem it necessary, they may lower the dividend or stop paying it altogether without breaking any contract with you. There are stocks that are considered highly safe, at least by comparison with other stocks. But there are no stocks that can match the safety of other vehicles like Treasury securities that have the backing of a government guarantee.

RISKS AND
DRAWBACKS

As has already been suggested above, you cannot buy a stock without taking a variety of risks. At the extreme, the company you pick can go bankrupt, costing you all, or practically all, of your investment. In addition to company, or business risk, there is market risk. You may choose a perfectly sound company whose earnings and dividends grow handsomely. But its stock price can go down anyway if stocks in general enter a period of disfavor.

As sophisticated as today's investors and market analysts may be, there remains an element of chance—luck, if you will—in stock market investing. In recent years, ways to hedge against some of the risks have been devised using options or stock-index futures. An awareness of all these risks is important. But it need not dissuade anyone with sufficient means at their disposal to pursue a carefully planned, disciplined strategy of investing in the stock market.

Stock prices may rise or fall in any given week, or month, or year. After the Great Crash of 1929, it took the Dow Jones average of 30 industrials, the best known measure of market trends, 25 years to get back to where it had been at its former peak. But over the history of the United States, the long-term trend of the stock market has been upward.

LIQUIDITY

Stocks as a class of investment are considered very liquid, with the very active markets that operate in this country. In usual circumstances, they can readily be bought and sold on short notice. This liquidity varies from stock to stock, however, depending on the amount of activity that takes place in it. A stock that consistently makes the active list on the New York Stock Exchange is regarded as much more liquid than a tiny unknown over-the-counter issue.

Stocks that have relatively small amounts of shares in public hands are often described as "thinly" traded. In issues like this, the price changes from one transaction to another can be very large. It should also be remembered that liquidity in the stock market is presumed, not guaranteed. In late October 1929, there were days when stocks were very illiquid.

TAX ADVANTAGES
AND DISADVANTAGES

Profits and losses on stocks are taxable at capital-gains rates in the year in which you sell. If you hold a profitable stock investment long enough to qualify for *long-term* tax treatment, the maximum tax rate is 20 percent—a primary attraction for long-term investing in the market. The minimum holding period to qualify for long-term status has been changed several times in recent decades. From the late 1970s it was one year, until 1984, when Congress set it at six months for assets purchased after June 23 of that year, effective through 1987. Dividends received by stockholders are taxable as ordinary income, except for any amounts that qualify for special exclusions under the current tax rules.

In the closing months of each year, brokers and other financial advisers frequently publish reports and booklets detailing tax-planning strategies for stock investors. These may contain some very helpful suggestions. However, you should evaluate them carefully, taking commission costs into account, and considering whether they might disrupt your long-term investment strategy.

Stocks, or mutual funds that invest in stocks, are candidates for use in individual retirement accounts, Keogh plans, and other tax-favored savings and investment programs.

LISTED STOCKS

DESCRIPTION

The shares of many corporations, including most large and well-established ones, are *listed* on stock exchanges. The largest of these, the New York Stock Exchange, traces its origins back to 1792, when a group of two dozen brokers and merchants reached an agreement on procedures for buying and selling securities. This pact was known as the "Buttonwood agreement," after a buttonwood tree on Wall Street that was a common meeting place for doing business.

The American Stock Exchange, two blocks away from the NYSE in New York's financial district, is home to hundreds of stocks, most of them representing smaller companies than the typical Big Board issue. In its early days, it was known as the "curb" market, because trading was conducted on the street outside a building where many brokers had offices. The Amex moved to indoor facilities in 1921.

There are also several regional stock exchanges around the country, from Boston to San Francisco and Los Angeles. Though they may vary greatly in size, all U.S. stock exchanges operate in pretty much the same way, governed by the securities laws and their own rules, and policed by the Securities and Exchange Commission and by themselves. The heart of their operations is a trading floor where activity in stocks and other securities is conducted.

Trading in any listed stock is conducted through a firm or individual known as a specialist, who acts as a meeting point for buy and sell orders. In the course of their business, specialists regularly buy and sell for themselves. Since they are in a position to know everything that is happening in the market for the stocks assigned to them, specialists might seem to have a big advantage over other traders on an exchange floor and the public. Indeed, some specialists make a lot of money, at least some of the time. But there are stringent rules covering their activity. They often must take great risks.

Specialists and the specialist system have their harsh critics. The National Association of Securities Dealers, which oversees the over-the-counter market, contends that it has a better system, in which two or more independent dealers act as competing market makers. However, the exchanges argue that the specialist system functions well because of the obligations imposed on the specialist to keep trading as orderly as possible.

In modern stock trading, furthermore, specialists have lost some of their "monopoly" status. Many stocks are listed on more than one exchange, with the various specialists linked electronically in what is called the Intermarket Trading System, which was introduced in 1978. Through this system a specialist operating at, say, the Philadelphia Stock Exchange may outbid the specialist in New York. Some independent investment firms aggressively seek to handle large block transactions in listed stocks away from exchange trading floors.

For many companies, having their stocks listed on an exchange confers a measure of status and respectability in the business world. It certifies that their enterprises meet the size and quality standards set by the exchanges as minimum requirements for listing.

HOW AND WHERE TO GET INFORMATION AND INVEST

Abundant information is available on just about any listed stock, from a broker or other investment adviser. Prices of all transactions are reported on exchange tickers immediately after they occur, and from there may be disseminated to individual investors in many ways— through computer services, for example, or in a telephone conversion between an investor and a broker. Tables of daily and weekly activity in listed issues are carried in many newspapers and the financial press.

The process of investing in stocks, of course, usually involves continuous gathering of information on the market, the economy and the companies of stocks you own or are considering owning. For regular statistics on the financial status of all or most listed issues, investors may subscribe to services such as the quarterly Moody's Handbook of Common Stocks or the monthly Standard & Poor's stock guide.

The typical investor cannot go onto an exchange trading floor and look over a specialist's shoulder as stocks are bought and sold. Access to exchange floors is generally limited to member brokers who own "seats" (a modern-day misnomer, since on exchange trading floors there is practically no place to sit down), employees of those brokers and the exchanges, and accredited visitors.

However, most stock exchanges seek to provide the public with ready access to information about their operations. They may offer guided tours, including a stop in a visitor's gallery that offers a view of the floor. The exchanges in New York are in fact tourist attractions that fascinate both active investors and people who have never owned a single share of stock.

COSTS OF BUYING, OWNING AND SELLING

When you buy or sell a listed stock through a broker, you can expect to pay a commission. If you, like many active investors, do a significant amount of your own research, you may incur significant costs for such things as subscriptions to financial publications and advisory services.

CAPITAL GAINS POTENTIAL

Some types of investments are "zero sum" games—that is, for every winner there must be a loser. But this is not necessarily the case with the stock market. Investor A can buy a stock at 5 and sell it at 10. Investor B, who buys at 10, can sell it at 15. As long as the price keeps rising, everyone is reasonably happy—including the brokers who collect commissions on all these trades.

The hope that this kind of thing can happen—that the majority of investors can profit—plays a big part in the mystique of the stock market. It is often referred to, with a distinct touch of cynicism, as the "greater fool" theory: No matter how ridiculously high a price you pay for a stock in a bull market, there is the hope that some "greater fool" will buy it from you later for an even higher price.

The cynicism is justified to the extent that the market rarely rises steadily and continuously to the delight of all. Even periods of extraordinary gains in stock prices can be punctuated by interim declines that severely punish investors whose timing is bad. Nevertheless, it is true that there is no theoretical limit beyond which stock prices cannot rise.

Within the spectrum of listed stocks, there are many choices for investors seeking capital gains. Though listed issues are by tradition the elite of corporate America, you can find speculative investments, as well as relatively conservative ones, on any stock exchange.

INCOME POTENTIAL

Many listed stocks are shares of long-established companies that pay generous dividends, and offer the hope of future dividend increases to help keep pace with inflation. Lots of listed companies pride themselves on their long histories of regular dividend payments. Stocks of such companies have a place in many an income-conscious investor's portfolio. However, next year's dividend of even the bluest blue-chip company is neither guaranteed nor contractually committed.

RISKS AND
DRAWBACKS

The market in listed stocks, notably at the New York Stock Exchange, has become increasingly dominated in the past two decades by investing institutions such as pension funds, bank trust departments and mutual funds. In the mid-1980s, almost half of all trading volume on the Big Board was accounted for by blocks of 10,000 shares or more. This has some important implications for individual investors.

The people who make investment decisions for these institutions may be intelligent, well trained, experienced professionals. But they are human, and they often are under considerable competitive pressure in their jobs. Many of them are generally exposed to the same body of Wall Street research. When a listed company announces some unpleasant surprise, it may come as a simultaneous shock to the whole community of investment managers. As disciplined as these managers may be, their response to bad news may be dramatic in the aggregate. So the price of any stock owned by many institutions can be unpredictably volatile.

Many investors consider listed stocks as a class to be superior in quality to over-the-counter stocks as a class. This generalization, of course, can have many exceptions. In addition, quality is no guarantee of stock market profits. At times, particularly when enthusiasm is running high, over-the-counter stocks may perform much better than those listed on the NYSE.

LIQUIDITY

A listed stock, under normal circumstances, is a highly liquid investment. The exchanges operate on a regular schedule, and when they are open investors can buy and sell most stocks whenever they choose, on short notice. Several things, however, can happen to limit or disrupt the liquidity of any given stock. Trading in any issue may be halted for a few minutes, a few hours or even several days when some development affecting the issuing company touches off an intense reaction among investors. If a listed company falls on bad times, an exchange may "delist" its stock. Such a stock may, or may not, subsequently find an active market in over-the-counter trading.

TAX ADVANTAGES
AND DISADVANTAGES

Listed stocks are subject to standard tax rules covering dividends and capital gains and losses. They may have a place in an individual retirement account, Keogh plan or other tax-favored savings and investment program.

OVER-THE-COUNTER STOCKS

DESCRIPTION

Thousands of companies whose stocks are traded in this country do not qualify for listing on an exchange, or do not opt for listing when they do qualify. Their shares are traded in the over-the-counter market, a network of dealers overseen by the National Association of Securities Dealers.

In years past, the over-the-counter market had a reputation as a pretty risky place for investors to operate. For the average investor, information about price trends and activity in over-the-counter stocks was less readily available than on listed issues. Over-the-counter dealers didn't always have to operate under the kind of close scrutiny that was focused on exchange trading floors. The merchandise they dealt in was, with a few exceptions, considered lower in quality than listed stocks. Trading in stocks was often less active than in listed issues, making them harder for the average investor to buy and sell at attractive prices.

There is a legendary story in the financial world about an investor who buys 100 shares of a little-known over-the-counter stock for 50 cents apiece. The broker-dealer who sells the investor the stock raises the price at which he is quoting it. Learning of the higher price, the investor buys 100 more shares for 75 cents. The broker raises his quote again, and the enthusiastic investor buys yet another 100 shares at $1. Shortly thereafter, the investor tells the broker he is ready to take some profits, and is interested in selling some of his stock. "To whom?" the broker replies.

This cautionary tale is still told on Wall Street. But there have been major changes in the over-the-counter market in the past couple of decades. The National Association of Securities Dealers Automated Quotations (NASDAQ) system, which began operating in 1971, provided a computerized hookup through which information is collected and distributed about the prices (*bid and asked* quotations) at which dealers offer to buy and sell many individual stocks.

A further step, in 1982, was the establishment of the NASDAQ National Market System, which provides for rapid reporting of prices of actual transactions, rather than bid and asked quotations, in over-the-counter trading of some stocks. By the mid-1980s, there were several hundred stocks in this system.

The NASD claims great progress in raising the quality, visibility and efficiency of its market. It argues that its arrangement of competing market makers—two or more dealers from different firms buying and selling the same stocks—has become an attractive alternative to the specialist system used on stock exchanges. Officials of the New York Stock Exchange, however, still refer to the over-the-counter market as "our nursery"—a place where stocks of smaller companies can be traded until they have a chance to grow sufficiently to qualify for listing. Many over-the-counter stocks are still regarded as more speculative than listed issues, if only because they have not yet had time to establish records as seasoned companies.

At the speculative extreme of the over-the-counter market is the specialized sector known as *penny stocks,* shares of companies usually involved in high risk ventures that trade at very low prices per share. When investors are in high spirits, penny stocks may fare especially well. In bear markets, they often fare especially poorly.

HOW AND WHERE TO GET
INFORMATION AND INVEST

In the past, particularly in the pre-NASDAQ days, investors often faced a problem finding good over-the-counter stocks and following their progress. Companies traded in the over-the-counter market must make the same regular disclosures about earnings and other material matters that are required of listed companies. But, because of their small size and sheer numbers, many over-the-counter companies got little or no coverage in the press, and few securities analysts kept tabs on them.

The information gap has narrowed in recent years, however. Where there was obscurity, some enterprising people concluded, there was probably opportunity. They began investment advisory services and mutual funds specializing in over-the-counter stocks. Today there are a great many brokers and advisers who specialize in searching out over-the-counter opportunities.

COSTS OF BUYING, OWNING AND SELLING

Costs can be a tricky question when you buy and sell over-the-counter stocks. Suppose you put in an order with your broker to buy 100 shares of an issue. If the broker obtains the stock from a dealer at another firm, you may be charged a commission just as you would with a listed stock. If, on the other hand, the broker gets the stock from the inventory of his or her own firm, there may be no stated commission. Rather, you will pay a cost in the form of a price concession.

Dealers in stocks seek to make a profit from a *spread*—the difference between what they are willing to pay for shares and the price they are willing to accept when selling them. The less actively traded the stock, the wider the spread is likely to be. Traders in penny stocks should be especially conscious of spreads.

The broker who takes your order must be compensated as well. This compensation can take the form of a commission, or it can take the form of a retail markup in the price you pay when you buy, or a markdown in the price you receive when you sell. Investors in over-the-counter stocks should never operate under the illusion that they can buy and sell these issues cost-free. As an official at one Wall Street firm put it succinctly, "sometimes we show the cost to you, and sometimes we hide it."

CAPITAL GAINS POTENTIAL

Over-the-counter stocks have a reputation as more volatile than listed stocks—prone to dramatic gains in good markets and equally dramatic losses in bad markets. Thus, the over-the-counter market is often said to be more attractive to speculators than conservative long-term investors. This generalization may have an element of truth, but it does not stand up as a blanket rule.

For one thing, the over-the-counter market is home to some well-established companies—notably insurance concerns and regional banks—that may be regarded as conservative investments. In addition, many knowledgeable investors regard the over-the-counter market as a likely place to search for long-term investment possibilities. Just about every successful company, they reason, begins life as a relatively small enterprise, and the best time to invest in it is when it is still small and unrecognized.

You cannot know in advance, of course, that any given small company will eventually grow to eminent status. But an industrious investor can search out, say, half a dozen promising issues and spread his or her money among them. If only one or two ever hit it big, the net reward may still be handsome.

INCOME POTENTIAL
Some relatively stable, high-yielding stocks trade in the over-the-counter market. If you want to invest in stocks for income, they may be perfectly acceptable candidates for you to consider. However, since so many issues are shares of relatively young companies, as a group they tend to offer lower yields than listed stocks. Stocks of new, small companies are not a logical place to put your money if you want or need to obtain maximum current income, with safety, from your assets.

RISKS AND
DRAWBACKS
The over-the-counter market has indisputedly grown in stature in recent years. Investing institutions that years ago would have bought only listed stocks now may well be active participants in over-the-counter trading. Still, the majority of issues tend to carry a higher degree of risk than a blue-chip company listed on the New York Stock Exchange.

Before you buy an over-the-counter stock, you may wish to determine why it is not traded on an exchange. It may be that the company qualifies for listing, but simply prefers to remain in the NASDAQ system. It may be that the company hasn't established the necessary record of profitability and popularity with investors. Or it may be that it simply doesn't have enough shares outstanding to be eligible for listing.

LIQUIDITY

Some over-the-counter stocks are highly liquid. They may be heavily traded every day in the NASDAQ National Market System, and for all practical purposes be as liquid as any stock traded anywhere. But among the thousands of over-the-counter stocks available, there are many others that do not have active markets. Before you buy a stock, it makes sense to check the number of shares outstanding and the typical daily or weekly volume of trading in those shares. You may also inquire how many dealers make markets in the stock you are considering.

TAX ADVANTAGES
AND DISADVANTAGES

The tax rules make no distinction between over-the-counter and listed stocks. OTC stocks, or mutual funds that specialize in them, may be bought by venturesome investors for their individual retirement accounts, Keogh plans or other tax-favored savings and investment programs.

NEW ISSUES

DESCRIPTION

Few events can create as much excitement in the investment world as the debut in the stock market of a hot new issue. Particularly in periods when the market is filled with enthusiasm and activity, new issues evoke images of fat profits in short periods of time.

In the classic script, here is how one of these dramas is played out: Hypothetical Corp.'s founders, having decided that the time is ripe to "go public," select an investment banking firm and consult with its experts. Together, they decide on the number of shares to offer, as well as the price per share they feel is justified by prevailing market conditions and by Hypothetical's operating record and prospects. For the sake of example, assume that Hypothetical's founders decide to sell 10 million shares (keeping another 10 million for themselves) at a price of $10 apiece.

The investment banking firm forms a syndicate of other brokers to distribute the offering to investors. A preliminary prospectus, known as a *red herring,* is drafted and circulated, and the offering is cleared by the Securities and Exchange Commission. The day of the initial public offering arrives amid much excitement. The 10 million shares are quickly snapped up by eager buyers, and as trading begins in them in the secondary market (usually the over-the-counter market), the price quickly jumps to $15.

Everybody is happy. Hypothetical's founders have raised a large chunk of new capital, and the stock they retained is worth $150 million on paper. The investment bankers and the members of their syndicate collect a fee from Hypothetical for their efforts. And the investors who bought at the $10 offering price have enjoyed a 50 percent paper profit on their investment in just a few hours.

Things do not always go so smoothly, of course. From the investor's point of view, the new issues game can involve great risk as well as reward. Once investors have more time to evaluate Hypothetical, and to study its earnings reports and other disclosures for a quarter or two, they may decide that the stock is really worth $5, not $15 or even the offering price of $10. When that happens, of course, people who bought in the initial period of euphoria repent their eagerness. Despite the risks, however, many financial advisers consider new issues an attractive means of seeking stock-market profits for investors who take the time to evaluate individual offerings carefully, and who do not permit their judgment to be overwhelmed by dreams of riches.

The ups and downs of the market for existing stocks tend to be magnified in the new issues market. When the stock market is booming, new-issues activity can reach a frenzied pitch, with buyers clamoring indiscrimately after every offering that comes along. By contrast, in bear markets, even quality companies with promising futures can have trouble attracting sufficient interest to bring off a successful offering.

HOW AND WHERE TO GET INFORMATION AND INVEST

Information about new issues is available from the brokers who sell them, and from some investment advisory services that specializing in tracking the initial-public-offering market and evaluating forthcoming offerings. Generally, when the best deals become available, ready demand for the stock exceeds the available supply. In these cases, brokers sell what stock they have to their best and most alert customers.

If you haven't done much business with a given broker before, it isn't sensible to expect him or her to come running to you with a big juicy block of the hottest new stock in years. In fact, if you receive an unsolicited pitch to buy a new issue from a broker whom you don't know, it is wise to ask yourself how many other knowledgeable investors might have already had a chance to look the deal over and have decided to pass on it.

"By their very nature, new issues can sometimes be a bit difficult to acquire in the initial offerings," says Norman Fosback, editor of the advisory letter "New Issues." To improve your odds, Fosback suggests advising your broker as far in advance as possible of your interest in a given scheduled offering. If that isn't enough, he recommends seeking out an office of the firm that is managing the offering, or officers of the company that is planning to go public. If you do a lot of business with a brokerage firm that regularly has access to new issues you want, and the firm consistently fails to produce them for you, Fosback says, "it is time to have a heart-to-heart talk with your representative."

COSTS OF BUYING,
OWNING AND SELLING

When you buy a new stock issue in the initial offering, as with underwritings of other types of new securities, you normally do not have to pay a commission. In this situation, brokers collect their fees from the issuing company. This difference from the standard procedure for trading in the secondary market adds to the allure of new issues. Of course, at some point you presumably will want to sell stock you acquired as a new issue. When that time comes, you can expect to pay a standard commission.

CAPITAL GAINS
POTENTIAL

The quest for capital gains is the driving force in the new issues market. Buyers may be motivated by a desire to "get in on the ground floor" with stocks they hope will appreciate greatly in value over the long term. Or they may be looking to turn a fast profit by buying at the offering and selling very shortly thereafter as secondary market trading in the stock begins.

There is nothing inherently immoral or unscrupulous about this latter strategy. However, brokers and issuing companies may not exactly encourage you to try to practice it regularly. Obviously, it could disrupt an offering if every buyer of a new issue immediately sought to sell his or her stock in the secondary market.

INCOME POTENTIAL

Buyers of a new issue may hope that someday the company in which they are investing will pay generous dividends. But most companies that go public are at a youthful stage in which they cannot and do not want to pay much money out in dividends. In fact, logic dictates that a budding company tapping the stock market for capital for the first time should invest as much of its available funds as possible for growth.

In any case, new issues, with the risks they carry, are not generally a suitable investment for people who want or need maximum current income from their assets, and are concerned with safety of their principal. An exception to these general rules may occasionally arise if a long-established private company in a mature industry decides for some special reason (say, the approaching retirement of its founder) to go public.

RISKS AND DRAWBACKS

Though you may feel you are getting "first crack" at a good investment when you buy a new issue, that is really not normally the case. Chances are that the owners of a company from its private days have acquired their stock for much less than the price at the initial public offering. This does not by itself mean that you, as a public investor, are necessarily getting a bad deal. But matters like this should be taken into account in evaluating a new issue.

This sort of information is normally included in the prospectus, which merits a close reading on several other counts. What do the company's past record, present financial condition and future prospects look like? What does the company plan to do with the money it is seeking to raise? How good are its chances of achieving its stated objectives? Typically, a section of the prospectus is devoted to specific discussion of the risks involved in investing in the company involved. When some experienced investors receive a prospectus on a forthcoming new offering, this is one of the first sections they subject to close scrutiny.

Even in cases when the issuing company is a solid, established entity, prices of new stock issues may be volatile in their first few days and weeks of trading. That is only natural, since many investors are simultaneously going through the process of getting acquainted with the issue and the issuer.

LIQUIDITY

Popular new issues are normally highly liquid—that is, there are likely to be many investors eager to bid for them once they begin trading in the secondary market. However, with many new issues, particularly those of small, untried companies, investors may take some degree of liquidity risk not normally associated with established, publicly traded stocks.

A stock that has been trading for some years tends to establish a certain identity for itself in the market. It comes to be considered relatively volatile or relatively stable, actively traded or inactively traded. These patterns can and often do change. But at least they provide an investor with something of a guide to what he or she is buying.

A new issue has had no opportunity to establish any such pattern. When you buy one, you have no past record to go on in assessing how actively traded it will be, say, a year from now and how readily the market will accommodate an order to sell your stock.

TAX ADVANTAGES
AND DISADVANTAGES

When you sell a stock bought as a new issue, you incur a capital gain or loss for tax purposes just as if you acquired the stock in the secondary market. The only difference is that there is no broker's commission to figure into your cost of buying when you compute how much you have made or lost.

New issues may fit into the investment strategies of a large individual retirement account, Keogh plan or other tax-favored savings program, if you choose to place such an account with a broker or other institution that can provide you with access to initial offerings. Conservative IRA or Keogh savers may choose to stick with less risky investments.

SHORT-SELLING

DESCRIPTION

"Buy low and sell high" runs the long-standing, if not particularly helpful, maxim about stock market investing. As the phrase implies, buying usually is the first step and selling occurs some time later. But suppose you think a stock's price is high now and will be lower later. You can simply wait, of course. Or you can seek to "sell high and buy low" through a process that is known as selling short.

In order to sell a stock you don't own, you have to borrow it first—normally from your broker. The typical broker stands ready to extend the stock on loan and conduct the whole transaction, once you have established a margin account with his or her firm.

Short-selling is a common practice, with a long history, in stocks and many other types of investments. Yet it retains a somewhat sinister image. People who, in effect, place a bet on declining stock prices are seen as scavengers, ghoulishly seeking to profit from unfortunate events. Selling short is also regarded, with some justification, as a high-risk proposition.

Actually, brokers and dealers who make markets in stocks and other securities regularly sell short as a routine part of their operations. While it is primarily a speculative stategy, short-selling has its conservative uses as well. Investors can sell short to hedge (offset risks to which some of their other holdings are exposed), or to "lock in" a paper profit on some stock they already own until the time when they wish to cash in that profit.

HOW AND WHERE TO GET
INFORMATION AND INVEST

Any good broker can provide you with information about short-selling procedures and techniques, and handle your orders. Part of the introductory process is establishing that your circumstances and finances are suited to short-selling, and opening a margin account for you (see the separate section of this chapter on investing on margin). Before you sell short, you may wish to consider alternative means of pursuing the same goal, such as options and stock-index futures.

COSTS OF BUYING,
OWNING AND SELLING

There are several costs involved in short-selling, all of which effectively reduce the return you can realize on a short position. There are the standard commissions to pay when you buy and sell. You must deposit a specified amount of cash or securities with your broker to meet margin requirements when you sell, and be prepared to meet sufficient deposits to comply with those margin requirements as long as your short position exists. If a stock pays a dividend while you have a short position in it, you are liable to pay an equivalent amount to the broker who lent you the stock.

CAPITAL GAINS
POTENTIAL

The standard goal in short-selling is to realize a profit from a decline in the price of a stock or other security. If you sell $10,000 worth of Hypothetical Corp.'s stock today, and "cover" your short sale by buying the same number of shares later for $8,000, you are $2,000 richer.

The risk of this stategy is usually high relative to the potential reward. In the instance described above, the most you can make is $10,000, even if Hypothetical Corp. goes bankrupt and its stock becomes worthless. But if Hypothetical discovers a new wonder drug, or anything else happens to make its stock price rise, there is no theoretical limit to your potential losses. For this reason, among others, some investment experts regard buying *put* options as an attractive alternative to selling short.

An entirely different strategy, known as "selling short against the box," can be used to protect paper profits you have on existing investments. Assume, for example, that you bought 100 shares of Hypothetical Corp. some time ago for $5 each, paying $500 excluding commissions. The stock now trades at $100 a share, and your investment is worth $10,000. You are eager to cash in your $9,500 profit, but you don't want to do so until a tax deadline—say, the end of the current year—passes. So you instruct your broker to sell 100 Hypothetical shares short at $100 apiece. As soon as you have set up this offsetting position, you will experience no further net gain or loss, no matter what happens to the price of Hypothetical's stock.

To be recognized as a valid transaction by the Internal Revenue Service, this kind of stategy must be planned carefully to conform to prevailing tax rules and court rulings. Furthermore, you should be aware of its drawbacks. Once you have sold short against the box, you cannot benefit from any further increase in the price of Hypothetical's stock. You are no longer entitled to receive any dividends Hypothetical pays. The transaction costs of the short sale actually reduce your eventual profit somewhat. In return, however, you have gained assurance that you will be able to realize a known profit at a time of your choosing.

INCOME POTENTIAL

Short sellers get no dividends or interest of any kind. In fact, because of the costs involved, short-selling is a "negative income" investment stategy. It is normally unsuitable for savers and investors who want or need maximum current income, with safety, from their assets.

RISKS AND
DRAWBACKS

Short-selling may play a useful—occasionally even necessary—role in the operation of professional investors and sophisticated individuals. Dealers in securities may take a short position as readily as they "go long" (have a net ownership position). Professionals may sell short to hedge their other holdings against risk. Or they may sell short as part of a process known as arbitrage—the simultaneous or near-simultaneous sale and purchase of similar or related securities to try to profit from temporary disparities in the prices of those securities.

If you could sell a stock to one broker for $6, and buy it immediately from another for $5, you would probably be eager to do so, in the process becoming an arbitrageur. Unfortunately, opportunities like this for the small investor are nonexistent, for all practical purposes. In many of its uses, short-selling requires the kind of elaborate facilities and large reserves of capital to which only investment pros have access.

LIQUIDITY

Short sales are routine transactions in the U.S. securities markets, which are usually highly liquid. Nevertheless, short-sellers face some special liquidity problems and concerns. Under the standard rules, a short sale can be made only on or immediately after an "uptick"—a rise of at least $1/8$ of a point in the price of the stock involved. Thus, when there is abundant evidence that a short sale is a good bet, it may be difficult for your broker to execute the sale at a favorable price.

Once the sale is executed, a second question immediately arises. As a short seller, you know that you must sooner or later buy back in to complete your transaction. If all goes well, you will have no trouble finding a willing seller in today's large and active securities markets. But there is always the chance of a "short squeeze."

Suppose that you are just one of many investors who have shorted a given stock. Savvy traders are aware of this large *short interest*. In fact, major stock exchanges report monthly on the number of shares of each stock that have been sold short and not yet repurchased. Many newspapers publish these lists.

If something happens to cause a given stock price to start rising, the "shorts" may very well scramble to try to cover their positions and limit their losses. This demand for stock can push the price up further. Owners of the stock, when they sense a short squeeze developing, naturally tend to become very choosy about what price they will accept. At the theoretical extreme, they have the "shorts" completely at their mercy.

When you sell short against the box, it should be noted, such matters are of no particular concern to you. Your net exposure in the market is zero.

TAX ADVANTAGES
AND DISADVANTAGES

To operate successfully, short sellers must have a good tax adviser or a thorough working knowledge of the tax rules. In multiple transactions particularly, those rules can be complicated, and may be changed in the future by Congress, the courts or the Internal Revenue Service.

Profits realized from going short are normally taxed at ordinary-income rates (they are almost always short-term transactions anyway). Losses are deductible only within limits set by the tax authorities. On the positive side, selling short against the box can be used to defer taking a capital gain from one year to the next, provided that you follow the rules correctly.

Short-selling is not allowed in individual retirement accounts, Keogh plans or other tax-favored savings programs. Most mutual funds and other pools of money that offer IRA and Keogh accounts are forbidden, by the rules under which they are organized, to sell short.

INVESTING ON MARGIN

DESCRIPTION

When you invest in securities, you do not necessarily have to put up the entire purchase price in cash. Instead, you can borrow part of the total from the broker with whom you are dealing. Investing in this way—"on margin"—is a tactic that can greatly increase your gains on profitable investments, and also multiply your losses when things don't go as you had hoped.

The traditional purpose of using margin is to gain *leverage.* With leverage, every dollar you put up works with the power of $1.50 or $2, or in the case of some speculative investments such as future contracts many times that amount. Example: You buy 100 shares of a stock selling at $20. The nominal price is $2,000 but, using a 50 percent margin loan from your broker, you put up only $1,000. In short order the stock rises to $30 and you sell. From the $3,000 proceeds, $1,000 is deducted to pay off the margin loan, leaving you with $2,000.

An investor who bought the stock in the hypothetical case above without using margin would have realized a gain of $1,000 on an investment of $2,000, or a return of 50 percent. The margin investor, by contrast, put up just $1,000 to earn $1,000, for a return of 100 percent.

Suppose, instead, that after the purchase at $20, the stock fell to $15 and was sold. The unmargined investor would show a 25 percent loss, while the one using margin would have just $500 left after settling the loan with the broker, for a net loss of 50 percent. At a stock price of $10, the margin buyer's investment would be wiped out.

In the real world, there are several complexities to consider in margin investing that the above example ignores: Commissions paid to the broker for buying and selling, interest on the margin loan, and the possibility of a margin maintenance call if the stock price declines. A margin call is a mandatory "request" from the broker, following the strict limits set by government regulators, securities exchanges and the brokerage firm itself, that you deposit additional cash or eligible securities as collateral in your margin account.

If you are unable or unwilling to put up this additional collateral, the rules require the broker to sell as much of your holdings as is necessary to bring your account back into compliance with margin limits.

There is a school of thought on Wall Street that margin investors should follow a simple rule to limit their losses in investments that aren't working out: "Never answer a margin call."

Leveraged investing like this sounds risky, and it is. However, it can have a useful place in an informed investor's strategies. After all, anyone who buys a house with a down payment and a mortgage is using leverage. It enables you to employ someone else's money to help pursue your financial objectives, while retaining the right to all the profits attained.

At times, depending on interest-rate levels and other prevailing conditions, you may consider using margin loans as a source of credit for other purposes, even to make a consumer purchase. Rates on margin loans are often substantially lower than those on, say, an unsecured consumer loan, because the stringent rules covering margin borrowing limit lenders' risks. In all cases, however, margin borrowers need to have a clear understanding of what is being used as collateral on their loans, and hence, what they stand to lose.

HOW AND WHERE TO GET
INFORMATION AND INVEST

Any good broker can supply you with information and the agreement form required to open a margin account. The process is somewhat different from applying for a credit card or consumer loan, in that the broker usually is not very concerned with your past credit history, how much you earn in your job, or why you want to borrow. If you can deposit a sufficient amount of eligible, marketable securities, that collateral speaks for itself.

COSTS OF BUYING,
OWNING AND SELLING

As was stated above, margin interest rates can be lower than rates on many other types of loans. Nevertheless, the burden of interest costs can be heavy. When you buy a security without using margin, it must generate enough earnings to cover your commission costs of both buying and selling before you can begin to profit from it. When you invest using margin, you must cover both the commission and interest costs before you begin to realize any return.

There is another, more subtle cost that sometimes arises in margin investing. If you are leveraged to your limit, a short-term decline in security prices may leave you no choice but to sell, even at a time when you may be absolutely convinced that market conditions are about to improve dramatically.

CAPITAL GAINS POTENTIAL

The usual purpose of investing on margin is to magnify your prospective capital gains. The Federal Reserve, which sets limits on how much margin can be used in buying stocks, has in recent years held the maximum level at 50 percent. Thus, using margin, the money you have available can be used to buy up to twice as many shares as you could acquire through an unmargined purchase. So margin can double your potential profit before subtracting the cost of the interest on the loan. With many other types of securities, margin requirements are even lower. Risks, it is imperative to remember, are similarly multiplied.

INCOME POTENTIAL

The typical margin investment runs counter to the purposes of investors who seek to maximize reliable current income from their capital. If the security you buy on margin produces any dividends or interest, they will be credited to your account just as if you owned the security outright. But seldom will that income be enough even to match the interest being charged against you on your margin loan. As a general rule, anyone who depends on investment income has no business taking the risks involved in margin investing.

RISKS AND DRAWBACKS

As the above discussions demonstrate, no consideration of investing on margin can proceed without a constant acknowledgement of the risks involved. With any heavily margined investment, the security you own needs only to lose a fraction of its market value to turn your investment into a total loss. Hence, it is axiomatic that any money invested on margin should be money you can afford to lose without any significant disruption of you other, basic financial plans and needs.

Margin investing, in addition, is by its very nature most suitable for short-term stategies. The longer the interest clock is ticking on a margin loan, the better your investments have to perform just to enable you to break even. The interest rate, by the way, is not fixed, but fluctuates with changes in prevailing open-market rates. So when you make a margin investment over any significant period of time, there is no way of knowing precisely in advance what your interest costs will be.

Investing on margin may restrict your maneuverability should unexpected opportunities come along. This can result in what economists call "opportunity costs"—benefits foregone because you were not in a position to take advantage of them.

LIQUIDITY

Margin accounts have some noteworthy flexible features. In contrast to, say, a home mortgage or bank loan, there is normally no set schedule for repayment of principal. Thus, you do not have to worry about early-repayment penalties should you wish to liquidate your position and close out the loan at any time. Once you have opened a margin account, unused credit is usually available to you whenever you want it, on short notice. Because of the risks involved, and the opportunity to accrue a mounting interest debt, ill-fated or ill-advised use of margin can leave you and your investments in a very illiquid position indeed.

TAX ADVANTAGES
AND DISADVANTAGES

Like other interest outlays, interest on margin loans is deductible for income-tax purposes in the year in which it is paid—within limits set by the tax authorities. These limits are designed to deter investors from transactions purely to gain a tax advantage. To cite one example, if you borrow money to buy municipal bonds, or borrow against an account in which municipal bonds are held, the normal tax treatment of interest may be suspended.

Also, you can run into a tax trap any time you take out a loan that even appears, by coincidence, to be used for certain investment purposes. Any margin invester, and any active investor who borrows money from any source, should consult a competent tax adviser or have a thorough knowledge of current tax laws and court rulings.

Profits and losses realized from securities owned on margin are subject to the usual capital gains taxes. The use of margin is not permitted in individual retirement accounts and other tax-favored savings plans.

INDEX INVESTING

DESCRIPTION

The game of trying to beat the stock market is as old as the market itself. Over the years investors big and small have devoted prodigious amounts of time and energy to it. Students of the market have developed countless approaches and theories with which to approach this challenge.

Some concentrate on fundamental analysis—the study of economic developments, trends in a given industry, and the factors that contribute to, or detract from, a given company's past, present and future earnings. Others practice technical analysis, using charts of past market fluctuations and "indicators," such as the ratio of short-selling to overall market activity or the amount of cash being held in reserve by investing institutions. They believe, essentially, that the best clues to the future direction of the market or an individual stock lie in the past and present behavior of the market or the stock itself.

Still others have gone far beyond these conventional disciplines. They have sought answers to the riddle of the stock market in astrology, fashion trends, even facetiously in the outcome of pro football's Super Bowl.

One school of thought, which has considerable support in the academic world, holds that while this activity may be a nice source of gainful employment to thousands of economists, analysts and financial advisers, it is otherwise pointless and unproductive. This doctrine is called the "efficient-market" hypothesis, or the "random walk" theory.

In sum, random-walkers believe that, at any given moment, all that is known and suspected about the future is already reflected in current stock prices. Thus, anything that can be predicted with better than 50-50 certainty isn't likely to be useful information for investment purposes, since the stock market has already "discounted" it—that is, adjusted its price level to take its presumed impact into account.

From this theory evolved the concept of the index fund, operating on an if-you-can't-beat-them-join-them principle. Index funds dispense with all the usual costly and time-consuming efforts to analyze and predict the market. They simply assemble a portfolio of stocks that duplicates the makeup of one of the leading measures of the market, such as Standard & Poor's composite index of 500 stocks.

Once they begin operating, they buy or sell only when stocks are added to or dropped from the index, as in cases where a company is absorbed through a merger.

Assuming that an index fund is properly constructed, an investor in it expects that his or her fortunes will rise and fall precisely, or very nearly so, with the ups and downs of the index. As you might expect, index funds are highly controversial within the investment world. People who have had a long history of success in stock-market investing sneer at them. Economists and security analysts naturally find the very idea abhorrent, since it implicitly declares that all the work on which they pride themselves, and from which they earn their living, is irrelevant. Some investment firms proudly cite independent studies of their long-term results that show that they have consistently outperformed indexes like the S&P 500.

The debate seems unlikely to be settled in the foreseeable future. But the random-walk theory has already had a substantial impact on the investment world. Many students of the stock market agree that the market is efficient to some extent. They contend, however, that it is still eminently worthwhile to search out areas in which inefficiencies exist. The paradox in all this is that if everyone came to believe totally in the efficient-market theory and stopped working so hard at analyzing it, the market would logically grow much less efficient than it is now.

You may well have any of a wide range of opinions about the efficient-market hypothesis. Whatever they are, if you invest in stocks you should be aware of it, becasie it influences the way many other market participants play the game. This includes not only pure index funds but "closet indexers"—investors and professional money managers who practice index investing to some extent without openly saying so, and perhaps, without admitting it to themselves.

HOW AND WHERE TO GET
INFORMATION AND INVEST

Index funds have traditionally enjoyed their greatest popularity with institutions such as pension funds. But they are available to small investors in the form of mutual funds as well as funds managed by some banks and brokerage firms. These organizations can provide you with prospectuses and other material that further explains index investing.

COSTS OF BUYING,
OWNING AND SELLING

By its very nature, index investing can and should be inexpensive. It is impractical to try on your own, unless you are very wealthy, but it is a relatively simple assignment for any competent manager of a large pool of money. The manager will have some costs, in handling paperwork, setting up the portfolio, and occasionally adjusting the portfolio for changes in the makeup of the index used. And of course the manager will want to charge a fee from the assets of the fund that is large enough to allow for some profit. Beyond that, however, costs should be low, since index funds need not pay for research, regular brokerage commissions or extensive trading operations.

When considering an index fund, you should check to see that the fees it charges are indeed low. Unless your investment expertise is extremely limited, it does not make sense to pay any large sales commissions or other up-front fees to invest in an index fund.

CAPITAL GAINS
POTENTIAL

Investors in index funds typically follow the conservative strategy of seeking long-term capital gains as the stock market rises over time— if it rises over time. As any examination of the past record of a market index will show, this is a reasonable hope over the long term—with some sharp fluctuations up and down to be expected along the way.

Some owners of individual stocks and other investments will obtain much better results than an index fund. Others, in the parlance of Wall Street, will "underperform" the indexes. In opting to go with an index fund, an investor gives up any realistic hope of "making a killing" in the market in return for the reasonable assurance that drastic losses also are unlikely.

You could theoretically trade in and out of an index fund in the hope of making short-term profits. But if your inclinations are speculative, there are many other vehicles—options and stock-index futures, to name two—that are designed more specifically to suit your purposes.

INCOME POTENTIAL

While index funds move up and down with the market, they produce an added source of gain in the form of dividends paid by companies in their portfolios. This yield is likely to be moderate—a sort of compromise between the low yields of the newer, growing companies represented in the index and the high payouts of the more mature stocks.

All this may be fine for an investor interested in obtaining a combination of growth and income. It also means that an index fund is a poor choice for people who want or need the greatest possible current yield from their investments.

For the typical index-fund investor with long term goals, it may well make sense to reinvest dividends automatically in order to gain growth of capital and the advantages of compounding. It should be easy to arrange this through the sponsor of the fund.

RISKS AND
DRAWBACKS

With an index fund, you eliminate one major risk of investing in stocks—the possibility of choosing the wrong stock. Every day the market as a whole does well, your investment will do well (if, for some reason this does not happen, it is time to investigate immediately).

In the process of eliminating business risk associated with owning a small number of individual stocks or other investments, you take on the nearest thing available to pure market risk. Every day the market does poorly, your investment will do poorly (if, for some reason, this does not happen, you may be pleased, but it is still time to investigate immediately).

To some investors, the idea of buying an index fund is repugnant. They see index investing as not just cautious, but downright timid, and mindless to boot. They would rather give investing their best effort, for better or worse, than simply buy a ticket on the market train and sit passively back in their seats.

Index investing appeals to many institutions such as pension funds because the managers of these funds have legal constraints on them mandating "prudence" in their role as fiduciaries, managers of other people's money. These constraints may also apply to an individual at times—for instance, if you are acting as an executor of someone's estate. At those times, it is advisable to get good legal advice about all investments you are considering. When you are operating on your own, with your own money, you do not have the legal obligations of a fiduciary.

LIQUIDITY

With an investment such as a mutual fund practicing index investing, liquidity should be no problem. You can buy or sell any time, on short notice. However, index investing is most suitable for money you can afford to set aside for long periods of time. If there is a reasonable chance that you will need to cash in your investment in an index fund at some unpredictable time in the near future, that date could coincide with a low point in stock prices, and consequently bring a poor or negative return on your investment.

TAX ADVANTAGES
AND DISADVANTAGES

Index investing involves the standard tax rules covering stocks—on capital gains, capital losses, and dividends. Since an index fund represents a nearly permanent portfolio, it should normally make few taxable capital-gains distributions to its investors.

If you reinvest dividends in an index fund, you should be aware that you are still liable for taxes on them for the year in which they are paid—unless the shares of the fund are held in some tax-deferred plan such as an individual retirement account. If you decide that it suits your temperament and long-term objectives, an index fund may be used for an IRA, Keogh plan or other tax-favored savings and investment program.

CONVERTIBLE SECURITIES

DESCRIPTION

Suppose, for a moment, that a situation arises in which you have some money to invest in securities, but you cannot decide whether common stocks or fixed-income securities offer the best deal for you. You could split the money down the middle, putting half in stocks and half in bonds. Or you might consider a sort of compromise form of investment known as a *convertible.*

Over the years, many corporations have issued convertible preferred stocks or convertible debentures (commonly referred to on Wall Street as convertible bonds). These securities carry a fixed interest or dividend rate, but may be exchanged whenever their owners wish—subject to any limits spelled out by the issuer—for a specified amount of common stock. As a result of their dual character, convertibles can provide their owners with fairly generous income, while at the same time giving them the hope of benefiting from rising stock prices.

They also may at times provide a degree of protection from adverse market conditions. If the price of Hypothetical Corp.'s common stock declines, the "conversion value" of its convertibles will drop, too. But in theory at least, the comparatively high yield of the convertible may act as a brake on any sharp decline in its price.

In considering convertibles, there are several reasons why investors should differentiate between those that are debentures and those that are preferred stocks. Debentures are debt issues that rank ahead of any preferred or common stocks as claims on the assets of the issuer. In addition, dividends paid on preferred stocks are largely free of tax to corporations that own the shares, but not to individual investors. This has the effect of making preferreds somewhat less attractive to individuals than competing fixed-income securities, all other things being equal.

Most, but not all, convertibles are issued with the common stock of the issuer as the underlying security. Special cases sometimes arise in which, say, an issuer that owns a large stock interest in another company may sell a bond or preferred stock that is convertible into the common shares of that other company.

HOW AND WHERE TO GET
INFORMATION AND INVEST

Investors can choose among several hundred convertible bonds and preferreds that are traded on stock exchanges or in the over-the-counter market. Any good broker should be able to provide you with information and handle your orders to buy and sell. Some brokers, in fact, make a specialty of following convertibles. There are investment advisory services, and mutual funds and other organized pools of money, that also specialize in convertibles.

COSTS OF BUYING,
OWNING AND SELLING

Brokers charge commissions to buy or sell convertibles, just as they normally do with stocks and bonds. Commission rates on bonds are traditionally lower than they are on stocks. So you may be able to trade convertible bonds at lower cost than you could convertible preferreds. There is usually no commission or other fee imposed when you elect to exchange a convertible for its underlying security.

CAPITAL GAINS
POTENTIAL

Some investors use convertible securities to pursue capital gains while retaining a measure of protection against stock-market risk. To see how this works, consider the following example. Hypothetical Corp.'s common stock is trading at $50. Hypothetical also has convertible preferred stock outstanding that allows its owners the right to obtain one common share at any time in exchange for each preferred share they hold. Because the Hypothetical preferred has a considerably higher yield, it is trading at $70.

The conversion feature has no immediate attraction, because exchanging a share of the convertible for a share of the common would leave you with a $20 paper loss. But it could produce a payoff in the future if the common stock rises in price.

Suppose the common does indeed rise, to $80. The preferred, exchangable one-for-one for the common, will naturally rise to at least $80 as well. Since it still pays a larger dividend than the common, in these circumstances it might rise to $90. If you sell the convertible in the open market, you will net a $20 gain, or 28.6 percent, on your original $70 investment.

That is smaller than the 60 percent profit an owner of Hypothetical's common could have realized during the same period. But you have been paid more generous dividends, and presumably taken less risk, while you owned the preferred than if you had owned the common stock instead.

INCOME POTENTIAL
Although convertible securities usually offer higher yields than common stocks of the same issuer, they also usually offer lower yields than you could obtain on straight debt securities that have no conversion features. Therefore, they may not be especially attractive for investors whose paramount objective is maximum current income from their assets. Straight fixed-income investments, of course, offer no protection from inflation. With a convertible, there is the hope of a rise in the price of the underlying common, and thus some chance of at least partial protection from inflation.

RISKS AND
DRAWBACKS
Some financial experts start their discussions of convertible securities with a warning—these investments should not automatically be thought of as a "best of both worlds" combination of stocks and fixed-income investments. In the active marketplace for all types of financial investments, any obvious benefits a convertible or any other security offers are likely to be reflected in the price the security commands at the time you wish to buy.

Indeed, some people see convertibles from exactly the opposite viewpoint—as a poor compromise that offers neither the capital gains potential of common stocks nor the kind of income available from a straight bond or preferred stock. This negative view is hotly disputed by advocates of convertibles who maintain that a diligent search of the markets can frequently turn up neglected convertibles that offer excellent investment value.

While convertibles are generally considered safer than common stocks, they are not without risk. If both the bond and stock markets drop, prices of convertibles can be expected to fall, too. Furthermore, when you buy a convertible, you are taking business risk with the issuer, just as you do if you buy the company's common stock or straight fixed-income securities.

Before you buy any convertible, you should check not only all details of the conversion privilege, but also any *call* provision—a statement by the issuer that spells out when, and under what terms, it may redeem the issue before its scheduled maturity date. Call provisions can have a material effect on the price of convertible securities with the passage of time.

LIQUIDITY

Convertible securities of large, well-known issuers generally enjoy fair liquidity. They may not be as actively traded as the common stocks of their issuers. However, if you own a convertible that is trading at or very near its conversion value, you normally enjoy the privilege of exchanging it at any time and without cost for the underlying common stock.

TAX ADVANTAGES
AND DISADVANTAGES

Dividends or interest received from convertible investments, and capital gains or losses realized from selling them, are subject to the standard tax rules covering securities. As noted above, dividends received by corporations are largely exempt from federal income tax. This exemption does not apply to individual investors.

When you exercise a conversion privilege, exchanging a convertible security for the shares of the common stock of the same issuer, you are not normally considered to have realized a capital gain or loss for tax purposes. This rule may not apply, however, in those relatively rare instances in which a security of one issuing company is convertible into the stock of some other issuer.

Convertibles, or a mutual fund or other investment company that specializes in them, may be suitable for an individual retirement account, Keogh plan or other tax-deferred savings program, particularly if you are a reasonably sophisticated investor and have an enduring interest in this segment of the financial markets.

CREDIT UNIONS

DESCRIPTION

In an era of rapid financial change, credit unions retain an old-fashioned appeal for many savers, investors and borrowers. They are non-profit cooperatives, owned by their members, which trace their origins to the 19th Century in Europe and the early 20th Century in the United States.

Credit unions have traditionally provided a convenient place to save, and at the same time a source of readily available credit at attractive interest rates. They can provide these services because their costs are usually very low. Some of the work required to operate them is customarily performed by volunteers, and they may have free access to office space and other facilities provided by a company or other organization whose employees participate in them.

Members of any credit union must share some common bond, and that bond is most commonly related tk their work. But credit unions can also be organized by people who live in the same community, or belong to the same religious organization or fraternal or civic group.

For many people, credit unions have an image as small-time institutions—a place to conduct simple transactions like saving via payroll withholding and borrowing to buy consumer items such as a car or furniture. To some credit-union members, in fact, smallness and informality can be a major part of their appeal. At a credit union where your face, or at least your name, is familiar, a check might be cashed or a loan obtained without elaborate security measures or extensive paperwork.

Some credit unions are anything but small-time. The Navy Federal Credit Union's assets surpassed $1 billion in 1982. With financial deregulation, credit unions have the option of offering a broad range of financial services—credit cards, automatic tellers, individual retirement accounts, even mortgage loans and discount stock-brokerage. More and more credit unions may expand into these areas in the future. Others may choose to stick with simplicity.

HOW AND WHERE TO GET
INFORMATION AND INVEST

Many people have ready access to a credit union where they live, work, worship or socialize. If you are interested but cannot find one readily that you are eligible to join, you can consult your state's credit union league. A trade association, the Credit Union National Association, has headquarters at P.O. Box 431, Madison WI 53701. It is possible to try to organize a new credit union, if you are willing to tackle the assignment.

Although saving at a credit union works in much the same way as it does at a banking or savings institution, credit unions operate under a different setup and hence a different terminology. Deposits you make are used to buy *shares*, commonly in units of $5, and the earnings you receive from your savings are called *dividends*. In credit unions that offer checking, checks are referred to as share drafts.

COSTS OF BUYING,
OWNING AND SELLING

If a credit union charges a fee to new members, it is typically nominal and of little concern. As a member and therefore an owner, you may receive a rebate on a loan, or other payment, at the end of a year in which a credit union's operating results turn out better than expected.

The main cost to consider is any opportunity cost you may incur by saving at or borrowing from a credit union without first doing some comparison shopping to see if other competing institutions like a bank a money market mutual fund offer better deals.

CAPITAL GAINS
POTENTIAL

Saving at a credit union, perhaps by regular deductions from your paycheck, is one means of working toward long-term growth of your assets. Unless your credit union offers a discount brokerage service, however, it is not a logical place to look for capital gains, particulary of the short-term variety.

INCOME POTENTIAL

Credit unions may offer a variety of ways to obtain income from your savings, including money market accounts. Their merits in this regard vary widely from credit union to credit union. A credit union that gets active support from a business or other employer, for example, may be able to offer yields competitive with, or better than, those available at other institutions. The situation may be very different at a poorly run or lethargically sponsored credit union.

RISKS AND
DRAWBACKS

All federal credit unions, and nearly all state-chartered credit unions, are covered by deposit insurance, usually up to $100,000 per account. However, in a few states, state-chartered credit unions are not required by law to be covered by this insurance. It makes good sense to inquire before joining any credit union exactly what its insurance arrangement is. At the same time, you may also ask what insurance, if any, the credit union provides or sells to cover loan balances in the event that you die or become disabled.

Many large employers enthusiastically support credit unions for their workers. As the Credit Union National Association says, "Employers often find that a credit union is an excellent, low-cost fringe benefit. A credit union frequently reduces or eliminates problems such as garnishment, wage assignments, company loans and salary advances."

A credit union, particulary a small or poorly run one, may not be the answer to all your financial needs. But is nevertheless may be worth considering joining, if only to gain access to it as a possible source of credit.

LIQUIDITY

Liquidity can be one of the prime selling points of a good, insured credit union. A credit union at your place of work can be the ideal place to maintain funds you may need to tap at short notice. Loans may be available without processing or qualifying delays.

Of course, if you invest in something other than a standard savings vehicle at a credit union, the liquidity of your assets may be affected.

For example, there are likely to be early withdrawal penalties on time deposits. In an uninsured credit union, you should be aware that you are taking liquidity risk, no matter how slight it may seem.

TAX ADVANTAGES
AND DISADVANTAGES

Though money your savings earns at credit unions is described as dividends, it is taxed in the same way as bank interest. If you are in a high tax bracket, you may be able to earn a better after-tax return, though at a somewhat greater risk, from tax-exempt securities such as municipal bonds.

Many credit unions actively promote individual retirement accounts, Keogh plans and other tax-favored savings programs. They can offer convenient payroll-deduction systems for accumulating your annual contribution to such a plan a little at a time. It makes sense, however, to check at the start, and monitor regularly thereafter, how the return offered by a credit union IRA compares with what you could earn at other competing institutions.

DISCOUNT BROKERAGE SERVICES

DESCRIPTION

On May 1, 1975, a historic change took place in the way brokerage firms competed for your business as an investor. Until then, all brokers operated under a fixed schedule of minimum commissions for handling orders to buy and sell securities. Whether you consulted extensively with your broker for investment advice and help in financial planning, or whether you used the broker simply to carry out decisions you made on your own, the price was the same.

Beginning on "May Day," however, the element of price competition was introduced to the securities business with the abolition of fixed commission rates. Over time, this produced a clear and understandable trend. The brokers competed hardest for the patronage of their biggest customers—in particular, investing institutions such as pension funds with huge pools of money to manage.

The commission rates brokers charged these institutions dropped significantly. At the same time, rates for small "retail" customers showed little, if any, decline, and in some cases actually rose. This helped create an opening, and a demand, for discount brokerage firms specializing in executing orders at relatively low cost. By the early 1980s, discounters had established a significant and growing presence in the securities industry, and banks, savings and loans and other financial institutions were entering the discount brokerage business by acquiring established firms or starting their own.

The typical discount brokerage firm advertises commission rates 50, 75 or even as much as 90 percent below those charged by full-service brokers, on sales and purchases of stocks, options and other securities. To do this profitably, it minimizes, or dispenses completely with, such other investment services as research and financial-planning advice. Its customer representatives usually work on salary, in contrast to the commission-sharing pay setup that is standard at full-service firms.

HOW AND WHERE TO GET
INFORMATION AND INVEST

Discount brokers are increasing in numbers and accessibility. The nearest one may be as close as your local bank or shopping center. Some discounters advertise heavily in newspapers and financial publications, and many have toll-free telephone lines through which they offer information and trading services.

It would be difficult and time-consuming to try to evaluate the relative merits of all the discount brokers seeking your business. However, it is sensible to do some comparison-shopping before picking one to deal with. Recommendations from friends or neighbors who are satisfied customers of a given discount broker can be especially helpful.

COSTS OF BUYING,
OWNING AND SELLING

The whole point of using a discount broker, obviously, is to save on the costs of operating as an investor. In one typical advertisement, a discounter offered to buy or sell 500 shares of a stock selling at $13 a share for $50, in comparison to one full-service broker's charge of $170 for the same transaction.

As a lure to new customers, discounters may offer promotional rates below their usual fee schedule on the first, or first few, orders you place with them. They also may offer special rates for active traders who conduct, or agree to conduct, a specified amount of business with the firm in a given period of time.

The benefits gained, of course, must be weighed against what you are giving up. Saving on commissions will do you little good if you do a poor job selecting investments without the help of a full-line broker. Particularly for investors who trade regularly and have large portfolios, it should be remembered that any broker, whether labelled discount or not, can negotiate on rates to keep the business of a valued customer.

As with full-service brokers, discounters' typical fees are skewed in favor of larger orders. That is logical, in the sense that any broker has some costs for handling each order that are fixed, whether a tiny odd lot or a big block of stock is involved. Also because of these fixed costs, discounters generally set a minimum fee for each order of, say, $40, or perhaps less. When you are dealing with a very small transaction, a full-line broker with whom you have a long-standing relationship may handle it, as a courtesy, for a smaller commission than a discounter's minimum fee.

CAPITAL GAINS
POTENTIAL

Whether you use a discount or full-service broker, you are selecting from the same universe of stocks, bonds and other investments with the same risks and rewards. By reducing your costs of buying and selling, obviously, you can enhance your chances of coming out ahead of the game, especially if you buy and sell regularly. But that principle applies only if you are capable of and comfortable with making your investment choices largely on your own, or with the help of advisers independent of a broker (see the chapter on investment advisory services).

Savings on commission dollars are of little or no value if the firm you deal with does a poor job of execution—that is, getting the best buying or selling price possible. When you trade through any broker, discount or otherwise, it is advisable to maintain close scrutiny of the firm's performance in this regard.

INCOME POTENTIAL

A discount broker that provides good execution and timely service can help investors interested primarily in maximizing their current income by reducing their costs of investing. If the execution is poor, or the service is slow, it can cost you in total return on your money.

Income-conscious investors should be aware that marketing efforts of many discount brokers are aimed primarily at traders in stocks, options, financial futures and other relatively fast-moving investments. Is a discount broker you are considering well set up to buy and sell bonds? Can it offer you the range of vehicles—for example, central assets accounts, unit trusts or mortgage securities—that a full-service brokerage firm has on its shelves? Will it get you as good a deal on, say, a municipal bond as a firm specializing in tax-free securities could? These and similar questions are pertinent to ask before deciding where best to shop for income-producing investments.

RISKS AND
DRAWBACKS

If you buy the wrong stocks, or the right stocks at the wrong time, you can lose money no matter where you bought them. If you buy them through, and on the advice of, a full-service broker, you can put the blame, in your own mind at least, on the broker. If you buy them through a discount broker, there may be no one to castigate but the blundering ignoramus standing before you in the mirror.

The point of this contrast, of course, is that discount brokerage is best suited for investors who have the knowledge, the time and the inclination to plot their own financial courses. If the markets are an impossible maze for you, or if you are too busy to spend much time figuring them out, you may be better off putting your efforts into finding a good full-service firm and an able, conscientious broker at that firm.

You do not need to confine yourself exclusively to one of the two alternatives. Many investors have accounts at both discount and full-service firms. Naturally, if you attempt consistently to pump a full-service broker for advice and ideas, and then act on those ideas through a discounter, the full-service broker isn't likely to work assiduously on your behalf for very long.

All that having been said, the quality of service offered by a discount broker remains an important consideration. You may not be paying first-class rates, but that doesn't mean you have to ride in the baggage compartment. Some bare-bones discounters may deal with you as an anonymous voice on the phone. Others may designate a single representative to handle all your business, and provide a broad range of financial services. You may well want to check on such details before opening an account.

LIQUIDITY

When you deal with a reputable discounter, you can reasonably expect your investments to be as liquid as they would be if you were operating through any other broker. Most discounters are members of self-regulatory organizations in the securities industry such as the National Association of Securities Dealers and some or all leading stock exchanges, as well as the Securities Investor Protection Corp., an organization that provides insurance in the event of a brokerage firm failure.

TAX ADVANTAGES
AND DISADVANTAGES

Dealing with a discount broker has no material impact on the tax status of your investments, other than affecting the size of the commissions that you add to your cost and subtract from your proceeds when you calculate your gains and losses for tax purposes. Some discounters aggressively promote individual retirement accounts, Keogh plans and other tax-favored investment programs.

DIVIDEND REINVESTMENT PLANS

DESCRIPTION

One of the long-standing attractions of putting your savings in a standard bank account has been automatic compounding of interest. It is convenient, and over time can make money grow at an impressive rate. The principle was once aptly described by Benjamin Franklin: "Money makes money. And the money that money makes makes more money."

For investors in mutual funds and many companies with publicly held common stock, a similar service is available through what is known as a dividend reinvestment plan. These plans originated in the mutual fund industry and, since the late 1960s, have proliferated among companies with publicly traded stock as well. By all accounts, they have proved popular with investors.

The plans allow shareholders to elect not to receive a check when dividends are paid periodically, but instead to have the money automatically reinvested in additional shares of the fund or company involved. They provide a convenient means for long-term investors to build up their stock or mutual fund holdings with dividends they might otherwise spend. For the small investor, they make it possible to make additional purchases of shares in amounts below what many stockbrokers would want to handle at anything less than a prohibitive commission cost.

Today these plans are a standard feature of mutual funds, including money market funds. It remains advisable, however, to verify details of how a given fund's plan works before investing. An alternative form of pooled investment, known as a unit trust, may also offer dividend reinvestment, either in units of the trust or in shares of a mutual fund advised by the same company that sponsors the trust.

Among publicly held companies, nearly all electric, gas and telephone utilities offer dividend reinvestment plans. So do hundreds of other large companies in a wide range of industries. Plans are somewhat less common among smaller companies.

Many companies give participants the right to make additional cash purchases of stock directly through their dividend reinvestment plans. Over the years, this has become an increasingly important attribute of these plans. Some companies also allow owners of their bonds and preferred stocks to automatically reinvest their interest or dividends in common shares.

HOW AND WHERE TO GET
INFORMATION AND INVEST

A stockbroker may not have much information to offer about dividend reinvestment plans, unless pressed for it by a customer. That is understandable, since the dividend reinvestment process bypasses the broker once investors have made their initial purchases of stock. However, independent investment advisory firms such as Moody's Investors Service Inc. and Standard & Poor's Corp. periodically publish lists of companies that offer them.

Probably the best source of information about dividend reinvestment plans is mutual funds and publicly held companies themselves. Mutual fund prospectuses usually give details of how their plans operate, and applications to open fund accounts include a section in which, by simply checking the appropriate box, the investor enrolls in the reinvestment plan for dividends, capital gains distributions, or both. Stockholders or would-be stockholders of individual companies can obtain information and an application by telephoning or writing to the investor relations department of the company in question.

Once a plan begins to operate, investments are made automatically, and are reported on periodic statements issued to the investor by whatever entity handles the record-keeping for the company or fund, be it the company itself or an agent bank.

COSTS OF BUYING,
OWNING AND SELLING

Low cost is one of the most attractive features of dividend reinvestment plans. Some companies impose a charge for handling dividend-reinvestment transactions. Many others do not, however, and thus investors are able to buy shares through these channels without paying the usual brokerage commissions or fund sales charges.

Some companies even offer a discount on the market price of stock acquired through dividend reinvestment. They do this to encourage participation in the plans, which provide them with a steady, inexpensive supply of capital, and help create a loyal following of long-term shareowners.

CAPITAL GAINS
POTENTIAL

Taking part in a dividend reinvestment plan does not affect the chances that the price of the stock or fund involved will rise or fall. But dividend reinvestment plans do have some features that can help enhance the gains an investor realizes. The power of compounding is legendary. If $10,000 is invested at a fixed annual interest or dividend rate of 12 percent in a security whose price doesn't change, it will increase to about $20,000 in six years. Since dividend reinvestment plans give their participants access to compounding, they can enhance the growth rate of an investor's portfolio.

At the same time, dividend reinvestment plans automatically allow their participants to apply a principle known as dollar cost averaging. In a world of ever-changing inflation rates, interest rates and volatile securities markets, the value of most types of investments is constantly fluctuating. In a program of periodic purchases such as a dividend reinvestment plan, similar amounts of money invested will buy more shares when the price of a security is low, and fewer shares when the price is high. Over a period of time, this means that an investor's average cost of purchase works out to less than the average price of the security over the same interval.

INCOME POTENTIAL

Dividend reinvestment plans can increase future income by helping money grow. They are not designed for investors who need maximum current income from their assets, since they divert money that would normally be received in the form of a check into the purchase of additional securities.

RISKS AND
DRAWBACKS

When you sign up for a dividend reinvestment plan, you are declaring, implicity if not explicitly, your optimism about the long-term future of the company or mutual fund offering it and the economy in which it will operate. These plans are of relatively little value to short-term traders looking for quick profits.

In fact, reinvestment plans actually tend to increase your market risk, as well as your potential reward; in a stock or mutual fund. If you accept dividends in the form of cash payment, you realize a partial return on your initial investment. If you elect instead to reinvest dividends, you are in effect keeping all your eggs in the same basket for an extended period of time, even as the quantity of eggs is growing. As with any investment involving market risk, investment advisers say it is important to monitor regularly the fortunes of any company or fund in which you are reinvesting dividends.

LIQUIDITY

Most dividend reinvestment plans are described as strictly voluntarily, and can be terminated at any time with the appropriate notice to the fund or company involved. Mutual funds stand continuously ready to redeem (that is, cash in) all shares, including full and fractional shares acquired through dividend reinvestment.

A corporation with a dividend reinvestment plan may offer to handle sales as well as purchases of stock for participants in the plan. Stock accumulated through dividend reinvestment can be sold at any time through a broker. However, fractional shares are generally not bought and sold in the public market.

TAX ADVANTAGES
AND DISADVANTAGES

Let's assume you own stock that paid $600 in dividends in a given calendar year, all of which went directly into new shares under a dividend reinvestment plan. Though you actually did not receive this $600, current law says you must pay tax on it as though you did. To support your participation in a dividend reinvestment plan, you must be able to meet this tax obligation from other sources of income.

However, if the investment is held through an individual retirement account, Keogh plan or other tax-deferred savings program, no current tax liability is incurred, since earnings under these programs are not subject to tax until withdrawals from them begin. Therefore, dividend reinvestment plans fit ideally into any tax-deferred retirement savings program.

A further exception, created by a tax law passed in 1981, applies to stocks of many utility companies. It allows participants in those utilities' dividend reinvestment plans to exempt up to $750 a year, or $1,500 for a married couple filing a joint return, from current taxation. This exception may or may not expire after 1985, depending on action by Congress.

FOREIGN CURRENCIES

DESCRIPTION

In a world where countless international business transactions take place every day, the values of the various countries' currencies fluctuate constantly against the U.S. dollar. Banks and other financial institutions handle vast amounts of foreign exchange, swapping one currency for another. Ups and downs in the dollar, the Japanese yen, the West German mark or the Swiss franc can have a powerful impact on government policies and financial and political relationships between countries.

Any place where so much money is changing hands is bound to attract investors' interest. There is a variety of ways in which you can seek to profit from changes in currency exchange rates. Whether you might want to pursue any of them depends on your circumstances, temperament and the financial means at your disposal.

Suppose you were worried about inflation and political trends in the United States, and thought that the value of the dollar was headed for a period of decline in the currency markets. You could simply take some of your dollars to a bank or foreign-exchange firm, and swap them for some other currency at the going rate. In the past, some U.S. investors have been attracted in particular to the Japanese yen, because of Japan's industrial successes, and the Swiss franc, because of the traditional economic stability and low inflation rates that have prevailed in Switzerland.

Such a straightforward investment in a foreign currency has its limitations, however. The bank or other foreign-exchange firm builds in a spread between its buying and selling prices of all currencies to cover its costs and profit. As a result, a foreign currency you buy must rise a certain amount against the dollar before you reach the break-even point.

For the conservative or income-minded investor, this proposition presents a problem because money invested this way earns no interest or dividends. For the speculative investor, at the same time, it does not offer a great deal of leverage—the opportunity to realize a large percentage gain in a relatively short period of time. Recognizing these circumstances, people in the financial world have devised several more complicated vehicles for foreign-currency investing.

One choice you have is to put your money in an interest-bearing account with a foreign bank. This, however, means taking not only currency risk but country risk—the political and business risks of investing outside the United States (see the following chapter on foreign investments). In addition, a foreign bank account does not offer the protection of U.S. federal deposit insurance.

There are some federally insured (up to $100,000) certificates of deposit denominated in foreign currencies available in this country. In the mid-1980s, Deak-Perera, a New York-based precious metals and foreign exchange firm, offered insured CDs in $5,000 minimum amounts, with the choice of two maturities (both less than a year) and three currencies—the mark, the yen and the Swiss franc. The interest rates on these CDs were all below the passbook savings rate on dollar accounts at U.S. depository institutions—as low as 1.75 percent to 1.875 percent on Swiss franc accounts.

For the speculatively inclined, there are both options and futures contracts traded in this country on certain foreign currencies. Investors considering a venture into either of these should have a thorough working knowledge of options and futures, both of which are discussed in separate chapters of this book.

HOW AND WHERE TO GET
INFORMATION AND INVEST

Choosing a currency investment that meets your needs may involve inquiring in widely disparate places. If you want to shop foreign banks, they may have U.S. offices that will be responsive to your inquiries. You may also investigate specialized precious metals and currency dealers for vehicles they have to offer. For information on currency futures and options, and execution of buy and sell orders in those securities, you may turn to a commodity or stock brokerage firm.

Before investing in currencies, it also makes sense to devote some study to how foreign-exchange markets work and what factors can influence the relative value of currencies. Such study may be daunting to any casual investor who is thinking of dabbling in this highly sophisticated and complex game.

COSTS OF BUYING,
OWNING AND SELLING

If you invest in a foreign currency through a standard vehicle such as an option or futures contract, your costs of buying and selling will be the standard commissions charged by brokers. If you pursue some strategy that involves actually exchanging your dollars for a foreign currency, you can expect to pay a cost that is built into the exchange rate set by the bank or other dealer that handles the transaction.

This cost can be difficult to evaluate, since the currency markets are constantly fluctuating. Anyone who has traveled abroad knows that the going rate can vary greatly, depending on the place you choose to exchange your money. Before making an investment commitment in currencies, you may wish to ask a bank or dealer how much it plans to collect on the deal.

CAPITAL GAINS
POTENTIAL

You can invest in foreign currencies in the hope of achieving large capital gains. A relatively small move in some foreign currency's value against the dollar may produce a big percentage profit in an option or futures contract on that currency. The risk you take in such a situation is normally great, and sometimes open-ended.

When you buy a foreign currency, you are purchasing only money—not any assets, such as real estate, or any participation in a business or other enterprise that can grow in the future. Sometimes, one currency can rise dramatically in value against another over a sustained period of time. But foreign-exchange markets are volatile, and generally require close and constant monitoring when you invest in them. For relatively conservative investors seeking long-term growth of their capital, investing in foreign currencies has some note-worthy limitations.

INCOME POTENTIAL

Many types of foreign-currency investments offer little or no potential for current income. A foreign bank to which American investors turn for safety and secrecy may even at times impose "negative interest," collecting a periodic fee on your account rather than paying you for the use of the money.

Certain foreign bank accounts may offer what appear to be alluring interest rates on deposits. In all cases of this sort, would-be investors should carefully consider the circumstances that encourage, or in fact impel, a bank to offer such a high rate in order to attract money. Savers and investors concerned with safety, as well as high income, should be especially wary of the risks, both real and potential, involved.

RISKS AND
DRAWBACKS

The foreign-exchange markets are volatile and unpredictable, subject to a wide variety of political, economic and psychological forces around the world. Governments themselves can have a powerful impact on the values of currencies by intervening—buying or selling large quantities of currencies from their reserves in an effort to halt or reverse a trend considered undesirable. Sometimes their efforts succeed, and sometimes they don't.

Speculators in the currency markets pit themselves against adversaries like government central banks, commercial banks and large multinational corporations. The currency department of a bank, for example, may employ a large staff, sophisticated facilities and great reserves of capital in seeking to help its large business customers "hedge" the currency risk to which they are exposed. An individual who enters this fray should be well-armed.

Some investors turn to currencies such as the Swiss franc for what they perceive to be a haven from risk. They may view the franc or some other currency as having some of the attributes of gold (see the chapter on precious metals). Whether you elect to invest in a foreign currency from this viewpoint depends to a great extent on your personal and political views of the future of the world.

LIQUIDITY

Currency exchange is normally a highly liquid process, and many currency investments can readily be bought and sold on short notice. When you select a particular vehicle, it makes sense to check whether it involves any exceptions to this general rule. Currency liquidity often comes at a price, however, in the form of the spread a bank or other dealer imposes between its buying and selling prices.

Travelers' checks denominated in foreign currencies are widely available for sale in this country. They are not investments per se, but can be money-management tools used by people who travel abroad a great deal. Such people can, for example, spread purchases of these travelers' checks over intervals to avoid the circumstance of settling for a single unfavorable exchange rate at a time when they need foreign currency for use. It is worth bearing in mind that sellers of travelers' checks benefit from the "float"—the free use of your money between the time you buy the checks and the time you spend them.

TAX ADVANTAGES
AND DISADVANTAGES

The treatment for tax purposes of a foreign-currency investment can vary widely depending on the form the investment takes. For example, interest earned on foreign bank accounts may be subject to special U.S. tax rules, and may incur a tax obligation in the foreign country as well. Some investments involving foreign currencies are used to avoid U.S. taxes. Their legality may be questionable, or subject to change in the future. Before embarking on any currency investment, especially a large one, you should have good tax advice or a thorough knowledge yourself of tax laws and prevailing tax rulings and tax treaties between countries.

Foreign currency investments have limited potential use, at best, for individual retirement accounts, Keogh plans and other U.S. tax-favored savings programs. For example, currency futures, like other futures contracts, are off-limits for IRAs and Keoghs. As a rule, foreign currencies do not fit the spirit of these programs as mandated by U.S. law. From the individual investor's standpoint, whatever currency investments have appeal may be best pursued separately from Keogh or IRA accounts.

FOREIGN INVESTMENTS

DESCRIPTION

From Swiss banks tk the gold mines of South Africa, foreign investments have always enjoyed a special mystique for Americans. In the
past, however, the typical individual investor was more likely to fanta-
size about investing abroad than to seriously consider attempting it.

In many cases there was, and still may be, good reason for this
reluctance. From many people's point of view, investment opportunities and risks may be abundant enough in the domestic economy.
Putting money to work in other countries means dealing with differing
laws concerning investor protection and disclosure of financial information, a different currency, and perhaps an unfamiliar economy as
well. It might also pose special tax problems and additional costs of
investing.

Nevertheless, beginning in the late 1970s, American financial experts began to look increasingly for foreign investment opportunities.
There are times, they realized, when money languishing in depressed
Wall Street markets might produce much better results in Tokyo,
Toronto or Zurich. The increased economic interdependence of the
industrialized countries and modern communications contributed to
sophisticated investors' eagerness to operate from an international
perspective. Financial links between countries grew as American financial-services firms expanded their overseas operations, and
some foreign firms moved into the U.S. marketplace.

Actually, people interested in stocks of foreign companies like Sony
of Japan or Britain's Rank Organisation have long been able to invest
in them in U.S. markets through a device known as American deposi-
tary receipts—documents issued by a U.S. bank that represent foreign shares held on deposit by the bank. Foreign governments have
sold numerous bond issues to American investors.

The number of choices has been widened in recent years by the
proliferation of investment companies, both mutual fund and closed-
end, that have foreign or international portfolios. These may be an
opportune choice for investors who want to invest internationally, but
who lack the capital and knowledge necessary to do it directly.

HOW AND WHERE TO GET
INFORMATION AND INVEST

U.S. brokers and other financial-services firms are devoting increased attention and research to overseas securities markets. They may be able to provide you with information and recommendations on specific governments, economies and companies, and to handle buy and sell orders for you. If you live in or near a large city, you may also be able to find a local office of, say, a Japanese brokerage house.

Information on funds that invest internationally can be obtained from brokers or the funds themselves. Reading fund prospectuses and other recent reports may be informative about the possible strategies and potential risks and benefits of foreign investments.

COSTS OF BUYING,
OWNING AND SELLING

Costs can be an important matter in buying foreign securities, and should be considered before you enter into any transaction. If your brokerage firm isn't a member of some foreign stock exchange, for example, you may have to pay a double commission each time you buy or sell.

Dealing in a different currency may mean actual and potential costs as well. Probably the most important of these to bear in mind is the currency risk involved in owning any security that is not denominated in dollars. You may, for example, obtain a 12 percent yield on an investment in some other country. But if the currency falls 12 percent in value against the dollar in a year's time, the whole return on the dollars you invested is negated.

When you buy foreign issues traded in this country, such as ADRs or the stock of a closed-end investment company specializing in foreign securities, you can expect to pay standard brokerage commissions. Like other mutual funds, open-ended funds with international portfolios may impose a sales charge when you buy, or they may be "no-load." Sponsors of all mutual funds normally collect an annual management fee from the assets of the fund.

CAPITAL GAINS POTENTIAL

Venturesome, knowledgeable investors may see foreign investing as a way to expand their opportunities for capital gains, particularly in times when the U.S. markets are in a slump. However, it should be noted that there is nothing inherently easy about picking the right time to move money from domestic investments abroad, or vice versa. Capital gains in an investment denominated in a foreign currency can be enhanced if the currency rises in value against the dollar during the time you own it. If the foreign security merely breaks even over a year's time, but the currency appreciates against the dollar, you can still emerge with a profit. Risk is similarly compounded.

INCOME POTENTIAL

Investors looking to maximize their income may consider securities of a foreign country in times when prevailing yields are greater abroad than they are in the United States. But people who need high income from their investments and safety of their principal should be wary of going this route. The results of even the most solid, prudent foreign investment may be disrupted by fluctuations in currency values.

If banks or other institutions of a foreign country are aggressively seeking your money by promoting extremely high interest rates, you should be especially wary. No entity seeking capital, whether in this country or abroad, will willingly pay returns that are way out of line with its competition in world markets without some important underlying reason.

The offer may come with a "story," e.g., "the government over there is subsidizing the banks so they can pay much better rates." In cases like these, you can usually assume that if the proferred reward were worth the risks involved, professional investors would have seized the opportunity long before you heard about it at a cocktail party or in an advertisement.

RISKS AND DRAWBACKS

Many people have learned first-hand the risks involved in uninformed and incautious foreign investing. They may have put money in a foreign bank just before the currency was devalued, or they may have bought shares of an ill-fated offshore mutual fund without considering that the reach of regulatory bodies like the Securities and Exchange Commission is limited beyond U.S. borders. At its most hazardous, foreign investing can pile country risk, both political and economic, and currency risk on top of business risk and market risk.

On the other hand, some large investors and investment companies seek to minimize risk by using foreign securities to diversify their holdings among several countries. They may hope, for example, that in times when American markets are declining, their investments in Hong Kong or London will do well enough to offset, or at least cushion, their overall losses. It should also be noted that sophisticated investors may hedge against currency risk using options or futures contracts on foreign currencies.

LIQUIDITY

Before you make a foreign investment, you should be reasonably confident of its liquidity. This may involve asking some questions and doing some research you wouldn't find necessary if you were investing in this country. In the worst case, of course, there are eventualities like a change of governments, with just possibly the seizure of foreign assets within that country's borders. More commonly, it may be wise to inquire into a given country's policies and restrictions on flows of money in and, especially, out. Investments in U.S.-based international investment companies and foreign securities whose shares are traded in this country are generally considered highly liquid.

TAX ADVANTAGES
AND DISADVANTAGES

Before you make a foreign investment, you should have a thorough knowledge of current U.S. tax laws that apply to your situation, and the tax laws applying to foreign investors in the country where you plan to put your money. These may significantly affect your prospective after-tax return on the investment. Securities of a foreign issuer, or shares of a fund with an international portfolio, may have a place in the individual retirement account, Keogh plan or other tax-favored savings program of an investor who is seeking to diversify the holdings of the plan as much as possible.

FUTURES CONTRACTS

DESCRIPTION

Futures contracts have been in use in this country for more than a century. For most of that time, they were mainly of interest only to business managers, farmers, and a relatively small community of professional traders and speculators. In the 1970s, however, as inflation accelerated, many newcomers were attracted to the market as a way to profit from rising commodity prices. Once the investing public got acquainted with futures, the concept was extended beyond agricultural and industrial commodities to many other types of investments.

In its simplest use, a futures contract is a very straightforward proposition. Consider the case of a farmer who has a wheat crop coming in some time in the future, and a baking company that will want to use that wheat to make bread. Both face an important uncertainty—what will the going price of wheat be at the time the crop is ready to be delivered?

To save themselves from having to operate under that uncertainty, they can agree on a price ahead of time. They then sign a contract under which the farmer agrees to deliver a specified amount of wheat to the baking company at a stated future date. Both parties are taking a gamble in this proposition. The farmer, in locking in a price in advance, takes the risk of missing out on any benefit from a subsequent rise in the price of wheat. The baking company stands to lose if the price of wheat falls.

Where there is risk, there is also opportunity. Investors who are in neither the farming nor the baking business may nevertheless have an opinion, and access to some information, about likely changes in wheat prices. They may seek to profit from that opinion or information by buying or selling a wheat futures contract on one of the nation's commodity exchanges.

Anyone who owns a futures contract makes a legal commitment to take delivery of the commodity or security covered by the contract, in the quantity specified, at the stated date. Anyone who sells a futures contract makes a similar commitment to make delivery. However, many participants in the futures markets have no intention of ever taking or making delivery. They enter into futures investments planning to close out their positions before the delivery date.

Nevertheless, every participant in the futures markets needs to be aware of the legal commitment involved. The standard nightmare vision of many a commodity trader is a row of trucks lined up before his or her house, filled with $100,000 worth of live cattle, and someone standing on the doorstep holding an invoice for $100,000 in cash.

In practice, alert, knowledgeable futures traders take steps to assure that this nightmare never becomes a reality. But there are plenty of other things that can occur in futures trading to disturb your sleep. It is a fast-moving, high-risk game. Many investors who do not have a high tolerance for risk never consider venturing into the futures markets. Many more who do take the plunge suffer losses and depart forever. Still, the active, vibrant futures markets that exist in this country attest to the fact that futures have a great allure for some investors who are armed with sufficient expertise and risk capital.

HOW AND WHERE TO GET
INFORMATION AND INVEST

Futures contracts are bought and sold, much like stocks, on a variety of exchanges around the country. Many securities brokerage firms do an active business in futures. In addition, there are brokerage firms that specialize in commodity research and handling futures transactions. A wide variety of information about futures is available from any of these sources.

There are many investment advisory services and newsletters that report on developments in the futures markets and assess the outlook for futures prices. Some emphasize "fundamental" factors—for example, weather and political trends that may affect the price of a given commodity. Others concentrate on "technical analysis," using charts of the behavior of the markets.

If you choose, you can have a broker trade futures contracts for you in a discretionary account—one in which the broker is empowered to make buy and sell decisions for you. Or you can entrust your money to a managed commodity service, a pool that operates somewhat like a mutual fund. Whatever course you take, you are exposing your capital to a great deal of risk.

COSTS OF BUYING,
OWNING AND SELLING

Futures brokers, like stockbrokers, charge commissions when you buy and sell. Since futures trading does not lend itself to long-term, "buy and hold" investing, it involves a lot of buying and selling. Futures brokers may charge "round-turn" commissions, collecting their fee only when you close out a position. Commission rates on futures may be significantly lower per transaction than they are on stocks. But commissions are nevertheless an important cost to take into account when you are evaluating whether futures are suitable for you.

Futures are normally traded on margin, just as stocks may be. But a futures account differs significantly from a stock margin account (see the investing on margin section of the chapter on common stocks). Minimum margin on a futures contract may be as low as 5 or 10 percent of the contract's nominal value. This margin is all you need to put up to invest.

Once you have invested, your account is screened daily to see that the money in it meets the minimum requirement. If it does not, you are required to pay in additional money. In the event that you do not do so, your broker will liquidate enough of your futures investments to meet margin requirements.

Suppose the broker closes out all your positions, and still does not raise enough money to bring you account balance up to zero. In that circumstance, which can easily arise, you are in debt to the broker for whatever other losses have been realized. This open-ended risk— the fact that you can lose more, sometimes much more, than your original investment—is a very important consideration to bear in mind in considering futures.

CAPITAL GAINS
POTENTIAL

Speculators generally trade futures contracts in the hope of achieving large capital gains in short periods of time. This hope exists because prices of many commodities and other investments covered by futures contracts are volatile, and because futures contracts offer great leverage.

Suppose, for the sake of illustration, that you choose to trade futures in a commodity called Example. Your broker informs you that a contract for delivery of 10,000 pounds of Example six months from now is currently trading at $10 a pound. Thus, each contract nominally represents $100,000.

You wouldn't dream, you say, of risking $100,000 on a single investment like this. Ah, replies the broker, but you don't have to. You need only put up 5 percent margin, or $5,000. Furthermore, he says, if you buy a contract and the price of Example rises just $1,000, or 1 percent, you will show a 20 percent gain on your investment. It needs to go up only 5 percent, to $105,000, for you to double your money.

That's all well and good, you say, but you have a friend who knows a lot about Example, and that friend thinks its price is likely to fall, not rise. In that case, says the broker, put up $5,000 to sell an Example contract, and you can double your money if the price falls to $95,000.

Once that basic arrangement is understood, its risk corollary is also readily apparent. Go *long* on Example, and it need only fall 5 percent in price to wipe out your money. If it drops 10 percent, you will have to come up with another $5,000 just to cover your losses. The identical risk applies if you opt to sell a contract and the price happens to rise.

There are many complex strategies available using multiple futures contracts in quest of capital gains. Some use one contract to partially offset the potential risks and rewards of another. These require a great amount of expertise, and are sometimes subject to a bewildering array of potential outcomes. As a general rule, any futures transaction that holds out the hope of significant capital gains also involves a great deal of risk.

INCOME POTENTIAL

Futures contracts pay no interest or dividends. They have very little to offer for investors who are concerned with safety of principal, and who want or need maximum current income from their assets. If you are are operating on a large scale, you may be able to arrange to make margin deposits in your futures account in the form of Treasury bills, or some other interest-bearing security. But whatever income is generated under such a setup is ancillary at best to the goal you pursue in futures investing. And it is not income that can be relied upon, since the margin deposited in your account is constantly at risk.

RISKS AND
DRAWBACKS

As a general rule, investors should steer clear of futures contracts unless they have a substantial amount of money that they are willing to put at great risk—including a reserve of cash they can use to cover losses beyond their original investments. In many instances, you may be able to pursue objectives similar to those offered by futures using options, which in some applications allow you to limit your risk to a known amount.

Even if you are so wealthy that you have become bored with dreaming up ways to get rid of all the money you have lying around, the futures markets merit a wary appraisal. When you invest money in futures, you are pitting your skill and wits against many people who play the game full time, with vast sources of information and capital backing.

Some people and institutions use futures to hedge against risk. A farmer, for example, might use them to sell part of a given crop at intervals, in order to avoid selling all of it at the worst price that prevails over a given period. For sophisticated individual investors, financial and stock-index futures, which are discussed in separate sections of this chapter, may have appeal in hedging strategies.

LIQUIDITY

New futures contracts are constantly being dreamed up, and old ones regularly fade from the scene. The ones that succeed, and last, are those that achieve enough popularity among investors to develop a liquid market. Among existing contracts, liquidity varies greatly in degree. Most experts agree that non-professional investors in futures should stick with the most liquid markets—those that show the greatest volume of trading, and the largest open interest (number of contracts outstanding).

No matter how large and active it is, any futures market can experience a bout of illiquidity when prices begin moving rapidly in either direction. That is because most of these markets have daily price change limits for each contract. Once a contract's price is "down the limit" on any given day, a speculator cannot sell until and unless a buyer can be found who is willing to pay a price within the specified limit. The liquidity of a futures market can also be affected by any change in minimum margin requirements imposed by government regulators or futures exchanges.

TAX ADVANTAGES
AND DISADVANTAGES

The tax aspects of futures trading can be complicated, particularly since the appearance and growth of financial and stock-index futures, and the evolution of many new investment strategies involving futures in combination with other types of investments, such as options. Before embarking on any venture involving futures, you should have access to good tax advice or a thorough working knowledge of current tax laws and rulings.

As the tax planning industry grew in the 1970s and early 1980s, strategies were developed to shift income tax liabilities from one year to another using multiple futures transactions. The government took exception to this practice and set up, in 1981 legislation, a special set of tax rules for futures transactions.

Most futures trading is short term. Nevertheless, the law provides that net profits on futures transactions are considered 60 percent long term and 40 percent short term. Since the maximum tax rate on long-term capital gains is 20 percent, and the maximum tax rate on short-term capital gains is 50 percent, you need only do a little arithmetic to determine that the maximum tax rate on futures profits is 32 percent.

At the same time, the law requires that all futures investments be "marked to market" at yearend for tax purposes. This means that any unrealized profits or losses from futures positions that are outstanding at yearend are figured into investors' tax accounts as though they had been closed out on the last trading day of the year.

Futures trading is not permitted in individual retirement accounts, Keogh plans and other tax-favored savings programs. Some sponsors of managed futures funds, which are typically organized as limited partnerships, seek IRA and Keogh accounts. These are suitable only for IRA and Keogh savers who can afford to take a high degree of risk.

COMMODITY FUTURES

DESCRIPTION

In the early 1970s, the United States entered a period of inflation shock. The root causes of the problem were, and still are, the subject of great debate. Experts pointed fingers of blame at any one of several decisions made by the U.S. government in its economic and political policies.

Whatever its origins, the accelerating rise in the cost of living began to manifest itself in surging prices of many agricultural, industrial and consumer commodities. Events the world over seemed to conspire to aggravate the situation. There were crop failures in many places—even the sudden disappearance of anchovies, which are used in feed for farm animals, from a normally productive fishing ground off the coast of South America.

The Soviet Union reached an agreement to make huge purchases of U.S. grain. And in 1973, the Organization of Petroleum Exporting Countries, a cartel of 13 nations that accounted for a large proportion of the industrialized world's energy supplies, flexed its new-found muscles and raised the price of oil dramatically.

This caused a lot of economic havoc in the United States. It helped touch off a steep decline in the stock market. But at the same time, it focused public attention on the markets in which commodity futures contracts are traded in this country. Stories spread of how traders in commodity futures were making fortunes riding the wave of inflation.

A decade later, the country appeared to have made great progress in subduing inflation. Double-digit annual increases in the cost of living were no longer the rule. But investors of many descriptions retained their awareness of the commodity futures markets, and the lure of speculative profits they hold.

The range of commodity contracts traded on the nation's commodity exchanges attests to the diversity of the U.S. economy: cattle, wheat, soybeans, oats, corn, hogs, lumber, plywood, gold, silver, copper, coffee, cocoa, cotton, sugar, crude oil, heating oil, gasoline, orange juice, and too many more to mention. Each market may have participants who specialize in a single commodity. At the same time, a trader who uses technical analysis as a guide may jump from market to market whenever and wherever his or her charts say opportunity beckons.

HOW AND WHERE TO GET
INFORMATION AND INVEST

Information about the rules and techniques of trading commodity futures is available in great quantity from any good broker, or from the exchanges that serve as their marketplaces. Sales literature, specialized periodicals and books that provide information and discuss commodity-trading strategies abound. Many brokerage and commodity firms, which handle buy and sell orders, and independent advisers track the markets and make recommendations to their customers. The U.S. government is an important source of information in many markets, with the weather and crop information it collects in the course of such endeavors as trying to help farmers and formulating farm policies.

Because commodity futures offer the potential for large short-term profits, the markets tend to attract at their periphery high-pressure salespeople, frequently operating by telephone, offering outlandish promises of potential rewards to people who may be unsuited for trading futures. All commodity propositions that come from an unknown "voice on the phone" should be evaluated with great care.

It is often said that there is no such thing as "inside information" in the commodity markets, in contrast to the stock market. Most all information that may affect the price of a given commodity is theoretically available to anyone with the energy, the resources or the luck to gather it, or stumble upon it. But that information can be very diverse.

Many participants in the commodity futures markets are large, sophisticated operators—for example, companies that use great quantities of a given raw commodity or commodities in the course of their operations—that have elaborate systems for gathering information. If you choose to venture into commodity futures, you should be aware that your are going up against such formidable adversaries.

COSTS OF BUYING, OWNING AND SELLING

Brokers charge the standard commissions to buy and sell commodity futures contracts. It may take only a small initial investment to get started in commodities, since contracts may be bought and sold on very low margin at a small fraction of their nominal value. But any good broker, before taking your order, should determine that you have adequate financial means to qualify you as a potential commodity trader. Some investment firms set minimum standards of annual income and liquid net worth (not counting the value of your house and personal possessions) that you must meet before they will open a commodity-trading account for you.

CAPITAL GAINS POTENTIAL

Farmers, businesses and other entities that deal regularly in a given commodity or commodities may use the futures markets for relatively conservative purposes, to hedge against unwanted risk of price fluctuations in those commodities. By contrast, individual investors who take part in the markets normally do so with but one purpose in mind—to speculate in hopes of capital gains.

Consider the case of a contract trading on the Chicago Mercantile Exchange for future delivery of 40,000 pounds of cattle. On one recent date, Barron's magazine reported, the price per pound was about 65 cents. So the total value of the contract was about $26,000. But a speculator could invest with minimum margin of just $900, and each one-cent move in the price per pound would translate into a $400 change in the value of the contract. Thus, if the price of cattle were to rise or fall 5 cents, a speculator could make or lose $2,000 on his or her initial investment of $900.

"Speculation" is not the most prestigious word in the English language. It suggests reckless, irresponsible use of money, excessive greed, and other non-virtues. In their minds, people often do not make any distinction between speculation and gambling. But many financial experts over the years have pointed out that there is a fundamental difference between the two. In gambling, some device is provided—say, a roulette wheel or a horse race—with the express purpose of creating risks for people to take with their money.

In speculation, on the other hand, a risk already exists, and mechanisms such as the futures markets are used to transfer that risk from someone who does not wish to bear it to someone—a speculator—who is willing to take it on. This argument should not be taken to minimize in any way the risks to which commodity speculators expose themselves. But it does make a case that speculators serve a useful economic function.

INCOME POTENTIAL

Commodity futures offer no prospect of any interest or dividend income. They are not suitable for investors who want or need maximum current income from their assets, or who are unwilling to take big risks.

RISKS AND
DRAWBACKS

If you do not have a substantial reserve of money that you are prepared to lose, speculating in commodity futures is almost certainly not for you. Among people who can meet that financial standard, most experts agree, there are many who are temperamentally unsuited for the game. Even the most successful commodity traders may incur frequent losses. In fact, it is axiomatic in the business that the best strategy for trading commodity futures is to take losses quickly, and let positions that are proving profitable run. To follow this line of action, you must have the self-discipline necessary to overcome the natural human inclination to cash in profits eagerly, and to hold on to losers in the hope of getting out even.

For most participants in the markets, trading commodity futures requires specialized knowledge. How many of us are in a position to reach an informed opinion about the factors likely to influence, say, the price of sugar in the future? How many of us can hope to know more about those factors than experts at the big food and soft-drink companies? A large number of commodity traders don't concern themselves overly with "fundamentals" like these, concentrating instead on technical analysis—using charts of past and present price fluctuations. But technical analysis is an art unto itself.

LIQUIDITY

Futures markets for the most common, well-known commodities are generally very liquid, except in periods when prices move up or down the daily limit. If you are considering some exotic, lesser-known commodity, it is best to check the recent volume of trading and the *open interest*—number of contracts outstanding—before assuming that you are getting into a liquid investment.

TAX ADVANTAGES
AND DISADVANTAGES

The general tax rules covering futures contracts, discussed in the opening section of this chapter, apply to investments in commodity futures. They do not apply, however, if you conduct futures transactions as part of a business or trade involving the underlying commodity.

   You cannot speculate directly in commodity futures in an individual retirement account, Keogh plan or similar tax-favored savings program. If you are considering some managed commodity-trading fund for your IRA or Keogh, you should have great faith in the fund managers' skills and integrity, and have other retirement planning programs to fall back on should the fund suffer losses.

INTEREST-RATE FUTURES

DESCRIPTION

As the investing public's awareness of the agricultural and industrial commodity futures markets grew in the mid-1970s, some enterprising people in the business came up with an idea—futures contracts on that old familiar commodity, money. Well, not money exactly, but securities that very closely represent money, like Treasury bonds and bills (described in a separate chapter of this book).

The cost of money to lend is reflected in the prevailing level of interest rates. Using futures on investments like Treasury securities, investors who own government securities can protect themselves against adverse changes in interest rates by taking "hedge" positions. And other people can seek to profit from those same changes in interest rates by speculating in interest-rate futures. Because interest rates have been very volatile for most of the decade since these futures contracts came on the scene, the markets for them have enjoyed rapid growth.

Their rise to popularity might have been even more dramatic if they weren't fairly complex vehicles for newcomers to understand and become comfortable with. Traders in interest-rate futures must first understand that prices of fixed-income securities rise when interest rates fall, and vice versa. Thus, if you buy a futures contract on, say, a Treasury bond, you are attempting to profit from a drop in interest rates. If you think rates are going up, and want to profit from that increase, you would consider selling a Treasury-bond futures contract.

If you owned some Treasury bonds and were fearful of a rise in interest rates, but didn't want to sell the bonds, you might consider selling a futures contract as a hedge. Assuming that rates did indeed rise, the increase in the value of your futures contract would work to offset the corresponding drop in the market value of your bonds.

Before speculating or hedging using interest-rate futures, it makes sense to consider the alternatives. There are interest-rate options, and even options on interest-rate futures (both of which are discussed in the Options chapter of this book) that can be used in pursuit of the same objectives, but that have some significantly different characteristics from futures contracts.

HOW AND WHERE TO GET
INFORMATION AND INVEST

The principle markets in which interest-rate futures are traded are the Chicago Board of Trade and the Chicago Mercantile Exchange's International Monetary Market. Information on these contracts is available from the exchanges or, perhaps more conveniently, from any securities or commodity broker who stands ready to take your orders to buy and sell.

Before venturing into interest-rate futures, you must be familiar with the nature and workings of the securities that underlie them. Futures contracts are traded not only on Treasury bills and bonds, but on other interest-bearing vehicles such as Government National Mortgage Association securities, or "Ginnie Maes" (discussed in the chapter on mortgage securities).

COSTS OF BUYING,
OWNING AND SELLING

When you trade interest-rate futures, you can expect to incur commission charges from the broker who handles your business. This cost should be borne in mind whenever you plan some strategy involving these vehicles, whether it is speculative or a relatively conservative hedging maneuver. Hedging may have some very helpful applications for you as an investor. So may complicated strategies using multiple transactions in interest-rate futures. But it should be noted that brokers who depend on commissions for their livelihood may have a natural inclination to recommend hedge investments and complex strategies because they bring in extra commissions.

CAPITAL GAINS
POTENTIAL

Interest-rate futures can be used to seek substantial capital gains from changes in interest rates. Consider the case of a contract for future delivery of Treasury bonds with a face value of $100,000 at a nominal, or *coupon,* interest rate of 8 percent. The going price of the bonds is quoted as a percentage of 100, to the nearest 1-32 of a dollar. Each rise or fall of 1-32 in the price represents a $31.25 change in the value of your contract.

For the sake of simplicity, assume that you expect interest rates to drop, and you can buy a T-bond futures contract at a price of 80, putting up $8,000 in margin. Prevailing interest rates on Treasury bonds do in fact fall, from 10 percent to 8 percent. That pushes the price of the contract covering a bond with an 8 percent coupon up to 100. The contract's actual value has climbed from $80,000 to $100,000, and you close out your position. Your profit: $20,000, or two times your original investment. Of course, if you had guessed wrong and interest rates rose, depressing prices of Treasury bonds, they wouldn't have to go very far to wipe out much, all, or more than all, of your original $8,000.

INCOME POTENTIAL

Like other futures contracts, interest-rate futures pay no dividends or interest. But sophisticated income-conscious investors may have occasion to use them, to hedge or for other purposes. Suppose, for example, that you expect to receive a lump sum of money several months in the future, and plan to invest that money in Treasury bonds once it comes into your hands. You find today's interest rates appealing, and are fearful that rates may fall before you receive the money you plan to invest.

You can buy a T-bond futures contract now that will assure you of getting today's rates at the delivery date set by the contract, since the seller of the contract has entered into an obligation to deliver the bonds at the price specified. If rates do in fact decline, you can simply take delivery of the bonds covered by the contract. If rates rise, you will lose money on your futures investment when you close out your position. But you will have the consolation of getting a higher rate on the bonds you wind up buying.

This hypothetical case ignores commissions, and assumes that prices of Treasury bonds and Treasury bond futures move on precisely parallel tracks. In the real world, there are commission costs to consider, and price fluctuations from market to market rarely match up exactly. Whatever appeal any strategy in interest-rate futures may have, it exists only for investors who know what they are doing and have enough capital at their disposal to operate with a great deal of flexibility.

RISKS AND
DRAWBACKS

Interest-rate futures may strike many individual speculators as more appealing than trading commodity futures. They may readily confess to a total ignorance of what makes the price of pork bellies or palladium rise and fall. At the same time, they may have some definite opinions about the outlook for interest rates. This situation can turn into a trap for the unwary, because predicting the future behavior of interest rates is much more difficult than it may appear.

Like other futures contracts, interest-rate futures expose speculators to open-ended risk. Operating on margin, you can lose much more than you put up. In some circumstances, people who want to speculate on interest rates, but to limit their risk to a known amount, may find interest-rate options or options on interest-rate futures preferable to interest-rate futures themselves.

LIQUIDITY

Some interest-rate futures have become highly popular with speculators, hedgers and professional money managers, and thus enjoy very liquid markets. This liquidity is presumed, but not assured, for the future. Liquidity can become a problem, however, when prices of interest-rate futures rise or fall the daily allowable limit. Both the daily limit and some other specifications of interest-rate futures contracts are subject to change by government regulators or authorities at the exchanges where the contracts are traded.

TAX ADVANTAGES
AND DISADVANTAGES

If you realize profits or losses from speculating in interest-rate futures, they are treated for tax purposes under the rules for regulated futures contracts discussed in the opening section of this chapter. The effective maximum tax rate on gains is 32 percent, and all positions are "marked to market" at yearend.

However, if you use interest-rate futures in hedging transactions, such as to protect yourself against a possible decline in the prices of bonds you own, any profits or losses may be subject to standard rules for capital assets rather than the special treatment accorded speculators in futures trading. Whenever you are considering a hedging maneuver or any other multiple transaction involving futures or options, you should have a thorough understanding beforehand of the tax consequences to which it can lead.

Though you cannot speculate in interest-rate futures in a tax-favored savings program such as an individual retirement account or Keogh plan, you may now or in the future find a managed pool of money for your IRA or Keogh that makes use of interest-rate futures for non-speculative purposes. In the mid-1980s, commodity exchanges and brokers were striving to attract increasing numbers of investing institutions such as pension funds and other professional money managers to interest-rate futures as a tool for managing risk.

STOCK-INDEX FUTURES

DESCRIPTION

Once the definition of commodities eligible for futures trading had been broadened to include items like bonds and foreign currencies, people in the futures business set to work creating futures contracts covering the stock market as well. They reasoned that these contracts would be a relatively simple product for investors to understand and embrace, since millions of those investors were already familiar with the workings of the stock market and often had strong opinions about the future direction of stock prices.

Furthermore, futures on a stock index can simplify the risks involved in "playing" the stock market. Speculators who believe strongly that the market is going to rise, and decide to buy stock-index futures, can proceed without worrying about which individual stock or stocks to pick.

There was one stumbling block to be overcome before stock-index futures could get rolling—the question of delivery. It wasn't possible to carry out physical delivery of a number such as Standard & Poor's index of 500 stocks, and it wasn't a practical proposition to effect delivery of the individual stocks that make up such an index each time a contract was settled. The problem was resolved by setting up arrangements under which stock-index futures are settled for cash.

In a few years' time in the early 1980s, futures were introduced on a half dozen market indicators—long established measures like the S&P 500 and the New York Stock Exchange composite index, as well as new ones devised specifically for the purpose of building futures contracts around them. At this writing, there were no futures contracts on individual stocks, but the possibility of creating them was being widely discussed.

HOW AND WHERE TO GET
INFORMATION AND INVEST

Commodity and securities brokers, or the various futures exchanges around the country, can provide you with information on stock-index futures. Before you venture into this market, you must have a feel not only for how futures work and the many forces than can influence stock prices, but also for the makeup of the various market indicators on which index futures contracts are based.

The oldest and best-known yardstick of market trends, the Dow Jones average of 30 industrial stocks, originated in the late 19th century. There is no futures contract on this average—Dow Jones Co., which publishes the Wall Street Journal and has many other operations in the information business, strenuously objected to having its name associated with any trading vehicle. But there are some that have been designed to track the venerable "Dow" fairly closely.

It is a common observation in the investment world that the Dow, made up as it is of a small sampling of blue-chip stocks, often gives a misleading or incomplete picture of what is happening in the general market. Over the years many broader indicators have been developed to provide what their sponsors claim to be greater accuracy. The argument over which indicator is the best continues, and is not likely to be settled soon.

This leaves would-be traders in index futures with a range of choices. They can choose among futures contracts covering indexes of varying volatility and other individual characteristics. Before deciding on index futures, they may also wish to consider the alternative of index options.

COSTS OF BUYING,
OWNING AND SELLING
Commodity and securities brokers charge the standard commissions on index futures trading. Furthermore, there are "opportunity" *costs* involved in speculative strategies using index futures rather than stocks, because futures provide no dividend income.

CAPITAL GAINS
POTENTIAL
It can be a tricky assignment, but you can buy or sell index futures in the hope of achieving large profits on a small initial investment in a short period of time. Suppose a given market index stands at 200.00 when you buy a futures contract that represents $500 times the current index number. The value of the contract is $100,000, but you need put up margin of only, say, $10,000.

The contract's price can move up and down in minimum "ticks" of .05, each of which represents $25. The first day you own the contract, it jumps to 201. At the close of business, your account is credited with a profit of $500. The next day, the contract moves up .50, to 201.50, and an additional $250 goes into your till. Over the next several weeks, the market goes through a series of up and down days, but gradually pushes upward, lifting the value of the contract to 210.00. With a $5,000 profit in your account, you decide to sell. Commissions excluded, you have realized a 50 percent return on your investment.

If you were bearish and sold this index future at 200, you could have realized the same kind of handsome result if the contract fell to 190. But if you guess wrong either way, the above example shows that a 10 percent move against you in the value of the contract would cost you half your capital. A 20 percent move in the wrong direction would wipe out all you put up. By that time, you would have heard from your broker with a call for more margin maintenance money. As the saying goes, index futures are a good way to find out fast whether you are destined to grow rich or poor.

INCOME POTENTIAL
Stock-index futures provide no hope whatever of dividends or interest. Even if you take delivery on a contract you have previously bought, you normally receive the proceeds in cash that must be invested elsewhere before it can generate any income. So stock-index futures cannot simply be used the way, say, a Treasury bond futures contract can to make a delayed purchase of an income-yielding investment.

Furthermore, index futures cannot be sold the way index call options can in hopes of enhancing your income from a stock portfolio. With call options, buyers pay a premium to sellers that can represent additional income to the seller if the call expires unexercised. There is no such premium in the futures markets. Though they do have relatively conservative "hedging" applications, index futures are generally unsuitable for people who seek maximum income, with safety, from their assets.

RISKS AND
DRAWBACKS

Many people have been wrong many times in their forecasts of the stock market. Just about everybody errs sooner or later in this guessing game. A large body of opinion holds that the market is a "random walk" that cannot be predicted, no matter how much you know or how hard you try. Other seasoned veterans who have beaten the market, and hope to keep doing so in the future, openly acknowledge that they do not know what stock prices will do in the next few weeks or months. They concentrate instead on looking for undiscovered values in individual stocks, and waiting patiently for that value to be recognized at some unknown time in the future.

Anyone who speculates in stock-index futures is attempting to overcome all these recognized difficulties. They are, in effect, operating on the belief or perhaps only the hope that the large potential rewards are worth the great risk involved.

"Hedgers," by contrast, may use index futures to transfer risks to which their stock investments are exposed to speculators. If you own a diversified portfolio of stocks, you can sell an index futures contract against it, expecting that ups and downs in either the futures contract or the prices of your stocks will offset a rise or fall in the other half of your hedged position.

You cannot, however, expect a perfect hedge. Even if you own shares of an index fund, set up to duplicate the performance of Standard & Poor's 500-stock index, and sell a futures contract on the S&P 500, you may experience disparities. As the Chicago Mercantile Index said in a descriptive pamphlet, "The contract does not move point-for-point with the actual index, but it stays close enough to act as an effective proxy for the index and, by extension, for the stock market as a whole."

LIQUIDITY

Markets for stock index futures are generally very liquid, with trading volume and open-interest (number of contracts outstanding) varying from contract to contract. As with futures generally, the most popular contracts are the most liquid and their liquidity in turn enhances their popularity. Unlike many other kinds of futures contracts, index futures typically have no limit to the daily fluctuations in their prices.

TAX ADVANTAGES
AND DISADVANTAGES

Profits or losses from speculating in index futures are treated for tax purposes under the rules for regulated futures contracts discussed in the opening section of this chapter. The effective maximum tax rate on gains is 32 percent, and all positions are "marked to market" at yearend.

However, if you use index futures in hedging transactions, such as to protect yourself against a possible decline in the prices of stocks you own, any profits or losses may be subject to standard rules for capital assets rather than the special treatment accorded speculators in futures trading. Whenever you are considering a hedging maneuver or any other multiple transaction involving futures or options, you should have a thorough understanding beforehand of the tax consequences to which it can lead.

You cannot speculate directly in index futures in a tax-favored savings program such as an individual retirement account or Keogh plan. However, you may find a managed pool of money for your IRA or Keogh that uses index futures for non-speculative purposes. In the mid-1980s, the futures industry was seeking to promote index futures as a risk-management tool for pension-fund managers and other fiduciaries.

INDIVIDUAL RETIREMENT ACCOUNTS

DESCRIPTION

They may disagree on almost everything else, but commentators on the investment scene are just about unanimous in their acclaim for individual retirement accounts. IRAs first appeared in 1975 as a retirement savings vehicle for workers not covered by pension plans at their place of employment. New legislation in 1981 extended eligibility for IRAs to all working Americans. By 1983, it was estimated that IRA contributions were running at about $40 billion a year.

IRAs are an instrument of U.S. tax policy designed to promote savings and investment, and to encourage individuals to prepare financially for retirement on their own initiative, at a time of considerable uncertainty about the long-term future of the Social Security system. Individuals may contribute all their earnings from employment each year, up to a maximum of $2,000, and deduct the amount of the contribution on their federal tax returns. For married couples filing joint returns, the maximum is $2,250 if only one spouse works, or $4,000 if both work and each has earnings of at least $2,000. Investment income does not count in determining your eligibility for an IRA.

Income produced by IRA money in the form of interest, dividends or capital gains is exempt from current taxation until withdrawals begin. Since IRAs are intended for retirement savings, a 10 percent penalty, in addition to regular taxes, is imposed on any withdrawals made before age 59. After that point, IRA investors may make withdrawals at a rate of their own choosing. The law says that withdrawals must begin at age 70 at a set rate based on the life expectancy of people in your age group.

IRA money can go into most traditional investments, and many of the newer types as well. Among the institutions that aggressively seek IRA accounts are banks, savings and loans, brokers, credit unions, life insurance companies selling annuities, mutual funds, real estate syndicators and packagers of mortgage-backed investments.

There are some investments that are excluded from IRAs either by their tax characteristics or by the 1981 law. Municipal bonds, for example, are unsuitable for IRAs because the interest they pay is already exempt from federal taxation. So are any other investments whose principal attraction is shelter from current taxes.

The law specifically bars IRA investments in *tangible assets* such as gold and collectibles. It should be noted, however, that devotees of gold can invest their IRA money in gold-mining stocks or mutual funds specializing in precious metals. On the other hand, there are some investments tailored especially for IRAs and other tax-favored accounts—for example, zero-coupon securities. Some mutual fund companies have set up funds specifically for IRA customers. More vehicles of this nature are likely to be offered in the future.

HOW AND WHERE TO GET INFORMATION AND INVEST

In their eagerness to get your IRA business, institutions ranging from your local bank or credit union to the big national financial-services companies stand ready to inundate you with information about these accounts. Their literature naturally tends to emphasize the benefits of their particular plans. Newspapers, books and magazines are filled with descriptions and analyses of IRAs and IRA investment strategies, particularly in the season leading up to the April 15 income-tax deadline.

Most IRA sponsors have standard application forms and procedures designed to simplify the process of opening and maintaining an account. Nevertheless, there can be many subtle differences in IRAs from institution to institution. Some important information may be available only by asking questions before investing on subjects such as what fees are charged and what procedure must be followed if you should decide later to move your account elsewhere.

COSTS OF BUYING, OWNING AND SELLING

Costs of IRA investing vary widely from institution to institution. In some cases, they can add up to a considerable amount. They are just one of several factors to be considered in deciding where to invest, but in no case overlook them. One institution may charge only a small annual fee of perhaps $15 or $20 to cover its costs of acting as custodian for your account. Another may impose a custodial charge several times that large, as well as separate fees for opening an account and closing it if you decide to move your money elsewhere.

These fees come in addition to the standard costs of investing. For example, if you buy and sell stocks through a brokerage firm IRA, you will be charged the usual commissions on each trade. If you put your IRA money into a time deposit at a bank or savings institution, and then wish to move it somewhere else before the deposit's maturity date, you can expect to face an early-withdrawal penalty.

CAPITAL GAINS
POTENTIAL

The obvious purpose of an IRA is to produce long-term growth of your capital for retirement. One way to pursue this goal is to invest in assets with the potential for capital gains, such as stocks or stock mutual funds. However, there is actually a disadvantage that comes with capital gains in an IRA. In standard investing, when you sell a stock or other capital asset at a profit after holding it for at least six months, 60 percent of the gain is excluded from taxation. Also, if you sell such an asset at a loss, at least some of that loss is deductible on your tax return.

But money in an IRA is treated differently. None of it is subject to any tax until withdrawals are made. When you do withdraw it, however, all of it is taxed as ordinary income regardless of whether it represents your original contributions, interest or dividends earned, or capital gains. Thus, IRA investments do not enjoy the favorable tax treatment normally accorded capital investments.

Partly for this reason, and partly because they want to minimize their risks, a large majority of IRA investors to date have shown a preference for interest-bearing investments with little or no capital gains potential, such as certificates of deposit and money market mutual funds. A notable minority, however, have chosen to invest for capital gains anyway, reasoning that they must hope for growth from that source to protect themselves from the erosive effects of inflation over the years in which their money is tied up in an IRA.

INCOME POTENTIAL

IRAs are plainly for people looking for income in the future, not the present. Even with the tax breaks they afford, they represent a drain on your current cash flow of at least 50 cents for every dollar invested. Therefore, if your situation requires that you maximize current income on your investments, it may be that an IRA is unsuitable for you. Nevertheless, you should be aware that not investing in an IRA can cost you money in the form of tax breaks foregone.

The way IRAs are set up under the law, a special situation exists for people between the ages of 59 and 70. In these years, the rules allow both contributions and withdrawals at your discretion. So for that period of your life, you can use an IRA as a sort of tax-favored savings account, within the law's contribution limits. If, for example, you had greater than unusual income in your 66th year, you might use an IRA to shift $2,000 of your earnings into the next year, when you expect much less money coming in.

RISKS AND
DRAWBACKS

IRAs are available in just about all degrees of risk. You can put all your money in government-insured Treasury securities or bank deposits, or you can let it all ride on a single speculative stock. Or, like many people, you can seek some middle ground. Since there is nothing in the law that limits the number of IRA accounts you can open, you can hedge your bets by investing half your contributions in something speculative and the other half in some low-risk vehicle.

The attractiveness of IRAs increases with your tax bracket. An IRA deduction is quite evidently more valuable to someone in the maximum 50 percent bracket than to someone with a small income taxed at a much lower rate. This results in what some observers consider the main flaw of IRAs—in their present form they are of the least benefit to the people who most need help preparing for their later years. At the high end of the income spectrum, an IRA may have minimal appeal for someone who is already gaining great tax benefits from other investments in, say, real estate.

There are special circumstances in which it may be advisable to pass up making an IRA contribution—for example, if you expect to buy a house or pay a college tuition bill in the immediate future, and need all the ready cash you can come up with. It is possible that savings plans modeled along the lines of IRAs will be created in the future for purposes such as these.

LIQUIDITY

IRAs have an image, partly deserved, as illiquid investment vehicles. After all, the rules state very clearly that you cannot withdraw any money from them before age 59 without incurring a regular tax obligation and a 10 percent penalty besides. But this penalty is not as severe as it may first appear. For a person in a high tax bracket, it can be offset within a very short time—roughly 5 to 15 years, depending on the return your investment produces by the benefits gained from tax-free compounding. For that reason, some investment advisers contend that IRAs are worth considering even for people who expect to need the proceeds in, say, 15 years to pay a child's college tuition.

If you become permanently disabled and are unable to continue working, the 10 percent penalty doesn't apply. If you die while money remains in your IRA, it passes to the beneficiary you have named.

For people past age 59, IRAs present no liquidity problem, assuming that the money is invested in some vehicle from which it can readily be withdrawn. For those below the age of 59, however, an IRA is indeed illiquid in the sense that it cannot substitute for a standard savings plan, providing a cash reserve for any emergency or opportunity that may unexpectedly arise.

TAX ADVANTAGES
AND DISADVANTAGES

Tax advantages—two of them—are what make IRAs tick. The first is the immediate deduction you get on your federal tax return for any contributions you make and the contribution may be made at any time up until your filing deadline for the year in question. Assume, for the sake of illustration, that you are in the 35 percent tax bracket and make a $2,000 contribution. In effect, Uncle Sam provides you with a $700 subsidy for that contribution. States that impose income taxes may or not recognize the contribution as a deduction. If they do, that increases the benefit.

The second advantage is tax-free compounding of the earnings your IRA investment accrues. Because the dividends, interest and-or capital gains are not taxed, all of them go to work immediately earning more money. Institutions that sponsor IRA programs regularly publish tables showing the dramatic difference this can make over time in the size of your retirement nest egg. This combination of incentives makes a powerful case for investing in an IRA.

INVESTMENT ADVISORY SERVICES

DESCRIPTION

In the modern world, investors face a complicated challenge planning strategies, studying the many forces that influence investment markets, and keeping abreast of rapidly changing developments within the deregulated investment world itself. They need information, expertise, and the time to evaluate all the alternatives.

For help, they may turn to a banker, a stockbroker, an insurance salesperson or other investment professional, in many cases with positive results. But there can be a limitation to the value of such a relationship in that these advisers often have a vested interest in encouraging you to take some specific course of action. Their livelihood depends to a considerable degree on emphasizing the merits of the products they sell, and deemphasizing the virtues of what the competition has to offer.

As a result, independent advisory services that sell information and advice with a presumed impartial viewpoint have found a wide audience. They may offer statistical reference material on stocks and other investments, or periodic newsletters analyzing the economy and the markets, or telephone "hotlines" with toll-free numbers for quick access to changes in their recommendations, or money-management services, or personal financial-planning consultations, or any combination of the above. Some companies specialize in selling charts of past performance of stocks or other investments.

Among the hundreds of services available today, some take a broad view of the investment scene. Others concentrate on one discipline, such as "technical analysis" of the stock market or the commodities markets. In the 1970s, advisers who recommended gold and other precious metals flourished as those markets boomed. There are even market letters that evaluate the other market letters, or keep track of the general trend in "advisory sentiment." Whether your interest is no-load mutual funds, real estate, or tax shelters, you can find a service or services aimed at you.

Successful investment advisers can attract a large and loyal, not to mention lucrative, following. Some have been known to exert a powerful influence on the markets simply by announcing that they have had a change of opinion.

This industry clearly couldn't thrive if it didn't meet a very real and legitimate demand. The best advisers are experienced, astute commentators admired by their subscribers and competitors alike. Some services provide the kind of in-depth statistical information that investors consider invaluable in making their own decisions.

However, it should be noted that investment advisory services vary widely in quality and value. Since many of them are keyed to the writer's temperament and view of the world, they may encourage you to follow strategies that are unsuited to your own needs. A letter that advocates frequent trading maneuvers, for example, may complicate your financial life rather than simplifying it. As a general rule, the more an adviser promises, the warier you should be. If anyone possessed a magic key to instant riches, it stands to reason that that person would be likely to use it for his or her own purposes rather than sell a copy of it to you.

HOW AND WHERE TO GET
INFORMATION AND INVEST

Many investment advisers advertise heavily in the financial press and the business sections of general-interest newspapers. They often sponsor or appear as guest speakers at investment seminars. If your name is on a mailing list that attests to your interest in investment matters, you probably also receive direct-mail solicitations from them as well.

It is a common practice among advisory services to offer short-term trial subscriptions at modest cost. Occasionally, you may come upon offers to get a sample look at 20, 30 or more different services by answering a single advertisement. A broker or friend whose opinions you value may provide helpful recommendations of advisory services. Public libraries usually subscribe to the biggest and best-known ones. Firms which provide statistical information about stocks and other investments include Moody's Investors Service, Standard & Poor's Corp., and Value Line, all with headquarters in New York City.

COSTS OF BUYING,
OWNING AND SELLING

Costs of subscribing to investment advisory services vary considerably, with most in the $100-$400 range per year. Some offer the choice of a basic newsletter service, or the letter and access to telephone "hotlines" for an extra charge. Prices of single copies or an introductory subscription to a newsletter are generally low. At the high end of the scale, an adviser whose opinions are much in demand may charge a hefty fee for even a brief individual consultation in person or on the telephone.

CAPITAL GAINS
POTENTIAL

Most investment advisers concentrate on recommending strategies for capital gains. Many but not all are directed at investors with large portfolios who trade fairly actively, since people in this category are naturally more inclined to seek regular investment advice than are conversative investors of the buy-and-hold school. One specialized category of advisers studies and recommends mutual funds and timing strategies for moving money in and out of, or switching it between different types of, those funds.

INCOME POTENTIAL

In recent years, with the heightened volatily of interest rates and the proliferation of new investment vehicles, advisory services in increasing numbers have begun offering information and advice for income-conscious investors. The categories they may cover include money market funds, bank money market deposit accounts and certificates of deposit, even real estate limited partnerships.

RISKS AND
DRAWBACKS

The merits or drawbacks of any given investment advisory service usually come down to your personal preference and interests. Reams of statistical material may be of great value to an avid student of investing with the time to make use of it, but lost on someone with limited interest in the intricacies of business finance.

A service that runs heavily to recommendations rather than background information may suit an investor who has limited time to spend on research and analysis. That investor must be willing, however, to take financial steps on the basis of the adviser's say-so, sometimes without even a full explanation of the opinions and reasoning behind the recommendation.

Some advisory letters mix their investment commentary with political opinions and analysis, philosophical musings and even ideological diatribe. If their audiences overwhelmingly disapproved of this, they would presumably stop doing it. But if you find such material inappropriate or irrelevant to your needs, it makes sense to consider the fact that it is part of a product for which you are being asked to pay money.

Firms that give investment advice must normally be registered as investment advisers with the Securities and Exchange Commission. The statement that they are so registered should not be taken to mean that the SEC has approved their methods or certified them as experts.

LIQUIDITY

As was pointed out above, you usually need to pay little or nothing to get samples of the work of a wide variety of investment advisers. And of course, if it provides you with information that helps improve your investment results, a good advisory service can pay a nice return on your subscription cost. Particularly if you are a small investor with a limited portfolio, it may be worthwhile periodically to try to calculate the benefits you gain from an advisory service and compare them with what the service costs you.

TAX ADVANTAGES
AND DISADVANTAGES

Some investment advisers specialize in analyzing tax shelters and tax planning strategies. Many evaluate investments for their suitability in individual retirement accounts, Keogh plans, and other tax-favored savings programs. Subscription fees charged by investment advisory services are normally deductible for federal income tax purposes in the year in which they are paid, provided that you actually have investments that you are buying, selling or monitoring.

Some investment advisers regularly hold seminars in popular vacation spots, combining a good deal of recreational activity with discussions and presentations on investment matters. The costs to those attending these seminars are usually considered deductible. But before claiming big tax writeoffs for attending this kind of affair, you should get the advice of a good tax adviser or have a thorough knowledge yourself of applicable tax laws and court rulings.

INVESTMENT CLUBS

DESCRIPTION

Individuals with relatively small amounts of money to invest face several obstacles. They do not have the kind of clout with a broker that a wealthy person or an investing institution enjoys. The cost of investing in small amounts is often disproportionately high for them, and the minimum amount required to buy several kinds of desirable investments may be beyond their means. They may find it especially difficult to diversify their holdings sufficiently to limit their risks.

One way to get around these disadvantages is to buy into a professionaly managed pool of money, such as a mutual fund or unit trust. But with such organizations, the investor has little to say in the investment decisions that are made. For an activist investor, an alternative possibility is to participate, with a dozen or so kindred spirits, in an investment club.

In the ideal, the membership of an investment club is made up of a compatible group of friends and neighbors who share not only a common interest in the securities markets, but similiar objectives with their finances. Each member might have some special expertise to contribute—in accounting, for example, or in law, or in intimate knowledge of an industry in which the club might choose to invest.

In the typical investment club, members contribute a set amount each month, and meet regularly to discuss the progress of existing investments and where new funds should be put to work. According to the National Association of Investment Clubs, a non-profit organization owned by its members, the first clubs of this kind got their start in the United States about 1900. Some individual clubs have operated continuously for decades, and there have been cases in which a club's total assets grew to more than $1 million.

HOW AND WHERE TO GET
INFORMATION AND INVEST

Any group of people with a desire to do so can form an investment club on their own. They should get good legal advice, however, in setting out a statement of operating rules, in making sure that any regulatory requirements are met, and in taking steps to protect against the misuse or misappropriation of club funds by any member. The NAIC, at 1515 East Eleven Mile Road, Royal Oak, MI 48067, offers its members standard forms and other materials designed to facilitate this process, as well as other information on investing.

COSTS OF BUYING,
OWNING AND SELLING

Investment clubs are faced with the usual costs of investing, including commissions to brokers. Commission costs may be lower for a club than they would be for its individual members investing on their own, since rate structures at most brokerage firms, including discount brokers, are skewed in favor of larger buy and sell orders.

Investment clubs, like individual investors, can save on commission costs by participating whenever possible in dividend reinvestment plans, which allow the purchase of a sponsoring company's shares at low or no cost, and sometimes even at a discount from market value. The NAIC sponsors its own dividend reinvestment program for some stocks.

The NAIC charges its members annual dues—as of 1984, $30 per club plus $6 for each member of the club. Payment of these dues includes coverage under a $25,000 fidelity bond, which protects against the misappropriation of club property by a member. For an additional fee, the association also offers extra bonding up to $1 million.

CAPITAL GAINS
POTENTIAL

The typical investment club pursues long-term growth of assets, usually through stocks offering the hope of capital gains, as well as compounding through reinvestment of dividends and interest earned. The NAIC suggests that clubs operate under four "conservative principles":

"1. Invest a set sum once a month in common stocks, regardless of general market conditions. This helps you obtain lower average costs.

"2. Reinvest dividends and capital gains immediately. Your money grows faster if earnings are reinvested. This is compound income at work.

"3. Buy growth stocks—companies whose sales are increasing at a rate faster than industry in general. The companies should have good prospects for continued growth. In other words, they should be stronger companies five years from now.

"4. Invest in different fields. Diversification helps spread both risk and opportunity."

Theoretically, you could operate an investment club with a much more aggressive strategy—say, buying options and trading stocks on margin. But such an approach would be fraught with perils for an organization that makes its decisions by committee, typically through monthly meetings. It might well also quickly destroy the club's sense of common purpose. Aggressive investors usually prefer to operate on their own.

The NAIC specifically suggests that people not form or join an investment club looking for short-term profits. "An investment club is an accumulating and building program," the association says. "It is not a get-rich-quick scheme."

INCOME POTENTIAL
Investment clubs, by their very nature, are more suited to the pursuit of long-term gains than to the realization of current income. They are designed primarily for people who can afford to put aside money for the future, not for people who want or need the highest possible current return from that money.

RISKS AND
DRAWBACKS
Investing by committee can be a very helpful discipline, fostering patience, providing a steady interchange of information and knowledge, and encouraging individual participants to stick with long-term strategies at times when their own whims and the prevailing emotions in the markets might tempt them to do otherwise.

However, it plainly requires a compatible group with shared objectives to succeed. Some investors have a highly individualistic temperament, and in fact relish the challenge of operating on their own. If you are a cantankerous contrarian scornful of most other people's ideas, you would probably not be an asset to an investment club, nor it to you. The NAIC offers information, advice, and other services to individuals as well as clubs.

Even if you determine that an investment club is suited to your goals, and find a group in which you are comfortable, you must be willing to pursue an investment stategy determined by that group, under the operating rules. There are standard market risks as well, and you must bear them in an investment club just as you would when investing on your own or through a mutual fund.

At the time you want to cash in some or all of your investments, the securities your club owns could be depressed in price. However, the investment-club concept attempts to apply several principles to minimize this type of risk. These include diversification, regular investing to produce a relatively low average cost, compounding of dividends and interest, and the use of the combined intelligence and expertise of all members of a given club in making investment decisions.

LIQUIDITY
The rules of a given investment club spell out procedures and circumstances under which a member can withdraw funds. Normally, they provide you with access to your money at any time that an emergency or unexpected opportunity arises. But investment clubs' strategies usually are set from a long-term perspective. Funds withdrawn early in a club's life may not have had the time necessary to show the benefits of that strategy. As a general rule, investment clubs are not a likely place for money you may need in the near future for ordinary expenses.

TAX ADVANTAGES
AND DISADVANTAGES
Tax considerations are important in setting up and operating an investment club. Whenever the club receives a dividend or interest payment, or sells a security at a gain or loss, a "taxable event" occurs. The way in which the club is organized determines how these tax obligations are met. Many, but not all, investment clubs are taxed as partnerships, with individual members paying their share of taxes, and taking their share of allowable deductions for the club's costs, each year. Some clubs can be treated as corporations, creating different tax consequences. The deductible costs normally include dues and other fees paid to the NAIC.

INVESTMENT MANAGERS

DESCRIPTION

The modern investment markets are dominated by professional money managers. These institutional operators invest the pooled assets of large numbers of individuals, with access to information, facilities and methods beyond most individuals' reach. Many Americans indirectly use these professionals' services in many ways—in their pension plans where they work, in the life insurance companies to whom they pay premiums, in college endowment funds, and more.

Professional money managers are eager to serve you directly as well. If you have only small amounts to invest, they will most likely try to interest you in buying mutual fund shares, unit investment trusts, annuities or perhaps an interest in a public limited partnership. If you are wealthy or just reasonably prosperous, you can choose from an even wider range of possibilities.

Banks offer money-management services through their trust departments. Brokerage firms offer package deals of just about every conceivable description, from low-risk to speculative. Money-managers who operate on their own seek individual accounts above specified minimums, which can range from $50,000 or $100,000 to $1 million or more.

If you have large sums to invest and are willing to take considerable risk in the hope of great reward, you might seek out a hedge fund—a type of private partnership that can employ strategies like short-selling and investing on margin to seek profits in the stock market. There are also services offered by brokers and commodities firms that concentrate on the options or futures markets. Or you may choose to set up a discretionary account with a registered representative of a brokerage firm, in which you agree to let the broker buy and sell without consulting you first.

The common factor in all these arrangements is that you turn the process of making investment decisions over to someone else. This may relieve you of a burden you aren't comfortable with on your own. It may allow you to rid yourself of the distractions of investment management and to devote full attention to a busy career in some other field of work. But it also means you are staking your fortunes and future on the integrity, judgment and wisdom of somebody else.

HOW AND WHERE TO GET
INFORMATION AND INVEST

Investment management services may be found at many types of financial firms. You may find profiles of individual operators in newspapers, magazines and the business press. Your physician, dentist, accountant, lawyer, or anyone you know who is an active investor may have a money manager to recommend. Most managers will eagerly solicit your business, provided that you meet their minimum investment requirements. If you have a relatively small nest egg, however, you cannot expect a red-carpet welcome from a high-rolling hedge fund.

COSTS OF BUYING,
OWNING AND SELLING

Money managers naturally want to collect a fee in some form to cover their costs of operating, and to permit them the kind of profit they believe their skills and efforts merit. These charges can take many forms, all of which have the effect of lowering the return you can expect on your investment. They may, like the sponsor of a mutual fund, charge an annual fee based on the amount of money they have under management. Or they may base their fee at least partly on the results they achieve for you—for example, a percentage of profits realized over a set minimum.

If you place your money in a discretionary account at a brokerage firm, you may have no charges to pay other than commissions on trades conducted on your behalf. In such instances, it is wise to be aware that this arrangement gives the manager a financial incentive to trade frequently.

CAPITAL GAINS
POTENTIAL

Many investment managers operate with capital gains as their primary objective, because that is where the biggest market for their services lies. Their strategies may be relatively conservative, stressing total return—growth through a combination of dividends and moderate appreciation. Or they may shoot for the sky with leveraged investments concentrated in just a few securities.

INCOME POTENTIAL

Investment managers may offer services for investors whose primary needs are current income from their assets with maximum safety of those assets. However, it does not require as much effort and expertise to invest in, say, a stable portfolio of Treasury securities as it does to make a killing in the commodities markets. When you are considering using the services of a professional to invest for income, it makes sense to compare what return you will receive after you have paid the professional's fees with, say, what you could earn putting the money yourself into low-risk, high-yielding investments.

RISKS AND
DRAWBACKS

The historical record shows that full-time investment professionals, with all the skills and tools at their disposal, do not enjoy some magically high probability of success in investing. At any given time, there are some professionals who earn wealth and acclaim for their prowess. But it is illogical to believe that the vast majority of them can consistently produce superior results. Neither is there anything in the record to show that professional investment managers are bound to achieve better results than knowledgeable individuals operating on their own.

Furthermore, it may be difficult to find a professional operation that exactly mirrors your financial needs and instincts. If you are able to find one, a good investment manager who understands your goals or employs strategies that appeal to you can be a precious asset, and a great help in achieving your objectives. Even when you are very pleased with the way things are going, however, it is only sensible to maintain regular contact with your investment manager and periodically review the progress of his or her efforts.

LIQUIDITY

In most cases, you are free to withdraw your money from the account of a professional manager on short notice. Before investing, you should determine whether a given manager imposes any constraints on your liquidity. If the manager is pursuing some long-term objective, investors who want or need to pull out of the venture early may forego the chance to share in the success of that strategy. Obviously, if the manager puts your money in illiquid investments, your account with the manager may be illiquid as well.

TAX ADVANTAGES
AND DISADVANTAGES

If an investment manager is going to serve you well, he or she must pursue strategies that fit your particular tax situation. For example, a broker who maintains a discretionary account for you shouldn't be conducting transactions that are ill-suited to a person in your tax bracket, or that contravene your other tax planning efforts.

Fees paid out of your pocket to investment managers are normally tax deductible investment expenses. However, commission charges that are passed through to you generally are taken into account for tax purposes only when you sell an investment and calculate whatever capital gains or losses have been realized. Since there is such a great variety of investment managers to choose among, it is important to have a thorough knowledge of the tax status of your account at the start.

Mutual funds and other professionally managed pools of money are aggressive bidders for individual retirement accounts, Keogh plans and other tax-favored savings programs. As the amount of money in any of these accounts grows over time, it is likely that investment managers will eagerly seek them as well.

KEOGH PLANS

DESCRIPTION

Keogh plans were created by Congress in 1962 to allow self-employed people access to retirement savings and investment programs similar to those available to individuals working for large corporations and other entities (the bill that got the whole process started was introduced by Rep. Eugene J. Keogh, D-N.Y.). Since their first appearance, they have been modified and enlarged several times.

Today's Keogh plans resemble individual retirement accounts in that they offer eligible savers two distinct tax advantages. Contributions to a Keogh account up to a specified maximum amount are exempt from current income taxes. And any money the account earns in the form of dividends, interest or capital gains is exempt from taxation, so that all of it can remain at work compounding the value of the account.

Like IRAs, Keoghs are taxed only when you begin withdrawing money from them, usually at age 59 or thereafter. Since Keoghs, like IRAs, are designed as retirement savings vehicles, withdrawals before age 59 are subject to taxation as ordinary income, plus a 10 percent penalty tax, except in special circumstances such as the death or disability of the account-holder.

You can invest your Keogh contributions in many places. Among the institutions that offer Keogh accounts are banks, savings and loans, brokers, credit unions, mutual funds, real estate syndicators and packagers of mortgage-backed investments.

Some investments are out of bounds for Keoghs either because of their inherent tax characteristics or because they are prohibited by law. Municipal bonds, for instance, don't make sense in a Keogh account because the interest they pay is already exempt from federal taxation. The same reasoning applies for tax shelters. The law expressly bars direct Keogh investments in "tangible" assets such as gold and collectibles. However, if you fancy gold, you can invest your Keogh money in gold-mining stocks or mutual funds specializing in precious metals.

Along with their many similarities, Keogh plans have some significant differences from IRAs. To be eligible to open one, you must have income from self-employment. If you have substantial income from that source, you may contribute a great deal more to a Keogh than an

IRA. Effective in 1984, Keogh plans were revised to set them up along lines closely resembling a corporate pension plan. This involved some complicated rules and procedural changes.

HOW AND WHERE TO GET
INFORMATION AND INVEST

If you have or expect to have employees in your self-employed endeavors, you should consult a knowledgeable adviser before starting a Keogh plan to ensure that you comply with the rules covering mandatory contributions for those employees. The adviser can also help in designing a plan that is organized to fit your circumstances to the best advantage. If you work on your own, as many self-employed people do, any good bank, broker, mutual fund or other financial institution should be able to supply you with a standard plan agreement that makes the task of opening an account relatively simple.

People who are covered by pension plans at work may have Keogh plans if they have self-employment income from second, or "moonlighting" jobs—for example, free-lance writing, consulting, serving as a director, or preparing other people's income tax returns. Within the limits set by the rules, self-employed people may have both an IRA and a Keogh plan. Investment income does not qualify as self-employment income, and therefore does not make you eligible for a Keogh.

As with IRAs, contributions to a Keogh account for a given year may be made any time up until the deadline for filing your income tax return for that year. But a Keogh account must be open by Dec. 31 of the year in question.

COSTS OF BUYING,
OWNING AND SELLING

When you open and manage your Keogh account, you may incur any of the standard costs of investing. For example, if you buy a "load" mutual fund, you will pay the sales charge, and the fund managers will collect their annual fee from the assets of the fund. In addition, the trustee of the account, such as a bank or brokerage firm, may impose separate Keogh charges for opening or closing an account, and for maintaining it year by year. These fees can vary considerably from institution to institution, and you should inquire about them before investing.

In 1984 the maximum annual contribution to a Keogh account for a self-employed individual was set at $30,000, or 25 percent of total income from self-employment, whichever is less. To complicate matters, the rules dictated that the amount of the contribution must be subtracted from your net earnings in calculating the total income base. So if you earned $10,000 and wanted to make the maximum deductible contribution, it would be not $2,500 but $2,000—25 percent of $10,000 minus $2,000, or $8,000. Starting in 1986, the maximum contribution is scheduled to be adjusted annually for inflation.

Owner-employees participating in Keogh plans may also make extra "voluntary contributions" of up to 10 percent of their self-employment income. These contributions are not deductible from current income taxes, but like other money in a Keogh plan can go to work earning money that is compounded tax-free.

CAPITAL GAINS POTENTIAL

The standard goal of Keogh investors is long-term growth of capital for retirement. One way to pursue this goal is to invest in assets with the potential for capital gains, such as stocks or stock mutual funds. When you choose to go this route, you must forego the favorable treatment taxable investors get when they realize long-term capital gains. When withdrawals are made from Keogh accounts, all the money is taxed under the same rules, regardless of how you earned it.

Because of these circumstances, many Keogh savers choose interest-bearing investments or vehicles like zero-coupon bonds. They pursue long-term growth through compounding, rather than capital gains. However, some others put their Keogh money in stocks or stock mutual funds anyway, on the theory that they will need investments that can produce capital gains if their Keogh plans are to keep ahead of, or stay even with, inflation.

INCOME POTENTIAL

Keogh plans, by their very nature, are designed to produce a nest egg for the future rather than current income. The contributions you make to them actually produce the opposite of current income—a drain on your current cash flow. If you require maximum current income from your capital to stay afloat financially, you may choose not to open a Keogh plan, even if you are eligible. When you do this, you should be aware that you may be foregoing some after-tax income in the form of the tax breaks accorded to Keogh savers.

RISKS AND
DRAWBACKS

With all their attractions, Keoghs may not be suited for every self-employed person in every circumstance. If, for instance, you are saving for your first home and expect to need every cent you can lay your hands on, you might choose to put off Keogh investing until that objective has been realized. Sophisticated investors willing to take risks may operate on the belief that they can do better for themselves putting their available money in a tax shelter than in a Keogh plan. But for most self-employed people, Keoghs merit serious consideration.

Once they have decided to start a plan, Keogh investors can go wrong by failing to follow and understand thoroughly the somewhat complicated rules covering them. For instance, an older self-employed person may not realize that he or she could be better off in what is known as a "defined benefit" Keogh plan.

Under the standard arrangement described above, most Keogh plans are defined contribution plans. That is, the amounts that can be contributed are determined by limits on the contributions. A defined benefit plan works from the other end, providing for calculation of contributions based on a maximum payout when you retire.

Keogh plans have many flexible features, but they may involve some inflexible legal commitments. If you have people working for you, you may have no choice but to include them in your plan, and to contribute to the plan each year. In managing money for your employees, you also have a legal fiduciary responsibility to operate prudently.

LIQUIDITY

Particularly if you are many years from retirement, Keogh plans are illiquid investments. Unless you die or become disabled, money in them cannot be withdrawn before age 59 without incurring regular federal income tax plus a 10 percent penalty tax. As with an IRA, this penalty may not be as severe as it looks at first. But Keogh plans are generally long-term commitments. If you have partners or employees participating in a Keogh plan with you, the individual plan may impose additional restrictions on early withdrawals.

TAX ADVANTAGES
AND DISADVANTAGES

With all the illiquidity problems and paperwork headaches they may cause, lots of self-employed people find Keogh plans very alluring because of the great tax advantages they offer. The up-front tax deduction on contributions mean that, if you are in the 50 percent bracket, Uncle Sam makes half your contributions for you. The second advantage, tax-free compounding, may be more subtle, but of very great benefit. As the United States League of Savings Institutions put it: "In effect it allows you to earn a market rate on a tax-sheltered investment...the longer you keep the money in your Keogh plan, the more valuable this benefit becomes."

Under the rules prevailing at the time this book was written, Keoghs had one tax edge over IRAs. On retirement, if you wish to take a lump sum distribution from a Keogh plan, it may qualify for "10-year forward averaging"—an arrangement under which you can spread the tax liability over the next 10 years. IRA distributions are not eligible for this treatment.

LIFE INSURANCE

DESCRIPTION

When young people finish school and embark on their own in the world, many investment experts recommend that they give life insurance first priority in their financial planning. Adequate life insurance should be obtained, they say, before you begin to consider other investments like stocks and bonds. But selecting the right policy, in the right amount, from the right insurance company, can be a challenging and bewildering task.

Life insurance in its purest form is not, strictly speaking, an investment. It is, like other forms of insurance, a consumer purchase of financial protection against misfortune—in this case, the possibility of your untimely death. But the insurance industry has developed many products that combine this protection with a savings or investment program.

The first question facing would-be buyers is how much life insurance they need. If you have many dependents who are used to a lush style of living, you may well need a lot. If you have none and don't expect to have any, you may need very little or none at all.

The second question is what form of insurance best suits your circumstances and temperament. Insurance that provides only for a death benefit, with no savings program, is known as *term* insurance. Premiums on term insurance are low relative to other types or, to put it another way, term insurance permits you to buy more coverage for your premium dollar. But term insurance premiums typically rise as the years pass and your statistical likelihood of dying increases. Over time the policy accumulates no surrender or cash-in value.

Whole life insurance, by contrast, combines death coverage with a savings program. The premiums are relatively high. But they usually remain level over the years, and a part of them goes into a cash value account that can serve as a savings reserve. This account may earn dividends that can be put to various uses—for example, to buy additional amounts of death coverage.

There are many variations on these two basic themes. A life insurance agent may offer a package that combines a term and a whole life policy, for example, or a whole life policy with a premium payment schedule set up so that is paid off over a specified number of years, or at the time you reach age 65.

With all its apparent flexibility, life insurance has come under some serious reevaluation in recent times. Relatively simple life policies with fixed death benefits were ill-suited for the inflationary climate that developed in the late 1960s and 1970s. Critics questioned the large up-front fees collected by companies and their agents when they sold many policies. Annual returns earned on policies with savings features lagged behind other choices available to an increasingly sophisticated public. Often, it was difficult for the life insurance investor to figure out what the actual return was, at a time when available yields on many other types of investments were published daily in the newspaper.

When the subject of whole life was raised, some advisers adopted the standard recommendation, "Buy term and invest what you save on premiums elsewhere." Others argued that that was too simplistic an answer. In any event, it was evident in the mid-1980s that the life insurance industry was under pressure to modernize itself. In 1960, according to the American Council of Life Insurance, a trade group, 5.2 percent of all ordinary life policies in force were terminated voluntarily by policyholders. By 1982, the figure had reached 10 percent.

"The life insurance business strongly seeks to minimize the lapsing of policies," the council said. One of the industry's responses was to develop new types of policies with names like adjustable, universal and variable life (discussed in a separate section of this chapter). Nevertheless, it faced a difficult task in attempting to offer new attractive vehicles without undermining the foundation of traditional policies on which it rested.

HOW AND WHERE TO GET
INFORMATION AND INVEST

Lots and lots of people would like to sell you life insurance, especially if you are a responsible and healthy sort of person, and therefore likely to make your premium payments regularly and unlikely to have a claim on your policy any time soon. By one recent count, there were more than 2,000 U.S. companies in the life insurance business.

These companies are typically represented by agents, salespeople who are constantly seeking out new customers. An agent you encounter may well be an exemplary person in every way, highly trained in all the nuances of insurance and other financial matters. Nevertheless, he or she may not be an absolutely impartial source of information. An agent who represents a single company has a natural human inclination to emphasize the virtues of that company's products. Agents who represent more than one company may have a natural human inclination to favor the policies of the company that pays them the biggest commissions.

Generally, one of the cheapest forms of life insurance is group term life. You may automatically qualify for this through your employer or some other organization of which you are a member. Many employers pay some or all of the premiums on a stated amount of coverage, and offer employees the right to buy additional coverage. In the few states where depository institutions known as savings banks operate, you may consider savings bank life insurance.

Booklets on life insurance prepared by the National Association of Insurance Commissioners and insurance trade groups should be available on request from any good agent. You may wish to check consumer publications for their latest evaluations of available life insurance products.

COSTS OF BUYING, OWNING AND SELLING

Since all life insurance is at least partly a consumer purchase, and since there are many, many companies prepared to offer you essentially the same product, cost is a paramount consideration in evaluating and buying life insurance. There are two cost components built into your premium—the cost of coverage itself, and the cost to cover commissions to salespeople and operating expenses of the insurance company.

It can be a complex process to calculate and compare those costs, especially if you are evaluating different types of policies. For help in this endeavor, you may consider checking with insurance regulators or consumer protection agencies in your state for information on standardized cost formulas under which companies are required to provide figures.

CAPITAL GAINS
POTENTIAL

Traditional life insurance policies offer no potential for capital gains as such. With term insurance, of course, you normally realize no investment return of any kind. With whole life, part of your premiums may go into an account that earns dividends, which provides for long-term growth of a cash value nest egg. But standard whole life is not a likely place to seek the kind of growth that can keep up with unpredictable rates of inflation. Some of the newer types of policies described in the following section of this chapter have features designed to provide access to capital gains through investment in stock funds.

INCOME POTENTIAL

Life insurance, by its very nature, involves foregoing some current income—the amount of the premiums you pay each year in return for financial protection of your dependents in the event of your early death, and possibly the expectation of some eventual future income. Instead of a lump-sum payment, you may arrange with an insurer for you or your survivors to receive periodic payments after you die or, alternatively, after you reach retirement age.

Such arrangements combine life insurance with annuities in one package. In fact, life insurance and annuities are really opposite sides of the same coin. Life insurance is designed to protect you against the risk that you will "die too soon," i.e., before you can fulfill financial responsibilities to your dependents, pay off mortgages and other loans, and meet other commitments. Annuities are designed to protect you against the risk that you will "die too late," i.e., outlive your savings.

RISKS AND
DRAWBACKS

Life insurance is considered a safe investment, in that the risk of an insurer failing to meet its commitments is regarded as low. To be eligible to sell policies, insurers must meet financial and other requirements set by state insurance departments. With modern health facilities and steadily increasing life expectancies in this country, the typical life insurance company does not have to take an enormous overall risk. It pretty well knows, from its actuarial tables, how many deaths to expect each year in this country. If some cataclysmic event killed a large percentage of the population, the insurance industry might face financial troubles, but that would be the least of anyone's worries in those circumstances.

Nevertheless, it makes sense to evaluate an insurance company carefully before buying one of its policies. Regulators may vary considerably in their diligence and ability from state to state. One of the most spectacular frauds in this country's recent history occurred at an insurance company, the Equity Funding Corp. of America. Unlike banks and brokers, insurance companies have no national organization with a pool of money to serve as a backup in case of trouble.

"The regulatory safeguards to protect or warn consumers against, say, an insurance company's shaky financial condition are rudimentary," Business Week magazine said in a 1984 editorial. "If the industry and the 50 states that regulate it cannot provide an urgently needed new safety net, public pressure will certainly cause the federal government to move in and take over."

The image of life insurance as a wise investment has plainly suffered some harm lately at the hands of inflation. Possibly, the new products the industry has developed will help it regain that lost luster. A return to relatively stable cost-of-living levels in this country would certainly help.

But the industry still clearly faces problems catching up with the financial revolution of the '70s and early '80s. At the time this book was written, investors' awareness of the choices open to them was rising significantly, and many financial services firms were scrambling to meet their needs. Yet one of the most respected insurance companies in the country was still sending out annual statements of account to policyholders that were indecipherable even to a full-time student of investing and personal finance.

LIQUIDITY

Life insurance is traditionally an illiquid investment, in several senses of the word. To buy it at an attractive price, you must do so long before you are likely to collect on it. Once you begin paying premiums in a whole life policy, it normally takes some years before you start realizing anything approaching an attractive return on your money.

Holders of older, existing whole life policies should be aware, however, of the availability of their cash values as a source of ready funds at low interest rates. Before inflation started raging, these policies were typically written with specified interest rates on policy loans of 5, 6 or 8 percent. Under the policy contract, you normally can tap any or all of the cash value in your policy at the stated interest rate whenever you wish. In the 1970s and early 1980s, many policyowners took advantage of this provision to borrow on their cash values and invest the money elsewhere at higher rates.

This might sound like a good deal for the insurance company, too— lending you "your own money," and collecting interest in the bargain. But it is not. In order to operate in orderly fashion, the typical insurance company counts on having the use of your money for its own investment plans, where it can earn competitive returns. In the mid-1980s, 5 or 6 or 8 percent was not a competitive return.

TAX ADVANTAGES
AND DISADVANTAGES

Life insurance has some attractive tax features. A whole life policy can give you access to tax-free compounding. In many situations, proceeds received from a life insurance policy aren't subject to federal income tax. But they can be subject to estate taxes. This is a matter of concern to anyone who expects to leave an estate large enough to be taxed. Life insurance is barred from (and anyway would not make much sense in) individual retirement accounts, Keogh plans and other tax-favored savings programs.

ADJUSTABLE, UNIVERSAL AND VARIABLE LIFE INSURANCE

DESCRIPTION

With the sweeping changes that took place in the U.S. economy and the financial-services industry in the 1970s and early 1980s, insurance companies in increasing numbers found it desirable or necessary to offer products designed to overcome the limitations of standard term or whole life insurance. Some of these were based on old concepts that had not previously gained wide acceptance; others were new ideas entirely.

The new breed of life insurance policies gives policyholders one or more of several options not usually available with "plain vanilla" coverage. It may, for instance, provide for variation in the size of premiums paid and amount of death benefit coverage, at the discretion of the policyholder. It may involve lower costs. It may provide a better return on the policyholder's cash value savings program than traditional policies. And it may allow the policyholder to decide how the money in that account is invested.

Three primary categories in this new generation of policies are adjustable, universal and variable life insurance. Adjustable life, as the name implies, gives its buyers the right to change the financial terms of the agreement as their needs or desires change. If they want to increase death benefit coverage, they may be able to do so by paying a bigger premium or shortening the length of the policy's duration. If they reach a point where their death benefit coverage needs diminish, they may reduce it and pay lower premiums.

Universal life, as the American Council of Life Insurance describes it, "is designed to permit a policyholder to pay premiums at any time, in virtually any amount, subject to certain minimums. The policyholder can also change the amount of insurance more easily than under traditional policies. In a universal life insurance policy the amount the cash value increases each year reflects the interest earned on short-term investments."

Variable life provides a set minimum guaranteed death benefit, and then in effect turns the policyholder loose to invest cash values as they accumulate in any one of several funds that work like mutual funds. The cash value fluctuates, depending on the investment results obtained, and the death benefit can increase if the fund produces a good enough return.

Now that the door has been opened to such new types of life insurance, more innovation in the future would certainly be no surprise. As the recent past has demonstrated, pure life insurance can be packaged together with variable annuities or mutual fund-style investing to produce a great variety of products. Presumably, it can be matched up with other investment vehicles as well. Today's diversity can add to the complexity of making decisions in buying life insurance, but it also gives would-be buyers helpful choices in a complicated world.

HOW AND WHERE TO GET
INFORMATION AND INVEST

In the mid-1980s, the number of life insurance companies offering vehicles like adjustable, universal and variable life was growing steadily. Some securities brokerage firms aggressively market them. Inquiries with a few agents and-or brokers should lead you toward the type of new breed policy you are interested in.

Consumer publications may be helpful in sorting out the pluses and minuses of these products, and evaluations of policies offered by individual companies. The American Council of Life Insurance, a trade group, invites written inquiries on any life-insurance matter. Its headquarters is at 1850 K Street NW, Washington DC 20006.

COSTS OF BUYING,
OWNING AND SELLING

Like its sister product, annuities, life insurance in its newer forms is becoming increasingly available at low, or no, up-front sales charges. These vehicles typically do call for a charge, however, if you want to get out of the deal before a specified amount of time has passed. Various other fees also may be imposed, and they bear close examination in the contract, prospectus or other legal document covering the policy before you invest.

CAPITAL GAINS
POTENTIAL

The new varieties of life insurance have introduced policyholders to the possibility of capital gains. Suppose, for example, that you buy a variable life policy, and specify that the amount of your premiums set aside in your cash value account be invested in a growth fund that holds stocks in its portfolio. If the fund does well, the gains it generates build up your cash value, and can increase the amount of death-benefit coverage provided by the policy.

This gives the policyholder the hope of at least some protection from inflation—an element largely lacking in many forms of traditional life insurance. You cannot obtain this potential advantage, of course, without taking a risk. If the fund performs poorly, you can suffer cash value losses. Some variable-life policies offer holders a choice between aggressive and conservative growth funds, as well as short-term money market funds and bond funds. They may permit you to spread the money in your account over several of the funds, and to switch the money between funds periodically.

INCOME POTENTIAL

New breed life insurance policies may offer ways to invest your cash value account that produce better yields than were heretofore available in conventional policies. With universal or variable life, you may have access to a competitive money market return on your money. But no form of life insurance is set up to compete with, say, Treasury bills as a short-term parking place for your money. Nor is it designed primarily as a vehicle for people whose sole concern is maximum current income to live on.

RISKS AND
DRAWBACKS

Whenever a life insurance policy permits you to earn market returns on your money, you must assume some degree of market and other risks. If you choose a stock fund for your variable life policy, your cash value can fall short of your hopes if the stock market and the managers of the particular stock fund do not perform well. If interest rates rise, cash value in a bond fund can decline.

If interest rates fall, and stay low for an extended period, money market investments may well produce a smaller return than you planned on. If you have bought a policy under an arrangement in which cash-value proceeds go to help pay premiums, you may be faced with higher-than-expected premium payments out of your pocket if the earnings generated by the cash value drop because of changing conditions in the investment markets.

All this has the effect of introducing elements of uncertainty to a vehicle that savers and investors have traditionally relied on for security. However, that security was already seriously eroded by inflation and volatile interest rates.

Many companies in the insurance industry have been somewhat cautious in their approach to writing new breed policies, in part because they do not want to provoke a large-scale exodus of money from traditional policies into the newer products. When the Northwestern Mutual Life Insurance Co. told its policyholders that it was developing a variable-life product in 1984, it declared: "Variable Life is not intended to replace sales of the company's other whole life products, but it will provide additional opportunities to certain segments of the insurance market."

LIQUIDITY

Many of the new breed life insurance policies are illiquid investments—in some cases, even more so than traditional life products. They are often designed to discourage early terminations of policies, a problem that has been plaguing the industry. The policy contract may spell out early-withdrawal charges for policies cashed in before a specified time period has elapsed. Thus, these modern policies should be evaluated as long-term propositions, and financed with money you do not expect to need in the near future.

With these newer policies and, in fact, with some traditional policies, many insurance companies have also taken steps to make it less attractive for policyholders to borrow against their cash value. When you take out such a loan, for instance, a variable life policy may specify that the amount borrowed is moved out of the fund in which it was invested and placed in a lower-yielding general fund.

TAX ADVANTAGES
AND DISADVANTAGES

Like conventional life insurance, new breed life insurance products can offer some significant tax features. Money earned in a policy's cash value account can enjoy the significant advantage of tax-free compounding. The Tax Reform Act of 1984 specifically made universal life insurance eligible for the standard tax benefits provided by other types of policies.

The new types of life insurance policies, like traditional ones, are ineligible for use in tax-favored savings programs such as individual retirement accounts and Keogh plans. They may, however, be considered separately from IRAs and Keoghs as part of your retirement planning.

LIMITED PARTNERSHIPS

DESCRIPTION

Limited partnerships have been a hot "new" item in the investment world over the last few years. At first, the ones that got the most attention were tax shelter deals, investing in things like real estate and oil and gas exploration. More recently, sponsors of these programs have begun to offer increasing numbers of partnerships designed to produce attractive income. Still others are used to create pools for trading in commodity futures. It would be no surprise if many additional uses for limited partnerships were devised in the future.

These investments bear some resemblance to mutual funds and closed-end investment companies. There are, however, very important differences in the way they operate. To understand them, it is first necessary to know how a partnership functions.

There are two basic types of organization in American business. One is the corporation, which has a legal identity of its own, pays taxes and assumes a broad range of legal and financial responsibilities. In the other form, the partnership, the burden of many of these obligations falls on the individual owners, rather than the business itself. If a partnership incurs losses beyond its financial means, for example, or loses a lawsuit, liability typically rests with the individual owners.

That is more risk than most passive investors would ever want to take. So the concept evolved of *limited* partnership, as opposed to *general* partnership. To attract capital from limited partners, general partners exempt them from some of the risks and responsibilities involved in the business. In return, limited partners generally agree to abide by whatever decisions general partners make.

In limited partnership investments, the firm that organizes and sells the venture typically names itself or an affiliate as the sole general partner. It then offers a piece of the action to limited partners as "units."

Many of today's limited partnerships are referred to as "private." They are not registered with the Securities and Exchange Commission, and generally are sold only to small numbers of wealthy investors. "Public" limited partnerships, by contrast, are registered with and reviewed by the SEC. As William Brennan, a finanical adviser specializing in tax matters, has pointed out, "reviewed" does not mean "approved."

Public partnerships are offered in pieces as small as a few thousand dollars. They are even marketed for use in individual retirement accounts. Whether public or private, limited partnerships may offer attractions that are hard to find elsewhere. But they also involve special risks that should be carefully evaluated and understood before you invest.

HOW AND WHERE TO GET
INFORMATION AND INVEST

Many large financial-services firms sponsor and sell limited partnership investments. There are also a large number of less-known organizations that specialize in them. If your financial status is such that you are a prime candidate for investing in limited partnerships, chances are that you will not have to look hard for information and prospective deals. It may well come to you, in the form of mail, telephone or in-person sales pitches.

Unless you already have a well-established relationship of trust with the salesperson who approaches you and the firm he or she represents, it makes sense to proceed very warily in these circumstances. The greater the promised benefits, the more investigation and evaluation should be made.

COSTS OF BUYING,
OWNING AND SELLING

The costs of investing in limited partnerships are generally high. Large up-front sales charges are common, and the general partner often collects a variety of fees once the venture is in operation. You should have a thorough understanding of all the fees you will, or might, be charged before you invest.

In some partnerships, there is a provision in the agreement that allows the general partner to call on you for additional capital under certain circumstances. Before entering into such a deal, you should be confident of being able to meet this requirement.

CAPITAL GAINS POTENTIAL

Many limited partnerships take substantial risks in the hope of achieving large capital gains. Some realize this goal; others do not. When people evaluate a partnership's prospects, they generally look into the sponsor's past record in similiar programs. But of course, past successes are no assurance of future ones.

In the process of evaluating a partnership investment, it is possible to get so preoccupied with all the trappings of the deal—its structure, potential tax benefits, and so forth—that you overlook the fundamental business question: Does the whole venture make economic sense? Is the price right? If you were a wealthy investor operating on your own, would you consider making the same commitment?

INCOME POTENTIAL

Limited partnerships investing in oil or real estate for income have become increasingly popular in recent years. These partnerships take fewer risks than many other types. For example, they typically buy properties for cash, using no borrowed money. Furthermore, your after-tax return on the payments you receive may be substantially enhanced through writeoffs for depreciation. However, conservative investors who want or need maximum income and safety of principal generally should not expect a limited partnership to offer the protection from risk available with such vehicles as Treasury bills or federally insured deposits.

RISKS AND DRAWBACKS

As a general rule, limited partnerships are moderate-to high-risk propositions. There have been cases when even large, well-respected sponsors of these packages have failed to deliver expected returns because of adverse business developments. There have also been highly publicized cases of outright fraud.

In addition, it is important to understand that, as a limited partner, you have little or no say in how a venture operates once you invest. In real estate, for example, it is common for units to be sold before the syndicate even has decided what properties to buy. Because of their illiquidity (see below), limited partnerships are generally not a suitable place for money you might want or need before the time when they are scheduled to be dissolved.

LIQUIDITY

Limited partnerships are notoriously illiquid. Once you have invested, it may be difficult or even impossible to get all your capital back before the partnership breaks up—typically, seven to 12 years after it begins operating. As this type of investment gains a broader market, it is possible that sponsors will devise ways to alleviate this problem. In any case, before getting into a partnership investment, it is wise to inquire what, if any, provisions have been made to permit you to get out early.

TAX ADVANTAGES
AND DISADVANTAGES

Many limited partnerships are set up to gain handsome tax benefits (see Tax Shelters). Some real estate programs, for example, produce no significant income in the early years, but provide investors with tax writeoffs for interest on mortgages and construction loans, and for depreciation of properties owned. Income-producing partnerships may use depreciation and other deductible costs to shelter some or all of the payments you receive from income taxes.

No matter what strategy a given program follows, it is important to understand that any "taxable event"—for instance, a capital gain—that happens with the venture normally goes into your personal tax accounts for the year in which it occurs. There may be unanticipated tax events that can disrupt the rest of your tax planning. As a limited partner, you may be relatively powerless to take any steps to prevent such things from happening.

Marketers of limited partnerships are aiming their efforts increasingly at individual retirement accounts, Keogh plans and other tax-favored savings programs. When considering a given partnership deal for, say, an IRA, it makes sense to consider how much of the package's benefits consist of advantages for taxable investors. These advantages may be negated in an IRA or other tax-deferred account.

MONEY MARKET DEPOSIT ACCOUNTS

DESCRIPTION

With the rise of money market mutual funds in the 1970s, banks and savings institutions were confronted with some formidable new competition. While decades-old regulations limited the interest rates and other attractions these institutions could offer their depositors, money funds could pay their shareholders whatever returns the fund managers could earn investing in the money markets.

It didn't take many years for government regulators to decide that banks and savings institutions should be allowed to offer a similar product. Thus, on Dec. 14, 1982, was born the money market deposit account—a savings vehicle on which interest rates are determined by open competition.

MMDAs proved to be an immediate hit. In their first six months of existence, they piled up much greater growth than money funds had achieved in a decade. The money funds suffered a setback, but survived the onslaught. Today the two types of vehicles are regarded as close rivals for savers' money, though there are some important differences between them.

At the start, banks and savings institutions were permitted to pay whatever rates they chose on an MMDA as long as there was at least $2,500 in the account. If the total fell below that, the maximum interest rate reverted to 5.5 percent. Government regulators announced plans, however, to lower this $2,500 cutoff point to $1,000 effective Jan. 1, 1985, and to zero on Jan. 1, 1986.

There are a few other restrictions as well. While savers can be allowed unlimited withdrawals from these accounts, no more than six a month can be "third party" or "pre-authorized" transactions—and of these six, no more than three can be checks written on the account.

The advent of MMDAs, along with other banking deregulation (see the chapters on certificates of deposit and NOW and Super-NOW accounts) changed the world of banking for customers as well as the institutions. In the days when all the institutions were limited to "the highest rate permitted by law," as they frequently noted in their advertising, customers evaluated them primarily on matters such as convenience and service. There wasn't much point to comparison shopping for yields. Today, rates and other terms available on MMDAs may vary significantly from one city to another, and between institutions in the same community.

HOW AND WHERE TO GET
INFORMATION AND INVEST

In their modern deregulated world, many banks and savings institutions compete aggressively for money market deposit accounts. Chances are you will be able to get the basic information you need on MMDAs with a few phone calls or visits to the institutions in your area. But it should be noted that the interest rates currently offered by a sampling of institutions do not necessarily tell you which one will ultimately provide you with the best return.

Rates on MMDAs are subject to change monthly, or even more frequently. Furthermore, banks may use different methods of compounding and crediting interest. Before signing on with any institution, it makes sense to inquire what formula, if any, it uses to set its MMDA interest rate, what methods of compounding and crediting it employs, and what effective annual yield you would earn on a given nominal interest rate. As one bank declared in an advertisement for its accounts, "astute investors watch yields, not rates."

Beyond that, a thorough study of any other limits or restrictions a given institution imposes is recommended. Is there, for example, a minimum dollar amount stipulated for each check you write against the account? Does the account give you access to other benefits and services at the institution, such as a no-fee checking account?

The process of gathering information about MMDAs does not stop once the account is open. If you are eager to receive the best possible return on your money, you may want periodically to compare what you are getting from your MMDA with what other institutions are offering.

Within a short time after the debut of MMDAs, some independent firms began collecting information on rates available at institutions across the country, and providing that information to their customers

and to newspapers and financial publications. You can make compar-
isons on your own, of course, by keeping an eye on bank advertising
and by periodically telephoning or visiting institutions in your area.

COSTS OF BUYING,
OWNING AND SELLING

The costs incurred in opening and maintaining an MMDA should be
nominal at most, given the competitive environment in which they
exist. If one institution sets some fee or other charge you feel is
excessive, you can easily look elsewhere or consider the alternative
of a money market mutual fund.

CAPITAL GAINS
POTENTIAL

As with other bank savings accounts, MMDAs offer no potential for
capital gains. However, they do offer the prospect of reliable growth,
with compounding, of the portion of your assets that you do not wish to
tie up in long-term investments. They also provide you with a measure
of inflation protection, since interest rates on MMDAs presumably will
rise with other short-term interest rates in periods when the cost of
living is increasing at a rapid pace. For people in a position to seek
growth with long-term capital gains tax advantages, many advisers
suggest looking to stocks, real estate or other investments once you
have established a liquid cash reserve that you feel is adequate to
your needs.

INCOME POTENTIAL

For income conscious savers and investors, MMDAs represent a
great improvement on the old passbook savings account. At the same
time, they retain the advantage of federal deposit insurance of up to
$100,000 per account.

Like money market mutual funds, which, though considered highly
safe, are not covered by federal deposit insurance, MMDAs may give
you access to current competitive interest rates. They do not, however, give you the opportunity to "lock in" a given return for any
appreciable period of time.

If your circumstances are such they you would like to assure yourself of today's prevailing rates for the next six months, the next year, or for that matter the next 25 years, it makes sense to consider such alternatives as time certificates of deposit and bonds.

Some banks and savings institutions offer premium interest rates for MMDAs with large deposit balances of say, at least $15,000 or $25,000. This is a point to check into if you have, or expect to have, large amounts of money to deposit in an MMDA.

RISKS AND DRAWBACKS

The advantage MMDAs offer when interest rates are high or rising— the fact that they tend to move with the general credit market—becomes a disadvantage when rates are low or falling. Ideally, you could use an MMDA to best advantage by moving money into it just before interest rates rise significantly, and shifting the money out into some long-term, fixed-income investment just as rates hit their peak and begin a decline. Unfortunately, predicting interest rate movements consistently and correctly is a feat that has eluded just about everyone, including the most esteemed experts. Furthermore, a given bank or savings institution that sets its MMDA interest rates by an unspecified method of its own choosing may be slow, in comparison with money market funds and its competition in the banking industry, to raise its payout when interest rates are moving up.

With an MMDA, you have every reason to expect convenience and good service. If that is not your experience at any particular institution, you might well consider moving the account elsewhere.

LIQUIDITY

MMDAs generally offer the attraction of great liquidity. You can use them to earn market returns continuously on any extra money you have until the moment when you need or want the money for some other purpose. Nevertheless, the liquidity of MMDAs is not quite flawless. For one thing, as long as government-mandated minimum deposits continue, the first $1,000 or $2,500 in an MMDA is effectively tied up in the account for as long as you wish to keep receiving a market rate of return on your money. Assuming that regulators proceed as planned to eliminate the minimum requirement, some banks and savings institutions may choose to set minimums of their own afterward.

A second, less important liquidity question involves the institution's method of crediting interest. For example, it makes sense to inquire at the start whether withdrawing all your money on, say, the 28th day of a month will mean losing all your interest for that month.

TAX ADVANTAGES
AND DISADVANTAGES

Interest earned from an MMDA is subject to federal and any applicable state and local tax as ordinary income. If you have a good-sized amount of money in an MMDA earning a generous rate of return, it is wise to bear in mind during the course of any given year that you are also probably running up a good-sized tax obligation.

MMDAs are theoretically suitable for individual retirement accounts, Keogh plans and other tax-favored savings programs. In the early years of MMDAs' availability, however, many banks and savings institutions have not promoted them for IRAs and other similar plans, but have stressed other types of deposits.

MORTGAGES

DESCRIPTION

When people make real estate investments, such as the purchase of a home to live in, they commonly finance a large part of the cost with a mortgage—a loan that uses the property involved as collateral. Their main motive in taking out such a loan is often quite simple: They couldn't possibly pay the entire price in cash. But that is by no means the only attraction of mortgage borrowing. The interest on the loan, which accounts for nearly all your periodic payments in the early years of a mortgage, is deductible on your income tax return.

Furthermore, mortgages give the buyer leverage. Consider the case of a $100,000 house, bought with a $20,000 down payment and an $80,000 mortgage. Should the value of the house rise to $120,000, the owner, using a traditional mortgage, gets all the profit. His or her equity ownerhip interest in the house rises to $40,000.

Leverage, as is pointed out in many other chapters of this book, usually increases risk to the same degree that it enhances potential reward. Indeed, if that $100,000 house falls in value to $80,000, the owner's equity drops to zero. Prices of houses, like any other unguaranteed investment, can decline at any time.

Why, then, is it considered perfectly prudent for conservative investors to use mortgage financing to buy a home, rental property or vacation cottage, even if they wouldn't dream of leveraging their other investments? Part of the answer lies in the special status of many real estate investments, which is discussed in the real estate chapter of this book.

Another factor is the way that mortgage-lending institutions traditionally operate. They do not usually want to expose themselves to any great risk of default on their loans, and so they go to some trouble to determine that anyone they approve for a mortgage is a good risk. It is a standard maxim in the residential real estate business that buyers applying for mortgages need not worry about whether they can afford to meet the payments in the future. If a reputable institution approves a loan, your statistical likelihood of defaulting is very low.

It should be noted, however, that rules like that one evolved when the standard mortgage carried a fixed interest rate and called for regular payments over the life of the loan. In recent years, mortgage lenders have begun to offer several new types of mortgages whose interest rates and other terms are not fixed. These loans generally involve significant risks to the borrower that do not exist with conventional fixed mortgages. The most important of these new vehicles is the adjustable-rate mortgage, or ARM, which will be discussed extensively in this chapter.

As many real estate investors are well aware, it is possible to obtain more than one mortgage on a property. A second mortgage may be used to increase leverage on the investment and obtain cash for other uses. In the booming California real estate market of the late 1970s, there were second mortgages, third mortgages, and fourth mortgages, and on and on. It goes without saying that in situations like this, each layer of debt compounds the risk to which the borrower is exposed, no matter how choice the property involved.

Conservative investors often take out new mortgages on appreciated property they have owned for a long time to pay for such expenses as the cost of a child's college education. An alternative to mortgage borrowing on residential property you already own is the home-equity access account, discussed in a separate section of this book.

HOW AND WHERE TO GET
INFORMATION AND INVEST

In simpler times, anyone in the market for a mortgage simply shopped the local financial institutions. Each had one standard, fixed mortgage deal to offer. You applied for the one or ones that looked most attractive, and then waited with the customary anxiety to find out whether you had been approved.

Now, with the spread of ARMs and other exotic mortgages, the investigation required is typically a lot more complicated. A single institution now may offer several different possibilities. Particulary for the first-time investor, it is more advisable than ever to have the advice and counsel of knowledgeable acquaintances or a professional in real estate finance as you evaluate your mortgage options.

If you buy through a real estate broker, that broker may provide a great deal of information about mortgages available in the immediate area. In most real estate transactions, it should be remembered, brokers are paid by, and represent, the seller of the property. Thus, the broker's advice and recommendations to you as a buyer should be considered with the understanding that the broker is not a disinterested bystander in the whole process.

COSTS OF BUYING, OWNING AND SELLING

Mortgages are generally costly to obtain, to keep up with, and even sometimes to get rid of. The long-lost era of the low-interest, fixed mortgage is fondly remembered these days, but even back then many borrowers had to devote a good portion of their life's labors to paying the mortgage bills.

Before you sign mortgage papers, you should ideally have at hand a written list of all the lender's fees, over and above the specified interest and principal to be paid. These may include charges for processing your application and evaluating you as a credit risk, fees mandated by local governments, and, perhaps most important of all, *points.* A point is 1 percent of the total amount of the loan.

Another angle to consider in committing yourself to a mortgage is the possibility that you may want to pay the loan off early. Even if you plan to put down permanent roots in the property you are buying, there is a chance that events could change those plans in the very near future. Thus, you should have a clear understanding before committing yourself to a mortgage of what penalties or other charges the lender will impose for prepayment of the loan.

CAPITAL GAINS POTENTIAL

Mortgages, with the leverage they provide, are an important tool available for use in seeking capital gains in any real estate investment. You pay a price for this leverage, however, in the form of the after-tax cost of the interest payments, points and other charges involved with the loan.

If you take out an ARM, or other exotic mortgage, it can have a significant effect in the capital-gain prospects of your real estate investment. The provisions of an ARM call for periodic adjustment of the interest rate on the mortgage. They may also specify a "cap"—a limit on the amount your periodic payments may increase.

This cap may also pose a hidden problem. In future years, if the prevailing level of interest rates rises significantly, the cap will prevent your payments from going up as much as open-market interest rates. But the mortgage terms may allow the lender to charge prevailing interest rates against your account anyway. If the maximum periodic payment doesn't cover the amount owed by this formula, the total you eventually must pay can be increased. This situation is known as *negative amortization.* If the market value of your property is not increasing while you are in these circumstances, your equity in the property can decrease with each payment you make.

Another type of modern home loan is known as a graduated-payment mortgage. The interest rate may be fixed, but the mortgage is set up to provide for low payments at the outset, with steps up in later years. Frequently, these loans also involve negative amortization in the early stages of their life.

Some lenders in the early 1980s offered what they called *shared-equity* mortgages. These gave them an interest in any profits realized from the eventual sale of a home. Shared-equity deals have become increasingly common in commercial real estate. But to date they have not been a smash hit with home buyers.

INCOME POTENTIAL

Of course, mortgages normally represent a drain on your cash flow. They are the opposite of an income-producing investment. But you can sometimes use them as a tool in investing for income—say, to finance the purchase of a property that generates rents. The proper role of mortgage borrowing in the financial plan of an investor seeking current income depends largely on the investor's particular situation, and on prevailing levels of interest rates.

For example, suppose you are nearing retirement and are shifting your assets around so that they will start yielding maximum current income once you leave your job. Should you pay off an existing mortgage on your home? Possibly, if the money needed to do it could not be invested elsewhere at a greater return than the interest rate on the mortgage. But most probably not, if the mortgage is an old loan at a low interest rate, and if safe, higher-yielding investment alternatives are available.

LIQUIDITY

For most every mortgage borrower, the loan payments are a heavy drain on cash flow at the start. In the 1970s, when rates on most mortgages were fixed and inflation was running high, many borrowers found that what seemed an onerous burden at first grew much lighter in only a few years' time.

Lenders suffered from those circumstances, but they learned a lesson from them. Today many set their rates on fixed mortgages at very high levels, or do not offer fixed-rate loans at all. They encourage borrowers to take on interest rate risk with adjustable-rate mortgages.

There is widespread concern that ARMs, with their growing popularity, could lead to a big increase in mortgage defaults in any future period when interest rates rise significantly. Whether or not those fears are ever realized, you should be aware, before committing yourself to any non-fixed mortgage, that it poses at least some element of risk to your future liquidity.

TAX ADVANTAGES
AND DISADVANTAGES

Borrowers love their mortgages most at tax time. The interest, every blessed penny of it, is deductible on their income tax returns. In your enthusiasm over this tax break, it is possible to forget that the after-tax cost of mortgage borrowing can still be significant. Furthermore, it is possible that the mortgage tax break may be curtailed in the future as efforts at tax reform continue.

MORTGAGE SECURITIES

DESCRIPTION

Mortgages—long-term loans used to purchase homes and other property, with the property used for collateral—are a time-honored tradition in American finance. Until recently, most home mortgages were issued and held over their lifetime by local institutions such as savings and loans. Individuals made up a large percentage of mortgage borrowers, but relatively few acted as mortgage lenders. Those that did usually confined themselves to making direct loans on homes they were selling.

The situation began to change in the 1970s, however, when interest rates grew more and more volatile, reaching previously unthinkable levels. The risks and rewards of mortgage lending—investing in mortgages—changed dramatically. As a result, a secondary market blossomed in which mortgages and securities representing pools of mortgages could be bought and sold, much like bonds, by investors. By 1983, according to the Public Securities Association, a trade group, the money for almost half the new loans issued on one- to four-family homes in the United States was provided by mortgage-backed securities.

To the newcomer, mortgage investing can seem bewildering at first. It is dominated by professionals such as pension fund managers. But the rapid growth of the market indicates that increasing numbers of individual investors are finding it attractive.

Typically, a mortgage-backed security is created when a middleman gathers together a large package of loans, then cuts the package up again into pieces for sale to investors. The investors thereafter receive their proportionate share of the interest payments on the mortgages and the principal payments as well.

Three big names in the business are government-sponsored companies and agencies known as the Federal Home Loan Mortgage Corp., the Federal National Mortgage Association and the Government National Mortgage Association. They are usually referred to by the nicknames Freddie Mac, Fannie Mae and Ginnie Mae, respectively. Other, private middlemen with no links to the government are appearing in increasing numbers.

Most mortgage securities are known as "pass-throughs," because the packager passes through monthly interest and principal payments directly to investors. A newer variation, which met with an enthusiastic initial response, is the "collateralized mortgage obligation," a corporate bond backed by mortgages, that typically makes payments of interest and principal to investors semi-annually.

HOW AND WHERE TO GET
INFORMATION AND INVEST

Since there are various issuers of mortgage securities, each with their own special setups, the best way to get information on these investments may be to consult a sampling of the brokerage firms and government-securities dealers who buy and sell them. Many brokers also can supply information about unit trusts investing in mortgage securities. In addition, some mutual fund companies have introduced funds specializing in this area. Prospectuses of funds and unit trusts can be informative about mortgage securities generally.

COSTS OF BUYING,
OWNING AND SELLING

Costs of buying and selling mortgage securities vary with the type of vehicle you choose and the broker or dealer with whom you deal. The firm that sells you such a security may charge you a flat fee, or it may earn its money on the transaction by setting a "spread" between its cost of acquiring the security and the price it charges you.

Mortgage-security unit trusts, like trusts of other types, generally carry a sales charge of about 4 percent. Mutual funds specializing in this field may also set a sales charge (one introduced in early 1984 charges 5 percent of the total invested) or they may be "no-load." In any case, a mutual fund's sponsor also collects an annual management fee from the assets of the funds.

The usual minimum investment for a mortgage security is $25,000—a steep ante for a good many small investors. However, an older mortgage security that has been partly paid off, or which was issued in times when interest rates were low, may be available for considerably less.

Some of the newer vehicles are available in denominations as small as $1,000. With unit trusts and mutual funds, the usual minimum is also $1,000.

CAPITAL GAINS POTENTIAL

Prices of interest-bearing investments, including mortgage securities, move up and down in the opposite direction from shifts in the prevailing level of interest rates. Thus, it is possible to realize a capital gain from a mortgage security after a period of falling interest rates. However, mortgage securities are aimed primarily at investors looking for a generous yield, not capital gains.

INCOME POTENTIAL

As stated above, the main allure of mortgage securities is generous yield. In the past, they have offered returns higher than Treasury bonds of comparable maturity, without any major sacrifice of safety or liquidity.

With many types of mortgage securities, some confusion is possible about periodic payments that are received. When homeowners make their monthly mortgage payments, they pay interest and a portion of the principal amount of their loans. Frequently, they pay off the whole loan well before its scheduled maturity date when they sell their houses and move.

The way many mortgage securities are set up, payments to investors also are part interest, part principal. Investors in these securities must be aware that the checks they are receiving represent not just earnings on their investments, but also a partial return of the money they put up in the first place.

This arrangement is fine with some investors, while others find it unwieldy. The problem can be averted if an investor selects a mortgage security, unit trust or mutual fund that provides for automatic and immediate reinvestment of the principal payments received in new mortgages. Some also provide for reinvestment of interest payments if the investor does not wish to receive them as current income.

RISKS AND
DRAWBACKS

The main risk in making any loan, mortgage or otherwise, is that the borrower will fail to make timely payments of interest and principal. In the extreme, the borrower may default completely. It is a risk to be borne prominently in mind whenever you are thinking of making a direct mortgage loan to another individual, or of investing in any uninsured package of mortgages.

But mortgage-backed securities generally carry some insurance against this risk, either privately or through government guarantees. The safest of all mortgage securities are those carrying "full faith and credit" guarantees of the federal government, since the U.S. government is widely regarded as the world's safest credit risk.

Prices of mortgage securities move up and down as interest rates fluctuate. So there is also a market risk in investing in them should you want or need to sell them before they mature. Also, like any fixed-income investment, mortgage securities carry an inflation risk. There is no way of knowing for sure at the time you buy how much inflation will erode the purchasing power of your money while it is invested.

LIQUIDITY

Since the market for major mortgage securities is large and growing, the liquidity of these investments is considered good to excellent. Many dealers and brokers trade in them regularly. Unit trusts and mutual fund shares can normally be sold at any time through the firm from which you purchased them.

However, it should be noted that, from an individual investor's point of view, the basic appeal of mortgage securities is as a long-term investment. They are not a logical place to put money you reasonably expect to need for other purposes in the near future.

TAX ADVANTAGES
AND DISADVANTAGES

Interest received on mortgage investments is taxable as ordinary income. People in high tax brackets may find they can get higher after-tax returns from tax-exempt bonds. Profits or losses realized on a sale of a mortgage security are taxed at capital gains rates. There is no tax liability, of course, on money you receive that represents a return of your initial investment.

Mortgage-backed securities are a suitable candidate for individual retirement account, Keogh plan or other tax-favored investment plan.

MUTUAL FUNDS

DESCRIPTION

Mutual funds are a staple item in the American investment diet, with millions of small investors and a substantial number of large ones as well. They are companies organized to pool and invest money received from their shareholders, providing benefits such as convenience and diversification that individuals might not be able to obtain through direct investment in stocks, bonds and other securities.

The first investment companies operated in Europe more than 150 years ago. "Investment trusts" enjoyed a boom in the United States in the 1920s, and then fell drastically from favor in the stock market crash of 1929 and the Great Depression that followed. Modern mutual funds trace their origins to the Investment Company Act of 1940, which spelled out detailed rules under which they were to operate.

The industry grew as the stock market prospered in the 1950s and 1960s, and then fell on difficult times in the bear markets of 1969-70 and 1973-74. Since then, it has enjoyed another period of heady growth, benefiting not only from a stock-market recovery but from expansion into other investment areas—the money markets, municipal bonds, and more.

The various types of mutual funds, discussed in separate sections of this chapter, share some important common characteristics. They are open-ended—that is, they stand ready every business day to sell new shares directly to investors and to redeem old shares for investors who wish to cash them in. (One exception to this rule occurs occasionally when a fund opts to suspend sales of shares to new investors. This action may be taken when directors and management of a fund feel it is receiving new money too rapidly to invest it effectively within its stated philosophy. In this situation, redemptions continue as usual.)

A mutual fund's price is set daily by its net asset value per share—the total worth of its investments and other assets divided by the number of shares outstanding. Tables of funds' net asset values are published regularly in many general-interest newspapers and financial publications. In recent years, fund "families" have evolved that allow their investors to switch money from a fund with one type of objective to another with a different strategy, at little or no cost.

HOW AND WHERE TO GET
INFORMATION AND INVEST

Some mutual funds employ salesmen to market their shares, or sell them through brokers who receive commissions for their efforts. Others (called "no-load" funds) depend primarily on advertising and word-of-mouth to attract shareholders. Abundant information is readily available on both types. Several independent firms publish directories of fund names, addresses and telephone numbers, and newspapers and magazines frequently profile individual funds. There are advisory services that specialize in rating fund performance and recommending individual funds. Information is also available from two trade associations: the Investment Company Institute, 1775 K Street N.W., Washington, D.C. 20006, and the No-Load Mutual Fund Association, 11 Penn Plaza 2204, New York, N.Y. 10001.

Once investors have identified a fund in which they are interested, they can obtain a prospectus, spelling out details of the fund's objectives and operations, and other information such as the most recent annual report, by request from the broker or salesman they are dealing with, or by telephoning or writing the fund itself. Applications to open an account with the fund typically are included in the prospectus—which, however dull, is generally considered must reading for would-be investors.

COSTS OF BUYING,
OWNING AND SELLING

So-called *load* funds marketed through salesmen or brokers impose a sales charge of up to 8.5 percent of the amount you put up when you invest. They usually set sliding scales under which the percentage charge decreases gradually as the size of the investment increases. A relatively new breed, called *low-load,* carries a smaller sales charge of perhaps 2 to 4 percent.

No-load funds, by contrast, collect no such commission and boast that 100 percent of the money you entrust them with goes to work for you. If you have the necessary investment knowledge and the inclination to do your own research and use your own judgment to select a fund, many investment experts recommend concentrating on no-load funds.

In any case, no fund is free of all costs. The investment advisers that operate them collect an annual management fee from the fund's assets. This is usually a percentage—say, one-half of 1 percent—of the total average assets in the fund over the period in question. You never have to pay this fee out of your pocket, but it has the effect of diminishing the return you get on your investment. When they buy and sell securities, funds also must pay brokerage commissions—although they and other investing institutions can generally command more favorable rates from brokers than small investors might be able to negotiate. Some funds may also charge redemption fees when you cash in your shares, in order to discourage investors from constantly moving their money in and out. Of course, mutual funds are not operated as charities. Any fees and sales charges you pay can be money well spent if the fund does a good job in managing your money.

CAPITAL GAINS POTENTIAL

Your chances of realizing capital gains depend on what kind of fund you choose. Some funds investing in stocks concentrate on smaller companies or speculative "special situations." They often show dramatic gains in rising markets, but may also be the worst performers of all when the stock market is falling. From these "aggressive growth" funds, the emphasis on capital gains (and concomitant risk) theoretically decreases in steps through several categories—growth funds, balanced funds, income funds, and money market funds. The latter, which invest in short-term interest-bearing securities, usually follow a policy of holding their net asset values stable while paying out regular interest income, and thus offer little or no hope of capital gains.

Over long periods of time, the top-performing funds have compiled outstanding records of capital gains. Among the hundreds of other funds available, there are others that have shown only fair or even poor results. Attempting to trade in and out of a fund for a quick capital gain is a speculative endeavor.

INCOME POTENTIAL

As with capital gains, the potential for income from mutual funds varies with the fund's objective and the skill of its management. Some, such as bond and money market funds, offer yields that are competitive with other investments aimed at income-conscious investors. Aggressive growth funds, by contrast, typically offer current yields that range from small to negligible. That is by design, since their emphasis is on capital appreciation and many of their shareholders have no interest in obtaining current income.

RISKS AND
DRAWBACKS

In offering their shareholders access to all the potential rewards of the securities markets, mutual funds also expose them to the standard risks that go with investing. They seek to help their shareholders limit risk by investing in diversified portfolios, so that a calamity afflicting one company in which a fund invests will have a much smaller impact on the fund's investors than it will on people who own that company's shares directly.

Still, if the stock market collapses, so will the net asset values of most mutual funds heavily committed to stocks. If rising interest rates push bond prices lower, bond-fund asset values will fall. There is always the hope that the managers of your fund will be adroit enough to maximize gains in good markets, and minimize losses when times are bad. There is also always the fear that the reverse will occur.

Investors can seek to hold down their risks by picking their spots carefully among funds that have solid records of past achievement and stated investment philosophies for the future that seem to make sense. But as the standard legal disclaimer notes, past performance is no guarantee of future results. The more conservative the fund, the lower the presumed risk. Money market funds, though they lack the government guarantee offered by such other investments as Treasury bills, are considered highly safe, barring some tumultuous event affecting the credit markets.

LIQUIDITY

By comparison with many other types of investments, mutual funds are generally highly liquid. Except under extraordinary circumstances described in the prospectus, they stand ready to sell or redeem shares for cash at short notice. In recent years, increasing numbers of funds have established services that allow you to redeem instantly by simply writing a check.

Many investors nowadays judge their funds not only by investment results, but by the services that they offer, and how well they perform them. With the wide array of no-load funds to choose from in today's market, there is no need to keep your money in a fund whose shareholder service is consistently poor.

TAX ADVANTAGES
AND DISADVANTAGES

Mutual funds pass substantially all their investment earnings—whether from dividends, interest or capital gains—directly through to their shareholders. Thus, tax rules affecting fund investments generally conform to those covering the types of securities the fund holds. If a fund earns and distributes interest from Treasury bonds, for example, the interest is taxable to the shareholders just as if they had received it through direct ownership of the bonds. Under the tax laws in effect at the time this book was written, all capital gains distributions by funds are considered to be long term—that is, subject only to taxes at favorable long-term capital gains rates of no more than 20 percent.

Most mutual funds, with the notable exception of municipal bond funds and short-term tax-free funds, are suitable for individual retirement accounts, Keogh plans and other tax-favored savings programs.

GROWTH FUNDS

DESCRIPTION

One of the biggest, and broadest, categories of mutual funds comes under the general heading of "growth funds." These funds seek appreciation of their shareholders' assets, employing any one of an almost limitless number of stategies in the stock market. For example, in the Hypothetical group of funds, there may be one fund that concentrates on well-established growth stocks—seasoned companies that have achieved widespread recognition, but still show fairly rapid and consistent earnings growth year to year. A second fund in the group may devote its portfolio to "emerging growth" issues, newer and smaller companies with bright promise but relatively little record of past achivement. A third fund may focus on "special situations"— for instance, companies the fund manager believes are about to emerge from a period of problems and gain a new following among investors.

In the Imaginary group of funds, at the same time, one fund may specialize in a "contrarian" strategy, buying stocks it considers overlooked by the majority of investors or selling at prices that reflect unfounded fears. A second may invest in a single industry or sector of the market, such as energy or high technology. A third may emphasize growth, but pursue income as a secondary objective.

Identifying the category into which a given fund falls is only the first step in evaluating it. For example, one aggressive growth fund may keep a fairly static portfolio of volatile stocks, paying little heed to short-term market fluctuations in quest of long-term gains. Another with the same stated objective may trade frequently, or try to outwit the market by switching a large portion of its assets into low-risk money market investments in times when it believes the market is about to decline.

The best growth funds have achieved handsome results for their investors over long periods of time. Occassionally, some growth funds run up dramatic gains in short periods as well. When this happens, enthusiasm for the most venturesome funds runs high, and investors typically pour new money into them in huge amounts. Recent history has shown that these circumstances amount to a danger signal—a sign that a bull market in stocks and stock funds may be approaching its last peak.

HOW AND WHERE TO GET
INFORMATION AND INVEST

A broker may offer you literature on several funds to choose among, or you may do your own research among no-load funds—reading prospectuses and annual reports to evaluate their objectives, the methods they use, and their past results. Many investment advisory services and financial publications publish tables ranking funds for both recent and long-term performance.

Once you have chosen a fund or funds, investing is normally a simple process of filling out an application, writing a check, and delivering them to a fund salesman or the fund itself. You can, if you wish, invest a large sum at once. Or you can start small, adding further amounts at regular intervals or whenever you have money available.

Many advisers recommend a program of regular investments, regardless or the prevailing market climate, because such an approach provides a form of discipline and gives an investor access to what is known as "dollar cost averaging." Suppose for example, that you open an account with the Hypothetical Growth Fund, investing $2,000 when the fund's net asset value is worth $10 a share. Six months later, with the fund shares at $11, you invest another $2,000. After another six months have passed, you put up another $2,000 with the fund at $9 a share. Shortly thereafter, the net asset value climbs back to $10.

The fund itself has gone nowhere since you bought it, but you are nevertheless a little bit ahead of the game. Your first investment bought 200 shares, your second 181.82 shares, and your third 222.22 shares. Your $6,000 has bought you 604.04 shares, worth $6,040.40 at $10 apiece. Over time, and particularly in the case of volatile funds, dollar cost averaging can yield significant benefits.

It obviously requires a long-term commitment to work, however. If you pick an inferior fund, it will not save you from realizing inferior results. Even with a good fund, there may be long bear markets for stocks during which you face the fear that in dollar-cost averaging you are merely throwing good money after bad.

COSTS OF BUYING,
OWNING AND SELLING

As with other types of mutual funds, growth funds may carry a sales charge or be "no load." Though no-loads are often considered preferable for informed investors, some growth funds with loads have excellent performance records. A second cost associated with all growth funds is the annual management fee collected by the funds' managers.

When they buy and sell stocks and other investments, growth funds pay brokerage commissions. These costs too come out of the funds' assets. For this reason and others, some investors take a wary view of growth funds that have high portfolio turnover rates.

CAPITAL GAINS
POTENTIAL

There are two ways of realizing capital gains in growth funds. By law, funds must pass gains they achieve when they sell securities through to their shareholders to avoid incurring a tax obligation. These are called capital gains distributions. Fund investors may elect to accept these distributions in cash, or to have them automatically reinvested in new fund shares. Most investors pursuing long-term growth opt for automatic reinvestment.

At the same time, fund shareholders hope that the prices of stocks still held in their fund's portfolios will rise, increasing the fund's net asset value per share, which is calculated daily. Unlike the capital gains distribution, over which the individual fund shareholder has little or no control, this kind of capital gain is realized at the investors' discretion, when he or she chooses to redeem (cash in) shares of the fund.

As a general rule, funds that aim for the greatest possible capital gains also involve the greatest risk of losses. If any growth fund is poorly run, or operates in a period of adverse market conditions, there is always the chance that an investor will realize no capital gains of any kind.

INCOME POTENTIAL

Even a highly aggressive growth fund is likely to produce some small income from dividends it receives and passes through to its shareholders. Some relatively conservative growth funds pursue dividend income as a secondary objective. Investors who seek long-term growth often choose to have these dividends reinvested automatically, along with capital-gains distributions.

Normally, yields available in growth funds are not competitive with returns offered by many other types of investments. Because of this, and because of the market risks they take, growth funds are not a logical choice for people who want or need maximum current income from their assets, and safety of their principal.

RISKS AND
DRAWBACKS

Growth investments almost always involve some risk, and growth mutual funds are no exception. In poor markets, net asset values of even the best-managed funds are likely to decline. Funds that rack up the most dazzling results in good times often show the biggest losses when the stock market turns sour.

In addition to market risk, there is a "fund risk." That is, you may have the bad luck to pick a fund that turns in a subpar performance even when the stock market in general is doing well. Studying funds' past performance records is of some help in trying to avoid this pitfall. But shifting market trends can turn last year's standout fund into this year's dud. Furthermore, the impressive gains shown in a fund's past record may have been achieved by a stock-picking genius who has since moved on to another job.

By definition, long-term growth is an objective that requires patience. You can, of course, invest in growth funds for short periods of time. But doing so is a chancy proposition at best. If you have money set aside for speculation, there are other alternatives that usually offer greater prospective rewards—for example, options or investing on margin.

LIQUIDITY

Growth funds, like other mutual funds, offer easy-in-easy-out liquidity. But they are not an ideal place to put money you may want or need for some other purpose in the near future. Many of the attractions of growth funds—the chance to profit from the long-term growth of the U.S. economy, dollar-cost averaging, and the compounding of reinvested dividends and capital gains distributions—require years to produce their potential results.

TAX ADVANTAGES
AND DISADVANTAGES

Gains or losses realized when you redeem shares of growth mutual funds are subject to standard tax rules covering capital gains and losses. Capital gains distributions are normally treated as long-term gains, provided that you hold your fund shares for a minimum period specified in the tax laws. Dividends paid out by growth funds are taxable as ordinary income. All growth-fund distributions are subject to taxation for the year in which they are made, even if you choose to have them automatically reinvested.

Growth funds are a candidate for individual retirement accounts, Keogh plans and other tax-favored savings programs. In these accounts, of course, you need not concern yourself with current tax liabilities. However, when considering a growth fund for an IRA or Keogh plan, you should be aware that these vehicles nullify the tax breaks accorded to long-term capital gains. When you eventually begin to take money out of an IRA or Keogh account, all the distributions are taxed as ordinary income.

BALANCED FUNDS

DESCRIPTION

Some mutual fund investors have more than one goal. They may, for example, want both fairly generous income from their savings and the hope of protecting those savings from inflation by means of capital appreciation. Such investors may look to a fund that seeks these dual onjectives, which may be described as a "growth and income" fund or "balanced" fund.

In times past, the textbook balanced fund might put 50 percent of its assets in blue-chip stocks, and the other 50 percent in high-grade, high-yielding securities like bonds and utility shares. If all went well, the blue chips rose in price, providing enough growth to keep up with inflation. The bonds and other high-yielding securities, at the same time, lent an element of stability to the portfolio and produced a satisfactory stream of income.

More recently, however, it has become a difficult proposition to achieve that kind of result with that kind of stategy. Frequently, blue-chip stocks failed to keep pace with inflation. And volatile interest rates sharply increased fluctuations in the prices of securities like bonds and utility stocks. At the time this book was written, balanced funds were not a particulary popular breed.

Nevertheless, balanced funds do offer conservative investors a sort of compromise alternative to making a choice between the stock market and the bond market. In a sense, they are roughly the mutual fund equivalent of a convertible bond, and, in fact, a given balanced fund may well invest in convertibles.

It is even conceivable, under circumstances like those that prevailed in the early 1980s, that balanced funds might attract some venturesome investors. Today stocks and bonds are both subject to considerable volatility, and professional investors spend a great deal of time debating which of the two is likely to produce the greatest total return in the future. In theory, at least, an investor could use a balanced fund to try to participate in a rally in either market, or both.

HOW AND WHERE TO GET
INFORMATION AND INVEST

The newspapers and airwaves have not been filled recently with advertisements trumpeting the virtues of balanced funds. But there are a fair number of them available, from brokers or on your own initiative in no-load form. Names and addresses can be found in any directory of mutual funds.

COSTS OF BUYING,
OWNING AND SELLING

Balanced funds, like other varieties of mutual funds, may carry sales charges of up to 8.5 percent of the money you put up, or they may be "no-load." The fund sponsor collects an annual management fee from the assets of the fund. In addition, a balanced fund must pay commissions when it buys and sells securities. However, since a balanced fund theoretically pursues a conservative investment strategy, it is likely to do less buying and selling than, say, an aggressive growth fund.

CAPITAL GAINS
POTENTIAL

These, days, there may be more potential for capital gains in balanced funds than their stodgy image might imply. Assume, for instance, that the Federal Reserve takes some action that causes interest rates to fall sharply from a high level. When rates fall, bond prices rise—and so the bonds in your balanced fund's portfolio shoot up in value. The drop in rates causes a rally in the stock market as well. The conservative stocks owned by your balanced fund don't rise as much as some high-flying issues, but they still fare quite nicely.

Naturally, the reverse can happen as well. A sharp rise in interest rates can inflict a lot of damage on the net asset value of a classically structured balanced fund. Managers of balanced funds know this, and since they may consider themselves committed to a conservative investment policy, they may have cleaned most of their long-term bonds out of their portfolios in favor of, say, low-risk stocks and Treasury notes with only a few years to go until maturity. Therefore, a would-be investor in a balanced fund should study its portfolio beforehand to evaluate how much capital gains potential it has in the event of rallies in either the stock or bond markets, or both.

INCOME POTENTIAL
Typically, balanced funds offer yields that exceed the income available from growth funds, but that fall short of current returns offered by straight "income" funds and other high-yielding investments. The income produced by a balanced fund can provide some cushion against whatever market risks the fund takes. Or at least it can be viewed as a kind of consolation prize in periods when the net asset value of a balanced fund is falling along with other mutual funds and stock and bond prices. However, investors interested in maximum current income at minimum risk are likely to find more attractive possibilities elsewhere.

RISKS AND
DRAWBACKS
As the foregoing discussions make clear, the typical conditions that used to make a balanced fund a low-risk investment have been, well, unbalanced in recent times. In the late 1970s and early 1980s, it was no longer possible to rely on bonds for stability.

Even in simpler times, balanced funds never caught on as a hot idea. When the markets are rising attention and enthusiasm naturally tends to focus on growth funds, particulary the most aggressive ones. When the markets are falling, all mutual funds, except money funds and perhaps some income funds, tend to fall out of favor.

Balanced funds also appear to suffer from a flaw common to investment vehicles that pursue more than one specific objective. In a balanced fund, the ingredients are mixed according to the fund manager's recipe. But individual investors, even with relatively modest amounts of money to work with, can pursue multiple or compromise goals on their own, setting up a program according to their own tastes. They can fine-tune risks and returns, for example, by putting some of their available assets in a growth fund, and the rest in Treasury bills or a money market mutual fund.

The increasing sophistication of the American public about financial matters does not appear to portend any bright future for balanced funds. But they will probably retain a following among people who want a convenient way to invest in a diversified portfolio that combines current income and some hope of inflation protection.

LIQUIDITY

Balanced funds enjoy the high liquidity offered by most types of mutual fund investments. They have traditionally been a popular choice for investors who want to enroll in withdrawal plans. Under these plans, investors elect to receive regular periodic payments from their fund accounts, hoping that dividends, interst and capital gains, however irregularly realized, will cover the payments received over time. For investors like these, and indeed for many others, the new volatility of interest rates and the bond market is an unwelcome development.

TAX ADVANTAGES
AND DISADVANTAGES

Balanced funds offer the hope of a mixture of capital gains, which may enjoy favorable tax treatment, and dividend and interest income, which does not. Like their other compromise features, this tends to make them especially attractive to no single category of investors.

However, funds that seek a combination of growth and income have developed a fan club of sorts for use in individual retirement accounts, Keogh plans and other programs in which current taxation is not a consideration. In fact, some balanced growth-and-income funds have been established in recent years specifically with IRA and Keogh investors in mind.

INCOME FUNDS

DESCRIPTION

The principle of mutual fund investing has been widely applied to the needs of people who are primarily interested in obtaining current income for their assets. A fund can assemble a portfolio of bonds, other fixed-income securities, high-yielding common stocks, or any combination thereof, and sell part interests in that portfolio to individual investors in the form of shares of the fund. In this way, investors can participate in a diversified package of income-producing investments that reduces their exposure to risk of default, or a dividend reduction or elimination, by any single issuer.

But in the late 1970s and early 1980s, when interest rates began to fluctuate widely, a troublesome problem arose for these funds and their shareholders. As prices of bonds and other high-yielding securities grew increasingly volatile, so did the net asset values of income funds. Owners of a single bond or unit trust could shut their eyes to short-term fluctuations in price, counting on receiving face value at maturity. But owners of income mutual funds did not have that consolation.

As managed portfolios of securities with varying maturities, mutual funds for income have no set maturity date of their own. As a result, interest-rate risk has become a constant factor in evaluating the investment merits of any given fund. This risk, in fact, comes in two layers.

In order for their income funds to perform well, fund managers must not only pick investments that offer attractive yields in relation to credit risk, but also choose those investments at the right time and in the right maturities. In order to achieve the best results on their investments, people who invest in income funds must also be skillful, or lucky, in the timing of their decisions to buy and redeem shares of the funds.

There is one readily apparent way for fund investors to dodge this whole problem. They can switch to money market mutual funds. But money funds seldom provide access to the yields available in long-term investments, which can sometimes look very tempting.

Many types of longer-term income funds are available today. Some take a broad approach, trying to maximize their holdings of long-term securities when interest rates appear likely to decline, and to take cover in less vulnerable money market securities when they foresee a rise in interest rates. Others focus on a single specific objective—high yield, say, or high quality. As long as interes rates remain volatile, however, investments in income funds will be exposed at least to some extent to the ups and downs of a difficult market.

HOW AND WHERE TO GET
INFORMATION AND INVEST

Brokers and fund sponsors can supply you with detailed information, including prospectuses, on the income funds they have to offer. In considering any given income fund, it is advisable to devote some close attention to the stategy the investment adviser employs. It should fit closely with your own preferences and desires concerning the extent of risk taken and the degree of reward sought.

COSTS OF BUYING,
OWNING AND SELLING

Income funds involve the standard costs of mutual fund investing. Some impose sales charges; others are "no-load." All fund sponsors collect annual fees from the fund's assets for their management services and costs such as commissions.

CAPITAL GAINS
POTENTIAL

Interest-rate risk may be an unpleasant fact of life for many investors. But it does carry with it the concomitant possibility of capital gains in times when rates decline. For example, in 1982, when rates fell significantly, some income funds appeared high on lists of the year's top performing funds. If a lasting decline in interest rates is ever achieved in this country (a long shot, maybe, but not a total impossibility), many income funds would produce enduring gains for their investors.

Before you buy an income fund in quest of capital gains, there are several questions to be asked. Do you strongly believe that interest rates are headed lower? Is the fund you have in mind in position to gain maximum advantage from such a drop? How long are you willing to wait to see if your expectations are fulfilled?

Some funds take an aggressive, high-risk approach to investing in bonds and similar investments. They may employ timing stategies, or they may climb out on the limb of credit risk, buying "junk bonds." Such funds are not suitable for, nor designed for, investors concerned primarily with reliable, steady income from their assets.

INCOME POTENTIAL
In the mid-1980s, many income funds offered alluring yields, especially by comparison to an inflation rate that had subsided to below 5 percent. But partly because of fears that inflation would revive, prices of high-yielding investments—and hence, net asset values of most income funds—still encountered periods when they declined substantially. In that climate, income funds did not come highly recommended for investors looking for "safe" places to put their money.

RISKS AND
DRAWBACKS
In times when inflation accelerates and interest rates rise, just about all investors in high-yielding securities suffer in one way or another. Owners of fixed investments like bonds or bond unit trusts have a choice in how they accept their financial misfortune. They can confront their losses directly, selling their existing holdings at a depressed price and putting what remains of the money into newer, higher-yielding vehicles. Or they can hold on, waiting to receive the face value at maturity—but letting inflation continue to erode the purchasing power of their money in the meantime.

Under these same conditions, owners of an income mutual fund face a different set of circumstances. Shares of an income fund do not have a face, or maturity, value. Their only value is the net asset value, which is recalculated daily to reflect all that has occurred.

In this regard, it may seem that a unit trust, a fixed portfolio of income-producing investments, holds a significant edge on a typical managed income fund. But advocates of income funds have a case of their own to make. They point out that unit trusts, as static investments, cannot be maneuvered to cope with, and benefit from, changing market conditions.

Managers of income funds take active steps to try to limit losses in bad markets and reap the greatest possible benefit from rising ones.

Your assessment of a given income fund may hinge largely on whether you believe the fund's managers can indeed succeed in that task.

LIQUIDITY

Like other mutual funds, income funds are highly liquid. You can normally redeem part or all of your investment on short notice at any time you choose. Some income funds, adopting a feature that first became popular with money market funds, allow you to redeem shares by telephone or simply writing a check. If a specific income fund does not permit this, but is a member of a fund "family" that includes a money fund, you may be able to switch the sum you want to redeem from the income fund to the money fund, and then immediately redeem by check.

Income funds may offer an additional advantage over bonds by paying interest and dividends more often—say, monthly, rather than the semiannual interval that is common with bonds. But no matter how much convenient access they provide to your money, income funds are not the most logical place to put cash you expect to need soon. Blame that limitation, like most others involved with income funds, on the risk of unexpected price declines in the modern credit markets.

TAX ADVANTAGES
AND DISADVANTAGES

Capital gains and losses, dividends and interest from income funds are all subject to the standard tax rules. As with other types of mutual funds, you may elect to have distributions reinvested. But taxable investors must pay taxes on those distributions for the year in which they are made, whether they actually receive the money in cash or not.

Income funds are a candidate for individual retirement accounts, Keogh plans and other tax-favored savings programs. Before you put IRA or Keogh money in an income fund, however, it makes sense to consider alternatives such as a money fund that involves less interest rate risk, and other vehicles such as zero-coupon investments that permit you to "lock in" a known dollar return for an extended period of time.

MUNICIPAL BOND FUNDS

DESCRIPTION

In the days when only rich people were in high income-tax brackets, most individual investors of relatively modest means had little incentive to invest in municipal bonds. The exemption state and local securities offered from federal income tax on the interest they paid was appealing to the well-to-do, but the relatively low yields available on them weren't especially attractive to most everyone else.

Then, in the 1970s, "bracket creep" went to work with a vengeance, pushing more and more people into high brackets as their dollar incomes rose with inflation. Eager to tap this growing potential, mutual fund sponsors sought and won, in 1976, the right to offer funds investing in municipal securities, passing through the tax benefit to shareholders in the funds.

Since then municipal bond funds have enjoyed a measure of success, accumulating several billion dollars in assets. However, soon after they made their debut, municipal funds ran into a problem that bedeviled many other kinds of income investments—volatile inflation and interest rates that caused wide swings in security prices. Sharp fluctutations in net asset values were not what many conservative investors had in mind.

Managers of municipal bond funds have responded to these circumstances in several ways. They try to manage their portfolios to catch upward movements in bond prices and to cushion the impact of declining markets on the funds' asset values. In addition, they have in recent years begun to offer "limited maturity" funds investing in relatively short-term municipal securities that aren't so sensitive to interest rate changes. The most extreme example of these is the tax-free money fund, which is discussed in a separate section of this chapter.

HOW AND WHERE TO GET
INFORMATION AND INVEST

Information about these funds, including prospectuses and application forms to open an account, is available from brokers or the funds themselves. Prices and net asset values of the funds are reported in newspapers' mutual fund tables. Some investment advisory services publish detailed information on these funds and evaluate them.

COSTS OF BUYING,
OWNING AND SELLING

Costs of buying shares of municipal bond funds vary widely from fund to fund. Some carry sales charges at or near the maximum 8.5 percent rate; some have "low loads" in the 2 percent to 4 percent range, and many others are no-load. Almost all of the load funds grant significant volume concessions to large purchasers. But investors who qualify for these may have the necessary capital to do their own direct investing in municipal bonds under attractive terms.

CAPITAL GAINS
POTENTIAL

As long as the credit markets in general, and the municipal bond market in particular, remain volatile, a well-timed investment in a well-managed municipal bond fund may produce capital gains to go with attractive tax-favored income. Of course, many investors for whom municipal funds are suitable would just as soon forego the chance to realize capital gains in return for less interest-rate risk.

INCOME POTENTIAL

The primary goal of a typical municipal bond fund is to realize the highest possible after-tax income for its investors, consistent with the amount of risk they are willing to take. Credit risk can vary greatly among municipal-bond issues. So some funds may concentrate on lower-quality issues in quest of the greatest possible yield, while others may emphasize quality and concede a few points in yield. What this means for the conservative investor is that the highest-yielding fund might not be the most desirable investment.

The key question for any yield-conscious investor, of course, is the after-tax return available on alternative investments. A broker or fund sponsor can provide you with tables useful in determining whether, in your tax bracket, a taxable fund or a tax-free fund best fits your circumstances.

RISKS AND
DRAWBACKS

In their early years of operation, municipal bond funds attracted surprising numbers of investors in low tax brackets. Apparently, some people wanted the emotional satisfaction of dodging the tax collector even if the real benefit to them was actually small or even nonexistent. Before investing in a municipal bond fund, or any other tax-favored investment, it makes sense to calculate whether you are giving up more in potential return from alternative vehicles than you are gaining in tax breaks.

Unit trusts investing in fixed municipal bond portfolios are a competitive alternative to municipal-bond mutual funds. At this writing, the trusts with a longer operating history had attracted much more money from investors than the funds. Trusts, like municipal bonds themselves but unlike mutual funds, can offer the promise of full repayment of principal at maturity. Mutual funds, with their continuously managed portfolios, have no maturity dates.

On the other hand, a managed fund may be able to maneuver its holdings to advantage as conditions change, while a unit trust has no such flexibility. With a no-load municipal bond fund, furthermore, you escape the sales charge—typically 4 percent—imposed when you buy a unit trust. When you are considering a municipal bond investment, it may be worth the time and trouble to look into a representative sampling of both funds and unit trusts.

LIQUIDITY

A no-load municipal bond fund is normally the most liquid of municipal investments. Fund shares can be bought and sold at any time, at short notice. By contrast, the selection of individual municipal bonds a given dealer has to offer may vary over time. If you want to sell a bond before maturity, it is possible that you may have trouble finding ready buyers at a price you consider satisfactory. New unit trusts are being brought out constantly, but if you want to cash in your investment in them early, you may also have to accept price concessions.

A fund, therefore, may have its greatest appeal to municipal bond investors who figure on committing their money for just a few years. People in these circumstances must be aware, however, that even in brief time periods the net asset value of a municipal bond fund may rise or fall significantly.

TAX ADVANTAGES
AND DISADVANTAGES

The exemption from federal taxes on the interest municipal bond funds earn and distribute can be very alluring—so alluring, in fact, that it can cause investors to overlook the risks that come with them, and some other fine points as well. If a municipal bond fund realizes profits from some source other than interest on municipal bonds, such as capital gains from trading, those profits are taxable to you, under the standard tax rules, for the year in which they are distributed.

People who live in places where there are significant state and local taxes on interest income should take note that municipal funds typically spread their holdings among securities from many states and localities. Interest from these sources is generally subject to state and local taxes where you live. There are some funds and unit trusts, by contrast, that invest only in securities of a given state or locality, thus giving their owners exemption from income taxes at all levels.

Municipal bond funds are unsuitable for use in individual retirement accounts, Keogh plans and other tax-favored savings programs. In an IRA or Keogh, the special tax status of municipal investments would be redundant. And when you started taking money out of your IRA or Keogh account, you would be in the utterly undesirable position of paying taxes on the "tax-free" interest you had earned.

MONEY MARKET FUNDS

DESCRIPTION

When the first money market mutual fund, the Reserve Fund, was organized in 1972, its debut went largely unnoticed. But within a few years, money funds were making headlines as one of the great success stories in the modern financial era. By the early 1980s, millions of investors large and small had many billions of dollars invested in money funds.

A money fund is organized along the classic lines of a mutual fund. It is a pool of money whose sponsors put that money to work, distributing the proceeds it earns to the funds' shareholders. Instead of stocks or bonds, however, money funds invest only in short-term securities in the credit markets—Treasury bills, perhaps, or large bank certificates of deposit, or commercial paper, or bankers' acceptances, or any other kind of low-risk, high-yielding security of relatively short duration that comes along.

Some money funds confine themselves to a single category, such as government securities or commercial paper. Others hold a mixture of many varieties. While just about all money funds operate in similar ways, and are considered safe investments as a general rule, there are gradations of risk, and variances in yield, from fund to fund.

A money fund should never be confused with a bank investment (the rough equivalent in banking is the money market deposit account). Still, many investors in the 1970s embraced money funds, as, in effect, a new and improved alternative to passbook savings accounts at banks and savings institutions.

With a money fund, they could put money in and take it back out, on short notice, whenever they wanted to, in relatively small amounts. The key difference was that, while the interest earned in a passbook account was limited by law, money funds could yield whatever they could earn in the open market. They brought together small investors and the many opportunities available in the short-term credit markets, which had long been perceived as the exclusive province of institutions and a few wealthy individuals.

Today, money funds' period of dramatic growth seems to be over. Their popularity helped induce regulators to create attractive alternatives such as the MMDA. Nevertheless, the funds appear to have established for themselves a prominent place in the investment world.

They may be used as a convenient, temporary parking place for idle funds, to keep money at work when it is not invested elsewhere. The process of doing this has been facilitated further with the advent of central assets accounts at many investment firms. Although many advisers regard money funds as best suited for short-term purposes, some savers also use them in pursuit of long-term goals.

HOW AND WHERE TO GET
INFORMATION AND INVEST

Information about money funds, including prospectuses and applications to open accounts, is available from the brokerage firms and mutual fund organizations that sponsor them. They have been widely written about in books, magazines and newspapers. Some investment advisory services and newsletters report regularly on developments involving and affecting the funds.

COSTS OF BUYING,
OWNING AND SELLING

The typical money fund, whether sponsored by a mutual fund organization or brokerage firm, imposes no charge either when you buy or when you cash in shares. If a given fund imposes such a charge, it makes sense to look elsewhere. The only standard cost is the annual fee collected from a fund's assets by the sponsor for its management services and to cover its costs of operating the fund.

If you use special features a fund offers, such as investing by bank wire or telephone switching privileges to and from other funds, however, you may incur fees for these transactions. If you expect to make use of any or all optional features a fund offers, you should have a thorough understanding of the costs involved before you invest.

CAPITAL GAINS
POTENTIAL

There is usually no potential whatever for capital gains in a money fund. The funds' managers seek to keep the net asset value at a constant level of, say, $1 a share. Most money fund investors want it that way. When you invest in a money fund, you should bear in mind that you are foregoing an opportunity you could seek in, say, stocks or real estate to achieve long-term capital gains at attractively low tax rates. Some investors nevertheless seem to favor money funds in their quest for long-term growth. They elect to have their dividends reinvested in new shares, thus gaining access to the long-term benefits of compounding.

INCOME POTENTIAL

Generous current income is, naturally, a primary attraction of money funds in periods when interest rates are high. Since no two funds have precisely identical portfolios, their yields may vary considerably. Many financial publications and newspapers publish weekly tables of individual funds' recent yields. You can normally get a current figure on any fund by telephoning the fund itself.

Whatever the current return is, it provides no assurance of future yield. If interest rates rise, a good money fund's yield should follow them up. But if interest rates fall, there is little a fund management can do to prevent the fund's yield from declining eventually as well.

An important point to bear in mind is that money fund yields usually follow interest rate trends with a lag. That is so because the amount of interest the fund can earn changes only as securities in its portfolio mature and are replaced with new ones offering different interest rates. The length of this time lag for a given fund depends on the average maturity of its portfolio.

Ideally, an investor wants to have his or her money in a very short-term fund when rates are rising, and in one with a relatively long average maturity when rates are falling. Some sophisticated investors and institutions invest directly in the money markets in periods of stable or rising interest rates; but move into money funds when rates are declining to take advantage of the funds' lag time.

RISKS AND
DRAWBACKS

Just how safe are money funds? The question has been the subject of much debate for as long as the funds have been operating. The record to date suggests that almost all funds are reasonably safe. Some, because of the special policies they follow, may be classified as highly safe.

But money fund investors should always bear in mind that no fund is directly insured or backed by the government. All the Treasury bills the fund owns may have government backing, but the fund itself does not. No matter what type of securities it buys, a fund can get into trouble if it guesses wrong about the direction of interest rates and extends its portfolio maturity just before rates rise.

In this circumstance, its yield can become increasingly unattractive in comparison to that offered by other funds. If large numbers of disenchanted investors redeem shares, the fund could be forced to sell securities in its portfolio at a loss to meet those redemptions, starting a vicious cycle.

A very few cases like this have actually occurred. In the most notable one, the sponsors of the fund paid in additional capital so that no fund shareholder suffered any loss. Today, many funds go to great lengths to forestall problem situations like this. They stick with investment strategies designed to minimize both credit risk—default by an issuer of securities they own—and maturity risk.

The safety record of the money fund industry is excellent. The only great threat to that record in the future would seem to be some tumultuous event in the credit markets, which would probably have a widespread negative impact on most other financial investments as well.

LIQUIDITY
One element in the great popularity of money funds is the exceptional liquidity they provide. Many funds have low minimum investments, typically $1,000; some set no minimum. Most offer a broad selection of methods by which you can redeem shares at any time, including unlimited check-writing for amounts of $500 or more per check (lower with some funds). There is no guarantee that every fund will always be so liquid in the future. But it is reasonable to expect that well-managed funds run by reputable sponsors will continue to offer this advantage, even in turbulent economic times.

TAX ADVANTAGES
AND DISADVANTAGES

Dividends paid by money funds are subject to federal tax as ordinary income. This tax obligation occurs even if you reinvest dividends rather than receiving them in cash.

In some states and localities, you may face a tax disadvantage with a money fund. For example, a state that taxes dividends but not interest may levy a tax on your money fund dividends, even though they actually represent a pass-through to you of interest the fund earned on its investments. A state may also demand taxes on dividends from government-securities money funds, even though government securities themselves are exempt from state and local taxes. At the time this book was written, funds of this type were pressing their case to have their dividends declared eligible for the same exception.

Money funds are a suitable, and popular, candidate for use in individual retirement accounts, Keogh plans, and other tax-favored savings programs. If you receive some payment that is eligible for a "rollover" into an IRA, a good money fund may be a convenient place to put the money while you decide how you ultimately want to invest it.

TAX-EXEMPT MONEY FUNDS

DESCRIPTION

Once money market funds and tax-free municipal bond funds became popular in the late 1970s, investors began to develop an appetite for a product that combined the attributes of both—a tax-free money fund. Such a fund would invest only in relatively short-term interest-bearing securities, to keep market risk to a minimum. Furthermore, it would limit selection of those securities to issues of state and local governments, so that the income it generated would be exempt from federal tax.

Mutual fund sponsors, sensing the possibilities of this type of vehcile, set about to form tax-exempt money funds. At first, they faced an obstacle: There was a limited selection of short-term municipal securities available. But this "raw material problem," as the investment management firm of T. Rowe Price Associates described it, soon began to resolve itself.

If investors wanted short-term securities, state and local government entities were pleased to offer them, at interest rates well below what they had to pay to raise long-term capital. Some issuers sold "revenue anticipation notes" to be paid off with future tax receipts or other revenue. Some offered floating-rate notes, securities whose interest rates were adjusted at intervals to keep them in line with prevailing market trends. Others chose a commercial paper format. By one estimate, the volume of municipal commercial paper outstanding quadrupled between 1982 and 1984.

So by the mid-1980s investors had a wide range of tax-exempt money funds to choose among. No two of these funds are precisely alike, but they generally fall into two distinct categories. The straight tax-exempt money fund, like a taxable money fund, seeks to keep its net asset value constant at all times, thus all but eliminating the risk of changes in its shareholders' principal values. The limited term tax-exempt fund buys securities of somewhat longer maturity in quest of higher yields, at the same time attempting to keep changes in its net asset value within a fairly narrow range.

HOW AND WHERE TO GET
INFORMATION AND INVEST

As new as they may be to the investment world, abundant information about tax-exempt money funds is readily available—in mutual fund guides, from some investment advisory services, and of course from the funds themselves. When you reach the stage of reading prospectuses, it is especially important to examine the investment policy any given fund follows, or may follow in the future. These funds may vary greatly in the degree of credit risk—quality of issuers—and the degree of market risk—exposure to price fluctuations—they take.

COSTS OF BUYING,
OWNING AND SELLING

Like taxable money funds, most tax-exempt money funds are "no load." It normally does not make sense to consider any tax-exempt money fund that imposes a significant fee when you buy or redeem shares. Sponsors of these funds cover their costs and earn their profits by collecting annual management fees from the assets of the funds.

Tax-exempt money funds may offer a variety of optional extra services such as telephone exchange privileges into other types of funds and redemption of shares by telephone or check-writing. If you plan to use any of these services, you should check beforehand what fees, if any, are involved.

CAPITAL GAINS
POTENTIAL

If the net asset value of a tax-free money fund changes between the time you buy and the time you redeem your shares, you will realize a capital gain or loss. It is possible to invest in a tax-free money fund for long-term growth through compounding, by automatically reinvesting your dividends. However, these funds are not designed to produce trading profits for their investors, nor are they especially well-suited to long-term growth objectives.

INCOME POTENTIAL

Like taxable money funds, tax-free money funds provide a means of keeping money at work earning interest, in a place where you have immediate access to it whenever you want to use it for something else. The pre-tax yields of these funds tend to be significantly lower than the return available on taxable money funds. Thus, the relative merits of taxable versus tax-free money funds depend largely on your tax bracket.

The yield you can get from a tax-exempt money fund is usually well below what you could earn from a long-term municipal bond fund (which, of course, also produces tax-free income). The difference amounts to the sacrifice you must make in return for a greater degree of stability and safety of your principal.

RISKS AND
DRAWBACKS

Tax-free money funds are considered highly safe investments. However, they do not have a long operating history to reinforce that opinion. Some of the types of securities in which they invest are also relatively untested.

In addition to minimizing market risk, tax-exempt money funds may seek to limit credit risk in several ways. They may stick with only the highest-quality issues. They can diversify their holdings among many issuers around the country, so that a default by any single issuer would not have a drastic impact on their portfolios. But people considering tax-exempt money funds should be aware that the extent of their diversification is limited to the municipal securities market. These funds cannot, like a taxable money fund, seek ultimate shelter in Treasury bills, since interest on bills is subject to federal income tax. However remote the possibility, any event that disrupted the short-term municipal market would very likely pose trouble for many tax-free money funds.

Safe or not, tax-free money funds are not a suitable place to look if you want to "lock in" a known dollar yield on your money for any extended period of time. If interest rates fall, prevailing yields offered by tax-free money funds will also come down sooner or later. It will be sooner if the fund has a relatively short average maturity of securities in its portfolio, later if the average maturity is relatively long.

LIQUIDITY

Tax-free money funds offer the standard, and substantial, liquidity advantages of short-term mutual funds. Money can be moved in and out of them easily, conveniently, on short notice whenever you wish. Many financial services firms that offer central assets accounts give their customers the option of keeping idle money in a tax-free fund rather than a taxable money fund. These general statements about liquidity, it should be noted, assume that the fast-growing market for short-term municipal securities proves to be, and remains, as healthy and liquid as the taxable money markets have been in the past.

TAX ADVANTAGES
AND DISADVANTAGES

Though these funds may be called "tax-free" investments because the dividends they pay are generally exempt from federal income taxes, the name can be misleading or confusing. The dividends may be subject to state and local income taxes. Futhermore, if you realize a capital gain or loss from an investment in a tax-exempt money fund, it is a "taxable event" as far as the Internal Revenue Service is concerned.

Tax-exempt money funds, like other investments involving state and local securities, are unsuitable for individual retirement accounts, Keogh plans, and other tax-favored savings programs.

NO-LOAD FUNDS

DESCRIPTION

Years ago, there was an accepted maxim in the investment business: "Mutual funds are sold, not bought." It was assumed that fund shares, like life insurance, needed a strong push from stockbrokers and trained salespeople working for fund organizations if they were to reach the large potential market of individuals who could benefit from them.

These brokers and salesmen naturally wanted to be suitably compensated for their considerable efforts. So the funds were sold with sales charges, up-front commissions, of up to 8.5 percent. If you as an investor put up $5,000, only $4,575 actually went to buy fund shares. The other $425 was the sales charge or *load*. The effective cost to the investor was even higher than 8.5 percent—$425 is 9.29 percent of $4,575.

As the fund industry and public awareness of it grew, some fund sponsors began to compete by offering their shares without sales charges. They dispensed with the usual sales force, relying on advertising, favorable publicity and word of mouth to get their message out. Knowledgeable investors, they reasoned, would respond enthusiastically to the idea of commission-free investing.

When they began to appear, "no-load" funds did not revolutionize the industry overnight. But as time passed, they gained an increasing share of the business. In the 1970s, some prominent fund organizations switched their funds from load to no-load. The trend gained further impetus with the dramatic success of money market funds, virtually all of which carry no sales charges of any kind.

Today there remain a good many popular and successful load funds. But no-loads have grown from a tiny segment of the industry to a prominent factor in it. The rise of no-load funds, indeed, has helped increase investors' awareness of the costs involved in other types of investments, creating competitive pressures to reduce or eliminate sales charges on some of those other vehicles as well.

HOW AND WHERE TO GET
INFORMATION AND INVEST

Finding and evaluating no-load funds is likely to involve some initiative and expertise on your part. It is illogical to expect a broker, insurance salesman or anyone else who makes a living from commissions to spend a lot of time gathering information and advising you about no-load investments.

But that doesn't necessarily mean the job has to be difficult. Your neighbor, your dentist or your rich uncle may have a fund to recommend. Many no-load funds advertise heavily. Numerous mutual-fund guides, advisory services and magazines publish extensive information about no-load funds, including their mailing addresses and telephone numbers. A representative sampling of these publications is available in most libraries and bookstores.

Upon your inquiry, a sponsor of a no-load fund should be eager to provide you with information—descriptive literature, a prospectus and a simple application with which you can open an account. If a given fund's response is sluggish or the information provided seems confusing or incomplete, you may well question what kind of service you could expect after you invested money in that fund.

COSTS OF BUYING,
OWNING AND SELLING

No-load funds would not have proliferated if fund organizations didn't find them profitable to operate. Once a fund attains any significant size, the annual percentage fee managers collect from the fund's assets can reward them handsomely. This fee can vary from fund to fund, and should not be neglected in your appraisal. You should also look closely at any other "miscellaneous" items in a fund's fee structure. A further point to consider—a no-load fund that does a lot of short-term trading will spend more of your money on brokerage commissions than one that follows a practice of holding investments it selects for relatively long periods of time.

In recent years some funds, no-loads among them, have set up arrangements in which they are permitted to use money invested in them by existing shareholders to pay promotional expenses in seeking new investors. This is a controversial practice. You may wish to inquire before investing whether a fund you are considering has adopted, or may adopt in the future, such an arrangement.

CAPITAL GAINS
POTENTIAL

Suppose you make indentical and simultaneous investments in two growth mutual funds, one of which is no-load and the other of which imposes the maximum sales charge. If both appreciate about 9 percent in value shortly thereafter, you will be 9 percent ahead in your no-load fund, but only at about the break-even point with your load fund.

This seems to give no-loads an obvious edge. And indeed it does if you are investing for the short-term. But some investors with long-term growth goals do not rule out all load funds as possibilities. There are well-managed load funds that have achieved superior results for their shareholders over time, even after the sales charge is taken into account. Conversely, there are no-load funds that have achieved disappointing results for their shareholders.

Suppose you were considering a bet on a race between two horses, one of which, No Load, was positioned some distance ahead of the other, Load, at the start. No Load has a clear advantage at the beginning. But you might want to consider the distance of the race, and the prospective speed of both entrants, before making your choice.

INCOME POTENTIAL

Among funds that invest for current income, rather than growth, the case for no-loads is especially strong. If there is only limited or no hope for appreciation in the net asset value of your fund, there is only limited or no hope assuming comparable yields that a load fund can produce results as good as those achieved by a no-load fund. These circumstances explain why all successful money market mutual funds are no-load.

RISKS AND DRAWBACKS

The presence or absence of a sales charge in itself tells you nothing about how well any given fund is managed. A no-load fund is no bargain if it can't achieve the investment objective it sets for itself. Some investors lack the time, the expertise or the inclination to make financial decisions on their own. For them, the advice of a paid broker or salesperson, especially one who can offer a wide variety of funds sponsored by different management companies, may be worth the price of a sales charge.

But many mutual fund investors actively enjoy the process of picking out funds on their own, and monitoring the progress of their investments. They wouldn't dream of paying somebody else to tackle that job.

LIQUIDITY

No-load funds appeal greatly to fund investors who are concerned with liquidity. Of course, an investment in any fund, load or no-load, can normally be redeemed whenever you wish, on short notice. But even the best load funds need to have your money at work for some indeterminate period of time just to realize enough earnings to recoup the cost of your sales charge. If you are considering buying mutual fund shares with money you might need for other purposes in the near future, it makes sense to consider no-load funds first.

TAX ADVANTAGES AND DISADVANTAGES

When you buy shares of a load fund, the sales charge is considered part of your purchase price. Like the brokerage commission on a stock purchase, it is built into the "cost basis" you use for calculating your profit or loss, for tax purposes, at the time you redeem (sell) your shares. With a no-load fund, this is obviously not a consideration.

No-load funds may be a very suitable candidate for individual retirement accounts, Keogh plans and other tax-favored savings programs. They may be used by activist IRA and Keogh savers who want to try to get the most mileage out of their money by switching from one type of fund to another as they feel changing conditions in the financial markets dictate.

NOW AND SUPER-NOW ACCOUNTS

DESCRIPTION

Earn interest on your checking account!

That alluring prospect, long a legal impossibility for Americans, began to become a reality in the 1970s when financial institutions came up with the idea of NOW (negotiable order of withdrawal) accounts. Negotiable orders of withdrawal functioned exactly like checks, and for all but technical legal purposes were in fact checks. But, in contrast to the standard checking account, the bank or savings institution paid interest on the balance in your NOW account.

At first, the maximum interest rate was limited to 5.25 percent. Then, at about the same time that they created money market deposit accounts in the early 1980s, regulators of banks and savings institutions authorized what came to be called Super-NOW accounts.

With Super-NOW accounts, banks and savings institutions were given the right to pay whatever interest rate they chose on balances over $2,500. On amounts up to $2,500, the top interest rate remained at 5.25 percent. Under a timetable set by regulators, this $2,500 cutoff point was scheduled to be reduced to $1,000 on Jan. 1, 1985, and to zero on Jan. 1, 1986.

Unlike MMDAs, Super-NOW accounts allow for unlimited check-writing. In practice, many institutions have designed their Super-NOWs along the lines of a traditional checking rather than savings account. For example, they may be offered with debit cards (a plastic substitute for a checkbook) and automatic lines of credit.

In their early years, Super-NOW accounts gained a following, but they did not attain the kind of popularity enjoyed by MMDAs. There were several reasons for this. First of all, banks and savings institutions offer significantly lower interest rates on Super-NOWs than on MMDAs, in part because the government requires these institutions to set aside a portion of deposits in Super-NOWS as a reserve. Also, many institutions imposed a number of fees on them.

Some savers concluded that their best money management strategy at a bank or savings institution was to keep a modest balance in a standard checking account, and put the rest of their ready cash in an MMDA. With a reasonable amount of careful planning, they reasoned, they did not need to settle for the compromises involved in a Super-NOW account. Just as with MMDAs, rates and other terms available on Super-NOW accounts may vary significantly from place to place and institution to institution.

HOW AND WHERE TO GET
INFORMATION AND INVEST

Many banks and savings institutions promote their Super-NOWs along with their MMDAs. Basic information on them should be readily available with a few inquiries at institutions in your area. If you determine that a Super-NOW has a place in your personal financial arrangements, it makes sense to do some extensive comparison shopping among competing institutions before choosing one. In today's deregulated world, any given bank or savings institution has a great degree of latitude in making the Super-NOW accounts it offers as attractive, or unattractive, as it wishes. NOW and Super-NOW accounts are available to estates, trusts and non-profit organizations, but not to businesses.

COSTS OF BUYING,
OWNING AND SELLING

Costs are usually an important consideration in evaluating NOW and Super-NOW accounts. Since an institution's own costs are increased when it must pay interest on money deposited in what amounts to a checking account, it may seek to recoup at least some of those interest outlays with things like per-check fees or service charges. You should have a thorough understanding of all actual and potential fees involved, and the circumstances in which they can be imposed, before opening a NOW or Super-NOW account.

CAPITAL GAINS
POTENTIAL

As with other bank deposits, there is no potential for capital gains in a NOW or Super-NOW account.

INCOME POTENTIAL

NOWs and Super-NOWs provide a way to gain income from your assets by earning interest on money you keep available for ready use. In that sense, they represent a potential improvement from the saver's point of view on older forms of checking accounts. However, rates offered even on Super-NOWs may not be competitive with those available on alternatives like MMDAs and money market mutual funds. In addition, the net income you realize from a NOW or Super-NOW may be reduced by fees and service charges incurred in your use of the account.

Some banks and savings institutions offer premium interest rates for Super-NOWs with large deposit balances of say, at least $15,000 or $25,000. This is a point to check into if you have, or expect to have, large amounts of money to deposit in a Super-NOW account.

Rates paid on Super-NOWs, like those on MMDAs, are subject to change monthly or even more frequently. When you are shopping for a Super-NOW, it makes sense to inquire how any given institution calculates the rate it will pay.

RISKS AND
DRAWBACKS

Business risk is considered negligible with NOW or Super-NOW accounts as long as the balance remains at $100,000 or less, since they are normally covered by federal deposit insurance up to that amount. It may seem a routine matter, but it is always wise to make sure that an institution in which you put your money is in fact a member of a federal deposit insurance program.

There are institutions that operate without this coverage. A few years ago, news stories about one small uninsured bank that failed told of shocked depositors who had assumed that their money was protected.

As was indicated above, Super-NOW accounts represent a kind of compromise between old-fashioned checking accounts and MMDAs. Before opening a Super-NOW account, it may be worthwhile to check prevailing rates and terms to see if you can do better dividing your money between a standard checking account and an MMDA.

For the sake of self-discipline and order, some savers and investors like to keep what they deem to be savings and what they deem to be spending money in separate and distinct places. People used to operating in this way may find the mixed savings and checking features of Super-NOWs to be a drawback, rather than an attribute.

LIQUIDITY

NOWs and Super-NOWs are considered highly liquid. In fact, they have a slight liquidity edge on MMDAs in that they permit you to write checks and make other third-party payments from them as frequently as you wish.

Their liquidity is flawed, however, by some of the rules covering them. As long as there is a minimum balance required for access to top interest rates, that amount of money is effectively frozen as long as you wish to gain the advantages of those rates. Also, some institutions may impose service charges when your balance falls below specified levels, which has the effect of limiting your options on your use of the money in a NOW or Super-NOW account.

TAX ADVANTAGES
AND DISADVANTAGES

Interest earned from a NOW or Super-NOW account is subject to federal and any applicable state and local tax as ordinary income. If you have a large amount of money in a Super-Now earning a fairly high rate of return and are treating the interest as bonus spending money, it is wise to keep in mind during the course of any given year that this interest is running up an extra tax obligation. Furthermore, in managing money in a NOW or Super-NOW account, you should be aware that fees incurred, such as per-check service charges, may not qualify as tax-deductible expenses.

NOW and Super-NOW accounts are ineligible for use in individual retirement accounts, Keogh plans and other tax-favored savings programs.

OPTIONS

DESCRIPTION

The idea of options is age-old, and has been used in countless types of business dealings. But the modern market in investment options traces its start to 1973, with the founding of the Chicago Board Options Exchange. Today there are several markets across the country in which investors and speculators buy and sell investment options of numerous kinds. All share some important common characteristics.

Options are contracts that give their owners the right to conduct a specified transaction, such as buying or selling a certain number of shares of a given common stock, at a set price within a stated period of time (typically a few months). They can be used for speculative purposes to try to achieve a big profit quickly or for conservative aims such as increasing income or "hedging" against risk.

Over the years, investment professionals have developed an imposing array of strategies, employing multiple transactions in options or in combinations of options and other securities, with exotic names like "spreads" and "straddles." The applications of options are too diverse to describe in any single discussion, especially with new ones being devised all the time.

Even in their simplest uses, options require a degree of investment knowledge and attention that goes beyond the likely means, needs and desires of some investors. Nevertheless, the success and growth of the options markets makes it apparent that many investors find them appealing and useful.

Like their close relatives, futures contracts, they provide a means of shifting risk from parties who are presently exposed to it but don't want to be to other parties who are willing to assume the risk in return for the chance at accompanying potential rewards. The major categories of options—calls, puts, stock index options, interest-rate options and options on futures—are discussed in detail in separate sections of this chapter.

HOW AND WHERE TO GET
INFORMATION AND INVEST

Before 1973, options were available only through specialized dealers. Since then, several exchanges have been established where options are traded continuously, much like stocks and bonds. These exchanges today dominate the business, although some dealer-traded over-the-counter options remain. Transactions in listed options are reported regularly in tables in financial publications and many general interest newspapers.

Options prospectuses and other descriptive material are available from the exchanges or most brokerage firms. Before you begin to trade in options, a broker is required to determine whether you meet specified suitability standards, and you will be asked to sign an agreement certifying that you understand what you are getting into. There are some mutual funds that incorporate options in their investment strategies.

COSTS OF BUYING,
OWNING AND SELLING

When you buy and sell options, you pay a commission to a broker, just as you would with stocks and many other types of securities. Since options are typically short-term vehicles, they involve a lot of buying and selling. Even though commission rates on options are normally well below rates on stocks, the cost of commissions can be very important in deciding whether options are for you, and what kinds of strategies you should employ with them.

Another significant cost in most option purchases is called the premium. When you buy an option, you are in effect buying time—time in which you hope the security covered by your option will move in a favorable direction for you. For this time, you must usually pay a premium that is built into the market price of the option.

For example, assume that the stock of Hypothetical Corp. sells today for $49. A call option carrying the right to buy Hypothetical stock for $50 is, at the moment, theoretically worthless. But the call option could begin to take on value in the future should Hypothetical's stock price rise above $50. So that call option today might sell, not for $0, but for a price that reflects its time value—say, $5.

The more time remains before the option expires, and the more enthusiastic option traders are about Hypothetical's prospects, the greater the premium is likely to be. As time passes and an option draws closer and closer to its expiration date, its time value steadily diminishes. Hence, all other things being equal, the premium of any given option has a natural tendency to shrink from week to week and month to month.

All other things are rarely equal, of course. Premiums fluctuate constantly with changes in stock and options prices, which rarely follow courses that are precisely parallel. You can calculate the premium at any given time by comparing the value of an option if it were to be exercised at the moment and the option's actual market price.

Still another, less apparent cost of owning options is the absence of any dividend or interest payments. Though they may represent a claim on a dividend-paying stock, options produce no income for their owners. Thus, when you invest money in options, you in effect forego the dividends or interest the money could earn if you employed it elsewhere. There are options strategies, discussed below, that are designed to enhance income.

On the other side of the coin, options can allow you to "play" the markets seeking big rewards, with relatively small commitments of just a few thousand, or even a few hundred, dollars. In many cases, the amount you need to put up is a great deal smaller than what would be required to buy a "round lot" (in the case of stocks, 100 shares) of the securities covered by an option.

CAPITAL GAINS
POTENTIAL

Without the hope of lucrative capital gains, the options market probably could not exist. Thanks to their great leverage, options provide speculators with a means of investing small amounts in the hope of earning large profits. Example: Suppose Hypothetical Corp. stock is trading at $50 when you pay $5 for one call option to buy it at that price. Since the standard option covers 100 shares, you put up $500 excluding commissions.

In a short time, Hypothetical's stock rises to $75. That's a nice benefit to common stock holders who bought 100 shares of Hypothetical at $50—a $2,500 profit on their $5,000 investment, or a return of 50 percent. But those results pale in comparison to what you gained from your investment in the Hypothetical call option.

At a stock price of $75, the option to buy Hypothetical at $50 has an inherent value of $25. You can exercise the option, and realize a $2,000 profit before commissions on your $500 investment, for a return of 400 percent. If the option has some further time to run, it will probably still be trading in the options market at a premium over its exercise value, so that if you sell the option instead of exercising it you could realize an even greater gain.

Of course, if this sort of thing happened all the time with any predict-able regularity, everyone who knew anything about options would be rich. That is not the case now, and nobody expects it to be that way in the future.

INCOME POTENTIAL

Unlike many other types of securities, options are not created by financial entities such as corporations or governments. Rather, they are written by investors who are willing to sell a partial claim on their investment holdings in return for a benefit—which in some cases is the income they receive from the buyer of the option in the form of a premium. However, as a general rule, options are unsuitable for con-servative small investors who depend on reliable, steady income from their investments.

RISKS AND DRAWBACKS

Options can be used for hedging—that is, limiting risk. In these cases, hedgers usually pay some relatively modest price in one form or another, which they look upon as a form of insurance premium insu-lating them against any bigger losses. If a hedging strategy is some-how miscalculated, however, there still can exist a chance of a larger loss than anticipated.

Risk is paramount in many other types of options transactions. The basic risk in simply buying a put or call, for instance, is that it will never appreciate in value, and eventually expire as worthless. This is a fate that befalls many, many options. Losses can be cut in such investments by selling an option in the options market before expiration when it still has some, even if only very little, market value.

In some other types of speculative options transactions, the risk in fact can be unlimited. One of these is the "naked" sale of a call option in which you grant the buyer a claim on a security you do not own. If markets go the wrong way, your loss can be many times your initial commitment. To be successful in many types of options transactions, you must accurately appraise beforehand not only the direction in which a given security's price is likely to move, but also the timing of that move.

LIQUIDITY

With the growth of the organized market for trading in options, these investments usually enjoy good liquidity in the sense that you can act quickly on any decision to buy or sell. But that does not mean you can count in every case on realizing in cash the current paper value of your positions in options. That is because even a moderate move in the price of an option's underlying security can be translated immediately into a big percentage change in the market value of the option.

TAX ADVANTAGES
AND DISADVANTAGES

Reacting to a period of confusion and what it saw as some abusive practices, Congress made a major overhaul of the tax treatment of options in the Tax Reform Act of 1984. For all options except those on stocks and small groups of stocks, it imposed the same rules that apply to commodity futures contracts. Speculators are subject to a maximum tax rate of 32 percent on their profits from non-stock options, and at yearend must "mark to market" all their outstanding positions, treating them for tax purposes as if they were closed out on the last business day of the year.

Options on stocks, however, continue to be treated like stocks themselves or any other ordinary capital asset, subject to the standard capital gains rules. The 1984 tax law shortened the holding period to qualify for favorable long-term treatment of profits from one year to six months. Since some listed options traded at any given time have lives of more than six months, this means that options traders can now buy puts and calls in quest of long-term gains taxed at a maximum rate of 20 percent.

The 1984 tax law was designed, in part, to curtail elaborate options transactions that had the effect of postponing income for tax purposes from one year to the next. Whenever you are contemplating some multiple options transaction, especially if you have some tax advantage in mind, you should get good tax advice or be thoroughly familiar yourself with current tax law and the latest Internal Revenue Service and court rulings.

Some options strategies and investments may have a place in an individual retirement account, Keogh plan or other tax-favored savings program. For example, you might choose to buy shares of a mutual fund that seeks income from options. Or, in a self-directed IRA with a brokerage firm, you might use options to hedge investment positions. However, speculating in options is generally regarded as a dubious strategy for most IRA and Keogh savers, since these accounts are designed as long-term savings programs.

CALL OPTIONS

DESCRIPTION

Calls, probably the best known and most easily understood species of options, are contracts that give their owners the right to buy a certain stock, at a specified price, within a stated time period usually ranging up to about nine months. Calls on many large, actively traded stocks are traded at the various options exchanges around the country.

Speculators may buy a call hoping to realize a large gain in a relatively short time on a small investment, if something happens that causes a significant rise in the price of the call's underlying stock. They may also adopt the especially risky strategy of selling "naked" calls on stocks they don't own. They hope to profit from the premium they receive on the sale of the call, in the expectation that the price of the underlying stock will not rise significantly before the call expires.

More conservative investors may "write" (sell) covered calls on stocks they own for a wide variety of other purposes. If they want to hold onto a stock they own, but believe it is likely to go nowhere or decline in the immediate future, they may sell a call to increase their income with the premium they receive. Or they may view the call as a hedge—a cushion against a decline in the price of their stock. One risk they take is that the option will be exercised, "calling" the stock away from them, in which case they have no choice but to deliver it.

As with other types of options, many traders in calls operate without intending ever to exercise them. Rather, they seek to profit from changes in the market price of the calls themselves in the secondary markets provided by the options exchanges.

HOW AND WHERE TO GET
INFORMATION AND INVEST

Information about calls and other options is available in the prospectus offered by the options exchanges, which can be obtained from any good broker. The exchanges and brokerage firms also have pamphlets and other literature devoted specifically to calls and the ways in which they can be used. At many brokerage firms, there are analysts who specialize in creating and recommending options strategies aimed at capitalizing on events affecting the stock market, such as takeover proposals.

COSTS OF BUYING,
OWNING AND SELLING

Brokers charge commissions to handle purchases and sales of calls. These are an important consideration, because calls are not "buy and hold" investments. Since the typical call has only a few months of life, regular activity in calls involves frequent transactions.

Because calls have time value, their price almost always carries a built-in premium over their present worth should they be exercised. As calls move closer to their expiration dates, this premium tends to shrink. Suppose you bought a call today carrying an exercise price slightly higher than the price at which its underlying stock is trading. If two weeks from now the stock price has not changed, the price of your call will likely have declined at least slightly.

Another cost involved in owning a call rather than its underlying stock involves the absence of dividends. The stock may offer a healthy yield, but the call has no claim on the dividend unless it is exercised before the "record date" stated in the declaration of the dividend.

CAPITAL GAINS
POTENTIAL

The standard reason for buying calls is to seek large capital gains, using a relatively modest amount of money and the leverage provided by the call. To see how dramatic the effect of this leverage can be, consider the example of an "out-of-the-money" call—one whose exercise price is far above the current market price of the underlying stock.

Hypothetical Corp. stock is selling today for $50 a share. You buy a call, due to expire in two months, on Hypothetical at $60 a share. Since investors see little chance that the call will ever have any exercise value, its price is only 50 cents. Your outlay on a call for 100 Hypothetical shares, therefore, is just $50.

Two weeks from now, Hypothetical announces that it has developed a new wonder product and expects to receive a major government contract for it. The stock jumps to $70 a share. Your little 50-cent call is now worth $10 if it were to be exercised. Furthermore, other options traders are so excited about Hypothetical and its product that they have bid the price of the call, which still has a month and a half to run, up to $13. You sell, receiving $1,300 excluding commissions. You realize a profit of $1,250, or 25 times your original $50 investment.

Of course, this is not the way things usually work out with deep out-of-the-money calls. The great majority of them expire worthless. You can take a lot of these little flyers without ever having any of them pay off.

At-the-money and in-the-money calls—those with an exercise price equal to or less than the going price of the underlying stock—tend to be less volatile and less risky, since their chances of expiring worthless are less. Once you have a good understanding of the way the relationship between call exercise prices and the prices of their underlying stocks works, you can plan call-buying strategies within a broad range of potential risks and rewards. Selling naked calls is a proposition suitable only for investors willing and able to take on risk in large and indeterminate amounts.

INCOME POTENTIAL

As mentioned above, buying calls is not normally a sensible way to try to generate reliable current income from your investments. But writing, or selling them, can produce income in the form of premiums received. This is not a risk-free strategy, however.

Suppose you own 100 shares of Hypothetical Corp. at $50, and are expecting Hypothetical's regular $1 quarterly dividend in a couple of weeks. Hypothetical's annual dividend yield of 8 percent is quite respectable, but you're not satisfied with it. You ponder the outlook for Hypothetical Corp. and the stock market, and decide that Hypothetical stock is unlikely to rise significantly in the near future.

So you sell a call on the stock at an exercise price of $55, and receive a $1 premium from the call buyer. Like magic, you have doubled the income you can get this quarter from your stock investment. But you are also taking some chances. If Hypothetical shares rise above $55, your stock could be called away from you at any time before the option expires, and you will have gotten no benefit from any of the stock's rise beyond the $55 exercise price. The call could be exercised before the dividend record date, preventing you from receiving the dividend. Furthermore, you involuntarily record a capital gain or loss for tax purposes when a stock is called away from you.

If, after selling a call, you become more and more uneasy about the prospect of its being exercised, you do have an out. You can buy an identical call in the open market, thus cancelling out your position. At the time you decide to do this, the going price of the call may be greater or less than the price you received when you sold the original one.

RISKS AND DRAWBACKS

The examples above illustrate that there are risks and drawbacks in varying degrees with any transaction in calls. However, it should also be noted that, with their flexibility, calls offer you a good opportunity to select an investment strategy that closely matches the precise degree of risk you want to take.

In any event, it is important not to let strategies in options distract you from your overall investment objectives. For example, if you sell calls in the hope of fattening the return from your income investment portfolio, the exercise of those calls can throw your other plans out of whack, bringing on the need to rebuild the portfolio and also possibly incurring tax liabilities you hadn't figured on.

LIQUIDITY

An active market in calls provides good liquidity for most of them whenever you want to buy or sell. On this score, it is worthwhile to check the "open interest" (the number of contracts outstanding) and the recent amount of trading volume on a call you are considering. The greater the open interest and volume, the better your chances are likely to be of buying or selling the call at a price close to that in the last transaction. Other factors that naturally influence the liquidity of a listed call include the size, volatility and trading volume of the underlying stock.

TAX ADVANTAGES
AND DISADVANTAGES

Profits and losses realized on calls you buy go into your capital gains and losses accounts for tax purposes. If your own a call for more than six months, these profits and losses are considered long-term with a maximum tax rate of 20 percent on gains. When you conduct transactions in calls on stocks you own, it can affect the way your holding period of those stocks is calculated for tax purposes. In addition, as described above, when a call owner exercises an option you sold, you may have to realize a taxable gain or loss on the underlying stock.

PUT OPTIONS

DESCRIPTION

Puts are a special kind of upside-down security with many unqiue characteristics. For the newcomer, it takes some study to understand their potential uses and what makes the markets in which they are traded tick.

Puts are contracts that give their owners the right to sell a specified stock at a set price within a given time period (usually up to about nine months). That means that a put's value tends to increase as the price of its underlying stock goes down, and to decrease when the stock goes up. Puts on many large, actively traded stocks are traded at the various options exchanges around the country. Speculators often buy puts seeking to profit from market declines. In this use, puts provide an alternative to short-selling. Hedgers, on the other hand, may buy puts as a cushion against declines in the prices of stocks they own.

Similarly, puts may be "written," or sold, with a variety of aims. Sellers may be primarily interested in gaining extra income, in the form of the premium received from the buyer of the put. Or they may use puts as a means of trying to acquire a stock at an effective price lower than the current market price. No matter what their ultimate aims, writers of puts must be prepared to fulfill their part of the bargain to buy the stock involved at the specified price any time owners of puts decide to exercise their option to sell.

HOW AND WHERE TO GET
INFORMATION AND INVEST

Information about puts and other options is available in the prospectus offered by the options exchanges, which can be obtained from any good broker. The exchanges and brokerage firms also have pamphlets and other literature devoted specifically to puts and the ways in which they can be used. At many brokerage firms, there are analysts who specialize in creating and recommending options strategies aimed at capitalizing on events affecting the stock market, such as takeover proposals.

COSTS OF BUYING,
OWNING AND SELLING

Brokers charge commissions to handle purchases and sales of puts. These are an important consideration, because puts are not "buy and hold" investments. Since the typical put has only a few months of life, regular activity in puts involves frequent transactions.

Because puts have time value, their price almost always carries a built-in premium over their present worth should they be exercised. As puts move closer to their expiration dates, this premium tends to shrink. Suppose you bought a put today carrying an exercise price a little below the price at which its underlying stock is trading. If two weeks from now the stock price has not changed, the price of your put will likely have declined at least slightly.

For sellers of puts, there are also margin requirements. That is, they must keep a specified amount of funds on deposit with a broker as assurance that they will be able to meet their obligation to buy the stocks involved whenever an owner of a put decides to exercise the option.

CAPITAL GAINS
POTENTIAL

There are numerous ways to seek capital gains by buying puts, or employing them in combinations with other options. The simplest is an outright purchase of a put in anticipation of a drop in the price of its underlying stock.

Suppose, for example, that Hypothetical Corp. stock is selling at $50 a share—a price you feel is too high based on the market outlook and the company's prospects. You buy a put giving you the right to sell 100 shares of Hypothetical stock at $50 a share any time in the next two months, paying a price for the put of $5, or a total of $500 excluding commissions.

Two weeks later, Hypothetical announces that it has unexpected production problems in its most profitable subsidiary, and that its profits will be lower than expected for the next two quarters. The stock drops to $40. Your put now has an exercise value of $10 a share, and because many option traders believe Hypothetical's stock could go still lower in the immediate future, it is commanding a price of $15 in the options market. You sell, receiving $1,500, for a profit of $1,000, again excluding commissions. You have realized a 200 percent return on your money on the basis of a 20 percent decline in the price of Hypothetical's stock.

Advocates of puts like to point out that someone who sells a stock short—borrowing it from a broker and selling it, hoping to buy it back later at a lower price—has less leverage than a put owner in a situation like this. They also note that risk in a short sale is theoretically unlimited, while put buyers can lose no more than their original investment plus their commission cost. Furthermore, put owners need not concern themselves with other problems of short selling such as margin requirements or covering dividends on their "negative" stock position.

Investors can also buy puts in order to protect paper profits they have already attained on stocks they own. Suppose, for example, that you bought a large number of Hypothetical shares years ago at an average cost of $5, compared to its present price of $50. For tax reasons, you do not wish to sell your stock this year, but you are extremely worried that Hypothetical stock will decline significantly before you will be ready to sell.

By buying puts covering some or all of your Hypothetical holdings, you can insulate yourself against this risk. The price you pay is the premium on the puts, say, $5 a share. In effect, you are giving up a part of your gain on your original Hypothetical investment in order to assure that the rest remains intact until the puts expire.

For an illustration of one slightly more complicated option strategy, consider a case in which Hypothetical is trading at $50 while awaiting word on whether government regulators will approve a whole new series of products the company wants to offer. A ruling from the regulators is due in two weeks.

You have no idea which way the ruling will go. But you are convinced that, either yea or nay, Hypothetical stock will react with a big move. You buy both a $50 call and a $50 put on Hypothetical shares, paying $5 for each, or a total of $10. If Hypothetical stock goes either above $60 or below $40 before the put and call expire, you will have a profit again, ignoring commissions.

INCOME POTENTIAL

Puts, like most other options, are generally unsuitable for people who depend on maximum, reliable current income on their investments. There are, however, strategies for attempting to gain increased income by selling puts. For example, if Hypothetical stock is selling at $52 and you believe it is very likely to stay there or go higher over the next several months, you could sell a put on the stock at, say, $50. If the stock behaves as you expect, the put presumably will never be exercised and you can pocket the premium you received for it as extra income. When you sell a put, however, you must always be prepared to buy the stock involved for the price specified, at any time of the put owner's choosing.

RISKS AND DRAWBACKS

The examples above illustrate that the risks of investing with puts are as diverse as their possible applications. Buyers of a put take the risk that the underlying stock will rise, driving down the price of the put and eventually rendering it worthless on expiration. Sellers of puts take the risk that they will have to buy the underlying stock at a time when it is inconvenient for them to do so. People on both sides of the market are constantly exposed to market risk.

Puts, like other options, are tools for shifting and balancing risk and reward. Generally, the greater the reward you are seeking, the greater the amount of risk you will have to assume. In puts, as in other options markets, you are matching wits with sophisticated investors who use computers and their own great expertise to monitor the market continuously, searching for opportunities. The perils of dabbling in such a game are readily apparent.

LIQUIDITY

An active market in puts provides good liquidity for most of them whenever you want to buy or sell. On this score, it is worthwhile to check the "open interest" (the number of contracts outstanding) and the recent amount of trading volume on a put you are considering. The greater the open interest and volume, the better your chances are likely to be of buying or selling the put at a price close to that in the last transaction. Other factors that naturally influence the liquidity of a listed put include the size, volatility and trading volume of the underlying stock.

Writing a put can have an adverse effect on the overall liquidity of your investment portfolio, because of margin requirements and the ever present possibility that the put will be exercised and you will be obligated to buy the underlying stock. Of course, you do not have to keep the stock—you can immediately sell it again. But its market price may be much lower than the exercise price set by the put, and you will incur commission costs as well.

TAX ADVANTAGES
AND DISADVANTAGES

Profits and losses realized on puts you buy go into your capital gains and losses accounts for tax purposes. When you conduct transactions in puts on stocks you own, it can affect the way your holding period of those stocks is calculated for tax purposes.

The tax implications of many transactions involving puts and other options can be complicated and should not be overlooked. An active participant in the market should have a good tax adviser or a thorough personal knowledge of the prevailing tax rules.

INDEX OPTIONS

DESCRIPTION

In the early 1980s, with trading well established in options on individual stocks, the major exchanges took the idea one step further. They introduced options on the stock market as a whole or, to be precise, on many of the leading indexes that measure trends in stock prices.

If speculators thought the market was about to rise, but were uncertain about which specific stock or stocks would do well, they could buy call options on a market index. If those same speculators anticipated a general decline in stock prices, they could buy put options on the same index. Investors who wanted to "hedge" a broad portfolio of stock holdings, creating for themselves a cushion against unfavorable market trends, could sell index options, in the process gaining extra income in the form of premiums received from the buyers of those options.

There was a hitch to this whole idea. When an option is exercised, someone must deliver the underlying security. But it would be cumbersome and difficult, if not impossible, to have to deliver all the stocks that make up a market index. So the rules of index options were written to specify that settlement would be done not with securities but with cash.

While this solved the basic problem, it also gives index options characteristics that differ significantly from those of standard stock options. For one thing, it means that any time a transaction requires you to deliver, you need to have the necessary cash on hand. If you don't have it, you might be forced to sell some other investment to raise the money.

For this and other reasons, investors familiar with options on individual securities should not assume that they are ready to play the index options game without some further study and experimentation on paper. A miscalculated move with index options can make a mess of your entire investment strategy.

HOW AND WHERE TO GET
INFORMATION AND INVEST

Detailed information on index options is readily available from most brokers and other financial services firms, and from the various exchanges where they are traded. Before you venture into trading in these securities, it is necessary to understand the makeup and traditional behavior of the various indexes used. No index on which options are presently traded exactly duplicates the market, and no two are exactly alike. Even casual followers of the stock market know that there are frequently days when, say, the American Stock Exchange market value index rises while, say, Standard & Poor's 500 stock composite index declines.

COSTS OF BUYING,
OWNING AND SELLING

Brokers charge commissions to handle buy and sell orders on index options. While these charges may seem relatively low in comparison to commissions on stock trades, they can add up quickly because most index option strategies involve frequent buying and selling.

Investors who take positions in index options that may require them to deliver cash must also meet margin requirements with their broker—that is, they must have specified amounts of cash or securities on deposit with the broker. These margin requirements should be thoroughly understood before you invest.

An important cost to buyers of index options is the premium they pay for the time value of the option. If a market index is at 200 and you wish to buy a put or call expiring in three months on that index at 200, you obviously will not be able to get it free—even though neither the put nor the call has any current exercise value.

The standard trading unit for index options is $100 times the current value of the index. Thus, each one-point move in the index means a gain or loss of $100. Your initial investment in the "at-the-money" put or call described in the paragraph above might be say, 5 points, or $500.

CAPITAL GAINS POTENTIAL

Buyers of index options hope to realize capital gains by profiting from a rise in the stock market with calls or a market decline with puts. Assume, for example, that you and a friend disagree sharply in your attitudes about the market outlook.

You are bullish, and your friend is bearish. You buy a call on an index at 200, and he simultaneously buys a put on the same index at 200, at a time when the index is precisely at 200. You each pay $500, plus commissions.

If, before the options' expiration date, the index rises to 210, your call will have an exercise value of $1,000, plus any remaining time value. You can sell your call, more than doubling your money. Your friend's put, at the same time, has no exercise value and appears increasingly likely to expire worthless. Because it still has a little time value, the friend is able to sell it for $25. He has incurred a 95 percent loss on his $500, plus commissions.

If, instead of rising to 210, the index fell to 190, the results would in theory be exactly reversed. The friend would more than double his money, and you would suffer a total or near-total loss.

There is a third possibility that these two people in this case cannot overlook. The index could simply hover around 200 for weeks, while the market value of both the put and call steadily shrinks as their expiration date approaches. In this case, both parties lose substantial amounts of their original investment. There are other, more complicated strategies for seeking capital gains by trading in combinations of index options. All come under the same general rule—your entire investment is at risk.

INCOME POTENTIAL

Sellers of index options can realize income by "writing" puts or calls. This comes in the form of the premium received from the buyer. Assume that you and your friend, in your disagreement over the market outlook, decide not to pursue separate option-buying strategies. Instead, the friend, being bearish, sells you through a broker a call on an index at 200 when the index stands at 200. Commissions aside, you invest $500, which is deposited in the name of your friend.

Subsequently, the index rises to 210. You could sell your call to someone else at a profit, but instead you decide to exercise it. Under the random selection process used in option trading, the exercise notice is assigned to your friend.

You are owed $1,000, and the friend must pay it to you. His "income" from this venture into index options thus turns out to be minus $500. This example illustrates that strategies aimed at realizing income from index options typically involve risk—even unlimited risk. Consider what your friend might owe you if the index rose to 250, or 300, or more. As a general rule, index options are unsuitable for investors who want or need reliable current income from their assets, and preservation of those assets.

RISKS AND
DRAWBACKS

The risks involved in index options are many and varied. In some cases, the degree of risk is known—100 percent of your original investment, but no more. In other cases, it is unknown and theoretically limitless. No investment using index options should ever be made without a thorough understanding of the risk, actual or potential, involved.

Index options can be used as a hedge against market risk. Say, for example, that you own a broad portfolio of stocks, and are worried about the near-term market outlook. You don't want to unload the stocks, because that would mean a big tax bill. So you buy a put option on the index that most closely resembles, in its makeup, the portfolio of stocks you hold.

If stocks in general fall, yours presumably will, too. But you will have the consolation of a profit on your put. If your fears aren't realized, you will be out the cost of the put, but your stocks presumably will be keeping you feeling happy and prosperous.

In practice, you cannot expect to find a perfect one-to-one hedge in index options or any similar investment. The markets aren't so neat and tidy. But a partial or approximate hedge still affords some degree of insurance, at the cost of the premium you must pay.

LIQUIDITY

The liquidity of index options—the degree of readiness with which a market can absorb your orders to buy and sell—varies from option to option. The options which enjoy the greatest liquidity are those that are most actively traded and have the largest "open interest" (number of contracts in existence).

At the time this book was written, the number of index options was proliferating. May new sub-index options were being introduced, covering individual sectors of the stock market such as a group of technology or telephone stocks. The overall market for index options seemed likely to keep growing in the future, but many observers expected some individual options to fall by the wayside for lack of interest, and hence lack of a liquid market. With all the other risks they take, many options traders prefer to stick with markets whose liquidity is established.

TAX ADVANTAGES
AND DISADVANTAGES

The 1984 tax law subjected index options to the same tax rules that cover futures contracts. Regardless of how long the holding period, profits and losses realized by speculators in index options are considered 60 percent long-term and 40 percent short-term. All outstanding holdings are "marked to market" at yearend, as though they had been sold on the last business day of the year.

These rules are in part designed to curb strategies for using index options to defer taxes or gain some other tax advantage. You should not attempt any such strategy without the advice of a tax expert, or a thorough personal knowledge of current tax laws and court rulings.

Index options may have a place in the individual retirement account or other tax-favored savings plan of a sophisticated investor who has accumulated a fairly large amount of money in the account. Conservative investors generally should look elsewhere for IRA opportunities.

INTEREST-RATE OPTIONS

DESCRIPTION

If you can buy and sell options on stocks and stock indexes, why not options on interest-bearing securities as well? That question took on special urgency in the 1970s, when interest rates began to fluctuate with unprecendented volatility in this country. Thus was born the market in interest-rate options—puts and calls covering investments such as Treasury bills and mortgage-backed securities.

At first glance, the whole idea might seem daunting for the average investor. For the uninitiated, it takes a lot of study just to gain an understanding of how interest-rate options work. Futhermore, unlike equity options, interest-rate options are based on underlying securities traded in markets that are unfamiliar to many individuals. Besides, if highly paid professionals have so much trouble predicting interest rates, what chance does an unsophisticated individual stand in such a game?

These all may be valid concerns. However, interest-rate options have a wide variety of potential uses, and it may be helpful to many people at least to be aware of them. It is possible to go through life paying no attention to the stock market, if that is your inclination. But most Americans, whether they want it that way or not, sooner or later find changes in interest rates affecting their lives.

In the interest-rate options market, a call option gives its owner the right to buy a specified security, such as a Treasury bond, at a specified price within a set period of time. A put provides its owner with the right to sell the same security under those same conditions.

To get an idea of how these options work, it is first necessary to grasp the relationship between prices of fixed-income securities and interest rates. When rates fall, prices of existing bonds and other fixed-income investments naturally tend to rise. When rates rise, prices of those investments can be expected to fall. Thus, a straight purchase of a call on a fixed-income security is, in effect, a bet that interest rates will decline. Buyers of puts, on the other hand, seek to profit from a rise in interest rates. There are numerous, more complicated investment strategies you can pursue with interest-rate options.

Perhaps the most intriguing aspect of interest-rate options is their potential usefulness, on occasion, for people who don't invest in the bond market and have no interest in speculation in any form. Suppose, for example that you plan to buy a home in a few months, and are worried that interest rates on home mortgages will rise between now and the time you expect to get a commitment from a mortgage lender. In this situation, you might buy a put on a mortgage-backed security that extends over that time interval.

If mortgage rates do in fact go up, the value of your put will increase, and the profit you realize on it can provide you with some extra money to cover the higher mortgage costs. If mortgage rates remain stable or fall, you will lose money on the put. But you can view that loss as merely the cost of "insurance" you wanted to have to protect yourself from unfavorable changes in the mortgage market.

This is admittedly something of an idealized example. Lots of prospective home buyers don't have extra money lying around to use in fancy hedging strategies. Nevertheless, it serves as an illustration of the uses imaginative, knowledgeable managers of money can find for interest-rate options.

HOW AND WHERE TO GET
INFORMATION AND INVEST.

Interest-rate options are traded on several exchanges in this country. Information on them is available from these exchanges, or from any good broker or other financial services firm that maintains an option department. These brokers stand ready to handle your orders to buy and sell interest-rate options.

COSTS OF BUYING,
OWNING AND SELLING

As with other types of options, commission costs must be taken into account in planning any strategy involving interest-rate options. Commission rates per trade in these securities may be substantially lower than, say, rates charged to buy and sell stocks. But many options maneuvers require frequent buying and selling, and commission fees can add up quickly.

CAPITAL GAINS
POTENTIAL

Speculators can use puts and calls on interest-bearing securities to try to achieve large capital gains in short periods of time, putting up relatively small amounts of capital. Those who believe interest rates are likely to fall can seek to cash in on that decline by buying calls. Those who think rates are going higher can buy puts or sell calls.

For example, consider a situation in which a given Treasury bond is trading at par, or face value. Its price, in the shorthand of Wall Street, is expressed as 100. Futhermore, assume that call options are traded giving their owners the right to buy $100,000 in principal amount of this bond. The call is precisely "at the-money"—that is, it has neither positive nor negative value at the moment should it be exercised. But it has time value, and so it trades at a price of, say, 3. To buy it, you pay a price of $3,000.

In short order, Treasury bond interest rates drop, and the value of the bond covered by your option rises to 106, or $106,000. Your call now has an exercise value of $6,000 and, since it still has some time to run, it is trading at 8. You decide to sell it in the options market for $8,000. Commissions aside, you have realized a profit of $5,000, or 167 percent on your original investment, on a 6 percent change in the price of the underlying bond.

Of course, if interest rates rose, held steady or even declined by only a small amount, your call would not have appreciated, but would have fallen in value with time. There are other strategies available to options speculators that involve as much risk as just about anyone would ever want to take.

INCOME POTENTIAL

Investors who own interest-bearing securities may use options to try to increase their income from their holdings. In the above example, the speculator who bought a call on $100,000 of a given Treasury bond paid $3,000 for that call. Put yourself now in the position of the seller of this call. The $3,000 premium you receive represents income over and above the interest you are earning from your $100,000 in bonds. To gain this income, however, you have taken the risk that, if rates fall, the call will be exercised and you will have no choice but to sell the bonds for the $100,000 price specified in the option contract.

RISKS AND
DRAWBACKS

Rarely does an option transaction present itself as neatly and cleanly as in the examples given above. With each type of interest-rate option contract, there is a separate set of rules and specifications a newcomer must master. Whenever you take a plunge into interest-rate options, you are swimming among some very big fish—sophisticated traders and financial institutions whose options specialists spend all of every business day monitoring the markets. They are armed not only with skill, experience and knowledge, but also with computer equipment that enables them to keep tabs on and respond to minute-by-minute fluctuations in the markets.

For anyone familiar with the forces that influence trends in the credit markets, it is not hard to form an opinion about whether interest rates are likely to rise or fall. The experience of recent years, however, has shown that it is quite hard to form a correct opinion. Generally, to operate with any success in interest-rate options requires that you have an appetite for risk-taking, as well as the financial means and temperament necessary to take setbacks in stride.

LIQUIDITY

As activity in interest-rate options has grown, highly liquid markets have developed for several of these contracts. As with any other type of option, the most liquid markets are usually those with the greatest volume of trading and the largest "open interest"—number of contracts outstanding.

TAX ADVANTAGES
AND DISADVANTAGES

The tax implications of investment strategies employing interest-rate options can be complex, and can have a material effect on the bottom-line results you achieve. Before venturing into interest-rate options, you should have a thorough knowledge of the prevailing tax rules.

The 1984 tax law subjected them to the same tax rules that cover futures contracts. Regardless of how long the holding period, profits and losses realized by speculators in interest-rate options are considered 60 percent long-term and 40 percent short-term. All outstanding holdings are "marked to market" at yearend, as though they had been sold on the last business day of the year. These rules are in part designed to curb strategies for using options to defer taxes or gain some other tax advantage.

Interest-rate options may have a place in the individual retirement account or other tax-favored savings plan of a sophisticated investor who has accumulated a fairly large amount of money in the account. Conservative investors generally should look elsewhere for IRA opportunities.

OPTIONS ON FUTURES

DESCRIPTION

If standard options and futures contracts in their many forms aren't enough to satisfy your appetite for financial sophistication and adventure, how about options on futures? These contracts are one of the most exotic forms of investment available. Indeed, they are probably far too exotic for many people who have limited capital to work with, little time to devote to investing, or anything less than a great willingness to take risk. There are some venturesome investors, however, who find options on futures appealing, in part because they bring the features of option trading to the commodity markets.

Although both options and futures are discussed extensively in separate sections of this book, it may be useful to provide a summary comparison of them here. Options and futures are two types of contracts that call for the future sale or purchase of some other investment or a commodity. A buyer of a futures contract takes on the legal obligation (temporarily, in most cases) to buy the underlying investment or commodity. A buyer of a call option, by contrast, acquires the right, but not the obligation, to buy the underlying security or commodity.

Speculators in futures contracts generally take on open-ended—unlimited—risk. Speculators in options, on the other hand, can limit their risk exposure. But options buyers must normally pay a premium over the contract's exercise value. And options are "wasting assets." As a futures contract nears its stated delivery date, its price tends to converge with the going price for the underlying commodity or security in the spot market. If an option gains no exercise value, its price tends to shrink toward zero as its expiration date approaches.

Options on futures are contracts that give their owners the right to buy (in the case of a call option) or sell (in the case of a put option) a specified amount of a given futures contract within a stated period of time. Options on several different types of futures contracts are traded, like options and futures, on various exchanges around the country. Thus, they are referred to as "listed" options.

Commodity dealers whose reputations range from excellent to dubious may offer unlisted commodity or futures options. These should be evaluated with great care, especially if they are offered in an unsolicited telephone call by some salesperson you don't know. Before considering investing in any unlisted option, you should be very confident of the integrity and financial stability of the firm that offers it. The remainder of this section discusses listed options only.

HOW AND WHERE TO GET
INFORMATION AND INVEST

Commodity and securities brokers, or the exchanges where options on futures are traded, can provide you with detailed information that explains how these investments work and any possible applications they may have for you. These brokers stand ready to handle your orders to buy and sell, provided that you meet any suitability criteria, such as a minimum liquid net worth, which they set.

Before you can reasonably hope to venture successfully into trading options on futures, you should have a good working knowledge of both the options and the futures markets. It might be fun to consider "taking a flyer" on something as sophisticated as options on futures—what a story to tell your friends!—but it could also be dangerous to your financial well-being. Most traders in options on futures operate with a great deal of expertise.

COSTS OF BUYING,
OWNING AND SELLING

If you trade options on futures, you can expect to incur the standard brokerage commissions. If you trade them often, or use them frequently in strategies combining them with futures positions, you can expect to incur a lot of brokerage commissions.

CAPITAL GAINS
POTENTIAL

Like futures and other options contracts, options on futures can provide a means of speculating for large capital gains in relatively short periods of time. Suppose a commodity called Example is trading at $100 a bushel, and each futures contract represents 1,000 bushels. The value of each contract, then, is $100,000.

Believing that Example is about to rise in price, you check with your broker and find a call option, expiring several months from now, that gives you the right to buy the Example futures contract at a price of

$100,000. Since the call has considerable time value remaining, it is selling at a price, or premium, of 5. Your cost to buy it is $5,000, plus commissions.

If the Example futures contract rises to $110,000 in value over the next two months, the price of your call option must increase to at least 10 its exercise value and will likely go even higher than that because it still has some time to run. Suppose it is trading at 12¹/₂ when you sell it, taking a $7,500 profit (again, ignoring commissions).

You have realized a 150 percent profit on just a 10 percent change in the price of the underlying futures contract. But wait, an experienced commodity trader might say at this point, if you had bought the futures contract directly on 5 percent margin, for the same initial outlay of $5,000, you could have made a $10,000 profit instead of $7,500.

True, an advocate of options on futures might reply, but you took less risk. If you had bought the futures contract, you might have lost more than $5,000 if the market went against you. Options, unlike futures, are not traded on margin and hence are not subject to margin calls.

There are many, many more ways to seek profits using options on futures. Some of them that go beyond simple purchases of puts or calls do involve open-ended risk. There also are strategies in which options can be used with other options or futures in transactions set up to "hedge," or limit, risk. No complicated or multiple maneuver in this or any other options or futures market should be attempted before you understand all its possible outcomes.

INCOME POTENTIAL

Like other options, options on futures pay no dividends or interest. But you can sell a put or call on a futures contract you own in an attempt to generate additional cash flow into your account. If the option you sell is never exercised, you collect the premium originally paid for it.

This is not a conservative way to seek reliable, steady income with safety, however. If your primary investment needs are high, steady income and safety, there is little likelihood that you would, or should, ever own a futures contract against which to sell an option.

RISKS AND
DRAWBACKS

As the foregoing discussion suggests, you don't have to venture far into options on futures to find yourself in very deep water. Simply picking an opportune spot in this game can involve a complex process of evaluation. You have to choose, first of all, among underlying futures contracts—not just the commodity involved, but the delivery month. Then you have to pick from among several "strike," or exercise, prices on available options. You also must consider whether the going premium, or market price of the option, is attractive. Ideally, you'd also like the option you choose to be actively traded, so that it can readily be bought or sold at a price close to the last transaction in it.

There is more special esoterica with which you must also be familiar. For example, the month stated in an option on a futures contract is typically the delivery month for the futures contract, not the expiration month for the option. Trading in a futures option may expire in the month before the futures contract's delivery month.

All this is not meant as a blanket statement that no one should pay any attention to options on futures. Rather, it is intended to suggest that anyone who is considering trading them should pay a lot of attention before he or she invests.

LIQUIDITY

Some options on futures enjoy active markets, and thus offer ready in-and-out liquidity. The degree of liquidity can vary from contract to contract. Unlike most futures contracts, options on futures are generally not subject to daily limits on the amount by which their price can change. As the Coffee, Sugar Cocoa Exchange in New York put it in a brochure describing options on futures: "Experienced futures traders will recognize the significance of still being able to trade in options even at times when futures prices have moved the maximum daily limit."

TAX ADVANTAGES
AND DISADVANTAGES

If you speculate in options on futures, your gains and losses are treated for tax purposes the same way futures themselves are treated. All gains are subject to a maximum tax rate of 32 percent, and all outstanding positions are "marked to market" at yearend for the purposes of computing taxes owed. If you engage in hedge transactions, different tax rules may apply, depending on your circumstances and the other investments involved.

The rules that bar direct speculation in commodities from tax-favored savings programs such as individual retirement accounts and Keogh plans make options on futures an unlikely candidate for these accounts. Exceptions to this rule may arise—for example, venturesome investors may consider for their IRAs some managed pool of money that uses options on futures as part of its strategy. For many conservative investors of modest means, options on futures are generally considered unsuitable either in or outside of a tax-favored investment account.

PASSBOOK SAVINGS ACCOUNTS

DESCRIPTION

Before the financial upheaval of the 1970s and '80s, passbook savings accounts at banks and other depository institutions played a central role in the savings and investment system in the United States. People relied on the convenience and safety of passbook accounts to accumulate money as a reserve against emergencies; for the down payment on their first car or first home; for other large expenses such as college tuition; and for eventual ventures into riskier, more ambitious investments such as stocks.

The interest you could earn on a passbook account was limited by law. As long as inflation and interest rates were low and there were relatively few competing vehicles, however, people still found them to be appealing ways to build a foundation, at least, for their financial plans.

As this book was written, there were still many billions of dollars on deposit in passbook savings accounts. Many people still use them for short-term savings goals. Lots of parents still choose them as a handy way to introduce their children to the virtues of saving. But by many standards—including potential for growth or income, flexibility, and tax status—passbook accounts in their present form are an idea whose time has passed.

They are outclassed in yield by a wide variety of vehicles that are considered just as safe, or even safer. Even though they provide banks and savings institutions with a seemingly cheap source of money, many of those cost-burdened institutions have lately taken steps actually to reduce the appeal of small passbook accounts.

The timetable for banking deregulation set by government authorities calls for the eventual elimination of interest-rate ceilings on all deposits. Depository institutions then would presumably be free to do whatever they wish to encourage a revival of passbook accounts, let them continue to languish, or actively seek to phase them out. The decision will be dictated largely by economic, political, financial and competitive circumstances prevailing when, and if, full deregulation takes effect.

As long as no active steps are taken to kill it off, a phenomenon as deeply rooted in American society as the passbook savings account seems unlikely to disappear from the scene any time soon. In the modern, highly competitive world, however, it will have to develop some new attractions if it is going to have a chance to thrive again.

HOW AND WHERE TO GET
INFORMATION AND INVEST

Opening a passbook savings account has always been a relatively simple process at any bank or savings institution. If you seek to do so these days, any conscientious banker will advise you of the many higher-yielding alternatives available, at no sacrifice in safety and in some cases at not much sacrifice in liquidity.

COSTS OF BUYING,
OWNING AND SELLING

In the old days, the only cost involved in putting your money in a savings account was the foregone opportunity to realize better returns elsewhere, usually at some extra risk. That, however, is now no longer true in all cases. In times of high interest rates and inflation, the "opportunity cost" involved in a 5.5 percent passbook account can be very high.

It has become an increasingly common practice among depository institutions to pay no interest at all on a passbook account when its balance falls below a specified minimum of $50, $100, $250 or even more. In some instances, institutions have even set what amounts to negative interest—monthly fees charged on accounts with very small balances. Whatever a given institution's minimums, they may be subject to change in the future for existing accounts.

When an institution sets such rules, it is in fact giving you a strong incentive to close out an old account with a few dollars sitting in it. Even at no interest, the institution finds that account a costly, unappealing burden to carry.

CAPITAL GAINS
POTENTIAL

There is no, and never has been any, potential for capital gains in a passbook savings account. Of course, you can still, as always, use a passbook account to seek long-term growth of your assets through regular deposits and compounding of interest. With an interest ceiling on passbook accounts of 5.5 percent in the investment climate prevailing in the mid-1980s, that is about the equivalent of entering the Indianapolis 500 with a Model T Ford.

INCOME POTENTIAL

Passbook savings accounts are interest-bearing vehicles. But people who want or need maximum current income from their investments, perhaps more than any other class of investors, should be aware of the many, more appealing alternatives not only in other types of bank deposits, but in Treasury securities and other highly safe vehicles.

Even at a uniform ceiling interest rate, not all passbook accounts produce the same effective yield. That is because individual institutions may use different methods of compounding, and of figuring balances over a given period of time for the purpose of calculating interest to be paid. In addition, interest may be credited differently at different institutions—say, monthly at one, quarterly at another.

RISKS AND
DRAWBACKS

With the guarantee of federal deposit insurance of up to $100,000 per account (assuming the institution where you bank is covered by that insurance), passbook savings accounts are safe. Safe, that is, from the risk of losing your principal and interest should the institution fail. Not safe, however, from the ravages of inflation and taxes.

Suppose you have $1,000 in a 5.5 percent passbook account, and earn about $58 in interest this year (compounding of interest raises your effective yield slightly above $55). Of this, you pay, for the sake of illustration, $18 in taxes. That leaves you with a net return on your investment of $40. Even if the cost of living rises just 4 percent over the year (certainly a low figure by recent standards), you have gained nothing in purchasing power.

From the viewpoint of some investment theorists, it may seem remarkable that there is any significant amount of money still on deposit in passbook accounts. Ignorance of the alternatives is certainly one explanation, but so is the inertia that a lot of people are subject to. Passbook accounts are probably still one of the simplest, and most widely understood, savings vehicles in this country.

LIQUIDITY
Passbook savings accounts are highly liquid. True, you can't write a check on one, as you can with a money market deposit account, NOW or Super-NOW account, or money market mutual fund. But the money is there for ready withdrawal in person, by mail, and increasingly these days, by telephone transfer into, say, your checking account at the same bank for immediate investment elsewhere.

The fact that passbook money can be so easily tapped makes it all the more striking that so much of it remains in these accounts at a time when other investments are so much more appealing. On the other hand, perhaps it explains why many passbook savers find it so easy to put off taking any action to move the money elsewhere: It's a little matter, involving some inconvenience, that can be taken care of tomorrow, or the next day, or the next.

TAX ADVANTAGES
AND DISADVANTAGES
The rising tax burden in this country has played a big part in the declining appeal of the passbook savings account. While higher taxes have enhanced the appeal of anything that can qualify for favorable tax treatment—whether tax-exempt bonds or securities offering the hope of long-term capital gains—those same taxes have taken an increasing bite out of the return the typical passbook saver realizes. All interest earned on passbook accounts is subject to federal taxation as ordinary income, and to any state and local taxes that may be levied on interest where you live.

Passbook accounts are legally eligible for use in individual retirement accounts, Keogh plans and other tax-favored savings programs, but hardly anybody thinks they are a good choice.

PRECIOUS METALS

DESCRIPTION

If money is defined as a store of value and a medium of exchange, some investors consider precious metals the ultimate form of money. Since ancient times, gold and silver have been revered for their beauty and relative scarcity, and used as trustworthy vehicles for conducting financial transactions and conserving wealth. They have long been among the most common materials used to mint coins.

In modern times, it has generally become the custom around the world to use paper money for transaction purposes. In many cases, this paper money originally was backed by a given quantity of gold or silver. But this kind of link has grown more and more tenuous in the late 20th Century.

So precious metals have evolved as separate investments, whose prices fluctuate regularly—and sometimes wildly—when stated in dollars or any other paper currency. Some investors put a great deal of trust in gold and silver as a repository of value that offers protection from the ills that can befall paper currencies—inflation, political instability, and changing values of currencies relative to each other in foreign exchange. In the view of some people, currencies have only relative value, while gold and silver are absolutes, or very nearly so.

Another commodity, platinum, has a shorter history in the realm of money and finance. But many people today classify it with gold and silver as a precious metal.

The means and methods available for precious metals investing today are just about limitless. You can buy gold, silver or platinum in the form of bullion—bars of various weights. You can buy gold and silver coins. You can buy the stocks of companies that mine or process precious metals, or shares of mutual funds that invest in these stocks. You can trade options or futures contracts that represent an interest in gold, silver or platinum.

HOW AND WHERE TO GET
INFORMATION AND INVEST

There are many companies around the country, and the world, that make a specialty of precious metals. Some are large, long-established enterprises esteemed for their consistent records of honesty, fair dealing and trustworthiness. The boom in precious metals investing in the 1970s and early 1980s attracted some less scrupulous operators into the game. When you are contemplating a precious metals transaction, as with just about any other kind of investment, it is important to have a thorough knowledge of the firm with which you are dealing.

In recent years, large numbers of banks, securities brokers and other financial services firms have greatly expanded the services they offer in precious metals. If you are interested in this market, chances are you will not have to look very far to get information on it and find a good sampling of brokers and dealers eager to compete for your business.

COSTS OF BUYING,
OWNING AND SELLING

The costs you may incur in investing in precious metals can vary widely, depending on the type of investment you wish to make. If, for example, you choose a "no-load" mutual fund that invests in gold- and silver-mining companies, the only cost involved may be the annual management fee that the fund's sponsor collects from its assets.

If, on the other hand, you want to buy bullion and bury it in your back yard—an idea that some people regard as eccentric, but which a good many others quietly practice—the costs can be numerous and significant. A sample list of possibilities: Dealer fees and commissions, shipping and handling charges, and sales or transfer tax. If you decide that a vault in some institution is really a safer place for your bullion than two feet under your lawn, you will probably have to pay annual storage fees. If you ever wish to resell bullion you have kept in your personal possession, you may have to pay for an assay to determine its weight, integrity and value.

Direct investments in precious metals produce no dividend or interest yield. This can work out to a significant "opportunity cost," especially in times of high interest rates. It obviously makes sense, whenever you are considering a precious metals investment, to determine all the costs involved beforehand, and take them into account in determining the return you expect to get on that investment.

CAPITAL GAINS POTENTIAL

There are many strategies available for seeking capital gains in precious metals. Typically, investors look to them first and foremost as a "hedge" against inflation. They buy for the long term, trusting that the value of gold or silver or platinum will rise at least enough to keep up with increases in the cost of living.

Short-term traders are active in the precious metals game, too, because precious metals prices have been highly volatile in recent times. Trying to catch short-term swings in precious metals, as in any commodity market, is usually a highly speculative endeavor, suitable only for people with the financial means and temperament to tolerate high risk.

INCOME POTENTIAL

In some of its forms, investing in precious metals produces "negative income." That is, it generates no dividends or interest, and may involve annual outlays such as storage charges. Obviously, however, if you own a gold mine you have access to a great deal of income if you regularly sell the metal that comes out of the ground. The actual discovery or purchase of a gold mine is, alas, a possibility open to very few people. But you can buy an interest in a mine or mines by investing in the stock of a company or companies in the precious metals business.

Some mining stocks pay high current dividends. The reasons for their high yields, however, may have something to do with risks—for instance, the expectation that a given company's mine is past its peak economical production, or political risk in the country where the mine is located.

For people who need maximum income from their assets, and maximum safety of those assets, precious metals are generally a chancy proposition at best. On the other hand, some conservative investors regard precious metals as the only truly safe investment in the long run.

Ultimately, how you view precious metals as an investment may come down to your personal economic and political philosophy. If some gold or silver or platinum hidden under your bed helps you sleep better at night, it may produce psychic income that is of great value to you.

RISKS AND DRAWBACKS

The reputation of precious metals as one of the best available hedges against inflation is firmly entrenched. Yet no single precious-metals investment can be expected to track precisely the Consumer Price Index or any other measure of inflationary trends. Precious metals prices are generally influenced not by changes in actual inflation, but by shifts in inflationary expectations among participants in the markets. For that reason, they can be highly volatile.

Though theory may argue that they ought to, all precious metals investments do not follow precisely parallel courses. There are times, for example, when stocks of silver-mining companies do better than silver bullion, and vice versa. Changes in interest rates, the politics of energy, and many other considerations may influence the precious metals markets. With all the mystique surrounding them, precious metals are also industrial commodities, used in business ranging from dentistry to electronics. So the present and prospective future state of the economy is often a relevant question for investors in these markets.

Furthermore, though it has gained much in stature in recent years, the idea of putting your money in gold or silver or platinum is not universally popular. Precious metals are often derided as "sterile" investments that help foster no innovation and create no new jobs. An investment in precious metals can be viewed, in effect, as a bet against future general prosperity. Even some eminent experts in the precious metals field have observed on occasion that they are not so sure they would want to live in a world where the price of gold was, say, $10,000 an ounce.

Still, precious metals appear to have won for themselves a lasting place in the financial establishment. It is common today for advisers not of the "gold bug" persuasion to suggest putting perhaps 5 or 10 percent of your available capital into some form of precious metals reserve. Like life insurance, this is a kind of investment in which most people hope not to realize a quick payoff.

LIQUIDITY

The market for most commonly accepted precious metals investments is so big, with so many participants, that you can usually expect good liquidity when you buy and sell them. There are, however, variations from this general rule. Whenever you are about to buy, it makes sense to know or find out under what conditions, and under what pricing terms, you can expect to sell. If the feared calamities that prompt some people to invest in precious metals ever occur, the prospective liquidity of those investments afterward is a matter of faith.

TAX ADVANTAGES
AND DISADVANTAGES

It is tough to find many government-sponsored tax incentives to invest in precious metals. Of course, stocks of gold-mining companies are subject to the same tax treatment as other stocks. Gold mutual funds, futures and options come under the usual tax rules for those types of securities.

Unlike many financial investments, however, a purchase of bullion or coins may incur a sales tax charge. Direct investments in precious metals are also expressly barred in tax-favored savings programs such as individual retirement accounts and Keogh plans. You can get around this prohibition, if you are so inclined, by putting your IRA or Keogh money in securities such as gold-mining stocks or shares of a mutual fund specializing in precious metals investments.

PREFERRED STOCKS

DESCRIPTION

Preferred stocks sound deceptively simple. They are securities, like common stocks, that represent part ownership of a corporation. They are described as "preferred" because they have the first right, before common stocks, to any money the corporation has available to pay out in dividends.

In practice, they do not always behave like stocks, and there are several reasons why an individual investor might not prefer them. While a preferred issue's dividend is generally more secure than that of a common stock, it is usually fixed. For that reason, a "straight" preferred tends to behave more like a bond.

But as a stock, it lacks some of the most important legal characteristics of a bond. When a company gets into trouble, investors who own its debt securities, such as bonds, normally have a claim on the company's assets. At the very least, they stand first in line to get allotments of whatever is left should the company be liquidated. Preferred stockholders in such situations remain owners, not creditors, of the company.

Furthermore, there are a great many details to consider in evaluating a preferred stock—voting rights, call provisions, sinking funds, cumulative arrangements for unpaid dividends, and more. Any and all of these can significantly affect the way the market values a preferred stock. If, as in many cases, it is a *convertible* preferred, it will have very different characteristics from a staight preferred (see the chapter on convertible securities). If, as in many cases, its dividend is adjustable, it will take on many of the characteristics of a money market investment (see the following section on adjustable rate preferreds).

A further deterrent to individuals contemplating preferreds is the tax status of dividends. Most dividends received by individuals are subject to income tax. But corporations are permitted to exclude a large share of the dividends they receive from taxes. Corporations buy and own a great number of preferreds, and thus usually help set the yields of these securities at levels that are relatively unattractive to individuals on an after-tax basis.

Thus, preferreds are most worthy of your consideration if you are involved in a corporation—say, an incorporated small business or a professional corporation.

HOW AND WHERE TO GET
INFORMATION AND INVEST

Preferred stocks trade, like common stocks, on stock exchanges and in the over-the-counter market. You can buy and sell them through brokers and other financial services firms. Some mutual funds and other organized pools of money include preferreds (most often convertible preferreds) in their portfolios.

COSTS OF BUYING,
OWNING AND SELLING

Brokers charge commissions to buy and sell preferreds, just as they do with common stock. Straight preferreds often have relatively "thin"—that is, inactive—markets, and thus you may have to pay an added cost when you buy and sell in the form of price concessions from the most recent trade.

CAPITAL GAINS
POTENTIAL

You can invest in non-convertible preferred stocks seeking capital gains. However, you should be aware that there are several factors that influence their prices that differ from the usual forces at work in common stocks. One primary reason for buying common stocks is the hope of future dividend increases. This hope does not exist with preferreds.

Since preferreds are held mainly by income-conscious investors, the ups and downs of interest rates tend to exert a stong influence on prices of preferred stocks. Like bonds, preferred stocks generally fall in value when interest rates rise, and increase in value when rates decline. The market for common stocks may also be influenced by changes in interest rates, but there the effect is less uniform and may be mitigated by other developments.

There are, however, some opportunities in certain preferreds for speculators seeking large capital gains. These can occur, for example, when a company is in trouble and has been unable to pay dividends on its preferred stock. In this situation, the preferred's price is likely to be depressed. A venturesome investor might buy such a preferred stock in hopes of profiting from an improvement in the company's fortunes. This type of speculation closely resembles buying "junk" bonds.

INCOME POTENTIAL

The main appeal of preferreds is their dividend yield. Before buying a preferred stock for income, however, you should consider your tax status, and the many alternatives available, such as perhaps an outstanding bond of the same company.

Some corporate investors use a system called "rolling over" to try to maximize their return from investments in preferred stocks. This involves buying a preferred just before the record, or ex-dividend, date, for a dividend payment, then selling the stock shortly afterward and moving the proceeds to another preferred that is about to go ex-dividend. The process is repeated as many times as possible, so that the corporate investor receives not just one, but two or three dividends from various preferreds each quarter.

This strategy involves market risks. For many reasons, including the amount of time, investment expertise, commissions and record-keeping involved, it is likely to be a chancy endeavor for an individual investor of modest means or a busy owner of a small business.

RISKS AND
DRAWBACKS

The potential risks and drawbacks of preferred stocks, as discussed above, can be many and complex for the individual investor. Benjamin Graham, the eminent authority on security analysis, described the basic form of preferreds as flawed, lacking the important attributes of either bonds or common stocks. However, Graham said that there was nevertheless the possibility of finding good investments for income in preferreds if the issuer's financial strength was unquestioned.

LIQUIDITY

Preferred stocks are typically not as liquid as common stocks because the volume of activity in them is less. When you want to sell straight preferred shares of a small or troubled company, willing buyers may be scarce, and you may have no choice other than to sell at a distress price.

This problem may be minimal or nonexistent with an actively traded preferred stock of a large, healthy company, however. Convertible preferreds, with their claim on the issuer's common stock, often enjoy good liquidity.

TAX ADVANTAGES
AND DISADVANTAGES

Tax considerations are paramount in considering preferreds. For individuals, dividends, capital gains and losses on preferreds are taxed in the same way as are dividends, gains and losses on common stocks. But corporations can exclude from taxes 85 percent of the dividends they receive. This makes preferreds especially attractive to corporate treasurers seeking to maximize the after-tax return on their employers' money.

As a result, preferreds may have considerable attraction for you if you can buy them for a corporation in which you are involved. If you cannot do so, you should be aware, before buying a preferred, that its relative risk and return are likely to be skewed against you by the fact that many other participants in the market get a better after-tax return on preferreds than you can. This situation also makes preferred stocks a questionable candidate at best for individual retirement accounts and other tax-favored savings plans for individuals.

ADJUSTABLE-RATE PREFERREDS

DESCRIPTION

As the volatility of interest rates increased in the 1970s and early '80s, some investors who had previously bought preferred stocks started to shy away from them. In the days of relatively stable rates, prices of preferreds didn't usually change much unless there was a significant change in the financial health of the issuer.

But volatile rates brought increased market risk. Prices of even the best quality preferreds could rise or fall significantly simply because of changes in the general level of interest rates. When rates rise, prices of existing fixed-income securities must fall to remain competitive in the marketplace with new ones that are being issued.

To counter that problem, a new type of investment was devised—a preferred stock whose dividend was adjusted regularly by some formula agreed upon in advance. Adjustable-rate preferreds quickly became a popular vehicle, combining some of the traditional features of preferreds with some elements of short-term money market investments.

Yields on these securities are adjusted each quarter, so that each dividend payment reflects prevailing market conditions. The calculation is usually performed through a formula based on yields offered by a predesignated U.S. Treasury security. Thus, yields of adjustable-rate preferreds fluctuate in a way roughly analogous to that of a money market fund.

In other respects, however, they retain the characteristics of a preferred stock. They represent ownership, not debt secured by any promise to repay. In addition, their yields for individual taxpayers may be relatively unattractive because corporations can buy preferreds and exempt most of the dividends they receive from taxes. Not long after the market for adjustable-rate preferreds began to blossom, some mutual funds were organized to invest in them. These funds direct their marketing approaches to corporations.

HOW AND WHERE TO GET
INFORMATION AND INVEST

Brokers and other financial services organizations buy and sell adjustable-rate preferreds, and can provide you with information on them. Prospectuses, annual reports and other material published by mutual funds investing in these securities can be instructive on the subject.

COSTS OF BUYING,
OWNING AND SELLING

As with many other types of securities, you usually pay no direct cost if you buy an adjustable-rate preferred at the time it is first offered for sale. In an underwriting like this, brokers who sell the security collect their fees from the issuer. When you sell, and when you buy an existing issue, there are standard brokerage commissions to be paid.

Costs of investing in mutual funds that concentrate on adjustable-rate preferreds vary. One such fund levies a straight one-time charge of $250 to open an account. Another sets a 1.5 percent sales charge that can be reduced to 1 percent or half of 1 percent on large orders. In addition, mutual fund sponsors collect annual management fees from the funds' assets, which has the effect of slightly reducing shareholders' return on their investment. A typical minimum initial investment in these mutual funds is $5,000.

CAPITAL GAINS
POTENTIAL

There is some possibility of capital gains in adjustable-rate preferreds, because their prices are subject to change day by day. If the financial status of an issuer improves dramatically, the price of any of its preferred stocks would be likely to rise. However, the adjustable dividend feature of these securities is designed specifically to keep price fluctuations to a minimum. Thus these securities, under ordinary circumstances, are not a logical choice for investors whose primary objective is capital gains. In fact, a mutual fund investing in adjustable-rate preferreds may actively seek to minimize the realization of either capital gains or capital losses.

INCOME POTENTIAL

Opportunities for income can be very good for corporations investing in adjustable-rate preferreds, or mutual funds specializing in them. Their dividend yields are generally attractive, and corporations can exempt most of the payouts they receive from federal taxes. Individuals who do not have corporate status lack this tax advantage, however, and they may obtain better results from a Treasury bill, money market deposit account or money market mutual fund.

Yields on adjustable-rate preferreds rise and fall with changing interest-rate conditions. Thus, if interest rates rise, shareowners will enjoy the benefits. But if interest rates fall, so will the yields of adjustable-rate preferreds. With these securities, it is not possible to "lock in" a given rate, as you can with a bond or other long-term, fixed-rate securities.

The income potential of adjustable-rate securities is also subject to business risk. That is, if an issuer gets into trouble, payment of dividends can be delayed or cease. The degree of this risk can be assessed using the letter rating assigned by the rating agencies. If no ratings have been assigned, the issue should be considered closely and cautiously. Mutual funds investing in these securities attempt to diffuse business risk by owning a diversified portfolio representing many issuers.

RISKS AND
DRAWBACKS

The chief drawback of adjustable-rate preferreds for individual investors, just as with straight preferreds, is their tax disadvantage. Because corporations' income from these investments is largely tax free, corporate investors are likely to be willing to accept a dividend-payout rate that is unattractrive to individuals, after taxes and risk are taken into account.

For investors concerned with safety of principal, adjustable-rate preferreds remove much, but not all, of the market risk associated with straight preferreds. When adjustable-rate preferreds are sold to investors, the issuer may set limits on the extent to which dividends can be adjusted in the future. If yields on other investments surpass the upper limit on an ARP's yield, its price can be expected to decline.

LIQUIDITY

As a security enjoying growing popularity, and flexibility with changing interest rate conditions, adjustable-rate preferreds usually enjoy good liquidity. Issues of large, healthy companies are likely to be the easiest to buy and sell. Liquidity may not be so good if the issuer is small, not well known in the investment world, or in financial trouble. Adjustable-rate preferreds may be traded on securities exchanges or through dealers in the over-the-counter market.

Liquidity is usually no problem with sound mutual funds that invest in adjustable-rate preferreds. These funds stand ready to sell or redeem cash in shares at short notice, and may even offer redemption privileges through check-writing, bank wire or telephone.

TAX ADVANTAGES
AND DISADVANTAGES

As stated above, the tax rules make adjustable-rate preferreds suitable primarily for corporations, rather than individuals. For this reason, they are not a likely candidate for individual retirement accounts. Capital gains and losses can be realized when you invest in these securities. These are subject to the usual tax rates for both long- and short-term capital gains and losses.

Mutual funds investing in adjustable-rate preferreds normally have reinvestment plans that allow investors to plow back dividends, and any capital-gains distributions, automatically into the purchase of new shares. This allows for growth of your assets through compounding. In reinvestment plans like this, the rules say that current taxes must be paid on dividends and other gains, even though a shareholder does not actually receive them in cash. However, this may not be a significant problem for a corporate investor in these securities, since a large part of dividends received by corporations is exempt from federal income taxes.

REAL ESTATE

DESCRIPTION

More than 350 years after the legendary purchase of Manhattan island for $24, real estate indisputedly remains many Americans' favorite investment. The love affair may be stormy at times, but it goes on and on. Real estate has romance—pride of ownership, and the dream of big profits—but it also has an element of practicality. While other investments may pale in the face of inflation, real estate seems to thrive on it. And while other investments may be only pieces of paper, real estate has utility, as long as people need a place to live and work and, for that matter, to take a vacation break from work. Real estate has durability, at least some of the time. Real estate has stability, at least some of the time. And real estate has tax advantages, just about all of the time.

In modern real estate investing, you can pursue almost any strategy you wish, whether it's speculative or conservative, long- or short-term. You can buy somebody else's package, or put together your own. Each of the major categories of real estate investments is discussed in a separate section of this chapter.

HOW AND WHERE TO GET
INFORMATION AND INVEST

Real estate is everywhere you look, and so is information on it—in books, magazines and newspapers, in the offices of real estate agents, in the offering documents and reports of companies and partnerships that want to invest your money for you in property. Theories of real estate investment strategies can be studied endlessly. In the practice of real estate investing, however, it's a general rule that the most valuable information you can lay your hands on is often that which you dig up yourself.

In most forms that it takes, real estate is bought and sold in thousands of local markets, each of them with their own special and often changing characteristics. Time spent studying one or a few of these markets can give you knowledge that isn't published anywhere. You may call on a broker or salesperson to help you find the right property, or you may rely on word of mouth, newspaper advertisements and your own initiative in your search.

COSTS OF BUYING,
OWNING AND SELLING

Real estate can be expensive to buy, expensive to own, and expensive to sell. The ownership costs, in fact, can be the most onerous and the most unpredictable. In direct real estate investment, there are property taxes, insurance, maintenance and repairs, and more. Your investment will likely consume a lot of your time as well as your money. If you can't or don't want to accommodate yourself to that prospect, you perhaps can hire somebody to take some or all of the responsibility off your shoulders. But paying that person, of course, will be another cost on your list.

You can keep your out-of-pocket expenses to a minimum by investing, say, in the stock of a company that in turn owns real estate. Even that arrangement simply makes you a part owner of an entity that probably is paying large real estate costs. With many types of real estate investment, however, tax breaks go a long way toward lightening the burden of the ownership costs.

CAPITAL GAINS
POTENTIAL

Whether they buy undeveloped swampland or a high-rise condominium, many investors take the plunge into real estate in the hope of realizing handsome capital gains. In old times and new, stories abound of people amassing large fortunes through real estate investment. The tools you can use to pursue capital gains in real estate include leverage and your own personal labor.

Leverage comes through the use of borrowed money, as with a home mortgage. Lenders almost always want interest payments for the use of their money, but they usually leave all the capital gains to you. Thus, if you can buy a $50,000 property with just $5,000 of your own funds, all you need is for the property to rise to $55,000 in value to double your original investment. Of course, leverage increases risk by the same amount that it enhances potential reward.

As for your own personal labor, a popular strategy used by energetic real estate investors is to buy properties in need of repair or improvement, put in the necessary work, and then seek to sell them again at a price that reflects their new "cream puff" status.

INCOME POTENTIAL

There are some ways to invest in real estate with the primary objective of income—for example, in selected real estate limited partnerships, or in real estate investment trusts. There are other strategies for combined income and capital gains goals—for example, buying a developed property that yields generous rental income while you wait and hope for appreciation of the value of the property.

Another approach among the almost limitless possibilities in real estate is to buy a multi-unit property, such as a two-family house, in which you plan to occupy one of the units and rent out the other or others. The standard aim in such a situation is to use the rental income from tenants to help cover your costs of both owning and occupying the property.

However, for the conservative investor concerned not only with dependable income but also with liquidity and maximum safety of principal, most real estate investments will not measure up to the standards of alternatives like U.S. government securities.

RISKS AND
DRAWBACKS

It is possible to become so entranced with all the opportunities open to you in real estate that you underestimate or overlook entirely some of its important risks and drawbacks. First of all, anyone who assumes that real estate in any form is automatically a low risk investment may do some reading on what happened to the Florida land boom in the 1920s, or check the record of the dismal performance of real estate investment trusts in the stock market of 1973-74.

After you buy a home in a prime neighborhood in a prime community, what might happen to the value of your investment if property taxes unexpectedly soared, a major local employer suddenly announced large layoffs, or any one of countless other unpleasant surprises arose? Each type of real estate has, along with its special attractions, its special drawbacks. Undeveloped land, for instance, may require little maintenance and attention, but you may have to wait years to learn whether you are going to earn any return on your investment at all. Business property may be depreciated for tax purposes, but a personal residence may not.

   Furthermore, since real estate attracts so many sophisticated specialists, your competition in this game can be formidable. Like many
other types of investment, real estate has its slick promoters ready to
sell you poor deals at rich prices. When prices are rising in a given real
estate market, human nature seems to dictate that people automatically assume the trend will continue indefinitely. While there is a good
case for choosing to invest in healthy markets, hoping for continued
gains, rather than depressed markets, hoping for some miraculous
turnaround, it makes sense to bear in mind that it is always possible to
pay too high a price for any investment, real estate included.

LIQUIDITY
Real estate, so goes the old axiom, is inherently illiquid. It is nearly
always tough to sell quickly, and doubly so when circumstances dictate that you must sell it quickly. This is true in a relative sense, but not
as an ironclad absolute. There are cases in which savvy investors
have earned handsome returns in hot real estate markets turning
properties over at a rapid pace (some call this practice "flipping").
Some forms of real estate investments, such as stocks of companies
that own or invest in real estate, have minimal liquidity problems.

   Normally, however, real estate has its greatest appeal for patient
investors with a long-term perspective. If you could somehow have
contrived to get in on the original purchase of Manhattan for $24 in the
early colonial days, you would be worth billions now. But you would
have had to wait a long, long time for the big payoff.

TAX ADVANTAGES
AND DISADVANTAGES
Real estate investments typically enjoy some bounteous tax advantages. They may offer large writeoffs against your current income in
the form of interest and-or depreciation deductions, and at the same
time give relatively benign tax treatment to any capital gains you
realize when you sell a property. Of course, you must generally pay
local property taxes each year on any real estate you own. But these
taxes also are deductible on your federal income tax return.

   The more sophisticated you get in your real estate dealings, the
more complicated the tax rules generally become. Ignorance or mis-

understanding of the tax rules can turn a whole investment sour.

Certain real estate-related investments may be appropriate for an individual retirement account, Keogh plan or other tax-favored retirement savings program. Others, like your own home, are ineligible for these accounts. Before considering a real estate proposition for such an account, it pays to make certain the deal does not involve significant tax benefits that would be negated by the rules covering IRAs, Keoghs and similar vehicles.

INVESTMENT PROPERTY

DESCRIPTION

How, in today's complicated financial world, can people starting out with a modest stake hope to grow rich? Many experts give the same answer they would have given 10, or 25, or 100 years ago—invest in real estate.

Perhaps you lack the resources to start out with anything more than, say, a small two-family dwelling, in bad need of repair and thus available at a distress price. Even from that kind of lowly beginning, veterans of the game declare, you can use your own hard work and acumen, plus leverage and real estate tax benefits, to achieve great financial success. The profits from your first property might provide a down payment for a larger one—say, a modest-sized apartment building. Over time, you might progress to large apartment complexes, shopping centers, hotels, and the fabled status of real estate tycoon.

Of course, if this path to prosperity were easily laid out on any map and free of all pitfalls, it would be a well-traveled one by now. Indeed, a great many fortunes have been built on real estate. But lots of other people have dealt themselves into the game and lost.

Investment properties are available in a wide variety of forms. For the speculatively inclined, there is undeveloped land. More conservative investors may concentrate on established commercial or residential properties, seeking to profit from a combination of rental income, appreciation and tax benefits. Each class of investment real estate has its distinctive attributes and hazards.

Individual investors in large numbers have found room to operate successfully in this huge and diverse market. But any large-scale investor must compete with a formidable array of professional and institutional adversaries, including pension funds, real estate limited partnerships and investment trusts, and wealthy foreign investors. For many reasons, the increased participation of such forces in recent years has been welcomed by experienced investors in real estate. However, it has also raised concern that their enthusiastic bidding for properties might sooner or later push prices to unrealistically, and dangerously, high levels.

HOW AND WHERE TO GET
INFORMATION AND INVEST

There is much to know about real estate—real estate law, real estate accounting, real estate finance, and more. If you confine yourself to investing in your own home and maybe some shares of a real estate investment trust, you need not know a great deal about these things. But if you plan to become an active direct investor in real estate, you will probably have to devote considerable study to the subject, or else have regular access to good advice.

Real estate rules and procedures vary greatly from state to state and community to community. And monitoring the various markets is a more complex assignment than following trends in stocks or mutual funds. But trade associations do publish some information on national price trends and activity, and there are newsletters and specialized periodicals devoted exclusively to real estate.

Scores of books have also been published on the subject. These range from the inspirational (a la "The Road to Riches in Real Estate") to the more modestly informational.

COSTS OF BUYING,
OWNING AND SELLING

Direct investment in real estate can, and usually does, involve many costs. If miscalculated or not properly managed, these costs can eat up much or all of the financial benefits you expected to gain. However, many of these costs can be offset to a great degree by tax advantages.

If you plan to invest on borrowed money, you can expect to find that lenders view loans on investment properties much differently from the way they look at credit for buyers of personal residences. For example, a lending institution may impose much stricter terms on the purchase of an unimproved lot than it would on a home mortgage. This difference arises from no unreasoning prejudice on the part of lenders, but rather from the general rule that loans on investment property are riskier than home mortgages.

Obviously, you cannot hope to buy a big shopping center or apartment complex if you have little cash and few other assets to pledge as collateral. But you can start looking at small properties with surprisingly small sums of money at your disposal. Vehicles like limited partnerships can give you access to the real estate market with as little as $1,000 to $5,000.

CAPITAL GAINS POTENTIAL

The hope of realizing large capital gains is the driving force behind many real estate investments. Properties of almost any kind are regarded as a primary way to become a beneficiary, rather than a victim, of inflation. Inflation aside, the dream endures of "making a killing" in real estate by, say, buying the right weed-infested vacant lot not long before a zoning change is voted that makes the property a prime candidate for high-rise development.

Succeeding at this type of venture involves a lot of attributes—including a sharp eye, an aggressive temperament and a willingness to take risks. The risks involved in real estate are not always as readily quantifiable as they are in many other types of investments, and hence they can be especially easy to overlook.

INCOME POTENTIAL

The right investment property, generally bought for cash rather than on credit, can produce generous rental income that may be largely sheltered from federal income tax by writeoffs for things like depreciation. Some real estate limited partnerships are set up along these lines, with income-conscious investors in mind.

In general, however, any real estate investment for income requires much more evaluation, and involves a greater degree of risk, than alternatives such as U.S. government securities. People who rely on their assets for maximum income and safety may well view real estate investments cautiously unless they are especially knowledgeable.

RISKS AND
DRAWBACKS

Along with the opportunities it presents, each kind of real-estate investment involves its own set of risks and drawbacks. Most experts on the subject agree, for example, that some people are simply not temperamentally suited to be landlords, with all the costs and aggravations they must face in that role. You can avoid the need to deal with tenants by buying unimproved land—but an investment like that may offer little or no prospect of any income to help cover costs like taxes and interest. Financial advisers say it is best to be psychologically as well as financially comfortable with a given real estate proposition before you invest.

Many real estate investors use leverage as a central part of their strategy. With leverage, it is possible to build up large holdings over time using relatively small amounts of money. But such edifices can be vulnerable to destruction by a single wrong move or miscalculation. Some of the richest real estate investors have gone broke in these circumstances.

LIQUIDITY

Some real estate properties are the quintessential illiquid investment. For example, a piece of undeveloped land in a remote area may be virtually impossible to sell on short notice. If you own a property in a community or region whose economic fortunes decline, you may find few potential buyers when you wish to sell. Investment properties of any description rarely can be bought with the confident expectation that they can readily resold at any time.

Accordingly, most investment real estate is not a suitable place to put money you cannot afford to tie up for a fairly long period of time. Unexpected problems arising at properties you own also can put a strain on the liquidity of your overall financial position.

TAX ADVANTAGES
AND DISADVANTAGES

The tax advantages of investment real estate are numerous and legendary. In fact, many tax shelters are set up based on real estate investments. Out-of-pocket costs like interest and property tax, maintenance and upkeep all are normally deductible on a property owner's tax return in the year in which they are paid. So is depreciation, which does not come out of the owner's cash flow.

If all goes well, owners of investment real estate hope eventually to realize profits at attractive long-term capital gains rates. Under the tax laws prevailing at the time this book was written, 60 cents of every dollar of long-term capital gains was exempt from federal tax.

All the alluring tax benefits that go with real estate cannot be assumed to be carved in stone, however. In 1984 legislation, for example, Congress tightened the rules somewhat covering how rapidly a real estate property could be depreciated for tax purposes.

Though some real estate investments may be impracticable or legally out of bounds for individual retirement accounts and Keogh plans, alternatives such as a real estate investment partnership may be a candidate for such a tax-favored savings program. When picking an investment for such programs, it obviously makes sense to steer clear of vehicles that already offer significant tax advantages that would be negated in an IRA or Keogh account.

REAL ESTATE INVESTMENT TRUSTS

DESCRIPTION

Real estate as an investment has traditionally suffered from two significant drawbacks. It is generally inaccessible to people with only a few hundred or a few thousand dollars to invest. And most real estate investments are illiquid, especially if an owner is forced to sell on short notice.

To counter these problems, Wall Street came up with the idea of the real estate investment trust—an enterprise that gathers together money from many investors and invests that money in real estate properties, or real estate loans, or both. An REIT resembles a mutual fund, in that it holds a diversified portfolio of investments, and distributes substantially all the income it earns in the form of dividends to those shareholders. Unlike mutual funds, however, REITs are not "open-ended"—that is, they don't constantly stand ready to issue new shares to investors. Instead, their shares trade like other common stocks on stock exchanges or in the over-the-counter market.

In their early days, REITS enjoyed a period of heady popularity, as a means for small investors to participate in the big-time commercial real estate market. In the recession of 1973-74, however, the prices of their stocks took a drastic drop as construction loans to builders and some other investments the REITS had made went sour. Many of the trusts didn't survive the debacle.

Those that did faced a long, difficult journey back to respectability in the investment world. By the mid-1980s, many of them had made considerable progress on that path. Many REITs today concentrate on owning quality commercial properties, rather than making risky loans. When they do wish to lend, they may opt to invest in government-backed mortgage securities.

Whatever their merits, it should be borne in mind that REITs do not constitute a direct investment in real estate. Rather, their shares represent part ownership of a real estate investment enterprise. Decisions about how, when and where to invest in real estate are made by the management of the company. The results an REIT investor achieves depend on the dividend income the management is able to earn for them, and on what value the market places on the shares of the REIT.

A relatively new form of REIT is the "self-liquidating" trust. This type of trust states its intention, at the time it is organized, of selling all its holdings, distributing the proceeds to shareholders, and dissolving at a specified future date, or possibly earlier at the discretion of management.

HOW AND WHERE TO GET
INFORMATION AND INVEST

Any good broker should be able to provide you with ample information on a sampling of actively traded REITs. You may, in fact, be able to find a broker that specializes in following the industry. Detailed information on individual REITs, including recent reports to shareholders, can be obtained by telephoning or writing the REITs themselves. Some brokerage firms and stock-market investment advisory services publish periodic reports on the state of the industry and given trusts within the industry.

COSTS OF BUYING,
OWNING AND SELLING

The costs of buying and selling REIT shares are the same as those associated with common stocks—commissions to any broker through whom you buy and sell, plus the time and money you expend on research in choosing and monitoring the progress of your investment. A great attraction of REITs is the low minimum investment involved. For an REIT selling at $15 a share, a "round lot" of 100 shares would cost you just $1,500, plus commissions. If you so choose, you can buy in even smaller "odd lot" quantities of shares. The exact minimum ante, of course, depends on the going market price of the REIT you select at the time you want to buy.

CAPITAL GAINS
POTENTIAL

In the past, there have been opportunities at times for significant capital gains in REITs. Some investors have made large profits speculating in REITs that emerged successfully from periods of trouble. A good many other investors who speculated in troubled REITs in the 1970s suffered losses.

A more conservative investor can buy shares of a healthy REIT hoping for long-term appreciation in the price of its stock stemming from several factors—future dividend increases as a result of higher rents received from properties the REIT owns; a rise in the market value of those properties; or simply increased enthusiasm among stock-market investors for REIT shares.

Some investors monitor REITs regularly, looking for instances in which a trust's share price is low relative to the apparent value of the properties it owns. They operate on the theory that sooner or later this value will be recognized in some way, whether by the market itself or through a development such as a takeover offer from some other company.

If a given REIT invests heavily in mortgages or mortgage-backed securities rather than property, the chances of significant capital gains may be less. But with any type of REIT, you may use automatic reinvestment of your dividends to seek long-term growth of your assets through compounding.

INCOME POTENTIAL

The income REITs can earn from interest on loans or rents on their properties can produce generous dividend yields for their shareholders. Like mutual funds, but unlike most other kinds of companies, REITs don't have to pay taxes themselves on the money they make, as long as they meet certain standards. One of those requirements is that they pass practically all their earnings through to their shareholders each year.

Unlike many other high-yielding investments, REITs may offer the hope of dividend increases as time passes. This may be an important consideration for inflation-conscious investors. However, REITs as a class are riskier propositions than Treasury securities, insured bank deposits and many other types of income-producing vehicles.

Their share prices fluctuate over time. And there is always the risk that an individual deal in which they are involved, or the whole real estate market in general, can run into stormy weather. Some REITs may be suitable investments for relatively conservative investors. But people whose highest priority is absolute safety may wish to look elsewhere.

RISKS AND
DRAWBACKS

People who owned REITs in the early 1970s know a lot about risk. The stock price of one large REIT fell from $26 in 1972 to $2 in 1974, and the annual dividend, which had been more than $2 a share, fell to as low as 13 cents. As it happened, that particular REIT survived, and later thrived once more. But others fell by the wayside.

Most of today's REITs are considered much sounder operations, run by experienced real estate people who are determined never to run the risk of another big shakeout. As one executive told Business Week magazine, "We've learned our lessons." Nevertheless, it should be borne in mind by any would-be REIT investor that the real estate business always involves some risks.

In the mid-1980s, REIT managements had to compete for good deals with investment partnerships, which attracted large amounts of money from investors because of the special tax advantages they could offer. Some experts feared that these partnerships were bidding prices of many properties up to unrealistic, and perhaps even dangerous, levels.

Some real estate investors prefer to invest on their own, seeking to gain the maximum return on their money and grow wealthy through the use of leverage, tax advantages and their own expertise. If your dreams and ambitions are on that kind of scale, REITs are probably not the most likely way to realize them.

LIQUIDITY

Liquidity is a prime selling point of REITs. It might take you months to find the right house, for example, and months to sell it again later. By contrast, REIT shares can normally be bought and sold in a matter of a few minutes, whenever you choose, with a telephone call or a visit to a broker's office. They provide investors who have a feel for the national economy with a means to move their money in and out of the real estate market whenever they believe the time is right to do so.

TAX ADVANTAGES
AND DISADVANTAGES

In order to gain the benefits that come with an REIT, you must forego many of the most attractive tax advantages of real-estate investing. As an investor in REITs, you get no direct access to deductions for depreciation, mortgage interest, or operating costs.

Although they cannot serve as pure tax shelters, REITs can have some reasonably attractive tax characteristics. Dividends you receive from an REIT normally are taxed as ordinary income. But in some cases, part of that dividend may be classified as a return of capital, which is not subject to current taxes. If a REIT sells a property at a profit, it may pass the profit through to shareholders as a long-term capital gains distribution.

When you sell REIT shares, any profit you realize is taxable under the standard capital gains rules. In computing profits or losses in these circumstances, you must reduce your original "cost basis" by the amount of any dividends received that were classified as a return of capital.

REITs, like stocks and mutual fund shares, are eligible for use in individual retirement accounts, Keogh plans and other tax-favored savings programs.

PERSONAL RESIDENCES

DESCRIPTION

One of the biggest and most important investments many Americans make is the purchase of a home in which to live. It is often the first financial goal young people set for themselves when they enter the working world. That goes today not just for married people starting families, but for many single people whose thoughts turn to their financial futures. As people's working lives progress, their homes typically continue to play a central role in their financial plans up to and including their plans for retirement.

Enthusiasm over homes has intensified over the past 20 years, during which inflation sent the price of the average American home from around $25,000 in the early 1960s to the neighborhood of $100,000 in the mid-1980s. People who bought houses because they simply wanted a place to live suddenly found themselves sitting on "investments" that attested to their shrewdness in personal finance. After a long career on Wall Street, a retired brokerage house executive confessed recently that his home in a New York City suburb was the best investment he had ever made.

Homes weren't always considered a sure-fire way to increase one's wealth. A couple of generations ago, it was common practice for homeowners to figure that their homes lost a certain amount of their resale value each year because they were gradually wearing out, like a car or any other consumer durable item.

There is no guarantee that house prices will keep rising in the future the way they have in the recent past. They can go up only as much as the means available to new homebuyers permits. It is possible to imagine, for example, that the relatively small number of people born in this country in the late 1960s and early 1970s will lead to a dropoff in the housing market some time in the 1990s, when that "baby bust" generation reaches typical home-buying age.

But at this writing the demand for home ownership in this country is far from fulfilled. Homes were desirable purchases long before they were regarded as investments comparable to stocks and bonds. They meet a basic need—shelter—and they can supply pride of ownership far beyond what any financial piece of paper can offer.

In today's market a personal residence, out of choice or of financial necessity, may well not be a separate single-family dwelling, but rather a condominium or cooperative apartment. The special benefits and risks that come with condos and co-ops are discussed in a separate section of this chapter.

HOW AND WHERE TO GET INFORMATION AND INVEST

The problem of matching up would-be buyers with homes they find appealing and affordable provides gainful employment to many people in the United States. They work as housing developers; real estate brokers in local communities; relocation counsellors for employers; and in government agencies that seek to help meet the public's housing needs. Any and all of these may serve as good sources of information in your search for a home. However, information from a builder who is eager to sell or a broker working on commission from the seller should be considered in the light of its source's financial motivations.

Perhaps even more so than in most other types of investments, your own initiative and energy can serve as a valuable tool in shopping for a house. Before or after making the rounds of a given community with a real estate broker, it may be rewarding or at least instructive to check classified ads, community billboards and other listing places for homes offered for sale "by owner."

Word of mouth can play a great part in any given housing market. Many a desirable house finds a buyer before it ever gets advertised or listed with a broker. Some enterprising people, in fact, shop for homes that aren't for sale. When they spot a property that looks ideal, they present themselves, by letter or in person, to the present owner, expressing their interest as potential buyers when and if the owner decides to sell.

COSTS OF BUYING, OWNING AND SELLING

For most homeowners, costs are a perpetual problem from the moment they make their first tentative foray into the market. By the simple law of supply and demand, the entry cost into the housing market seems to sit forever at the margin of great financial pain. When you look at, say, an $80,000 house today, you may yearn for the world of, say, the late 1940s, when families formed after World War II were shopping for $8,000 properties. But in that day, $8,000 looked to many buyers like a commitment they couldn't possibly meet.

Once the preliminary contracts are signed, the clock starts running on many other costs. Buyers must usually begin shelling out right away for building and pest inspections, legal advice, mortgage application fees, home insurance, and so forth. Maintenance and repair costs can arise, predictably and unpredictably, from the moment you move in.

When it comes time to sell and move onward and upward, or just onward, you are faced with more costs. If you choose to sell through a broker, you can expect to pay a commission of 6 percent or possibly more of the price you get, unless you can find an agent who will represent you for less or a flat fee. If you choose to try to sell on your own, you still have outlays for advertising and other expenses, in addition to giving yourself a demanding assignment.

CAPITAL GAINS POTENTIAL

Homes have earned, over many years, a reputation as an exceptionally good vehicle for achieving long-term growth of your assets. With a good property, purchased with the help of a fixed mortgage at a reasonable interest rate, homeowners have several forces working in their favor.

First of all, there has been housing inflation, which frequently has exceeded the overall rise in the cost of living. Secondly, there is leverage—the fact that you may put up only, say, 20 percent of the purchase price, but enjoy 100 percent of any appreciation in the value of your home. Furthermore, even if a given house does not rise significantly in value, you can slowly but steadily build your equity in it with the portion of your mortgage payments that goes to reduce the amount of the loan outstanding.

As desirable as these circumstances may be, however, growth of capital stemming from an investment in your own home can be less flexible in its uses than, say, gains from investment properties, stocks, or other investments. It may be difficult to unlock for other uses, unless you are able and willing to take on additional debt in the form of a new or additional mortgage. In an effort to address this problem, many banks and financial services firms have begun to offer home equity loan accounts, which are described in a separate section.

In strong housing markets, you can seek relatively short-term profits in single-family housing units, perhaps hoping to leverage your way to owning and occupying a dwelling you could never otherwise afford. Such endeavors require a good deal of energy, a reasonable amount of expertise, and a willingness to take risk beyond what the conservative homebuyer is usually exposed to.

INCOME POTENTIAL

Homes normally create a significant drain on their owners' cash flow, even in cases where the purchase can be made without a large and expensive mortgage. They may, of course, be rented out to others at rates that cover much or all of the owner's after-tax outlays for interest, maintenance, insurance and other costs. But people who buy homes with the intention of renting to others generally have capital gains in mind as their primary investment objective.

Some experts argue that single-family homes are a less reliable source of income than many other real-estate alternatives. Older people who want to achieve maximum after-tax income from their assets sometimes consider selling homes they own to relatives (for example, grown children) and leasing them back, in order to have more flexible use of those assets. Such strategies require careful evaluation, and in many cases the advice of a professional adviser, before they are undertaken.

RISKS AND
DRAWBACKS

The range of potential problems and drawbacks that can come with home ownership is almost limitless. Insurance can, and often must, be obtained to protect yourself against the most common calamities, such as fire. But it is left for homeowners themselves to bear the considerable responsibilities of keeping up with the ravages that time and nature almost inevitably inflict on a house.

A savings bond, bank certificate or other financial investment may repose quietly in your possession for many years without giving you a moment's trouble. A house, you may confidently expect, will make constant demands on your time and your pocketbook. The trouble is worth the reward, both psychic and financial, for most people but perhaps not for everybody.

LIQUIDITY

As the foregoing discussion indicates, houses are generally illiquid investments. Surprise problems with a foundation, a roof, or anything in between indeed can put a strain on the overall liquidity of your finances. Most people view their commitments to them in terms of years.

TAX ADVANTAGES
AND DISADVANTAGES

Government policies have long sought to encourage home ownership in this country through attractive tax benefits. These start with deductibility on your federal income tax return of all mortgage interest and property taxes paid.

When you sell a house at a profit, you realize a standard capital gain. But any federal tax obligation on this gain can be deferred indefinitely if you purchase a house of equal or greater worth within time limits set by the tax rules. People over 55 are also eligible for a one-time exemption, up to specified limits, on profits realized from the sale of a principal residence.

Certain people who use a portion of their homes for business may qualify for a "home-office" deduction. This is subject to stringent rules and limitations. Otherwise, homeowners cannot avail themselves of some tax breaks available on investment property, such as deducting ordinary utility and maintenance costs, and depreciation, on their tax returns.

You cannot use an IRA, Keogh plan or similar tax-favored savings program to invest in a personal residence. But homeownership can be a central element in your overall preparation, financial and otherwise, for retirement.

CONDOMINIUMS AND COOPERATIVE APARTMENTS

DESCRIPTION

In the 1960s and 1970s, as home prices soared and suitable places to build new single-family houses began to grow scarcer in some areas of the country, an old idea rose to new popularity in the United States. In new and existing multi-family housing, residents were given the opportunity to invest in a form of shared ownership.

The most common setup of this type is the condominium, in which individual investors buy apartments or town houses and a share of common facilities in the building or complex, such as hallways, grounds, driveways, and possibly a swimming pool or clubhouse. Condos, as they came to be called, found a market with single people, small families, retirees—a broad range of the population. They offered the financial and tax benefits of property ownership to people who could not afford a desirable single-family house or did not want the burden of upkeep that comes with ownership of a single-family home.

A variation on the condo theme is the cooperative apartment building. In this arrangement, investors do not buy an individual apartment or apartments. Rather, they buy shares in the property as a whole, which carry the right to use of a designated part of the property. Because this arrangement can have some important legal and personal complications, it has been less popular to date in this country than condominiums, except in a few areas like New York City.

For the young family, condos can provide the answer to the problem of affordable housing. They are also common as second, or vacation homes (see the separate section of this chapter on that subject). They also may provide a means for someone operating with relatively little capital to invest in real estate in quest of rental income and capital gains.

In the last two decades, condos as a class of real estate investments have had some dramatic ups and downs. Periodic "condo crazes" in many parts of the country have led to overbuilding, and resulting gluts in which many units stood unoccupied. But they appear to have established for themselves a prominent and lasting place in the U.S. real estate market.

HOW AND WHERE TO GET
INFORMATION AND INVEST

Developers of condominiums generally are not shy about advertising their projects. If you inquire at the manager's or sales office of any building or complex that looks appealing to you, you may obtain literature and a chance to inspect a variety of housing units that are actually for sale, or models of units scheduled to be built. The more aggressive the sales pitch you receive, the more carefully you should evaluate it. As with other types of real estate investments, the best deals as a rule sell themselves quickly by word of mouth or are snapped up in short order by people who actively shop the market.

Shopping for a condo involves checking on many details that are not involved in buying a single-family home. Since you are buying not just an apartment or town house, but also an interest in the entire complex, you must assess the physical, legal and financial condition of the complex as a whole in addition to the unit or units that interest you.

COSTS OF BUYING,
OWNING AND SELLING

As with most real estate investments, costs of buying, owning and selling are an important consideration in condominiums. With a condo, you avoid the need to buy a lawn mower, ladder and other paraphernalia of single-family home ownership. But in lieu of those costs, you must pay regular fees for upkeep of common facilities and other expenses. Before committing yourself to a purchase, it makes sense to check what this fee amounts to, whether it can rise in the future and by how much, and under what circumstances the condo association may and is likely to levy special assessments on owners.

CAPITAL GAINS
POTENTIAL

A carefully chosen, well-timed investment in a condominium can produce handsome rewards in the form of capital gains when you sell. But condos involve all the standard risks of real estate investing, plus some special ones of their own. If you buy in an area where the potential for overbuilding exists, for example, you may have trouble realizing much of a profit offering your used unit for sale at a time when many new units are going begging, and developers are having trouble finding buyers even for units they offer to construct to the precise specifications of would-be owners.

One strategy used by many real estate investors in quest of large profits is to acquire an existing property, residential or otherwise, with rental tenants, and convert it to condo or co-op status. This kind of venture usually requires a lot of time, effort and expertise, and is best embarked on only with good legal advice or a thorough knowledge of applicable laws, local zoning restrictions and similar matters.

INCOME POTENTIAL

Some investors buy condos with the intention not of living in them, but of renting them out to others. The rental income they receive may go a long way toward covering their costs of ownership while they wait for hoped-for capital gains. It may even produce net after-tax income for the investor.

But income from a condo is not usually as reliable as, say, the yield on a Treasury bill or money market fund. At times it may be hard to find a new tenant to replace a departing one. In a market where the supply of rental housing substantially exceeds demand from would-be tenants, there may be downward pressure on rents generally. People who want or need steady, maximum income from their assets might well consider other alternatives.

RISKS AND
DRAWBACKS

In return for the convenience and other attractions they offer, condominiums and cooperative apartments have drawbacks that may be significant for some people. A given complex may have a long list of rules that, say, ban pets, specify the color of paint on the exterior of all dwellings, and impose a wide variety of other restrictions on the way residents live their lives.

If you buy a condo to live in, you must be prepared to abide by these restrictions and submit to future collective decisions the association makes. This kind of situation is perfectly acceptable to some people, but borders on the intolerable for others.

If you buy a condo as an investment, planning to rent it out, you will be responsible to see that your property and tenants comply with the rules. Some condominium complexes have eligibility requirements for tenants that may limit your potential rental market. Some condo associations and co-op buildings do not permit rentals at all.

Investing in a condo in real estate has some parallels to buying stocks through an investment club. The success of the venture, and the return you realize on your investment, may depend to a great deal on whether you and your fellow investors are a congenial or contentious group.

LIQUIDITY

A home of any kind is a relatively illiquid investment. When you want to sell, market conditions may be such that buyers are lined up at the door the moment you put it up for sale. Or they may be such that it is difficult to find a buyer, even at what you consider a sacrifice price, for weeks or months.

Condos and co-ops may present some extra liquidity problems. The rules governing a given complex or building may specify that you can sell only to buyers approved by the other owners. They may limit the methods you can use to advertise your unit for sale. Any and all such restrictions should be thoroughly understood before you invest in the first place. As the Real Estate Investing Letter, a newsletter on real estate matters, put it, "Condo investors need to buy with the idea of selling in mind."

TAX ADVANTAGES
AND DISADVANTAGES

One primary appeal of condos and co-ops is the fact that they make the tax advantages of home ownership available to apartment and townhouse dwellers. Most renters cannot take tax deductions on any of their monthly payments. But owners of condos and co-ops can deduct mortgage interest and property taxes they pay on their federal income tax returns. They may also be able to deduct that portion of their monthly maintenance or dues payments that goes to pay interest or taxes for the complex or building as a whole. If you invest in a condo as a property to rent out to others, you may also gain access to deductions for other maintenance and upkeep costs, as well as depreciation.

Under normal circumstances, you cannot buy a condo or co-op for an individual retirement account, Keogh plan or other tax-favored savings program. The IRA and Keogh rules prohibit borrowing in such plans. Even in the absence of such strictures, it would make little sense to use a condo for an IRA or Keogh, since doing so would nullify the current tax advantages condos and co-ops offer taxable investors.

HOME EQUITY LOAN ACCOUNTS

DESCRIPTION

In the past couple of decades, many homeowners in the United States have enjoyed the satisfaction of watching the value of their investment increase sometimes dramatically in a relatively short time. Inflation might have eroded the value of the cash in their wallets, the money in their checking accounts and some of their other investments. But the typical home or other real estate investment worked out very well as an inflation "hedge," and often produced a nice real return over and above the inflation rate.

While they congratulated themselves on their sagacity in owning real estate, however, many homeowners also felt a sense of frustration. Sure, their net-worth calculations looked nice with all that extra home equity in the assets column, but otherwise what good did the paper profits do them? Their choices for cashing in on it were limited at best.

They could sell their houses and translate their profits into cash. That was fine if the circumstances were right—say, on retirement, when they planned to move to a less expensive place anyway. If the circumstances weren't right, they would most likely need to plow all the proceeds back into some other dwelling, whose price would presumably be inflated as well.

They could stay put and take out a second mortgage. But second mortgages are limited in flexibility, and their interest rates are usually quite high. As the years passed, the regular required payments on a second mortgage might wind up consuming a considerable share of the money raised.

So a lot of homeowners wound up sitting on a lot of paper wealth. In recent years, brokerage firms, banks and other financial institutions noticed that enormous untapped source of credit, and saw an opportunity. They introduced a vehicle known as a home equity loan account.

These accounts are open lines of credit, granted to the homeowner once the residence has been appraised and the homeowner approved as a credit risk, that allow the homeowner to borrow against the equity in the home. The money is available at the homeowner's discretion, for any purpose. The credit line can usually be tapped instantly by means of a credit card, checkbook or telephone request.

Lenders ventured into this market with fairly cautious rules. The credit line maximum is typically only a percentage of the owner's total equity, and the house itself stands as collateral. Under these circumstances, some lenders in home equity accounts may offer attractive interest rates and very flexible arrangements for repayment of the loan.

Home equity accounts have the potential for use in financing such things as improvements to the house itself, other real estate investments, or children's college tuition. They usually make less sense, however, as a way of financing consumer purchases.

The significant costs of opening a home equity loan account militate against their use for minor or frivolous purposes. More important, anyone who opens such an account should always bear in mind that should things go wrong, the lender could foreclose on the house. People who know or suspect that they might have trouble managing easily available credit should approach these accounts very warily.

HOW AND WHERE TO GET
INFORMATION AND INVEST

At the time this book was written, home equity loan accounts were spreading in many areas of the country, but were not available in all states. A few inquiries at financial institutions where you live should provide you with basic information on whether these accounts are available to you, and what restrictions, if any, regulatory authorities in your state put on them. In addition to owners of single-family dwellings, people with condominiums, cooperative apartments, and some other types of real estate investments may find these accounts available.

The process of opening an account may involve several steps— completion of an application, an appraisal of your home, and a check of your credit status by the lender. Once the account is open, you decide when and how much of your available credit line to borrow, and what to use the money for. One limitation on this: If the account is with a brokerage firm, you are not permitted to use the borrowed money to buy securities.

COSTS OF BUYING, OWNING AND SELLING

The costs of opening a home equity loan account are usually considerable. For that reason, it may be unwise to go through the process unless you expect to use the money for some specific purpose during the term of the account. There will normally be an appraiser's fee, a fee for processing the application and other charges for opening the account. These may be separate or bundled together, but in any case they will probably add up to at least 2 percent of the total amount of the credit line.

If the amount of the credit line is $75,000, that works out to $1,500 up front. Some lenders charge substantially more. Lenders may also collect a small annual maintenance charge, typically in the $20 to $40 range, while the account is open, whether you have borrowed from your credit line or not.

Another cost that can't be forgotten, of course, is the interest on any money you borrow. The interest rate is normally not fixed, but fluctuates depending on market conditions. Before opening an account, and whenever you tap it, you should have a clear understanding of how the interest rate is calculated.

At the outset, it may also be wise to consider the possibility that your application to open an account will be turned down. Before applying, you should inquire what charges, if any, you will incur for processing of the application if you are refused.

CAPITAL GAINS POTENTIAL

A home equity loan account may be used to increase your leverage in the investment in your property. For example, you might tap it to build an addition or otherwise improve the property, increasing its market value without putting in a significant additional amount of your own capital. Extra leverage, of course, heightens your risk if you run into other financial problems or if, for whatever reason, the market value of your house declines.

INCOME POTENTIAL

There may well be some benefits from a home equity loan account for people who seek to get the greatest possible income from their assets. For instance, the money from such an account might be used to pay off an existing high-interest mortgage. In general, however, conservative investors whose primary concern is conservation of their assets should give careful consideration to the risks involved before opening an account.

RISKS AND DRAWBACKS

Home equity loan accounts are best suited for people who are good managers of credit and have substantial assets other than their homes. These accounts can give such people access to a relatively inexpensive source of credit without disrupting their other financial plans. If you have limited other means at your disposal, however, tapping the equity in your home can pose considerable risks. Events beyond your control, such as a layoff from your job or an unexpected decline in the market value of your house, could suddenly put you in a tight spot. However well-heeled you are, when you borrow against a home equity loan account, you are exposing what is probably one of your most prized assets, your house, to at least some degree of extra risk.

LIQUIDITY

As described above, a home equity loan account is designed to make a frozen asset—your stake in a piece of real estate property—liquid. In addition, the account may offer you several advantages in managing your cash flow and overall debt load. For example, if you want to pay off an outstanding balance on a home equity loan account at any time, you can ordinarily do so without incurring any prepayment penalty or other cost. Conversely, some accounts allow you to make regular repayments of interest only. With a conventional mortgage, regular payments represent interest and a part of the principal of the loan.

Nevertheless, there are occasions that could arise when a home equity loan could put a severe strain on your liquidity. When you sell a property, for instance, the loan balance—interest and principal—comes immediately due, just as it does with a mortgage. The account may also specify that the lender can "call" an outstanding loan at certain times, requiring full payment on relatively short notice.

TAX ADVANTAGES
AND DISADVANTAGES

Interest payments made to home equity lenders, like mortgage interest payments, are tax deductible for the year in which you make them. Fees paid to obtain a loan or line of credit are also normally deductible. Especially for people in high tax brackets, this reduces the burden of the effective cost of borrowing through a home equity loan account.

VACATION HOMES

DESCRIPTION

A cottage at the seashore, a condominium at a ski resort, a pillared mansion in some sunny clime or a modest cabin in the woods—such second, or vacation homes, are the dream of many Americans. Vacation homes are often thought of as luxury consumer purchases. But for people who have the means and inclination to take on the trouble, expenses, responsibilities and risks involved, vacation homes can be fruitful investments as well.

Like any other direct real estate investment, a vacation home offers the hope of long-term appreciation in value, and accordingly may serve as a "hedge" against inflation. If you choose to rent out your property to others at least part of the time, it can produce rental income. In addition, vacation homes can offer their own special set of tax benefits.

In recent years the condominium principle has been applied extensively in the construction of second, or vacation homes. The benefits and risks involved in condominiums are discussed in a separate chapter.

In many areas of the country, developers and sellers of vacation property have taken the condominium idea one step further by selling *time shares* in condos. With these you buy, say, a $1/52$ interest in a condo that entitles you to use it for a week each year. If you don't wish to vacation in the same place at the same time every year, you may be able to swap your right of occupancy for someone else's in another place.

On paper at least, this may be an attractive alternative to paying out rent or motel or hotel bills every time you take a vacation. But in practice, time shares have their limitations, and may be subject to abuses by unscrupulous promoters. Ownership of time-share properties is so diffuse that any single owner may have little say in the way the property is managed and maintained.

HOW AND WHERE TO GET
INFORMATION AND INVEST

The ideal vacation home investment is made in a place you already know and like. The area may be far from your principal residence, but it is a valuable aid in picking a good property to know the local market and have a sense of going real estate values in that market. Friends, classified advertisements, or established and reputable real estate brokers may be able to steer you toward attractive properties in any area that interests you. Direct mail and telephone solicitations from salespeople you do not know, for properties in places with which you are unfamiliar, should be regarded very cautiously.

COSTS OF BUYING,
OWNING AND SELLING

Naturally, the purchase price of a well-built, comfortable place with a breathtaking view in a popular vacation spot is going to be high. Furthermore, once you have bought, you will face the many, sometimes unpredictable costs that go with direct ownership of any property—taxes, maintenance, insurance, payments on any loans you take out to finance the purchase, and so forth. When you sell, a broker's commission and other fees may take a big bite out of your proceeds.

CAPITAL GAINS
POTENTIAL

A lot of people have made a lot of profits investing in vacation properties. It can be an exhilarating vision indeed to imagine yourself buying property in a place that has not yet been discovered, and then watching its value soar as funseekers from all over discover the area's charms.

There are some special risks involved, however, in seeking profits from vacation properties. To be sure, some vacation spots seem to be eternally popular. But others that are considered "paradise" today may be shunned by future vacationers. One way that this can happen, perversely, is through real estate development itself. When a once-virgin vista is covered with condominiums and shopping centers, people may be dismayed to find that the place where they used to "get away from it all" now has all that they want to get away from.

Values of vacation homes also may be more sensitive to the ups and downs of the economy than other forms of real estate such as primary residences. Renters play an important role in many vacation-area real estate markets, and if the general state of the economy is poor at any given time, the supply of renters can contract significantly. Beyond that, owners who are in economic straits may be quick to dump vacation properties, while holding out to the very last before they put their primary residences on the market.

INCOME POTENTIAL

If you choose to rent out, rather than occupy, a vacation home you own, especially in its peak season, the resulting income may go a long way toward covering your costs of ownership. This may mean giving up some of the psychic income you derive from enjoying the place yourself. On the other hand, it makes a great deal of sense to seek rental income in this way if, for example, a given vacation home is a year-round dwelling that you intend some day to use as your retirement home. The net annual return you realize from renting out a vacation home may be greatly enhanced by tax breaks (see p. 317).

RISKS AND
DRAWBACKS

For many people, it may be difficult to assess with dispassion the investment merits of a vacation home. From an emotional standpoint, it is quite a different process from, say, choosing between a banker's acceptance and a Treasury bill. If you plan to spend a lot of time at the place, in fact, the investment merits are only a partial element in the decision to buy or not to buy, and later to sell or not to sell.

Upkeep can be a continuous and costly problem with vacation homes. Renters, as a general rule, do not take care of property to the extent that owners do. Even if they are conscientious about keeping a place clean and repairing damage they cause (as not all renters are), short-term occupants generally have no incentive to take any action to prevent or correct long-term maintenance problems that arise.

If a property is unoccupied for any period of time, it tends to become especially vulnerable to villainous forces like rot, pests and vandalism.

You can, and many owners of vacation homes do, retain representatives to care for a vacation home in your absence. If you do, this adds to your cost of ownership.

Investors in vacation homes may be well aware of these pitfalls and problems before they buy. If they aren't, chances are they will quickly perceive them afterward. This knowledge does not deter a lot of people from proceeding eagerly with investments in vacation homes.

LIQUIDITY

Vacation homes tend to be very illiquid investments. They may be very hard to sell on short notice, especially if a lot of other property owners nearby also want to sell. There may be exceptions to this general rule with the right property, in the right area, at the right time. But it normally makes sense to consider a vacation home a long-term investment, unsuitable for money you may want or need any time in the near future for other purposes.

TAX ADVANTAGES
AND DISADVANTAGES

Vacation homes may offer many attractive tax advantages, both short- and long-term. It is conceivable that some of these advantages will be reduced or eliminated in the future—a possibility to be borne in mind when you are considering making a purchase.

Mortgage interest and real estate taxes are in all cases deductible on your tax return for the year in which you pay them. Other expenses are not, if you keep the property only for your personal use. If you rent it out some of the time, however, proportional amounts of costs like maintenance, insurance and even depreciation may be deductible.

If you rent it out all of the time, or nearly all of the time (current tax laws and rulings should be checked on the time limitations), you may even be able to deduct costs that exceed the rent received. In these circumstances, you have, in effect, your own personal tax shelter.

Vacation homes, like most other direct real estate investments, are excluded by law from individual retirement accounts, Keogh plans and other tax-favored savings programs. But they can play a role in your other financial and personal preparation for retirement.

REPURCHASE AGREEMENTS

DESCRIPTION

Suppose a friend of yours owns a fistful of U.S. government securities and, for one reason or another, is short of cash. The friend wants or needs to raise cash for a short period of time, but does not wish to sell any of those securities outright. You step up and volunteer to buy some of the securities from the friend on Date X with the express agreement that the friend will buy them back, say, a month later on Date Y. For the use of your money, the friend agrees to pay a higher price for the securities on Date Y than you paid on Date X.

This two-part transaction is known as a repurchase agreement. In practice, the use of "repos" is most common at the highest levels of the banking system and among securities dealers and investing institutions. Until recently, few individuals knew, or had any great need to know, what a repo was.

Since the advent of money market mutual funds, however, many individuals have found themselves investing indirectly in repos if a money fund whose shares they own has some of them in its portfolio, as many of them do. In the early 1980s, banks and savings institutions dealing with the public developed the idea of the "retail repo," an account with a life of a few days to just under three months that was generally advertised as "backed by U.S. government securities." No matter who sells them, retail repos are not covered by federal deposit insurance.

A repo can be seen as a form of loan, the interest on which is the difference between the price the "lender" pays to buy on Date X and the price received on Date Y. Its actual legal status may be much more complicated than that. But assuming that the repurchase agreement is completed as agreed upon, one party has effectively employed it to gain the use of another party's money in return for a payment resembling interest.

Some money market funds, including those with a "government securities only" policy, make a regular practice of buying repos—that is, act as lenders receiving interest. Others do not, preferring to confine themselves to direct ownership of Treasury bills.

The practice of selling retail repos to customers of banks and savings institutions has dwindled with the introduction of federally insured money market deposit accounts and other new vehicles. However, it is possible that other forms of repo investments of concern to individuals will appear in the future. In all cases, an investor in repos should be confident about the security that underlies the transaction (no problem, presumably, with Treasury bills) and also about the financial soundness of the seller of the repo.

HOW AND WHERE TO GET
INFORMATION AND INVEST

If you contemplate investing in a money market mutual fund that is authorized to invest in repos, it is advisable to understand how they work and what policies the fund follows in regard to them. Basic information should be included in the fund's prospectus, and the fund should be able to answer any further questions you might have by mail or telephone.

As of the time that this book was written, retail repos, with their lack of federal deposit insurance, appeared to have little appeal in comparison with the alternative insured accounts available at banks and savings institutions. Should a repo proposition be offered to you by any such institution, it merits wary evaluation. Before investing, you should certainly have a clear understanding of your claim on the account and the underlying security should the seller of the repo run into trouble.

COSTS OF BUYING,
OWNING AND SELLING

When you invest in a money fund that buys repos, your costs will normally be the same as those involved in any other money fund— namely, the annual management fee and expense charges collected by the fund's sponsors from its assets. With any other kind of repo arrangement that might arise, no significant fees to the seller would appear to have any economic justification.

CAPITAL GAINS
POTENTIAL

Repos are normally transacted between two parties, both of which seek to avoid capital gains and the attendant risk of capital losses. Though there is normally a price difference between the original sale and the repurchase, the amount of the difference is treated as interest rather than a capital gain.

INCOME POTENTIAL

Lenders such as money market mutual funds sometimes regard repos as an appealing way to invest for income. With repos, they may be able to keep the maturity of their portfolios very short, so as to retain maximum flexibility in their investment strategy in times when they are concerned about the outlook for interest rates generally. Often, these funds can obtain a higher yield for their shareholders than funds investing all their assets directly in Treasury bills.

When the buyer and seller, at the time a repo is originated, set a stated price for the closing of the transaction, they also effectively set a fixed interest rate for a period in which other open-market interest rates are subject to day-by-day, hour-by-hour and even minute-by-minute fluctuations.

RISKS AND
DRAWBACKS

For several reasons, including the sophistication required to operate and negotiate in the money markets, direct investment in large-denomination repurchase agreements on Treasury securities is not a practical proposition for the typical individual investor. After the failure of some small government securities dealers in the early 1980s, complex questions were raised about the legal status of repos and the rights they conveyed on all the parties involved.

In the case of one small insolvent bank that had sold about $350,000 in retail repos, the Federal Deposit Insurance Corp. held that the Treasury securities backing the repos were assets that should be used to pay off the bank's depositors in insured accounts, not the holders of the repos. However, the ruling was based on a technicality involving the way the repos were set up by that particular bank.

Repos bought by a prudent, well-managed money market fund from government securities dealers of recognized reputation are considered highly safe. However, investors who are especially meticulous about minimizing risk may choose to stick with funds that invest directly in Treasury bills or, for that matter, they may opt to buy Treasuries directly for themselves.

LIQUIDITY

In day-to-day practice, repos of the kind normally bought by money funds are considered very liquid. In fact, the money funds and other institutions who deal in them may use them as a tool to maintain a high degree of flexibility and liquidity in their money management strategies. The government-guaranteed Treasury securities that stand behind them contribute to this liquidity.

However, repos themselves are not guaranteed by the government. So in times of strain in the credit markets, the liquidity of a given repo may be significantly affected by the way it is legally written, by court rulings, and-or by the financial soundness and integrity of the individual or institution that originated it.

TAX ADVANTAGES
AND DISADVANTAGES

Earnings from investments in repurchase agreements are normally treated as interest, taxable at ordinary-income rates. Barring some future court ruling or change in the tax laws, investors in repos on government securities do not have access to the exemption from state and local taxes enjoyed by investors on interest received directly from Treasury securities. Money funds that invest in repos may be a candidate for an individual retirement account, Keogh plan, or other tax-favored savings program.

SALARY REDUCTION PLANS

DESCRIPTION

Although individual retirement accounts and Keogh plans may have received more publicity, another type of tax-favored vehicle for retirement savings and investment began to attract increasing interest in the early and mid-1980s. It is known in the pension and financial planning business as a 401(k) plan, after the section of the Internal Revenue Code that authorizes it. Since 401(k) is neither a catchy nor an informative name, sponsors increasingly have come to refer to these arrangements as "deferred payment," "salary redirection" or "salary reduction" plans.

In many ways, a salary reduction plan resembles a standard pension plan. To be eligible to participate in one, you must work for an employer that has chosen to make it available to employees. If you are interested in participating in such a plan, but none is offered at your place of work, your employer may be responsive to requests that one be established. Business owners usually consult a qualified adviser before organizing a plan, to ensure that it is set up in compliance with the rules.

What differentiates a salary reduction plan from an ordinary pension plan is the fact that employees may elect to take contributions to a 401(k) plan in lieu of a portion of their salary—hence the phrase "salary reduction." This, of course, has the effect of diminishing participants' take-home pay, but it also correspondingly reduces their current income for federal tax purposes. Once a contribution is invested, it goes to work earning interest, dividends or capital gains that compound tax-free until you make withdrawals, usually on retirement. Thus, a contribution to a salary reduction plan works very much like a contribution to an IRA or Keogh plan.

Furthermore, a 401(k) may offer attractive features not available with an IRA. For one thing, an employer may offer to kick in a matching contribution of, say, 50 cents for every dollar you invest. For another, you may be able to put more in a salary reduction plan each year than the $2,000 IRA maximum. A 1983 survey by Towers, Perrin, Foster Crosby, a management consulting firm, found that typical higher-paid employees were contributing 4.9 percent of their annual salaries, and lower-paid employees 3.4 percent.

Like other employer pension plans, a salary reduction plan does not prevent you from having an IRA as well. But many workers have current commitments that limit the amounts they can put into deferred savings plans, and so may need to choose between a 401(k) contribution or an IRA contribution in any given year. Making this choice usually requires a careful consideration of the pros and cons of each, in the light of your individual circumstances.

HOW AND WHERE TO GET
INFORMATION AND INVEST

To determine whether you can and want to take part in a salary reduction plan, the first place to inquire is the personnel or employee benefits department of the company or other entity where you work. By the mid-1980s, many large companies offered such plans. Some others, however, were holding off awaiting establishment of more specific rules and guidelines from the Internal Revenue Service.

Pending that word from the IRS, specific provisions of existing 401(k) plans varied widely from employer to employer. For example, one company might offer you only the right to invest your money in its stock. Another's plan might give you a series of mutual funds or similar pools with a variety of investment strategies from which to choose and the right to switch from one fund to another at specified intervals.

Once you have determined that are eligible and wish to take part, arrangements for contributions may be made through some convenient arrangement such as regular payroll deductions. If you are on the point of taking a new job, it may be appropriate in the course of your inquiries about fringe benefits to ask whether your prospective employer offers a 401(k) plan.

COSTS OF BUYING,
OWNING AND SELLING

Costs should not be a significant factor in a salary reduction plan. However, in evaluating your employer's individual plan, it may make sense to check whether any administrative fees are imposed, say, if you choose to move your money from one investment fund to another within the plan.

CAPITAL GAINS
POTENTIAL

Beyond its current tax advantages, the purpose of a salary reduction plan is obviously to build a nest egg for your future. This may achieved to a considerable extent through capital gains on investments made in your plan, as well as long-term growth of your money through tax-free compounding.

If your plan requires you to invest your money in shares of the employer's common stock, the question of the potential for long-term appreciation in the stock's price becomes very important. Fortunately, in many cases employees are in a pretty good position to evaluate their employers' prospects. Through their own observation and conversations with fellow employees, they may acquire a good feeling for the company's chances of future success.

INCOME POTENTIAL

As the name implies, salary reduction plans don't do anything to enhance the current income flowing into your household. They diminish it. The extent to which you contribute to a plan and whether you take part in it at all depends on your ability and willingness to sacrifice a certain amount in your current standard of living. But the tax advantages lessen this sacrifice, by lowering your current tax bill. Matching contributions by your employer, if any, may also make a plan so attractive that you may conclude you cannot afford to pass it up.

RISKS AND
DRAWBACKS

With all the tax-favored savings programs available today, it is possible to build up, in a relatively short period of years, a substantial retirement nest egg. That's all to the good, most any financial adviser would say—especially if your retirement is a good distance away, you can benefit greatly by doing as much saving and preparation for it now as possible.

There is, however, an element of risk involved in committing a large portion of you assets to long-term, tax-favored vehicles. Implicit in such investments is a measure of faith and optimism about the long-term future of the U.S. economy. Furthermore, you will eventually want to begin withdrawing money from your savings plans, incurring taxes as you do. If that day is far off in the future, there is no way of knowing for sure what tax rates will prevail in this country then.

Salary reduction plans can present a few potential pitfalls for unwary participants. Before you sign up to take part, financial experts suggest that you ask whether it will have any effect on other, separate pension or profit-sharing benefits you might be eligible to receive from your employer. It also makes sense to determine whether, and how, it may affect your Social Security standing.

LIQUIDITY

Like IRAs and Keogh plans, salary reduction plans are basically illiquid, long-term investments. With 401(k) plans, however, there are some liquidity pluses and minuses that set them apart from those other types of accounts.

If you are willing to pay the penalties involved, you can make early withdrawals at any time from an IRA or Keogh plan. This option is not generally available with salary reduction plans. However, early withdrawals from a 401(k) plan may be permitted, without penalty, in case of "hardship." Just what constitutes a hardship depends on how your employer defines it, and on any future definitions issued by the Internal Revenue Service. In a 401(k), you may be permitted to borrow money from the plan—a practice not permitted with IRAs and Keoghs.

If you leave your job, you may take the money accumulated in a 401(k) plan as a taxable distribution. Alternatively, you may "roll over" the proceeds into a similar plan offered by a new employer or into a rollover individual retirement account, a special form of IRA to which the annual $2,000 contribution limit does not apply.

TAX ADVANTAGES
AND DISADVANTAGES

Salary reduction plans give you the alluring benefits of reduced current federal income tax liabilities, and tax-free compounding of your savings as they grow. Most financial advisers agree that these breaks make a strong case for participating, if you have access to a salary reduction plan, to as great an extent as you can afford. They say this principle may hold even if the state or locality in which you live—as some do—taxes 401(k) contributions as though you received them as ordinary income.

Eventually, of course, you will have to pay taxes on all money you withdraw. Periodic distributions are taxed at ordinary income rates. However, if you take your proceeds in a lump sum, you may spread it out for tax purposes over a period of 10 years. At the time this book was written, this "forward averaging" option was not available to people taking lump-sum distributions from IRAs.

TAX SHELTERS

DESCRIPTION

The phrase *tax shelter* can have many meanings in the financial world. Brokers and bankers use it in their promotional material to describe individual retirement accounts. Dealers in tax-exempt municipal bonds may trumpet their wares as tax shelters. And certainly, an investment in a home may provide you and your family with shelter from taxes as well as from the elements.

This chapter, however, discusses tax shelters under a narrower definition—investments specifically designed to give individual investors access to tax writeoffs that exist in certain businesses such as real estate and oil and gas. Most are set up as limited partnerships. The typical customer for one of these programs is an individual in a high tax bracket who is looking for some legal way to reduce his or her annual income tax bill. In some cases, tax shelter investments offer these investors the prospect of being able to deduct much or all of the money they put up, or even more than they put up, on their tax returns for the year in which they invest.

There is a legal basis for this type of investment. Government tax policies set up to encourage investment in businesses like energy exploration or cattle breeding provide for liberal tax breaks as an incentive. After a diligent and timely search, you may find a good selection of attractive, sound deals available.

However, there can be many pitfalls in tax shelter investing. The field has attracted more than its share of unscrupulous promoters engaging in outright fraud. In one case, a grand jury charged that sponsors of a program that purported to be engaging in tax-advantaged maneuvers in government securities never conducted any such transactions. Other sponsors have put together programs offering huge writeoffs that the government contends are based on sham transactions or unrealistic valuation of properties. At the time this book was written, the Internal Revenue Service was mounting an intensive campaign against what it deemed "abusive" tax shelters. The Tax Reform Act of 1984 closed many loopholes on which exotic forms of tax shelters were based.

No matter what kind of tax shelter you are considering, and no matter how reputable the firm that is offering it, experts in the field say it is essential to assess the investment merits, as well as the tax attractions, of the deal. As a general rule, the IRS recognizes as legitimate tax shelters only those ventures that take authentic business risks. In other words, a tax shelter should be evaluated not solely on the basis of the initial tax breaks it affords, but on the ultimate after-tax return you can reasonably expect or hope to realize from it, and on the degree of risk involved in trying to realize this return.

HOW AND WHERE TO GET
INFORMATION AND INVEST

It is axiomatic in the financial world that the general public never gets word of some of the best tax shelter propositions. These plums are supposedly snapped up by investment professionals as soon as they become available. However, since there is such great public demand for this kind of investment nowadays, there are still plenty of places to shop for them.

A banker may be able to point you in the right direction, and chances are that any good broker or other financial services firm can offer you information and a choice of investment products. There is a growing number of newsletters and advisory firms that specialize in reporting on and evaluating tax shelters.

Some tax shelter promoters advertise heavily and use direct telephone marketing, notably in the latter stages of the year when potential customers are most conscious of tax matters. Programs you learn about in this way may not automatically be bad deals, but they should be evaluated with great caution.

Furthermore, experts generally agree that the end of the year is an inopportune time to consider tax shelters. For one thing, the pressure of a tax deadline makes it difficult, if not impossible, to evaluate an investment carefully on its overall merits. For another, it may not be possible to realize the full tax benefits available for a given year if you invest in December.

COSTS OF BUYING,
OWNING AND SELLING

The sales charges and promoter's fees in tax shelters can be large, and are often an important consideration in evaluating a tax shelter. It may, in fact, take a detailed study of the prospectus or other descriptive material just to determine what your costs, actual and potential, may be.

So-called "private" tax shelters are normally restricted to investors who can meet lofty income and net worth standards, and may require a minimum investment of $50,000 or more. "Public" programs, registered with the Securities and Exchange Commission, also typically set minimum financial standards for investors, but they tend to be much lower. The minimum investment in these vehicles may be as low as $5,000.

If you are investing significant amounts, or are considering a tax shelter operating in a business with which you are unfamiliar, advisers say it is wise to have a disinterested professional such as an accountant examine a deal before you proceed. This usually will involve paying a fee to the evaluator, but the cost may turn out to be a small price to pay for the value received.

CAPITAL GAINS
POTENTIAL

In addition to offering attractive tax deductions in the early years, many tax shelters are set up with the aim of realizing income or profits in a form that is attractive for tax purposes—such as a long-term capital gain. For example, in a real estate program there is normally the hope that properties owned by the partnership can ultimately be sold for a price higher than their original cost.

However, investors rarely consider tax shelters with the sole objective of capital gains. A shelter that carries large up-front costs and promises only tax breaks but no profits in the early years of its operation is obviously not a likely place to look for speculative, short-term gains.

INCOME POTENTIAL

Essentially, tax shelters are for people who want to lower their taxable income, not increase it. Because of the risks they usually involve, they are unsuitable in general for investors who want or need maximum current income from their assets, as well as maximum safety of those assets.

However, some limited partnership programs, operating in fields such as real estate, are set up to produce relatively high current income from sources such as rents. This income may be partly, largely or even wholly sheltered from tax by accompanying writeoffs for such things as depreciation. On occasion, if a tax shelter plan goes wrong or you need to get out of it earlier than you planned, it can produce unwanted taxable income.

RISKS AND
DRAWBACKS

As the foregoing makes clear, tax shelters often involve significant investment risks. In addition, claiming deductions from a tax shelter may greatly increase the chances that the Internal Revenue Service will audit your return. The audit may focus on the shelter itself, or it may cover every line on every page of the return. For this reason, investors in tax shelters must be prepared to go through the rigors and inconvenience of the audit process.

Many tax shelters use methods that have the effect of deferring tax liabilities, not eliminating them. Thus, if you invest in a shelter in any given year, it may well complicate your tax circumstances and planning in future years. With all the costs and problems they may pose, however, many investors plainly consider well-conceived tax shelters to be an attractive alternative to paying income taxes at top rates.

LIQUIDITY

Tax shelters are generally considered illiquid for several reasons. Some programs may offer no easy way for investors to withdraw from them before their scheduled dissolution date, perhaps 10 years after the original offering. In cases in which you are able to get your money out early, doing so may forfeit some or all of the original tax benefits and cause other tax problems. As a general rule, money you expect you might need on short notice should not be invested in tax shelters.

TAX ADVANTAGES
AND DISADVANTAGES

Tax advantages are obviously what make tax shelters tick. But they can present tax problems as well. For instance, the government has imposed what is known as the *alternative minimum tax* as a means of ensuring that large numbers of well-to-do people do not escape taxation entirely. If you derive large writeoffs and long-term capital gains from tax shelters and other investments, the situation may arise in which your tax liability is greater under the alternative minimum tax than it would be calculated the regular way. Because the method of computing the alternative minimum tax differs significantly from the standard procedure, it can turn your other tax planning upside down.

By their very nature, tax shelters are unsuitable for use in individual retirement accounts, Keogh plans and other savings programs that have their own, separate tax advantages.

U.S. GOVERNMENT SECURITIES

DESCRIPTION

There is no such thing as a risk-free investment. But among the countless entities around the world to which you can entrust your money, the government of the United States is generally considered the safest bet by far. This precept held true even in recent years when the government's deficit—the gap between amounts it took in and the amounts it spent—widened to what many experts considered a dangerous degree. Even if it couldn't balance its checkbook, the government still sat atop a huge and powerful economy. If it ever ran short of dollars, it only needed to turn to itself for a fresh supply.

Some investors don't trust any government. They put their faith instead in what they consider tangible assets, most notably gold. To the great majority of the world's investors, however, U.S. goverment securities represent the ultimate in quality.

Because the government is so big and so prone to borrowing, these securities are available in vast amounts. You can put your money in them for periods as short as a few days (in fact, a few seconds if you have the means and inclination) or periods as long as 20, 25, or nearly 30 years. You can invest as little as $25, in a savings bond, or millions at a clip.

Although they are all nominally interest-paying vehicles, the various types of government securities each have distinctive characteristics of their own. The main categories—Treasury bonds and notes, Treasury bills, government agency securities, and savings bonds—are discussed in separate sections of this chapter.

There are many mutual funds, unit trusts and other packaged pools of money that invest in government securities. Some are specifically set up to invest only in government securities.

HOW AND WHERE TO GET
INFORMATION AND INVEST

The government itself provides abundant information about its securities, and sells most of them directly to investors (see the separate sections that follow this chapter for specifics). Alternatively, you may learn about them and invest in them through a bank, broker or other financial services firm.

COSTS OF BUYING,
OWNING AND SELLING

When you invest in government securities directly through the government's distribution channels, you normally pay no commissions or other fees. When you buy and sell through a bank or broker, however, you are likely to be charged a fee, depending on the institution's policy and your standing as a customer.

When dealers in existing government securities handle buy and sell orders, they seek to cover their costs of operations and risk, and to make a profit, by maintaining a "spread." That is, the price at which they offer to buy is slightly lower than the price at which they stand ready to sell. Because the market for government securities is so large, with many competing dealers, spreads tend to be narrow.

CAPITAL GAINS
POTENTIAL

Government securities appeal primarily to investors interested in income and safety. Nevertheless, in times when interest rates are volatile, they can present the possibility of capital gains, and the attendant risk of losses. That is because prices of fixed-income securities rise when interest rates fall, and fall when interest rates rise.

Assume, for example, that you paid $100,000 for a long-term Treasury bond at a time when market conditions set the interest rate at 10 percent. Some time afterward, prevailing rates on long-term Treasury bonds drop to 8 percent. Since your bond now offers a more attractive rate than is available on new comparable bonds, investors will naturally bid the price up until the effective yield of the bond is in line with the rest of the market.

This valuation process goes on continuously, minute by minute, whenever the credit markets are operating. If you want or need to sell your bond at a time when interest rates are lower than they were when you bought it, you may thus realize a capital gain on your investment.

Dealer firms and speculators who trade actively in government securities regularly realize gains and losses. They are generally sophisticated operators, armed with large amounts of capital. Smaller but still venturesome investors who want to try to play this game can consider interest-rate futures.

INCOME POTENTIAL

Government securities are a prime candidate for any investor who wants a combination of current income and maximum safety. Because of their high credit standing, however, government securities usually offer somewhat lower yields than those available on debt securities of other issuers, even solid blue-chip corporations.

In assessing the relative risks and rewards of various debt securities, investors who live in states and localities that levy taxes on interest income should keep in mind that interest on government securities is exempt from state and local taxation.

RISKS AND
DRAWBACKS

As was pointed out above, the U.S. government securities are considered virtually free of credit risk. However, investors in them are exposed to interest-rate risk and inflation risk. For example, suppose you buy and Treasury bond maturing in 20 years carrying a 10 percent interest rate. At the time you buy, inflation is running at about 5 percent.

Soon afterward, inflation accelerates to 12 percent and interest rates on new Treasury bonds soar to 15 percent. The market value of your bond drops as rates rise. If you want or need to sell the bond immediately, you will incur a capital loss.

Of course, you can opt instead to hold the bond to maturity, at which time you will receive the face amount of your principal and avert a capital loss. But every year you keep it, earning 10 percent interest, while inflation is running at more than 10 percent, you are losing purchasing power.

It should also be pointed out here that, however much wisdom lies in a conservative investment strategy, it is possible to be too cautious with your money. If you can afford to take some risks with your capital, investments like stock or real estate may offer potential rewards much larger than you can expect from government securities. This may prove especially true in inflationary times.

LIQUIDITY

Most government securities (with the exception of savings bonds in the first few years after purchase) are highly liquid. In cases in which the government does not stand ready to redeem them for you, you can usually expect to find large numbers of willing buyers and sellers in the secondary market.

If you have a sum of money that you expect to need soon, but that you wish to keep at work in the interim, Treasury bills or a money market mutual fund specializing in short-term government securities may suit your needs very well.

TAX ADVANTAGES
AND DISADVANTAGES

Interest earned on government securities is subject to tax as ordinary income on your federal tax return. But it is exempt from state and local taxation. Capital gains and losses realized on government securities are subject to the standard capital-gains tax rules. Savings bonds have some special tax advantages.

A small number of Treasury bonds, known as "flower bonds," have a unique feature that can be useful in estate planning. These are bonds whose interest rates are below prevailing market levels, and thus whose market prices are below *par* or face value. Upon your death, however, the government will redeem them for the face amount, before their maturity date, for the purpose of payment of estate taxes.

Government notes, bonds and bills, or pooled investment vehicles like mutual funds that specialize in them, are suitable for use in individual retirement accounts, Keogh plans and other tax-favored savings programs. They may have great appeal for IRA and Keogh savers whose primary concern is safety. However, if you live in a state or city that levies high taxes on interest received, you should be aware that the benefit of government securities' exemption from state and local taxes may be nullified in a tax-deferred savings plan.

FEDERAL AGENCY SECURITIES

DESCRIPTION

As the other sections of this chapter indicate, when the government wants to raise money for most of its disparate needs, it does so by selling Treasury securities. However, there are a variety of specialized government agencies or government-sponsored organizations that raise capital by selling debt securities of their own. Typically, these are agencies created by Congress to serve a particular function, such as providing credit to home buyers or farmers.

The list includes well-known names like the Tennessee Valley Authority, and less familiar ones like the Federal Home Loan Banks, the Federal Farm Credit Banks, and the Inter-American Development Bank. Also part of this market are certain mortgage-backed securities sponsored or approved by government agencies and government-sponsored organizations.

"Agencies," as they are spoken of in Wall Street shorthand, are generally considered very safe securities with appeal for many income-conscious investors. However, it is important to realize that they are not Treasury securities, and that they may be different in several important respects from Treasury issues.

Some are backed by the full faith and credit of the United States, but others are not. In those cases, the guarantee of the issuing agency, and the implicit commitment of Congress, usually stands behind them. Unlike Treasury securities, some agency issues do not offer the advantage of exemption from state and local income taxes on their interest payments.

Furthermore, issuers do not generally sell agency securities directly to investors, the way the Treasury does with its securities. Rather, they sell them to investment bankers (typically a syndicate of banks and brokerage houses), who in turn sell them to investors in underwritings similar to those employed to issue new securities of corporations, states and municipalities.

To compensate for these differences, agencies traditionally offer somewhat higher yields than Treasury securities with comparable maturities. Agency issues are available in a wide range of maturities, from a few months to many years. Many mutual funds and other organized pools of money that pursue income as an objective—including money market funds—invest in agency securities.

HOW AND WHERE TO GET
INFORMATION AND INVEST

Brokers, bankers and other financial services firms can supply you with information on agency securities. After these issues are sold in initial underwritings, they are continuously traded in an active secondary market involving dealers and some stock exchanges. Financial publications and some general interest newspapers publish tables of available agency issues and their recent prices or bid-and-asked quotations.

Some study may be necessary to learn which of the available agency securities best suits your needs. A good, continuing relationship with a broker or banker is likely to be helpful in gaining access to the most attractive deals at reasonable cost.

COSTS OF BUYING,
OWNING AND SELLING

The market for federal agency securities has traditionally been dominated by institutions dealing in large amounts in each transaction. For that reason, individual investors may have to pick their spots carefully to avail themselves of an opportunity in an agency issue that is attractive in comparison to Treasury securities.

As with other types of securities, if you buy from a member of a syndicate handling a new issue of agencies, you normally have to pay no commission or other charge. The investment banker collects a fee from the issuer. In other transactions, however, you may incur charges in the form of a flat fee, a commission or a dealer's "spread" between buying and selling prices. This naturally has the effect of reducing the ultimate return on your investment.

Minimum investments may vary from as little as $1,000 to as much as $25,000, depending on the specific agency security you are interested in. As in other markets, buyers and sellers in small amounts often must expect to accept price concessions to make it worth a broker's time and trouble to handle your order.

CAPITAL GAINS
POTENTIAL

Prices of agency securities, like other interest-bearing investments, have a natural tendency to rise when interest rates fall, and to fall when interest rates rise. Thus, if you sell an agency issue before it matures, you may realize a capital gain if rates generally have fallen since the date of your purchase or a loss if rates have gone up. However, individual investors do not normally enter the agencies market in quest of capital gains as a primary objective.

INCOME POTENTIAL

Agency securities usually offer attractive income, with a presumed high degree of safety. Before investing in these issues, however, it makes sense to calculate the return you expect to get, after any and all transaction costs and taxes, and compare it with what is available in Treasury securities.

Also, if you are willing to tolerate some relatively small degree of risk, it may be useful to see how much yield you sacrifice under prevailing market conditions if you choose agency securities over competing vehicles such as top-rated corporate bonds. An institution such as a government securities mutual fund that can operate on a large scale in the credit markets may use agency securities to try to enhance its yield over competing funds that buy only Treasury issues.

RISKS AND
DRAWBACKS

Investors who make a practice of limiting risk to an absolute minimum may view agency securities that aren't backed by the full faith and credit of the federal government with some degree of caution. However, it seems unlikely in any but extreme circumstances that the government—including Congress, the Federal Reserve and other regulatory agencies—would sit idly by while a government-sponsored organization defaulted on its debts.

LIQUIDITY

As a rule, most individual investors should buy agency securities with the intention of holding them to maturity. Though you can sell them at any time in the secondary market, the costs of doing so, particularly in small amounts, may materially reduce the return you get from the investment. Since the selection of maturities in agency issues is so broad, you should be able to choose specific securities that fit your circumstances and minimize the possibility that you will need to sell out early.

TAX ADVANTAGES
AND DISADVANTAGES

Interest received from investments in federal agency securities is subject to taxation as ordinary income on your federal income tax return. In the case of some agency issues, the interest is exempt from state and local taxation; with others, it is not. Obviously, if there are significant state and local taxes on interest where you live, it makes sense to determine the precise tax status of a given agency security before you invest. If you buy and sell agencies in the secondary market, any profit or loss you realize is subject to the standard rules covering capital gains and losses.

Agency issues, or mutual funds that invest in them, may be a candidate for a conservatively managed individual retirement account, Keogh plan or other tax-favored savings program.

U.S. SAVINGS BONDS

DESCRIPTION

From the days of World War II, U.S. savings bonds long enjoyed a unique place in the spectrum of choices available to investors. They were safe, they were convenient, they encouraged long-term savings, and they were patriotic to boot. Maybe they were a bit stodgy and small-time for some big investors' tastes, but almost nobody had a bad word to say about savings bonds.

Then came the inflation, high interest rates, and economic upheaval of the 1970s and early 1980s, and the introduction of a wide range of new investment vehicles by private firms seeking to attract the saver's dollar. The savings bond program started to suffer and, patriotic or not, became something of an embarrassment. Financially, the bonds were simply not a good deal. All this became increasingly evident to the authorities in Washington, and they did something about it. As of Nov. 1, 1982, they subjected savings bonds to an overhaul.

The basic bond sold since then is the Series EE bond, which carries an interest rate that "floats" up and down based on a formula linked to interest rates on five-year Treasury notes. Series EE bonds are sold in seven denominations, ranging from $50 to $10,000. Their stated maturity is 10 years, although in the past the government has usually permitted extensions beyond that.

There are no periodic interest payments with EE bonds. Rather, the interest is produced by a gradual increase in the redemption value of a bond over time. When you buy EE bonds, you pay just half the face amount printed on the bond. Thus, the minimum investment is $25.

One other class of savings bonds, designated HH, is also available. HH bonds cannot be bought for cash, but they can be obtained in exchange for EE bonds and-or older series E bonds and savings notes known as "freedom shares." Unlike EE bonds, HH bonds pay current interest at a flat rate of 7.5 percent a year. In theory, the EE bonds are designed for accumulation of a nest egg, and the HH bonds for use when you want to start drawing current income on that nest egg, say, at retirement.

Before buying savings bonds, an investor should compare their merits with other modern interest-bearing vehicles such as Treasury bonds, notes and bills, money market funds and money market deposit accounts, and zero-coupon investments (which operate on an interest-by-appreciation principle similar to that of EE bonds). These may offer higher yields, with equal or only slightly reduced safety, although perhaps not all the tax advantages of savings bonds. Regardless of how you evaluate today's savings bonds, however, most investment experts readily agree that the new ones are an unquestionable improvement over the old.

HOW AND WHERE TO GET
INFORMATION AND INVEST

In its eagerness to promote sales of savings bonds, the government has made it very easy to get information on them and purchase them. EE bonds are available at banks and savings institutions, and in many cases through your employer as a sponsor of a payroll savings plan. EE bonds can be redeemed, or cashed in, at any time six months or more after their issue date at many banks and savings institutions.

HH bonds can be obtained in exchange for E, EE and freedom shares bonds through any Federal Reserve bank or branch, or at the Bureau of Public Debt, Washington, D.C. 20226. A request for such an exchange will usually by forwarded to these agencies by a bank or other institution that sells savings bonds. HH bonds also are redeemable from six months after their issue date at Federal Reserve banks and branches and the Bureau of Public Debt.

COSTS OF BUYING,
OWNING AND SELLING

There are no commissions, management fees or other investment costs associated with buying, owning and selling savings bonds. The main cost to consider in evaluating them is any "opportunity cost" you may effectively be paying by owning them instead of some other type of investment. Even the new, improved models of savings bonds available since 1982 offer only limited protection from inflation should it return to high levels like those that prevailed in the late 1970s.

CAPITAL GAINS
POTENTIAL

Though Series EE bonds are designed for investors seeking long-term growth of their savings, there is no potential for capital gains as such with savings bonds. Rather, EE bonds grow through an accumulation of interest that is neither paid out nor taxed until the bonds are redeemed for cash.

The rules that determine what that interest rate is are fairly complicated. Once a bond is held for five years, the rate is calculated by taking 85 percent of the average market yield of five-year Treasury notes during the life of the bond. The government has set a guaranteed floor rate of 7.5 percent in these circumstances. If the bond is redeemed before five years, however, the interest rate is lower. It is set at 5.5 percent after one year, rising in steps after that to the five-year cutoff point.

Buying savings bonds regularly through arrangements such as the payroll savings plan can provide some help in building a nest egg over the long term by making savings automatic. But this feature is by no means unique to savings bonds—"forced" savings are available with payroll withholding or any other regular commitment, whether it involves a credit union, an investment club, a salary reduction plan, premiums on a whole life insurance policy, or any other of a wide variety of investments.

INCOME POTENTIAL

Series EE bonds are not a logical place for money from which you want or need current income. In fact, they are not suited for any funds that you may need to lay your hands on in the near future, because their optimum payoff does not take effect until five years after their issue date.

Series HH bonds, on the other hand, do offer current income. Whether they are desirable for a given investor depends in part on a comparison of their fixed 7.5 percent interest rate with prevailing yields on other, alternative investments. In this comparison, questions of safety and tax advantages should also be taken into account.

RISKS AND
DRAWBACKS

The government advertises savings bonds as safe and indestructible. It guarantees both the principal and the interest earned, and promises to replace them without charge if they are, in the time-honored words, "lost, stolen, mutilated or destroyed." That does not necessarily mean, however, that they are risk-free. If you buy a Series EE bond, hold it for four years in which inflation runs at a very high rate, and then must redeem it to pay an unexpected bill, you may be very disappointed at the amount of purchasing-power punch your investment packs.

When you consider that the yield of a Series EE bond is based on 85 percent of the return offered over the same period by another government and government-guaranteed security, a five-year Treasury note, you might naturally conclude that the savings bond suffers from a built-in disadvantage. The two are not strictly identical, of course. For one thing, savings bonds are easier to buy and to accumulate in small amounts. Furthermore, the U.S. Treasury says it saves billions of dollars in interest each year by borrowing through the savings bond program rather than having to raise the same money in the open market. Thus, there is a value judgment in considering savings bonds that investors must make for themselves.

LIQUIDITY

Savings bonds are highly liquid, in the sense that you can easily claim your principal and interest after you have held them for specified periods of time. But for short periods of time after you buy them, their liquidity is not so good. For instance, if you want your money back only a year after buying an EE bond, the floating-rate interest formula does not apply—you receive just 5.5 percent interest on your original investment.

TAX ADVANTAGES
AND DISADVANTAGES

Savings bonds offer some appealing tax advantages. There is no federal income tax due on interest from a Series EE bond until you cash it in or it reaches final maturity, at which time you may be in either a higher or lower tax bracket than you are now. If you exchange them for HH bonds, the tax on the interest earned by the EE bonds is further deferred until you cash in the HH bonds.

Interest on HH bonds is subject to federal tax in the year it is received. However, both EE and HH bonds, like other Treasury securities, are exempt from state and local income taxes. This can be an important consideration if you live in a place where state or local government levies a high tax on interest income. Both EE and HH bonds are fair game for state and local estate taxes when you die. But they pass directly to a surviving co-owner or beneficiary, provided you have named one, without being subject to probate.

Savings bonds are not a logical candidate for individual retirement accounts, Keogh plans and other tax-deferred savings plans because they already have tax-deferral features of their own. They may, however, be used as a supplement to other savings and investment vehicles for retirement.

TREASURY BILLS

DESCRIPTION

When safety is the watchword, many investors the world over think immediately of Treasury bills. Like other securities backed by the full faith and credit of the U.S. government, they are regarded as the best credit risk around. If a default were to occur, it would come under extraordinary circumstances indeed. Furthermore, since they have very short lives, Treasury bills involve relatively little market risk in times of volatile interest rates.

T-bills, as they are known in Wall Street shorthand, are sold regularly by the Treasury through the 12 regional Federal Reserve Banks and the branch offices of those banks. Three-month and six-month bills are auctioned weekly, and 12-month bills every four weeks. They are available in minumum amounts of $10,000 and multiples of $5,000 above that point.

T-bills are a bellwether investment in the short-term money market. When their prevailing yields rise or fall, returns on other vehicles like large bank certificates of deposit and commerical paper tend to move in the same direction. Though large institutions and professional investors play a dominant role in the Treasury bills market, many individual investors buy them directly as well. For people who lack the $10,000 minimum ante or do not want to take the trouble to invest directly in bills, there is a wide selection of money market mutual funds that invest only in goverment securities. Some of these confine themselves strictly to T-bills.

HOW AND WHERE TO GET
INFORMATION AND INVEST

Federal Reserve banks and branches can provide you, on request, with detailed information about the procedures they set for investing in bills through their facilities. Bills can also be bought and sold through commercial banks, brokers and other financial services firms. Investment advisory services and newsletters frequently publish how-to articles on T-bills. A booklet, "Buying Treasury Securities at Federal Reserve Banks," is distributed at no charge by the Federal Reserve Bank of Richmond, Bank and Public Relations Department, P.O. Box 27622, Richmond, VA 23261.

Investors who wish to participate in T-bill auctions submit tenders, accompanied by a check in the appropriate amount, to their district Federal Reserve bank or branch, following procedures prescribed by the district bank. These tenders, which can be delivered in person or by mail, may be in either "competitive" or "non-competitive" form. Competitive tenders specify the terms at which the bidder is willing to buy, and may be rejected by the Treasury if it so chooses. Investors who submit non-competitive tenders, by contrast, agree to accept the average rates set at the auction. The Treasury, under usual practice, accepts all non-competitive tenders.

For all but the most sophisticated individual investors, the standard recommendation is to submit a non-competitive tender. If you put in a competitive bid, you run the risk of seeking too high a return, and having the bid rejected, or of aiming too low and getting a return below that accorded to non-competitive bidders.

Once your bid is accepted, you do not receive a T-bill certificate. Rather, the goverment establishes a computer account in the name you have specified, and sends you a receipt confirming the details of the transaction. Once such an account has been established, it can be used to arrange for automatic "rolling over" of your investment—buying new T-bills as existing ones mature.

COSTS OF BUYING, OWNING AND SELLING

When you buy T-bills directly from the goverment and redeem them at maturity, there is normally no commission or other fee to be paid. Banks and brokers, on the other hand, generally impose a flat fee for each transaction. No matter how you acquire a Treasury bill, you can expect to incur a fee and accept some price concession if you want to cash it before its maturity date. The goverment does not handle such transactions. So you will have to sell in the secondary market maintained by private financial institutions.

CAPITAL GAINS
POTENTIAL

Brokers and firms specializing in the huge goverment securities market may trade T-bills hour by hour or even minute by minute seeking profits on changing T-bill prices. It is not practicable, however, for individuals to try to take part in this high-risk, largely unregulated game. Most individual investors buy T-bills for income and to avoid risk.

Of course, if circumstances dictate that you want or need to sell a Treasury bill before it reaches maturity, you may well realize a capital gain if interest rates have fallen since you bought—or a loss if rates have risen.

INCOME POTENTIAL

Treasury bills appeal to most investors as a reliable source of generous income, particularly in times when interest rates are high. Like some other types of money market securities (and savings bonds, for that matter), they do not provide periodic, separate interest payments. Instead, they are sold at a discount from their face value, and are subsequently redeemed at full face value. The difference between the purchase and redemption prices constitutes the interest income you receive on your investment.

This system may be confusing to a newcomer. To see how the process works, consider this example: You submit a $10,000 non-competitive tender in good order for a given auction, accompanied by a certified check for $10,000. Your bid, for a 12-month bill, is accepted at the average rate for that auction of 10 percent. A few days later, you receive a $1,000 check from the government.

This looks like the payment of your interest, but it is not. It is a return of excess funds you submitted. In actuality, the government has sold you a T-bill for $9,000, promising to pay you back the $9,000 plus $1,000 in interest, 12 months hence. Thus, the actual investment yield on your T-bill is not 10 percent ($1,000 on $10,000) but 11.11 percent ($1,000 on $9,000). In evaluating returns available on Treasury bills, it is important to understand at all times whether a rate being mentioned is the theoretical *discount* rate (10 percent in this example) or the actual investment yield (11.11 percent in this example).

RISKS AND DRAWBACKS

When you invest in T-bills, you need not worry much about the safety of your money. In recent years, because the government has had to borrow so much, T-bills have provided generous returns. In the future, whenever interest rates or inflation worries are high, T-bills will probably offer attractive returns as well.

They are not, however, the perfect investment for all seasons and purposes. For people whose primary goal in investing is long-term growth, they do not offer the hope of profits taxed at attractive long-term rates. Since T-bills are short-term investments, they do not provide you with a means of "locking in" a known yield for long periods of time. Furthermore, income-conscious investors who are willing to take a small degree of credit risk can choose among a variety of interest-bearing vehicles that normally carry higher yields than T-bills do.

All that having been said, Treasury bills seem likely to retain a unique and valued place in the spectrum of Ameican investments for the foreseeable future. They answer a widespread demand for safety, income and flexibility in the process of managing money.

LIQUIDITY

With their standing as safe short-term investments, Treasury bills are considered highly liquid. Investors who buy them can choose to tie up their money for as little as three months, or less if they buy in the secondary market. In emergencies, T-bills can be sold in that same secondary market before maturity.

Ideally, however, T-bills should be bought with the intention of holding them until they come due, in order to minimize costs that can substantially reduce the return you get from them. Idle cash that may be needed on very short notice can be put instead, at very little increase in risk, in an insured money market deposit account, or a money market mutual fund that invests solely in government-guaranteed securities like T-bills.

TAX ADVANTAGES
AND DISADVANTAGES

Interest earned on Treasury bills is subject to federal income tax as ordinary income (so is any short-term capital gain realized on the sale of bills before they mature). But the interest is exempt by law from state and local income taxation. This is a clear-cut advantage for people who live in states or cities that levy significant taxes on interest income. On the other side of the coin, people who live in places where interest is not taxed at the state or local level may wish to bear in mind that yields on T-bills reflect to a certain extent a tax benefit that is of no use to them.

T-bills may be appropriate conservative investments for individual retirement accounts, Keogh plans and other tax-favored savings program, provided that it can be arranged for the custodian of such a plan to invest in them under attractive circumstances. One readily apparent way to do this is to put IRA or Keogh money in a money market mutual fund that invests in T-bills.

TREASURY BONDS AND NOTES

DESCRIPTION

Treasury bonds and notes may be thought of as longer-lived cousins of Treasury bills. Notes and bonds have many of the same attributes as bills—the safety of the full guarantee of the federal government and its power to collect taxes and regulate the money supply; a fairly generous and assured return; and direct availability at no commission cost from the government. Like Treasury bills in the short-term money market, Treasury bonds and notes are the trend-setting investments in the longer-term credit market.

For all the similarities, government bonds and notes have some significant differences from T-bills. The most obvious is their maturities. Notes may be offered with lives of two to 10 years, and bonds from 10-plus years up to as much as about 30 years. The longer the maturity, the more exposure a Treasury security has to the risks of inflation and interest-rate fluctuations. For this reason, Treasury bonds usually, but not always, offer higher yields than notes, and notes higher yields than bills.

Unlike bills, which are sold at a discount and redeemed at their face value, notes and bonds pay interest periodically (normally twice a year). The government does not maintain book-entry accounts with bonds and notes, but sells them for delivery to investors. You may choose to keep possession of them yourself or arrange for some financial services firm, such as a bank or broker, to hold them for you.

The minimum investment in notes and bonds is lower than for bills. In the case of notes with maturities of less than four years, it is usually $5,000. With other notes, and with bonds, it is just $1,000. This helps make them a practical possibility for almost all savers and investors.

HOW AND WHERE TO GET
INFORMATION AND INVEST

You may buy existing notes and bonds at any time, and in just about any maturity you wish, through a bank or broker. If you prefer to buy directly from the government, you will have to arrange to monitor information on forthcoming issues on your own. New two-year notes are generally sold monthly, and other notes and bonds at longer, and occasionally irregular, intervals.

General interest newspapers and financial publications often carry reports on these offerings. Or you may make inquiries at the Bureau of Public Debt, Washington, DC 20226, or at your district or branch of the Federal Reserve, which acts as the selling agent for Treasury securities. The Federal Reserve bank or branch may be willing to put you on a mailing list for information on future offerings of notes and bonds.

Once you have decided that you want to buy some of a given issue, you must submit a tender form, or a letter containing all the specific information required, to the Federal Reserve bank or branch. In this tender you state how much of the issue you want to buy, and you enclose a check or some other approved form of payment.

Sophisticated investors may submit a "competitive" tender, declaring the price they are willing to pay or the yield they are willing to accept, depending on which method is being used in a given auction. Competitive bidders run the risk of having their tenders rejected by the government, or alternatively of choosing a less favorable return than other bidders get at the same auction. To avoid these risks, you can submit a "non-competitive" bid, agreeing to accept the average price or yield that results from the auction. All non-competitive bids are normally accepted.

When a note or bond matures, you may present it to your Federal Reserve branch or bank in person or by mail for redemption. Alternatively, you may deliver it to the branch or bank as payment for some new Treasury security.

COSTS OF BUYING,
OWNING AND SELLING

Whenever you conduct a transaction involving Treasury bonds or notes directly through the government, you incur no costs other than any postage you may have to pay. Whenever you have a bank, broker or other financial services firm handle the transaction for you, you can expect to be charged a fee. If you want some institution to keep and safeguard any notes and bonds you own, it may impose a custodial charge.

CAPITAL GAINS
POTENTIAL

Because prices of existing Treasury bonds and notes fluctuate constantly with changes in credit conditions, moving in the opposite direction from interest rates, it is very likely that you will realize a capital gain or loss whenever you sell a bond or note in the secondary market before maturity. In times of volatile interest rates, this gain or loss can be considerable.

Professional government securities dealers regulary realize gains and losses as they buy and sell bonds and notes. It is impracticable for individual investors operating with relatively small amounts of capital even to try to outwit them in this high-risk game. If you have the means and inclination to speculate on future changes in the credit markets, you may consider options or futures on government securities.

Like other fixed-income securities, Treasury bonds and notes have important limitations for investors seeking long-term growth through capital appreciation. They cannot grow the way that, say, a stock or real estate investment can.

INCOME POTENTIAL

Treasury bonds and notes generally offer attractive, assured income for savers and investors who want to "lock in" a given yield for a period of years. People interested in short-term income may evaluate the possibility of buying in the secondary market a note or bond that is nearing maturity, and compare what they can earn that way against alternatives like Treasury bills.

When you submit a non-competitive bid in an auction of new Treasury securities, you cannot determine in advance the precise yield you will get. It is set by the results of the auction. However, except in especially turbulent periods, you can usually make a reasonably accurate guess.

With the extreme degree of safety from credit risk that they offer, Treasury bonds and notes often carry somewhat lower yields than many competing investments that are almost as safe. Before buying Treasury bonds and notes, enterprising investors may want to check such alternatives as government-backed mortgage securities to see if they offer any significant yield advantage.

RISKS AND DRAWBACKS

Even the longest Treasury bonds on the market are considered all but immune for the risk of default. But that cannot protect investors from interest-rate risk. If rates rise, all existing conventional bonds and notes must fall to make their yields to current buyers competitive with yields of newly issued bonds and notes. So you can lose some, even possibly a significant amount, of your original capital if you want or need to sell a note or bond before it matures.

Many investors are aware of that risk, of course, and so they buy bonds and notes only with money they can afford to keep tied up until the maturity date. Still, even these investors are not entirely *safe*. They are exposed to inflation risk. In theory, an "inflation premium" that takes the prospect of future inflation into account is built into the yield of a note or bond at any time when it is bought. But that premium covers only expected inflation, not unexpected inflation.

Sometimes investors around the world get quite emotional in their quest for quality and safety, and flights of money into Treasury securities can occur. When this kind of demand exists, it may have the effect of significantly lowering the returns available on Treasury securities from what is available in alternatives that are nearly as safe. In assessing Treasury securities at any given time, it may be worthwhile to consider whether there is a high fear element in the going price and whether you believe that fear is fully justified.

LIQUIDITY

Treasury bonds and notes are easy to buy under favorable terms even in small amounts. They offer a wide choice of maturities, and when they come due you can use them to "roll over" your money into new Treasury securities. They are highly marketable, since millions of investors have great faith in the issuer.

However, when you buy notes or bonds, you should be aware that the government does not stand ready to redeem them before maturity. If you want or need to sell a bond or note early, you must turn to a banker or broker for access to the secondary market. Selling this way may involve fees and accepting some price concession that effectively reduces the return you get on your investment.

TAX ADVANTAGES
AND DISADVANTAGES

As with most other government securities, interest on Treasury bonds and notes is subject to federal income tax but exempt from state and local income taxation. If you sell at a profit or loss, capital gains tax rules apply.

Their stature helps make bonds and notes good candidates for an individual retirement account, Keogh plan or other tax-favored savings program. One potentially attractive approach for IRA and Keogh investors, at only a small sacrifice in safety, is to buy a zero-coupon package backed by government securities.

UNIT TRUSTS

DESCRIPTION

Unit trusts are one of the most versatile investment vehicles available to the individual investor. They provide a means of investing small or, if you choose, not so small amounts of money in diversified portfolios of many types of securities. Unit trusts are similar in many ways to mutual funds, and in practice are often spoken of as "funds." But the two should not be confused. The portfolios of mutual funds are managed, with securities bought and sold whenever the fund managers feel it is appropriate. A mutual fund theoretically has an indefinite life.

Most types of unit trusts, on the other hand, have fixed portfolios that do not change once a trust has been assembled. For that reason, most trusts exist only until the securities in their portfolio mature, and are liquidated at that point. To keep a full supply of merchandise on their shelves, most sponsors of unit trusts constantly create new series to offer as existing ones approach maturity.

The first step a brokerage firm or other securities dealer takes in creating a trust is to buy a selection of a specific type of security—say, municipal bonds. Once it has assembled this package, it breaks it up into *units* typically priced at about $1,000 apiece, which it then offers for sale to the public.

In addition to municipal bonds, the unit trust concept has been used with corporate bonds, government securities, money market securities and other interest-bearing vehicles. It has also been employed with common stocks of electric and telephone utilities, and to set up "index funds" of stocks designed to duplicate the performance of a leading index of overall stock market trends. New uses for unit trusts will doubtless be devised in the future.

HOW AND WHERE TO GET
INFORMATION AND INVEST

Like mutual funds, unit trusts are sold by prospectus—a document that spells out the trust's methods and objectives, and all the legal and other details involved in investing in them. These prospectuses and other descriptive material are readily available from any good broker or other financial services firm.

Prospectuses for all types of financial products are notoriously ponderous reading, although efforts have been made in recent years to make them easier to pore through and understand. In any case, investors should give a prospectus a close inspection before committing their money. If any salient point in the document is unclear, it should be straightened out with the broker or other dealer involved before you invest.

COSTS OF BUYING, OWNING AND SELLING

Unit trusts generally carry sales charges that are imposed at the time you invest. Depending upon the sponsor and the type of securities a trust contains, the charge can range from less than 1 percent to 4 or 5 percent of the total amount invested. This expense, and any other fees as described in the prospectus, should be taken into account when you are considering the merits of a unit trust against some other vehicle with the same objectives.

Unit trusts, with their fixed portfolios, have an advantage over mutual funds in that their managers need not go to the trouble and expense of monitoring the markets and regularly buying and selling securities. Normally, this difference should be reflected in minimal management fees with unit trusts, as compared to the annual fees collected from a mutual fund's assets by fund sponsors.

The typical minimum investment in a unit trust is $1,000. If you are able to invest a considerably larger amount, the trust may provide for a volume discount on the sales charge.

CAPITAL GAINS POTENTIAL

Most unit trusts are designed with income-conscious investors in mind. The quest for capital gains usually involves timing decisions of the kind that are not possible with a fixed portfolio of securities. Nevertheless, there is usually some possibility of capital gains or losses with unit trusts, particularly if you sell before the trust reaches the point of maturity. That is because prices of fixed-income investments like municipal bonds fluctuate with changes in the prevailing level of interest rates. When rates rise, bond prices decline. When rates decline, bond prices rise.

You can normally sell or redeem units you own through the sponsoring firm at any time of your choosing. The price you receive is determined by the current market value of the securities in the portfolio, and thus could be higher or lower than your original purchase price.

If you invest in a unit trust that owns stocks, a capital gain or loss is likely regardless of when your investment is cashed in. If the trust invests, say, in utility or preferred stocks, capital gains may be incidental to the trust's investment goals. On the other hand, if the trust invests in an index-fund portfolio of stocks, capital gains are a primary objective.

INCOME POTENTIAL

Many individual investors choose unit trusts as income-producing vehicles. Trusts allow them a broad range of choices in regard to safety, maturity and other matters of primary concern to people looking for current yield from their assets. Like mutual funds, unit trusts seek to minimize risk by spreading their owners' money out over a diversified portfolio.

A sponsor of a trust may set a policy of paying out interest and-or dividend income monthly. This can be a convenient feature for investors who depend on a steady stream of income to meet their routine costs of living.

Though trusts have a fixed number of units, their sponsors still can, and usually do, offer reinvestment plans for dividends and interest. Participants in these plans may have the option, for example, of having their money automatically reinvested in a mutual fund or other vehicle run by the same sponsor. Reinvestment, of course, means forgoing current income.

RISKS AND
DRAWBACKS

Unit trusts are a passive investment, in some senses. Once their portfolios are set up, they typically have no managers on duty to try to take advantage of changing market conditions or financial developments affecting issuers.

With a unit trust, you do not have to pay the price of hiring such a manager. But you should be aware that the trust probably is not set up to realign its portfolio should the fortunes of any or all of its holdings take a turn for the worse. Diversity of holdings provides a cushion against this risk, but it still exists.

Furthermore, a fixed portfolio of, say, bonds, is automatically exposed to interest-rate risk. At a mutual fund, by contrast, managers may seek to shift the maturity of the portfolio and take other steps to try to maximize benefits in periods of falling interest rates, and minimize the damage when rates rise.

For particularly conservative investors, there are unit trusts that invest only in top-rated or government-guaranteed securities. There are short-term trusts with minimal exposure to interest-rate risks. There are also trusts that carry insurance on investments such as municipal bonds in their portfolios, or on the portfolio itself.

LIQUIDITY
Most sponsors of unit trusts say they plan to make markets in the units after they are sold, offering to buy and sell them whenever you are so inclined. They usually do not promise to do this under all circumstances, however. You also may have the choice of redeeming units through the trustee. It is worthwhile to verify beforehand what rights you legally have, and what options you can reasonably expect to have, should you choose to redeem early.

Several other choices may exist with unit trusts. Commonly, they offer dividend or interest reinvestment programs, and they may also permit exchanges at a low or no fee into other trusts or investment programs in the sponsor's product line.

All this adds up to reasonable liquidity. Still, unit trusts other than those specializing in short-term money market securities are probably not an ideal place for funds that you simply want to "park" for a short period of time, or that you could well need for other purposes in the near future. After all, it takes a certain amount of time for the trust just to earn you back what you pay up front in sales charges.

TAX ADVANTAGES
AND DISADVANTAGES

Gains, losses and investment income from unit trusts are generally subject to the same tax rules that apply to gains, losses and investment income from the type of securities owned by the trust. One popular area of concentration for trusts is municipal bonds, the interest income from which is exempt from federal income taxes. In most states and localities where interest income is heavily taxed, unit trusts have been developed with portfolios of local municipal bonds that are exempt from state and local taxes as well.

A good many unit trusts owning taxable investments have been formed with the explicit aim of appealing to savers for individual retirement accounts, Keogh plans, and other tax-deferred savings programs.

WARRANTS

DESCRIPTION

Let's suppose you have some money set aside for speculation in the stock market. You are leery of the costs of investing on margin, and you don't have the time you feel is necessary to trade options. In such a situation, you might investigate warrants.

In many respects, warrants closely resemble call options. They are securities that, in their most common form, entitle their owners to buy a specified amount of a given stock at a stated price. Unlike call options, which usually only have a few months of life, warrants typically run for periods of several years. They may even be specifically labeled "perpetual."

Warrants have some other important differences from calls. A call is created when one investor sells it to another. Warrants, by contrast, are issued by corporations, normally covering their own common stock or, in a few cases, other securities they have outstanding.

This implies a distinct difference in motivation on the part of the seller. Investors who sell calls hope those calls will expire worthless. But a corporation that issues warrants may well have a strong interest in seeing that its warrants don't expire worthless. Such an event naturally tends to tarnish a company's image in the investment world. So, in a case where a warrant is nearing the point of expiration without any exercise value, the company may take action to extend the life of the warrant. You can never assume that such things will happen, but they often do.

When you are shopping for a call option, you can find one on just about any well-known stock you can name. Warrants, on the other hand, are relatively scarce, and exist only for companies that at some point have chosen to sell them as part of their stategy for raising capital. Warrants often are created as a kind of throw-in on a larger financial deal. For example, a company may issue them as a "sweetener" when it is selling stock or bonds, in order to help it obtain an advantageous price or interest rate on those other securities.

In one recent period, Allan S. Lyons, an analyst who specializes in warrants, options and convertible securities for Value Line Inc., counted fewer than 100 warrant issues outstanding that he considered worth monitoring regularly. Still, he said, "worthwhile profit opportunities are found among them."

WARRANTS

HOW AND WHERE TO GET
INFORMATION AND INVEST

Warrants are traded, like stocks, on stock exchanges or in the over-the-counter market. Any good broker can provide you with information on them and buy and sell them for you. On occasion, you may obtain warrants automatically from a company when you invest in some other security issued by that company. For example, when a small, untested company is going public, it is a common practice to sell "units" consisting of a combination of stock and warrants. After the offering is completed, investors are normally able to buy and sell the common shares and warrants separately.

Some investment advisory services offer information and advice regarding warrants. You also may be able to find a broker who makes a specialty of following these securities.

COSTS OF BUYING,
OWNING AND SELLING

When you obtain newly issued warrants in connection with the purchase of some other security, there may be a temptation to think of them as a free extra. Actually, you are paying a price for them in the form of a higher price, or lower interest rate, for the other security than it would probably command without the presence of the warrants. If you buy and sell existing warrants through a broker, you can expect to pay commissions.

Furthermore, warrants, like options, have a time value. For this value, you must normally pay what is called a premium over the exercise value of the warrant at present. For example, suppose that Hypothetical Corp.'s stock is trading at $20. If you wish to buy Hypothetical warrants giving you the right to buy Hypothetical for $20 any time in the next two years, you may have to pay a price of, say, $7 per warrant. As time passes and the warrant draws nearer to its expiration date, the prevailing premium tends to shrink.

There is also an "opportunity" cost to consider with warrants, since they pay no dividends. When you invest in warrants, you give up the income your money could earn if it were put instead in some high-yielding security or bank account.

CAPITAL GAINS POTENTIAL

Warrants often provide a means of seeking large capital gains with a relatively small investment. Like call options, warrants give their owners a measure of leverage. To see how this works, consider a case in which Hypothetical Corp.'s stock is selling at $20. You buy a warrant giving you the right to buy Hypothetical stock at $25 any time in the next two years, paying $5 per warrant. Thus, your cost for 100 warrants is $500 excluding commissions.

In a year's time, Hypothetical stock rises in price to $40. The warrant has an exercise value of $15, and since it still has a year to run, it is trading at $20. In this instance, owners of Hypothetical have doubled the value of their investment, while your warrants have quadrupled.

Of course, to gain this kind of leverage, you take significant risk. If Hypothetical's stock remains stuck at, say, $23, from the day you buy its $25 warrants, you can lose your entire investment, while owners of the common stock who bought at $20 may reap a small profit, plus any dividends paid in the interim.

There is also the possibility of capital gains if you own any warrant at a time when its issuer changes its terms—say, by extending its expiration date to make it more attractive to investors.

INCOME POTENTIAL

Since they pay no dividends or interest, warrants are by their very nature unsuitable for investors who want or need maximum current income from their assets. Since they are typically speculative investments, they are not a logical choice for people whose primary concern is to preserve their capital.

RISKS AND DRAWBACKS

Sophisticated investors may use warrants in combination with other securities for hedging or other complex purposes. Otherwise, investing in warrants generally means taking moderate to high risks with your money. One special element of risk involves the warrant's premium. At the time you buy, other investors who are bullish on the warrant's underlying stock may have bid the price of warrant up to a very high premium. When you want to sell some time later, this general enthusiasm may have waned, and the premium may have contracted significantly.

Another peril may arise if the issuing company's circumstances change significantly—say, in some form or reorganization or merger. In these cases, new management may take great pains to see that owners of the company's stocks and bonds are satisfied, but may regard the existence of the warrants as nothing more than a nuisance. Warrant holders normally have no claim on a company other than the exercise provisions spelled out in the warrant, and no say in any corporate decisions that are made.

LIQUIDITY

Liquidity of warrants varies from issue to issue. Actively traded warrants of well-known issuers may be every bit as liquid as a common stock. Of course, a warrant that has no exercise value and expires is just about absolutely illiquid. You may be able to obtain a very small price for it from some other investor who is looking to cover a "short" position.

TAX ADVANTAGES
AND DISADVANTAGES

Capital gains and losses on warrants are taxed in the same manner as gains and losses in stocks and similar securities. Aggressive investors may choose to use warrants in a self-directed individual retirement account or other tax-favored savings plan. More conservative investors should probably look elsewhere for appropriate vehicles for their IRAs.

ZERO-COUPON INVESTMENTS

DESCRIPTION

One of the many innovations that appeared on the investment scene in the early 1980s was the zero-coupon bond—a fixed-income security that pays no current interest. The idea might seem paradoxical at first. "Zero" doesn't sound like an investment goal that anyone would want to shoot for. But it has proved to be highly popular with investors, most notably those who don't have to worry about current income taxes.

Novel as the concept may be, it actually works under a principle that is familiar to anyone who has ever bought a U.S. savings bond. A zero-coupon security is sold for a price below its face value, and produces earnings by rising to that face value at maturity.

Corporations may issue zero-coupon bonds directly, but the federal government does not. However, an institution such as a brokerage firm can create a package of zero-coupon investments by buying a block of interest-bearing government securities—say, Treasury bonds. It then sells investors receipts of varying maturities (from a few months to almost 30 years) that represent part interests in the package. When interest is paid on the underlying Treasury bonds, the broker does not pass it through to the zero-coupon owners, but uses it to pay off that portion of the receipts that are reaching maturity. The zeros with the longest maturity are paid off when the underlying bonds mature.

What is the point of such a complicated arrangement? First of all, zeroes provide a known return at a set future date on a saver's investment. They serve as an automatic compounding machine. With a conventional bond, the interest rate is known in advance, but its owners have no way of knowing what return they will be able to get in the future when they seek to reinvest the interest payments they receive.

The return available on a zero-coupon investment depends on the prevailing level of interest rates at the time you buy. At a rate of about 11 percent, an initial investment of about $5,000 would grow to $50,000 in 20 years.

Zeros are available on a variety of interest-bearing investments, including Treasury bonds, municipal bonds and bank certificates of deposit. Before buying them, investors should consider the safety and stability of both the firm offering to sell them and the issuer of the underlying security. They should also consider their tax circumstances.

HOW AND WHERE TO GET
INFORMATION AND INVEST

A growing number of financial institutions, such as brokerage firms, sell zero-coupon investments. They will probably be eager to provide you with information and examples of the zeros they have available. Zeros are also the subject of increasing attention in the financial and general interest press.

COSTS OF BUYING,
OWNING AND SELLING

If brokers sell zeros as part of, say, an underwriting of new municipal or corporate bonds, there may be no direct cost to you when you buy, since brokers receive compensation from the issuer in an underwriting. If you buy zeros in the secondary market (that is, from a broker buying and selling existing zeros) you can expect to pay a cost in the form of a commission or, more likely, in the form of a "spread" between the prices at which the broker buys and sells. If you sell a zero before its maturity date, similarly, you can expect to incur a cost in the form of this spread.

At the time you wish to buy, it might pay to do some comparison-shopping among several institutions for similar zero-coupon deals to minimize cost and maximize your return. The minimum investment to buy a zero is usually quite small—as low as a few hundred dollars.

CAPITAL GAINS
POTENTIAL

There is some theoretical capital gains potential in zero-coupon investments, since the value of all fixed-income securities rises and falls with the general level of interest rates. If you sell a zero-coupon investment before maturity, at a time when interest rates are significantly lower than they were when you bought, you might well realize a profit. But for most investors, this possibility is incidental to their purposes in buying and owning zeros. These securities are not designed as short-term trading vehicles for the average investor.

Rather, they are designed to provide growth in their owners' assets through the compounding of implied interest, in much the same manner as U.S. savings bonds. Financial advisers say they are especially well suited for cases in which an investor wants to accumulate a known sum for some anticipated event, such as retirement or a child's entering college.

INCOME POTENTIAL

Zero-coupon investments defer the payment of any proceeds until they are sold or mature. Thus, any zeros other than those with very short maturities are unsuitable for investors who want or need maximum current income from their assets.

RISKS AND
DRAWBACKS

If you own a zero-coupon investment backed by a security that yields taxable income, you must pay taxes each year on the amount of implied interest accrued, even though you do not actually receive any money. Several ways to get around this problem are discussed in the section on taxes below below.

Furthermore, it is important to understand that with some zeros you are investing your money with an intermediary, the packager of the zeros, not with the issuer of the underlying security. A zero-coupon receipt on a Treasury bond, for example, is not issued by the government but by the firm from which you buy it.

This does not necessarily imply any great risk. In the standard arrangement, the packager keeps the underlying Treasury bonds on deposit in an escrow account with a third party, such as a bank, and those Treasury bonds carry the usual federal guarantees covering both principal and interest. But any buyer of a zero should be aware of the distinction.

If you buy a zero from an uninsured issuer, you are exposed to credit risk just as if you owned an interest-paying bond of the same issuer. Furthermore, early redemption of such a security, under call provisions or for the issuer's sinking fund, can result in a change of the maturity status of your zero-coupon investment.

The risk of owning any security, no matter how safe, is magnified to some extent whenever all the earnings produced by that security are plowed back into it rather than paid out to you. If you own a bond directly that defaults 10 years after you bought it, you at least have 10 years of interest payments to show for your investment. If you own it under an arrangement like a zero under which no current payments are made, all your investment and proceeds remain tied up in it until you sell or the security matures.

LIQUIDITY

Zeros typically cannot be redeemed before their maturity date. If you need the money you have tied up in them, the firm from which you bought them or some other institution probably will be making a secondary market in them, and thus would be willing to buy them from you at a price somewhat below their paper worth at any given time.

As long as a secondary market is functioning, zeros thus have some degree of liquidity. But the typical investor who buys a zero intends to hold it to maturity. Hence, zeros are not a logical place for money that you reasonably expect to need before the maturity date.

TAX ADVANTAGES
AND DISADVANTAGES

As stated above, zeros present a potential problem for taxable investors. Though they pay no current interest, the tax rules treat them just as though they did, and you must pay taxes each year on the implied interest out of your other current funds. A zero backed by a municipal bond does not carry this obligation, however, because interest on such a bond is not subject to federal income tax. If there is state or local taxation of interest where you live, you may be able to find a municipal-bond zero that is exempt from these taxes as well.

Furthermore, you can dodge the tax problem by buying zeros other than municipal-bond ones for an individual retirement account, Keogh plan, or other tax-deferred savings plan. Many financial experts consider zeros an ideal vehicle for IRAs and similar programs. They also frequently recommend them for situations in which you can legally arrange for their implied interest to be charged to a dependent such as a child whose income is not large enough to incur a tax obligation, or who is in a low tax bracket.

THE INVESTOR'S ANNUAL: 1984

CONTENTS FOR THE INVESTOR'S ANNUAL: 1984

HOW TO READ THE STOCK TABLES

Just as cooks use recipes and travelers use road maps, serious investors learn early on how to read stock tables to glean a great deal of information in a short time. Because of varying space requirements and other factors, the tables to which an investor has access may differ somewhat in format from one newspaper or financial publication to another. But the annual tables that follow in this book are typical of the breed.

Reading from left to right, the table begins with the name of the company in question—in most cases, abbreviated to save space. The abbreviation, it should be noted, is not the same as the one- to four-letter "ticker symbol" by which a stock is identified on exchange tickers and in many computerized investment information services.

After the name may appear a single letter (a notation explained in the footnotes at the end of the table) and/or a number, which is the dividend rate per share. The first full column of figures gives the number of shares of the stock, in hundreds, traded during the year. Next comes the price-earnings ratio—the latest stock price divided by the company's most recently reported annual earnings per share. This is a commonly used tool for gauging the degree of investors' enthusiasm about a stock's prospects that is already reflected in its price.

The remaining columns show the highest and lowest prices reached by each stock during the year; the price of the last trade before the end of the year; and the net change, in both absolute dollar and percentage terms, from the closing price the previous year. As a further aid in understanding the two over-the-counter tables, it is recommended that readers consult the discussion of the over-the-counter market in the Common Stocks chapter of this book.

NEW YORK STOCK EXCHANGE COMPOSITE TRADING DECEMBER 31, 1984

NEW YORK (AP) -New York Stock Exchange issues trading for 1984. The net change and percentage change is from the previous year on issues listed prior to Jan. 1, 1984.

Stock	Div	Sales (hds)	PE	High	Low	Last	Net Chg.	Pct. Chg.
— A—A—A —								
AAR	.48	53038	14	23½	16⅛	18½	+ 1¼	+ 7.3
AGS		48126	10	30½	9⅜	12⅞	— 15⅜	— 54.4
AMCA	1	11085	......	22	13½	14¾	— 6⅞	— 31.8
AMF	.50	147187	81	17⅞	13⅛	14½	— 1½	— 9.4
AMF pf	5e	7029	......	51¾	49⅝	50⅛	....	....
AMR		1379575	6	41¼	24¼	36⅛	....	....
AMR pf	2.18	18747	......	20⅜	18¼	19⅜	— ⅜	— 1.9
AMR pf	2.13	108873	....	41½	27½	36⅞	— 1⅛	— 3
ANR pf	2.67	4558	......	25¼	22⅞	23⅜	— ⅞	— 3.6
ANR pf	2.12	3810	......	23	19	19⅝	— ⅞	— 4.3
APL		11617	3	14⅜	8½	10½	— 3⅝	— 25.7
ASA	3	153355	....	69¾	44¾	48⅛	— 7⅜	— 13.3
AVX	.32	69636	10	30⅛	16	17½	— 9⅝	— 35.5
AbtLab	1.20	569351	13	48¾	36¾	41¾	— 3½	— 7.7
AccoWd	s.44	35584	19	23⅜	16½	22¾	+ 4½	+ 24.7
AcmeC	.40	38200	......	27¼	12½	13	— 12¼	— 48.5
AcmeE	.32b	6559	13	12⅛	8¼	9⅜	— ⅜	— 3.8
AdaEx	2.11e	24413	......	18¾	15	16⅝	— 1¼	— 7
AdmMl	.32	9185	8	18⅞	11⅞	15⅞	— ⅛	— .8
AdvSys	.81t	38009	16	21½	8⅝	10⅛	— 11⅛	— 52.4
AMD		1168347	13	41⅛	25⅛	29½	— 4⅛	— 12.3
Advest	.12	22374	......	14⅛	6⅞	7⅝	— 3⅞	— 33.7
Aerflex		18689	9	15⅝	8¾	10	— 5	— 33.3
AetnLf	2.64	540547	30	39	27¼	36½	+ ½	+ 1.4
AetnL pf	2	29	......	82½	63⅛	78¾	— 1¼	— 1.6
AetL pf	5.87e	65281	......	58¾	52⅜	54⅜	— 2⅞	— 5
Ahmns	1.20	340828	12	34½	15¾	26⅜	— 4⅜	— 14.2
Aileen		17421	......	5⅜	2⅝	2¾	— 1⅞	— 40.5
AirPrd	1.20	178268	10	48⅜	36½	46	+ 1⅜	+ 3.1
AirbFrt	.60	43443	10	30½	13	18½	— 11¼	— 37.8
AlaMoa	.50e	62467	......	4¼	1⅝	4	+ 1⅞	+ 88.2
AlaP pf	2.97e	29791	......	27⅛	21	24½	....	....
AlaP pfA	3.92	2478	......	31	26¾	30	....	....
AlaP dpf	.87	6982	......	7¼	6	6⅞	....	....
AlaP pf	9	1720	......	71	61½	67	+ ½	+ .8
AlaP pf	11	2706	......	101	85¼	97	+ 4¾	+ 5.2
AlaP pf	9.44	1494	......	74⅛	63½	74⅛	+ 5⅛	+ 7.4
AlaP pf	8.16	940	......	64¾	57	62½	+ 3½	+ 5.9
AlaP pf	8.28	652	......	64½	56	61½	+ ½	+ .8
Alagsc s	.92	4580	8	13⅜	11¾	12⅝	+ 2⅜	+ 23.2
AlskAir	.14	96742	9	17¼	9¼	15⅛	+ 1	+ 7.1
Alberto	.54	6019	18	22⅝	15¾	20⅝	+ 3¾	+ 22.2
Albtsns	.68	81458	12	29½	22½	29	+ 1⅞	+ 6.9
Alcan	1.20	612310	10	41¼	23½	28¾	— 11	— 27.7
AlcoStd	1.20	41711	11	36⅝	27⅛	30⅜	— 4⅜	— 12.6
AlexAlx	1	178584	....	25⅝	17	22½	+ ⅜	+ 1.7
Alexdr		49221	23	28½	16⅛	20½	+ 4⅛	+ 25.2
AllgCp	1.08b	28998	8	87⅛	62⅝	77⅝	+ 13¾	+ 21.5
AlgCp pf	2.86	7980	......	26¾	23	25⅜	— ⅞	— 3.3
AlgInt	1.40	48815	23	34	18¾	22¼	— 10⅜	— 31.8
AlgIn pf	2.19	10052	......	22⅝	15¼	17⅝	— 4¼	— 19.4
AlgI pfC	11.25	9628	......	93½	81	89¼	— 3¾	— 4
AllgPw	2.70	232711	8	30	24⅝	28¾	+ 2	+ 7.5
AllenG	.60b	32079	10	26	15¾	17⅛	— 6¾	— 28.3
AlldCp	s1.80	391080	8	37½	28¼	34½	— 2⅝	— 7.1
AldCp pf	6.74	13152	......	64⅝	53⅞	60⅛	— 4⅛	— 6.4
AldCp pf	12	2007	......	113	99	104¼	— 9¼	— 8.1
AldC pf	12.49e	30908	......	107½	100¾	102⅛	— 2¾	— 2.6
AlldPd		18147	......	23½	8¾	19½	+ 10¾	+ 122.9
AlldStr	2	298663	8	56½	38	49½	+ 1¾	+ 3.7
AllisCh		74432	......	17⅜	5⅛	5⅞	— 10¾	— 64.7
AlisC pf		6256	......	40	24	25⅜	— 10¼	— 28.8
ALLTL	1.84	21545	8	25¼	20	24⅛	— ½	— 2
ALLT pf	2.06	357	......	33	27	31¼	— 1½	— 4.6
AlphPr	.40e	2520	18	27	20¾	21¼	— 5⅛	— 19.4
Alcoa	1.20	690663	9	48⅝	30¾	37	— 7⅞	— 17.5
Amax	.20	208669	....	27¾	15½	16¼	— 7½	— 31.6
Amax pf	3	731	......	43⅜	32½	32½	— 8¼	— 20.2
AmHes	1.10	676384	9	34⅛	22⅞	24⅜	— 4⅝	— 15.9
AHes pf	3.50	565	......	144	101	104	— 21	— 16.8
AmAgr		121755	....	3	1¼	2¾	+ ¾	+ 37.5
ABakr		17010	10	19	14	17⅝	+ 3½	+ 24.8
ABrand	3.75	120249	9	65⅛	52⅞	64¼	+ 5	+ 8.4
ABrd pf	1.70	8	......	53½	52	53¼	— 1½	— 2.7
ABrd pf	2.75	17875	......	28½	24⅝	25⅞	+ ⅝	+ 2.5
ABrd pf	2.67	637	......	65⅞	53	65⅞	+ 6⅜	+ 10.7
ABdcst	1.60	387948	10	77¼	50¼	63⅛	+ 7½	+ 13.5
ABldM	.86	9585	11	26½	19½	24⅛	— ½	— 2
ABusPr	.56	7516	12	23⅝	17¾	20¾	— 1	— 4.6
AmCan	2.90	211064	12	55	40⅛	50½	+ 3⅝	+ 7.7
ACan pf	2.80	2437	......	24¼	21¼	23½	+ ¾	+ 3.3
ACan pf	3	15680	......	48	36	42	+ 1¼	+ 3.1
ACan pf	13.75	4725	......	109	103	106	....	....
ACapBd	2.20	15698	......	19⅝	16¾	18⅝	+ ¼	+ 1.4
ACapCv	6.56e	7913	......	33¾	25⅛	26⅝	— 4⅞	— 15.5
ACentC		18909	3	14¾	6½	6¾	— 6¾	— 50
ACyan	1.90	352590	11	53⅛	42⅛	50	....	....
ADT	.92	125586	20	29¾	18¾	20¼	— 5	— 19.8
AElPw	2.26a	790042	7	21⅜	15⅛	21⅛	+ 4	+ 23.4
AmExp	1.28	1759642	20	39	25	37⅝	+ 5	+ 15.3
AFamil	.64b	52531	12	25	13¾	23¼	+ 5⅛	+ 28.3
AGnCp	.90	576612	9	26¼	19⅜	26⅛	+ 3⅜	+ 14.8
AGnl wt		103293	....	9¼	5⅝	8¼	....	....
AGnl pfA	6.31e	66353	......	57	51⅜	53⅛	— ⅝	— 1.2
AGnl pfB	5.95e	41576	......	72⅞	57½	71¾	+ 7⅞	+ 12.3
AGn ipf	3.25	1227	......	55¾	43½	55¼	+ 5½	+ 11.1
AGn pfD	2.64	218386	....	53	39½	52¼	....	....
AHerit	1.08	2688	12	30¾	25¼	29½	+ 3¾	+ 14.6
AHoist		22224	......	14⅜	7½	8⅛	— 5	— 38.1
AHome	2.64	622019	12	55¾	46¾	50½	+ ⅞	+ 1.8
AHme pf	2	61	......	247¼	210¾	229¾	+ 2¼	+ 1
AHosp	1.12	482610	9	42¾	26¼	28¾	— 10⅞	— 27.4
Amrtch	6	530925	8	78	62⅜	76¾	+ 12¼	+ 19
AInGrp	.44	465266	15	73	50⅞	68⅛	+ 3⅞	+ 6
AIGp pf	5.85	548	......	125	112½	122½	....	....
AMI	.60	858590	12	28⅛	20⅛	20⅛	— 3⅞	— 16.1
AmMot		387387	....	8⅛	3¼	3½	— 2¾	— 44
ANtRs	s2.22	165955	8	39⅝	27¾	39¼	+ 8¾	+ 28.7
APresid	.74t	143873	4	36⅝	22⅞	32¾	+ 2⅞	+ 9.6
ASLFla		28645	7	15¼	9	10¾	— 3⅝	— 25.2
ASLFl pf	2.19	18613	......	19	15	17½	— ⅞	— 4.8
AShip	.80	29222	26	16	10	12⅝	— 1	— 7.3
AmStd	1.60	184506	10	33¼	22⅞	30⅜	— 1⅛	— 3.6
ASteril	.33i	137283	14	23⅜	15⅛	22	+ 3⅞	+ 21.4
AmStor	.64	117545	8	41⅛	26½	40	+ ⅜	+ 1
AStr pfA	4.38	19942	......	50	46⅛	50	....	....
AStr pfB	6.80	4458	......	53¼	51	51⅝	....	....
AT&T	1.20	4153610	13	20¼	14⅞	19½	+ 1⅝	+ 9.1
AT&T pf	3.64	60955	......	36½	30½	33⅞	+ 1⅛	+ 3.4
AT&T pf	3.74	42684	......	37⅞	31½	34⅜	+ ¾	+ 2.2
AWatr	1.60	11540	6	41	27	36⅝	+ 7½	+ 25.8
AWat pf	1.43	130	......	51½	35	45	+ 7½	+ 20
AWat pf	1.25	341	......	12	10	10½	— ¼	— 2.3
AWa 5pf	1.25	415	......	12½	10	11	....	....
AmHotl	2.48	24743	11	27½	20¼	26½	+ ¾	+ 2.9
ATrPr	5.35e	12809	......	65¾	53¾	64⅞	+ 9⅝	+ 17.4
ATrSc		21366	......	9¼	4⅜	7⅜	— ⅛	— 1.7
ATrUn	5.35e	7836	......	72½	58¼	71⅝	+ 9¾	+ 15.8
Ameron	1.60	2445	7	35½	26½	28½	— 6⅝	— 18.9
AmesD s	.20	64531	14	30½	17	26⅞	+ 3⅛	+ 13.2
Ames pf	5.32	4435	......	83	60	78½	....	....
Ametek	.80	60103	13	30¼	21½	24½	— 3½	— 12.5
Amfac	1.44i	52080	5	30⅜	18¾	19⅜	— 10⅛	— 34.3
Amfesc		20374	5	20	10½	11⅛	— 6¾	— 37.8
AMP s	.64	520011	16	39½	26⅛	33⅜	— 4¾	— 12.5
Ampco	.30	53367	44	24	14½	16	— 1⅝	— 9.2
Amrep s		16400	6	14¾	12⅞	13⅛	— 2⅞	— 18
AmSth	1.40	15720	7	24½	19	24⅛	+ 2⅛	+ 9.7
Amsted	1.60	36420	16	37	25⅝	36¾	+ 5	+ 15.8
Anacmp		169919	....	7¼	1⅜	2⅛	— 4½	— 67.9
Analog s		86165	17	30	19⅝	23⅝	— 5⅜	— 18.5
Anchor	1.48	140892	17	35¾	19¼	20⅛	— 14⅞	— 42.5
AnClay	1.32	28605	17	35⅝	24½	35½	+ 7	+ 24.6
AndrGr	.20	10762	21	12	9½	9⅞	— 1⅝	— 14.1
Angelic	.56	35622	10	23¾	16¼	17¾	— 4⅞	— 21.5
Anheus	2	307265	10	74⅜	53¾	72½	+ 10	+ 16
Anheu pf	3.60	49485	......	54¼	44	52½	+ 4¼	+ 8.8
Anixtr	.28	74022	21	25	13¾	17⅜	— 6⅞	— 28.4
Anta	9c	3671	......	29⅛	13½	15⅛	— 9⅞	— 39.5
Anthem	.04	54062	13	17¼	8⅞	13¼	— 2	— 13.1
Anthny	.44b	7121	7	16⅝	10⅞	12¾	— 1⅜	— 9.7
Apache	.28	86036	10	14⅝	9¼	10⅛	— 1⅞	— 15.6
ApchP wt		37275	......	4	½	⅝	— 2⅞	— 82.1
ApchP un	2e	81872	......	20¼	15⅛	15¼	— 4⅜	— 22.3
ApPw pf	8.12	645	......	66	55½	61	+ 1¾	+ 3

ApPw pf 7.40	1804	......	60	50	55	....	....
ApPw pf2.65	7870	......	24½	21	24	+ 1	+ 4.4
ApPw pf 4.18	1721	......	31⅞	27¼	31	....	....
ApPw pf3.80	2252	......	29½	26	29	+ 1¼	+ 4.5
AplDta 1.12t	31537	17	31	17¾	29⅛	— ⅜	— 1.3
ApplMg 1.14t	59601	60	29⅛	8	9⅝	— 17⅝	— 64.7
ArchDn .14b	506164	16	23½	15⅜	19⅛	— ⅞	— 4.4
ArizPS 2.60	380814	6	22⅝	14½	22	+ 2⅝	+ 13.6
AriP pf10.46e	5184	......	91½	71	86¼	— 2¾	— 3.1
AriP pf 3.58	8637	......	28⅜	23	27½	+ 1	+ 3.8
AriPpf 10.70	1172	......	95¾	79	84¼	— 8¾	— 9.4
ArkBst .40	37953	7	27¼	13⅛	15⅞	— 10⅝	— 40.1
Arkla 1.08	375477	14	27⅝	16	16¾	— 5⅜	— 24.3
ArlnRt	51003	......	1¼	¼	9-32	—15-32	— 62.5
Armada	2900	25	13¾	9⅝	11⅝	+ 1	+ 9.4
Armco .20j	270762	....	23⅜	9	9¾	— 11⅛	— 53.3
Armc pf2.10	6099	......	33½	18	18⅜	— 11¾	— 39
ArmsR s .48	26133	7	19⅞	15⅜	18⅝	+ 1¾	+ 10.4
ArmWln 1.20	133667	10	34	22¼	33⅝	+ 6	+ 21.7
ArmW pf3.75	120	......	34	29½	32	+ 1	+ 3.2
AroCp 1.20	4034	9	28	18⅜	28	+ 6	+ 27.3
ArowE .20	37527	7	29⅜	13¼	15½	— 11¾	— 43.1
Artra .22	6382	......	22⅞	16	16¾	— 3	— 15.2
Arvin s	36910	8	19⅞	19⅛	19⅝	+ 3½	+ 21.7
Arvin pf 2	376	......	46½	34⅜	46½	+ 6½	+ 16.3
Asarco .30j	126147	....	34½	18½	19	— 11	— 36.7
AshlOil 1.60	98549	......	29½	20¾	24	— 4½	— 15.8
AshlO pf4.50	4904	......	40¼	33⅜	39¾	+ 1¾	+ 4.6
AshlO pf3.96	3840	......	40⅜	31½	35	— 4	— 10.3
AsdDG 2.60	199087	8	61½	45⅛	51¼	— 7⅜	— 12.6
AsdD pf 4.75	20705	......	98	73	84½	— 11½	— 12
Athlone 1.60	6124	15	28¾	18⅜	19⅛	— 4¾	— 19.9
AtCyEl 2.48	53357	7	25	19⅞	24⅛	+ ⅞	+ 3.8
AtlCE pf5.87	18	......	86	67	86	+ 5	+ 6.2
AtlRich 3	1321718	17	52½	40⅝	44⅛	+ ⅞	+ 2
AtlRc pf 3	108	......	347¾	283	291½	— 3	— 1
AtlRc pf3.75	742	......	38⅞	32½	34½	— ½	— 1.4
AtlRc pf2.80	1115	......	125	97	105¾	+ 3⅝	+ 3.6
AtlasCp .50j	11570	......	20	14½	14¾	— 3	— 16.9
Augat .32	124334	14	44¼	18¾	22⅜	— 17⅜	— 43.7
AutoDt .62	172256	18	40¼	29½	39	+ 3½	+ 9.9
AvcoCp 1.20j	577443	10	49½	24	49⅜	+ 17⅝	+ 55.5
Avco pf3.20j	14440	......	98¾	52	98¾	+ 36½	+ 58.6
AVEMC .60	4059	11	23½	15⅝	18⅞	— 1½	— 7.4
Avery .60	77933	14	32	23	32	+ 4¾	+ 17.4
Aviall n	7260	6	15	10	12¼	....	....
Avnet .50	356948	14	49⅛	27	34⅞	— 11⅛	— 24.2
Avnet pf 1	2	......	144¾	144¾	144¾	— 15¼	— 9.5
Avnet pf2.50	2	......	415	415	415	— 88¼	— 17.5
Avon 2	639177	10	26	19¼	21⅞	— 3¼	— 12.9
Aydin	32216	9	42¾	18	21⅛	— 19⅝	— 48.2

— B—B—B —

BMC .48	38878	15	25	10¼	12⅝	— 6⅛	— 32.7
Bairnc s .50	34641	11	31⅝	18⅝	27¼	+ 5	+ 22.5
Bkrlntl .92	425391	17	23½	15	16⅝	— 2⅝	— 13.6
Baldor .36	14038	15	26⅜	18⅜	20⅝	— 5⅞	— 22.2
viBaldU	123700	....	3¼	⅝	⅝	— 1⅞	— 75
BldU pf	2083	......	11¼	2	2⅞	— 7¾	— 72.9
BallCp 1.28	22313	11	45½	28½	45	+ 13¾	+ 44
BallyMf .20	442579	145	23⅛	11⅝	11⅝	— 8	— 40.8
BallyPk	23649	10	15⅝	7⅜	9	— 3½	— 28
BaltGE 3.20	211958	7	40⅝	30¼	40⅝	+ 9	+ 28.5
Balt pfB4.50	283	......	41¾	36½	41½	+ 2½	+ 6.4
BncOne 1	41170	9	26¼	20¾	25⅝	+ 2¼	+ 9.6
BncCtr n	1690	......	11⅝	8⅝	9	+ ⅜	+ 4.4
BanTex .20	76728	24	6⅛	3¾	4½	— 1½	— 25
Bandag 1.10	46418	11	55½	38	52½	— 3	— 5.4
BkBos 2.40	88230	6	43⅞	29	39¾	— ¾	— 1.9
BkBos pf3.95e	9840	......	53⅛	43	46½	....	....
BkNE dpf5.72e	7426	......	56	49	52	— ⅝	— 1.2
BkNY 2.04	74612	6	36¾	26¼	35½	+ 2¾	+ 8.4
BnkVa s 1	33251	8	25	15⅝	24⅜	+ 8	+ 48.9
BnkAm 1.52	723751	10	23⅛	14½	18⅛	— 2¾	— 13.2
BkAm pf5.21e	100041	....	52½	40	42½	— 7¾	— 15.4
BkAm pf8.43e	55130	......	86	66	68¾	— 11	— 13.8
BkAm pf2.88	60751	......	21⅛	11¼	14¼	— 5⅞	— 29.2
BkARty 2.40	19798	8	29⅞	22⅝	29⅛	+ 3¾	+ 14.8
BankTr 2.70	285183	6	58¼	37¾	54¾	+ 9⅝	+ 21.3
BkTr pf 2.50	9706	......	23⅝	19¼	21¼	....	....
BkTr pf 4.22	11433	......	39	35	36	+ ¼	+ .7
Banner .06e	12897	19	12⅞	7½	10⅛	— ⅝	— 5.8

Bard .44	148890	10	37¾	19	22½	— 12	— 34.8
BarnGp .80	12639	7	23½	18	21⅝	— 1⅛	— 4.9
Barnet 1.36	86914	8	44	32½	43⅞	+ 4⅞	+ 12.5
Barnt pf2.38	5201	......	46	35	45½	+ 4⅛	+ 10
BaryWr .60	29556	13	33⅝	21¾	22¼	— 7¾	— 25.8
BASIX .12b	34811	11	12⅛	8⅝	10⅝	— 1½	— 12.4
Bausch .78	221095	16	27⅞	17½	25¾	+ ¾	+ 3
BaxtTr .33	1217407	10	24⅞	11¾	13⅛	— 10⅛	— 43.5
BayFin .20e	13372	16	25½	16⅝	24¼	+ 6⅜	+ 35.7
BayStG 2.60	8232	8	30	19¾	28⅜	+ 7¾	+ 37.6
Bearing 1	11387	11	39¾	28⅜	33½	— 4½	— 11.8
BeatCo 1.70	717698	8	36	24⅞	28	— 3⅞	— 12.2
Beat pf 3.38	11528	......	65½	46½	54	— 5	— 8.5
BectnD 1.20	95441	13	41¼	30¾	39⅝	+ 2⅞	+ 7.8
Beker	104748	....	12	4¾	5¾	— 3	— 34.3
Beker pf	4	......	9⅞	9⅞	9⅞	....	....
BeldnH .40	13523	13	20¾	12½	17¼	— 3	— 14.8
BelHwl .56	97314	13	30½	19¼	26½	+ 2½	+ 10.4
BelHw pf.67	18476	......	30	19½	26	+ 2⅛	+ 8.9
BellAtl 6.40	471015	8	83	65⅝	80⅜	+ 15⅛	+ 23.2
BCE g 2.28	105826	....	27⅛	22⅜	26⅞	— ⅛	— .5
BellInd .32	25865	10	35⅜	19⅝	22⅛	— 13⅛	— 37.2
BellSo s 2.60	940517	8	35⅞	27¼	34	+ 6	+ 21.4
BeloAH .72	25995	15	50¼	35¾	42⅛	+ 3¾	+ 9.8
Bemis s .88	6438	11	27¼	20¼	26⅜	+ 5⅞	+ 28.7
Bndx pf 4.04	1578	......	85½	73	81½	— 3½	— 4.1
BenfCp 2	91063	9	35½	23	33¾	....	....
Benef pf 4.30	1011	......	35¼	30¼	33⅝	....	....
Benef pf4.50	182	......	37½	32	34	— 1	— 2.9
Benef pf5.50	z4140	......	152	104½	150½	+ 5	+ 3.4
Benef pf2.50	369	......	20¾	17	20¼	+ ½	+ 2.5
BengtB .15e	77669	8	8¼	3¼	3⅝	— 2⅜	— 39.6
BergEn	33497	9	16¼	7⅛	14	+ 1¾	+ 14.3
Berkey	21071	11	8⅛	3⅞	4	— 4	— 50
BestPd .24	399897	12	19¼	10⅝	11¾	— 6¾	— 36.5
BethStl .60	466871	....	29½	14¼	17½	— 11	— 38.6
BethSt pf 5	26931	......	59⅞	37¼	40¾	— 17½	— 30
BethSt pf2.50	49522	......	29¾	18⅝	20⅞	— 8⅛	— 28
Beverly .32	194166	19	34	19½	31½	+ 6¾	+ 27.3
BigThr .80	205865	17	24⅞	18¼	20⅞	— ⅝	— 2.9
BlackD .64	393440	12	28⅝	17¼	23½	— 2⅞	— 10.9
BlckHP 1.68	10633	7	27¾	20	27	+ 4⅝	+ 20.7
BlairJn .56	84959	9	40	14¼	15⅞	— 13⅝	— 46.2
BlckHR 2.40	70584	11	50	37	44½	— 4	— 8.2
Boeing 1.40	937193	15	59½	35⅝	56⅝	+ 12⅞	+ 29.4
BoiseC 1.90	192018	11	45	32½	40⅝	— 3⅛	— 7.1
BoiseC pf 5	19004	......	57¾	46	52⅝	— 3⅜	— 6
BoltBer .10	33112	25	27⅜	15¾	21	— ⅝	— 2.9
Borden 2.72	130264	9	65	49⅞	64¾	+ 8¼	+ 14.6
BorgWa .92	274150	9	25⅞	16⅞	21⅜	— 3⅜	— 13.6
Bormns	10496	......	8⅜	4¼	5½	— 1⅛	— 17
BosEd 3.24	82104	8	35½	24⅞	34⅝	+ 6¼	+ 22
BosE pf 8.88	422	......	73	63	73	+ 3	+ 4.3
BosE pr 1.17	9917	......	10⅛	9	9⅞	....	....
BosE pr1.46	3995	......	12⅜	10½	12⅜	+ ¾	+ 6.5
Bowtr n .36e	190032	10	25⅛	14⅞	20½	....	....
Bowtr wi	370	......	21¼	16⅜	21¼	....	....
BrigSt 1.60	46795	10	31⅞	25½	29	— 2⅛	— 6.8
BristM 1.60	672820	16	52⅝	41	52⅜	+ 10⅛	+ 24
BrstM pf 2	589	......	110½	90¼	110½	+ 21½	+ 24.2
BritLnd	5105	38	6	3¼	3¾	— ¼	— 6.3
BritPt 1.76e	78199	6	30	21¾	22⅝	— 1	— 4.2
BritT pp	295159	....	12⅜	9½	12⅜	....	....
Brock .08j	54235	......	7½	2⅝	3	— 3¾	— 55.6
Brckwy 1.32	16297	......	18⅛	14⅝	17¼	+ ⅜	+ 2.2
BkyUG 3.12	32514	8	36	28	35½	+ 3⅛	+ 9.7
BkUG pf2.47	754	......	22½	19⅛	22	+ 1¼	+ 6
BkUG pf3.95	3206	......	33½	29	31	— ¼	— .8
BwnSh .20	9454	5	20⅞	13	17	— 2⅝	— 13.4
BrwnGp 1.36	92772	10	33	22¾	27⅜	— 4½	— 14.1
BrwnF 1.08	189498	14	44½	26½	37	— 6	— 14
Brnswk 1	222115	8	36¼	23¾	33⅞	+ 5	+ 17.3
BrshW s .48	49361	16	39¾	25½	34½	+ 6⅝	+ 23.8
BucyEr .44	108790	....	19¼	12	14⅜	— 3	— 17.3
Bundy .80	10613	7	23¼	13⅞	17	— 4	— 19
BunkrH 2.16	3908	......	17¾	15½	16¾	— ¼	— 1.5
BurlInd 1.64	239555	12	37	23	25⅜	— 9¾	— 27.8
BrlNth s1.40	533104	7	50	35	47	— 2½	— 5.1
BrlNo pf .55	3594	......	7⅜	6⅜	6¾	+ ⅛	+ 1.9
BrlN pf 2.13	6869	......	21¼	19	20¼	+ ⅛	+ .6
BrlN pf5.43e	175877	....	50¾	44½	48⅝	+ 1	+ 2.1

Burndy	.84	40482	14	20½	12¾	14½	− 5⅛	− 26.1
Burrgh	2.60	609719	11	59⅞	44⅜	56¾	+ 6⅜	+ 12.7
Butlrln	.52	23793	......	20¾	12⅛	17¼	− 3¼	− 15.9
Buttes		16443	......	12⅜	3⅞	4⅞	− 5⅞	− 54.7
Butes pf	2.10	1851	......	15	11	11¾	....	....
— C—C—C —								
CBI In	1.40a	52394	10	33⅞	24⅛	25	− 4⅝	− 15.6
CBS	3	267513	9	87¾	61½	72⅜	+ 6⅛	+ 9.3
CBS pf	1	11	......	58½	44¼	55	+ 12	+ 27.9
CCX		25659	10	10¼	4¼	5¼	− 4¼	− 44.7
CCX pf	1.25	z7760	......	10⅜	8¼	9½	+ ¼	+ 2.7
CIGNA	2.60	626234	19	45½	27	44⅜	+ ⅝	+ 1.4
CIG pf	2.75	30434	......	29⅛	23⅜	27½	− 1¼	− 4.3
CLC		12144	......	9½	4¾	4⅞	− 4¼	− 46.6
CNA Fn		40937	13	32	21	32	+ 10⅞	+ 51.5
CNAI	1.20a	7825	......	10½	8⅞	9⅞	....	....
CPC Int	2.20	176151	14	41⅞	34¼	40	+ 1½	+ 3.9
CP Ntl	1.40	19968	8	19	14⅝	19	+ 2¼	+ 13.4
CSX	1.04	686233	7	26¼	18⅜	24	− ¾	− 3
CSX pf	7	157	......	156	117	141	− 9½	− 6.3
CTS	1	37188	13	33¾	22	33⅛	+ ⅜	+ 1.2
C 3 Inc		94986	42	15½	6¾	10⅞	− 4⅝	− 29.8
Cabot	.92	65782	9	28⅞	22⅝	26⅝	+ 1⅝	+ 6.5
Caesar		241023	13	13⅝	8¼	9⅞	− 1⅝	− 14.1
CalFed	.32	341406	4	23¾	11⅜	16	− 5¼	− 24.7
CalFd pf	4.75	11947	......	42¾	32¾	41¾	....	....
Callhn	.25r	28097	81	24⅛	13½	14½	− 7⅝	− 34.5
Camrnl	.12	39951	......	20	11⅝	12½	− 7⅛	− 36.3
CRLk g	.40	140702	....	30⅜	16⅜	18¼	− 8⅛	− 30.8
CmpR g	.16t	16881	......	9⅞	4	4¼	− 4	− 48.5
CpR pf	g2.50	512	......	14½	12¼	12⅜	....	....
CamSp	2.50	80248	12	72⅛	54¼	69½	+ 8½	+ 13.9
CdPac	g1.40	67038	......	43	28⅛	38	− 2⅜	− 5.9
CanPE	g .80	15518	......	20⅛	14¼	18½	− ¾	− 3.9
CanIR	68c	693	12	59½		28¼	....	....
CapCits	.20	61445	15	174½	123½	164⅝	+ 20⅝	+ 14.3
CapHld	1.54	101146	10	44	30⅛	43	+ 5⅞	+ 15.8
CapH pf	10.80e	16030	......	108¾	100½	101½	− 1⅞	− 1.8
Caressa	.42	57936	12	18⅜	8½	15⅝	− ⅛	− .8
Carlng g	.48	33642	......	18⅜	11	11⅜	− 6⅝	− 36.8
Carlisle	1.02	35226	10	36½	24⅛	33⅞	+ 6⅛	+ 22.1
Carnat	2.40	340663	14	81⅞	50¾	81½	+ 25½	+ 45.5
CaroFt	.36	50061	11	31½	13⅞	22¼	− 7¾	− 25.8
CarPw	2.60	314604	7	26⅛	19¼	25⅜	+ 3⅜	+ 15.3
CarP pf	2.67	1748	......	23¾	19⅝	21¾	+ ½	+ 2.4
CarTec	2.10	31321	10	58¼	36⅝	40	− 13¾	− 25.6
Carrol	.07	30402	13	10⅜	7⅛	8¾	− 1⅜	− 13.6
CarsPir	1.20	34181	17	40¼	30⅜	37¾	+ 4¾	+ 14.4
CartHw	1.22	560132	45	32¼	18¼	23⅝	+ ⅛	+ .5
CartWl	.48	36183	10	27⅞	19⅜	27⅝	+ 6¾	+ 32.3
CascNG	1.20	12751	9	15⅛	9¼	14¾	+ 5¼	+ 55.3
CastlCk		226636	....	19⅝	9⅛	12⅞	− 4⅞	− 27.5
CstlC pf	2.50	30881	......	33¾	15¾	22⅛	− 9⅜	− 29.8
CatrpT	.50	753083	....	52¾	28⅜	31	− 16¼	− 34.4
Ceco	.76	10220	9	25¾	16	20¼	− 4¾	− 19
Celanse	4.40	149547	7	82	62¾	81⅛	+ 12⅛	+ 17.6
Celan pf	4.50	1652	......	38¾	34	37¾	+ ¾	+ 2
Cengy n	.01e	36754	18	15	7½	8¼	....	....
Centel	2.38	67486	9	38½	30⅝	37⅝	+ 2½	+ 7.1
Centex n		16816	......	26½	17	22⅞	....	....
CenSoW	1.90	459077	6	22⅞	16⅞	22¾	+ 3¼	+ 16.7
CenHud	2.84	37862	6	25⅝	16⅛	25⅜	+ 2⅜	+ 10.3
CHud pf	2.92e	6605	......	26¼	20¼	23¼	− 2¼	− 8.8
CenIlLt	2.14	35530	8	23⅝	18½	23¼	+ 2⅜	+ 11.4
CnILt pf	4.50	108	......	41¾	36	40½	+ 3	+ 8
CnILt pf	2.87	816	......	27	24¼	26⅛	+ 1⅛	+ 4.5
CnILt pf	2.62	640	......	27	21¾	27	+ 5¼	+ 24.1
CnIlPS	1.60	147878	7	17⅞	14	17¼	+ 1⅜	+ 8.7
CnLaEl	1.96	66183	6	22¼	17⅝	22⅛	+ 3¾	+ 20.4
CLaEl pf	4.18	1904	......	33¾	29⅛	32¾	+ ⅞	+ 2.8
CeMPw	1.40	90768	4	14¾	7⅞	9¾	− 4¾	− 32.8
CnSoya	.84	44671	11	17½	14	16	+ 1⅛	+ 7.6
CVtPS	1.90	22581	5	17¼	10⅞	17⅛	+ 1½	+ 9.6
CentrDt		45810	......	17⅜	7¾	11⅛	− 3⅞	− 25.8
CntryTl	.78	19203	8	9¾	7¾	9¼	+ ½	+ 5.7
Cenvill	2.60	10159	8	25	18⅝	21¼	− 2⅛	− 9.1
Crt-teed	.60	36583	11	23½	15½	21¾	+ 1½	+ 7.4
CessAir	.40	117415	388	27¾	17	19⅜	− 5¼	− 21.3
Chmpln	.40	664542	10	28⅞	16⅞	22¼	− 6⅝	− 22.9
Chml pf	1.20	2812	......	29	19	23⅞	− 5	− 17.3
Chml pf	4.60	19245	......	56⅞	43¼	50¾	− 5½	− 9.8
ChamSp	.40	120077	10	12	8	8¼	− 2⅜	− 22.4
viChrtC	.50i	148978	....	12⅞	1	1	− 10¼	− 91.1
viCht wt		30822	......	6⅛	¼	¼	− 4⅜	− 94.6
viChrt pf	.82i	25022	......	11⅛	1½	1⅝	− 8⅞	− 84.5
Chase	3.65	374750	5	52¾	35⅝	47¾	+ 2¼	+ 5
Chase pf	6.75	3683	......	63	52½	54½	− 1½	− 2.7
Chase pf	7.60	5869	......	70⅞	60½	60½	− 2	− 3.2
Chase pf	5.25	10820	......	44	36⅝	40¾	....	....
Chase pf	6.57e	92957	......	58	48	52¾	− 2¾	− 5
Chase pf	6.20e	36224	......	57⅞	51	52¼	....	....
Chelsea	.66	9115	8	19	13⅝	18	+ 1⅛	+ 6.7
Chemed	1.48	46237	11	36⅝	24⅝	26⅝	− 9⅞	− 27.1
ChNY s	2.36	319465	6	35⅞	23½	34½	+ 5¼	+ 18
ChNY pf	1.87	2289	......	35¾	23⅝	33⅝	+ 4¼	+ 14.5
ChNY pf	6.57e	76912	......	58¼	48	53¾	− 2	− 3.6
ChNY pf	5.99e	32926	......	56⅜	46	50½	− 3⅞	− 7.1
Chespk	1.24	12733	16	39½	31¼	33⅝	− 5⅞	− 14.9
ChesPn	1.92	265895	11	39⅞	32⅛	33⅝	− 3½	− 9.4
Chevrn	2.40	905494	7	40¼	30	31¼	− 3⅜	− 9.7
CNWst		115599	10	43¼	18¾	26½	− 17	− 39.1
ChiMlw		12762	81	195¾	94¾	186¼	+ 89¼	+ 92
ChiMl pf		3040	......	74⅞	47	66½	+ 17¼	+ 35
ChiPnT		35491	7	25¼	16	19¾	+ 3⅝	+ 22.5
ChkFull	.33t	18275	142	15	7¾	8½	− 3¾	− 30.6
ChrisCr	.48t	27611	......	35¼	24⅝	33½	+ 3⅜	+ 11.2
ChCft pf	1	216	......	11¼	10¼	10¼	− ¼	− 2.4
ChCft pf	1.40	20	......	234	187	215	+ 42	+ 24.3
Christn		14689	......	10⅝	5	9⅛	+ 3¾	+ 69.8
Chroma		61100	......	13⅞	9⅜	10¼	− 1⅜	− 11.8
Chrm pf		4904	......	54¾	42	46	− 7	− 13.2
Chryslr	1	1752530	4	33¾	20⅞	32	+ 4⅜	+ 15.8
Chubb s	2.20	172433	11	53	34⅞	52½	+ 6⅝	+ 14.4
Church	.80	263552	17	30½	21¼	30⅛	+ 5⅝	+ 23
CinBell	3.12	9511	7	43	35⅛	42½	+ 1⅞	+ 4.6
CinGE	2.16	216830	6	15⅜	8⅞	14¾	+ 1⅞	+ 14.6
CinG pf	4	399	......	31	24	29	+ 2	+ 7.4
CinG pf	4.75	210	......	33½	24⅜	32	+ 1¾	+ 5.8
CinG pf	9.30	1592	......	65¼	50	61	+ 4	+ 7
CinG pf	7.44	1195	......	52½	39	48½	+ 1½	+ 3.2
CinG pf	9.28	1444	......	64½	48	62	+ 4	+ 6.9
CinG pf	9.52	502	......	65⅝	50	63	+ 5¼	+ 9.1
CinG pf	10.20	1260	......	77	58⅛	75	+ 9¼	+ 14.1
CinG pf	12.52	1203	......	86½	66	86	+ 5	+ 6.2
CinMil	.72	55190	32	34⅞	20	21	− 11¾	− 35.9
CirclK	.74	82461	14	33¾	20¾	31⅝	+ 6⅛	+ 24
CirCity	.08	89124	13	29½	11⅝	21⅜	+ 5⅛	+ 31.5
Circus		36720	11	19¾	13½	17⅝	+ 2⅜	+ 15.6
Citicrp	2.06	1095197	6	40½	27⅜	38¾	+ 1⅝	+ 4.4
Citicp pf	8.33e	61340	......	86	68½	71½	− 7¼	− 9.2
Citcp pf	A9.95e	29318	......	99¾	75½	84	− 11¼	− 11.8
Citcp pf	B9.02e	9120	......	101	97¼	97¼	....	....
CityInv	2	573227	9	44½	32	38⅞	+ 1¼	+ 3.3
CtyIn pf	1.31	6	......	83½	71	79¼	+ 9¾	+ 14
CtyIn pf	2	1747	......	68	49½	60	+ 1¼	+ 2.1
CtyIn pf	2.87	103794	....	26¼	21¾	24⅜	− 1	− 3.9
Clabir	.72b	16939	......	11⅝	6⅛	6⅝	− 4⅝	− 41.1
ClarkE	1.10	94903	13	39	23⅝	24⅞	− 12⅞	− 34.1
ClayHm		24191	15	13⅜	10⅛	13¼	+ 4⅛	+ 45.2
ClvClf	1	37152	......	26	17	17⅛	− 7½	− 30.5
ClevEl	2.52	427911	5	20¼	13¾	19½	+ ⅞	+ 4.7
ClvEl pf	7.40	2389	......	59¼	46½	54½	− 1	− 1.8
ClvEl pf	7.56	1289	......	60	47	54½	− ⅞	− 1.6
ClvEl pf	12.89e	4345	......	97	77⅞	81¾	....	....
Clevpk	.60	13593	......	17¼	10⅛	12½	− 2¼	− 15.3
Clvpk pf	2.23	18069	......	17¼	15¼	16¾	+ ⅞	+ 5.5
Clvpk pf	1.84	8406	......	20½	14¾	15⅞	− 3¾	− 19.1
Clorox	1.20	241990	10	31	22½	28¾	+ 2¼	+ 8.5
ClubM n		27125	......	17¾	14¾	16	....	....
CluettP	1	57673	8	30⅞	22½	27⅞	− 2⅛	− 7.1
Cluet pf	1	4235	......	19⅜	14⅝	17½	− 1¼	− 6.7
Coachm	.40	97180	6	29¾	12¼	17⅜	− 8⅝	− 33.2
Coastal	.40a	157188	6	39¼	23½	28¼	− 5¼	− 15.7
Cstl pf	1.19	421	......	38	24¼	31	− 2¼	− 6.8
Cstl pf	1.83	595	......	39	24½	29⅜	− 3⅛	− 9.6
CocaCl	2.76	696352	13	66	49	62⅜	+ 8⅞	+ 16.6
Coleco		539583	....	22¼	9⅝	12⅛	− 7⅜	− 37.8
Colemn	1.20	25995	9	37¾	25¼	26½	− 10½	− 28.4
ColgPal	1.28b	790908	10	26½	20½	24⅞	+ 3⅜	+ 15.7
ColgP pf	4.25	139	......	49½	39	41	....	....
CollAik	1.20	100551	7	39⅜	27½	38½	+ 1½	+ 4.1
ColFds s	.16	49331	12	16⅞	9⅞	15	+ 2	+ 15.4

ColPen	1.40	137613	9	31⅜	20⅜	27½	+ 3½	+ 14.6
Coltlnd	2.50	117724	11	57	39⅞	51½	− 2	− 3.7
ColGas	3.18	145728	7	37½	27	34	− 1¼	− 3.5
ColGs	pf5.48	1815	......	52¾	48¾	49⅞	− ⅛	− .3
ColGs	pf5.12	8563	......	49	45½	46	− 1½	− 3.2
ColGs	pf5.68e	17643	......	55	48	50⅜	− 3⅞	− 7.1
CSO pf	3.45	6168	......	26½	21¼	25½	+ 2	+ 8.5
CSO pf	2.42	282	......	18¾	15⅞	18	+ 1¾	+ 10.8
CSO pf	o15.25	199	......	105½	96	104½	+ 9½	+ 10
CSO pf	n15.25	1005	......	106	95	106	+ 11	+ 11.6
Combln	2.08	113932	10	43½	27¼	38⅛	− 2⅛	− 5.3
CmbEn	1.84	146443	12	35⅝	25¾	32⅛	+ ⅜	+ 1.2
Comdis	.20	242603	11	21½	8	11⅛	− 7⅞	− 41.4
ComMtl	.36	28722	13	26¾	15½	17⅜	− 5⅛	− 22.8
Comdre		783141	3	49⅜	16¼	16⅜	− 25⅛	− 60.5
CmwE	3	1122825	7	28⅞	21½	27⅞	+ 1⅞	+ 7.2
CwE wtA		41	......	9½	7½	9	− ⅜	− 4
CwE wtB		7	......	7¾	7⅝	7⅝	− 1⅛	− 12.9
CwE pf	1.42	794	......	28¾	21¾	27½	+ 1⅞	+ 7.3
CwE pf	1.90	11757	......	16¼	13	14¾	+ ¼	+ 1.7
CwE pf	2	4103	......	16¼	13¼	15⅜	+ ⅞	+ 6
CwE	pf12.75	1286	......	103¾	93½	100¼	− 5⅜	− 5.1
CwE	pf11.70	2065	......	95¾	80	89⅝	− 8⅛	− 8.3
CwE	pfB8.40	1187	......	79	65	70¼	− 8¾	− 11.1
CwE pf	8.38	1363	......	65	53⅜	63½	+ 2⅜	+ 3.9
CwE pf	2.37	11071	......	21¾	18⅜	20¾	− ¾	− 3.5
CwE pf	2.87	5252	......	24⅝	20⅞	23½	− ½	− 2.1
CwE pf	8.40	1669	......	65½	54½	63	+ 2½	+ 4.1
CwE pf	7.24	2392	......	57	46	54	− 1	− 1.8
ComES	2.32	12738	5	25½	16¼	24½	+ 5⅛	+ 26.5
ComES	pf9.80	329	......	88¼	78¾	80	− 5½	− 6.4
Comsat	1.20	164943	10	34½	20¾	25⅞	− 6⅞	− 21
CPsyc s	.24	149029	23	30	16⅞	26⅝	+ 3⅝	+ 15.8
Compgr	.55e	13079	11	39½	26	30⅛	− 2½	− 7.7
CompSc		96234	10	21⅜	11	14	− 5⅜	− 27.7
Cptvsn		317252	32	46¼	29	37¼	− 6⅛	− 14.1
ConAg s	.87	53313	13	27½	19¾	27⅜	+ 4⅝	+ 20.3
Conair	.24b	44555	12	22⅜	13¼	21⅛	+ 3⅛	+ 17.4
ConnE	s1.52	2940	7	18¼	12⅝	17⅛	+ 4½	+ 35.6
CnnNG	2.40	5411	9	25	19½	24½	+ 3⅞	+ 18.8
Conrac	.40	33052	6	18⅝	10⅜	14¼	− 1½	− 9.5
ConsEd	2.12	551441	7	31¼	22⅝	30¾	+ 5⅞	+ 23.6
ConE pf	6	65	......	190	145	190	+ 35½	+ 23
ConE pf	4.65	3280	......	40½	35	39	− 1	− 2.5
ConE pf	5	2813	......	44¾	38	42½	+ 2	+ 4.9
ConsFd	1.44	242302	10	34⅞	25	31¾	+ 5¾	+ 22.1
ConF	pf4.32e	24708	......	54½	50⅜	52½	+ 1½	+ 2.9
CnsFrt s	1	120354	11	30	20⅛	28¾	− 1⅜	− 4.6
CnsNG	2.32	104697	8	42¼	31	41¾	+ 7⅞	+ 23.3
ConsPw	1.08i	612666	2	16⅛	4⅛	4⅝	− 9½	− 67.3
CnP	pfA4.16	512	......	29	13	20½	− 5½	− 21.2
CnP	pfB4.50	1397	......	30	13¼	22	− 5¼	− 19.3
CnP	pfC4.52	144	......	51⅞	26	30½	− 18½	− 37.8
CnP	pfD7.45	2596	......	50	23¼	37	− 8	− 17.8
CnP	pfE7.72	4467	......	51	25¾	35½	− 10	− 22
CnP	pfG7.76	4773	......	52	25	36½	− 9½	− 20.7
CnP	prV 4.40	16131	......	28½	11½	19¼	....	....
CnP	prU3.60	21332	......	23¾	9¼	15¾	− 6	− 27.6
CnP	prT3.78	16141	......	25¼	10¼	17¼	− 5½	− 24.2
CnP	pfH7.68	1751	......	51	25⅜	36	− 9½	− 20.9
CnP	prR 4	15589	......	25⅞	11¼	18	− 6	− 25
CnP	prP3.98	13984	......	26	10⅞	18¼	− 6	− 24.7
CnP	prN3.85	12033	......	25¼	10¼	18	− 5¼	− 22.6
CnP	prM2.50	5896	......	17	7¼	12⅛	− 3⅜	− 21.8
CnP	prL2.23	7758	......	15⅜	7	10⅞	− 3½	− 24.3
CnP	prS4.02	15817	......	26½	11	17¾	− 6½	− 26.8
CnP	prK2.43	7949	......	17⅜	7¼	11½	− 4	− 25.8
CntlCp	2.60	269369	5	37⅛	23½	36¾	+ 9¼	+ 33.6
CtlC	pfA2.50	15	......	79	59	79	+ 20	+ 33.9
CtlC	pfB2.50	4	......	78	61	78	+ 19	+ 32.2
Contlll		19131	......	7¼	4⅞	5¾	....	....
Contll rt		166263	....	2⅞	⅜	¾	....	....
Cntlll	pf2.81i	36299	......	51¼	12	36½	− 13⅛	− 26.4
CtllHd n		162780	....	4½	⅜	½	....	....
ContTel	1.72	426259	9	24⅝	18	22¼	+ ⅞	+ 4.1
CtData	.66	697756	11	48½	24⅜	35¼	− 10	− 22.1
CnDt pf	4.50	150	......	39½	33	35½	− 3	− 7.8
Conwd	1	27347	12	33⅞	22¾	30⅛	+ 6⅜	+ 26.8
viCookU		33091	......	4⅞	1	1⅛	− 3⅛	− 73.5
Coopr	1.52	167343	14	37⅞	26	28⅜	− 6⅜	− 18.3
Coopl	pf2.50	4	......	223	198	198	− 27	− 12
Coopl	pf2.90	17516	......	38⅞	30	32¼	− 4¾	− 12.8
CoopLb	.06e	324192	3	27	10⅜	13¼	+ 2¼	+ 20.5
CoprTr	.40	38306	8	19	12⅝	17⅜	+ 1½	+ 9.5
Coopvis	.40	399104	13	24⅜	11⅞	16½	+ 1¼	+ 8.2
Copwld	.58	13290	10	23¼	11⅝	12⅜	− 8¼	− 40
Cpwld	pf2.48	5619	......	29½	19¼	20	− 7⅛	− 26.3
Cordura	.84	25907	15	23⅝	16½	22⅞	+ 2	+ 9.6
Coreln	.52	12929	11	14⅞	10⅞	12⅝	− 1¾	− 12.2
CornG	2.56	93296	16	74¼	59½	69	− ¾	− 1.1
CorBlk	1	63740	25	31¼	22⅝	31	+ 7½	+ 31.9
Cowles	.40	17932	37	45⅞	23½	45¾	+ 22¼	+ 94.7
CoxCm	.34	101493	17	54⅞	39⅛	49⅜	+ 4¼	+ 9.4
Craig		2383	......	8⅜	4¼	6⅝	− ⅞	− 11.7
Crane	1.60b	74905	22	40¾	27	35	+ 4½	+ 14.8
CrayRs		190124	16	59⅜	38½	52½	− 3⅛	− 5.6
CrockN	.40	81321	......	30⅜	16¼	25⅜	+ ½	+ 2
CrckN	pf2.18	6467	......	23¾	15¼	18⅛	− 3	− 14.2
CrmpK	1.20	6524	9	23¾	19¼	21⅛	− 2⅜	− 10.1
CrwnCk		51261	13	45¾	34¾	45¼	+ 7⅞	+ 21.1
CrwZel	1	208068	11	38¾	27¾	33⅞	− 2¾	− 7.5
CrZel	pf4.63	10903	......	51½	43	46¾	− 2⅝	− 5.3
CrZel	pfC4.50	12103	......	63½	50	55⅜	− 6⅜	− 10.3
Culbro	.60	4478	6	26¼	18¼	23	....	....
Culinet		140064	33	47¼	24¼	45	+ 4¼	+ 10.4
CumEn	2.20	90091	4	88¼	61¼	77⅝	− 2⅞	− 3.6
Currlnc	1.10a	7922	......	10½	8¼	10⅛	+ 1⅛	+ 12.5
CurtW	1.20	6892	9	49½	30¼	31¾	− 16¼	− 33.9
Cyclops	1.10	13334	10	39⅜	27½	39¼	+ 3½	+ 9.8
			— D—D—D —					
DamonC	.20	50580	35	19⅞	10⅛	11⅝	− 3¾	− 24.4
DanaCp	1.28	255513	8	31⅛	21⅛	26⅝	− 1⅜	− 4.9
Danahr		34508	......	7⅞	4⅜	7	+ 2½	+ 55.6
Daniel	.18b	35898	......	13¾	8½	10¾	+ ⅝	+ 6.2
DartKr	4.24	283567	10	87¼	64¾	85¼	+ 18⅝	+ 28
DataGn		512463	19	59¾	38	58¾	+ 21½	+ 57.7
Datpnt		463214	19	30½	13⅛	20¼	− 7¼	− 26.4
DtaDsg	.20	38203	9	12¼	8⅜	8⅝	− 2¾	− 24.2
Dayco	.24	32988	6	19⅛	12⅛	15⅛	− 1¾	− 10.4
Dayc pf	4.25	z4220	......	98	77	89	+ 9	+ 11.3
DaytHd	.74	545066	12	37¼	26⅛	31½	+ ⅜	+ 1.2
DaytPL	2	183090	7	16¼	11⅝	15¼	+ 1⅞	+ 14
DPL pf	7.48	288	......	55⅝	45¼	53	+ 1½	+ 2.9
DPL pf	7.70	629	......	58½	45	55¼	+ 1¼	+ 2.3
DPL pf	7.37	966	......	55½	45	52¾	+ 2¾	+ 5.5
DPL	pf12.50	1170	......	96	75⅜	96	+ 8½	+ 9.7
DPL	pf11.60	890	......	91⅛	75	82	− 15	− 15.5
DeanF s	.48	19481	15	29⅜	19⅜	27	+ 5¼	+ 24.1
Deere	1	456558	19	40⅜	24⅝	29¾	− 8¾	− 22.7
DelmP	1.92	147943	8	22⅜	17⅛	22	+ 2¾	+ 14.3
DeltaAr	.60	589855	8	45⅞	27	43⅝	+ 3⅞	+ 9.8
Deltona		17297	......	9½	4¼	4⅞	− 4⅛	− 45.8
DlxChk	1.76	78533	15	58	35½	57	+ 17⅛	+ 43
DenMf s		20881	10	24⅛	22¼	22⅝	− ⅝	− 2.7
Dennys	.72i	225469	15	42¼	30¼	42⅛	+ 5⅝	+ 15.4
DeSoto	1.40	9560	10	34⅜	26½	33¾	+ 2	+ 6.3
DetEd	1.68	498824	7	16⅛	11½	16	+ 2¼	+ 16.4
DetE pf	5.50	114	......	87¼	67¼	84¼	+ 6¼	+ 8
DetE pf	9.32	732	......	69	59	67	+ 3	+ 4.7
DetE pf	7.68	1133	......	58	47½	55	+ 3½	+ 6.8
DetE pf	7.45	1861	......	57½	46	52	+ 2	+ 4
DetE pf	7.36	1754	......	56	45⅛	54	+ 3	+ 5.9
DE pfF	2.75	6261	......	24	19⅞	23⅜	+ 1¾	+ 8.1
DE prR	3.24	5665	......	24¾	20	23⅝	+ 1½	+ 6.8
DE pfQ	3.13	10774	......	24⅛	19⅜	22¾	+ 1⅜	+ 6.4
DE pfP	3.12	1634	......	24½	19	22¾	+ 1⅞	+ 9
DE pfB	2.75	3488	......	23½	19¼	22½	+ 1⅛	+ 5.3
DE pfO	3.40	7903	......	25¾	19⅞	24¾	+ 1⅛	+ 4.8
DE pfM	3.42	11540	......	25⅞	19½	25⅛	+ 1¾	+ 7.5
DE prL	4	3949	......	30	24¼	28¾	+ 1	+ 3.6
DE pfK	4.12	4265	......	30¾	24⅛	29⅝	+ 1⅜	+ 4.9
DE	pfJ15.68	1419	......	115	96	111½	− ¾	− .7
DE pfi	12.80	1971	......	100⅞	86	97⅛	+ 2⅛	+ 2.2
DetE pf	9.72	5380	......	83½	72½	80½	+ 4	+ 5.2
DetE pr	2.28	4122	......	17⅞	13¼	17⅛	+ 1¼	+ 7.9
Dexter	.80	33782	11	25⅛	17¾	19¼	− 2¾	− 12.5
DiGior	.64	39983	21	15	9⅜	13¾	+ ¾	+ 5.8
DiGio pf	.88	z6120	......	23	17	23	+ 1½	+ 7
DiGio	pf2.25	1518	......	27⅝	21¾	26⅛	+ ⅛	+ .5
DiamS	1.76	885450	57	22⅝	16¾	17¾	− 2⅛	− 10.7
DiaSh pf	4	14457	......	38⅞	34¾	35	− 2⅜	− 6.4
Diebld	1.20	76326	11	88½	65¼	71¾	− 5⅞	− 7.6

Digital		1203422	14	111¼	70⅜	110¾	+ 38¾	+ 53.8
Disney	1.20	981187	22	68½	45¼	59⅞	+ 7¼	+ 13.8
DEI	2.60	8398	5	40	30	36¾	+ 5⅝	+ 18.1
Divrsln		28986	3	6⅞	3⅞	4½	+ ¼	+ 5.9
Dome g	.12	227350	....	16⅞	6½	7	— 6⅝	— 48.6
DomRs	2.72	415572	8	29¼	20⅜	28⅞	+ 6¾	+ 30.5
Donald	.66	10760	8	24⅜	16	17½	— 6	— 25.5
DonLJ	.28	163437	18	30	14⅜	29⅞	+ 13⅞	+ 86.7
Donley	1	136574	15	49¼	32	49	+ 10½	+ 27.3
Dorsey	1.20	41442	10	38½	23¼	23⅞	— 10⅜	— 30.3
Dover	.82	134205	12	40	28½	34¼	+ 4¼	+ 14.2
DowCh	1.80	904875	10	34½	25¾	27½	— 5⅞	— 17.6
DowJn	.72b	140659	21	51⅜	35⅛	41¾	— 6⅞	— 14.1
Dravo	.50	46569	......	15	10⅞	11⅜	— 2¾	— 19.5
Dresr	.80	463772	15	23⅜	15¼	18¼	— 2½	— 12
DrexB	2	4513	......	18	14¾	18	+ ½	+ 2.9
Dreyfus	.50a	57378	11	40	23¼	37¾	+ 14¼	+ 60.6
duPont	3	746979	8	52⅞	42⅜	49½	— 2½	— 4.8
duPnt pf	3.50	3665	......	34¼	30⅝	32¾	+ ¼	+ .8
duPnt pf	4.50	5544	......	44	39	42½	+ ¾	+ 1.8
DukeP	2.48	394329	7	30⅛	22¼	29	+ 3⅞	+ 15.4
Duke pf	6.75	127	......	120	95	120	+ 16½	+ 15.9
Duke pf	8.70	928	......	76½	64	70½	+ 1⅞	+ 2.7
Duke pf	8.20	1545	......	69½	59½	65	....	....
Duke pf	7.80	2520	......	67	57	61½	+ 1	+ 1.7
Duke pf	2.69	6469	......	25	21⅝	23¾	+ ⅛	+ .5
Duke pf	3.85	3724	......	32⅝	28	32⅛	+ 1	+ 3.2
Duke pf	11	3249	......	100⅜	89¼	97	— 1	— 1
Duk pfN	8.84	1734	......	84¼	77½	83½	+ 1¼	+ 1.5
Duk pfM	8.84	2824	......	74	64½	71½	+ 1¼	+ 1.8
Duke pf	8.28	1535	......	69¼	60½	66	— ¼	— .4
DunBrd	1.88	284637	20	67½	51⅛	65⅝	+ 3⅝	+ 5.9
DuqLt	2.06	211320	7	16⅜	11½	15⅛	+ 1⅝	+ 12
Duq pfA	2.10	2470	......	18¾	14	16⅜	— 1⅛	— 6.4
Duq pf	1.87	389	......	14¾	11¼	14⅜	+ 1⅜	+ 10.6
Duq pf	2	568	......	15⅜	12¼	13¾	— ⅛	— .9
Duq pf	2.05	441	......	15½	12	15	+ 1	+ 7.1
Duq pf	2.07	567	......	17	12½	14⅞	— ⅛	— .8
Duq pfG	2.10	203	......	16¼	13	15¼	+ ⅞	+ 6.1
Duq prK	2.10	1733	......	16½	12⅞	15¼	+ ½	+ 3.4
Duq pr	2.31	1420	......	17¾	13⅞	16¾	— ¼	— 1.5
Duq pr	2.75	620	......	25¼	22	24	....	....
Duq pf	7.20	992	......	55	43⅛	51¼	— ¾	— 1.4
DycoPt	.28	15600	7	18½	8½	9⅞	— 7¼	— 42.3
DynAm	.20	17069	12	22¾	17½	22¾	+ 3⅞	+ 20.5
— E—E—E —								
EGG	.48	93378	18	36⅛	26⅛	31⅝	— ⅞	— 2.7
E Syst	.50	242014	12	33⅞	21¾	24	— 7½	— 23.8
EagleP	1.04	26725	9	26⅞	20⅝	23½	— 2⅜	— 9.2
Easco	.44	59884	......	22⅞	12	16¼	— 5¼	— 24.4
EastAir		251167	....	7¾	3½	4⅛	— 2⅜	— 36.5
EAL wtO		16911	......	4½	1⅜	1½	— 1¾	— 53.8
EAL wtA		24180	......	1¾	½	9-16	—1 1-16	— 65.4
EsAir pf		5967	......	13½	6⅞	11½	+ ⅜	+ 3.4
EAir pfB		16376	......	15½	6¾	11¼	— 1	— 8.2
EAir pfC		13157	......	19½	9¾	13½	— 3	— 18.2
EastGF	1.30	159602	9	27⅞	19¼	25¾	+ 1¾	+ 7.3
EastUtl	1.94	46873	6	18	12½	18	+ 3⅛	+ 21
EsKod	3.20a	1221152	14	78	60¼	71⅞	— 4¼	— 5.6
Eaton	1.20	163858	9	56½	37¾	53⅛	— 2⅛	— 3.8
Eaton pf	10	50	......	210	164½	210	+ 2	+ 1
Echlin	.76	142996	11	27¼	20¼	25⅛	+ 1⅜	+ 5.8
Eckerd	1	213695	12	29¾	20¼	28¾	+ 1	+ 3.6
EdisBr	1.60	21770	8	43	32½	33½	— 8¼	— 19.8
EDO	.24	43825	12	19¾	13	16¾	— 1⅛	— 6.3
Edward	.80	78033	16	29⅛	18½	24⅛	+ ⅛	+ .5
EPG dpf	2.35	10256	......	22⅞	19¼	21⅝	+ ⅛	+ .6
EPG pf	3.75	5595	......	29⅝	25⅛	28	....	....
EPG pr		20009	......	28	23⅞	27⅛	+ ½	+ 1.9
ElToro n		31429	12	14⅝	9	11	....	....
Elcor	.36	5439	......	15⅝	8⅛	8⅜	— 5⅜	— 39.1
ElecAs		15631	......	8⅝	2⅝	3¼	— 3½	— 51.9
EMM		29435	14	8¾	4⅜	4¾	— 3¼	— 40.6
EMM pf	1	2004	......	10¼	7¾	8¼	— 2⅛	— 20.5
Elctsp s	.08	31434	24	24	19⅛	21	+ 2⅝	+ 14.3
Elgin	.80	9407	11	19⅜	11¼	12⅞	— 4⅛	— 24.3
Elscint		104478	31	20	5⅝	7½	— 11	— 59.5
EmrsEl	2.60	246199	14	71¾	58⅛	69½	+ 3	+ 4.5
EmRd s	.94t	94174	16	10⅝	5½	10	+ 3⅜	+ 50.9
EmryA	.50	243519	10	26	11¾	17⅜	— 8¼	— 32.2
Emhart	1.40b	89518	9	31½	24½	29½	+ 1⅜	+ 4.9
Emht pf	2.10	48	......	110	95½	105	— 1½	— 1.4
EmpDs	1.76	8180	7	19¾	14¾	18⅞	+ 2⅜	+ 14.4
Emp pf	.47	927	......	4¾	3¾	4¼	— ¼	— 5.6
Emp pf	.50	417	......	4⅞	4	4½	+ ⅜	+ 9.1
Emp pf	.92	291	......	8¼	7	8	+ ⅜	+ 4.9
EnExc		107285	....	9-16	⅛	5-32	—17-32	— 77.3
EnglCp	.72	99519	15	39⅛	22⅝	28	— 10½	— 27.3
EnisBu	.56	7588	11	29	18¼	29	+ 6⅞	+ 31.1
Enserch	1.60	264894	18	22¾	17½	21	— 1¼	— 5.6
Ensch pf	10.32	800	......	103	97	101	— 1	— 1
Ensch pf	6.25e	30064	......	58⅜	51½	54½	— 3½	— 6
Ensch pf	11.23e	11994	......	107	91⅜	98⅜	....	....
Ensrce		87347	20	3¼	1⅞	2	— ⅝	— 23.8
Entera	.21i	52406	......	21⅜	9⅛	10	— 5¼	— 34.4
EntxE n	1.25e	13819	......	20	16⅜	16⅞	....	....
Entexln	1.30	54134	7	21¾	16	20¼	— ⅜	— 1.8
Equifax	1.70	13576	14	35⅛	23¼	34⅛	+ 6⅝	+ 24.1
Equimk		23803	......	5⅞	3	4⅛	— ¾	— 15.4
Eqmk pf	2.31	2235	......	18¼	11⅛	14⅜	— 2⅝	— 15.4
EqtRs s	1.72	40540	6	38⅝	28½	36	+ 5½	+ 18
Equitc n	.12	9429	7	14⅜	9½	10⅜	....	....
Erbmnt	.20e	62870	15	14½	8⅞	11⅜	— 1½	— 11.7
EssBs n	.09e	17896	10	15⅛	12⅝	14⅞	....	....
EssexC	.80b	9619	10	22⅛	15⅜	20¼	+ 1¼	+ 6.6
Estrlne	.72	33024	12	34⅜	20⅝	25⅛	— 4	— 13.7
Ethyl	.85	149900	11	33¼	20	32	+ 6½	+ 25.5
Ethyl pf	2.40	67	......	174	104	174	+ 36	+ 26.1
EvanP	1.07t	50411	......	11	3	3⅝	— 5⅞	— 61.8
Evan pf	1.40	3737	......	10⅞	7	7¼	— 3⅜	— 31.8
Evan pf	2.10	731	......	14½	11	11⅛	— 2⅛	— 16
ExCelo	1.60	45240	10	41	30	37⅛	— 1⅝	— 4.2
Excelsr	1.81e	3050	......	16	13⅜	15½	....	....
Exxon	3.40	2321766	7	45½	36⅛	45	+ 7⅝	+ 20.4
— F—F—F —								
FH Ind		19905	6	12⅞	6¼	7¾	— 4⅛	— 34.7
FMC	2.20	141026	8	62	41½	56⅜	+ 10¼	+ 22.2
FMC pf	2.25	2962	......	76½	51¾	67½	+ 9½	+ 16.4
FabCtr	.28	12528	15	13⅝	9⅝	12½	+ ⅝	+ 5.3
Facet		15962	......	16⅛	9⅛	11¾	— 3⅞	— 24.8
Fairchd	.80	58193	9	19¼	15	16¾	— 1¾	— 9.5
Fairc pf	3.60	12725	......	39	33⅞	36⅜	— 1¼	— 3.3
Fairfd	.16	41959	10	16¾	9⅝	14⅝	+ ⅜	+ 2.6
FamDlr	.22	85710	20	29¼	16¼	24⅜	+ 3⅝	+ 17.5
Fanstl n	.60e	14675	12	19⅜	14⅝	15	....	....
FrWstF		4245	5	33⅝	27¼	29	— 2¼	— 7.2
Farah	.88	49896	8	28¼	14⅜	19⅜	— 5⅝	— 22.5
FayDrg	.20	54115	15	13¾	8⅜	10⅛	— 3⅛	— 23.6
Feders		50793	9	7½	4¼	5½	— ⅜	— 6.4
FedlCo	1.64	40482	7	35⅛	29¼	34⅛	+ 3⅜	+ 11
FedExp		672090	22	47	27¾	34½	— 11¾	— 25.4
FdMog	1.52	34055	9	37½	29⅜	31	— 6	— 16.2
FedNM	.16	1053795		25¼	10⅞	15⅜	— 7⅝	— 33.2
FedPB s	.70	47798	7	27	16⅝	21	— 1⅞	— 8.2
FPap pf	1.20	68	......	63	45	50	— 5	— 9.1
FedRlt	1.44	14765	15	21¼	16	20¼	+ 2⅞	+ 16.6
FdSgnl	.80	21530	17	19⅝	13⅞	15	— 2½	— 14.3
FedDSt	2.40	252491	8	55¾	42⅝	51⅝	— 2	— 3.7
Ferro	1.20	41596	8	38½	22¼	24⅜	— 8⅞	— 26.7
Fldcst	2	16577	10	39	25¼	31	— 5¾	— 15.6
FinCpA	.20	1274899		24⅜	4	7⅞	— 12⅜	— 61.1
FinCp pf	.60	1105	......	5¾	3½	5	— ⅝	— 11.1
FinCp pf	6.74e	59762	......	48	14¼	32	— 14½	— 31.2
FnSBar		18355	......	9¼	2½	3½	— 4⅝	— 56.9
Firestn	.80	256275	9	22⅝	15¾	17	— 5¼	— 23.6
FtAtlln	.88	38199	8	25¾	19	24	+ 3¾	+ 18.5
FtAtl pf	6.20e	9770	......	57¼	50¼	54½	....	....
FBkSy	s1.48	65938	7	29⅜	21¼	26⅜	— ½	— 1.9
FBkFla	1.20	9249	11	33	24⅛	31½	+ 6¾	+ 27.3
FBost	.60a	94716	10	56	34⅜	54⅝	+ 12⅞	+ 30.8
FstChic	1.32	291969	15	27	18⅝	21⅜	— 4	— 15.8
FChi a pf	5.82e	31327	......	57	44½	45	— 8¾	— 16.3
FChi pfB	8.67e	19077	......	87⅝	70	70½	— 12¼	— 14.8
FChi pfC	8.20e	15124	......	104⅝	87	87¼	....	....
FtBTex	1.30	90523	13	20¼	13¼	14⅝	— 4¼	— 22.5
FtBTx pf	5.87e	19503	......	56	40	41½	— 11⅜	— 21.5
FtBTx pf	2.48e	16452	......	51	38½	38½	....	....
FtCity		40073	14	21	11¾	18¼	+ 5¼	+ 40.4
FFedAz		148471	....	18⅞	10¾	13⅝	+ 1½	+ 12.4
Flntste	2.34	159310	7	45¼	30¼	43	+ 1⅜	+ 3.3
Flntst pf	2.37	28064	......	30⅜	21	26⅝	— 1⅞	— 6.6
FtMiss	.24	99810	9	13¾	7¼	8⅞	— 3⅛	— 26

FNStB	2.88	22040	6	46⅞	31¼	46⅞	+ 5½	+ 13.3
FNStB	pf11.70e	5293	......	107⅜	90⅛	98¾	— 4½	— 4.4
FstPa		88910	100	7½	4½	6	— ⅝	— 9.4
FstPa	pf2.62	50890	......	28⅛	20¼	25½	— ¼	— 1
FtUnRl	1.84	33755	13	28¾	20	26¼	+ 3	+ 12.9
FtVaBk	.84	34159	8	20	14¾	19⅛	+ 2⅝	+ 15.9
FtWisc	1.20	15653	7	24¾	16	24¾	+ 4⅜	+ 21.5
FWisc	pf6.25	898	......	52½	45⅞	50½	....	....
Fischb	1	31586	18	55½	30¼	32½	— 18	— 35.6
FishFd	.05e	21861	......	12⅛	8¼	10⅛	+ ⅛	+ 1.3
FltFinG	2.40	24702	8	57¾	40½	57⅛	+ 9⅜	+ 19.6
FltFin wi		....	......	28⅛	20¼		....	— 100
FltF	pf4.63e	13211	......	47½	42½	42½	— 1¾	— 4
FleetEn	.36	371750	10	30¾	14⅛	26⅜	— ¼	— .9
Flemng	.88	57763	13	35⅜	22¼	34⅛	+ 5¼	+ 18.2
FlexiV	.80	36303	12	30⅞	23¾	29⅞	+ 1⅛	+ 3.9
Flexi	pf 1.61	4704	......	12⅝	10¼	12⅝	+ 1¼	+ 11
FligtSf	.20	43585	20	35	19½	34⅝	+ 5⅝	+ 19.4
FloatPt		100211	11	36¾	12½	19⅝	— 16⅜	— 45.5
FlaEC	.16a	8256	12	36⅞	29¾	34⅜	+ 1⅛	+ 3.4
FlaPL	3.76	315497	9	45⅝	35¼	44¾	+ 4½	+ 11.2
FlaPrg	2.16	245945	9	24¼	18¾	23¾	+ 3½	+ 17.3
FlaStl	.40	27362	12	24⅞	11⅝	13⅜	— 6⅝	— 33.1
FlwGen		58090	......	10¼	3¼	4¼	— 5¼	— 55.3
Flowr s	.38	40047	17	17½	11½	16⅝	+ 3⅜	+ 25.5
Fluor	.40	323795	1475	23⅜	14½	14¾	— 2½	— 14.5
FooteC	2.20	8545	10	54½	43⅜	51	+ 2½	+ 5.2
FordM	1.60a	1891678	3	51⅜	33	45⅝	+ 3¼	+ 7.7
FtDear	1.36	10281	......	12	10¼	11⅞	+ ⅝	+ 5.6
FtHowd	1.64	72919	14	63½	45¼	59⅛	+ 4⅜	+ 8
FostWh	.44	73396	11	16⅝	10	11⅛	— 4⅜	— 28.2
FoxStP	.68	15432	13	12¾	6⅝	8¼	— 2¾	— 25
Foxbro	1.04	46196	61	40½	27	30	— 5¼	— 14.9
FMOG	1.81e	97305	......	11⅝	5⅛	8¼	+ 3	+ 57.1
FrptMc	.60	372830	13	25¾	13½	16¾	— 3⅜	— 16.8
Frigtrn	.60	63210	15	34⅜	20⅞	30	+ 4⅛	+ 15.9
Fruehf s	.60	104448	6	33⅝	19	22⅝	— 8⅜	— 27
Fruhf pf	2	17829	......	40¼	25	27⅞	— 9⅛	— 24.7
Fuqua	.40	49127	9	31½	20	31½	+ 4¾	+ 17.8
Fuqa pf	1.25	181	......	49½	35	48	+ 6	+ 14.3

— G—G—G —

GAF	.10e	123988	....	25¾	15	24½	+ 7⅞	+ 47.4
GAF pf	1.20	13862	......	32	20	31	+ 9½	+ 44.2
GATX	1.20	61508	......	34½	25¾	33¼	+ ¾	+ 2.3
GATX	pf2.50	262	......	44	33¼	42	+ 2	+ 5
GATX	pf5.24e	11185	......	51⅝	49¼	50	....	....
GCA		208994	14	41¼	19⅛	24½	— 11½	— 31.9
GEICO	.88	62249	10	65⅝	48⅞	58	— ⅛	— .2
GEO		59924	......	10⅛	4	4¾	— 3⅝	— 43.3
GF Cp		17413	......	13⅞	5⅞	6	— 2⅜	— 28.4
GTE	3.08	719027	8	43⅞	34⅞	40⅝	— 3⅛	— 7.1
GTE pf	2.50	460	......	37⅞	31¼	35⅝	— 1⅞	— 5
GTE pf	2	919	......	25	21½	24¾	....	....
GTE pf	2.48	11600	......	22¾	19⅝	21¾	+ 1⅛	+ 5.5
GalHou		17261	......	10	4⅞	5¾	— 1⅜	— 19.3
Ganett	1.48	264424	18	50¾	33⅜	47	+ 7⅝	+ 19.4
GapStr	.50	50847	11	23⅝	17½	20⅝	— ⅜	— 1.8
Gearht	.40	88063	13	30⅝	10⅝	11¼	— 9⅝	— 46.1
Gelco	.56	55542	14	23¼	13⅜	16¾	— 4¼	— 20.2
GemCa		3492	128	65¼	53⅝	65¼	+ 5¼	+ 8.8
GemIn	4.85e	5640	......	16	11⅝	12	— 3¼	— 21.3
GnCorp	1.50b	80617	15	40	30¼	34¼	— 5⅛	— 13
GAInv	3.05e	22582	......	22⅝	15⅞	16⅞	— 4¾	— 22
GnBcsh	1	7035	8	45¾	29¾	42	+ 4¼	+ 11.3
GCinm s	.40	59509	9	28	16¾	26¾	+ 4¼	+ 18.9
GCn pf s	.46	14929	......	27	16¾	26	+ 4⅜	+ 20.2
GnDat s		67513	19	21	12½	15⅜	— ⅝	— 3.9
GnDyn	1	462959	10	69¾	42	69½	+ 11⅜	+ 19.6
GenEl	2.20	1411169	12	59⅜	48¼	56⅝	— 2	— 3.4
GnFds	2.50	260884	9	59⅞	45⅛	55⅞	+ 4½	+ 8.8
GGth	.60	48350	112	31½	23	30¼	+ 6¼	+ 26
GGth wt		36420	......	12½	6½	8¾	+ 1¾	+ 25
GGth	pf 1.90	6094	......	31¼	26⅛	30¼	+ 3	+ 11
GnHost	.40	112432	2	22	12¼	17⅝	+ 3⅝	+ 25.9
GnHous	.24	20775	11	19½	8⅞	9¾	— 7	— 41.8
GnInst	.50	409487	16	34⅝	15½	16¼	— 16¼	— 50
GnMills	2.24	205513	12	60	41⅝	50⅞	— 1⅜	— 2.6
GMot	4.75r	1915582	5	82¾	61	78⅜	+ 4	+ 5.4
GM E n		39452	......	42½	33	42⅜	....	....
GMot	pf3.75	4430	......	39	33¾	36½	+ 1⅜	+ 3.9
GMot pf	5	6752	......	52¼	44½	50⅛	+ 3⅝	+ 7.8
GNC	.16	43302	12	13½	3⅞	5⅛	— 8	— 61
GPU		284219	7	11⅝	7¼	11½	+ 3¾	+ 48.4
GenRe	1.44	256288	22	68¼	46¼	63¾	— 4¾	— 6.9
GnRefr		14388	5	9½	5	8¼	+ ⅝	+ 8.2
GnSignl	1.80	99824	13	54	39⅝	47	— 3¾	— 7.4
GTFI	pf 1.25	752	......	11½	9¾	11¼	+ ½	+ 4.7
GTFI	pf 1.30	627	......	12	10	11½	+ ⅞	+ 8.2
GTFI	pf 8.16	745	......	68½	61⅝	65½	— 1½	— 2.2
Gensco		59683	8	8⅜	5¼	5⅝	— 2¼	— 28.6
GnRad	.10	183061	16	39	13⅞	15⅜	— 21⅝	— 58.4
Genst g	1	93284	......	25¼	15	20¼	— 4¼	— 17.3
Gst pf	1.68	630	......	22	16½	19⅞	— 2⅜	— 10.7
GenPt	s 1.02	154237	15	33¾	24	31¾	+ 1¾	+ 5.8
GaPac	.80	596517	12	25¾	18	25	+ ¼	+ 1
GaPc	pf2.24	17600	......	36¾	33	36¾	+ 1⅞	+ 5.4
GaP	pfB2.24	2281	......	35¾	32¼	35½	+ 3¾	+ 11.8
GaPc	pfC2.24	1014	......	33	30¼	32½	+ 2¼	+ 7.4
GaPw	pf3.44	12621	......	27¾	22⅞	26¼	+ ¼	+ 1
GaPw	pf3.76	8547	......	30⅛	25½	28⅛	— ⅛	— .4
GaPw	pf2.56	5734	......	22	17¼	19¼	+ ⅛	+ .7
GaPw	pf2.52	2331	......	21	17	19⅝	+ ⅝	+ 3.3
GaPw	pf2.75	7120	......	24¼	21¼	22	— 1¼	— 5.4
GaPw	pf7.80	3780	......	62½	52	59	+ ½	+ .9
GaPw	pf7.72	407	......	61¾	51¼	58	+ ½	+ .9
GerbP	s1.16	107513	10	32	20½	24¾	— 3½	— 12.4
GerbSc	.12	55395	18	31½	18	29	+ 2¼	+ 8.4
GerbS s	.12	86876	13	21¼	12	15⅞	— 1⅞	— 10.6
GiantP		8917	......	10⅝	6¾	9⅛	+ 2¼	+ 32.7
GibrFn		148957	5	11⅞	5¾	9½	— ⅞	— 8.4
GiffHill	.52	59543	15	26¼	16¾	24⅜	+ 6¼	+ 34.5
Gillette	2.60	205804	11	58½	42⅝	56⅝	+ 8	+ 16.5
GleasC		12522	......	17¾	11⅛	12¾	— 1	— 7.3
GloblM	.24	175383	....	9¾	4½	4⅝	— 3¼	— 41.3
GlobM	pf3.50	31693	......	26	17¾	19¼	— 5¾	— 23
GldNug		252644	10	15⅜	8⅛	9⅜	— 3⅝	— 27.9
GldN wt		95546	......	6⅛	1¾	2	— 3	— 60
GldWF	.20	204268	6	25¼	11	23¾	+ 1⅝	+ 7.3
Gdrich	1.56	141478	6	36⅜	24⅝	27	— 3⅜	— 11.1
Gdrch	pf7.85	548	......	83	73½	83	+ 9	+ 12.2
Gdrch	pf .97	394	......	11	8¼	9½	+ ½	+ 5.6
Goodyr	1.60	684576	7	31½	23	26	— 4⅜	— 14.4
GordnJ	.52	41398	7	21⅝	13¾	16½	— 4⅞	— 22.8
Gould	.68	365780	12	36½	19	21⅛	— 9⅛	— 30.2
Grace	2.80	183004	10	46⅞	36½	39¾	— 5½	— 12.2
Graingr	1.24	49347	13	66	47	57⅜	— 4⅛	— 6.7
GtAFst	.40	95675	8	13¾	8⅛	13⅜	+ 3¼	+ 32.1
GtAtPc		126882	9	18	11⅝	16	+ 3¾	+ 30.6
GtLkIn	.90a	10139	9	39⅞	27½	37⅜	+ 3⅜	+ 9.9
GNIrn	1.85e	4186	6	21½	15½	15⅝	— 3⅛	— 16.7
GtNNk	1.52	211637	7	43¼	31	35½	— 5½	— 13.4
GtNNk	pf4.75	7541	......	67½	51½	57½	— 6½	— 10.2
GtWFin	.88	461634	10	26⅜	16½	25⅜	+ 3⅜	+ 15.3
GWHsp		84584	33	19¾	9½	13⅞	+ 3¾	+ 37
GMP	1.72	5841	9	15½	11¼	15	+ 1	+ 7.1
Greyh	1.20	300062	12	26¼	18⅝	24¼	— 1⅛	— 4.4
Greyh	pf4.75	164	......	42	37½	42	+ 1	+ 2.4
Grolier		76334	5	5	2¾	3⅛	— 1¼	— 28.6
GrowG	.40b	23507	15	20	12⅞	18¾	+ 1	+ 5.6
GrubEl	.08	27443	10	9⅝	6¾	8	— 1½	— 15.8
Grumn	1	129703	7	29⅝	21¾	27⅛	+ 2⅞	+ 11.9
Grum	pf2.80	12845	......	26¼	23⅝	25⅝	+ 1⅛	+ 4.6
Gruntal	.16	14459	22	8½	4¼	4¾	— 3½	— 42.4
Guardl	.32	38115	13	23½	14½	23	+ 2½	+ 12.2
Guilfrd	.68	32914	7	32	20	21¾	— 8⅞	— 29
GlfWst	.90	566511	8	35	25⅛	28⅜	— 1¾	— 5.8
GlfW pf	5.75	216	......	62	56	57¼	— 2¼	— 3.8
GulfRs		50854	5	24¼	12	12⅝	— 7½	— 37.3
GulfR	pf .20	17	......	34	27	29	+ 4	+ 16
GulfR	pf1.30	749	......	30	16⅝	17½	— 8	— 31.4
GlfStUt	1.64	395122	6	13⅞	10	13	+ ¼	+ 2
GlfSU	pf4.40	421	......	38	30½	31	— 5	— 13.9
GlfSU	pf4.52	z910	......	35	32½	34	— 3½	— 9.3
GlfSU	pf5.08	z1370	......	39½	34½	35½	— 3⅛	— 8.1
GlfSU	pf5.69e	4248	......	50¾	39	41¾	....	....
GlfSU	pr3.85	6017	......	30½	24	27¾	+ ¼	+ .9
GlfSU	pr4.40	5125	......	33¾	27	31¼	....	....
GlfSU	pf8.80	1876	......	76⅝	55¾	65	— 7¾	— 10.7
GAero	.55e	124306	8	20¼	12⅞	13¾	— 2⅝	— 16
Gulton	.60	9131	12	18⅛	14	14¾	— 1¾	— 10.6

— H—H—H —

HRT n		9853	......	7	4¼	5¼	....	....

HallFB	1	106239	....	26	19¼	24⅛	+ 1	+ 4.3
Halbtn	1.80	925341	10	44	27⅛	28½	− 11⅞	− 29.4
Hallwd	.08	85143	......	1½	¾	1⅛	− ⅛	− 10
Halwd pf	.56	12391	......	8½	5¾	7⅞	....	....
HamrP	2.04	55381	8	55⅜	38¾	47⅛	+ ⅜	+ .8
HanJS	1.47a	14691	......	13½	11½	13¼	+ ⅜	+ 2.9
HanJI	1.84a	8734	......	18¾	15⅝	18⅝	+ 1	+ 5.7
Hndlm s	.92	53638	14	41	21⅛	39¾	+ 13⅜	+ 50.7
HandH	.66	28321	16	20	15½	16¼	− 1½	− 8.5
Hanna	.40	26482	12	24¼	16¾	18	− 2⅝	− 12.7
HarBrJ	1	74595	13	45	23⅞	44⅞	+ 17⅞	+ 66.2
HarInd	.92	23403	17	49	32½	47⅝	+ 10⅝	+ 28.7
Harnish		61170	7	12⅛	7⅜	8¾	+ ¼	+ 2.9
HrpRw	.80	11443	16	29⅞	14½	28¼	+ 7¼	+ 34.5
Harris	.88	229506	12	42⅝	22¾	27⅛	− 13	− 32.4
HarGr n		15213	......	15	10⅝	12¼	....	....
Harsco	1.28	37858	12	25	19	24	+ ¼	+ 1.1
Hartmx	1.12	53811	9	32¾	23½	28½	− 3⅞	− 12
HattSe	1.80	2892	11	16¼	13⅞	16¼	+ ¾	+ 4.8
HawEl	s1.64	32263	9	21¼	15⅝	21	+ 5⅜	+ 34.4
HayesA	.10e	20047	8	11¾	8	10⅞	+ ⅜	+ 3.6
Hazletn	.36	66658	46	34⅝	15¾	27⅜	+ ⅜	+ 1.4
HazLab	.32	10590	17	13½	9	9⅞	− 2⅜	− 19.4
Hecks	.28	62653	26	15⅞	9⅞	10½	− 4½	− 30
HeclaM	.20e	151935	30	23½	13¼	13⅝	− 5⅛	− 27.3
Heilmn	.48b	97768	9	30½	14⅜	17⅛	− 12⅝	− 42.4
Heilig	.36	24625	11	21¾	15⅝	18¾	− 2⅜	− 11.2
Heinz	1.60	209296	12	45	32	43	+ 5	+ 13.2
Heinz pf	1.70	52	......	99	77½	97	+ 17	+ 21.3
HelneC		25734	5	32⅛	12¾	16	− 14⅞	− 48.2
HelmP	.34	150031	24	25⅞	18	20	− ⅛	− .6
HemCa		5709	......	5⅝	3⅝	4⅞	− ⅛	− 2.5
HemInc	.90e	1513	......	12⅜	11	11¾	+ ¾	+ 6.8
Herculs	1.60	329869	9	38	27¼	33⅞	− 1⅞	− 5.2
HeritC	.05e	30706	32	19	13⅜	18⅜	+ 1⅞	+ 11.4
HeritC pf	1.50	1878	......	23¼	18¾	23	+ 2⅞	+ 14.3
Hershy	1.40	77804	12	41¼	28¼	38⅝	+ 7	+ 22.1
Hesston		18125	......	24⅞	5¼	5⅝	− 16⅛	− 74.1
Hestn pf		2465	......	25	9	9⅛	− 13¼	− 59.2
HewlPk	.22	1304752	13	45½	31⅛	33⅞	− 8½	− 20.1
Hexcel	.60	23473	18	30	17½	28	+ 7	+ 33.3
HiShear	.50	17650	......	17½	12	15⅞	+ 1¾	+ 12.4
HiVolt	.15	28247	9	12½	8⅛	9½	+ ⅜	+ 4.1
Hilnbr s	.51	33425	11	23⅞	17½	21	− 4	− 16
Hilton	1.80	147317	15	58	45½	57⅝	+ ⅝	+ 1.1
Hitachi	.28e	149855	12	44⅛	31	34⅜	− 1⅝	− 4.5
Holiday	.90	334159	13	51¾	35¼	43¾	− 3¾	− 7.9
HlidyA	1.70t	24	......	65	55½	64½	− 15½	− 19.4
HollyS	1	32854	12	75	45¼	72	+ 11¼	+ 18.5
HomeD		303445	32	27⅞	12	17¾	− 8½	− 32.4
HmFSD		307649	7	20⅜	11¾	19¼	+ 5¼	+ 37.5
HmeG pf	1.10	7422	......	9⅜	8	8⅝	− ⅝	− 6.8
Hmstke	.20	321444	28	36¾	20½	21½	− 8¼	− 27.7
HmstF n	.40	15939	4	20⅞	8¾	11⅝	....	....
Honda	.40e	105633	10	60¼	41½	48½	....	....
Honwll	s1.90	498894	10	67½	46⅜	63¼	− 1¾	− 2.7
HoovrU	1.04	34177	9	28⅛	19⅛	23⅜	− 2½	− 9.7
HrznBn	1.12	20175	8	26⅜	18	26⅛	+ 6	+ 29.8
HrzBn pf	2.98e	1910	......	26	20	23½	....	....
Horizon		40942	......	10	3⅞	4½	− 4¼	− 48.6
HospCp	.50	666417	12	48¾	35¾	37¾	− 1¾	− 4.4
Hotelln	2.60	13569	13	28⅝	21⅞	27¾	+ 4⅞	+ 21.3
HoughM	.96	30025	13	35¼	20¾	33⅝	+ 10½	+ 45.4
HouFab	.40	38756	12	19	13⅝	19	+ 3	+ 18.8
HousInt	1.75	288064	8	34⅜	24	32¾	+ 2	+ 6.5
HoInt pf	2.37	197	......	75	54½	72¼	+ 1¾	+ 2.5
HoInt pf	2.50	617	......	50½	36	50½	+ 6	+ 13.5
HoInt pf	6.25	5427	......	72½	61	69	− 1¼	− 1.8
HouInd	2.48	534481	6	22½	17⅝	22½	+ 3⅛	+ 16.1
HouNG	2	595655	10	63¼	40¼	40¾	− 2	− 4.7
HouOR	2.19e	10101	......	20	9¾	9⅞	− 8⅜	− 45.9
HowlCp	.40	9334	20	23¼	11	15¼	+ 3⅝	+ 31.2
Hubbrd	2.20	25008	11	26	20½	24½	+ 1½	+ 6.5
Huffy	.40	31336	8	16⅜	9⅞	12⅜	− 3⅝	− 22.7
HughTl	.48	290823	....	21⅜	12½	13½	− 7⅜	− 35.3
HughSp	.32	20665	8	25¼	17¼	17¼	− 7¼	− 29.6
Human	.68	681785	12	33	21½	23½	+ 1½	+ 6.8
HuntMf	.44	10289	15	24¾	17½	23	+ 2⅞	+ 14.3
HuttEF	.80	305745	20	39⅛	23⅞	29¼	− 5¾	− 16.4
Hydral	1.92	6664	8	23¼	18¼	22¼	+ ¾	+ 3.5

— I—I—I —

IC Ind s	1.30	154586	8	28¾	21	28¾	+ 4⅞	+ 20.4
IC In pf	3.50	1569	......	84¼	62¾	83	+ 11¾	+ 16.5
ICN		86065	51	9¾	4⅞	9¼	+ 2⅛	+ 29.8
ICN pf	2.70	1206	......	25⅜	22½	25⅜	....	....
INAIn	1.92	5398	......	17⅛	14	16⅜	+ ⅜	+ 2.3
IRT Pr	s1.60	10403	10	19⅜	13⅞	18¾	+ 2½	+ 15.4
ITT Cp	1	1425761	8	47⅜	20⅝	29⅜	− 15⅜	− 34.4
ITT pfH	4	121	......	87½	46	57	− 26⅛	− 31.4
ITT pfJ	4	312	......	79	44	51½	− 24	− 31.8
ITT pfK	4	4243	......	76	40	52	− 20½	− 28.3
ITT pfO	5	4278	......	71	44½	55½	− 10½	− 15.9
ITT pfN	2.25	1303	......	58¾	28	39¾	− 16½	− 29.3
ITT pfI	4.50	1647	......	80	42⅛	54⅛	− 21⅜	− 28.3
IU Int	1.20	151415	22	25⅝	15¼	16⅜	− 6¾	− 29.2
IdahoP	3.28	62896	7	38½	30¾	38¼	+ 4¾	+ 14.2
IdealB		42103	......	26	13⅛	13¾	− 9¼	− 40.2
IllPowr	2.64	450568	6	23⅞	17⅝	23¾	+ 3¾	+ 18.8
IlPow pf	2.04	1347	......	16⅞	13½	16	....	....
IlPow pf	2.10	270	......	18¼	14½	18	+ ¾	+ 4.4
IlPow pf	2.13	595	......	18	14½	16½	− 1¼	− 7
IlPow pf	2.21	1382	......	17¾	15	17¾	+ ¼	+ 1.4
IlPow pf	2.35	820	......	19½	15⅝	18⅝	− ⅛	− .7
IlPow pf	4.12	2579	......	33½	27¼	32	+ ½	+ 1.6
IlPow pf	3.78	3385	......	31	25	30½	+ 1½	+ 5.2
IlPow pf	5.75	70	......	50	49¾	49¾	....	....
IlPow pf	4.64e	21385	......	45½	37½	39¼	− 3⅞	− 9
IlPow pf	5.83	3041	......	50½	45⅜	48¼	− 1⅞	− 3.7
IlPow pf	4.47	5935	......	36	28⅞	35	+ ⅜	+ 1.1
IlPow pf	4	7693	......	32	25½	31	− ¾	− 2.4
ITW s	.64	27887	15	29⅞	21¼	28¼	+ 1	+ 3.7
ImpChm	2	442755	13	37⅛	27¾	34	− 3½	− 9.3
ImplCp		89175	......	9⅜	5⅜	9⅜	+ ¼	+ 2.7
INCO	.20	438020	....	15¼	8⅝	12⅜	− 2¼	− 15.4
IndiM pf	7.08	643	......	54	45	50¼	+ ¼	+ .5
IndiM pf	7.76	727	......	59½	49	55⅝	+ 1⅝	+ 3
IndiM pf	8.68	3210	......	66⅛	54½	63½	+ 3¼	+ 5.4
IndiM pf	12	598	......	102½	91½	97⅛	+ ⅝	+ .7
IndiM pf	2.15	2012	......	17⅛	14	16⅜	+ ¾	+ 4.8
IndiM pf	2.25	4185	......	17¾	14⅝	17⅛	+ 1⅛	+ 7
IndiM pf	3.63	6009	......	28½	23⅛	26¾	+ ⅛	+ .5
IndiM pf	2.75	838	......	23¼	20½	22¼	− ¾	− 3.3
IndiGs	s1.88	7103	6	25⅝	16½	23¾	+ 7¼	+ 43.9
Inexco	.14	151590	16	15	5½	6	− 4⅜	− 42.2
Infmtc		47721	14	24¼	13¼	16⅞	− 3⅛	− 15.6
IngerR	2.60	99229	......	55¾	35½	45½	− 6⅞	− 13.1
IngR pf	2.35	10465	......	35	27¾	31½	− 2	− 6
IngrTec	.54	3608	19	15½	10⅞	13¾	− ⅛	− .9
InldStl	.50	154494	....	32¾	19⅞	23¼	− 7¾	− 25
InldSt pf	4.75	10806	......	48½	38⅝	42⅝	....	....
Insilco	1	62712	10	21⅞	14	18¾	+ ⅛	+ .7
InspRs		54468	......	12¼	4⅛	4⅝	− 6⅝	− 58.9
IntgRsc		105317	6	29½	11⅞	14⅜	− 11⅝	− 44.7
IntgR pf	3.03	21723	......	33½	19	21⅝	− 10⅜	− 32.4
IntgR pf	6.63e	5505	......	54¼	42	46	− 8	− 14.8
IntgR pf	4.25	29650	......	42½	25¼	29⅝	− 8⅜	− 22
IntRFn		19693	......	18¼	7¼	8¼	− 6¾	− 45
ItcpSe	2.10a	9462	......	18½	15⅞	18	− ⅛	− .7
Interco	3.08	71182	9	68	55	59¾	− 6¾	− 10.2
Inter pf	7.75	1547	......	146½	120	128	− 14½	− 10.2
Intrfst	.60	305317	6	18⅞	9½	10¼	− 6⅜	− 38.3
Intrlk	2.60	19616	6	51⅛	41	44½	+ 1⅛	+ 2.6
Intmed		46441	......	19¾	8¾	9¼	− 5⅞	− 38.8
IntAlu	.72	9945	9	21⅞	14¾	18¾	− ¼	− 1.3
IBM	4.40	2874291	12	128½	99	123⅛	+ 1⅛	+ .9
IntFlav	1.12	150599	15	29¼	22⅞	28	+ ¾	+ 2.8
IntHarv		637749	....	13⅝	5⅛	8⅛	− 3⅜	− 29.3
IntHr wt		106883	....	9⅜	2⅞	5¼	− 2⅝	− 33.3
IntH pfC		7684	......	44½	23½	42¼	+ 7	+ 19.9
IntH pfA		5408	......	50⅝	20¾	31	− 12¼	− 28.3
IntH pfD		17793	......	28	17¾	25¾	....	....
IntMin	2.60	196853	11	49	32⅞	37⅛	− 6¼	− 14.4
IntMn pf	4	175	......	35¾	30¼	34	....	....
IntMult	1.76	32763	8	33	23	25⅝	− 5⅞	− 18.7
IntPapr	2.40	571775	11	59⅞	46	53⅞	− 5⅛	− 8.7
IntRc s		66236	14	12½	9¼	12¼	+ ¼	+ 2.1
IntNrth	2.48	184660	8	42½	32¾	42¼	+ 2¾	+ 7
IntNt pf	6.40	z1640	......	75	68½	69	− 2¾	− 3.8
IntNt pf	6.84	216	......	74	67½	68½	− 4	− 5.5
IntNt pf	8.48	102	......	87¾	82¼	84	....	....
IntNt pfJ	10.50	2190	......	148½	126	143½	+ 6	+ 4.4
IntNt pfH	10.50	4832	......	96¾	86¼	94⅛	+ 2⅝	+ 2.9

IntpGp	s 1	42793	11	36	24⅜	34⅜	+ 8⅜	+ 32.2
IntBakr		30015	......	17¼	10	16½	+ 2½	+ 17.9
IntstPw	1.90	25707	7	19⅜	15⅞	18⅞	+ 1¼	+ 7.1
InPw	pf 2.28	365	......	20	16¾	19	+ ¾	+ 4.1
IowaEl	1.90	29736	8	18⅜	14¼	18	+ 3⅛	+ 21
IowllG	2.60	36457	7	27⅝	21½	26¾	+ 2¼	+ 9.2
Iowlll	pf2.31	1831	......	19½	17	19⅛	+ ⅞	+ 4.8
IowaRs	3.08	27319	7	30⅜	25	30	+ 1¼	+ 4.4
Ipalco	2.92	99885	8	33¾	26	33⅛	+ 5	+ 17.8
IpcoCp	.34	21516	9	14⅝	9¾	10½	— 1⅞	— 15.2
IrvBk	s 1.84	54134	6	34¼	23⅛	32⅛	+ 5¾	+ 21.8
IrvBk	pf5.19e	28427	......	54	42¾	45	— 5¾	— 11.3
			— J—J—J —					
JWT	s 1.12	36188	11	27⅜	25¼	26½	+ ⅜	+ 1.4
JRiver	.56	129676	8	35⅞	23½	28¾	— 6⅝	— 18.7
Jamswy	.10	65127	9	19	12½	18⅜	+ 1⅞	+ 11.4
JapnF	1.15e	45473	......	15	10⅜	12⅛	— 1⅛	— 8.5
JeffPl	s 1.32	105372	10	41¼	23¾	40¼	+ 15⅛	+ 60.2
JerC	pf 4	169	......	29½	24½	29½	+ 2½	+ 9.3
JerC	pf 9.36	198	......	64	54¼	64	+ 2	+ 3.2
JerC	pf 8.12	449	......	55½	46½	55	+ 1½	+ 2.8
JerC	pf 8	1351	......	55	47	53⅞	+ ⅞	+ 1.7
JerC	pf 7.88	1103	......	54½	45½	54½	+ 3½	+ 6.9
JerC	pf13.50	548	......	98½	88½	95	+ 3½	+ 3.8
JerC	pf 11	523	......	92¼	76⅜	88¼	+ 8¾	+ 11
JerC	pf 2.18	4456	......	16¼	12¾	15⅞	+ 1⅜	+ 9.5
Jewlcr		12057	17	8	5⅞	6⅝	— ½	— 7
JohnJn	1.20	1041848	14	42⅞	28	36⅛	— 4¾	— 11.6
JohnCn	1.86a	30873	9	49⅜	37½	41⅜	— 7	— 14.5
Jorgen	1	4901	14	30⅜	21⅞	23⅞	— 5⅜	— 18.4
Josten	s .80	38177	13	22½	20¼	22⅛	+ 3⅜	+ 18
JoyMfg	1.40	108316	14	32⅝	21¾	25¼	— 5	— 16.5
			— K—K—K —					
KDI	.20	28101	10	10⅛	6¾	9	— ⅞	— 8.9
KLM	s	99417	11	14¾	9⅜	12⅞	+ ⅜	+ 3
KMI	pf 4.50	4864	......	39⅝	33	36¼	— 1⅞	— 4.9
K mart	1.24	1010838	8	37⅝	26¾	35¼	+ 2	+ 6
KN Eng		68294	13	36⅛	23¾	29	+ 4⅞	+ 20.2
KaisrAl	.60	218324	41	22½	12¾	14⅝	— 5⅛	— 25.9
KaiAl	pf4.12	22	......	69	45	49	— 24	— 32.9
Kai	57pf4.75	24	......	68	54	55½	— 20½	— 27
Kai	59pf4.75	19	......	68⅛	53	55¼	— 20¾	— 27.3
Kai	66pf4.75	34	......	70¾	52	53½	— 21½	— 28.7
KaisCe	.20	49800	......	25¼	14⅝	17⅛	— 4½	— 20.8
KaiC	pf 1.37	2856	......	22½	15¼	16⅝	— 2½	— 13.1
Kaneb	.40	231755	....	16½	8⅝	9¼	— 5⅛	— 35.7
Kaneb	pf12.63e	2230	......	101⅜	87	87¾	— 7¼	— 7.6
KCtyPL	2.36	133223	4	20½	14¼	19⅞	+ 1⅛	+ 6
KCPL	pf3.80	z3930	......	30	25	28	— ½	— 1.8
KCPL	pf4.35	155	......	33½	29	32½	— ½	— 1.5
KCPL	pf4.50	217	......	36½	29¼	34	— 1¼	— 3.5
KCPL	pf2.20	886	......	18	14¼	17	— ⅜	— 2.2
KCPL	pf2.33	937	......	19¼	15½	17½	— ½	— 2.8
KCSou	1	52507	11	60	36½	45⅜	— 12⅛	— 21.1
KCSo	pf 1	484	......	15	10¼	12¾	+ 1	+ 8.5
KanGE	2.36	250868	5	19	12½	17¼	....	....
KanPLt	2.76	71660	7	35¼	27⅝	33½	+ 3½	+ 11.7
KaPL	pf2.32	5087	......	22¼	18	20	+ 1⅛	+ 6
KaPL	pf2.23	2252	......	20⅞	17¼	18¾	— ½	— 2.6
Katyln		70575	......	33⅞	17¾	23⅜	— 6¾	— 22.4
Katy	pf 1.46	1278	......	86	49	62	— 15½	— 20
KaufBr	.40	89325	9	17½	10¾	15½	+ ½	+ 3.3
Kauf	pf 1.50	2031	......	16¾	12⅞	14½	— 1⅛	— 7.2
Kauf	pf 8.75	8077	......	83¾	68	74	— 6	— 7.5
Kellogg	1.76	142833	12	42¾	27	40	+ 7⅝	+ 23.6
Kellwd	1	15965	6	31⅝	21⅝	25¾	— 2¼	— 8
Kenai		16312	......	4¾	1	1¼	— 2¾	— 68.8
Kenmt	.80	39276	18	35¼	19⅜	21	— 10½	— 33.3
KyUtil	2.36	56651	8	25	20⅜	24⅜	+ 1⅝	+ 7.1
KerrGl	.44	21024	......	18½	11	12⅜	— 4¾	— 27.7
KerG	pf 1.70	1491	......	26⅝	18⅝	20	— 4¾	— 19.2
KerrMc	1.10	335873	13	36⅜	26⅜	27⅞	— 2¾	— 9
KeyBk	1.10	16766	8	23¼	16½	23¼	+ 4	+ 20.8
KeyCn	n	2390	......	6¾	2½	3⅛	....	....
Keyslnt	.48b	25762	18	22⅞	14	16¾	— 4⅜	— 20.7
Kidde	1.20	62141	19	35¼	26¼	28⅞	— 3	— 9.4
Kid	prB 4	444	......	80½	61¾	66	— 7½	— 10.2
Kid	pfC 4	1130	......	81	62	65	— 8½	— 11.6
Kidde	pf1.64	802	......	54½	42¼	43¼	— 6¼	— 12.6
KimbC	s2.20	127262	9	48¾	39⅜	47⅝	+ 1⅝	+ 3.5
KnghtRd	.76	157847	14	31	21¼	29¼	+ 2¾	+ 10.4

Koger	2.30	20570	74	26¾	17¾	25⅛	+ 2½	+ 11.1
Kolmor	.32	45317	12	34	16¼	17¼	— 15⅛	— 46.7
Kopers	.80	164154	17	23⅝	17⅛	18	— 3¾	— 17.2
Kopr	pf 4	229	......	35	30½	34½	+ 2	+ 6.2
Koppr	pf 10	5022	......	103½	96¾	100	....	....
Korea	n	40291	......	16	12⅝	14⅛	....	....
Kroger	2	194959	12	39½	29⅛	39¼	+ 2¼	+ 6.1
Kubota	.52e	133	27	31	25¼	26½	+ ¼	+ 1
Kuhlm	s .60	11799	10	18½	10¼	17⅛	+ 6⅝	+ 63.1
Kyocer	s.14i	18372	28	67½	44⅞	55¾	+ 1¾	+ 3.2
Kysor	.60	16560	5	19⅞	13	16⅝	— 3¼	— 16.4
			— L—L—L —					
LN Ho	2.84e	6759	9	26⅞	22⅝	26⅝	+ 3¾	+ 16.4
LFE		21484	......	15⅜	7⅜	12½	+ 2	+ 19.1
LFE	pf .50	226	......	10	6¼	8½	....	....
LLE Ry	2.22e	114096	....	17⅛	12	15	+ 2⅞	+ 23.7
LLCCp		3529	......	5⅞	2	2¼	— 2⅜	— 51.4
LLC	pf	797	......	11⅞	8	10⅜	— 1¼	— 10.8
LTV	.19i	832155	....	19⅞	8⅞	9⅞	— 8½	— 46.3
LTVA	.43t	760	......	30½	14	14⅜	— 12⅝	— 46.8
LTV	pf 5	290	......	60⅛	45½	46	— 13½	— 22.7
LTV	pf 3.06	80279	......	31½	18¼	21¼	— 8⅞	— 29.5
LTV	pf 5.25	13666	......	69	50½	55	....	....
LTV	pf 1.25	40239	......	17¾	13	14¼	....	....
LQuint		80305	13	18⅞	10½	10¾	— 7¼	— 40.3
LacGs	s 1.70	15729	7	24¼	15⅝	24	+ 8⅜	+ 53.6
Lafarge	.20	45486	......	12⅞	8⅛	8⅜	— 3⅛	— 27.2
Lafrg	pf2.44	12568	......	31⅞	23¾	25	— 4⅝	— 15.6
Lamaur	.24	12259	4	18⅞	12⅜	14¾	— 3	— 16.9
LamSes		14354	......	3⅞	1¾	2½	— ¾	— 23.1
Lawtln	s .56	62306	13	14½	10½	11½	— 1¾	— 13.2
LearPt	.20	82729	13	26¼	13½	21¼	— 4¼	— 16.7
LearP	pf2.87	14652	......	29⅜	20⅛	23¾	— 3	— 11.2
LearSg	1.80	69197	9	49½	37½	44¼	— 1⅛	— 2.5
LearS	pf2.25	111	......	120	95	109¼	— 2¼	— 2
LeaRnl	s .36	12777	12	19⅛	14	15¼	— 2¾	— 15.3
LswyTr	1.50	52878	10	39½	24½	29½	— 9½	— 24.4
LeeEnt	.80	11749	13	28	20⅛	25¾	+ 2	+ 8.4
LegMas	.20	14956	16	13⅞	9	9⅝	— 1½	— 13.5
LegPlat	.44	22280	9	21¾	15½	18⅞	— 1⅛	— 5.6
LehVal		37580	......	5	2⅛	2¾	— ⅛	— 4.3
LVln	pf	357	......	38½	25	26⅝	— 3⅜	— 11.3
Lehmn	2.98e	81654	......	19½	13⅝	15	— 3⅝	— 19.5
Lennar	.20	39918	16	19⅜	9⅞	12⅝	— 4⅝	— 26.8
LeucNt		8524	5	33¾	16	28¾	+ 11¾	+ 69.1
Leucd	pf 2	12554	......	35	20	31½	+ 9½	+ 43.2
Leucd	pf6.79e	8916	......	53¾	50	53	....	....
LeviSt	1.85	221652	11	43⅛	23	25¼	— 16⅜	— 39.3
Levitz	.72	105152	9	43⅜	25¾	36¾	— 6⅛	— 14.3
LOF	1.32	39334	8	50	38¾	44⅞	+ 6¼	+ 16.2
LOF	pf 4.75	3187	......	79	62	71¾	+ 9½	+ 15.3
LibtyCp	.72	11811	13	26⅝	21	22⅝	— ¼	— 1.1
Lilly	3.20	327444	10	67⅝	53	66	+ 8⅛	+ 14
Limited	.24	334893	20	28	15¼	27	+ 2½	+ 10.2
LincNt	s1.84	167061	9	41½	26¼	39	+ 6⅜	+ 19.5
LincN	pf 3	258	......	161¼	114½	157¼	+ 27¾	+ 21.4
LincPl	2.24a	4608	......	21	18⅛	20⅝	+ ⅛	+ .6
Litton	2	276403	9	80	56¼	64⅞	— 5¾	— 8.1
Litton	pf 2	2256	......	25½	16½	20½	+ 3¾	+ 22.4
Lockhd	.45e	751416	9	48¾	30⅛	44	+ 4	+ 10
Loctite	.80	35064	13	42¾	30⅝	34	— 7½	— 18.1
Loews	s 1	58168	8	106½	70½	105	+ 30⅜	+ 40.7
LomFin	1.16	106488	13	32¾	19	31¾	+ 6⅜	+ 25.1
LomMt	3.36e	11511	10	33⅜	24⅜	32⅞	+ 3¾	+ 12.9
LnStar	1.90	59200	10	29¼	17⅝	26	— 2⅛	— 7.6
LoneS	pf4.50	3	......	112	112	112	+ 4	+ 3.7
LoneS	pf 5.37	7207	......	53	44	49¼	....	....
LILCo	.50i	691382	2	11½	3¾	6⅞	— 3½	— 33.7
LIL	pfB3.75i	438	......	33	16	25½	— 7½	— 22.7
LIL	pfE3.26i	832	......	30	14½	22¼	— 6¾	— 23.3
LIL	pfI 4.31i	78	......	65	35	57¾	— 3	— 4.9
LIL	pfJ6.09i	1195	......	53½	21½	40	— 8½	— 17.5
LIL	pfK6.22i	1563	......	55½	23¾	41	— 8¼	— 16.8
LIL	pfX2.62i	35739	......	23¼	8½	17⅛	— 4⅞	— 22.2
LIL	pfW2.64i	19656	......	23¾	9	17¾	— 4⅛	— 18.9
LIL	pfV2.62i	26397	......	23½	9½	17⅝	— 4¼	— 19.4
LIL	pfU3.19i	20500	......	28	11¼	20⅝	— 5¾	— 21.8
LIL	pfT2.48i	19492	......	23	8⅞	16⅜	— 4¾	— 22.5
LIL	pfS7.35i	1757	......	65	27¼	50	— 11¼	— 18.4
LIL	pfP1.82i	7302	......	17⅛	6	12⅝	— 3⅜	— 21.1
LIL	pfO1.85i	9901	......	18	7	14⅞	— 2	— 11.9

LongDr	1.28	34504	12	49¾	34	44¼	− 4⅜	− 9
Loral	.48	177473	16	29¾	18½	26⅛	+ 1⅜	+ 5.6
LaGenl	.54	10092	9	15	11	11⅝	− ⅛	− 1.1
LaLand	1	268697	10	34⅞	22¼	31	+ 3⅞	+ 14.3
LaPac	.80b	136430	26	29⅝	17	21⅞	− 3½	− 13.8
LaPL pf	4.80	1062	......	31½	28⅞	31	....	....
LaPL	pf3.16	8380	......	24	16⅝	22⅝	+ ¼	+ 1.1
LouvGs	2.44	75585	8	28¼	22⅝	25⅞	+ 2¼	+ 9.5
Lowst s	2	12607	6	49¾	36	46⅝	+ 3⅜	+ 7.8
Lowes	.32	209561	15	25⅛	16¼	24¾	+ 2⅜	+ 10.6
Lubrzl	1.16	128156	13	24½	18¼	21⅜	− ½	− 2.3
Lubys s	.54	15285	18	32	26⅜	27	− 1⅜	− 4.8
LuckyS	1.16	188459	9	19¾	15⅜	17⅞	− 1	− 5.3
Lukens	.40	11543	142	16⅜	10⅛	11⅜	− 2¾	− 19.5
— M—M—M —								
MACOM	.22	334294	21	21¾	13⅛	19¼	− ⅝	− 3.1
MCA	.88	341277	19	46⅜	34⅜	39⅝	− 2⅞	− 6.8
MCorp	1.32	107899	6	29¼	16⅝	20¾	− 6	− 22.4
MCor wi		58	......	24	22	22	....	....
MCor	pf3.50	691	......	42	34	37½	− 2½	− 6.3
MDC	.32	41601	9	13	7⅜	11⅛	− ⅞	− 7.3
MEI	.44	64853	15	40	31½	37⅜	+ 2	+ 5.7
MGMGr	.44	75235	31	13¼	9¼	12¼	− ⅜	− 3
MGMGr	pf.44	12039	......	12	9	11¼	+ 1¼	+ 12.5
MGMUa	.20e	223591	17	16½	10⅞	12	− 2⅝	− 17.9
MGMu wt		29071	......	5¼	2⅛	2⅝	− 1¼	− 32.3
MGMHo	.60a	30801	13	25¾	17½	20⅛	− 3¾	− 15.7
MB Lt g	.83t	4070	......	28¼	17⅞	19¼	− 4¼	− 18.1
Macmil	1	71376	15	47	25	46½	+ 18⅜	+ 65.3
Macy	1.04	383311	10	53⅞	38½	40⅞	− 11⅜	− 21.8
Macypf	4.25	334	......	41½	37	37⅝	− 3⅜	− 8.2
MadRes		57199	......	19¾	11⅞	12¾	− 4¾	− 27.1
MagiCf	.80	100889	6	43⅝	24	35⅜	− 1¼	− 3.4
MgtAst		88564	......	29½	17¾	27⅛	+ 9¼	+ 51.8
Manhln	.30b	33995	6	26	12½	15⅛	− 9¾	− 39.2
ManhNt	.32	14012	15	20¼	13⅝	15¾	− 3⅛	− 16.6
ManrC s	.15	51621	17	18¾	10½	17¼	+ 4⅞	+ 39.4
MfrHan	3.20	458779	4	41½	22½	36⅝	− 1⅜	− 3.6
MfrH	pf6.57e	68056	......	59	41	47¾	− 7⅛	− 13
MfrH	pf5.89e	80356	......	57	40	43¾	− 10⅞	− 19.9
vjManvl		145688	4	13⅝	5⅝	5⅞	− 5⅛	− 46.6
vjMnvl pf		17911	......	28¼	18¼	19¼	− 5⅞	− 23.4
MAPCO	1	162905	10	30¾	21	26⅛	+ 1¾	+ 7.2
Marntz		6839	......	4⅞	3	3⅛	− ⅞	− 21.9
Marcde		33475	......	2⅞	1	1⅛	− 1½	− 57.1
MarMid	1.60	34122	6	28¾	19¾	28½	+ 3¾	+ 15.2
MarM	pf5.32e	37805	......	51½	40¾	42⅜	− 6⅛	− 12.6
Marion	.52	85557	31	43½	27¼	43¼	+ 4½	+ 11.6
MarkC	.32	24439	34	14⅝	9¾	10	− 4⅛	− 29.2
Mark pf	1.20	4466	......	19⅝	14¾	15½	− 4	− 20.5
Marriot	.54	117635	16	80¼	58½	75¾	+ 4½	+ 6.3
MrshM	2.40	223893	43	59⅜	35¾	59	+ 9¼	+ 18.6
MartM	1.34	294113	....	46⅜	30¼	44½	+ 8¾	+ 24.5
MrtM	pf4.88	30831	......	74	55	71½	+ 8¾	+ 13.9
MaryK	.12	125245	11	16⅝	8⅝	9⅛	− 6⅛	− 40.2
Masco	.56	263145	13	33⅞	22½	28	− 5¾	− 17
MassMr	.16	24597	13	12½	7¼	11⅛	− ⅜	− 3.3
MasM	1.80	27823	12	18¼	15⅜	18¼	+ ⅞	+ 5
MaseyF		153414	....	6⅛	2¼	2¾	− 1¾	− 38.9
MasCp	2.88	8669	......	25⅜	20⅜	24⅞	+ 2	+ 8.7
MasInc	1.32	11073	......	11⅞	9⅞	11	− ⅜	− 3.3
MatsuE	.45r	91482	10	80⅛	54⅜	61½	− 12½	− 16.9
Mattel		398009	....	13⅝	4⅞	10¼	+ 5¼	+ 105
Matel wt		58011	......	10⅛	2⅞	7	+ 4⅝	+ 194.7
Mattl	pf2.50k	45550	......	30¾	13¼	25⅝	+ 12¼	+ 91.6
Maxam		48187	6	15½	9¼	12¾	+ 1¾	+ 15.9
MayD s	1.72	207010	8	43⅛	30¼	38⅛	+ 2⅜	+ 6.6
Maytg	2.60a	55684	10	55	36¼	44¾	− 6½	− 12.7
McDr	pf2.20	11456	......	32½	25⅛	26	+ ⅛	+ .5
McDr	pf2.60	18352	......	23¼	20⅛	20⅞	+ ⅜	+ 1.8
McDerl	1.80	354673	24	31⅝	23¾	24⅜	− ½	− 2
McDrl wt		49359	......	12	6¼	7¼	− ¾	− 9.4
McDld	.20	7655	15	11¼	6½	7¼	− 2¾	− 27.5
McDnl s	.82	482529	12	55⅞	48½	51⅝	+ 4⅝	+ 9.8
McDnD	1.62	241503	9	73¾	47⅝	72¼	+ 13	+ 21.9
McGEd	2	67431	13	42	31⅜	38⅛	− 3¼	− 7.9
McGrH	1.24	193671	15	48¾	34	42¾	+ ½	+ 1.2
MGH pf	1.20	11	......	155	135	135	− 16	− 10.6
McInt g		5220	......	33¾	19¾	26½	− ¾	− 2.8
McKess	2.40	52460	10	44¼	32⅜	38¼	− 1⅝	− 4.1
McK pf	1.80	171	......	69	54	62½	− 1½	− 2.3
McLean		65534	10	15½	10	11¼	+ ½	+ 4.7
McLea wt		52550	......	6½	3⅝	4	....	....
McNeil	.90	13206	9	25½	18¾	23½	+ 4⅛	+ 21.3
Mead	1.20	188419	8	41¼	27⅛	34¼	− 4½	− 11.6
Mesrux	.24	69925	13	22	12¾	18⅜	+ 1¾	+ 10.5
Medtrn	.76	150223	8	44½	24½	27	− 14½	− 34.9
Mellon	2.60	97793	8	52	33½	46¾	− 4¼	− 8.3
Mellon	pf2.80	10260	......	26⅜	22⅝	24½	− ⅞	− 3.4
Melvill	1.32	255662	11	45½	30¾	37¼	+ 2⅜	+ 6.8
MercSt	1.20	35994	10	59	40¼	56½	+ 1½	+ 2.7
Merck	3.20	441252	14	97½	78¼	94	+ 3⅝	+ 4
Merdth	.80	20198	13	56¼	39	54½	+ 10½	+ 23.9
MerLyn	.80	1625822	113	36⅜	22	27	− 5	− 15.6
MesaOf		337256	....	3⅛	2	2⅞	+ ½	+ 21.1
MesaPt		858253	5	22	12¾	18¼	+ 4⅞	+ 36.5
MesaR	1.76e	69026	......	35⅜	24⅝	31	+ 5⅛	+ 19.8
Mesab	.81e	40165	7	9	5½	6¼	− 2	− 24.2
Mestek		3396	......	6½	2¼	2⅞	− 2⅝	− 47.7
MtE	pfC3.90	129	......	28	21¾	27	+ 2	+ 8
MtE	pfF8.12	172	......	54½	46	52¼	+ 2¼	+ 4.5
MtE	pfG7.68	910	......	53	44½	51	+ 2½	+ 5.2
MtE	pfJ8.32	520	......	56	47½	54½	+ 3½	+ 6.9
MtE	pfI 8.12	504	......	55	45½	53	+ 3	+ 6
MtE	pfH8.32	243	......	56	48½	55	+ 5	+ 10
MexFd	.13e	80688	......	4	2⅝	2¾	− ⅝	− 18.5
MhCn	pf2.05	4579	......	18⅞	16⅜	18½	+ 2⅛	+ 13
MhCn	pf3.19	3394	......	25¼	22¼	25¼	+ 1⅞	+ 8
MchER	1.38	3561	8	16½	11⅞	15⅞	+ 3⅞	+ 32.3
Micklb s	.06	8075	9	6⅜	4⅛	4¾	− 1¼	− 20.8
Midcon	2.36	100423	8	42½	32⅝	41¼	+ 6¼	+ 17.9
MidSUt	1.78	1011841	5	14¾	9¼	13¾	+ ⅜	+ 2.8
MidRos	1	44193	18	25⅝	17	17⅞	− ⅞	− 4.7
MWE	2.68	26102	10	27¼	22	26¾	+ ¾	+ 2.9
MiltnR	.40	13252	12	18¼	11¼	12¼	− 5¼	− 30
MMM	3.40	488876	13	85½	69¼	78⅝	− 3⅞	− 4.7
MinPL	2.56	42802	7	30	23¾	29⅜	+ 3⅛	+ 11.9
MisnIns	.38j	105782	....	27	7¼	8⅝	− 18⅛	− 67.8
MoPSv	1.20b	15549	6	19⅞	15	19¾	+ 2¼	+ 12.9
MoPS	pf2.44	710	......	20¼	17¾	20	+ ¾	+ 3.9
MoPS	pr2.61	1886	......	22⅜	18¾	20½	+ ¼	+ 1.2
MoPS	pf4.13	1106	......	33⅛	28¾	32¼	+ ¾	+ 2.4
Mitel		272731	....	16½	4	5⅞	− 7⅞	− 57.3
Mobil	2.20	1552631	8	32⅛	23⅛	27⅛	− 1⅝	− 5.7
vjMoblH		49803	......	5⅛	½	9-16	—3 7-16	− 85.9
ModCpt		23866	......	9⅞	5⅞	6¼	− 1½	− 19.4
Mohasc	.40	33136	9	24	16¼	22⅝	+ ⅞	+ 4
MohkDt		245834	....	16¾	8½	10⅞	− 4⅛	− 27.5
Monrch	.80	9972	22	24¼	14⅝	14¾	− 8¾	− 37.2
Monsn	s2.30	482998	8	53⅞	40⅝	44	− 8⅝	− 16.4
MntDU	2.56	18261	7	30¼	26	29⅛	+ ⅜	+ 1.3
MonPw	2	285742	8	30⅜	16⅝	19¼	− 10⅛	− 34.5
MonSt	1.80a	14791	......	17¼	14⅞	17	+ ⅝	+ 3.8
MONY	.80	30593	8	8⅞	6¾	8⅜	+ ¾	+ 9.8
MooreC	2	17941	12	45¾	34¾	45¼	+ 2¾	+ 6.5
MoreM	1.04	37958	11	25½	18⅝	22	− 1¼	− 5.4
MorM pf	2.50	4891	......	28⅞	23½	24¾	....	....
Morgan	4.40	330842	7	80¾	56½	78½	+ 11⅛	+ 16.5
Morgn wi		288	......	39⅞	28¼	39¼	+ 5⅝	+ 16.7
Morgn	pf7.77e	41243	......	84⅜	75¾	76¾	+ ½	+ .7
MorKnd	1.40	37700	9	34¼	26⅞	34	+ 5⅞	+ 20.9
MorseS	.80	35583	8	33	18⅛	19¼	− 13½	− 41.2
MtgRty	1.64e	44074	10	18	12	17½	+ 2⅛	+ 13.8
Morton s	.64	134111	12	31½	20	27⅜	+ 1⅞	+ 7.4
Motrla s	.64	1111010	10	46⅞	29¼	33¾	− 11⅝	− 25.6
Munfrd	.54b	16156	11	24¼	16¼	20⅞	+ 2⅛	+ 11.3
Munsng		5098	15	23⅜	14	17½	+ 3⅝	+ 26.1
MurphC	1.40	58992	9	43	26	39½	+ 3½	+ 9.7
MurpO	1	120516	10	38½	24½	26	− 3½	− 11.9
MurryO	1.20	17790	10	24⅝	18⅜	19½	− 2¾	− 12.4
MutOm	1.44e	10548	......	13	11	12½	+ ¼	+ 2
MyerL n		10317	......	11⅞	3⅝	4¼	....	....
— N—N—N —								
NAFCO	.80b	11405	17	25⅝	16	17⅞	− 5¾	− 24.3
NBD	2.40	46801	7	51⅜	39⅝	51⅜	+ 6¼	+ 13.9
NBI		127932	12	28¼	14¼	18	− 8¾	− 32.7
NCH	.72	19884	11	20½	16½	17½	− ½	− 2.8
NCNB	1.32	102253	9	36½	23	35⅞	+ 8½	+ 31.1
NCR s	.80	743727	8	33	20⅝	26⅝	− 5⅜	− 16.8
NI Ind		100335	7	24½	13	17⅜	− 5⅝	− 24.5
NL Ind	.20	319982	79	17	10⅜	11	− 4¾	− 30.2
NUI	2.32	2511	7	33	25¼	32¼	+ 6⅛	+ 23.4

NVF		82662	......	2½	⅞	15-16	− 1 1-16	− 53.1
NWA	.90	238804	9	49	33½	40¾	− 4	− 8.9
NabscB	2.48	276561	11	54	38½	51¼	+ 10¼	+ 25
Nalco	1.20	159875	14	33¼	21	26½	− 4½	− 14.5
Nashua		35359	8	29⅜	20	28⅜	+ 3¼	+ 12.9
NatCan	1	46212	8	37½	27½	31⅜	+ 3½	+ 12.6
NCan pf1.50		94	......	65	51	61	+ 15	+ 32.6
NtCnv s	.36	100876	15	18⅛	11⅛	14¾	− 2	− 11.9
NatDist	2.20	106599	13	30	22¾	26⅛	− 1¼	− 4.6
NDist pf4.25		z2100	......	87¼	73⅞	87	+ 12	+ 16
NDist pf2.25		103	......	33	26¾	32	+ 4	+ 14.3
NDist pr1.85		11151	......	19¼	16¼	17⅛	− 1	− 5.5
NtEdu s		60704	12	20⅝	12½	13⅝	− 4⅜	− 24.3
NatFGs	1.88	18073	6	29⅛	16⅛	26	+ 9⅝	+ 58.8
NFG pf	2.30	2460	......	22	19½	20½	− ¾	− 3.5
NatGyp	1.76	99044	6	40	27	38⅝	+ 1⅛	+ 3
NtHom		23791	......	5¼	2½	2¾	− 1⅝	− 37.1
NII	.25	200418	....	37⅝	23⅛	28	− 7	− 20
NII pf	5	10996	......	77	56	61	− 11¼	− 15.6
NMedE	.52	512350	12	25⅝	17⅝	23⅜	+ ⅜	+ 1.6
NMineS		7850	......	12⅞	6⅜	8⅜	− 1⅜	− 14.1
NtPrest	1	15640	12	29¼	20¾	25	− 3½	− 12.3
NtSemi		1524753	12	19¼	9½	11⅞	− 3¾	− 24
NtSvIn s	1	39580	10	29¾	21⅛	26⅞	+ 1⅛	+ 4.4
NStand	.40	7792	8	17¾	11⅞	14⅛	− 2¼	− 13.7
Nerco n	.32e	10853	7	11⅝	10	10⅞	....	....
NevPw	2.76	51445	8	29¼	21¾	28¾	+ ⅞	+ 3.1
NevP pf	1.60	712	......	14	11½	13½	....	....
NevP pf1.74		7976	......	17¾	14⅝	16⅛	+ ⅛	+ .8
NevP pf2.30		373	......	20½	17½	19⅝	+ 1	+ 5.4
NevP pf1.95		956	......	16⅞	14⅛	16⅜	+ ⅛	+ .8
NevSvL	.50	15403	5	14¾	8½	11¼	− 3¼	− 22.4
NEngEl	3.60	87625	6	40¾	28⅝	37	− 2	− 5.1
NEnP pf2.76		2190	......	26¼	21¼	24⅜	− 1⅜	− 5.3
NJRsc	2.04	18191	7	26⅜	19	26	+ 2	+ 8.3
NYSEG	2.44	282404	6	23	14¾	23	+ 2⅞	+ 14.3
NYS pf	3.75	224	......	30	24	28½	....	....
NYS pf	8.80	586	......	69	55½	64½	− 1½	− 2.3
NYS pfA3.03e		16395	......	26	19¾	23	− 1¾	− 7.1
NYS pf	2.12	2462	......	17½	13½	16½	+ ¼	+ 1.5
NYS pfD3.75		3396	......	29½	24	28	+ ¾	+ 2.8
Newell	.50	25979	10	17⅝	13¼	15⅝	+ ¼	+ 1.6
Newhal	.48	20694	26	40⅞	28⅝	39¾	+ 10⅞	+ 37.7
Newhll	4.78e	5703	......	16¾	11	12¾	− 1¾	− 12.1
NwhlRs	2.55e	6350	......	12	7¼	8½	− 2½	− 22.7
Newmt	1	131336	29	54⅞	31	35⅞	− 14⅞	− 29.3
Nwpark		72193	......	6⅝	1⅜	1⅝	− 4½	− 73.5
NiaMP	2	399406	6	17¾	12	17⅜	+ 1⅝	+ 10.3
NiaMpf	3.40	477	......	27⅛	22	25½	− 1½	− 5.6
NiaMpf	3.60	633	......	28¾	22½	27¼	....	....
NiaMpf	3.90	240	......	31½	24¼	28¼	− ¾	− 2.6
NiaMpf	4.10	704	......	33¼	26	31	....	....
NiaMpf	4.85	464	......	38	30¾	35½	− ¾	− 2.1
NiaMpf	5.25	438	......	42	34	39	+ ½	+ 1.3
NiaMpf	6.10	1033	......	49½	38½	44½	− 1½	− 3.3
NiaM pf2.76		16917	......	25	19⅛	21½	− 2½	− 10.4
NiMpf	10.60	343	......	92½	75	87¼	− 5¼	− 5.7
NiaMpf	7.72	1087	......	62	48⅜	54½	− 2½	− 4.4
NiagSh	2.23e	9814	......	21½	15⅝	16⅜	− 4⅜	− 21.1
Nicolet	.06e	34373	23	17¾	10⅝	15¼	....	....
NICOR	3.04	130110	15	29⅝	24¼	29	+ 2½	+ 9.4
NICO pf1.90		51	......	28⅜	24	28⅜	+ 1⅝	+ 6.1
NoblAf	.12	189568	35	19	12½	13¼	− 3½	− 20.9
NorfkSo	3.20	212813	8	64¼	48½	58⅝	− 4½	− 7.1
Norlin		11606	......	38⅝	17¼	17⅞	− 11⅛	− 38.4
Norstr	2.20b	20693	8	38½	29¾	36¼	+ ⅜	+ 1.1
Norstr pf4.75e		27521	......	50	43	43⅜	− 3¼	− 7
Nortek	.08	30083	7	17⅜	12	15⅛	− 1½	− 9
NACoal	1	9486	6	54	42	48⅜	− ¾	− 1.5
NAPhl s	1	43475	9	40½	28½	38½	− ¼	− .6
NEurO	1.56e	14945	9	21⅞	13⅝	14¼	− 2⅝	− 15.6
NoestUt	1.48	539334	5	14¾	10⅝	14¼	+ 2	+ 16.3
NIndPS	1.56	595633	7	15⅛	10⅞	11¾	− 2⅞	− 19.7
NIPS pf4.63e		10949	......	48⅛	42½	43½	+ ½	+ 1.2
NoStPw	3.24	148794	7	44¼	33⅝	41¾	+ 3¾	+ 9.9
NSPw pf3.60		283	......	33½	28	30½	+ ½	+ 1.7
NSPw pf4.08		809	......	35¼	30	32⅞	+ 1⅝	+ 5.2
NSPw pf4.10		1399	......	36½	31⅝	33¼	+ ⅝	+ 1.9
NSPw pf4.11		668	......	35⅛	31	34	+ 1⅛	+ 3.4
NSP pf	4.16	401	......	36½	32	35	+ 2	+ 6.1
NSPw pf	4.56	1503	......	41	34⅝	39½	....	....
NSPw pf6.80		1107	......	58½	51	56¼	+ 1¼	+ 2.3
NSP pf	10.36	734	......	103	96⅞	101½	− ¾	− .7
NSPw pf7.84		881	......	66¾	56½	64	+ 2	+ 3.2
NSPw pf	8.80	1145	......	75½	62¾	70½	....	....
NSPw pf	7	1039	......	60	51	57⅝	+ 1⅛	+ 2
NorTel	.40	481080	....	42¼	29⅞	34⅛	− 4⅞	− 12.5
Nthgat g		16721	......	5½	2⅞	3⅛	− 1⅜	− 30.6
Nortrp	s1.20	81234	11	39½	23⅝	35¼	+ 6½	+ 22.6
NwCP pf5.44e		6736	......	47	40⅛	42½	+ ½	+ 1.2
NwtInd	2.68	293556	17	62¼	40⅞	49	− ⅞	− 1.8
NwtP pf2.50		1986	......	22½	19½	19¾	− 2	− 9.2
NwtP pf2.36		6906	......	21¾	19⅜	20⅜	+ ¾	+ 3.8
NwStW		22883	......	25⅞	8⅞	10¼	− 14	− 57.7
Norton	2	69258	12	38¼	30¾	35⅞	− 1⅜	− 3.7
Norwst	1.80	176341	12	33⅞	21½	23	− 10⅝	− 31.6
Nwst pf6.15e		42568	......	58¼	48½	48½	− 6½	− 11.8
Nwst pf5.91e		5770	......	57⅞	50	50½	− 4⅜	− 8
Novo	.29e	211808	9	61⅜	20⅞	23¾	− 32¼	− 57.6
Nucor	.36	49624	12	44¼	26	32¼	− 10½	− 24.6
NutriS	.32	50432	......	12⅛	4⅝	5½	− 6⅜	− 53.7
NYNEX	6	597437	8	75⅞	58⅝	74¼	+ 12¾	+ 20.7
			— O—O—O —					
OakInd		97540	......	6¾	2	2½	− 3⅜	− 57.4
Oak pf	2.62i	40	......	40	22½	22½	− 50¾	− 69.3
OakiteP	1.52	1798	10	27⅞	23⅛	26⅞	+ 2⅞	+ 12
OcciPet	2.50	891451	7	35¾	24⅜	28	+ 3⅛	+ 12.6
OcciP wt		41059	......	17	9¾	11¼	....	....
OcciP pf2.16		112	......	55⅝	39⅝	45⅜	+ 6	+ 15.2
OcciP pf3.60		130	......	112⅞	80	95⅞	+ 15⅝	+ 19.5
OcciP pf	4	152	......	111	78	92½	+ 14½	+ 18.6
OcciP pf2.50		4360	......	23⅞	20	20⅞	+ ½	+ 2.5
OcciP pf2.12		6440	......	20⅝	17⅛	17⅜	− ⅛	− .7
OcciP pf2.30		4402	......	22⅛	18⅛	19⅛	+ ⅞	+ 4.8
OcciP pf	6.25	9211	......	51⅛	49¼	49⅞	....	....
OcciP pf15.50		170627	....	113	105⅝	108	+ ½	+ .5
Occi pf	14.62	18761	......	108⅛	101¼	104¾	+ 2⅞	+ 2.8
OcciP pf	14	z7620	......	107	100	105½	+ 5⅛	+ 5.1
ODECO	1	72111	13	34½	22	22	− 5¾	− 20.7
Ogden	1.80	100029	14	30½	24⅛	28¼	− 1⅞	− 6.2
Ogdn pf	1.87	126	......	85	71⅜	81½	+ 13½	+ 19.9
OhioEd	1.84	550153	5	14⅛	9⅜	13½	+ 1¼	+ 10.2
OhEd pf3.90		314	......	30	22½	27⅝	− ⅞	− 3.1
OhEd pf4.40		192	......	33½	25⅜	31	− ½	− 1.6
OhEd pf4.44		302	......	33	25⅛	30¾	− 1¾	− 5.4
OhEd pf4.56		311	......	34	26½	32⅝	+ 1⅝	+ 5.2
OhEd pf7.24		856	......	53½	41	51	+ 4¼	+ 9.1
OhEd pf7.36		1413	......	55	42	50½	− ½	− 1
OhEd pf	8.20	952	......	60⅜	45	56	....	....
OhEd pf1.58e		12975	......	30	25½	30	....	....
OhEd pf3.50		6318	......	26¾	18¼	24⅝	+ ⅛	+ .5
OhEd pr3.92		7211	......	28⅛	21	27⅞	+ 1⅛	+ 4.2
OhEd pf1.80		3426	......	14⅝	10¾	14⅛	+ ⅜	+ 2.7
OhEd pf9.12		177	......	65	51	61	+ ¾	+ 1.2
OhEd pf	8.64	1147	......	62	47½	58	....	....
OhE pf	10.48	375	......	87½	76	83¾	− 1¼	− 1.5
OhE pf	10.76	977	......	91	77	85½	− 1½	− 1.7
OhMat s	.40	69294	18	17¼	12¼	15	+ 1⅛	+ 8.1
OhP pf	8.04	199	......	61¼	52	58¼	+ 1⅜	+ 2.4
OhP pfB7.60		2186	......	61½	51½	57	− ⅛	− .2
OhP pfC7.60		1055	......	62	52	56¼	+ ¼	+ .5
OhP pfH	3.75	1409	......	29½	25½	28	....	....
OhP pfG2.27		2442	......	18¾	15	17⅝	+ ½	+ 2.9
OhP pfA	14	1553	......	106	98	104¼	+ 2¾	+ 2.7
OhP pfF	14	361	......	106¼	98½	103⅝	+ 2⅛	+ 2.1
OhP pfE8.48		2739	......	69⅛	56	64	+ 1	+ 1.6
OhP pfD7.76		1988	......	61¼	51¼	58¼	+ ¾	+ 1.3
OklaGE	2	223721	9	23½	19⅛	22¾	+ 1¾	+ 8.3
OklaG pf	.80	631	......	8¼	7	8	....	....
Olin	1.50	75730	8	33½	25⅛	30	− ¾	− 2.4
Omark	1.08	31686	19	37	20⅜	37	+ 12⅛	+ 48.7
Omncre	.69i	81344	8	31⅞	5¾	7⅝	− 21¾	− 74
Oneida	.80	10702	9	23⅞	14	14⅝	− 7⅞	− 35
ONEOK	2.56	30856	8	32	26½	28⅞	− 1⅝	− 5.3
OranRk	2.04	38343	8	25⅜	19¼	24¾	+ 3⅞	+ 18.6
Orange	.53t	71742	14	13⅞	5½	10¼	+ 4¼	+ 70.8
OrionC	.76	36164	233	30	19½	21	− 6¾	− 24.3
OrionP		106217	27	16½	8⅛	8⅞	− 4⅝	− 34.3
Orion pf	.50	3771	......	12	6½	7	− 2⅜	− 25.3
Orion pf	2.75	15538	......	30⅛	24	26	....	....
OutbM s	.64	88703	9	29⅝	18⅜	28½	+ 3⅝	+ 14.6
OvrhDr	.60	24349	9	21¼	13¾	19½	+ 1⅞	+ 10.6

OvrnTr	.64	82723	12	31⅜	17	27⅝	— 2⅝	— 8.7
OvShip	.50	69318	8	21⅞	13⅞	14¼	— 6	— 29.6
OwenC	1.40	214039	9	38⅞	25⅛	32	— 4½	— 12.3
OwenIll	1.68b	234356	8	46¼	31¼	40¼	+ 2⅞	+ 7.7
OwnIl pf	4	63	......	77	75	76	— ½	— .7
OwnIl pf4.75		280	......	135	96	119	+ 10	+ 9.2
Oxford s	.40	44644	6	20⅜	10½	10⅞	— 7⅛	— 39.6
— P—Q —								
PHH	.88	86847	10	36¼	18	24⅞	— 11⅛	— 30.9
PPG	1.44	228749	8	38	24¾	32⅞	— 2	— 5.7
PSA	.60	45799	......	24¾	15	21	— ¾	— 3.4
PSA dpf1.90		18714	......	19⅞	13¼	16½	— 1	— 5.7
PacAS	1.50	9514	......	12⅝	11⅛	12⅜	+ ¼	+ 2.1
PacGE	1.72	777043	7	17¼	12⅜	16⅜	+ 1½	+ 10.1
PacLtg	3.32	129497	12	41⅞	30⅞	41⅝	+ 5⅜	+ 14.8
PcLum	1.20	67920	13	29	20½	24⅞	— ⅝	— 2.5
PacRes	.05r	15773	......	10¾	5¾	6	— 4½	— 42.9
PacRs pf	2	5726	......	20⅝	13¾	13⅞	— 6¼	— 31.1
PacSci	.40	30392	11	19	11⅞	14¼	— 3	— 17.4
PacTele	5.40	734638	8	71⅛	52½	68⅞	+ 13⅜	+ 24.1
PacTin	.40	1699	10	13¼	9½	9⅞	— 3	— 23.3
Pacifcp	2.32	194362	7	25¼	21	24⅞	+ ⅜	+ 1.5
Pacif pf	4.07	7652	......	32¼	27½	31¾	+ 1⅛	+ 3.7
PainWb	.60	213330	36	38⅞	23⅝	27½	— 7½	— 21.4
PalmBc	1.20	27853	10	39	24⅝	37⅞	+ 8¼	+ 27.9
PanABk	.66	7449	9	24½	20½	21	— 3½	— 14.3
PanAm		701559	....	9¼	4	4⅝	— 3½	— 43.1
PanA wt		84882	......	6	1¾	2	— 3⅛	— 61
Pandck n	.20	52692	13	22⅝	13½	15⅛	....	....
PanhEC	2.30	249392	10	40	31	37¼	+ 1⅛	+ 3.1
PantPr		368728	13	6⅞	3	4	— 1⅝	— 28.9
Paprcft	.80	30777	13	16⅝	12	15⅛	+ ¾	+ 5.2
Pardyn		177345	47	18¾	10¼	14	— 3⅝	— 20.6
ParkE s		37115	11	26	12½	15½	— 5¼	— 25.3
ParkDrl	.16	153840	....	12⅝	6	6¼	— 2¾	— 30.6
ParkH	1.12	105782	10	36¾	25¼	31½	— 4⅛	— 11.6
ParkPn	.52	36476	26	21⅜	12½	15⅝	— 3⅜	— 17.8
Parson	1	129013	15	32⅜	20¼	31½	+ 6⅞	+ 27.9
PatPtrl		119420	....	7⅛	1½	1⅝	— 2	— 55.2
PayINW	.34	58424	15	24⅛	14	23¼	+ 5⅛	+ 28.3
PayNP	.60	51284	11	20	11¾	11⅞	— 5⅞	— 33.1
PayCsh	.16	238258	13	25	13½	15⅞	— 7⅝	— 32.4
Peabdy	.20	50414	......	14⅛	6¼	6⅝	— 7¼	— 52.3
Pengo		35904	......	1⅞	15-32	11-16	—13-16	— 54.2
PenCen		240137	41	50¼	36⅝	47	+ 9½	+ 25.3
PenC pr5.27		30338	......	122	94	114¾	+ 17¼	+ 17.7
Penney	2.36	437705	7	57⅛	46	46⅜	— 10¼	— 18.1
PaPL	2.48	184107	8	25⅝	19½	25⅛	+ 4½	+ 21.8
PaPL pf4.40		186	......	36½	30½	33½	+ ½	+ 1.5
PaPL pf4.50		455	......	37½	30	33½	— ½	— 1.5
PaPL pf8.60		241	......	67	57¾	63¾	+ ¾	+ 1.2
PaPL dpr3.42		3337	......	27⅜	23¼	26⅛	....	....
PaPL dpr2.90		2463	......	23⅞	20	23¼	+ 1¼	+ 5.7
PaPL pr8.40		352	......	65½	56½	63	— ½	— .8
PaPL dpr3.25		2924	......	26⅛	22⅜	25⅜	+ ½	+ 2
PaPL dpr3.75		3597	......	29¾	25¼	28⅛	+ ⅝	+ 2.3
PaPL pf9.24		2297	......	84½	65⅛	79¼	+ 2⅝	+ 3.4
PaPL pr	11	513	......	97½	81¾	88¼	— 1¼	— 1.4
PaPL pr	13	651	......	102	94½	99½	— ½	— .5
PaPL pr	8	417	......	62	54½	58½	....	....
PaPL pr8.70		1185	......	68	58½	65	+ 3	+ 4.8
Penwlt	2.20	55833	10	42¼	31½	39	— 1½	— 3.7
Penw pf2.50		143	......	62	48¼	57	— 6	— 9.5
Penw pf1.60		3263	......	24¾	20	22¼	— 1¼	— 5.3
Pennzol	2.20	372155	10	45⅜	30¾	44½	+ 10½	+ 30.9
Penz pfB	8	1034	......	83	72	79¼	— 4¾	— 5.7
PeopEn	1.06	141151	7	15½	9⅛	15⅜	+ 5⅝	+ 57.7
PepBoy	.36	28059	13	33⅛	23¼	29½	— ½	— 1.7
PepsiCo	1.68	644132	20	45¾	34½	42⅞	+ 4⅝	+ 12.1
PerkEl	.56	368183	16	31⅛	17⅞	26⅛	— 3¼	— 11.1
Prmian	1.22e	97861	6	10½	7¾	7¾	— 1¾	— 18.4
PeryDr	.28	19656	13	18½	12⅜	17⅝	+ 1½	+ 9.3
Petrie	1.40	59119	14	37½	26½	31¼	+ 3⅜	+ 12.1
PetRs	3.53e	14987	......	32⅜	26¼	26¾	— 2⅛	— 7.4
PetRs pf1.57		7289	......	17⅜	14	14⅝	— 1	— 6.4
PtrInv	1.03e	10373	......	8⅛	4⅝	4⅝	— 2⅝	— 36.2
Pfizer	1.32	1054912	14	42⅜	29⅜	42¼	+ 6½	+ 18.2
PhelpD		194295	....	27⅞	12⅞	13⅞	— 11⅜	— 45
Phelp pr	5	14348	......	48¾	34	36	....	....
PhibrS	.54	1098041	10	34¾	20¾	32	+ ⅛	+ .4
PhilaEl	2.20	623553	6	16	9	14⅞	+ ½	+ 3.5
PhilE pf3.80		553	......	29½	22	26	— ½	— 1.9
PhilE pf 4.30		164	......	32½	24	30	....	....
PhilE pf4.40		449	......	33	25	30½	+ ½	+ 1.7
PhilE pf4.68		352	......	34	25½	33	+ ½	+ 1.5
PhilE pf	7	1111	......	50½	40	50	+ 2¾	+ 5.8
PhilE pf8.75		1284	......	62½	50¼	58	— ¼	— .4
PhilE pf14.63		51	......	100	100	100	....	....
PhilE pf 1.33		21429	......	10¼	6½	9¼	....	....
PhilE pf7.85		1372	......	55¾	43	52¼	+ ⅛	+ .2
PhilE pf1.28		21786	......	10⅛	6⅝	9⅜	+ ⅜	+ 4.2
Phil pf 17.13		1580	......	116½	97	110½	— ⅝	— .6
PhilE pf15.25		1239	......	106½	87	103¼	— ¾	— .7
PhilE pf9.52		455	......	72	55	67¾	— 1¾	— 2.5
PhilE pf9.50		1293	......	67	51	62¼	+ ¼	+ .4
PhilE pf7.80		1680	......	56	44	52⅛	— 1⅜	— 2.6
PhilE pf7.75		303	......	56½	40½	51½	+ ½	+ 1
PhilSub	1.32	12110	11	20	15¼	17½	+ ⅜	+ 2.2
PhilMr	3.40	659291	10	83¼	62⅛	80⅝	+ 8⅞	+ 12.4
PhilpIn	.48	66503	10	17¾	10⅜	17¾	+ 1¾	+ 10.9
PhilIn pf	1	241	......	42	26	42	+ 3½	+ 9.1
PhilPet	2.40	1473010	8	56¼	33⅜	44¾	+ 10¼	+ 29.7
PhilVH	.40	65229	9	28½	16¼	25	+ 2⅜	+ 10.5
PiedAvt	.28	111418	8	39	27½	36	— ⅛	— .3
PieNG	2.32	8864	8	32	23⅜	31⅜	+ 5⅛	+ 19.5
Pier 1		30336	4	21	14	14¾	— 2⅞	— 16.3
Pilsbry	1.56	238204	10	45¾	33	44½	+ 8⅛	+ 22.3
Pioneer	1.24	348912	7	33	21¾	31¼	+ 4½	+ 16.8
PionrEl	.17r	11406	41	29⅞	17	20⅞	— 7⅞	— 27.4
PitnyB	1.04	206297	11	36¼	26½	35½	+ 2⅞	+ 8.8
PitnB pf2.12		5087	......	72	53¼	70	+ 5⅛	+ 7.9
Pittstn		128670	....	16½	9⅜	9⅝	— 4⅜	— 31.3
PlanRs	.20	62153	11	17¾	8⅝	13¾	— 3⅜	— 19.7
Plantrn	.16	31996	12	24½	12⅜	13⅛	— 11⅜	— 46.4
Playboy		21268	3	13¼	7½	11¼	+ 2⅜	+ 26.8
Plesey	1.02e	2089	11	35¼	23¼	23½	— 8	— 25.4
PogoPd	.60	40118	16	23⅜	16⅛	16⅛	— 4⅜	— 21.3
Polarid	1	236904	21	34¾	25⅜	27¾	— 5¾	— 17.2
Pondrs	.40	126909	8	24⅞	11½	13½	— 7⅝	— 36.1
PopTal	.80	16405	15	26¾	15	15¾	— 10⅞	— 40.8
Portec	.40	21938	......	19⅜	13¼	18¼	+ 2⅜	+ 15
Portr pf	5.50	110	......	86	72¼	73	— 8	— 9.9
PortGE	1.82	129504	5	17½	13	16⅜	+ 3⅛	+ 23.6
PoG pf	11.50	218	......	96½	90	93½	+ 2½	+ 2.8
PorG pf	2.60	1588	......	21¾	17½	20⅛	+ 1	+ 5.2
PorG pf	4.40	8567	......	33¼	28¼	31½	+ 1	+ 3.3
PorG pf	4.32	6838	......	32½	28¼	31¼	+ 1½	+ 5
PotItch	1.56	30933	11	38	25¾	28⅞	— 9⅛	— 24
PotIth pf12.38		6340	......	106½	101	103¾	+ ½	+ .5
PotmEl	1.94	226086	8	25½	19⅛	25¼	+ 3⅜	+ 15.4
PotEl pf2.44		99	......	74½	56½	74½	+ 12⅜	+ 19.9
PotEl pf4.50		550	......	41½	36	39	+ 1	+ 2.6
PotEl pf4.04		2479	......	36	31	34½	+ 1½	+ 4.6
PotEl pf4.23		422	......	42¼	38¾	42¼	+ 1¼	+ 3.1
Premrl	.54	18287	16	37¼	25¼	31½	— 2¾	— 8
Prel wi		....	......	24¾	16¾		....	— 100
Primk s	2	41849	6	35¾	23	33	+ 7	+ 26.9
PrimeC		572411	16	21½	11¾	18	+ ⅜	+ 2.1
PrimM	.12	55506	20	25½	16	25¼	+ 4½	+ 21.7
ProctG	2.60	569012	11	59⅞	45⅝	57	+ ⅛	+ .2
PrdRsh	.28	32503	20	14⅜	7¾	10½	— 2⅜	— 18.4
Proler	1.40	6418	8	47¼	31	36¼	+ 1½	+ 4.3
PSvCol	1.92	336704	8	19⅝	16¼	19⅜	+ ⅞	+ 4.7
PSCol pf7.15		824	......	60	51¾	56¾	+ 1¾	+ 3.2
PSCol pf2.10		4827	......	18¾	16¼	18⅜	+ ⅜	+ 2.1
PSInd	1	397183	2	13¼	6⅞	7	— 4⅝	— 39.8
PSIn pf	3.50	382	......	25	19¼	23⅛	— 1⅞	— 7.5
PSIn pf	1.04	3588	......	8¼	6	7⅝	— ⅜	— 4.7
PSIn pf	1.08	2222	......	8	6⅛	7	— ⅛	— 1.8
PSIn pf	7.15	987	......	50	36⅞	42½	— 1½	— 3.4
PSIn pf	9.44	2241	......	66¾	49⅝	58	— 2¼	— 3.7
PSIn pf	8.52	3007	......	58	44½	51	— 3¾	— 6.8
PSIn pf	8.38	3037	......	57	43	50	— 1	— 2
PSIn pf	9.60	2215	......	66¼	50¾	62	+ 2¼	+ 3.8
PSIn pf	8.96	1539	......	60	46¼	54½	— ½	— .9
PSvNH	.53j	272541	1	12⅞	3½	3¾	— 7¾	— 67.4
PSNH pf.69j		2346	......	19	6	9¼	— 8⅜	— 47.5
PNH pfB.70j		7442	......	19¼	6⅜	9	— 8⅞	— 49.7
PNH pfC1.06j		8228	......	28	8½	13½	— 12½	— 48.1
PNH pfD.94j		7601	......	24	7	11½	— 11¾	— 50.5
PNH pfE.96j		15366	......	25	7	11⅞	— 11⅛	— 48.4
PNH pfF.81j		8934	......	21¾	5¾	10	— 9¾	— 49.4

PNH pfG.86i		16913	......	22½	7⅜	10⅝	− 9⅞	− 48.2
PSvNM	2.88	160862	9	26⅝	19½	24⅜	− 1	− 3.9
PSvEG	2.72	464328	7	27⅛	20⅛	26¾	+ 4	+ 17.6
PSEG pf1.40		1313	......	13¼	10⅛	12½	+ 1	+ 8.7
PSEG pf4.08		1062	......	33¾	28	33½	+ 2½	+ 8.1
PSEG pf4.18		786	......	35	28½	32	− ¼	− .8
PSEG pf4.30		1508	......	35	29⅜	33	− ¼	− .8
PSEG pf5.05		601	......	41	33½	38½	+ ¼	+ .7
PSEG pf5.28		946	......	43⅝	35⅞	40⅛	− ⅜	− .9
PSEG pf11.62		2040	......	103	92	97½	− 2½	− 2.5
PSEG pf12.80		1882	......	109	97¼	101⅛	− 5⅝	− 5.3
PSEG pf13.44		5240	......	111¾	101	103⅜	− 4¾	− 4.4
PSEG pf 2.17		4719	......	18¼	15	16¾	....	....
PSEG pf6.80		779	......	56½	46½	53	− ⅛	− .2
PSEG pf2.43		4789	......	20¾	16⅝	19	− ¼	− 1.3
PSEG pf12.25		439	......	104½	96	96½	− 4	− 4
PSEG pf7.70		4556	......	66⅝	53	59¾	+ 1¾	+ 3
PSEG pf7.80		5886	......	66¾	55	60	+ ½	+ .8
PSEG pf8.08		144	......	64	55	60	+ ¾	+ 1.3
PSEG pf7.52		2746	......	62¼	51½	56	− 2⅛	− 3.7
PSEG pf7.40		2466	......	62¼	51	58½	+ 1½	+ 2.6
PSEG pf9.62		831	......	79	65⅜	72½	− ½	− .7
Publick		20056	......	4⅛	2½	2¾	− ⅝	− 18.5
Pueblo	.16	25973	7	13⅜	7¾	9⅝	+ 1½	+ 18.5
PR Cem		4739	5	12¼	6⅝	6⅞	− 1⅞	− 21.4
PugetP	1.76	166822	8	15	9¼	13½	− ¾	− 5.3
PulteHm	.12	183767	21	27	10⅛	18½	− 6¼	− 25.3
Purolat	1.28	48552	16	65½	23⅞	28¾	− 33¼	− 53.6
Pyro		102441	7	9¾	5½	8⅛	....	....
QuakO	2.48	129707	11	75⅛	54⅝	72⅛	+ 13⅛	+ 22.3
QuakO s		136824	....	38⅛	27¼	38⅛	+ 8⅝	+ 29.2
QuaO pf9.56		1025	......	97¼	90½	96¼	+ 1¼	+ 1.3
QuakSO	.80	85050	13	19⅞	15	18⅛	+ ⅝	+ 3.6
Quanex		45418	41	12½	6⅜	7¾	− 2⅜	− 23.5
Questar	1.60	81386	9	32⅞	23	29⅞	+ 3½	+ 13.3
QkReil	.20e	31232	13	20½	14	15½	− ¼	− 1.6
				— R—R—R —				
RBInd	.16	42757	......	24	6¼	9⅛	− 13⅝	− 59.9
RCA	1.04	823296	11	40	28⅝	36⅛	+ 1⅜	+ 4
RCA pf	3.50	369	......	34	29	30½	− 2	− 6.2
RCA pf	4	5487	......	91	67¾	82	+ 3	+ 3.8
RCA pf	2.12	46936	......	31⅜	24⅝	28¾	+ 1	+ 3.6
RCA pf	3.65	99220	......	34⅛	29¾	32⅝	+ 1⅜	+ 4.4
RLC	.20	28791	10	12⅛	6¼	8⅜	− 3¼	− 28
RPC n		37835	......	4⅝	3	3⅞	....	....
RTE	.56	26865	7	16⅞	12¼	15	− 2	− 11.8
RalsPur	.92	675220	13	36⅛	25	35¾	+ 8	+ 28.8
Ramad		362762	29	11	5⅛	5¾	− 4⅛	− 41.8
Ranco	.84	6031	8	21	16½	17⅞	− 2¼	− 11.2
RangrO		126569	....	11⅜	4½	4¾	− 6⅝	− 58.2
Raycm	.44	65313	15	83⅜	47½	52⅛	− 25⅞	− 33.2
Raymk		10136	......	17⅛	8⅞	13½	+ ⅜	+ 2.9
Raythn	1.60	496269	15	48⅞	34¾	40⅛	− 3	− 7
ReadBt	.40	116815	56	13⅝	7⅝	8⅜	− 3⅞	− 31.6
RdBat pf2.13		6200	......	23½	16⅜	16⅞	− 6	− 26.2
RdBat pf3.34e		11485	......	25	20	21	− 2	− 8.7
RltRef	1.35e	6476	10	13½	9½	13½	+ 2⅛	+ 18.7
RecnEq		57946	13	15⅞	9	12⅜	+ ⅛	+ 1
Redmn	.30	98084	14	18	8	9¾	− 7½	− 43.5
Reece		5993	13	10½	7½	8¾	....	....
Regal		27411	......	2⅛	11-32	¾	− ⅝	− 45.5
ReichC	.80	28410	9	35⅝	23	32½	− ¾	− 2.3
RepAir		163132	6	5¾	3¼	5⅜	+ 1⅝	+ 43.3
RepA wt		22065	......	2¼	1⅛	1⅜	+ ⅛	+ 10
RepCp	.60	19842	11	41½	25⅞	41	+ 9½	+ 30.2
RepGy	.56	21048	9	19½	8½	18¾	+ 10	+ 114.3
RepNY	1.60	36374	7	40¾	31½	39½	+ 3	+ 8.2
RNY pf	2.12	6344	......	22	17½	21½	+ 2¼	+ 11.7
RNY pfC3.13		3416	......	26	20¾	24⅝	+ 1⅛	+ 4.8
RNY pfA6.69e		16647	......	58⅜	52	55¾	− ½	− .9
RNY pfB4.47e		6902	......	52¾	40	47	....	....
RepBk	1.64	57620	7	32⅜	21½	27⅝	− 3¼	− 10.5
RepBk pf2.12		2466	......	29¾	20¼	25¼	− 3⅝	− 12.6
RepBk adj5.31e		7526	......	104⅞	88½	88⅞	....	....
RshCot	.32	21354	22	18⅞	14	16¼	+ 1⅛	+ 7.4
Revco	.80	472490	10	37½	22½	24⅛	− 10½	− 30.3
vjRever		15518	......	13½	9¾	11¼	− ⅛	− 1.1
Revlon	1.84	715887	11	40⅞	28⅝	34½	+ 1½	+ 4.6
Revln pf		64	......	23	20½	22	+ ½	+ 2.3
Rexhm	.70	11247	8	24¼	17¾	19¼	− ⅞	− 4.3
Rexnrd	.40	81777	11	20¾	11¾	14	− 4⅛	− 22.8
Reynln	3.40	736798	10	72½	52⅞	72	+ 11¼	+ 18.5
Reyln pf4.10		56806	......	48¾	45½	47¾	+ 1¾	+ 3.8
Reyln pf		9521	......	107½	100½	103⅞	+ 1⅝	+ 1.6
ReyMtl	1	134275	7	41⅝	26	33½	− 6	− 15.2
ReyM pf4.50		722	......	88½	58¼	73	− 12	− 14.1
RchVck	1.48	65026	9	30⅛	24¼	27⅞	+ ¾	+ 2.8
RiegelT	1.80	21982	......	34⅞	18¾	19½	− 10⅜	− 34.7
RiteA s	.41	186201	16	27¼	17½	25⅜	+ 3⅛	+ 14
RvrOk n		1212	14	6¼	5½	6	....	....
Robshw	1.12	23720	7	35⅞	25	29½	− 4⅛	− 12.3
Robtsn	1.60	33176	15	48½	36⅜	38¾	− 7¼	− 15.8
Robins	.76	158105	14	23¼	12	19⅞	− 2¼	− 10.2
RochG	2.20	63152	5	19⅞	12¼	18⅞	+ 1⅜	+ 7.9
RochTl	2.44	34062	9	33¼	27½	32⅞	+ 2⅝	+ 8.7
Rockwl	1	477218	9	33⅝	23	30⅜	− 2⅝	− 8
RkInt pf4.75		19	......	332	267	287	− 25	− 8
RkInt pf1.35		116	......	118	83	106	− 12¾	− 10.7
RohmH	2	73623	9	69¼	48⅛	63⅞	+ 3⅛	+ 5.1
RohrIn		63051	8	46⅛	27¼	43	+ 6⅜	+ 17.4
RolCm	n.20e	29742	26	17¼	10⅞	17⅛	....	....
RolinE	s.02i	43738	......	14⅞	6	14⅞	+ 7¼	+ 95.1
Rollins	.46	54196	15	13½	6⅞	9½	....	....
Ronson		19230	......	6⅛	2⅛	2⅜	− 1⅜	− 36.7
Roper	.64	36811	7	25	12⅝	14⅝	− 8	− 35.4
Rorer	1.08	93074	12	34⅛	25⅛	25¼	− 5	− 16.5
Rowan	.08	438730	....	14⅝	8⅝	9	− 2⅝	− 22.6
RoylD	2.87e	690894	4	54⅝	41¼	49⅜	+ 4⅜	+ 9.7
Rubrmd	.84	36776	17	45¼	32⅝	44½	+ 5⅜	+ 13.7
RussB n		52136	12	21½	13	17	....	....
RusTog	.76	22220	8	20	15½	15¾	− 1¾	− 10
RyanH	1	69989	14	35⅝	17⅜	26	− 9	− 25.7
RyderS	1.08b	124860	9	58⅞	38⅛	48⅝	− 9⅝	− 16.5
Ryland	.60	50275	12	27⅝	12½	21¼	− 5⅜	− 20.2
Rymer s		10613	4	20	8½	10¼	− 7½	− 42.3
				— S—S—S —				
SCM	2	57242	9	43½	33⅝	42⅛	+ 6⅛	+ 17
SFN	1.28	77729	28	43½	23⅞	43⅜	+ 7⅝	+ 21.3
SL Ind	s.20b	5581	10	12¼	7⅝	10¼	+ 1½	+ 17.1
SPSTec	.80	19876	11	30	19½	21¼	− 3⅜	− 13.7
Sabine	.04	62129	20	26	15	15½	− 5	− 24.4
SabnRy	2.85e	29203	......	23	16	16½	− 5	− 23.3
SfgdBs	.24	46527	14	18½	11⅜	14¼	− 3¾	− 20.8
SfgdSc		36592	81	10	5¼	7¼	+ 1⅛	+ 18.4
SfgdS wt		13292	......	2⅞	5-16	1⅜	+1 3-32	+ 388.9
SafKln	.40a	30216	18	41¾	29¼	35⅜	+ 1⅜	+ 4
SafKln s		33519	20	27¾	19½	26⅜	+ 3¾	+ 16.6
Safewy	1.60	327716	9	29¼	21¼	27⅛	+ 1⅜	+ 5.3
Saga	.44	83900	13	35½	24⅝	33¼	+ 2	+ 6.4
StJoLP	1.60	10618	7	20	15¼	19	+ 3¼	+ 20.6
SPaul	1.20	11678	......	10⅜	9	10⅛	+ ¼	+ 2.5
Salant	.30i	10261	......	12½	6½	7⅛	− 4¾	− 40
SallieM	.16	184786	15	34½	21	26½	+ 1½	+ 6
SallM pf4.07e		45521	......	53¼	49¼	52	....	....
SDieGs	2.10	241427	7	23¾	17⅝	22⅞	+ 3¼	+ 16.6
SJuanB	.82e	96788	9	10⅜	6¾	7⅝	− 2¼	− 22.8
SJuanR		5701	16	10⅞	8½	9⅜	+ ⅛	+ 1.4
Sandr s	.56	184976	14	51	35¼	35⅞	− 14⅜	− 28.6
SAnitRt	1.94	9476	12	24⅜	18¾	20¾	− ⅞	− 4
SFeSoP	1	737383	10	26⅝	20¼	25¾	− ½	− 1.9
SgtWel	1.40	3174	16	34¼	24¼	33	+ 6½	+ 24.5
SaulRE	.20	8426	43	17⅜	12⅞	16⅞	+ 3⅜	+ 25
SavElP	1.60	18832	7	19⅜	13⅜	18½	+ 4⅞	+ 35.8
SavE A	1.34	600	......	20⅛	14⅝	20⅛	+ 5⅝	+ 38.8
SavE pf	1.28	1627	......	11⅛	9⅝	10¼	....	....
Savin		54653	......	8⅛	3⅝	5⅛	+ ⅛	+ 2.5
Savin pf1.50		3563	......	11⅞	8½	10	− ⅝	− 5.9
SCANA	2.05	188163	8	23⅝	17¼	23⅝	+ 5⅞	+ 33.1
SchrPlo	1.68	269053	10	40	33	36	− 1¼	− 3.4
Schlmb	1.20	1181921	10	55	35⅞	38⅛	− 11⅞	− 23.8
SciAtl	.12	172265	20	15⅜	7¼	10⅝	− 4⅜	− 29.2
Scoalnd	.76	100457	11	29	19¼	24¾	− 1¼	− 4.8
ScotFet	1.80	124384	29	59⅛	39⅞	58	+ 15¼	+ 35.7
ScottP	1.12	232740	10	34⅞	25¼	34⅝	+ 3	+ 9.5
Scottys	.52	41230	9	16¼	11⅜	13⅛	− 1⅛	− 7.9
Scovill	1.52	163855	14	39½	20⅛	39¼	+ 10⅝	+ 37.1
Scovil pf2.50		110	......	93½	56	93½	+ 29¼	+ 45.5
SeaCnt n	.42	17557	5	30	18⅛	29½	....	....
SeaCt pf1.46		3476	......	11⅜	9½	10½	+ ¼	+ 2.4
SeaC pfB2.10		5107	......	15	12⅛	14¾	+ 1¾	+ 13.5
SeaC pfC2.10		10249	......	15	12	14½	+ 1	+ 7.4
SeaLd n	.48	254964	....	21½	14⅝	18¾	....	....

SeaCo n		31100	......	5⅜	2⅝	3¾	....	....
Seagrm	.80	153779	9	40⅜	30	40¼	+ 4	+ 11
Seagul		26628	19	21½	12½	17⅞	+ 1⅝	+ 10
SealAir	.40	40835	14	28¾	18⅞	24	+ 1	+ 4.4
SealPw	1	32673	8	32½	19¾	25⅞	— ¾	— 2.8
SearleG	.52	440401	23	65½	37½	64⅞	+ 21	+ 47.9
Sears	1.76	1456442	8	40⅜	29½	31¾	— 5⅜	— 14.5
Sears pf	6.68e	36454	......	102⅝	97	99⅝	....	....
SecPac	2.44	185948	7	53¾	38	51½	+ ½	+ 1
SelgLt	.30j	14083	10	22¼	12½	13⅝	— 7¾	— 36.3
SvcCp s	.40	59362	15	32¼	20⅜	29	+ 5¾	+ 24.7
Shaklee	.72	80427	13	22	11⅜	13⅝	— 7⅜	— 35.1
Shawln	.50	47311	7	22¾	10⅞	18⅝	— 2⅞	— 13.4
ShellO	2	382385	10	61½	39	55⅝	+ 15⅝	+ 39.1
ShellT	2.12e	33171	4	39½	28½	30½	— 2¼	— 6.9
ShelGlo	.70	77545	7	29½	17¼	27⅞	— 1⅜	— 4.7
ShelG pf	1.40	233	......	30¾	18½	30	....	....
ShelG pf	3	13	......	99⅜	66⅝	66⅝	— 28⅜	— 29.9
Shrwin	.76	118064	10	32⅜	22¼	28	+ 1¾	+ 6.7
Shoetwn		27171	9	9⅜	4½	6	— 3	— 33.3
Showbt	.60	12076	12	18⅞	12	12¾	— 2¾	— 17.7
SierPac	1.60	38869	7	16⅜	12¾	16¼	+ 1¼	+ 8.3
Signal	1	436611	14	35¾	24½	33⅛	+ ⅛	+ .4
Signl pf	4.12	8560	......	58	48¾	56½	— ⅜	— .7
Signl pf	2	357	......	70	50	66	+ ½	+ .8
Singer	.10	183562	14	35⅞	20⅜	29⅜	+ 1¾	+ 6.3
Singr pf	3.50	2004	......	30¾	26¼	28⅞	+ 1¾	+ 6.5
Skyline	.48	60100	23	19⅛	12¼	16	— 1¾	— 9.9
Smithln	.32	155917	18	21⅜	9¾	10½	— 10⅝	— 50.3
SmkB	2.80	445782	9	60¼	50	52¼	— 4¼	— 7.5
Smuckr	.96	9759	15	56¼	36⅛	55	+ 14½	+ 35.8
SnapOn	1	76134	13	37½	27	34¾	+ 4	+ 13
Sonat	1.85	143014	7	38	27	33⅞	+ 1	+ 3
SonyCp	.16e	912311	11	17⅜	12¾	14	— 1⅝	— 10.4
SooLin	1.20	5907	9	29½	22¾	23⅝	— 2¾	— 10.4
SourcC	3.10	9078	......	35⅞	27¾	35¼	+ 4½	+ 14.6
SrcCp pf	2.40	1976	......	20½	18	20¼	+ ⅜	+ 1.9
SCrE pf	2.50	255	......	22⅜	19⅝	22⅜	+ 2⅜	+ 11.9
SoJerln	2.44	10358	8	27¾	22	27⅜	+ 5⅛	+ 23
Soudwn	.50b	14068	10	48⅜	38¼	43⅛	+ 2⅜	+ 5.8
SoetBk	1.20	80994	8	26½	22	25¼	+ 1½	+ 6.3
SoetPS	1.65t	6360	13	12¾	5⅞	7⅜	— 4⅝	— 38.5
SCalE s	2.04	747868	7	24⅜	17⅛	22¾	+ 2⅞	+ 14.5
SouthCo	1.92	882679	6	18⅞	14⅜	18⅞	+ 2½	+ 15.3
SolnGE	2.48	26495	7	34¼	25½	33½	+ 5⅞	+ 21.3
SNETl	2.72	73716	9	36¼	27¾	36	+ 1½	+ 4.4
SoNE pf	3.82	4277	......	36	31½	33⅝	+ ⅝	+ 1.9
SoNE pf	4.62	919	......	49½	41⅝	42	— 5	— 10.6
SoRy pf	2.60	1685	......	24⅜	21⅞	23¾	+ ¾	+ 3.3
SoUnCo	1.72	48159	16	31	21¼	25¾	+ 2½	+ 10.8
Soutlnd	.92	267779	8	36½	23	27⅛	— 5	— 15.6
SoRoy	.08	189573	10	19¼	11⅝	12	— 4¾	— 28.4
Soumrk	.20	148768	4	10¾	6¼	6¾	— 3⅛	— 31.6
Somk pf	7.15e	17525	......	54½	48	49	— 4	— 7.5
SwAirl s	.13	273515	13	29½	14¾	22	— 5¼	— 19.3
SwtFor		216014	....	22½	13	15⅞	+ ⅜	+ 2.4
SwtGas	1.20	36363	13	14⅜	10⅝	14	+ 1¼	+ 9.8
SwBell	5.60	562683	8	71½	55	70¾	+ 11⅞	+ 20.2
SwEnr	.52	27154	14	27⅞	19¼	20	— ½	— 2.4
SwtPS	1.88	161785	8	22	17	20⅞	+ 1⅛	+ 5.7
Sparton	.52	16586	20	21	11½	14¾	— 5¼	— 26.3
SpectP		30762	23	28¼	18	22¼	— 3⅜	— 13.2
Sperry	1.92	625215	8	50	33¾	41⅝	— 5½	— 11.7
Springs	1.52	23551	7	40¼	30½	33¾	— 6	— 15.1
SquarD	1.84	121097	11	41½	31⅛	39⅜	— ⅝	— 1.6
Squibb	1.60	338184	15	54⅜	37½	53⅞	+ 8¼	+ 18.1
Staley	.80	140856	16	26¼	17¾	20¾	— 3¼	— 13.5
StBPnt	.54	69135	10	22⅝	16½	18⅝	— 1¾	— 8.6
StMotr	.32	87767	8	22	13	13¼	— 5⅛	— 27.9
StOlnd	3	1108662	7	60⅝	48⅛	52⅞	+ 2⅛	+ 4.2
StdOOh	2.80	683579	7	50½	40	42	— 2¾	— 6.1
SOOh pf	3.75	z6230	......	78	73½	74¾	+ 1¼	+ 1.7
StPacCp	.40	26347	8	18¼	9¾	18	+ ½	+ 2.9
Standex	.52	38544	10	17	11	15	+ 1¼	+ 9.1
StanWk	.96	136205	10	29½	19½	25⅞	— 1⅜	— 5
Starrett	1	2945	11	30⅜	23⅝	29½	+ 1	+ 3.5
StaMSe	1.20a	10970	......	10¼	8¾	9⅞	+ ¼	+ 2.6
StaufCh	1.44	285391	34	25¾	15¾	17½	— 7½	— 30
Steego	.12	15995	......	4⅝	2⅞	3	— 1¼	— 29.4
Sterchi	.76	4021	9	17½	14¼	16¾	— ⅜	— 2.2
StrlBcp	.72	9093	10	12¼	9⅜	10¼	....	....
SterlDg	1.16	375791	12	30	23½	28⅞	+ 1¾	+ 6.5
StevnJ	1.20	99403	14	23¼	15¼	17½	— 2½	— 12.5
StwWrn	1.68	26682	18	36	25⅝	29	+ ⅝	+ 2.2
StkVC pf	1	1553	......	12	8½	10¾	....	....
StoneW	1.60	6793	8	43¼	32⅛	40¼	+ 1	+ 2.6
StoneC	.60	73270	23	43¼	25¾	31¼	— 8⅝	— 21.6
StopShp	1	124967	9	53⅛	32¼	41¾	— 6¼	— 13
StorEq	1.84	9707	14	18¾	15⅛	17⅞	+ 1	+ 5.9
vjStorT		549768	....	14⅝	2	2¼	— 11⅜	— 83.5
Storer	.40	125037	....	47¾	30¼	46½	+ 9⅛	+ 24.4
StrtMt n		8008	......	20⅜	20	20⅜	....	....
StridRt	.80	48323	9	27⅞	14⅛	15	— 12⅞	— 46.2
SuavSh	.22j	13585	......	9	3⅞	4½	— 3⅝	— 44.6
SunBks	1.20	91347	10	30⅜	21¾	30⅜	+ 3⅞	+ 14.6
SunCh	.48	13888	20	33	24¼	29	— 1¼	— 4.1
SunEl		38450	......	20⅜	7½	8⅜	— 9⅞	— 54.1
SunCo	2.30	322700	12	59½	43⅜	46⅛	+ 2⅜	+ 5.4
SunC pf	2.25	962	......	122	89½	96¼	+ 5½	+ 6.1
Sundstr	1.80	84580	14	52	34⅜	44½	— 4¼	— 8.7
SunMn		108721	12	15⅞	7⅝	8	— 3¾	— 31.9
Sunstat		10572	5	10¼	6¼	6⅜	— 1⅞	— 22.7
SuprVl	.68	151227	11	33¾	23½	31⅝	+ 2⅜	+ 8.1
SupMkt	.42	74479	14	34⅜	19¼	33¾	+ 10⅛	+ 42.9
Swank	.90	9146	9	19¼	14	15¼	— 2¾	— 15.3
Sybron	1.08	42502	11	23	16⅛	19½	— 2½	— 11.4
Sybrn pf	2.40	1861	......	38¼	28½	32	— 3¼	— 9.2
SymsCp		30207	18	15⅞	10	11¾	— 4¼	— 26.6
Syntex	1.60	417221	12	56¼	37¾	48⅝	— 4⅝	— 8.7
Sysco	.36	72639	15	38⅜	25¾	33¾	— 2¾	— 7.5
			— T—T—T —					
TDK	.29e	25635	17	62	35⅜	39⅞	— 7⅛	— 15.2
TECO	2.20	187867	8	30½	24	29¾	+ 2⅞	+ 10.7
TGIF		58739	14	15⅞	7⅞	8⅜	— 5½	— 39.6
TNP	1.19	6257	7	14¼	11⅜	13¾	+ 1	+ 7.8
TRE	1	43852	14	36	17	20	— 10¼	— 33.9
TRW	3	123847	10	82	58⅜	72½	— 7⅛	— 8.9
TRW pf	4.40	165	......	179½	134	156	— 17¾	— 10.2
TRW pr	4.50	247	......	152	110	133¼	— 12	— 8.3
TacBoat		42960	......	14½	3½	4¼	— 7⅜	— 63.4
TaftBrd	1.12	50191	14	70	49¼	62⅜	+ 6⅜	+ 11.4
Talley		35167	11	15⅜	9¾	14	+ 2½	+ 21.7
Talley pf	1	6309	......	17⅞	13½	16	+ 1⅜	+ 9.4
Tambrd	3.20	81173	12	61⅞	46⅝	59⅝	+ 1⅜	+ 2.4
Tandy		957334	9	43⅜	23¼	24¼	— 19⅛	— 44.1
Tndycft		8532	12	16⅛	11⅞	13	— 1⅞	— 12.6
Tektrnx	1	115408	8	78¾	51⅛	57¾	— 16¾	— 22.5
Telcom		10338	5	3⅜	2⅛	2¾	— ¼	— 8.3
Teldyn		288366	13	302⅜	147¼	246	+ 78¾	+ 47.1
Telrate	.32	57293	25	23¼	13½	16¼	— 6⅝	— 29
Telex		287599	12	36⅛	18⅝	35⅞	+ 10	+ 38.7
Templn	.50	146706	10	37¾	25⅜	37⅝	+ 4⅞	+ 14.9
Tennco	2.92	658400	8	44¾	32⅜	37⅞	— 3⅛	— 7.6
Tenc pr	11	21779	......	97¾	87½	94½	+ 3½	+ 3.9
Tenc pr	7.40	6372	......	76	65	73½	+ 7⅛	+ 10.7
Terdyn		239830	14	39⅜	21¼	26	— 10	— 27.8
Tesoro	.40	113665	17	20⅞	9⅝	10	— 4	— 28.6
Tesor pf	2.16	8190	......	36⅜	20⅞	21⅛	— 5¾	— 21.4
Texaco	3	1267753	8	48⅜	31½	34⅛	— 1¾	— 4.9
TxABc	1.52	25658	9	42⅞	33¾	34¼	— 4½	— 11.6
TexCm	1.56	141141	7	48¼	36¾	39	— 2⅜	— 5.7
TxEst s	2.20	232392	9	35½	26⅛	29½	+ ⅜	+ 1.3
TxET pf	2.40	4595	......	23¼	20⅝	21	— ⅞	— 4
TxET pf	2.87	6420	......	25¾	24¼	24⅝	— ⅜	— 1.5
TxET pf	6.38e	26279	......	58	52	53½	— 2⅞	— 5.1
Texlnd	.80b	20736	16	40⅜	25	27¾	— 7¼	— 20.7
Texlnst	2	414385	9	149½	111¾	119½	— 19⅛	— 13.8
Texlnt		177516	....	5⅝	1	1⅛	— 4	— 78
TexOGs	.18	825989	11	27⅞	17	17⅞	— 6¼	— 25.9
TxPac	.40	5378	17	39	32	32¼	— 4¾	— 12.8
TexUtil	2.36	631715	6	28⅛	20¾	26⅜	+ 3⅛	+ 13.4
Texfi In		25524	......	8¼	2	2⅝	— 4¾	— 64.4
Textron	1.80	233304	13	43½	25⅞	33⅞	+ 1¼	+ 3.8
Textr pf	2.08	2854	......	47¼	28¾	36⅜	+ ⅞	+ 2.5
Textr pf	1.40	340	......	38	23¾	29¾	+ ¾	+ 2.6
Thack		9415	......	9⅞	5⅛	6⅜	— 2⅞	— 31.1
Thack pf	4.15	1364	......	28¼	23¼	25⅛	— 1⅛	— 4.3
ThermE		29342	24	22⅜	13¾	20	— 2	— 9.1
ThmBt	s1.24	29132	14	38	28¼	35⅜	— 1⅞	— 5
Thomln	.68b	11266	11	18⅞	12⅜	18¼	+ 5⅛	+ 39.1
ThmMed	.40	57585	7	26½	13¼	15⅛	— 2⅜	— 13.6
Thrifty	.52	114077	14	21⅜	11½	19⅞	+ 2⅜	+ 13.6

Tidwtr	.90	152385	...	29½	17¾	19⅝	−2⅛	−9.8
Tidwt	pf9.16e	6502	...	103½	99½	100⅝	...	...
TigerIn		177360	...	9	4⅞	6⅝	+⅞	+15.2
Time	.82	376154	13	50⅝	33¾	42¾	−9¼	−17.8
TimI	pfB1.57	1418	...	88½	60½	77½	−12½	−13.9
Timplx		47977	19	21⅞	12	18½	−1	−5.1
TimeM	1.36	184262	12	45⅝	28¼	40⅜	+2⅞	+7.7
Timken	1.80a	24969	12	67¼	49¼	52	−12¾	−19.7
TodShp	1.32	20865	6	35⅛	28¾	30⅞	−¼	−.8
Tokhm	.60	24128	10	31	22¼	27⅜	+2⅛	+8.4
TolEdis	2.52	134269	5	18⅞	13⅜	18⅞	+⅞	+4.9
TolEd	pf 3.72	377	...	25¾	24⅝	25⅜	...	...
TolEd	pf 3.75	5983	...	26½	22	25½	...	...
TolEd	pf3.47	4742	...	25⅝	20	23⅝	+1	+4.4
TolEd	pf4.28	3411	...	32	25⅛	29⅞	+1⅜	+4.8
TolEd	pf2.36	3642	...	18¼	13¼	16½	+⅛	+.8
TolEd	pf2.21	1491	...	17⅜	13½	15⅜	+½	+3.4
Tonka	.40	10527	...	48¾	23	41	+18½	+82.2
TootRol	.48	8834	11	34½	16	31	+13¼	+74.7
Trchm s	1	97304	11	34¼	18⅜	31¼	+9⅞	+46.2
Trch	pf11.38e	25080	...	109¾	92⅜	103	−1¾	−1.7
ToroCo	.20	26960	9	13¾	9⅞	12⅞	+1¼	+10.8
Tosco		187196	...	5⅛	1	1	−4	−80
Towle	.33i	20834	...	23	11⅜	11¾	−9⅝	−45
Towle	pf .44	1171	...	15¾	8⅜	8¾	−6¼	−41.7
ToyRU		399920	21	52⅞	31¾	38⅝	+2⅝	+7.3
ToyR	wi	575	...	35¼	21⅛	26⅛	+2⅛	+8.9
Tracor	.34	70513	13	27⅛	18½	26¼	+¼	+1
TWA		617979	8	14	7⅝	10½	−1	−8.7
TWA	pf 2.25	37953	...	15⅛	11⅜	13⅝	...	...
TWA	pfB2.25	50070	...	24½	16½	20	−⅝	−3
Transm	1.64	247420	13	30¾	20⅞	26⅛	−5	−16.1
TranInc	2.22	6542	...	18⅞	16¾	18⅝	+⅜	+2.1
TARlty	1e	3237	...	12½	10¾	11⅝	−¼	−2.1
Transco	2.04b	207060	10	55⅛	33½	52	+14¼	+37.8
Trnsc	pf3.87	24893	...	59⅝	42½	56	+11⅝	+26.2
TranEx	2.20	38331	...	25¾	19	22⅜	+1½	+7.2
Transcn		35851	5	17⅛	6½	8¼	−5¾	−41.1
TrGP	pf6.65	583	...	71¾	63	71¾	+2⅝	+3.8
TrG	pf 10.32	478	...	92¼	80	88¼	+⅝	+.7
TrGP	pf8.64	492	...	87¾	77	86	+1½	+1.8
TrGP	pf2.50	4014	...	24	20	22⅜	+⅜	+1.7
TrnsOh		13380	19	12	6⅛	9¼	−⅜	−3.9
Tranwy	1.80	27446	9	38⅞	28	33	−4	−10.8
Trnwld	.40	420568	19	32½	23⅝	31	...	...
Twld	wtA	30073	...	16½	9⅞	14⅝	−¼	−1.7
Twld	pf 2	4495	...	28⅛	22½	28	+3½	+14.3
Twld	pf 1.90	16511	...	17⅝	14¾	16¼	−¼	−1.5
Travler	1.92	547918	9	38¼	25½	37¼	+5½	+17.3
TriCon	5.59e	105759	...	26⅞	21⅝	24⅞	−⅝	−2.5
TriCn	pf2.50	846	...	23½	20¼	22¾	+1½	+7.1
TriSoln		20679	10	6⅝	5	6⅛	−⅛	−2
TriaInd	.40	9296	40	22⅝	12¾	16¼	+2⅝	+19.3
TriaPc	1	16245	8	29⅝	20¾	27	−¼	−.9
Tribune	.84	135653	14	34⅞	24	34½	+3⅞	+12.7
Tricntr	.36e	6825	9	6⅜	4¼	4⅜	−¾	−14.6
Trico	.16	26762	20	10⅝	5⅝	6⅛	−3⅜	−35.5
Trinty	.50	61707	...	25½	13¼	17	−6⅜	−27.3
TritEng	.10b	24825	16	19⅞	11¼	15⅜	−1⅜	−8.2
TritE	pf 1.10	11581	...	11½	8⅜	10⅛	...	...
TucsEP	2.60	106776	9	41¾	33⅝	41½	+3½	+9.2
TullJM	.52	8289	9	16¾	10¾	11½	−2⅞	−20
TwinDs	.80	3882	10	23⅜	16	16⅞	−4⅜	−20.6
TycoLb	.80	73814	9	37⅞	25½	34	+6	+21.4
Tyler	.70	23119	8	31	23⅛	29⅜	+⅜	+1.3
— U—U—U —								
UAL	.50e	725702	6	46¾	28	44	+7¼	+19.7
UAL	pf 2.40	116228	...	31¾	24	30¾	+3¼	+11.8
UCCEL		39813	30	12⅝	7⅞	12⅜	+1⅞	+17.9
UGI	2.04	39525	12	23⅛	16½	22¾	+5	+28.2
UGI	pf 2.75	451	...	23½	19½	22½	+1¼	+5.9
UNCRes		138198	...	11⅛	3	9¼	+3¾	+68.2
URS	.40b	11945	13	14⅞	10	11⅜	−2⅜	−17.3
USFG	s 2.08	310861	8	30⅞	17⅝	27½	−⅛	−.5
UniDyn	.60	39380	8	19⅜	12¾	15⅝	−⅛	−.8
UniFrst	.20	5602	12	20⅜	13⅛	15¼	−3⅜	−18.1
Unilvr	2.06e	215	8	55½	45	50¾	−1¼	−2.4
UniNV	4.20e	58618	8	92⅛	75	88	+6	+7.3
UCamp	s1.64	188776	9	42¼	30⅞	35⅜	−5⅞	−14.2
UnCarb	3.40	695369	13	65¼	32¾	36¾	−26	−41.4
UnionC		27770	...	7½	4⅜	4½	−1¾	−28
UnElec	1.72	351054	6	16½	12	16½	+3⅝	+28.2
UnEl	pf 3.50	215	...	27	21	26¼	+1	+4
UnEl	pf 4	579	...	31	25½	29¾	−¼	−.8
UnEl	pf 4.50	357	...	34	28⅛	33¼	+¼	+.8
UnEl	pf 4.56	2081	...	34½	27½	34⅜	+1⅜	+4.2
UnEl	pf 6.40	391	...	49	39½	48	+2¼	+4.9
UnEl	pfM 4	9480	...	29⅞	24½	29⅞	+1⅝	+5.8
UEl	pfL 8	1372	...	59½	48½	57¾	+1⅝	+2.9
UnEl	pf 2.98	19300	...	23⅜	18⅛	22⅞	+1¾	+8.3
UnEl	pf 2.13	6225	...	17½	13⅛	16⅞	+1⅝	+10.7
UnEl	pf 2.72	1761	...	23¾	19⅞	22½	+2⅝	+13.2
UnEl	pf 7.44	2437	...	56½	45	55⅜	+5⅜	+10.8
UEl	pfH 8	669	...	60	49	58¾	+1¼	+2.2
UnPac	1.80	500435	15	52¾	34¼	40⅞	−9⅞	−19.5
UnPc	pf7.25	17805	...	115	82	92¾	−19¼	−17.2
Uniroyl	.03e	333995	6	18	9¾	13¾	−3¼	−19.1
Unryl	pf 8	1289	...	66	53½	66	+7	+11.9
UnitDr		14288	50	6⅞	3⅜	3½	−2	−36.4
UnBrnd		45745	8	21¾	10¼	10¾	−4¾	−30.6
UBrd	pf	5866	...	17⅞	9⅝	10⅝	−2¼	−17.5
UCblTV	.14	41998	140	31⅛	20⅞	30¾	+5¼	+20.6
UnEnrg	2.48	119959	12	29	22⅛	27⅛	+2¼	+9.1
UIllum	2	77131	3	23⅞	9	13¾	−6⅞	−33.3
UIllu	pf 3.97	3392	...	28¼	19	24	−2	−7.7
UIllu	pf 2.20	1081	...	17	11	15	...	...
UIllu	pf 4	2448	...	28	20⅛	24¼	−2¾	−10.2
UIllu	pf 1.90	9245	...	13⅛	10	12¼	...	...
UnitInd	.52b	32773	11	25	15⅝	19⅞	−4½	−18.5
UnitInn	.22	4314	24	41⅛	32⅞	36½	+3½	+10.6
UJerBk	1.56	14539	8	34⅜	25½	32¾	−⅜	−1.1
UtdMM		39243	8	17⅛	9¾	15¾	+3⅛	+24.8
UPkMn		7185	1	3⅛	2⅛	2⅜	+⅛	+5.6
UsairG	.12	381079	7	35	22	33¼	+1½	+4.7
USGyps	3	118743	6	65¼	45	59⅜	+⅛	+.2
USGy	pf1.80	258	...	57	40½	53	+¼	+.5
USHom	.14i	294871	...	13	5⅛	6¼	−5¼	−45.7
USLeas	.76	32360	9	38⅜	28¾	34⅞	−1⅛	−3.1
USShoe	.86	173737	11	37¾	23	26⅝	−11	−29.2
USSteel	1	782008	...	33¼	22	26⅛	−4¼	−14
USStl	pf6.49e	72908	...	58⅛	49¾	51	−¼	−.5
USStl	pr12.75	43261	...	157	115¾	128⅛	−18⅛	−12.4
USStl	pf2.25	77140	...	31½	22⅞	26⅞	−2½	−8.5
USTob	1.44	102937	14	43	31¼	38½	−1⅜	−3.4
USWest	5.40	643767	8	70⅞	55⅝	70½	+14⅞	+26.7
UnTch	s 1.40	583523	8	41⅝	28½	36¼	...	...
UTch	pf 2.55	98466	...	35¾	27¾	32½	−½	−1.5
UniTel	1.92	473245	9	22¾	17⅜	22¼	+1⅛	+5.3
UniTl	pf1.50	124	...	32½	26½	31½	+½	+1.6
UniT	2pf1.50	307	...	27	21½	27	+1¾	+6.9
UWR	s 1.28	7489	9	17	12	15⅞	+1⅞	+13.4
Unitrde	.20	33987	18	36⅞	22	27⅛	−5⅛	−15.9
Univar	.68b	12366	12	24	14¾	17⅛	−3⅝	−17.5
UnivFd	1.04	22389	14	27⅜	18⅞	23⅝	−2⅜	−9.1
ULeaf	s .92	35036	8	22	15¼	19⅞	+2¾	+16.1
Unocal	1	1275391	9	43¼	30	37	+5⅜	+17
Upjohn	2.56	296521	12	72⅛	45	70⅛	+10⅞	+18.4
USLIFE	1.04	119462	10	35¾	23⅞	33⅞	+5	+17.3
USLF	pf3.33	263	...	33½	30¼	30⅝	−2⅜	−7.2
USLF	pf2.25	11007	...	34¼	25	33	+4½	+15.8
UslfeFd	1.04a	7237	...	9¾	8⅜	9¼	−¼	−2.6
UtaPL	2.32	161458	10	25⅛	20⅜	22	−1⅞	−7.9
UtPL	pf 2.80	2084	...	25¼	21⅜	23⅜	...	...
UtPL	pf 2.90	9202	...	25⅞	21⅜	24	−1	−4
UtPL	pf 2.36	3737	...	21½	17⅝	19½	−⅝	−3.1
UtPL	pf 2.04	4991	...	19	15⅜	17½	−¼	−1.4
— V—V—V —								
VF Corp	1.12	178756	7	32½	21¾	26⅝	−3½	−11.6
Valero	.33i	338192	...	23⅞	5⅞	6¼	−14⅝	−70.1
Valer	pf3.44	11900	...	26	14	16⅛	−8¾	−35.2
ValeyIn		13932	...	5⅞	2¼	2½	−2¾	−52.4
VanDr	s .92	14668	5	24⅛	14⅞	19¾	+1¼	+6.8
Varco		28097	...	7¼	2¼	2½	−4⅛	−62.3
Varco	pf1.50i	2778	...	20½	5⅞	7¾	−11¼	−59.2
Varian	.26	193793	14	58½	30¼	37⅜	−17⅝	−32
Varo	.40	22571	8	15½	9½	10⅛	−3¾	−27
Veeco	.32	52255	13	26⅝	17¾	20½	−5	−19.6
Vendo		13373	...	6⅞	3⅝	4⅜	−2	−31.4
VestSe	1.20a	10961	...	10⅝	8¾	10	+¼	+2.6
Viacom	.42	75668	12	34¾	23¾	32½	−¼	−.8
VaEP	pf 5	134	...	42	36½	41	+2¾	+7.2
VaEP	pf7.72	815	...	62½	54	59	+2	+3.5

VaEP pf8.84	3065	......	71	60½	66	+ 1½	+ 2.3
VaEP pf8.60	122	......	78½	67¾	75½	+ 4¼	+ 6
VaEI pf 8.60	636	......	79½	67¾	76½	+ ½	+ .7
VaEP pf9.75	3005	......	77⅝	68½	75	+ 3	+ 4.2
VaE pfJ7.72	1676	......	62¾	52½	59	+ 2	+ 3.5
VaEP pf7.20	1921	......	58½	49⅛	55¼	+ 2⅞	+ 5.5
VaEP pf7.45	2068	......	61	51¾	58½	+ 1⅞	+ 3.3
Vishay 1.85t	8541	11	20⅞	14⅞	18	— 2	— 10
Vornad	11697	13	38¾	25⅝	35½	+ 8¾	+ 32.7
VulcnM 2.44	10819	10	73¾	58	69⅜	+ 1½	+ 2.2
— W—W—W —							
WICOR 2.30	14454	6	27¾	20¼	26⅞	+ 5¾	+ 27.2
WabR pf4.50	154	......	49	34½	44¼	— 1¾	— 3.8
Wachv s .92	66102	10	29¾	20⅝	28⅜	+ 6⅛	+ 27.5
Wackht .60	12497	10	25½	16⅝	17	— 4¾	— 21.8
Wainoc	47986	117	9⅞	6¼	7	— 2¼	— 24.3
WalMrt .21	512769	22	47	30¼	37⅞	— 1⅛	— 2.9
WlMrt pf	641	......	99	68	88	+ 2	+ 2.3
Walgrn .88	109862	16	45¼	28⅝	45	+ 6¾	+ 17.7
WkHRs g1.40	25203	......	22⅞	15⅝	18⅝	— 3⅝	— 16.3
WalCSv .45	24735	16	32⅛	23¾	31⅜	+ 1½	+ 5
WaltJ s 1.20	124305	7	32⅞	22	31⅞	+ 3	+ 10.4
WaltJ pf 1	265	......	9¾	7½	9¼	+ ¾	+ 8.8
WaltJ pf1.60	509	......	42¾	29½	42	+ 3½	+ 9.1
Warnco .88	76218	7	28⅜	18	18	— 9¼	— 33.9
WrnCm .50i	519475	....	29⅝	17	20⅜	— 6½	— 24.2
WarnrL 1.48	491237	13	36⅛	28¾	34¾	+ 5⅛	+ 17.3
WashG s1.56	30227	7	18½	14¾	18⅜	+ 2⅞	+ 18.6
WshNat 1.08	39723	11	28⅜	15⅝	21⅝	— 2¾	— 11.3
WasN pf2.50	185	......	50	30½	40¼	— 3½	— 8
WshWt 2.48	43225	7	20⅝	16	18½	— 1⅛	— 5.7
Waste .80	405185	16	47⅞	27¼	43⅞	— 2½	— 5.4
WatkJ s .32	90730	12	27½	18	21	— 6⅝	— 24
WayGos .20	3104	10	13⅞	8¾	9⅝	— 3¾	— 28
WayG pf1.60	460	......	28	20¼	20¼	— 6¾	— 25
WeanU	9489	......	10⅜	4	5½	— 3	— 35.3
Wean pf.95k	293	......	12	9½	11	+ 2	+ 22.2
WebbD .15e	112309	15	24⅛	12⅛	21½	+ 2½	+ 13.2
WeisMk .64	6852	14	37¼	29⅞	37	+ ⅞	+ 2.4
WellsF 2.16	158299	7	49¾	30⅞	47⅛	+ 7½	+ 18.9
WelF pf5.03e	40546	......	50	40	43⅝	— 2⅜	— 5.2
WelFM 2.80	20553	10	28⅞	22⅞	25⅝	— 1¾	— 6.4
Wendy s .28	428473	14	20½	13⅛	16⅝	+ 1	+ 6.4
WestCo .44	20731	9	28⅜	16¼	17⅝	— 8⅜	— 32.2
WPenP pf4.50	273	......	40	34	38¼	+ 3¼	+ 9.3
WstPtP 2.20	58335	6	53½	34⅜	36	— 15½	— 30.1
WstctT g1.04	3314	......	12⅝	9⅞	11⅜	— ¾	— 6.2
WnAirL	138677	....	5½	2⅝	3¼	— 1	— 23.5
WtAir wt	27214	......	2¼	¾	⅞	— ¾	— 46.2
WAir pf 2	16332	......	18	8¼	11⅛	— 1⅜	— 11
WAir pf 2.14	8809	......	13⅜	8¾	12⅛	....	....
WCNA	200822	....	11⅛	4	4⅝	— 4⅞	— 51.3
WCNA pf7.25	6113	......	53½	47	48⅞	— 3⅝	— 6.9
WPacI	4883	6	109	81	101	+ 19	+ 23.2
WUnion 1.40i	305394	....	39¾	8⅛	8¾	— 27¾	— 76
WnUn pf4.60i	630	......	89	26⅝	28½	— 56⅝	— 66.5
WnUn pf4.90i	227	......	98	29½	30½	— 67	— 68.7
WUn dpf1.18i	15535	......	9⅝	3½	3⅝	— 5¼	— 59.2
WUn pf .87i	15193	......	15½	5⅝	6	....	....
WUTI pf 6i	397	......	48⅜	23	23	— 22¼	— 49.2
WUTI pf2.56i	4857	......	20⅜	8	8	— 11	— 57.9
WstgE s 1	765441	9	28⅜	19¾	26⅛	— 1¼	— 4.6
Westvc 1.32	69000	8	40½	31¾	37¼	— 1¾	— 4.5
Weyerh 1.30	484173	16	35½	25	29⅛	— 4⅝	— 13.7
Weyr pf 2.80	26873	......	45	34¾	40	— 3½	— 8
Weyr pr4.50	17609	......	50⅞	43⅝	47¾	— 1¼	— 2.6
WhelLE 5.75	z6630	......	92	74¼	82	— 1	— 1.2
WhelPit	26812	......	35⅝	13½	13⅝	— 14⅛	— 50.9
WhPit pf 6	244	......	43	31½	34	— 4¾	— 12.3
WhPit pf 5	316	......	38	25	26⅞	— 6⅛	— 18.6
Whirlpl 2	222708	9	50	36½	46½	— 2	— 4.1
WhitC 1.50	82455	9	47½	24⅛	29	— 18¾	— 39.3
WhitC pfA 3	70	......	49	47¼	47¾	— ½	— 1
WhitC pfC 3	1022	......	45½	36⅝	39	+ ¼	+ .7
Whitehl	44532	8	41¾	17⅝	21⅝	— 16⅞	— 43.8
Whittak .60	238704	7	22¼	14½	21⅞	+ 3⅜	+ 18.2
Wiebldt	4678	......	9	6⅝	7¾	— ⅜	— 4.6
Wilfrd n	9795	......	10⅞	8	9⅞	....	....
William 1.40	249732	7	31⅞	22¾	29¾	+ 2⅛	+ 7.7
WilmEI	54331	......	10⅜	2	2½	— 6⅜	— 71.8
WilshrO .10	19829	17	10⅞	6¼	6¾	— ½	— 6.9
WinDix 1.68	28867	11	34	25¾	31⅞	+ 3	+ 10.4
Winnbg .10e	205221	14	15½	7¾	15½	+ 2¼	+ 17
Winner	44609	14	15⅝	5⅛	6¾	— 8¾	— 56.5
WinterJ	5145	......	10¼	3¾	4¼	— 4¾	— 52.8
WiscEP 2.28	200906	7	33⅝	25¼	31⅛	+ 3⅝	+ 13.2
WisE pf 8.90	1465	......	79	68⅝	75	— 1	— 1.3
WisE pf 7.75	1704	......	68	59½	66	+ 1	+ 1.5
WisG pf 2.55	2780	......	25⅜	23⅛	23¾	— ⅞	— 3.6
WiscPL 2.56	39428	8	30⅞	25⅝	29¾	+ 1¼	+ 4.4
WiscPS 2.56	26236	7	32⅞	24¼	31¼	+ 3½	+ 12.6
Witco 1.48	62344	8	39½	27⅝	34	— 1¼	— 3.5
Witco pf2.65	6	......	215	185	185	+ 6	+ 3.4
WolvrW .24	69930	15	17⅜	9½	10½	— 4⅞	— 31.7
WoodPt .72	50546	14	27½	18⅝	20⅜	— 3⅛	— 13.3
Wolwth 1.80	211152	9	38⅞	29⅞	37	+ 1⅞	+ 5.3
Wolw pf 2.20	568	......	54¼	42½	52⅜	+ 2⅞	+ 5.8
WrldAr	8164	......	5¼	2⅜	2¾	— 1¾	— 38.9
Wrigly 1.80a	12464	11	60	45	59¾	+ 7⅛	+ 13.5
Wurltzr	7212	......	8⅝	3⅛	3¼	— 5	— 60.6
WyleLb .32	51840	10	25⅜	10¾	14⅞	— 10	— 40.2
Wynns .60	11768	7	20½	16½	18⅝	— ⅞	— 4.5
— X—Y—Z —							
Xerox 3	691270	11	51⅛	33¼	37⅞	— 11⅝	— 23.5
Xerox pf5.45	57494	......	50½	45¼	48½	+ ⅜	+ .8
XTRA .64	47797	9	36¼	19	23¼	— 10⅜	— 30.9
ZaleCp 1.32	14576	8	31¾	24	25⅞	— 4⅜	— 14.5
ZalepfA .80	70	......	24	19¼	21½	— 2	— 8.5
Zapata .84	241355	13	24⅞	15¼	16⅜	— ½	— 3
Zapat pf 2	1	......	210	210	210	+ 15	+ 7.7
Zayre .40b	163288	12	49	31¾	44½	+ 1¼	+ 2.9
ZenithE	314166	7	38⅝	19½	19¾	— 15¾	— 44.4
Zero .40	16613	18	27⅝	18	23⅞	— 2⅛	— 8.2
ZurnIn 1.32	34249	11	30½	21⅛	26	— 1¼	— 4.6

Copyright by The Associated Press 1984.

AMERICAN STOCK EXCHANGE COMPOSITE TRADING DECEMBER 31, 1984

NEW YORK (AP) - American Stock Exchange issues trading for 1984. The net change and percentage change is from the previous year on issues listed prior to Jan. 1, 1984.

Stock	Div	Sales (hds)	PE	High	Low	Last	Net Chg.	Pct. Chg.
— A—A—A —								
ADI n		9846	19	7¼	3⅞	5¼	...	...
ADI wt		1319	...	3¾	1⅝	2¼	...	...
AIC Ph		1052	...	3⅜	¾	⅞	-2	-69.6
ALLab n	.20	8568	9	15¾	8¼	9⅜	...	...
AMC n	.12	3752	11	14¼	12	13⅞	...	...
AM Intl		33291	...	3¼	2½	3¼	...	...
ATTFd n	5.52e	26250	...	71¾	58	71¾	...	...
AcmePr		3512	26	6½	2⅛	4⅜	-1⅛	-20.5
AcmeU	.32	7622	11	16¼	8½	9¾	-6⅜	-39.5
Action		48850	37	16⅞	9⅝	14⅞	+2⅞	+24
Acton		20386	...	9¼	3⅞	4¼	-2⅜	-35.8
Actn wt		3197	...	3⅞	5-16	½	-2	-80
AdmRs		12680	2	3⅝	1½	1½	-1	-40
AdRusl	.14	26138	19	25½	15⅞	24¼	-1¼	-4.9
Adobe	.24	28462	10	24¼	15	15½	-4¼	-21.5
Aeronc		24103	7	8⅜	4½	6¾	+1¼	+22.7
AfilHsp	.44	1645	8	25⅛	16½	19⅝	-5⅛	-20.7
AfilPub	.80	5687	15	50⅞	38½	47⅝	+9⅛	+23.7
AirExp		16782	10	9¾	6	8⅛	+1¼	+18.2
Alamco		18863	7	5¼	2⅝	3⅛	-1⅝	-34.2
Almito n		53	...	75⅜	72	73¼	...	...
AlbaW	.15i	8891	8	14	6⅜	7⅛	-6⅜	-47.2
AlgC wt		22	...	81	59½	81	+24¼	+42.7
AlnTre		601	...	4½	2	2⅛	-2½	-54.1
Aloha	.48r	4203	1	9¼	6	6⅛	-⅜	-5.8
Alphaln	.05	32105	13	22¼	9½	11⅜	-10¼	-47.4
Altex		28932	...	1⅝	½	1¼	-¼	-16.7
Altex wt		4158	...	⅜	⅛	⅛	...	...
Alcoa pf	3.75	1969	...	34¾	28⅝	31	-1	-3.1
AlzaCp		55653	50	22	11	19	+2½	+15.2
Amdahl	.20	288057	17	20¼	9½	13⅜	-5	-27.2
Amedco	.08	30850	...	17	6½	8⅛	-6⅞	-45.8
AmBilt	.15	6067	5	7¼	4¾	7	+1½	+27.3
AmCap		9695	...	9⅝	4	4½	-4⅛	-47.8
AContrl	.92a	404	10	37½	30	37¼	+3½	+10.4
AExp wt		27932	...	27	12¼	25	+3½	+16.3
AFruc A		2422	...	7⅞	5⅝	6⅞	...	...
AFruc B		2248	...	7½	5⅝	6½	...	...
AHlthM		26226	6	12¼	7¼	7⅝	...	...
AIsrael		8263	2	7⅛	4	4½	-3	-40
AMzeA	.52	9717	8	19⅞	12⅝	15⅝	-1	-6
AMzeB	.52	2018	8	18½	12¾	15⅜	-⅞	-5.4
AMBld		56452	...	3⅛	½	1 3-16	-1 13-16	-60.4
AMotl s	.16	114200	12	21¾	12½	21⅜	+4⅝	+27.6
AmOil		11117	20	10⅜	3	4	-4⅝	-53.6
APetf	3.20	6038	13	64¾	53½	60⅝	+5⅝	+10.2
APete rt		968	...	1-64	1-256	1-256	...	...
AmPln v		10627	...	8⅜	⅜	½	-8	-94.1
APrec s	.24	4633	16	17⅝	10⅝	15½	+4¾	+44.2
AmRlty		4083	5	8½	6⅜	6⅝	+⅛	+1.9
ASciE		11047	...	6⅞	3	3⅜	-1⅞	-35.7
Ampal	.06	42966	4	3⅜	1¾	1¾	-1⅛	-39.1
Andal		15151	9	5⅜	3½	5⅛	+⅞	+20.6
AndJcb		9280	...	11⅞	3¼	3½	-6¾	-65.9
Andrea	.72	1252	12	16	9	10⅛	-1¾	-14.7
Angles n		10892	9	14⅝	6¼	6⅞	...	...
Angel wt		4339	...	3¾	¾	⅞	...	...
Anglo v		24278	...	3	⅞	1⅛	-⅝	-35.7
ArgoPt		28736	...	9¼	3⅜	3⅝	-2	-35.6
Arley n		1686	...	7¾	5½	5½	...	...
Armtrn		4074	7	12⅝	6½	6¾	-4¼	-38.6
ArrowA	.20	5152	8	12⅞	9¼	9⅝	-1⅝	-14.4
Arundl		15851	32	24	9⅝	19	+7¼	+61.7
Asmr g	.15	51681	...	11⅝	6½	7⅛	-4⅝	-39.4
Astrex		7194	...	12⅝	8⅛	10⅜	+¼	+2.5
Astrotc		137265	...	3⅞	2¼	2½	...	...
Astrot pf	1.80	1409	...	17¾	14⅞	16½	+⅜	+2.3
AtlsCM		53739	...	2½	9-16	¾	-1½	-66.7
Atlas wt		3400	...	5½	3¼	3¼	-1½	-31.6
Audiotr	.05e	5355	12	7½	4¼	4⅜	-2⅜	-35.2
AutoSw	1a	12466	19	49⅞	32⅝	48	+9⅛	+23.5
Avondl s	.80	4759	6	25¾	13⅝	16	-7¾	-32.6
— B—B—B —								
BAT	.12e	295044	...	4¼	2½	4⅛	+1½	+57.1
BDM	.15	8593	17	35	21⅛	27	...	...
BRT		2545	7	3¾	1⅞	2⅛	-1	-32
BSN		22394	26	5⅞	3½	4⅞	-⅛	-2.5
BTK		6903	...	3⅜	⅛	5-16	-2 5-16	-88.1
Badger	.40e	2510	12	11¼	7¼	9¼	+¾	+8.8
Baker		1438	...	9¾	7½	9¾	+⅝	+6.9
BaldwS	.32a	4506	...	9¼	7½	8⅞	-¼	-2.7
BalyM wt		10530	...	7¼	2¼	2½	-3	-54.5
BanFd	2.08e	3299	...	24¾	21	22½	-½	-2.2
Banstr g		7102	...	6⅞	4⅝	5½	+⅜	+7.3
BnkBld	.40	3361	23	10	6⅛	7	-1¾	-20
Barco	.60i	3232	36	5⅞	3½	3⅝	-1⅜	-27.5
BarnEn		4901	53	6¼	2½	2⅝	-2¾	-51.2
Barnwl	.20	1798	...	13¾	7¾	8⅛	-5⅜	-39.8
BaryRG		12333	...	6⅜	4⅛	4⅛	-⅞	-17.5
Baruch	.34t	5071	14	15½	10⅝	10⅝	-2⅝	-19.8
Beard		9652	...	10½	4¾	5¼	-4⅝	-46.8
BeefCh		22196	...	4¾	1¾	2	-2⅜	-54.3
BeldBl n	1.80	2390	...	22½	13¼	13½	...	...
Beltran		13291	19	8⅞	3½	4¼	+⅜	+9.7
Beltr wt		1034	...	2¾	⅜	⅝	-¼	-28.6
BnfStdA	.30c	14633	...	50	25¾	38	+12¼	+47.6
BnfStdB	.30c	8763	...	50¼	25⅞	39	+12⅞	+49.3
BergBr	.32	102017	15	27⅝	19	22½	-1½	-6.3
BethCp	.49t	1158	...	5⅝	3¼	3¼	-1¾	-35
BicCp	.60	14459	7	30¾	12½	22⅞	+10⅝	+86.7
BigV	.40	5137	26	12⅜	9¼	11⅛	+⅜	+3.5
Biltrite	.15	3037	...	6⅜	4⅝	6⅛	+1½	+32.4
BinkMf	1	4102	11	24	19⅛	22½	+2⅝	+13.2
BioR B		916	...	17¼	14	14¼	-2⅜	-14.3
BioR A		2541	...	17	14⅛	14½	-2⅜	-14.1
Blessng	.80b	1960	6	26	17⅝	22¼	-3⅜	-13.2
BlockE		21350	...	3½	¾	1¼	-⅝	-33.3
BlountA	.45	16323	7	17¼	9⅞	15	...	...
BlountB	.40	5492	7	17	10¾	14⅞	-⅝	-4
BolarP	.05	15674	21	32	17½	24	+⅞	+3.8
BowVal	.20	16258	...	20¾	12½	12⅞	-7⅞	-38
BowlA s	.44	906	9	11⅛	9⅛	9¾	-¾	-7.1
Bowmr		14248	16	4⅝	2½	2¾	-1⅛	-29
Bowne	.44	67570	14	19	12	15	-1⅞	-11.1
BradNt		51198	...	15¼	5⅛	8⅝	-4¼	-33
Brscn g	1.60	14735	...	33⅝	21¾	22¾	-8⅛	-26.3
Braun s		2071	7	16¼	11¼	13⅝	-1	-6.8
BrnFA	.88	6694	9	30	22¾	27⅝	-2¼	-7.5
BrnFB	.88	55312	10	32⅞	23¼	31	-1½	-4.6
BrnF pf	.40	1565	...	3⅞	3⅛	3⅝	...	...
Buckhn		3084	...	4	2⅜	2½	-1	-28.6
Buckh pf	.50	2450	...	4¾	3⅜	3¾	-¼	-6.3
Buell	.50	4844	7	32⅞	18¼	31⅞	+12⅝	+65.6
— C—C—C —								
CDI s		6788	8	17⅜	11½	14⅞	+1⅜	+10.2
CHB	.20b	4345	9	13½	9¼	9¾	-2¼	-18.8
CMI Cp		22730	...	9¾	4½	7¾	+2¾	+55
CRS	.34	9148	15	22¼	13⅝	15¾	-6¼	-28.4
CaesNJ		18330	11	19¾	9⅛	9⅞	-4⅞	-33.1
CagleA		8143	7	8¼	3¾	7⅞	+4⅛	+110
CalRE	1.24	8351	12	13⅛	10	10¾	-⅜	-3.4
Calmt n	.60	7849	24	25	18⅛	21⅜	...	...
Calprop	.80t	2835	3	9	6⅜	8⅜	+1¾	+26.4
Camco	.32	10241	10	14¼	9⅞	11¾	...	...
Campnl		4894	...	4½	2	2⅛	-2¼	-51.4
CMarc g	.28	30198	...	23½	13⅜	14⅝	-6¼	-29.9
CdnOcc	.50	7748	...	24¼	18½	19¼	-3¾	-16.3
CWine		9043	10	36¼	25⅞	32¼	+1⅜	+4.5
Cardiff		2916	...	6¾	4½	5	+⅛	+2.6
Cardil		3134	...	5¼	2⅛	2¼	-1¾	-43.8
CareB		2266	12	12⅛	7⅜	8¼	-3¾	-31.3
CareA	.10e	2553	12	11	6⅝	8¼	-1¾	-17.5
CareEn		31479	17	11¾	5¼	8½	-1¼	-12.8
CaroP pf	5	238	...	43⅜	36	38	-1	-2.6
Casblan	.66t	15584	3	8¼	3½	3⅞	-2⅜	-38
CastlA s	.80	4393	8	17¼	14⅞	16	-⅜	-2.3
CasFd	2.20a	1527	...	34⅛	25⅝	27¼	-4⅝	-14.5
CastInd		6974	...	9	4⅝	6¼	-1⅜	-18
Centenl		7896	...	1½	⅞	15-16	-5-16	-25
Centl pf		1995	...	2⅛	1⅜	1⅜	-⅜	-21.4
CenM pf	3.50	288	...	27¼	20⅜	23¾	-2	-7.8
CentSe	1.70e	4677	...	14¾	11	12¾	-1¾	-12.1
CenS pfC	1.25	z1250	...	54	47	51	-2	-3.8
CenS pfD	2	84	...	25¼	22½	24¼	...	...
CtryFa	.15i	1813	178	20½	14⅜	16	-3¼	-16.9

Cetec	.20	7492	9	11¼	6⅞	7½	—	3⅞	—	34.1
ChmpH		125283	14	5⅝	2½	3¼	—	1⅛	—	25.7
ChmpP	.72	4678	10	17½	12⅛	13⅜	—	1⅛	—	7.8
ChrtMA	.20	67841	19	34	18½	33	+	14⅞	+	82.1
ChrtMB	.20	1591	18	32	18¾	32	+	13⅞	+	76.6
ChrtM pf	.75	430	......	6½	5⅝	6¼	+	½	+	8.7
ChiRv	1.20	2292	9	19⅝	14½	17¼	+	¼	+	1.5
ChfDv g		6317	......	15	9⅝	10⅛	—	3⅛	—	23.6
ChftD pf	4.75	z1100	......	46	37½	37½	—	7	—	15.7
ChftD pf	4	z400	......	42	35	36	—	7½	—	17.2
Chiltn s		22647	20	20⅝	9⅛	18¾	+	4⅞	+	35.1
Citadel		36354	6	16⅝	11⅝	15⅞	+	3⅜	+	27
CitFst	1b	5633	8	27⅜	18⅞	26¼	+	5½	+	26.5
CitFst pf	2.50	233	......	38¼	27⅞	38¼	+	7	+	22.4
CtyGas	1.20	2080	11	21½	17	21	+	3½	+	20
Clarmt	1.45e	2701	......	38½	28⅛	36⅛	+	5⅞	+	19.4
ClarkC	.28e	1100	8	9¼	6¾	8⅜	+	½	+	6.4
Clarost	.70e	3195	10	34¼	21¼	30¾	+	3¼	+	11.8
Clopay	.16	1412	10	19½	13⅝	17¼	—	⅝	—	3.5
Cognitr		12035	......	12⅛	3½	4	—	6⅞	—	63.2
Cohu	.20	7007	8	10¼	6¾	7⅝	....		....	
ColF wt s		7149	......	4	2	3⅜	....		....	
Comfd n		13025	3	15¼	8¾	11¾	....		....	
Comin s		5124	......	16⅜	8½	9	—	6⅝	—	42.4
ComA pf	1.62	443	......	14	12	13½	....		....	
ComdrC		88629	......	6⅛	½	¾	—	5¼	—	87.5
Compo	.20	22592	8	11⅜	7¼	8⅞	....		....	
CompD		3372	7	12⅜	6¼	9½	+	2¾	+	40.7
CmpCn		78402	13	20½	7½	11⅞	—	8⅝	—	42.1
CmpFct		11294	21	9½	5½	6	—	1⅛	—	15.8
Cnchm	.50e	3043	9	22	11⅞	15⅜	—	2	—	11.5
ConcdF		5293	5	12¼	6⅞	9½	+	1⅝	+	20.6
Connly		1672	7	9¾	5⅛	7¾	+	1⅜	+	21.6
ConrHm		9963	7	18	12	16½	....		....	
Conqst		55982	40	11¾	5⅝	6⅞	—	1⅞	—	21.4
Conq wt		15812	......	7½	2	2¼	—	2½	—	52.6
ConsOG		49753	4	11⅜	8¼	9	+	⅛	+	1.4
ConOG wt		5480	......	13-16	⅛	⅛	—	⅜	—	75
viContA		45446	......	9⅜	3⅞	8⅜	+	4⅜	+	109.4
viCntA pf		10133	......	11⅝	4⅞	10¾	+	5⅞	+	120.5
ContMtl		11739	7	34⅞	12¼	17¾	—	13⅝	—	43.4
CookInt	.50e	8203	283	14¼	7¾	14⅛	+	6⅛	+	76.6
Cordn v		5282	......	4⅞	¾	1¼	—	3½	—	73.7
CntCrd	.24r	18936	18	10¼	5⅝	6⅝	—	1½	—	18.5
Courtld	.06e	5535	......	2⅜	1⅜	1⅜	—	5-16	—	18.5
Crwfrd		4430	......	2⅞	⅝	11-16	—	1 11-16	—	71.1
CrstFo	.15e	2075	8	12¼	7⅜	8½	—	3½	—	29.2
Cross	1.32	22558	14	32½	23¾	27	—	5⅜	—	16.6
CrowlM	1	1320	7	31	19⅝	29⅞	+	8¼	+	38.2
CrnCP	.40i	5861	......	22⅝	10¾	11	—	6⅞	—	38.5
CrCPB	.40i	2875	......	18¼	8	8	—	7¾	—	49.2
CwCP pf	1.92	1659	......	28½	16	17⅝	—	6⅝	—	27.3
CrownC		2304	7	9½	4¾	6⅜	—	1	—	13.6
Crownl	.28	8300	6	14¼	8½	11⅛	—	2¼	—	16.8
CrutcR		46484	3	4⅛	1	1⅜	—	2¾	—	66.7
CrystO	.27i	172371	....	17	2⅞	3¼	—	11⅛	—	77.4
Cubic	.39	28959	9	27¾	13¾	15⅝	—	8½	—	35.2
Curtice	.80	4585	10	28	21⅝	27¾	+	1¾	+	6.7
CustEn		13203	......	9⅞	9-16	13-16	—	7 13-16	—	90.6

— D—D—D —

DWG	.30t	27122	8	3⅞	1⅞	2¼	—	1	—	30.8
DaleEn	.32	7671	8	26	15¾	25	+	7¼	+	40.9
DamnC		959	......	9⅛	5¾	6	—	1⅜	—	18.6
Damson		37112	3	10¼	3¾	4	—	5¼	—	56.8
Dam wtO		5753	......	3¾	1-16	⅛	—	3⅛	—	96.2
Dams pf	2.50	6877	......	32¼	18¼	20⅛	—	10⅛	—	33.5
Dams pf	3.75	191	......	23⅛	20¼	21	....		....	
DataPd	.16	177876	10	31½	13⅜	15¼	—	13¼	—	46.5
Datarm		9558	......	10¾	3⅜	4⅞	—	4¾	—	49.4
DeRose		2597	8	9½	3¼	4⅞	—	3⅜	—	40.9
Decrat s		2858	9	6⅝	4¼	5⅛	+	⅛	+	2.5
DelLab	.52	1724	9	31⅛	20⅞	27¼	+	2¼	+	9
DelVal	1.68	4654	8	14¾	11¾	13¾	—	⅝	—	4.3
Delmed		175208	....	11⅝	2¼	2¾	—	6⅛	—	69
Dsgntrn	.23t	4594	10	7½	4	4¾	—	2¾	—	36.7
Desgnl	.92t	2833	15	11½	7¼	7⅞	—	¾	—	8.7
DevlCp		8890	8	16	9⅝	13¾	+	1¾	+	14.6
Diag A		16074	15	10½	5⅝	6⅞	—	2	—	22.5
Diag B		7434	15	10	5⅜	6⅞	—	1⅛	—	14.1
DiaBth	.20	6228	9	12	8	9¾	—	⅜	—	3.7
Digicon		33334	......	9⅞	2	2¼	—	5½	—	71
Digic wt		6614	......	2⅞	¼	⅜	—	1⅜	—	78.6
Dillrd s	.20	28023	12	41⅞	21⅝	38¼	+	10¼	+	36.6
Diodes		10962	7	7⅞	3¼	4	—	2⅝	—	39.6
DirAct n		13957	6	9½	6	6½	....		....	
Dixico	.17e	13051	10	8¼	5¼	7⅛	+	½	+	7.6
DomeP		520251	....	3 11-16	1 9-16	1⅝	—	1¾	—	51.9
Domtr	g1.40	7772	......	28¼	22⅛	25¼	+	⅞	+	3.6
Downey		8303	4	11¾	6⅞	9⅜	—	¾	—	7.4
Driller		4556	......	4⅜	1⅛	1¼	—	2½	—	66.7
DrivHr		407	27	24⅞	13⅝	24½	+	7⅞	+	47.4
Ducom	.80	12446	26	43⅞	26	27¼	—	14¾	—	35.1
Dunlop		235079	....	¾	⅛	5-16	—	¼	—	44.4
Duplex	.84	5298	10	27⅜	22½	27¼	+	¾	+	2.8
DurTst	.40a	15764	13	22⅞	13	13¼	—	5¾	—	30.3
Dynlct	.25e	54023	11	14¼	9¾	11⅛	—	1⅜	—	11
Dyneer	.80	2450	8	21⅞	17½	18⅜	—	1¾	—	8.7

— E—E—E —

EAC	.40	7327	12	12⅛	6⅛	6½	—	4	—	38.1
EECO	.32	9502	25	15¾	11⅞	15¼	+	1⅜	+	9.9
EaglCl		48763	14	8¾	2⅛	2⅜	—	6⅜	—	72.9
EstnCo	1	3202	6	23¾	14⅝	18⅛	+	2	+	12.4
Estgp	6.96e	5495	4	39	33⅜	39	+	¾	+	2
EchoB g	.12	235381	....	11⅛	6¼	8⅞	+	1⅜	+	18.3
ElAudD		14735	......	4¾	1¾	2⅛	—	1⅝	—	43.3
ElcAm	1.40	2751	5	22¾	15⅛	16¾	—	3	—	15.2
ElecSd		3076	14	5⅞	3½	3¾	—	1⅛	—	23.1
Elsinor		55465	18	11⅛	5⅞	6¼	—	2¾	—	30.6
EmMd n		462	......	12⅝	11½	11⅝	....		....	
EmCar		3236	3	6½	2⅞	3	—	2½	—	45.5
EngMgt		20185	......	2⅜	¼	½	—	⅞	—	63.6
EnrSrv		3621	......	4¼	⅞	1	—	1½	—	60
Enstr pf	.50e	6453	......	6½	3⅛	3⅛	—	2	—	39
Ero In s		3823	10	10½	5½	10½	+	4¾	+	82.6
Espey	.40	18770	6	38	19½	20¾	—	10¾	—	34.1
Esprit		8261	10	9¼	1½	1⅞	—	6¼	—	76.9
EsqRd	.72e	2508	8	34¾	24⅜	34	+	5¾	+	20.4
EtzLav	.20e	4495	20	36¾	22⅛	34⅜	+	2⅞	+	9.1
EvalRs		14676	13	10	3⅞	5½	—	2⅛	—	27.9
EvrJ B	.10	1450	......	12¼	7⅝	8¼	—	1⅛	—	12
EvrJ A	.20	7696	......	12⅛	7	8½	—	¾	—	8.1
Excel n	.30e	5127	5	8¾	6¼	8⅜	....		....	
ExplSv		4526	38	4¾	2⅝	2⅝	—	⅛	—	4.5

— F—F—F —

FPA		7958	17	12⅞	8¼	9⅛	—	1¾	—	16.1
FabInd	.40	6552	7	20⅜	14⅝	15½	—	2	—	11.4
FairmC		744	......	5⅛	2	2⅜	—	1¼	—	34.5
FtConn	1a	780	7	11½	9½	10	—	½	—	4.8
FtFSL n	.60b	461	13	24½	18¾	24½	....		....	
FWymB	.80	5964	8	13⅞	11	11½	—	2	—	14.8
FischP		11531	13	17⅜	12¼	13⅛	—	2⅜	—	15.3
FitcGE	1.40	6881	3	19⅞	8⅜	8⅞	—	9⅞	—	52.7
FitGE pf	4	950	......	28¾	22¾	24⅞	—	2⅜	—	8.7
FlanEn		3697	......	12⅛	8⅛	8⅞	—	2⅜	—	21.1
FlaRck	.70	12344	8	32¾	23⅛	31⅞	+	5⅝	+	21.4
Fluke	1.27t	14957	11	31½	22⅝	26	—	4½	—	14.8
Foodrm		3568	......	10⅜	6¼	8¾	—	⅞	—	9.1
FooteM		1955	......	10¼	7¼	8	—	1⅛	—	12.3
Foote pf		518	......	34¾	28½	30	—	1⅜	—	4.4
FthillG		43182	......	8¼	4½	7¾	+	¾	+	10.7
FordCn	g 7e	1345	......	101¼	62½	97	+	27¾	+	40.1
ForstC A	.15	2715	340	21¼	15	20⅜	+	1½	+	8
ForstC B	.09	2382	342	22⅜	15	20½	+	1½	+	7.9
ForestL		46191	30	32¼	11¼	15⅞	—	11⅛	—	41.2
Fotomt		32519	......	2½	¾	15-16	—	9-16	—	37.5
Frantz	1	1224	14	37	29	32½	+	2⅞	+	9.7
FrdHly	.20i	1739	12	9¼	4¼	4⅜	—	4½	—	50.7
FreqEl		19512	15	32½	14	16¾	—	8¾	—	34.3
Friedm	.28b	2542	11	9⅝	7¾	8¼	—	⅝	—	7
FriesE n		1662	9	5½	5	5⅛	....		....	
Friona	.50	8972	9	16½	9⅞	15¾	+	3¾	+	31.3
Frisch s	.22	3292	15	16⅜	12	15⅝	+	⅛	+	.8
FrntHd	.15i	56981	......	15	8¼	13⅞	+	1¼	+	9.9
FrtA wt	.17t	3544	......	8⅞	4⅝	6¼	+	¾	+	13.6
FurVlt n		18294	12	16¾	10¾	14	....		....	

— G—G—G —

GNC En		12768	......	13⅛	3¼	4¾	—	6½	—	57.8
GlExpt		12931	6	11	3½	6½	+	2¼	+	52.9
GlEx rt		778	......	1¼	⅜	7-16	....		....	
GRI		12007	10	9⅞	4¼	4½	—	5	—	52.6
GTI		7705	20	6⅝	2½	3	—	2⅞	—	48.9
GalaxC		18704	6	21½	9⅝	12½	—	6¾	—	35.1

GalxyO		95135	......	3⅞	1½	2¼	+ ¾	+ 50
Garan	1.20	6496	7	33	24⅜	25¾	− 3½	− 12
GatLit	.05e	17626	16	18⅞	10	11⅞	− 3¼	− 21.5
Gaylrd		2959	14	10⅝	7	7⅞	− ½	− 6
GelmS		6261	16	16¼	9¾	10½	− 3¾	− 26.3
Gemco		8275	72	6¼	2⅝	2⅞	− 2⅞	− 50
GDefns	.88	35443	9	21⅜	12½	13⅞	− 7⅛	− 33.9
GnEmp	.20e	3796	8	5¼	2⅝	2¾	− 1⅜	− 33.3
GnMicr	.10	7209	12	17¾	11½	14	− 1½	− 9.7
Genisco		11235	......	10⅜	2⅞	3⅞	− 4⅜	− 53
GenvDr	.20	5610	12	17½	11⅛	12¾	− 4⅝	− 26.6
GeoRes		5508	4	12⅜	7¼	8⅜	− 2⅜	− 22.1
GeoR wt		450	......	2	1⅜	2	....	....
GeoRs pf	1	4526	......	11	8¼	8½	....	....
GiantFd	.80	23735	10	30	19¼	28½	+ 6	+ 26.7
GntYl g		11199	......	21¾	8⅝	10	− 8⅝	− 46.3
Glatfl s	.88	9796	5	24⅝	16½	22⅛	+ 5½	+ 33.1
Glnmr	1b	8357	9	31¾	22⅛	24⅞	+ 2⅝	+ 11.8
GlbNR n		23171	24	6½	2¾	4¼	....	....
Gloser	.44	5892	9	16½	10⅛	13½	− 2⅜	− 15
GoldW		12002	......	11¼	4¾	5	− 3⅞	− 43.7
GldFld		46167	......	1⅝	⅞	15-16	− 9-16	− 37.5
Goldm	pf2.50	5592	......	24⅞	18¼	24½	+ 4½	+ 22.5
GorRup	1.12	2717	10	27⅝	23	25¾	+ 1¼	+ 5.1
GouldT	1.40r	1699	8	25¾	19¾	23⅛	+ 1⅛	+ 5.1
GuldT	pf3.25	78	......	30¼	26½	30¼	....	....
GrahCp	.32	1116	......	13	8⅝	11⅝	+ ¼	+ 2.2
GrndAu	.40	4879	10	27⅜	15⅞	16⅞	− 5½	− 24.6
Grant	.62t	10425	8	12¼	8⅛	8⅞	− 3⅛	− 26
Grant wt		1610	......	3⅛	1	1⅛	− 2	− 64
GrTech		15219	15	18¾	9¾	13	− ½	− 3.7
GtAml	.60	4297	23	32	23⅜	31¼	+ 6⅛	+ 24.4
GrtLkC	.40	64303	14	38⅝	24	33¼	− ⅝	− 1.8
Grenm s		20929	7	17⅝	6 1-16	13⅛	+ 4¾	+ 56.7
Greiner		4300	233	8⅛	4⅜	7	+ ½	+ 7.7
Gross	50c	1977	......	77⅛	27⅛	29⅛	− 30⅞	− 51.5
GrdCh	.50b	7674	9	12¼	8⅛	11	− ⅛	− 1.1
GlfCd g	.52	303400	....	16	10⅞	11½	− 2⅜	− 17.1
Glfstr	.30	16969	12	28⅛	19½	24⅝	+ 1⅛	+ 4.8
— H—H—H —								
HMG	.60a	1166	......	17¼	12	12¼	− 4¾	− 27.9
HUBC n	.60a	1794	11	13¼	9¼	12½	....	....
Hamptl	.93t	2576	7	10¾	7½	10	+ 1⅝	+ 19.4
Hanfrd	.90	4127	11	32½	24¾	32⅜	+ 1⅝	+ 5.3
Harvey		8856	......	2⅞	1⅛	1⅜	− 1⅜	− 50
Hasbro	.30	52096	9	62¼	23	54¼	+ 27¼	+ 100.9
Hasbr pf		11857	......	30½	22½	26⅝	....	....
Hasting	.40a	1776	7	46⅝	25⅛	38⅜	+ 9¾	+ 34.1
HawaiA		9120	6	10⅜	4⅛	7½	+ 2⅞	+ 62.2
HlthCr	n1.96e	9242	7	19⅞	14½	19½	....	....
HlthCh		24867	8	9⅝	5½	6⅛	− 2⅛	− 25.8
HlthEx		25900	36	19⅞	11¾	14½	− ¼	− 1.7
HelthM	.56	3346	8	13⅞	10⅛	11⅝	+ ⅞	+ 8.1
HeinWr	.20e	2521	11	8⅜	6⅛	8	+ ⅝	+ 8.5
Heinick	.10	11968	10	13¼	7⅞	11⅛	+ 2⅜	+ 27.1
Heizer	13.75c	151279	....	18	2¼	2⅝	....	....
Heldor		6394	7	5½	2⅝	3⅛	− 1½	− 32.4
Heliont		51299	30	24¾	5¼	5¾	− 16½	− 74.2
HelmR		24158	......	2⅝	⅝	¾	− 1½	− 66.7
HershO		13734	19	8⅝	4¼	4⅜	− 2⅜	− 35.2
Hindrl		5320	40	5	2⅞	3⅝	+ ⅜	+ 11.5
Hiptron		5281	18	14	9¼	10¼	− 2⅝	− 20.4
Hofman		6553	8	8⅛	2¼	3¼	− 3⅜	− 50.9
HollyCp	.12e	18728	16	13⅜	6½	8	− 2⅞	− 26.4
Horml	1.08	7448	10	33½	25¼	30½	− ½	− 1.6
HrnHar	.71t	159723	13	22¼	8⅝	10½	− 9⅛	− 46.5
HrnH wt	.27t	22535	......	10½	2¼	2⅝	− 6¾	− 72
HouOT	1.43e	153804	.....	9⅞	4½	4¾	− 4⅝	− 49.3
HovnE		7261	9	14¼	8	13	+ 1¾	+ 15.6
Howlln	.20e	2053	7	11⅞	6½	10	+ 3⅛	+ 45.5
HubelA	1.36	2782	11	36⅞	28⅞	36¾	+ 4¼	+ 13.1
HubelB	1.36	14929	11	36½	28¾	36¼	+ 4⅝	+ 14.6
Hubbl	pf2.06	693	......	48	38	48	+ 6⅜	+ 15.3
HudGn	.40	2792	14	21⅝	16¾	20½	+ 1½	+ 7.9
Husky g	.15	38921	......	10	7¼	8½	....	....
— I—I—I —								
ICH	.25	39569	12	82⅜	24¾	74	+ 45¾	+ 162
ICO		13469	10	9	4¾	5⅜	− ¼	− 4.4
IPM	.05r	5093	8	5¼	2⅛	2⅝	− 1	− 27.6
IRT Cp n		3441	18	11¾	6⅝	7⅜	....	....
ISS	.12	1526	15	6½	4⅛	4⅜	− 1⅜	− 23.9
ImpGp	.12e	43965	......	2⅜	1 13-16	2 1-16	+ 1-16	+ 3.1
Implnd		25895	......	3½	1⅞	2⅜	....	....
ImpOil	g1.60	42354	......	34⅜	25⅜	32	+ 2¼	+ 7.6
InPL pf	4	z2490	......	34½	32	32½	− ⅞	− 2.6
Inflght		11320	9	10⅝	6½	6⅞	− ½	− 6.8
Instron	.28	4273	27	21⅜	16½	18½	− ⅛	− .7
InstSy		134361	10	3¾	1⅞	2	− 1	− 33.3
InsSy pf	.25t	3240	......	3⅞	2⅛	2¼	− ¾	− 25
IntCty g	.40	11065	......	9½	6⅞	7¼	− 2	− 21.6
Intrcle	.77t	3935	11	9⅜	5⅝	8⅜	+ ⅝	+ 8.1
Intmk	.12	8096	17	17¼	11	12	− 3⅛	− 20.7
IntBknt	.04i	96319	......	6	2⅞	3½	− 1¼	− 26.3
IntBk wt		29143	......	3	1	1⅛	− 1	− 47.1
IntCtrl	.30	16288	9	18¼	13½	16¾	− ¾	− 4.3
InHyd n		13088	26	17¼	8⅜	8¾	....	....
IIP	.87e	1656	20	11⅞	8¼	10½	+ 2¼	+ 27.3
IntPwr	.12i	1714	41	8⅜	3½	4⅛	− 2¾	− 40
IntProt		2923	......	4¾	1¾	2¼	− 1⅝	− 41.9
IntSeaw		1440	102	11	6⅝	7⅛	− 1⅝	− 18.6
IntDta		19026	......	8⅞	1⅛	1⅛	− 6¼	− 84.7
Ionics		7066	10	25	16¾	21½	+ 2⅜	+ 12.4
IroqBrd		8447	13	29½	17⅝	29⅜	+ 7¼	+ 32.8
Isaly n	.08	7292	23	5½	3	3¼	....	....
— J—J—J —								
Jaclyn	.50b	7475	8	17¾	10¾	13½	+ 2⅛	+ 18.7
Jacobs		6561	......	10¼	5⅜	5⅝	− 3¾	− 40
Jensen		4185	7	17⅛	10⅜	15	....	....
JetAm		18567	1	7¼	2⅞	2⅞	− 3½	− 54.9
JetA wt		4525	......	3⅜	⅝	⅞	− 1¾	− 66.7
Jetron	.49t	7169	15	7½	3⅞	7½	+ 3	+ 66.7
JohnPd		15895	......	10	2⅞	4	− 5⅛	− 56.2
JmpJk n		4173	5	7¼	5	5⅛	....	....
Jupiter		772	5	29¾	21⅝	28¼	+ 5⅜	+ 23.5
— K—K—K —								
KnGs	pf4.50	197	......	37½	28¼	34¾	+ 1¾	+ 5.3
KapokC		12234	......	5⅝	1⅛	2½	− 3	− 54.5
KayCp	.20	3515	17	14⅞	10	11	− 3	− 21.4
KearN n	.40	1688	7	16⅜	9¾	11⅝	....	....
Kentrn		13681	16	8¾	3	3½	− 4⅞	− 58.2
Kenwin	.80	537	7	18⅝	14¼	15⅞	+ ¼	+ 1.6
Ketchm	.58t	7249	28	21	10½	15¼	− ⅜	− 2.4
KeyCo	.20	3062	......	9½	5¾	6⅛	− 2½	− 29
KeyPh	.20	203712	15	20¼	8	9⅜	− 8⅛	− 46.4
Kidde wt		15267	......	6⅜	2¼	2⅝	− 2⅞	− 52.3
Kilern		1392	26	4½	3⅛	3⅞	− ⅛	− 3.1
Kinark		8127	8	5⅞	3⅜	3¾	− 2	− 34.8
KingR	.20	5192	23	39⅝	18¾	37¼	+ 13½	+ 56.8
Kirby		64469	......	7⅜	3	3¼	− 2¾	− 45.8
Kit Mfg		2683	15	5⅝	3½	4⅛	− ¼	− 5.7
KleerV	s.02r	8520	......	3⅞	2⅜	3¼	− ⅛	− 3.7
Knogo		18424	14	18⅛	8⅞	10⅞	− 5¾	− 34.6
Knoll		24095	12	16½	8⅞	11¼	− 4¾	− 29.7
KogerC	2.20	22812	143	26⅝	21	24¼	+ 1⅛	+ 4.9
— L—L—L —								
LSB		8573	......	3	1⅛	1¼	− ¼	− 16.7
LaBarg	.06	6529	......	4⅞	2½	2½	− 1½	− 37.5
LaPnt		3791	7	7⅜	2¾	5½	+ 1⅛	+ 25.7
LakeS	g.15e	7932	......	41⅝	23⅝	25⅜	− 11⅞	− 31.9
LndBn n	.54	898	10	14⅞	11⅞	14	....	....
Ldmk s	.16e	10339	......	15¾	11	15⅜	+ 2¾	+ 21.8
Laser		11281	36	17⅞	9½	10⅜	− 5½	− 34.6
Laurn n		538	......	10⅞	8¾	10½	....	....
LazKap		1242	......	6½	3¾	4¾	+ 1¼	+ 35.7
LeePh		7318	12	3¾	2⅛	2¾	+ ½	+ 22.2
Lehigh		2190	14	44½	25¼	43⅛	+ 10⅜	+ 31.7
LeisurT		16075	19	8⅛	3¾	4⅝	− 3⅜	− 42.2
Levitt n		2275	5	9⅜	5	5⅛	....	....
Litfld		3965	......	5	2½	2¾	− ⅞	− 24.1
Lodge		6907	......	4¼	1¾	1⅞	− 2	− 51.6
Logicon	.20	18711	17	31	18	25⅞	− 3⅞	− 13
Lorimr		75090	16	35	20	30¼	+ 8¼	+ 37.5
LouisCe	1	8215	20	70½	30¼	70⅜	+ 40⅛	+ 132.6
Lumex	.08	22813	17	21⅞	8⅝	13¼	− 5⅞	− 30.7
LundyE		10751	17	12¾	6½	10	− 1¼	− 11.1
Luria	.41t	16245	10	16¾	10⅝	13⅛	− 1⅞	− 12.5
Lydal s		6419	4	13¼	9⅞	12½	+ 2½	+ 25
LynCSy	.10	26776	18	26½	12⅝	25⅞	+ 12½	+ 93.5
LynchC	.20	3056	15	10⅝	8¾	9¾	+ ½	+ 5.4
— M—M—M —								
MCO Hd		21455	7	15¼	11⅝	13½	− ⅝	− 4.4
MCO Rs		27778	14	3⅝	1¾	1⅞	− 1¾	− 48.3

MSA n	.48e	1666	......	9⅛	7⅜	8⅜	....	....
MSA wt		1481	......	2⅛	1	1⅛	....	....
MSI Dt	.40	18069	5	21⅜	9⅛	9¾	— 9⅛	— 48.3
MSR		20357	......	5⅝	3	3	— 1	— 25
MacSc n	.14	18139	23	17⅜	8½	11	....	....
Macrod		18592	......	2⅞	¾	13-16	—1 15-16	— 70.5
MePS	1.40	4520	2	26	12¼	12¼	— 13⅝	— 52.7
Malart	g.70e	1623	......	15¾	10¼	10⅜	....	....
Mangd s		6473	62	35	13⅝	24¼	+ 10⅞	+ 81.3
MrthOf		10630	10	9¾	5¼	5⅜	— ⅝	— 10.4
Mardq v		26850	......	9-16	1-16	1-16	— 3-16	— 75
MarkPd		12751	47	5¼	3⅝	5⅛	+ ⅝	+ 13.9
Marm	pf2.35	6496	......	22½	21¼	21¾	....	....
Mrshln		26311	8	33¾	18¾	23⅛	— 8⅝	— 27.2
MartPr		5645	13	15⅜	6¾	14¾	+ 6	+ 68.6
Maslnd	.20a	4008	7	13⅜	8½	10⅞	— 1	— 8.4
Matec		5296	16	8⅞	5	6¼	+ 1	+ 19.1
MatRsh	.12	26825	16	26½	12⅜	15¼	— 10⅛	— 39.9
MatSc n		11683	......	12⅜	8¾	10⅝	....	....
Matrix s		44892	22	24¾	14⅛	21	— ⅛	— .6
MayEng	2	6113	13	18	12⅛	13⅜	— 4⅜	— 24.6
Mayflw	.80b	21207	9	25½	13⅛	25⅛	+ 10	+ 66.1
McCO n	2e	22616	......	11¾	8	8¾	....	....
McDow		4291	......	9⅛	4½	5¼	— 2½	— 32.3
McRae A		1231	......	4	2⅛	2⅜	— 1⅝	— 40.6
McRae B		957	......	5⅛	2⅜	2⅜	— 2	— 45.7
Medalst	.05e	12385	7	13½	7¾	8⅞	— 2⅛	— 19.3
Media	1.08	20803	12	65⅝	52	65	+ 8¼	+ 14.5
Mediq	.20	6741	16	17	12⅜	15½	— ⅛	— .8
MEMCo	1.16	1949	11	29⅜	20½	26⅞	+ 6⅜	+ 31.1
MercSL	.37t	9499	5	11⅞	5⅜	6⅛	— 3¾	— 38
MetPro	.15	3753	12	10¼	7⅞	9⅛	....	....
Metex		3324	11	15⅝	11¼	13⅛	— ⅜	— 2.8
MetroC		3928	34	23⅜	13⅞	21	+ 5½	+ 35.5
MchGn		89050	19	9⅝	4⅝	5¾	— 3⅜	— 37
MidAm	.44	2173	11	11	8⅛	9⅝	+ ⅛	+ 1.3
Midlnd	.40	2051	7	21½	13⅜	19⅝	+ 1⅝	+ 9
MinP pf	5	z7500	......	44¼	38½	42½	+ 1½	+ 3.7
MinP	pf 7.36	608	......	62¾	53⅝	58½	+ ½	+ .9
MinP	pf 8.90	439	......	74¾	65¼	72	+ 2	+ 2.9
MissnW	.23r	2064	13	9⅛	7⅛	8⅛	+ ⅝	+ 8.3
MtchlE	.24	103629	11	25½	14½	15⅝	— 7⅞	— 33.5
MiteCp	1	1127	10	41¾	33	41¾	+ 6⅜	+ 18
MonMg	.56	2150	8	10⅞	8⅞	9⅞	....	....
MonP	pf4.40	110	......	38¼	31¼	36½	+ 3¼	+ 9.8
MonP	pf4.50	174	......	41	33	36	— 1¼	— 3.4
MoogB	.20b	3386	13	17⅞	10½	11	— 6⅜	— 36.7
MoogA	.28b	24494	13	17⅝	10½	10⅞	— 6⅝	— 37.9
MtgGth	1.44e	14967	12	18⅛	12⅞	17¾	+ 2¾	+ 18.3
Mortrn		16418	......	4¼	11-16	1	— 2½	— 71.4
Motts	.20	1275	40	12¾	10⅝	12¼	+ 1¾	+ 16.7
MtMed		14527	11	14	2⅞	4	— 8⅝	— 68.3
MovStr	.60	1369	7	21	15	20⅜	+ 5⅜	+ 35.8
MovieL		2352	......	8⅝	4¼	5⅜	— 2	— 27.1
Murpln		5956	......	5¼	3	·4⅛	— ½	— 10.8
MuseAr		34754	......	16¼	3⅝	5⅛	— 11	— 68.2
Muse wt		5418	......	2¾	1-16	5-16	....	....
Myerln	.28	6055	9	10¼	7⅞	9⅝	+ ⅜	+ 4.1
— N—N—N —								
Nantck		10977	8	10¼	5½	6⅛	— 3⅞	— 38.8
NtGsO	.40b	1940	7	14	10⅞	13	+ 1¾	+ 15.6
NtPatnt	.10	154084	15	33⅝	12½	16⅜	— 12½	— 43.3
NelsLB		7226	......	3	1	1¼	— ¾	— 37.5
NHamp	.80	14548	36	58	25½	48¼	+ 3⅝	+ 8.1
NMxAr	.79t	4170	16	19⅝	11⅛	17½	+ 2¾	+ 18.6
NPlnRt	.96	9833	14	13¾	10⅞	13⅝	+ 1½	+ 12.4
NProc	1.21e	30732	8	21½	13	15⅜	— 4¾	— 23.6
NY Time	.52	135774	16	39	21⅞	38⅜	+ 10⅜	+ 37.1
NewbE	.25e	8339	4	9¾	4⅝	5	— 4	— 44.4
Newcor	.32	3122	13	16⅛	10¾	13	— 1⅞	— 12.6
NwpEl	1.50	1282	8	14⅞	11⅞	13⅜	— ½	— 3.6
Nexus		3514	......	3⅛	¾	1⅛	— 1½	— 57.1
Nichols		21306	5	10½	5⅛	7½	— 3	— 28.6
Noellnd		2535	......	5⅜	2¼	2½	— 2¾	— 52.4
Nolex		8203	12	3½	2¼	2¾	— ⅜	— 12
NordR n		12357	8	13⅞	10	13¼	....	....
NoCdO g		8401	......	18	13⅝	14¾	+ ⅜	+ 2.6
NIPS	pf 4.25	1121	......	35	29¾	31⅝	— ¼	— .8
NuHrz n		2310	5	5¾	3⅛	3¾	....	....
NuHr wt		446	......	1⅝	¾	⅞	....	....
NuclDt		8294	15	10⅜	5⅞	8⅝	+ ⅞	+ 11.3
Numac		16948	......	14⅛	9½	10¾	+ ¼	+ 2.4
— O—O—O —								
OEA		7695	11	27¼	16¼	17¼	— 7	— 28.9
Oakwd	.08b	14634	13	22½	14⅛	19⅞	+ 2½	+ 14.4
OdetA n		723	34	5¼	4	4⅜	....	....
OdetB s		3306	41	6⅞	4¼	5⅜	— ⅜	— 6.5
OhArt	.24	1110	17	18⅞	9	16⅝	+ 5⅜	+ 47.8
Ollalnd	.40	2470	15	22	16⅞	20¼	— 1⅝	— 7.4
Olsten	.30	13296	12	20⅝	13¾	18⅜	+ 2½	+ 15.8
OOkiep		3831	......	15⅞	3⅛	3½	— 9⅞	— 73.8
Openh n		1728	25	6¼	3¾	5¾	....	....
OriolH A	.50	3223	9	10⅛	5¼	5¾	— 1	— 14.8
OriolH B	.60	2839	9	9¼	5⅜	5⅝	— 1	— 15.1
Ormand		4280	9	4	1	1⅛	— 1½	— 57.1
Orrox		9369	......	5⅜	2¼	2¾	— 1½	— 35.3
OSullvn	.60b	1911	12	35	21⅝	29⅞	+ 3⅜	+ 12.7
OverSc		173	......	7⅞	6¼	6¼	— ¾	— 10.7
OxfrdF	.42t	5875	10	10¾	6⅛	7⅛	— 3	— 29.6
OzarkH	.20	73773	7	12	7⅝	9⅝	— ⅝	— 6.1
— P—Q —								
PGEpfA	1.50	4195	......	12⅝	10⅛	12⅛	+ ⅜	+ 3.2
PGEpfB	1.37	1247	......	11⅝	8⅞	10⅝	— ⅛	— 1.2
PGEpfC	1.25	887	......	10⅝	8½	10¼	+ ½	+ 5.1
PGEpfD	1.25	5369	......	10⅜	8⅝	10¼	+ ⅞	+ 9.3
PGEpfE	1.25	10264	......	10⅜	8¼	10¼	+ ⅝	+ 6.5
PGEpfG	1.20	5540	......	10⅛	8	9⅝	+ ¼	+ 2.7
PGEpfF	4.34	7566	......	33½	28⅛	33	+ ⅝	+ 1.9
PGEpfZ	4.06	20593	......	31⅝	26¾	31	+ ⅞	+ 2.9
PGEpfY	3.20	22948	......	26¼	21⅛	24⅞	+ ⅜	+ 1.5
PGEpfW	2.57	15604	......	21¼	17⅛	20⅛	+ ¼	+ 1.3
PGEpfV	2.32	12968	......	19¼	15⅝	18¼	+ ½	+ 2.8
PGEpfT	2.54	12430	......	20¾	17	19½	— ⅛	— .6
PGEpfS	2.62	8585	......	21⅛	17⅜	20¼	+ ⅛	+ .6
PGEpfH	1.12	2991	......	9½	7⅜	9	+ ½	+ 5.9
PGEpfR	2.37	11902	......	20⅜	15¼	18⅝	+ ¼	+ 1.4
PGEpfP	2.05	10590	......	18¼	13⅝	16¾	+ ⅞	+ 5.5
PGEpfO	2	8977	......	16½	13¼	15⅞	+ ½	+ 3.3
PGEpfM	1.96	6509	......	16	13¼	15½	+ ⅜	+ 2.5
PGEpfL	2.25	1293	......	17⅞	14⅞	17⅛	+ ⅜	+ 2.2
PGEpfK	2.04	8750	......	16¾	13⅝	16	+ ⅛	+ .8
PGEpfJ	2.32	872	......	18½	15	18⅜	+ 1¼	+ 7.3
PGEpfI	1.09	2667	......	9	7⅜	8⅝	+ ¼	+ 3
PGTrn	1.12	15548	6	20	14½	20	+ 3⅜	+ 20.3
PacLt	pf4.36	502	......	37¾	31	34⅛	— ⅝	— 1.8
PacLt	pf4.40	283	......	36¾	30	35⅞	+ 1¾	+ 5.1
PacLt	pf4.50	779	......	37⅝	31½	34¾	— 1	— 2.8
PacLt	pf 4.75	404	......	41	34	39¾	....	....
PacLt	pf7.64	1409	......	63¼	54¼	59½	+ 1¼	+ 2.2
Pacif pf	5	144	......	42	35½	40¾	+ 2¾	+ 7.2
Page g		20804	......	2¾	⅜	11-16	— 1½	— 68.6
PallCp	.40	50705	19	38¼	27¼	33	— 4	— 10.8
Pantast		9825	12	11¼	5⅛	6½	— 2⅞	— 30.7
ParaPk		1471	15	7½	3½	7	+ 3	+ 75
ParkC	s.60a	1806	8	23⅜	15⅜	18¾	+ ¼	+ 1.4
PatTch		33605	20	17¾	10¼	11	— 1¾	— 13.7
PayFon		4262	20	5⅜	2¼	2¾	— 2⅜	— 46.3
PUMG	.12e	1300	11	7½	5⅞	7⅜	+ ¾	+ 11.3
PEC Isr	.82t	180	23	15¼	7¼	11¼	....	....
PeerTu	.40b	1947	14	11¾	8½	8¾	— 1⅞	— 17.6
PenEM	1.20a	1949	9	42¼	32¼	38⅜	+ 4⅜	+ 12.9
PenTr	1.20	3885	9	25	15½	18	— 6¾	— 27.3
PE Cp	.25r	20089	7	2⅝	1⅛	1⅛	— 1⅜	— 55
PenRE	2.40	6139	9	31½	26	31	+ 4¾	+ 18.1
PenobS	.40	731	......	11⅜	8¾	9¾	— 1	— 9.3
Penril	.20	10178	9	14⅝	10¼	12	— ⅝	— 5
Pentrn v		10110	......	1 13-16	13-16	⅞	— ¼	— 22.2
PeriniC	.80	10961	12	33¾	23	27¾	— 5¼	— 15.9
Perinl n		7787	31	14⅜	10⅜	11⅝	....	....
PetLw		159547	....	12¼	3	4½	— 6⅝	— 59.6
PetL wt		45864	......	3⅜	5-16	5-16	—2 5-16	— 88.1
PetLe	pf1.65	9317	......	11½	6⅜	7⅛	— 3¼	— 31.3
PetLe	pf2.28	11354	......	15	7¾	9¼	— 5	— 35.1
PetLe	pf3.33	13763	......	23⅞	12¾	14	— 10	— 41.7
PhilLD	.22e	23039	2	2⅝	1¾	1⅞	— ⅝	— 25
PicoPd		19522	......	12⅜	3½	4	— 7	— 63.6
Pier 1 wt		5269	2	6	2½	2⅝	— 2	— 43.2
PionrSy		16463	42	12⅜	5	5⅞	— 5¾	— 49.5
PitWVa	.56	4151	10	7¼	4⅞	5⅜	— 1⅜	— 20.4
PitDM	.40	3176	......	17⅝	11	12⅝	— 3	— 19.2
Pittway	1.80	1644	11	70¼	57	70	+ 9⅞	+ 16.4
Pizzaln	.08e	18838	7	14½	6⅞	7¾	— 6⅜	— 45.1

PlcrD g	.30	8791	......	20¼	13⅛	17⅛	— 2⅛	— 11
PlantIn		9057	......	2½	¼	⅜	— 1⅝	— 81.3
PlyGm s		8141	12	14⅛	7½	13⅜	+ 5⅜	+ 67.2
PlyR A		699	......	3½	2¼	2⅜	— ⅜	— 13.6
PlyR B		664	......	3½	2¼	2½	....	....
PneuSc	1a	1296	11	32	21½	21¾	— ½	— 2.2
PopeEv		40109	19	9⅛	4⅜	4⅞	— 3	— 38.1
PortSys		17755	63	14⅛	7⅜	8¾	— 3¾	— 30
PostlPr		3919	16	16⅜	12	16	+ 2⅜	+ 17.4
PowerT	.16b	6890	39	23⅛	11⅞	20¾	+ 8¾	+ 72.9
PrairO g		2504	......	30¾	18⅝	27¾	+ 7¼	+ 35.4
PrattL	.92	3177	7	24¾	18⅛	19¾	— 1⅛	— 5.4
PrattRd	.20	2359	115	9¼	6⅛	6⅞	— 1⅞	— 21.4
PratR pf	.66	327	......	7⅞	6⅝	6⅞	— ⅝	— 8.3
PremRs		6706	......	1⅜	½	¾	— 3-16	— 20
PresR A	.80	102	7	11⅜	9	11¼	+ 2⅛	+ 23.3
PresR B	.80	3276	6	8⅞	6½	8⅞	+ 1⅜	+ 18.3
Presid		9367	18	6	3⅜	3⅞	— ⅝	— 13.9
PrpCT s		5951	11	20½	15⅝	19¼	+ 1⅞	+ 10.8
ProvEn	2.04	1449	7	25¾	18½	25⅜	+ 6⅜	+ 33.6
PSCol pf	4.25	130	......	35½	30½	33¼	— 1¼	— 3.6
Pgt pfC	2.34	2210	......	18⅜	14¾	18¼	+ ⅝	+ 3.6
Pgt pfE	4.38	6055	......	33	25⅞	31¼	....	....
Pgt pfD	2.34	1176	......	18⅞	15⅜	18½	+ ⅜	+ 2.1
PuntaG		6651	......	10⅛	4⅞	5¼	— 2⅞	— 35.4
Queb g s	.28	1340	......	19½	10	18½	+ 6½	+ 54.2
— R—R—R —								
RAI	.35t	8357	13	11	5	6¾	— 2⅝	— 28
RMS El		2418	......	6¼	3⅞	4	— 2¼	— 36
RTC	.12j	5166	......	10⅞	3¼	3⅝	— 4⅞	— 57.4
Ragan	.12	4615	23	16¾	13⅞	16	— ½	— 3
Ransbg	.72	39693	......	20	12½	16⅝	— 2	— 10.7
Ratliff		3071	......	4⅜	¾	1¼	— 2⅛	— 63
Raven	.42	4630	8	15¼	10½	12⅞	— 1¼	— 8.8
Raymln	19c	5131	......	29¾	10⅝	11¼	— 17⅝	— 61
RlEst n	1.72	6063	9	16⅝	11⅝	14⅛	....	....
REst wt		5168	......	3	1⅜	2¾	....	....
RtlncT		1329	11	7¼	6	7	....	....
Redlaw		6485	......	2⅞	1⅜	2⅛	+ ⅛	+ 6.3
RegalB	.56	7077	9	17⅜	10½	11¾	— ¾	— 6
Resrt A		96805	17	47⅛	27⅝	36½	— 1¾	— 4.6
Resrt B		681	19	47½	30½	41¼	+ 1½	+ 3.8
RestAsc		12397	8	9½	5⅝	5⅝	— 2⅛	— 27.4
RexNor		4221	8	4⅞	3¼	3¼	— ½	— 13.3
RibletP	.20	25209	13	18	9⅝	10¼	— 3½	— 25.5
RchTC v		4894	......	6	2⅛	2⅛	— ⅜	— 15
RchT pfv		1848	......	9½	5	7¼	+ 2¼	+ 45
RioAl g	.55	2677	......	17	10¼	15	+ ¼	+ 1.7
RioGDr		8599	......	4⅜	⅞	1¼	— 1⅜	— 52.4
Rckwy s	.52	12185	16	20½	11⅞	19¼	+ 2⅜	+ 14.1
Rogers	.12	9152	12	35¾	20½	23¾	— 11⅞	— 33.3
RoonP n		11277	......	7	2	2⅞	....	....
RoyPlm		8070	......	5⅜	3⅜	3⅞	+ ⅝	+ 19.2
Rudick	.56a	938	13	29⅞	20	25⅝	+ ⅜	+ 1.5
Rudck pf	.56	188	......	29⅝	22¼	26	+ ½	+ 2
RBW		6000	6	5⅜	3⅞	5¼	+ ⅝	+ 13.5
Russell	.30	31134	11	18	11¼	14⅜	— 2¾	— 16.1
Rykoff	.50	31666	11	18⅞	10⅛	18⅜	+ 2⅛	+ 13.1
— S—S—S —								
SFM		1416	......	6⅜	4⅜	4⅝	— ½	— 9.8
SMD		8657	......	6¼	3½	4¼	+ ⅛	+ 3
SPW Cp		3053	......	6⅞	3½	3¾	— 2⅜	— 38.8
Sage		14446	10	15	7	7⅛	— 7⅞	— 52.5
Salem	.37t	1469	......	11¾	7½	7¾	— 2⅛	— 21.5
SCarlo		2365	......	4⅛	⅝	1⅜	— 1½	— 52.2
SDgo pf	.88	658	......	7⅜	6¼	7¼	+ ⅜	+ 5.5
SDgo pf	.90	428	......	7¾	6½	7⅜	+ ½	+ 7.3
SDgo pf	1	344	......	8½	7¼	7¾	— ¼	— 3.1
SDgo pf	9.84	241	......	76½	67¼	75¼	+ 1¾	+ 2.4
SDgo pf	7.80	840	......	62½	52¾	60	+ 1¾	+ 3
SDgo pf	7.20	670	......	57¼	49	55½	+ 2½	+ 4.7
SDgo pf	2.47	1452	......	21¼	17¼	20½	+ 1¼	+ 6.5
SDgo pf	4.65	3501	......	36¾	31½	36	+ ¾	+ 2.1
SDgo pf	2.68	1401	......	22½	18⅛	22	+ 1⅝	+ 8
SanJW	2.65	838	7	44½	31⅛	44¼	+ 13⅛	+ 42.2
Sandgte	.80	6022	10	36	20⅜	26	+ 5⅝	+ 27.6
Sanmrk	.43t	7986	12	6¾	3½	4½	— 1⅜	— 23.4
Saund B	.15	833	5	5⅝	4⅛	4⅞	— ⅜	— 7.1
Saund A	.20	3001	5	5⅝	4⅜	5	....	....
Sceptr n		1601	......	5¼	3⅞	4	....	....
Scheib	.56	7523	10	21⅞	14	18⅜	— ⅛	— .7
SchoolP		826	4	3½	1¾	2	— ⅞	— 30.4
Schwab	.48	1703	8	13½	10¼	11½	+ 1⅛	+ 10.8
SciMgt	.10	23821	......	16¼	3⅝	4⅞	— 10⅛	— 67.5
SciLsg		16051	14	35	22¼	27	+ ¾	+ 2.9
Scope	.36	1732	10	39	30	35⅜	— 1½	— 4.1
ScurRn		2190	......	16⅞	11	13⅜	— 1¼	— 8.5
SbdCp	.50	1055	7	46½	34	46⅛	+ 8⅞	+ 23.8
Seaport		3556	10	3⅛	1⅛	1¼	— 1½	— 54.5
Seapt pf		221	......	7½	5	5	— 2¾	— 35.5
SecCap	.16e	21130	8	13⅝	10	13	+ 2⅞	+ 28.4
SeisPro		3457	......	6½	2½	2¾	— 2¼	— 45
SeisDlt		33662	......	9⅝	11-16	13-16	— 6 7-16	— 88.8
Selas		3648	......	6½	3⅛	5⅝	+ 1¾	+ 45.2
SeligAs		1919	11	4⅞	3⅜	4⅛	+ ⅝	+ 17.9
Semtch		3850	......	7⅛	2¼	2⅜	— 3½	— 59.6
Srvisco	.44	1539	9	16¼	11⅞	13	— 3⅛	— 19.4
Servo		3627	......	14¾	7⅜	8⅞	— 3⅛	— 26
Servotr	.62t	3891	7	10	5¼	8⅞	— ½	— 5.3
Seton s	.12	5401	11	18¾	14¾	15⅞	+ 7¾	+ 95.4
ShaerS	.60e	5206	4	14⅛	8⅛	10⅜	— 1⅜	— 11.7
Sharon		9055	......	3½	1¼	1¼	— 1½	— 54.5
Shopwl	.16b	8093	56	15	9½	11¾	— 2⅛	— 15.3
Siercn	.40	5862	10	15⅞	10⅛	12⅛	— 2⅛	— 14.9
Sifco	.20	2815	24	8⅞	5⅜	6⅝	— ¾	— 10.2
SikesA s	.20	9887	9	13½	8	9⅞	— 2⅜	— 19.4
Silvrcst		8240	......	9¼	4⅛	4¾	— 3	— 38.7
SimcoS	.12j	1272	......	5¾	2½	2⅞	— 1¾	— 37.8
SmthA	.48	12344	6	20¾	10⅜	13⅞	— 5⅝	— 28.8
SmthB	.48	5831	5	18½	9¾	11⅜	— 6⅛	— 35
Snyder	2	9533	11	16¼	12⅞	13¼	— 2¾	— 17.2
Solitron		20485	16	9¼	5⅛	6⅜	— ⅞	— 12.1
SoTex		3818	......	2⅛	11-16	13-16	— 7-16	— 35
SoetCap	.35e	504	......	11⅝	8⅛	8¾	— 2¾	— 23.9
SCEd pf	1.02	6608	......	9¼	7⅝	8¾	+ ½	+ 6.1
SCEd pf	1.06	5448	......	9½	7¾	9⅛	+ ⅝	+ 7.4
SCEd pf	1.08	2056	......	9⅝	7¾	9⅛	+ ½	+ 5.8
SCEd pf	1.19	2352	......	10⅜	8½	10¼	+ ¼	+ 2.5
SCEd pf	4.08	1528	......	42	33	41⅝	+ 4⅛	+ 11
SCEd pf	1.45	10576	......	12¾	10½	12⅛	+ ⅛	+ 1
SCEd pf	1.30	402	......	37⅛	27¾	37	+ 5¾	+ 18.4
SCEd pf	12	5331	......	105⅜	94½	102	....	....
SCEd pf	8.54	1257	......	77¾	69	69¼	— 5½	— 7.4
SCEd pf	2.30	5514	......	20	16¾	18¾	....	....
SCEd pf	2.21	6781	......	19⅛	16	18⅛	+ ⅝	+ 3.6
SCEd pf	7.58	3237	......	64	53½	62	+ 2	+ 3.3
SCEd pf	8.70	2081	......	72½	61	68⅝	+ ⅝	+ .9
SCEd pf	8.96	2374	......	77	64½	72	+ 2	+ 2.9
Sprkmn		30944	9	16½	6½	7½	— 5¾	— 43.4
Sprk pf	1	2518	......	10¾	6⅞	7½	— 2½	— 25
Spectro	.14	13251	12	27⅞	15½	26⅝	+ 6⅝	+ 33.1
SpedOP		3605	83	6⅛	3½	5	— ⅛	— 2.4
Spencer	.24	13972	20	15	10¼	12¼	— ⅛	— 1
SqrD wt		4421	......	4	2⅝	3⅝	....	....
StHavn	.08	5084	40	10⅛	4⅜	5¼	— 3⅜	— 39.1
StHav wt		1449	......	3⅞	1⅛	1½	— 1⅞	— 55.6
StdMet v		2687	......	10⅞	3¾	4¼	— 5	— 54.1
StdPrd	.80	28760	5	26⅜	13½	19⅞	— 4⅞	— 19.7
StdShr	2.79t	1798	9	68	53	68	+ 14⅛	+ 26.2
Stanwd		2928	14	11⅞	8¼	8⅞	— 1⅛	— 11.3
StarrtH		8162	19	17⅞	11⅝	15⅛	+ ¾	+ 5.2
Statex		4517	......	12¼	6¾	9	— ⅝	— 6.5
Statx pf	2.55	106	......	25	20¼	22	....	....
Stepan	.68	6808	11	18⅝	14½	16½	+ ½	+ 3.1
StrlCap		972	......	6¼	4¼	4¼	— ¾	— 15
SterlEl		8939	10	4	1⅝	1¾	— 1½	— 46.2
StrlExt		7090	11	16⅞	4⅝	16⅛	+ 11⅝	+ 258.3
SterlSft	.08e	18624	25	13⅞	5⅝	6¼	— 6½	— 51
StrutW		7176	......	4⅜	1¾	2⅛	— 1¼	— 37
SumitE		8608	......	9	5¼	6⅜	— 1⅜	— 17.7
SumtE pf	1.80	1861	......	15¾	11½	12¼	— 2⅝	— 17.6
SunCty		3306	8	10¾	6⅜	10¼	+ 1⅞	+ 22.4
SunSL n		2462	10	11½	5	7⅝	....	....
Sunair	.24	12145	11	14⅞	5¾	6	— 6⅛	— 50.5
SunJr	.48	2080	13	17⅝	11⅛	13¼	— 1¼	— 8.6
SuprFd	.44b	21101	10	27⅝	16¼	23¾	— 3	— 11.2
SupCre		37097	......	4⅝	½	11-16	— 2 15-16	— 81
SupInd	.05e	15988	9	14⅞	6½	8⅞	— 4¼	— 32.4
SuprSr	.32	10951	9	13⅞	10⅝	12¾	+ 1½	+ 13.3
Susqueh		19503	11	6⅝	3¾	4⅞	+ ⅛	+ 2.6
Swantn		24178	......	10¼	4	4¾	— 5¼	— 52.5
SwftE n		1179	......	2½	1½	1⅞	....	....

Swiftln	1.20	17977	11	32¾	19½	25	— 5¼	— 17.4
Synaloy	.38t	6679	......	9⅝	5	5⅞	— 2¼	— 27.7
SystEn	.16	2638	15	14	9⅞	13⅛	+ 2⅞	+ 28.1
— T—T—T —								
T Bar	.51t	12125	21	11⅛	6½	6¾	— 1⅝	— 19.4
TEC	.06e	2454	17	12	7½	8¼	— 2⅛	— 20.5
TIE		572948	11	28⅜	5½	7⅜	— 19⅝	— 72.7
TII		12131	41	17¼	6⅞	9	— 6¼	— 41
TabPd s	.20	9288	10	18⅝	13	15	— 1	— 6.3
TandBr		7324	......	17	6⅝	7⅝	— 9⅝	— 55.8
Tasty	.40	2870	12	13	9⅞	11⅝	+ 1⅛	+ 10.7
Team		4550	......	8	2¾	3½	— 2	— 36.4
TchAm		20129	......	5⅞	1⅞	1⅞	— 3⅝	— 65.9
TchSym		25165	14	20¼	13⅛	16½	— 3⅛	— 15.9
TechOp		4385	15	53¾	33⅛	52¼	+ 14¼	+ 37.5
TechTp		22543	7	9⅜	3¾	4⅝	— 3⅜	— 42.2
Techtrl	.30	13286	8	18⅜	7½	14⅞	+ 1⅜	+ 10.2
Tchnd n		1920	......	4½	1⅝	2	....	....
TejonR	.30e	2048	74	108⅜	76	101⅞	+ 5⅞	+ 6.1
Telecon		24254	......	9⅛	2	2⅜	— 6¼	— 72.5
Telflex	.44	11349	14	32	21¼	27¾	— 3	— 9.8
TelDta	.36a	18205	9	13⅞	8¼	9⅛	— 2¼	— 19.8
Telsci		17604	55	18⅝	7⅝	8⅞	— 3⅝	— 29
Telesph		72637	......	5⅞	2¼	3⅛	— 2⅛	— 40.5
Tenney s		4902	12	4⅞	3½	4⅜	....	....
Tensor		1586	......	10¾	5⅛	5⅛	— 4⅛	— 44.6
TexCd	g1.20	3002	......	33	25½	27	— 6⅛	— 18.5
TexAir		89432	4	9⅞	5⅝	9⅛	+ 2½	+ 37.7
TexAE	.39t	48204	5	10⅛	5⅛	6⅜	+ ⅝	+ 10.9
TexAE pf		5254	......	22¼	16½	18⅜	....	....
Txscan		48543	8	20	3¼	5	— 13¾	— 73.3
ThorEn		4377	13	3½	2	2⅛	— ⅛	— 5.6
ThrD B	.06	2973	13	9¼	4½	4¾	— 4⅝	— 49.3
ThrD A	.10	2878	13	9	3¾	4¾	— 4⅜	— 47.9
Tidwell		12402	......	11¾	2½	3½	— 7¾	— 68.9
TolEd	pf4.25	307	......	33	23	28⅝	+ ⅛	+ .4
TolEd	pf8.32	z5660	......	60½	47	55½	— 2½	— 4.3
TolEd	pf7.76	367	......	56	42	52	— 2	— 3.7
TolEd	pf 10	202	......	72½	56	65½	— ¾	— 1.1
Tortel		7866	10	9	4⅞	7⅜	+ ⅝	+ 9.3
TotlPt g	.24	18939	......	13¼	7⅞	9	— 1⅜	— 13.3
TotPt wt		3223	......	2⅞	⅝	11-16	—1 13-16	— 72.5
TotPt	pf2.88	239	......	27	22	24⅝	— ⅞	— 3.4
TrnsLx	.10	5249	9	13⅛	8⅜	9⅛	— 2½	— 21.5
TrnsTec	.56	12823	8	19¼	11¼	13⅝	— 3	— 18
Tranzon	.40	2981	7	19	13⅜	13¾	— 1⅛	— 7.6
TriSM	.40e	2709	6	15⅝	7⅞	8⅜	— 5⅛	— 38
TriaCp	.69t	1016	148	9⅝	6⅞	7⅜	....	....
TriHme		2781	8	7¼	3¾	4½	— 2½	— 35.7
Tridex		14611	......	14¼	3¾	4⅓	— 4⅝	— 52.9
TubMex		19772	5	4⅜	2½	2½	— 1⅛	— 31
Tultex	.44	17698	10	14⅞	10⅜	10⅝	— 3½	— 24.8
TurnC s	1.10	5204	8	24⅜	19½	22¾	+ 3¼	+ 16.7
Tyler wt		14922	......	7	3½	4⅛	— 1¾	— 29.8
— U—U—U —								
UNA		1461	7	4½	2½	2¾	— 1⅜	— 33.3
USR Ind		7092	......	7	2	2¼	— 2½	— 52.6
Ultmte		95588	12	24⅜	12⅝	16⅜	+ ⅛	+ .8
Unicorp		246869	....	15-16	½	11-16	— 1-16	— 8.3
Unicp pf	.75	2044	......	12¾	11½	12¼	....	....
Unimr n		32096	......	11⅛	9¼	9⅜	....	....
UAirPd	.54b	2216	9	19⅜	14⅛	16¼	— ¾	— 4.4
UnCosF	1b	673	7	36¼	33¼	34⅝	— 1¼	— 3.5
UFoodA	.10	14414	15	3½	1⅝	1¾	— 1⅜	— 44
UFoodB		12991	14	3⅜	1¼	1⅝	— 1½	— 48
UtMed	.65t	3994	16	16⅞	10½	12¾	— 2⅞	— 18.4
USAG wt		4751	......	21	10½	19½	+ 1⅛	+ 6.1
USAG pf	3	130	......	100	78½	82	— 12½	— 13.2
UStck n		9899	28	11⅛	5¼	10¾	....	....
UnitelV	.94t	8389	12	10	6⅛	6⅞	— 1⅜	— 16.7
UnityB		2692	14	19⅜	16⅞	19¼	+ 2⅜	+ 14.1
UnvCm		7110	15	13⅜	7⅞	11⅞	+ 1⅜	+ 13.1
UnivRs		65239	......	10⅝	5⅞	7⅛	+ ¼	+ 3.6
UnivRu	.80e	2665	6	23⅜	15	16	— 5	— 23.8
UnvPat		16410	......	18¾	9½	11⅜	— 5⅜	— 32.1
— V—V—V —								
VST n		159	......	10	9½	9½	....	....
VallyR	1.92	1351	10	20½	14¾	20¼	+ 5¼	+ 35
Valmac		1342	16	29⅝	18⅝	29⅝	+ 9⅜	+ 46.3
Valspr s	.44	9552	10	20⅜	15¼	19¾	+ 2	+ 11.3
Verbtm		237821	....	16⅞	4¾	6¼	— 10¾	— 63.2
Verit		1565	11	5½	2⅝	2¾	— 1⅛	— 29
VtAmC	.40b	9154	9	19½	14¾	18¼	+ ¼	+ 1.4
VtRsh		9302	......	10⅝	3⅜	3½	— 5¼	— 60
Verna		2732	......	1½	⅜	7-16	— 9-16	— 56.3
Vernit	.20	27389	9	17¼	11⅛	12⅛	— 4⅞	— 28.7
Vertple	.10	4077	......	8⅛	3⅞	4	— 1⅜	— 25.6
Viatech		1893	......	8⅛	4⅝	8	+ 2⅞	+ 56.1
Vicon		6839	10	10½	5⅝	5⅞	— 3⅞	— 39.7
Vintge		5485	35	8⅞	2¾	3⅛	— 4	— 56.1
Virco	.04r	2424	8	16¼	10⅞	16¼	+ 5⅛	+ 46.1
Valntl n		1553	......	59	42	56½	+ 14¾	+ 35.3
VisualG	.28	1952	10	7⅞	6⅛	6⅜	— ½	— 7.3
Voplex	.36	9086	11	13⅞	8	8⅞	— 4¼	— 32.4
VulcCp	.40a	1987	8	16¼	12⅜	15	+ ¼	+ 1.7
— W—W—W —								
WTC		7812	18	9⅝	6¼	7	— 1	— 12.5
Walbar	.40	10888	10	22¾	17⅜	18⅜	— 1⅛	— 5.8
Walco	.40	5048	7	15	10½	11	— ¼	— 2.2
WangB	.16	854392	16	37⅝	23	25⅞	— 9¾	— 27.4
WangC	.11	1898	16	37⅜	23	25⅝	— 10	— 28.1
WrnC wt		27568	......	6⅛	¾	¾	— 4⅞	— 86.7
WshHm		5578	5	12½	5⅛	10½	— ¼	— 2.3
WshPst	.80	23945	14	85	60¾	80¼	+ 7	+ 9.6
WRIT	1.60	9084	16	24	17	23⅝	+ 6	+ 34
Watsc A	.20	860	4	8¾	6¾	8	....	....
Watsc B	.16	2017	5	9¼	6⅞	8½	+ 1⅝	+ 23.6
Wthfrd		36238	......	8⅜	2⅝	3⅝	— 4⅛	— 53.2
Wthfd	pf2.63	2575	......	27	13¾	13⅞	— 12¾	— 47.9
Webcor		25957	......	9⅞	1¾	2¼	— 6¾	— 75
Wedco		1114	7	5¾	3⅝	3¾	— 1⅝	— 30.2
Wedtc n		4286	11	14½	11⅝	12¾	....	....
Weiman	.12	1369	37	5⅛	3⅛	4¾	+ ⅛	+ 2.7
WeldTb	.10	1903	......	14	7	7⅝	— 6⅛	— 44.5
Weldtrn		9509	13	11⅝	6¾	11⅝	+ 3¼	+ 38.8
Wellco		518	......	7	4⅜	5⅛	— 1⅛	— 18
WelGrd		7502	......	5⅞	2¼	2¼	— 2⅜	— 51.4
Wesco	.58	2914	6	22⅝	15¾	21¾	+ 4⅜	+ 25.2
Wespc v		9568	......	10⅛	¾	⅞	— 7⅝	— 89.7
WTex	pf4.40	127	......	38½	31⅝	36	— 1½	— 4
WstBrC		17444	13	13⅞	7¾	13⅞	+ 3⅝	+ 35.4
Wstbr g	.20	8857	10	13½	8¼	8⅞	— 3⅛	— 26
WDigitl		193221	17	11⅞	5⅞	8⅝	— ⅜	— 4.2
WtHlth n		3193	......	8½	7⅞	8⅛	....	....
WIRET	1.50e	2912	14	17⅞	14⅞	17⅜	....	....
WstnSL	1.23e	24370	6	29	16	24¼	+ 5½	+ 29.3
WhEnt s		32376	16	18⅜	9½	15¾	+ 2¾	+ 21.2
Wichita		9629	......	6½	3⅜	3½	— 1	— 22.2
WillcxG		15558	6	10½	7⅛	8⅜	....	....
WilsnB		3080	......	4¼	1	1⅝	— 2⅛	— 56.7
Winklm	.50	2767	11	15½	12⅛	14	+ 1	+ 7.7
Wintln	2.16	3788	......	23¾	19⅝	21⅞	— 1	— 4.4
WisP	pf 4.50	z9420	......	40	35¼	38	+ 2	+ 5.6
WolfHB	.10e	781	14	5⅝	2¾	3	— 2	— 40
Wdstrm	.40	1875	8	10¼	8	8¼	— ½	— 5.7
WkWear	.52	6622	6	16½	11	12⅞	— 2⅛	— 14.2
WwdeE	.44t	40894	15	6⅞	2¾	3	— 2⅝	— 46.7
WWde	pf1.80	8067	......	17¼	12⅝	12¾	— 2½	— 16.4
Worthn	.50	3146	12	36⅝	27¾	31⅞	+ ⅞	+ 2.8
Wrath s	.02	22882	......	19	12	18	+ 5	+ 38.5
WrgtH	g.05e	18648	13	7⅝	3½	4	— 2¼	— 36
— X—Y—Z —								
YankCo		26662	5	17¼	5⅜	5½	— 11¼	— 67.2
Yardny	.08	4230	10	5⅞	4⅛	4⅛	— 1¼	— 23.3
Zimer	.10	24908	21	14⅛	5⅝	7½	— 5½	— 42.3

Copyright by The Associated Press 1984.

OVER-THE-COUNTER QUOTATIONS NASDAQ

NATIONAL MARKET DECEMBER 31, 1984

NEW YORK (AP)—Over the Counter NMS trading for 1984. The net change and percentage change is from the previous year on issues listed prior to Jan. 1, 1984.

		Sales (hds)	PE	High	Low	Last	Net Chg.	Pct. Chg.
				— A—A—A —				
AEL s		9343	2	24	15¼	22¼	+ 1⅝	+ 7.9
AFG		58650	11	22½	12¾	18½	— ½	— 2.6
ASK		93899	29	20¼	13	17	+ ¼	+ 1.5
ATE		9000	44	6¾	3¾	4	— 2¾	— 40.7
AarnRt		14675	16	19½	14	17¼	— 1	— 5.5
Acadln	.20b	172957	....	15⅜	8	9⅞	— 4⅜	— 30.7
Acelrtn		31045	13	12¼	8½	10	— 1¾	— 14.9
AcuRay	.20	59340	12	25⅜	14⅜	18¾	— 6⅝	— 26.1
AdacLb		147236	....	11	2¾	4¼	— 5⅛	— 54.7
Adage		41056	10	18	6¼	7¾	— 7¼	— 48.3
AdvCir		38073	8	9½	5	7⅛	....	....
Aequtrn		16991	......	4⅜	2¾	3½	....	....
AflBsh	.80	39644	7	19⅞	13½	14¾	— ¾	— 4.8
AgcyRt	t	38400	14	27¼	15¼	25¾	+ 1¾	+ 7.3
AirMd	.10e	16395	6	13¼	9	10¾	+ 1¾	+ 19.4
AirWisc	t	46715	12	16⅝	7¾	8⅝	— 4	— 31.7
AirCal		28911	7	14⅜	5⅞	7¼	— 4½	— 38.3
AlskMt	.25r	15136	......	17¾	11	15¼	+ 1	+ 7
AlskPc	.55r	20674	10	25¼	15¾	24⅜	+ 7	+ 40.3
AlexB s	1.20	55370	10	39½	24½	35¾	+ 10⅜	+ 40.9
Alfin		21586	16	19½	10½	18¼	+ 3¾	+ 25.9
Algorex		39420	52	32¼	5⅞	7¼	— 20½	— 73.9
AlegWt		38186	29	17	10¾	13¼	+ 1⅛	+ 9.3
AllegB s	.40	42095	10	20¾	13½	16⅜	+ ⅛	+ .8
AlldBn	.84	149062	8	25¾	20⅜	21⅜	— ½	— 2.3
Allnet		46777	79	7⅛	1¾	2⅜	— 3⅛	— 56.8
AlpMic		57142	6	18½	5¼	7	— 8	— 53.3
Altos		166490	12	12¾	6⅞	9½	— ¼	— 2.6
Amcst s	.40	64473	14	26⅜	17½	18¼	— 3½	— 16.1
AWAirl		79076	......	12½	4⅞	7⅞	— 3⅞	— 33
AmAdv		37289	4	17¼	8½	9¼	— 1	— 9.8
ABnkr	.50	74388	7	15¾	10	11½	— 2¼	— 16.4
ACarr s		60378	7	20½	8⅛	13½	— 6	— 30.8
AContl		33225	8	11¾	4¾	6⅛	— 4⅞	— 44.3
AFdSL s	.60	13347	......	17⅞	11	13¾	— 2	— 12.7
AmFrst	t	9270	14	7¾	6	7¼	....	....
AFletc	1.48	25175	7	37¾	27¼	36	+ 5½	+ 18
AGreet	.58	337366	14	34¼	21½	31	+ 4½	+ 17
AmInLf	.40e	54524	6	13⅜	8¼	9⅜	— 2	— 17.6
AMagnt		24657	21	13½	6	7⅝	— 5⅛	— 40.2
AMS		8331	......	21¼	12½	17¾	— 2½	— 12.3
ANtlns	1.08	61779	7	30¾	21⅜	30¼	+ 8¾	+ 40.7
APhyGp		25215	32	9⅛	5⅜	6	....	....
AQuasr		169132	....	7⅞	1⅞	1 15-16	—5 9-16	— 74.2
ASecC s	1.02	15670	8	21⅛	14½	17	— 2⅛	— 11.1
AmSoft		19408	14	19½	11	15½	— 2½	— 13.9
ASolar		128243	25	8	2⅞	3	— 3	— 50
ASurg		178436	....	5	½	⅝	— 3⅝	— 85.3
Amritr	3.08	44605	8	58¼	40½	57⅝	+ 9⅛	+ 18.8
Amrwst		33957	......	20¾	12¼	17¼	+ 5	+ 40.8
Amgen		42202	......	8¼	3¾	5	— 2¼	— 31
AmskB	.54e	53852	31	22⅞	16	22½	+ 6⅛	+ 37.4
Ampad	.60	19579	14	26	16¼	24¼	+ 7½	+ 44.8
Anadite	.10	7698	......	12⅛	5⅛	5½	— 6	— 52.2
Anlogic	.77	147961	13	25	9	11¼	— 12	— 51.6
Analyl		26090	......	14½	4½	4⅞	— 6½	— 57.1
Anaren		27546	19	12¼	7⅝	9⅛	— 1¾	— 16.1
Andrew		45333	17	39½	28½	35½	— 3½	— 9
Andros		16850	12	10	4⅝	7	— 1¾	— 20
Apogee	.12	26967	19	11¾	6⅞	8⅞	— 1½	— 14.5
ApoloC s		553018	35	29¼	15⅝	20½	— 1⅛	— 5.2
AppleC		1864211	28	34⅜	21¾	29⅛	+ 4¾	+ 19.5
AplBio		44446	40	31½	16½	28½	+ 10½	+ 58.3
ApldCm		31516	23	18½	8½	12½	— 6	— 32.4
ApldMt		91413	13	39¾	21¼	27	— 11½	— 29.9
ApldSlr		40083	16	16⅜	9⅝	10	— 5⅞	— 37
AplS wt		5044	......	4½	⅛	⅛	— 4	— 97
Archive		29690	23	10¼	3⅝	3⅝	— 6⅛	— 62.8
ArgoSy		28241	20	21½	14	18	— 4	— 18.2
ArizB	.80b	49689	10	21	15⅝	20¾	+ 4¼	+ 25.8
Artel		21297	45	9¼	6¼	7¼	— 1⅝	— 18.3
AsdHst	.12	77330	16	17½	10½	13⅝	+ ⅝	+ 4.8
Astrosy		38739	9	8¾	5⅜	5⅝	— 1⅞	— 25
Atcor	.40	11291	7	17¾	10¼	13¼	— 2½	— 15.9
Athey	.80b	698	12	16	13	15⅛	....	....
AtlAm	.40b	5664	11	17¾	11¼	17½	+ 4¼	+ 32.1
AtlntBc	.80	32905	9	28	22⅞	26	+ 3	+ 13
AtlnFd		39512	50	11⅛	7¾	9½	— ¼	— 2.6
AtlFin		31462	......	12	8¼	9⅜	+ ⅝	+ 7.1
AtlRes		35138	14	34¾	22½	31¾	+ 2½	+ 8.6
AtSeAr s		20991	10	11¼	5	10½	+ 1¼	+ 13.5
Austron		11141	18	6⅛	3¼	3½	— 1⅜	— 28.2
AtwdOc		30784	31	19¾	15¾	16	— 1¼	— 7.2
AutTrT		33029	40	25¼	7¼	8½	— 13¾	— 61.8
Autmtx		71976	......	21½	5½	5¾	— 14¾	— 72
Auxton		31261	23	17¾	4½	6½	— 11	— 62.9
Avacre		17707	......	13¼	3¼	10	+ 5¼	+ 110.5
AvntGr		47770	21	26	11½	11¾	— 11	— 48.4
Avntek		217895	25	26	16½	20½	— ⅜	— 1.8
Avatar		35613	......	18½	13	16	+ 3	+ 23.1
AviatGp		54055	4	17¾	11¼	16¼	+ 2¼	+ 16.1
AztcM	.20	12919	39	10¼	4¼	4¼	— 4	— 48.5
Aztch		8117	......	5	1¾	2	— 1⅝	— 44.8
				— B—B—B —				
BBDO	2	28220	12	46½	32¾	44¼	+ 6¼	+ 16.5
BFI Cm		25478	12	8½	1⅝	2	— 6	— 75
BIW Cb	.10a	5050	......	10	4¾	5⅜	— 3⅞	— 41.9
BPI Sy		75081	11	10½	1⅝	2⅜	— 7⅞	— 76.8
BRCom		27352	9	23¼	10	11	— 9¾	— 47
BairdC	t	17458	15	10¾	5	6⅜	— 3⅝	— 36.3
BaltBcp		38005	......	17⅝	14	17½	....	....
Bancokl	.90	14467	5	24½	16¾	17⅞	— 6⅜	— 26.3
BcpHw	1.24	21142	7	26¾	18	26¼	+ 2	+ 8.3
Banctec		29290	......	17	5	6¼	— 8	— 56.1
BangH	.80	39886	3	13⅞	5½	6¾	— 7⅛	— 51.4
BkNE	2.84	14769	7	59¾	41	58¼	+ 12¼	+ 26.6
BkMAm	1	34694	7	16¾	9¾	11	— 4½	— 29
Bankvt		6575	19	15⅝	8¼	10	— 3¾	— 27.3
BantaG	.64	50006	9	28¼	16¾	26¾	+ 4⅞	+ 22.3
BaronD		18205	10	11¼	6⅞	7¼	— 3¾	— 34.1
Barton		13396	......	6¼	2⅜	2½	— 2¼	— 47.4
BsTnA	.15b	12381	......	15	6	9	— 2⅜	— 20.9
BasAm		33712	8	13⅜	7	7⅛	— 3⅜	— 32.1
BsetF	.80a	33886	10	49¼	30	35	— 11½	— 24.7
BayBks	2.20	38699	8	44¾	33½	43⅛	+ 4½	+ 11.7
Bayly	.12	19493	13	15	6¼	6½	— 6⅞	— 51.4
BlFuse s		24562	......	18½	8	10¼	+ 2¼	+ 28.1
BellNt		46924	2	23½	4¾	5¾	— 15¾	— 73.3
BnchCf		16121	8	11⅛	5½	6½	— 4½	— 40.9
Benhan		45236	......	16⅛	4⅜	15¼	+ 9¾	+ 177.3
Benhn wt		27301	......	10⅛	1⅜	9¼	+ 7⅜	+ 393.3
Berkley	.32	17521	......	16	12	14¾	+ 1¼	+ 9.3
BesiCp		89453	......	3 5-16	7-16	½	—1 11-16	— 77.1
BetzLb	1.20	157402	14	39	27¼	32¼	— 5½	— 14.6
BevHS		63988	......	27	4¾	7¼	— 16½	— 69.5
Big B		14194	18	13¼	8⅞	10⅞	— 2⅛	— 16.3
BigBite		14089	......	3⅜	1 1-16	1½	— ⅜	— 20
BigBear		20080	6	13	8	9¾	— 1	— 9.3
Billings		66084	......	14½	3¼	7¼	+ 1⅛	+ 18.4
Bindly		21412	16	22	13½	19⅞	+ 2⅛	+ 12
BioRes		104778	....	14⅜	3⅝	4¾	— 5¼	— 52.5
Biogen		67613	......	14	4¼	5½	— 5¼	— 48.8
Biosrc		27245	......	9¼	4⅝	5⅛	— 3⅛	— 37.9
BiotcR		14085	......	12¼	6¼	7¼	— 1	— 12.1
BirdInc		38617	......	11	5	8⅝	— 1¼	— 12.7
BishGr		10543	14	10½	4	7	— ¾	— 9.7
BlissAT	t	147146	....	5⅛	7-16	⅝	— 4⅛	— 86.8
BoatB s	1.50	12256	7	33½	23½	27½	— 1	— 3.5
BobEvn	.30	70128	17	23¾	14¾	18	— 4¾	— 20.9
BoltTc	.16	20423	16	15¾	7½	7½	— 7¾	— 50.8
BstnDig		4813	21	15½	7½	8¾	— 5¾	— 39.7
BstnFC	.10e	41788	10	15½	9	15¼	+ 3¼	+ 27.1
BraeCp		17210	50	14¼	8¾	9½	— 2¾	— 22.4
Brenco	.24	39013	......	10⅝	4¾	4⅞	— 4¾	— 49.4
BrwTom	t	206088	....	7⅛	3⅛	3⅜	— 2⅝	— 43.8
Bruno	.28	41250	18	20⅝	12¾	20½	+ 5¾	+ 39
Buffton		59190	12	1⅝	⅞	1⅝	+ ¼	+ 18.2
BuildTr		17927	9	22¼	13	19¾	— ¼	— 1.3
BurlCt		73821	10	24¼	14¼	14½	— 8¼	— 36.3
Brnhm	.18e	35136	16	19½	14¼	17½	+ ¾	+ 4.5
BurrBr		12441	12	24¾	15¾	15¾	— 7¾	— 33
BMA	1.94	16824	8	49¾	35¾	49¾	+ 11⅝	+ 30.5
Businld		84673	......	13¼	3½	4	— 6½	— 61.9
				— C—C—C —				
C COR		21628	89	13	6	6¼	— 4	— 39
CP Rhb		130531	20	15¼	5¾	8	— 4⅝	— 36.6
CBTBc	.56	2706	13	25	16	19½	+ 3¼	+ 20
CBT	1.80	27054	7	35½	24	35¼	+ 7½	+ 27
CML		18160	13	13	6½	8½	— 4¼	— 33.3
CPI		59977	10	27¼	14⅝	14⅞	— 10⅛	— 40.5
CPT		261561	8	16¾	5⅞	6⅜	— 6½	— 50.5
CSP		16055	20	13¼	5⅞	6¼	— 5¾	— 47.9
Cache		79465	325	10¼	2¾	3¼	— 5⅜	— 62.3
CACI		81929	......	8⅞	2⅝	4⅞	— 3⅜	— 40.9
CbrySc		83521	......	19⅞	16⅝	18⅞	....	....
Calibre		4509	......	9	1¾	2¼	— 5¾	— 71.9
CalAmp		60806	5	17⅞	3	3¾	— 6⅜	— 63

CalMic		84631	14	19¼	6¾	8⅞	— 10⅛	— 53.3
CalSlv g		52034	......	7⅞	2⅞	3¼	— ⅛	— 3.7
CallonP		55068	6	9	2⅞	3⅛	— 4⅜	— 58.3
Calny	.16	25743	14	10¾	7¼	8⅜	— 1⅜	— 14.1
CanonG		63111	9	22¾	13¾	18¾	— 2½	— 11.8
CapFSL		19101	......	8⅛	5⅜	8	....	....
CapCrb		115355	....	6¼	1⅜	1½	— 3½	— 70
CardDis	.02e	9053	14	18⅝	12	13¾	— 3¾	— 21.4
Cardio s		46655	......	12¼	2⅝	12⅛	....	....
Carolin		67506	......	10½	1¾	1⅞	— 3½	— 65.1
Cartert	t	60802	8	10¾	6¼	8¾	— 1¼	— 12.5
Caseys		10422	13	14¾	10¼	14⅛	+ 2⅜	+ 20.2
Cencor		4023	9	20¼	13	16½	+ ¾	+ 4.8
CntrBc	1.80	41718	10	29½	18½	28	+ 1¾	+ 6.7
Centcor		41435	......	16¼	8	9	— 4	— 30.8
CenBcp	2.05b	11454	8	41	30	36½	+ 6¼	+ 20.7
CnBshS	1.32	8289	7	25¼	20⅛	24¾	+ 2	+ 8.8
CFdBk	1.12	11514	9	28⅞	18¾	28¾	+ 4⅝	+ 19.2
Centran	.60	42703	5	33¾	18½	33½	+ 14½	+ 76.3
CerbrA	.12	16337	7	11½	4¾	5⅝	— 5⅝	— 50
Cermtk		20249	8	10½	3¾	4¼	— 4½	— 51.4
Cetus		64062	175	14	8⅝	8¾	— 2⅛	— 19.5
ChadTh		3461	......	5	¾	1⅜	— 3⅝	— 72.5
ChncCp		6159	3	9	4	4⅜	— 4⅝	— 51.4
ChapEn		55376	60	7¼	4⅜	6	+ 1	+ 20
ChrmS s	.18	89718	18	17¾	10¼	17¼	+ 3½	+ 25.5
ChkPnt		36515	17	17	8¼	13	+ 1	+ 8.3
ChkTch		16359	......	8½	4¾	7	+ ¾	+ 12
ChLwn s	.38	70920	18	31¼	22	27¼	....	....
Chemex		34634	......	7¾	2¾	5⅞	— ¾	— 11.3
ChryE	.12e	8303	7	19½	10½	11	— 8	— 42.1
ChiChi		522226	18	25⅛	10	12¼	— 11⅜	— 48.1
ChiPac		19750	......	88½	68	81¼	....	....
Chomer		15417	25	22¾	13¼	20	+ 1	+ 5.3
Chronr		50636	......	19½	6½	7¼	— 11¾	— 61.8
ChrDw s	.38	17478	13	14⅞	9⅞	14⅛	+ 2	+ 16.5
Chyrn s	.10	77938	18	13¾	8⅛	10	+ ⅞	+ 9.6
Cintas	.09e	18092	22	27	19¾	26⅛	+ 4¾	+ 22.2
Cipher		192532	23	27½	14½	22	+ 2¼	+ 11.4
Ciprico	t	10220	13	12¼	8⅜	8⅝	+ ¼	+ 3
Circon		18650	46	15¾	4	6	— 8¾	— 59.3
CtzSGa	.76	152860	9	19¾	12⅞	19⅜	+ 5	+ 34.8
CtzFid s	.92	32502	10	27⅛	18⅞	27	+ 6	+ 28.6
CtzUt A	t	15476	13	31½	24	28½	— ¾	— 2.6
CtzUt B	1.80	4744	13	30	21	28¼	+ 3¼	+ 13
CityFed	.20e	170123	3	13¼	8¼	9⅞	— 1¼	— 11.2
CtyNCp	.88b	16154	9	29½	22	24	— 2¾	— 10.3
ClairSt	s.05i	46700	20	27½	7¼	26¾	+ 17⅝	+ 193.2
ClarkJ	.88	19203	13	29	21½	25¾	+ ½	+ 2
ClearCh		11783	17	15½	9¾	15	....	....
ClevtRt	1.52	9962	15	21	14	19⅜	+ 5	+ 34.8
Clthtme		17726	13	13¾	6¾	9¾	— ¼	— 2.5
CoastF		42990	......	15½	11½	14	+ ¼	+ 1.8
CobeLb		31757	15	20¼	8¼	10	— 8	— 44.4
CocaBt	s.56a	13403	14	32½	18	26½	+ 3	+ 12.8
Coeur	t	22650	51	23¼	13	13⅜	— 5⅞	— 30.5
Cogenic		48472	......	5⅜	3	3⅜	— ⅝	— 15.6
Cohrnt s		85067	11	24¼	11½	18½	+ 4¼	+ 29.8
ColabR		56003	......	10⅜	3⅝	4⅛	— 2⅝	— 38.9
Colagen		59997	44	14¾	7⅞	11⅜	— 3⅜	— 22.9
Collins		17991	10	7¾	4⅞	5⅛	— 2⅛	— 29.3
ColLfAc	.92	11884	10	29⅝	22⅛	28¾	+ 4⅞	+ 20.4
ColrTle		134403	11	18¼	13⅝	16⅜	— ¾	— 4.4
ColoNt s	.70	28896	6	18¾	15	16	— 2⅜	— 12.9
ColDta		29680	......	12	½	¾	....	....
Comair	t	29396	12	15¼	8½	12¾	+ ½	+ 4.1
Comcst s	.12	80356	15	20⅝	11¼	20⅛	+ 4½	+ 28.8
Comdta	.16	193605	21	25¾	10¼	13¾	— 9¾	— 41.5
Comdial		180814	....	12½	2	2⅝	— 7¾	— 74.7
Comerc	2.10	54050	8	34⅞	26	34	+ 3⅝	+ 11.9
CmceU	.92	21260	8	27½	20	27	+ 2¼	+ 9.1
CmlShr	.50a	16223	10	17¾	10¼	11½	— 5¼	— 31.3
CwlthF	1.34e	11600	6	11½	7½	8½	— 2	— 19
CmwTl	1.50	3152	6	26	18½	25½	+ 6	+ 30.8
ComAm		103198	....	8¾	3¾	4⅛	— 4⅜	— 51.5
ComInd	.36	87727	14	27¼	16½	17½	— 9	— 34
ComSy s		30477	9	16	7¾	9¾	— 3	— 23.5
CmpCrd		35191	67	25¾	13	25½	+ ½	+ 2
Compaq		332511	74	14⅞	3½	6⅝	— 5⅞	— 47
CmpoT	.01r	6907	17	14¼	6¾	13⅛	+ 6⅜	+ 94.4
CompC	.40	163563	18	25¾	16¾	24¾	+ 2	+ 8.8
Cmpcre		38437	16	17	5¼	7	— 9¼	— 56.9
Compcp		68923	......	7¾	⅜	1¼	— 6⅜	— 83.6
Compus		53627	8	5¼	2¾	2⅞	— ⅞	— 23.3
CCTC		83197	......	16¾	9	12¼	— 4	— 24.6
CmpAs		91598	19	29½	14¾	19⅜	— 4⅝	— 19.3
CptAut		18489	......	9¾	3⅞	4⅛	— 2⅝	— 38.9
CmpDt	.08	12264	10	16¼	8	10	— 5½	— 35.5
CptEnt		16243	15	6½	3¾	4	— 2	— 33.3
CmptH		21556	9	15¼	4½	7⅛	— 6⅝	— 48.2
Cmpldn		43436	......	7⅞	3¼	7⅛	+ 3⅞	+ 119.2
CmpLR	.12	48973	17	24	5½	7¾	— 15	— 65.9
CmptM		182764	13	12	2⅝	3¼	— 8	— 71.1
CmpPd		45979	19	18⅝	13⅞	16⅛	— 1⅝	— 9.2
CmpRs	.01e	5592	......	7⅝	2⅝	2⅞	— 4½	— 61
CmTask	.05	8741	17	17⅛	12¼	15⅛	— ⅛	— .8
CptUsg		16522	......	15	3	3¾	— 8⅞	— 70.3
Cmputn		33407	......	9¼	3¾	5½	— 3¼	— 37.1
Cptcft		14182	73	8¾	4½	5⅛	— 3⅛	— 37.9
Cmsrve		49542	......	7½	1	2⅝	— 3	— 53.3
Comshr		29941	29	13¾	6	6¾	— 6¼	— 48.1
Cmpshp		31041	......	12½	2½	3¾	— 8¼	— 68.8
Comtch		75442	63	6⅞	⅝	1¼	— 4½	— 78.3
Concptl		43043	17	12¼	6¾	9	— ⅛	— 1.4
Conifr s		7409	7	22	16½	21¼	+ 2¼	+ 11.8
CnCap	3.36a	50192	......	29½	23¼	25¼	— 3¾	— 12.9
CCapR	1.68a	13298	7	20½	15½	16½	— 4	— 19.5
CCapS	3.36	42528	8	29¼	23¼	25¼	— 4	— 13.7
ConFbr		9058	4	11	6¼	7⅝	— 1¼	— 14.1
CnPap	s1.28	26120	11	35¾	25⅛	35¾	+ 10	+ 38.8
ConsPd	.08e	25557	11	9¼	4¾	5⅜	— 3¾	— 41.1
Consul		61649	115	14⅞	4½	5¾	— 7⅞	— 57.8
CntlBcp	2.04b	9990	7	32½	26½	31¾	+ 2¼	+ 7.6
CtlHlth		21672	14	11¼	6⅛	10	+ 3¼	+ 48.2
CtlHltC		30148	28	9¼	3¼	3⅜	— 3	— 47.1
CntInfo	t	35280	5	9¼	4½	6⅝	— 2½	— 27.4
CtLasr		16226	......	10	4¾	5¾	— 3	— 34.3
Convgt		1476875	150	27⅜	4⅝	6	— 17¾	— 74.7
Convrse		53736	7	24¼	15	16½	+ ¼	+ 1.5
CoprBio		64804	38	9⅛	2¾	3	— 2⅞	— 48.9
Coors B	.40	218087	11	21⅝	12	16⅛	— 4⅛	— 20.4
Copytel		25232	......	41¾	22½	25¾	— 5½	— 17.6
Corcom		19091	7	13¾	6¼	6¼	— 7¼	— 53.7
Cordis		235117	8	24¼	6¾	8¼	— 13¼	— 61.6
CoreSt	2.08	70880	7	45⅜	29¾	44⅛	+ 13⅛	+ 42.3
Corvus		127669	20	9½	2¾	3	— 5¼	— 63.6
Cosmo		94653	7	18	4¾	5½	— 9	— 62.1
CrkBrl	.14	29114	14	24	11¾	14	— 7¼	— 34.1
CrimeC	t	120455	....	16¾	1⅛	1 9-16	—10 15-16	— 87.5
Cronus		18704	10	14¼	9	12⅞	+ 1	+ 8.4
CrosTr	.80	147985	73	30¼	16⅛	24¼	— 4⅝	— 16
CwnBk		32102	13	19½	9	9½	— 9½	— 50
Crump	.44	20862	16	18⅜	10⅝	18⅛	+ 7⅜	+ 68.6
CullnFr	.94	26545	......	34¼	22¼	24½	— 5⅜	— 18
Cullum	.56	51223	10	18¼	12¼	16¾	+ 2¼	+ 15.5
Cycare		11838	17	21	15¾	19¼	+ ¾	+ 4.1
— D—D—D —								
DBA		21545	13	14	7	11	— 1½	— 12
DEP		17840	13	8	6¼	7⅛	— ⅞	— 10.9
DaisySy		235003	36	28½	17½	26	+ 3¾	+ 16.9
DalasF		83766	27	25½	11⅛	23¾	+ 11	+ 86.3
DmnBio		33901	14	10½	4⅜	4½	— 3½	— 43.8
DartGp	.13	9578	15	109	57	86	+ 23	+ 36.5
Datcrd	.24	40094	16	17⅜	11⅛	16½	+ 2⅛	+ 14.8
Dta IO		141851	14	23¼	8¾	11⅜	— 10⅛	— 47.1
DtSwtch		157515	....	34	4	6⅛	— 23⅞	— 79.6
Datpwr		7904	15	8	3¼	4	— 3¼	— 44.8
Datscp		7498	27	18¼	11	13	— 5¼	— 28.8
Dtasth		15935	9	10½	3	3½	— 6⅜	— 64.6
Datum		36526	12	8⅝	4¾	5½	— 2⅞	— 34.3
Dawson		12994	27	10¼	5½	5⅞	— 2⅝	— 30.9
DebSh	.15e	33292	10	23½	13	16¾	— 4¼	— 20.2
DecisD		109567	14	13⅛	8½	12⅜	+ 1⅜	+ 12.5
DeklbA	.72	98114	9	28⅛	19¾	20⅞	— 5⅝	— 21.2
Delchm	.28	22701	11	14½	9⅝	14½	+ 2¼	+ 18.4
DeltaDt		15366	18	3⅜	1⅛	1¼	— 1⅛	— 47.4
Deltaus		25841	......	4⅞	1 5-16	1½	— 2⅝	— 63.6
Denelcr		49684	......	11⅜	3¾	5½	— 3	— 35.3
DentMd		111553	....	14	3½	6¼	— 6½	— 51
DetecEl		11400	103	9¼	3¼	4⅛	— 4⅞	— 54.2
DiagDt		34742	......	7¼	2¾	3⅛	— 1⅜	— 30.6
DiagPr		13307	18	13¾	7	8¾	— 2¾	— 23.9
Diasonc		429725	....	9	1⅞	2⅞	— 5⅜	— 65.2
Diceon		21717	10	19	11	11¾	— 3½	— 23
Dicmed		35138	18	15¾	9½	10⅜	— 1⅞	— 15.3
Diglog		11040	......	10¾	2¾	3¾	— 3½	— 48.3
DigtCm		71488	10	31½	12¼	12¾	— 17	— 57.1
DigitSw		813769	16	34¾	17	22½	— 9¼	— 29.1
Dionex		25501	23	29¼	21½	25¾	— 3	— 10.4
DistLog		14753	10	14	3¾	6	— 7¾	— 56.4
Dvfood	.34	962930	12	19¼	8	9¾	— 7⅜	— 43.1
DocuOl		67730	113	15	3½	4½	— 7⅝	— 62.9
DlrGnl	.20	89424	17	21¼	10⅛	20¾	+ 6¾	+ 48.2
DomB	1.20	33848	8	26½	18½	25½	+ 4⅜	+ 20.7

DrchH	.20	12297	......	21¾	12	13	— ¼	— 1.9
DoylDB	.88	40583	17	22	13¾	17¾	— 1¼	— 6.6
Drantz	.15e	4025	10	16	9½	10⅛	— 5⅜	— 34.7
Drexlr		25711	62	16½	8¾	10½	— 4¼	— 28.8
DreyGr		60387	16	24¼	11¼	13¾	— 9½	— 40.9
DuckA s	.32	31064	4	19¼	12½	13½	— 3½	— 20.6
DunkD	.32	28836	13	26½	18⅛	23½	+ ⅝	+ 2.7
Duriron	.56	25026	21	14¼	9½	9⅝	— 4⅜	— 31.3
DurFil	.16	24711	14	16¼	10¼	12⅞	— 1⅝	— 11.2
Dynscn	t	71577	......	14½	3¼	3⅝	— 10⅜	— 74.1
Dyntch s		64799	14	20¼	11	18½	....	....
Dysan		273615	....	25	4	9½	— 14½	— 60.4
— E—E—E —								
EH Int		21328	......	4¾	1⅝	2½	— ⅛	— 4.8
EIP	.12	7959	19	13¾	9½	13	....	....
EaglCpt		130152	....	9⅛	5-16	½	— 7	— 93.3
EaglTl		125761	....	5¾	3⅜	5	+ 1⅛	+ 29
EagT wt		17211	......	10¾	3½	9¼	+ 5½	+ 146.7
EarlCal		12708	......	9½	3⅝	5¾	— 1¼	— 17.9
EconLb	1.04	127210	10	31⅜	21½	27	— 4⅜	— 13.9
EdCmp	.12	34005	19	14¼	5½	9⅛	— 2⅛	— 18.9
Educom	.08i	15745	36	5⅞	3⅝	4	— ⅝	— 13.5
Eikonx		13260	......	14½	5	9⅝	+ ⅛	+ 1.3
ElChic		23397	9	14¾	7⅝	7¾	— 4⅞	— 38.6
ElPas	1.46	184481	5	14½	10	13	— ⅜	— 2.8
Elan	.07e	27550	......	12⅝	7¼	7⅝	....	....
Elbit g		23085	......	12⅞	8¼	8⅞	— 2¾	— 23.7
Eldon	.16b	6576	11	16¼	12¾	13¾	— 1¼	— 8.3
EldrM		9374	......	5⅜	3¾	4⅝	....	....
ElecBio		87092	11	11¼	4½	5¾	— 5¼	— 47.7
ElCath s		54373	52	21¼	6½	17¼	+ 7¼	+ 72.5
EleNucl		58698	......	10¾	5½	9¼	— ¼	— 2.6
ElcRnt		39899	14	20¼	13½	19	....	....
ElModl		86745	......	18⅛	10	17⅞	+ 5⅞	+ 49
ECplsr s		15785	15	16	9¼	13½	+ 1	+ 8
ElctMis		7053	......	12½	4¼	5½	— 2¾	— 33.3
ElronEl		39471	5	13¼	8	8¼	— 4½	— 35.3
Emcor		30326		2¼	½	¾	— 1¼	— 62.5
EmpAir		29150	6	9½	5¾	7½	— ⅛	— 1.6
Emulx s		187211	9	23⅞	6⅝	8	— 13½	— 62.8
Endta		7412	12	12¾	5½	7	— 3¾	— 34.9
Endvco		10067	11	7⅜	4⅜	6⅜	+ 1¾	+ 37.8
EndoLs		59533	......	8⅝	1	8	....	....
Endl wt		17449	......	8⅞	½	8¼	....	....
EngCnv		51712	......	42	20⅞	30¼	— 9¼	— 23.4
EnFact		12351	......	11¾	7¾	8⅜	— ¼	— 2.9
EngOil s		33819	8	10 5-16	4⅜	4⅝	—3 3-16	— 40.8
EngRsv		106212	......	12¾	⅝	13-16	—4 15-16	— 85.9
Engph s	.22	2657	14	12¼	9	12	+ 1⅝	+ 15.7
EntPub		15290	13	13½	8¼	12½	+ 2¼	+ 22
EnzoBi		52793	107	26½	11¾	15	— 10	— 40
Equat		133220	56	24	12⅝	17¼	— 2⅞	— 14.3
EqtOil	.20	34451	10	9¼	5⅞	6⅛	— 1⅜	— 18.3
EricTl	.94e	158442	7	50	27	28¾	— 21¼	— 42.5
EvnSut		80318	13	31½	11	13¼	— 17	— 56.2
ExcalTc		35921	......	6¼	7-16	9-16	—4 3-16	— 88.2
Exovir		41815	......	12⅛	2½	10⅝	+ 7⅝	+ 254.2
— F—F—F —								
FDP		17963	11	17¾	6	7¾	— 5¼	— 40.4
FMI	.02r	123266	13	9½	5	5⅜	— 2⅛	— 28.3
FamHl s		15327	......	1¾	1⅛	1¼		
FarmF	t	52495	21	19⅜	13½	19	+ 1⅛	+ 6.3
FrmG	1.52	204168	11	52½	34¼	49⅝	+ 7⅞	+ 18.9
FedGrp		66911	15	25½	14½	21	+ 3¼	+ 18.3
Feroflu		63010	33	10¼	4¾	5	— 4¼	— 45.9
Fibron		13027	50	14⅜	6¾	14⅛	+ 5½	+ 63.8
Fidlcr	2.40	33235	9	45¾	35¾	45½	+ 6¾	+ 17.4
FifthTh	2.20	9782	9	58	48	58	+ 9½	+ 19.6
Figgie	.68	30076	7	27¼	21⅛	22¾	— 3¾	— 14.2
Filmtec		26252	27	18¾	11½	13	....	....
Filtrtk	.40	14021	12	15¾	12	14¼	— 1½	— 9.5
Finalco	.20	16035	9	6⅞	3¼	3½	— 2	— 36.4
Fingmx		77260	......	9½	4¾	6½	— 1⅞	— 22.4
Finigan		40758	26	10¼	5	8⅞	— ⅞	— 9
FAlaB s	1	44011	8	24½	17⅛	21¾	+ 3⅜	+ 18.4
FtAFin	.72	8462	4	29	22½	25½	— 1½	— 5.6
FtATn	1.10	36180	8	25⅞	18⅜	25½	+ 5½	+ 27.5
FtBnOh	2.80	6474	7	51	38½	50	+ 7½	+ 17.7
FtColF		9254	5	17½	9½	12¾	— 3	— 19
FComr	1.20	12826	11	26¾	20⅜	23	— 1	— 4.2
FDataR		50918	19	19¾	11⅜	19¾	+ 5⅞	+ 42.3
FExec		644615	8	15⅛	7⅞	11⅝	— 2	— 14.7
FFdMic		86437	4	9⅞	5⅝	9⅜	+ ¾	+ 8.7
FFdCal		27492	......	16¼	10	14¼	+ ½	+ 3.6
FFFtM	.20e	13233	......	26⅛	17	18¼	— 2¾	— 13.1
FtFnCp	.80	12958	5	20½	11¾	18	....	....
FFnMgt		8513	23	18	13⅛	18	+ 3¼	+ 22
FtFlBk	.40	33271	7	22⅜	17	22⅛	+ 3⅝	+ 19.6
FJerNt	1.80	19126	6	32½	22⅜	30	+ 2½	+ 9.1
FMdB	1.60	31045	9	32½	21⅜	31	+ 7¾	+ 33.3
FNtlCin	2.60b	7154	9	54	38½	53½	+ 8½	+ 18.9
FNtSup	.02e	22655	......	17¾	7¾	13¼	— ¾	— 5.4
FRBGa	.96	26407	9	29	23½	27¼	+ ¾	+ 2.8
FtSvFla	.40b	19966	......	24¾	14⅛	20½	+ 3⅞	+ 23.3
FSvWis		13826	......	14	7¼	8¼	— 5¼	— 38.9
FtSecC	1.10	51543	27	23	15	19¾	— 1⅜	— 6.5
FTenNt	1.60	40848	8	30⅞	21⅛	29¾	+ 5½	+ 22.7
FtUnC s	1	105209	9	35	23	35	+ 7	+ 25
Flakey		71221	......	9⅜	4⅛	6⅜	+ 2¼	+ 54.6
Flexstl	.48	16773	8	17⅝	10	13¼	— 2¾	— 17.2
FlaFdl	.20e	133088	17	17¾	13⅛	15⅞	+ ⅝	+ 4.1
FINFl s	.72	53324	8	29¾	22⅞	29¼	+ 6¼	+ 27.2
FlowSy		17381	31	19	11⅝	13¾	— 5¼	— 27.6
Flurocb	.20	18714	11	14¼	9⅛	11⅞	— 2	— 14.4
Fonar		138437	....	6⅞	2⅝	4¼	— 1⅛	— 20.9
FLion	.07	24703	22	14½	8¼	14½	+ 4¼	+ 41.5
FLion A	.09	56875	21	14	8	13¾	+ 3	+ 27.9
ForAm	.96	38550	15	29½	21¼	28¾	+ 1½	+ 5.5
ForestO	1	23232	12	29⅛	18⅞	19	— 3⅜	— 15.1
FortnF		54060	9	22¾	12½	15	— 5¼	— 25.9
FortnS		220357	....	7⅛	1⅞	2⅝	— 4⅜	— 62.5
Forum	.06	182789	17	8	4¾	6⅞	+ ⅞	+ 14.6
Foster	.10	74549	16	8⅛	5¼	6¼	....	....
Foxmyr		78552	16	26¾	20	22¼	— 1¾	— 7.3
Fremnt	.48	160300	25	20⅞	10⅞	17⅜	+ 3⅛	+ 21.9
Fudrck		51812	500	17½	9⅛	10	— 6½	— 39.4
FulHB s	.30	49913	10	20	11¾	14⅝	— 5¼	— 26.4
— G—G—G —								
GTS s		31455	9	10⅞	6¼	10⅛	+ ¾	+ 8
Galileo		13979	13	14¾	7¼	13	+ 1¼	+ 10.6
GamaB	.10	24472	28	10½	6½	7½	— 2¼	— 23.1
Gandlf g		28672	......	14¼	9⅛	11⅝	+ 2⅜	+ 25.7
Garcia		49311	......	8⅜	1⅝	1¾	— 6	— 77.4
Genetch		65857	201	42¼	28¾	34¼	— ¼	— .7
GnAut		27517	......	13⅞	5⅛	5⅜	— 5⅝	— 51.1
GnHme		46307	10	11¾	5¾	7¼	— 2½	— 25.6
GenetE		14585	......	5⅝	1⅜	3½	— 1½	— 30
GenetL		7595	15	6¼	3¾	3¾	— ¼	— 6.3
GenetS		177480	....	10¾	4½	5½	— 3⅜	— 38
Genex		117367	....	17¼	4¾	5⅜	— 7⅝	— 58.7
Genova	.10e	7804	13	5½	3	5	+ 1⅝	+ 48.2
GaFBk		109117	....	10¾	7⅜	10½	....	....
GerMd s	.08	16091	22	6½	3¾	4⅞	....	....
GibsG	.21	193833	12	28¾	18	27¼	+ 6¼	+ 29.8
GigaTr		14228	19	25	14	14¾	— 9¼	— 38.5
GlenFd		243015	4	11⅝	6¾	8⅞	— ⅞	— 9
GldCorr		6660	......	10¾	9¾	10¾	....	....
GdTaco		25079	......	7⅜	¼	5-16	—4 9-16	— 93.6
Gotaas		112448	7	14⅝	10	13⅞	+ 2⅜	+ 20.7
Gott		8759	11	14¼	9¼	10¾	— 2¼	— 17.3
GouldP	.76	38878	13	21¼	14½	15¼	— 2¾	— 15.3
Graco	.44	22618	9	15¾	10	10¾	— 4¾	— 30.6
Grantre		30269	17	9⅜	5⅜	6¾	— 1¼	— 15.6
Graphl		11510	14	9⅞	6⅛	9⅞	+ 2⅛	+ 27.4
GrphSc		572613	....	9⅛	3⅛	5½	— 1	— 15.4
GWFSB	.48e	25029	......	17¼	8½	15	+ 3¼	+ 27.7
GBayCs		11443	19	25	9½	10⅝	— 10⅞	— 50.6
GreenT		34073	7	23¼	12¼	15¼	— 4¾	— 23.8
Gtech		50267	36	13¼	5¾	12½	+ 4¼	+ 51.5
Guilfrd		39838	11	21¼	13¼	14½	— 6	— 29.3
GlfBdc		552079	90	15¾	6¾	15⅜	....	....
GlfNuc		8108	......	3¾	1¾	1¾	— 1¼	— 41.7
Gull	.05e	16200	12	10¾	6¾	8¾	— ½	— 5.4
— H—H—H —								
HBO s	.16	151895	23	25	15⅛	17⅛	— 2⅛	— 11
HCC	.06e	10486	12	14¾	7	7⅜	— 5¼	— 41.6
HCW	.10	9238	5	14¾	4	4¾	— 10	— 67.8
HMO Am		19146	......	16¾	8¾	10¼	....	....
Haber s		17471	......	19⅜	12	12¾	— ¾	— 5.6
Hadco		19614	7	11½	5	5⅝	....	....
Hadson		54340	......	5½	2	2⅜	— 2	— 45.7
HaleSy		18893	10	8¼	4½	5⅝	— 1½	— 21.1
Halmi		79648	......	1⅝	15-16	1¼	— ¼	— 16.7
HamOil	.10	101450	19	19	12⅝	14⅛	— 1⅛	— 7.4
HarpG	.34	18715	13	35	22¼	28¾	— 1¾	— 5.7
HrtfN s	1.60	70441	6	26⅞	19	26½	+ 1½	+ 6
Hathwy	.20	4066	10	10¾	8	9¼	— ½	— 5.1
HawkB	.28	13124	10	17	8	8¼	— 8½	— 50.7
HlthA s		96531	20	31	8⅞	17	+ 8⅛	+ 91.6
HlthCS s		12740	30	18	5⅝	16	+ 10½	+ 190.9
Hlthln		15020	20	15½	7	7¾	— 2½	— 24.4
Hlthdyn		343933	....	21¾	1⅞	2⅞	— 16⅛	— 84.9
HechgA	.16	24214	19	21¼	13½	20¾	+ 2¾	+ 15.3
HechngB	.10	19854	19	21¾	14	21¼	+ 3½	+ 19.7

HelenT		38871	9	10⅞	5⅝	6⅞	— 3⅛	— 31.3
Helix		14026	11	29½	17½	25	......	......
HenrdF	.84	14060	12	40	28¾	35¼	— 2¼	— 6
HeritBn	1.60	19288	11	43¾	28	43¼	+ 9½	+ 28.2
Herley		11911	26	6½	3⅝	4⅜	— 1⅜	— 23.9
HiberC s	1	12990	8	21½	17¼	19½	+ 1½	+ 8.3
Hickam		11446	16	12¼	7	10¼	......	......
Hogan		145662	32	23½	7¾	11¾	— 11½	— 49.5
HmFAz		35561	14	15¾	9½	15	+ 1⅜	+ 10.1
HomeHl		164611	49	9⅛	4½	7⅜	— 1⅜	— 15.7
Hmecft		47491	......	17½	5¼	8	......	......
HonInd	.56	10651	11	23¼	15¼	16¾	— 5	— 23
HookDr	1	9593	12	29¼	18	20½	— 8¾	— 29.9
Hoover	1	123808	10	29⅞	19¼	28⅞	+ 2	+ 7.4
HorzInd		17970	6	14¼	3½	4	— 9½	— 70.4
HwBNJ		53217	7	18	11¼	17½	+ 2½	+ 16.7
HungTg		16959	24	9	3⅝	4⅜	— 2⅝	— 37.5
HuntJB		29827	18	21½	16½	20¼	+ 1¼	+ 6.6
HntgRs		20403	19	10¾	7	8¾	......	......
HuntgB	1.48b	24171	8	36¼	25¾	36	+ 6½	+ 22
Hurco		11446	......	19	3½	4½	— 12½	— 73.5
Hybritc		67262	275	23	11	16½	— 2¼	— 12
HydeAt		30735	5	11¾	3	4⅞	— 3⅞	— 44.3
Hyponx		21077	8	13	4¼	5	— 8	— 61.5
HytekM		14815	12	15¼	5¾	6¼	— 8⅛	— 56.5
— I—I—I —								
ILC		7675	13	10½	7¼	7¾	— 2½	— 24.4
IMS Int	.30	107634	16	38	21¾	36¼	+ 8¼	+ 29.5
IPL Sy		19718	......	6¼	1⅛	1⅜	— 4⅛	— 75
ISC		151303	15	16¼	7½	9⅛	— 3¼	— 26.3
Icot		95091	......	5⅛	2⅞	4	+ ⅛	+ 3.2
Imunex		32608	......	9	4	6¼	......	......
Imuno		18433	46	6¼	2⅜	2¾	— 2½	— 47.6
Imugen		19909	24	4 9-16	1⅝	2⅛	— 1⅞	— 46.9
Inacmp		17453	21	12	2¾	3⅝	......	......
IndpHlt		53264	15	36½	17¼	19	— 2¼	— 10.6
IndiN	1.40	24546	5	34¾	21½	33	+ 10⅜	+ 45.9
InfoRsc		52438	39	28	20	24	— 1½	— 5.9
Inftrn		41300	12	40	14½	19	— 18	— 48.6
Infraln		4424	23	10¼	7	7	— 1¾	— 20
InstNtw		23742	......	31½	14	18¾	— 1¼	— 6.3
Intecm		337743	33	19¾	6⅞	9	— 9⅛	— 50.3
IntgGen		25654	......	6½	2⅞	3⅝	— 2⅜	— 39.6
ISSCO		24549	25	22¾	11¾	17	— 4½	— 20.9
IntgDv		75184	46	15	7¾	11	......	......
Intel		1467337	15	43½	24¾	28	— 14	— 33.3
IntlSy		128366	8	22½	7	8⅝	— 10⅜	— 54.6
IntrTel		39412	......	5⅞	1½	1¾	— 3⅜	— 65.9
Intrnd		26032	......	15	3⅛	13¼	......	......
Intdyn		20856	......	16⅛	7¼	8¼	— 1¾	— 17.5
IntrfFlr	.16	36603	10	28½	6½	9¼	— 19¾	— 68.1
Intrfac		13153	9	8⅞	5⅝	5¾	— 3⅛	— 35.2
Intgrph		406301	31	57¾	32¾	55	+ 16½	+ 42.9
Intrmgn		68096	......	7⅜	3½	5¼	— 1⅜	— 20.8
Intmec		39889	22	18¾	13	15⅞	— 1⅝	— 9.3
Intrmet		9043	32	9⅜	5⅞	6	— 2½	— 29.4
InCapE		8510	......	9½	2¼	2⅞	— 5⅛	— 64.1
IntClin		83720	17	27	10½	12¾	— 10½	— 45.2
IGame		61412	11	20	11	14⅞	+ 3⅞	+ 35.2
IntKing	t	33858	12	19	11¼	16½	— 1	— 5.7
IntLse		18970	10	16¼	10½	13	— 1½	— 10.3
InMobil		63307	......	10⅝	4⅝	6⅝	— 1⅝	— 19.7
IRIS		116193	....	4	15-16	1 3-16	—1 15-16	— 62
IT Corp		16549	19	18½	12	16½	+ 1¼	+ 8.2
IntTotal		19659	......	6⅝	2⅜	3⅞	— ⅝	— 13.9
Invcre	.01e	34156	7	11½	3¼	4¼	......	......
Iomega		122783	8	8½	3⅝	7⅞	+ 2½	+ 46.5
Isomdx		8157	33	15	8¾	11¼	— 1¼	— 10
Itel		165069	....	6¼	2¾	5¼	+ ¼	+ 5
Itel pf		5954	......	27¾	20½	26¼	+ 5¼	+ 25
— J—J—J —								
JBRest	.24	20067	11	16¼	10⅜	14⅜	+ ¼	+ 1.8
Jackpot	t	26502	65	7⅛	2⅝	3⅞	— 2⅛	— 35.4
JackLfe		77449	6	32½	20	30	+ 6	+ 25
JamWtr		35685	21	27¾	12½	16¼	— 1¾	— 9.7
JefSmrf	.40a	34493	9	25¼	15	19	— 6¼	— 24.8
JefMart		59543	11	10¾	5¼	6⅝	— 3⅝	— 35.4
Jerico	.12	285871	12	18⅞	11⅞	17	— ¾	— 4.2
Jify s		109473	....	4	5-16	7-16	—3 1-16	— 87.5
JhnAm	.30a	18714	12	12⅛	7⅜	7⅝	— 2⅝	— 25.6
JonIcbl	t	13984	13	5⅞	3⅜	4	— 1	— 20
Jonel A	t	20361	12	5⅝	3	3⅝	— 1¼	— 25.6
Josphsn	.50	36386	......	16¾	6½	7	— 8¾	— 55.6
Juno		13242	11	23½	15¼	20½	+ 2	+ 10.8
Justin s	.30i	20264	7	16⅛	11	13⅞	— ⅝	— 4.3
— K—K—K —								
KLA s		103595	41	20¼	11½	16¾	— ½	— 2.9

KV Phr		16296	......	12¼	4¼	4⅝	— 4⅝	— 50
Kaman	.56	32927	9	24¾	18½	22¼	— ½	— 2.2
Karchr		71247	9	32½	13⅞	14¾	— 13¾	— 48.2
Kasler	.60t	34719	22	19	11¼	14½	— 2¼	— 13.4
Kaydon		36336	10	8¼	3½	6⅞	......	......
KelyJn		128624	....	14½	¾	1 7-16	—10 9-16	— 88
Kemp	1.80	55736	19	46¼	29¼	44	+ 4⅛	+ 10.3
KyCnLf	.80	21696	9	35	17¾	34½	+ 13½	+ 64.3
Kevex		25816	14	9¼	4½	5½	— 3½	— 38.9
KeyTrn		64234	8	24¼	7½	9½	— 13¾	— 59.1
KeyCm s		17802	......	15	5	6	— 6½	— 52
Kimbal	.54	11915	13	29½	19¾	29⅛	+ 7⅞	+ 37.1
Kimbrk		12230	50	11½	5½	6	— 2¾	— 31.4
Kincaid		14270	8	12¾	5½	7	— 5¼	— 42.9
Kinder s	.06	172471	22	17¼	9¾	15⅛	+ 1⅝	+ 12
viKoss		8765	......	4	11-16	11-16	—2 11-16	— 79.6
Kroy	.06	70982	11	28¼	8¾	11¾	— 15	— 56.1
Krugr s	.32	84416	13	14	7¼	13¼	+ 4¾	+ 55.9
Kulcke	.16	126009	14	29⅛	17¾	26	+ 2	+ 8.3
— L—L—L —								
LDBrnk		43558	5	12¼	7⅜	8⅜	— 2⅜	— 22.1
LJN		40629	6	16	5¾	6⅝	— 1½	— 18.5
LSI Log		254207	23	23¾	9¾	12½	— 7½	— 37.5
LTX		60369	18	21¾	14	19¼	+ 1¼	+ 6.9
LaPete s		38198	......	15¼	7	14¼	+ 4⅞	+ 52
LaZ By	1.04a	22342	7	48½	26½	34¼	— 12	— 25.9
LadFrn	.12a	43199	6	17¾	12⅜	13½	— 3⅜	— 20
Laidlw	.16	28286	16	13¾	9	12	+ 1	+ 9.1
LamaT	.80	13802	8	17⅛	10½	12¼	— 2¾	— 18.3
Lancast	.68	31658	10	20	13¾	15½	— 2½	— 13.9
LndBF	.60	84413	9	15¼	12⅝	13⅜	— ¾	— 5.3
LdmkS		15769	......	10½	3½	6⅛	......	......
LaneC	s.80a	22366	9	39⅝	29¾	39	+ ¾	+ 2
Langly	.25e	10442	11	9⅞	4⅝	6¼	— 3	— 32.4
Lawsn s	.28	36209	16	25¼	18¾	24¾	+ 1	+ 4.2
LeeDta		151426	7	22	5½	6¾	— 11½	— 63
Leiner		16749	15	14	10¼	13⅛	......	......
LewisP	.28b	19405	12	11½	7⅛	7⅛	— 2⅝	— 26.9
Lexicon		147727	....	5	2 1-16	2 15-16	—15-16	— 24.2
Lexidta		34427	156	8⅞	2⅞	3⅛	— 3¾	— 54.5
Liebrt	.07	54397	22	23½	15¼	21¼	+ ¼	+ 1.2
LfInvs	.24	3962	10	42¼	34⅞	42	+ 6¾	+ 19.2
LfeCom		54216	44	7¼	4¼	6⅛	......	......
LilyTul	.20	213585	12	17⅛	7⅛	13¾	......	......
LinBrd		219109	20	24¾	17	24⅜	+ 2¼	+ 10.2
LincTel	2.20	8507	7	29½	22¾	29½	+ 2	+ 7.3
Lindbrg	.16	6352	23	9⅜	4⅛	4⅝	— 4⅜	— 48.6
LizCla s		149864	14	26½	12⅜	25½	+ 8½	+ 50
LocalF		29580	12	22¾	11¾	14¼	— 4¾	— 25
LongF	1.28	17342	11	30½	20¼	21½	— 4¾	— 18.1
Lotus		424410	12	40	15¼	24	— 7	— 22.6
Lynden		6949	6	25¼	17	19¾	— 3½	— 15.1
Lypho s		48190	28	16	10¼	13⅞	+ 1¼	+ 9.9
— M—M—M —								
MCI		3589090	19	16¼	6	7½	— 6⅞	— 47.8
MIW		3396	23	5⅜	4	5⅛	+ ¼	+ 5.1
MPSI s		9525	29	17	5¾	6	— 11	— 64.7
MTS Sy	.32	8130	11	31	18½	23	— ½	— 2.1
MTV		104096	....	18½	13	18⅜		
Macrg s		16705	5	12⅝	5¾	10¼	+ 3¼	+ 46.4
MachTc		37603	13	11½	4⅞	6¼	— 4	— 39
MackTr		270751	18	21¾	12⅝	14⅛	— 7⅛	— 33.5
MadGE	2.20	10726	8	22⅞	18¾	22½	+ 2	+ 9.8
MagCtl		15554	17	15½	9⅜	11¼	— 2¾	— 19.6
MajRt		100483	17	11	7⅛	8⅛	+ ⅛	+ 1.6
Malrite	.01e	35565	50	13	7½	12	......	......
MgtSci		257318	27	30	8½	11½	— 16¾	— 59.3
Manitw	.80	32270	13	24½	17¼	18¾	— 2⅞	— 13.3
MfrsN	2	37030	6	45½	29⅛	44⅝	+ 7⅞	+ 21.4
Marcus	.28e	9205	10	15¼	11⅜	14⅛	+ ¼	+ 1.8
Margux		15745	......	9¾	5¾	6½	— 2½	— 27.8
Marqst	.05e	27346	15	10¼	6¼	7	— 2	— 22.2
MrldN	1.60	50237	8	44¼	29½	44	+ 9½	+ 27.5
Mscoln		33939	12	28	17¾	27¾	......	......
Masstor		218377	....	10½	2⅛	3⅞	— 4⅜	— 53
MathBx		23372	16	13	8⅜	10⅛	......	......
MatrxS	.10	16991	15	38¾	23¼	28	— 9¼	— 24.8
Maxcre		146371	44	29	11¾	25¼	+ 13¼	+ 110.4
Maxwel		15017	16	21¼	8¾	8¾	— 11¾	— 57.3
MayPt		149548	....	9	3⅞	4⅛	— 4⅞	— 54.2
MaynOl		28223	......	6¾	3½	3⅞	— 2⅞	— 42.6
McCrm	.88	109485	8	34¼	28¼	32	+ 1¾	+ 5.8
McFad		18824	13	12¼	9⅝	9⅞	— 1⅜	— 12.2
McFarl		40879	13	17½	11	12¼	— ⅜	— 3
Medex	.05	14777	15	13½	5⅝	6	— 6¾	— 52.9
MedCre		55149	......	17½	5⅜	5⅝	— 11⅜	— 66.9
MedclSt		19281	......	17¼	3⅜	14	+ 10⅝	+ 314.8

Medflx		28035	24	19½	12¼	15¾	+1½	+10.5
Megdt s		8190	9	7	4⅛	5½	-⅝	-10.2
Mentor		59704	26	16½	8¼	11¼	-2	-15.1
MentrG		137305	39	25¼	15⅝	18⅞	......	......
MercB	s1.92	15814	7	33	23⅝	33	+6¼	+23.4
MercBk	1.68	20577	9	44½	32	43¾	+9	+25.9
MrchCo		6330	......	14	8⅜	13¼	+⅜	+2.9
MerSv	.88	8991	7	23½	16	23	+5	+27.8
MrdBc	2.40	20505	8	40¾	28¼	39	+7¼	+22.8
MrdB pf	2.50	3182	......	30	21½	29⅜	......	......
MerrlB	1	4238	......	22¼	17	21½	+4½	+26.5
MeryG s		47416	5	22¼	11¼	11¾	-2½	-17.5
MetrAir		17996	15	11⅛	3⅝	10⅞	+6⅝	+155.9
MetSL	.60	13389	3	15⅜	8½	9⅞	-3⅛	-24
Micom		167135	19	47½	24⅝	29¼	-13¾	-32
MicrD		43313	31	10¼	3¼	3⅜	-5⅛	-60.3
MicrMk		17033	12	16⅞	9⅜	10¼	-6⅜	-38.3
Micrdy	.06	42112	13	10¾	4⅜	4⅞	-4⅜	-47.3
MicrTc		176912	22	40½	13¾	27¼	......	......
Microp		70144	20	13½	4	4⅞	-5½	-53
MicrSm		15480	9	6⅞	3⅞	4½	-1⅜	-23.4
MdPcA		29616	100	14½	4⅜	5	-7⅜	-59.6
MdStFd	.40	17694	12	26¾	17	18	-7	-28
MidBk	s1.12	47178	7	29⅜	21¼	29⅜	+5¾	+24.3
MdwAir		105764	....	12¼	3⅜	4	-7¾	-66
MillTch		7572	......	4⅞	1¼	1⅝	-2¾	-62.9
MillHr	.44	104504	17	36¼	20½	34⅝	+7¾	+28.8
Millicm		11552	......	12	3⅜	4	-5½	-57.9
Millipr	.44	174337	17	35⅜	25¾	35¼	+6¾	+23.7
Miniscr		117809	50	12½	2¾	3	-7⅞	-72.4
Minstr s		92363	18	19⅞	10½	19	+7¼	+61.7
Mischer		2852	6	14	10½	12¼	-½	-3.9
MGask	.01e	45598	18	18⅛	9⅜	15	+⅝	+4.4
MoblC A		14410	23	9	5⅜	7⅞	......	......
MoblC B		71773	24	9¾	5⅝	8	-⅞	-9.9
Modine	1.40	5575	5	36	24½	35¾	+7¼	+25.4
Moleclr		28628	363	16¼	6	7¼	-4¾	-39.6
Molex	.03	88861	15	42¾	26¼	29¼	-10⅛	-25.7
MonCa	1.40	74679	......	46	28⅞	44⅛	+9	+25.6
Moncor	.33i	43482	......	6¼	2¾	3	-2⅝	-46.7
MonfCl	.35e	8212	5	19¾	13½	18	+3¼	+22
MonAnt		14301	......	15½	8	8¾	-3¼	-27.1
Monolit		378804	10	30¾	12⅜	13⅞	-14½	-51.1
MonuC	1.30	11796	13	29⅛	21⅛	28⅛	+4⅜	+18.4
MorFlo	.01	14350	6	18⅜	10½	15⅜	-2⅝	-14.6
MorKg	.12e	8585	17	12¼	8	9⅞	-1⅜	-12.2
Morrsn	.48	94747	11	19⅛	13⅛	16⅞	-1¼	-6.9
Moseley		108178	95	7	4	4¾	-¼	-5
MotClb	.20	10776	4	20	12⅜	12¾	-1⅞	-12.8
Multmd	.60	75091	17	42½	29¾	36¾	-½	-1.3
Mylan s	.10i	173832	39	37⅜	8⅛	25⅜	+16⅝	+190
— N—N—N —								
NCA Cp		14556	18	15	5½	8	-6	-42.9
NMS		23444	......	4¼	2¼	2⅞	-½	-14.8
NapcoS		5634	12	14	7	12½	+3½	+38.9
NBnTex	.84	19830	10	27	19½	20¾	-1½	-6.7
NtCty s	1.90	88054	7	38¾	18⅝	38⅛	+17⅝	+86
NtCptr	.24	26165	16	21¼	14¾	21¼	+2¼	+11.8
NData	.44	165996	12	20⅜	6⅝	9¾	-10	-50.6
NHlthC	.30e	6789	16	23½	17½	20¾	+3¼	+18.6
NtLumb		15210	28	10¼	4½	5	-5¼	-51.2
NMicrn		153927	....	16½	3¼	4⅝	-11¼	-70.9
NTech	t	18788	......	7½	2¾	3⅛	-3⅝	-53.7
NatrBty		28187	26	9⅛	3⅛	4⅜	-4⅛	-48.5
Naugle		52703	......	20½	5½	5¾	-13¼	-69.7
Naug wt		7884	......	3¾	1⅜	1⅜	......	......
NelsnT	.20	18087	19	12¾	7½	7⅝	-3⅝	-32.2
Nelson		63204	......	20	6¼	8	-9¾	-54.9
NwkSec		46461	20	7⅞	4¾	7½	+⅝	+9.1
NetwkS		261815	36	29	15¾	22½	+1⅞	+9.1
NtwkEl		12601	......	8½	2¾	4	-2	-33.3
Neutrg s	.20	7351	33	38½	18¼	34	+13½	+65.9
NBrunS		24341	30	9⅜	6⅝	8	-⅜	-4.5
NE Bus	.48	18272	21	35	26½	31½	-3	-8.7
NHmpB	.80	14937	......	23½	15⅜	22⅞	+4⅞	+27.1
NJNat	s1.12	15035	9	23½	15	23½	+5⅞	+33.3
NYAirl		52048	37	7½	3¼	4¾	-2¾	-36.7
NY A wt		6199	......	2	⅛	3-16	-1 9-16	-89.3
NwldBk	.05i	14463	......	11½	7½	10¼	......	......
Newpt s	.06	61116	29	24¾	16¼	23¼	+2⅝	+12.7
NwpPh		108910	....	7⅝	2¾	5⅝	-⅝	-10
NiCal g	t	65782	......	8⅜	2⅝	3⅛	-3¼	-51
NickOG		32769	......	5⅛	⅜	⅝	-3¼	-83.9
Nike B	.40e	250208	12	16⅜	6⅝	7⅞	-6⅝	-45.7
Nordsn	.66	6022	13	19½	12	17½	+½	+2.9
Nordstr	.40	141346	16	38½	26½	31	-4¾	-13.3
Norsk B	.12e	37691	......	41¼	30½	37⅞	+3½	+10.2
Norstan		36469	27	10½	5½	5¾	-3¼	-36.1
NAtlIn s		33034	19	13½	6½	8	-4⅜	-35.4
NestSv		57095	......	12½	6¼	7¾	-2⅛	-21.5
NwNG	1.44	47834	9	16⅝	12¾	16⅜	+3	+22.4
NwtFn	1.16	15416	9	39⅞	28⅛	39	+8½	+27.9
NwNL s	.80	105396	11	29⅛	17⅜	28½	+11⅛	+64
NwstPS	2.10	7777	8	20⅝	16¼	20⅜	+2⅞	+16.4
Novmtx		16636	450	8¾	3⅛	4½	-3½	-43.8
Noxell	.92	62163	17	48½	31⅝	45⅜	+7⅝	+20.2
NuclPh		134915	35	11	5	5¼	-2	-27.6
Numrax		33562	49	15½	4¾	8¼	-5	-37.7
NutriF		40659	32	10½	4	9¼	......	......
NuMed		22971	10	12	8½	9¾	-½	-4.9
— O—O—O —								
OCG Tc		39792	......	7¼	2	2⅜	-3½	-59.6
OakHill		20955	5	7	3⅛	3⅜	-3⅛	-48.1
ObiRec		25835	......	8	2¼	2⅝	-4½	-63.2
Oceaner		44794	......	8⅞	3⅜	3⅝	-2⅝	-42
Ocilla s		26232	13	15¼	8½	14½	+3½	+31.8
OffsLog		20695	......	11	1⅞	1⅞	-8¾	-82.4
OgilM s	.92	60678	14	36¼	22⅜	35¾	+10⅛	+39.5
OhioBc	2.52	763	7	50¾	46	50¾	+3¾	+8
OhioCa	2.68	68346	19	49	34¾	46⅝	+1	+2.2
OldKnt s		22709	7	23¼	13¾	22½	+7¼	+47.5
OldRep	.88	36228	6	36½	28¾	30⅛	-6⅜	-17.5
OldS pfC	2.60	5434	......	21⅛	18¼	19⅞	......	......
OneBcp	.13e	43593	......	17	9½	16¾	......	......
OnLine		8614	......	18	3¾	4¼	-13¼	-75.7
Onyx		180237	....	11¼	1⅛	1⅜	-8⅛	-85.5
OpticC		46209	12	25	13½	16	-6	-27.3
OpticR		119791	25	39½	22½	30¼	+¼	+.8
Orbanc		13493	......	18	10½	14½	-2¼	-13.4
Orbit		86543	11	7⅞	5⅛	6	-1¼	-17.2
OrfaCp		13891	......	8¼	3¾	5¼	......	......
Oshmn	.20	29200	12	23½	14	16⅞	-6¾	-28.6
OttrTP	2.68	13842	7	28⅜	23	27⅞	+3⅛	+12.6
OvrExp		21510	6	26½	9¼	10¾	-11¾	-52.2
OwenM	.36	13845	9	16	11¼	12½	-2¾	-18
Oxoco		56091	4	9⅛	3⅜	3½	-4¾	-57.6
— P—Q —								
PLM	.12	7776	5	9½	5¼	6	-3¼	-35.1
PNC	2.32	79645	8	46⅞	36⅛	46¼	+3⅜	+7.9
PabstB		155449	....	11	5½	10	+1⅝	+19.4
Paccar	1.20a	42554	7	60	38½	44⅝	-13⅛	-22.7
PacFst		61004	......	12¼	7	8⅜	-1⅛	-11.8
PacTel	.80	21866	15	20¼	10	14½	-5¾	-28.4
PacoPh		39641	15	23⅝	12⅞	13¼	-5	-27.4
PancMx	.13	13192	14	8¼	5⅞	7¾	+½	+6.9
Pansph		85455	12	21⅛	10⅝	14⅛	-7	-33.1
Parisan		12797	11	16¼	9½	9½	-6¾	-41.5
ParkOh	.60	30574	......	20¼	12¾	14¼	-½	-3.4
PatntM		33126	......	6⅛	4	4¾	......	......
Patrkl		40433	26	12¼	5⅜	7⅜	-2	-21.3
PaulHr		21593	9	19½	11⅜	13	-3⅜	-20.6
PaulPt		18418	46	16⅝	5½	6⅞	-9½	-58
PayN	.60	275562	15	26⅞	14⅜	22½	-3⅜	-13
Paychx		27724	23	12¼	7½	9⅜	-2⅝	-21.9
PeakHC		77833	20	25½	9¾	13⅛	+2¼	+20.7
PearlH		145079	15	24⅜	15⅛	22¾	+2⅞	+14.5
PegGld	.06r	79742	......	14¼	5⅞	6¾	-6⅜	-48.6
PenaEn	2	10272	5	26½	16	26	+7⅝	+41.5
Pentar	.76	33373	8	29⅛	21¾	28⅞	-⅛	-.4
PeopEx		300733	19	22⅝	7⅝	10⅛	-10¾	-51.5
PeopRt		194803	2	8¼	¼	⅜	-7	-94.9
Percept		9351	......	15	6¼	7¼	-6½	-47.3
PersCpt		23400	67	10⅛	4¾	8	+⅝	+8.5
Petrlte	1.12	36547	13	32½	24½	26¼	-2	-7.1
Phrmct		48773	......	22	4	6	-11	-64.7
PSFS		575699	4	12⅛	6⅞	8⅝	-2⅝	-23.3
PhilGl	.48r	686113	....	17⅜	12¾	15⅝	+1¼	+8.7
PhnxAm		22136	3	12¼	2¾	3	-9¼	-75.5
PicSav		316276	16	24⅛	14⅜	19⅞	......	......
PicCafe	.60	40311	11	24⅜	13⅜	18⅝	+5¼	+39.3
PionHi	.92	120420	15	33½	23¼	32	+2	+6.7
PionSt s	.12	19461	5	13½	7½	7½	-4⅞	-39.4
PoFolk		23155	16	16⅝	8¾	10	-3⅜	-25.2
PlcyMg		116404	35	31	22	27¾	-¼	-.9
Porex		65600	29	29	17⅜	24	+3¼	+15.7
PosiSl		13269	......	7⅞	3⅝	7¾	+2⅞	+59
Powell		21233	19	4⅝	1¾	1⅞	-2	-51.6
Powrtc		14413	15	22	12¾	15¾	......	......
PwConv		20941	40	8⅞	5¼	7¼	-1⅝	-18.3
PrecCst	.16	19171	20	33⅝	19¾	32	+6¾	+26.7
PrpdLg		9533	68	9½	4¼	6¾	......	......
Preway	.38i	47790	......	11¾	2⅞	3⅛	-6⅝	-67.9
Priam		146429	13	11¾	3⅞	4¾	-6	-55.8
PricCm		15294	......	15⅛	5⅛	15	+9⅞	+192.7

PricCo s		162023	33	48¾	23¾	41¾	+	9⅜	+	29
Prtronx		33015	7	29	12½	14	—	13	—	48.1
ProdOp	.16	49919	14	7⅞	4⅜	4¾	—	2	—	29.6
ProgCp	.16	17345	11	37¾	29¾	34½	—	2¼	—	6.1
ProptTr	1.20	15648	15	14½	11¾	14	+	¾	+	5.7
Protcol		22029	......	10¾	1⅝	2	—	6	—	75
ProvIn		37218	......	17¾	12⅜	15	+	2⅛	+	16.5
PullTrn		114006	16	5 11-16	2 13-16	4¼	—	5-16	—	6.8
PurtBn	.40	23208	28	27	12⅝	14¾	—	9¾	—	39.8
QMS s		79377	......	16⅝	7¼	13¼	+	3⅜	+	34.2
Quadrx		74965	......	7⅞	3⅛	4⅛	—	2¾	—	40
QuakrC	.68	6460	11	28½	20¼	25½	—	2	—	7.3
QualCre		59302	39	12¼	7	11⅝	+	2⅜	+	25.7
QualSy		25711	83	17½	1¾	2½	—	12⅛	—	82.9
Quantm		104742	13	23½	15¼	21	+	2¼	+	12
QuestM		70761	......	7¼	2¾	3⅛	—	3⅞	—	55.4
Quixote		28808	13	15¼	8¼	10½	—	3	—	22.2
Quotrn		676734	10	22½	7¼	8	—	12¼	—	60.5
— R—R—R —										
RAX		23260	15	18¾	8¾	10½	—	7¼	—	40.8
RPM s		50789	14	14	9¾	13¾	+	1	+	7.8
RadSys		63531	14	18¾	9¼	14	—	4	—	22.2
RadtnT		39187	52	17¾	6¾	7¾	—	4½	—	36.7
Radice		46875	7	11	6¼	8¾	—	1⅞	—	17.6
Radion		9430	17	11¼	7	10¼	....		....	
Ragen		46861	......	7¼	2⅝	5⅞	....		....	
Rainr	1.76	60434	8	49⅝	34¼	47⅞	+	8¾	+	22.4
Ramtek		39030	......	12¼	3½	4⅞	—	5⅞	—	54.7
RayEn	.24	15659	7	17½	11¾	13½	—	1¼	—	8.5
Readng		22575	......	22¾	13½	19¾	+	3⅜	+	20.6
Recotn		19954	9	10⅞	5½	5⅝	—	4¾	—	45.8
RedknL	.64	14113	9	35¾	26⅞	28½	—	½	—	1.7
Reeves		118900	....	12¾	3¾	5½	—	5½	—	50
RgcyEl	.20	125629	66	14	5⅝	6⅝	—	4⅞	—	42.4
Regis s	.09	20160	17	20½	11	13	—	⅜	—	2.8
Rehab		55629	33	23½	10¾	22⅝	+	9⅝	+	74
Reliab		32488	9	15¼	8⅞	9¾	—	5¼	—	35
Renal		12379	22	10¾	3⅞	4⅛	—	5⅝	—	57.7
RpAuto	.44	13265	17	10⅜	7¼	8⅛	—	2¼	—	21.7
RpHlth		76719	7	17	9⅞	11¼	—	2½	—	18.2
RestrSy		7569	15	14½	9	12¾	+	3½	+	37.8
Reuterl	.15e	20668	12	14	9½	11	—	⅞	—	7.4
ReutrH	.09e	109224	8	21¼	16½	20¼	....		....	
Rexon		29895	......	13⅜	3⅝	4	—	7¾	—	66
ReyRey	1.24	38106	9	40¼	25¾	33	—	6¾	—	17
Rhodes	s .20	33999	9	12¼	7⅝	12⅛	+	⅞	+	7.8
Ribilm		28476	......	12	6	8¼	—	¼	—	2.9
RichEl		8482	17	22½	15⅞	20¾	+	4	+	23.9
Ritzys		23762	......	9	1⅞	2	—	6¾	—	77.1
Rival	.80	38411	37	12¾	9⅝	11⅞	+	1¼	+	11.8
RoadS s	1	203103	12	35¼	23½	30½	—	3⅞	—	11.3
Robesn	t	21175	......	10⅛	5¾	6	—	3	—	33.3
RobNug	.06	16480	11	20	11¼	13¾	—	5½	—	28.6
RobVsn		37211	......	13¾	5⅞	9½	+	⅝	+	7
Rockor		67050	20	15⅛	8⅛	14¾	+	1⅞	+	14.6
RosesSt	.28a	3234	8	24	14	17½	—	1½	—	7.9
RoseSB	.28a	27821	9	26½	15	19¾	—	2¾	—	12.2
Rouse	.92	42491	13	37¾	28¾	34	+	2¼	+	7.1
RoyBGp		6492	......	6⅝	1½	1¾	—	3½	—	66.7
RoyInt		39787	16	18½	11¼	18	+	5½	+	44
RoyPlm		23261	......	9¾	5¾	8½	....		....	
RoylRs		19695	11	13⅜	7⅜	7¾	—	4⅛	—	34.7
RoylAir		8362	8	8½	5	7½	+	1¼	+	20
RustPel		19495	16	18⅜	11¼	13¾	—	¼	—	1.8
RyanFa		36734	27	23¾	15½	18½	—	4¾	—	20.4
— S—S—S —										
SAY Ind		20579	20	11¼	7¾	9	....		....	
SCI Sy		187896	15	25½	10¾	14	—	8½	—	37.8
SEI		49872	21	27	10½	14¼	—	11¼	—	44.1
SFE	.10r	30060	13	21½	7	7¾	—	13¼	—	63.1
SP Drug	t	16100	14	14¾	7⅝	14¾	+	3½	+	31.1
SRI	.68	56043	16	20	12¼	17¾	+	1¾	+	10.9
Safecrd		55317	22	13⅞	5⅝	13⅛	—	⅛	—	.9
Safeco	1.50	163655	8	35¼	26¾	33	+	5⅜	+	19.5
SafHlth		22588	32	17¾	7	15½	+	2½	+	19.2
StJude		57442	8	19¼	7¾	8¾	—	10½	—	54.5
StPaul	3	304891	....	67¾	38	53⅝	—	6⅞	—	11.4
SalCpt		48305	11	6	1⅞	3¼	—	2⅝	—	44.7
SanBar	.05r	12166	......	11¼	4¼	7	+	½	+	7.7
SandChf		8303	13	12⅛	6¾	7¼	—	1¾	—	19.4
Satelco		14791	......	6	⅝	¾	—	5¼	—	87.5
SatelSy	.12	6154	9	10¼	5¾	6¼	—	2½	—	28.6
SavnF	1.60a	8239	11	45	32¾	35¾	—	3½	—	8.9
SvBkPS	.72	20656	7	28½	18¼	27¾	+	5¾	+	26.1
ScanOp		40527	11	12½	6¼	7⅛	—	2⅞	—	28.8
ScanTr		16977	19	18¾	8¼	12¼	—	4¾	—	27.9
Scherer	.32	45463	20	17⅝	8⅝	10	—	6⅝	—	39.8
SchlmA	.36	10602	8	18½	15	16⅜	—	⅞	—	5.1
Scimed		10259	67	12½	5	8	—	4	—	33.3
SciCmp	.28	9636	7	12	4½	5	—	7	—	58.3
SciInc s		2946	13	7⅞	4¼	7¾	....		....	
SciMic		24386	5	8⅞	3¾	3¾	....		....	
SciSft		30698	14	23¼	9¼	10½	—	11½	—	52.3
SciSySv		30266	19	12	2¾	4	—	7¾	—	66
Scitex		37038	14	24	14	15¾	—	5½	—	25.9
SeaGal		70862	12	11¼	7⅛	7⅜	—	1⅜	—	15.7
Seagate		1072571	7	17	4	5	—	8⅞	—	64
SecTag		24205	......	8⅛	2⅛	2¼	—	5¾	—	71.9
SEEQ		94187	......	14	4¼	5¾	—	5⅞	—	50.5
Seibel	.80	55407	......	30¾	17¾	19¾	—	1¾	—	8.1
Semicn		13495	5	13	7¾	8⅛	—	4⅞	—	37.5
Sensor	.05	579624	22	24½	5⅝	7⅝	—	15⅞	—	67.6
SvcMer	.08	518829	8	16⅝	10⅝	11⅞	—	4¼	—	26.4
Svmast	1.12	94468	20	36½	26¾	27¼	—	5½	—	16.8
Servico	t	11346	6	22 5-16	12¼	15	+	¾	+	5.3
SvcFrct		23041	7	11⅜	4⅝	5½	—	2¼	—	29
SevOak	.16	71683	12	17¼	11⅝	13⅝	—	1½	—	9.9
ShrMed	.48	250563	21	34⅝	21¼	27	—	6¼	—	18.8
Shwmt	s1.68	72315	7	34⅝	22½	30⅞	+	2⅝	+	9.3
Shelby	.16	42936	17	18	11⅞	17	+	4¾	+	38.8
Sheldhl		37957	9	19¼	9½	15	....		....	
Shoney	.16	119817	22	35⅛	20	31⅞	+	8⅜	+	35.6
ShonSo s		20940	11	16¾	11	13⅜	—	1⅝	—	10.8
Shpsmt	.10e	7641	10	12¼	4¾	4¾	—	6¾	—	58.7
Silicon		79264	9	15	6¼	7¼	—	6¾	—	48.2
SiliconS		74692	15	27	9½	12	—	5¼	—	30.4
SilicVal		31841	12	29¼	13	14¾	—	10¾	—	42.2
Silicnx		36641	11	18¾	11⅝	13½	—	2¼	—	14.3
Siltec		46604	17	17½	6¾	9	—	8½	—	48.6
SimpIn	.80	22552	10	16½	11¼	13⅜	—	2⅜	—	15.1
SippIn		26936	11	17⅜	10½	15¼	—	¾	—	4.7
SisCp		3801	413	9¼	3¼	4⅛	—	4⅜	—	51.5
Sizzler		43649	11	18¾	8¾	15	+	2½	+	20
Skipper	.06	17633	12	11¾	8	10⅛	+	⅝	+	6.6
SloanTc		5929	11	8¼	2⅝	4	—	3¾	—	48.4
SmithL		107107	8	11	2⅞	3⅜	—	6⅞	—	67.1
SmithF		5273	7	9½	6⅛	7⅝	—	1	—	11.6
Society	1.70	27601	7	36½	28½	36	+	6¼	+	21
SoctySv		80841	......	13½	8⅞	11¾	....		....	
Softech		31315	40	15¾	5¼	7¼	—	7¾	—	51.7
SoftwA		48488	14	16½	9¼	16	+	3⅝	+	29.3
SonocP	1.20a	20375	......	46½	37½	39¼	—	4¾	—	10.8
SonrFd		27079	14	34¾	16	16½	—	17½	—	51.5
SoBost	.40	42089	6	24⅛	14	23¾	+	7¾	+	48.4
SoHosp		28999	11	5¼	3½	4	—	½	—	11.1
SthdFn	.52	226830	....	38⅜	19½	31¼	+	4¼	+	15.7
Soutrst	.88	18125	15	23¼	14¾	22¾	+	6⅜	+	38.9
Sovrgn	.10	98596	13	9⅝	5¼	8⅜	....		....	
Sovran	1.68	95428	9	38⅞	25¼	38⅝	+	1⅞	+	5.1
SpcMic		11916	......	5⅝	1¾	2⅛	—	3½	—	62.2
SpanA	.05e	6496	12	8¼	3	3⅛	—	4⅜	—	58.3
Specd s		74535	15	16⅛	8½	11	—	4⅛	—	27.3
Spctran		17644	......	13	5½	12	+	4¼	+	54.8
SpecCtl	.05	21202	14	10⅞	5½	5½	—	4⅛	—	42.9
SpertiD		10351	......	9¾	1⅞	3¾	+	1⅛	+	42.9
Spire		24012	113	14¾	8¾	14¾	+	5⅝	+	61.6
StafBld	.20	27741	15	10½	5⅜	5⅞	—	2½	—	29.9
Standy s	1	21529	6	25¼	19⅜	21¾	+	2	+	10.1
StdMic		163210	103	25⅛	16	18½	—	6⅝	—	26.4
StdReg	1.16	10006	13	44¼	29¼	44¼	+	12¾	+	40.5
Standun		12231	......	10¾	4⅝	4¾	—	4½	—	48.6
Stanho	s1.20	9238	9	23¼	17	20½	+	2¾	+	15.5
StarSr s		37701	......	19¾	1⅛	9	+	7⅞	+	700
StaStB	1.06	54760	8	46¼	28¼	46	+	17	+	58.6
StateG	.15b	35358	7	10	4¾	5	—	3⅛	—	38.5
Steiger		29002	13	11¾	6	6¼	—	4⅜	—	41.2
SternrL		5833	13	5¾	3⅞	4¼	—	1⅛	—	20.9
StewStv		19880	27	15⅝	9⅝	11⅞	—	3⅜	—	22.1
StwInf	.72	15877	9	29	16¾	22¾	—	6¾	—	22.9
Stifel		26835	123	8⅞	5	6⅛	—	2⅛	—	25.8
StockSy		16424	18	9½	5¾	9	....		....	
Stratus		102648	53	14	7¾	9½	—	2	—	17.4
StrwC	s .90b	21622	11	57	31½	51	+	17	+	50
Stryker		21339	18	30¼	18¾	24½	—	3¼	—	11.7
StuartH	.05	8574	14	7⅛	3⅛	3⅜	—	1⅜	—	28.9
Subaru	1.68	35921	12	120½	72¾	114½	+	30¼	+	35.9
SubrB	1.84	23967	8	43⅝	31⅝	43¼	+	9⅜	+	27.7
Summa		89026	......	8	2½	2¾	—	4	—	59.3
SumtHl	.09e	81692	16	9	6	7⅞	+	1⅜	+	21.2
SunCst		37610	......	5½	1¼	1⅜	—	2⅝	—	65.6
SunMed		7983	15	16¼	6½	6½	—	7	—	51.9
SunSL	t	116735	2	26	8¼	10	—	12⅞	—	56.3
SupRte	.12e	18704	17	16¼	11¼	15¾	+	1½	+	10.5
SupSky		5365	24	14	7½	8¾	—	4⅜	—	33.3

Suprtex		30177	200	11	3½	4	— 3¾	— 48.4
SuprEq		9984	......	10⅝	5	10⅛	+ 2⅜	+ 30.7
Sykes		143227	....	5¼	1	1⅜	— 2⅞	— 67.6
SymbT		28261	......	12¼	6	9⅜	— ½	— 5.1
Syncor		18451	150	7¾	2½	3	— 2¼	— 42.9
Syntech		41492	......	12	6¼	8¾	— ⅝	— 6.7
Syntrex		57988	12	10¼	3¾	3¾	— 5¼	— 58.3
Syscon	.24	11954	10	19¼	11½	13⅛	— 4⅞	— 27.1
SyAsoc		26998	15	25⅜	14¼	15¾	— 7¼	— 31.5
Systln		44701	......	18	3½	7	— 8½	— 54.8
Syslntg		17769	12	11½	6¾	7¼	— 3	— 29.3
SystGn		14265	12	10½	6¾	7⅛	— 2⅝	— 26.9
Systmt	.04i	34823	30	22	12	16⅜	— 4⅝	— 22
SCT Cp		95773	21	29½	14	15¾	— 11½	— 42.2
— T—T—T —								
TBC		20348	10	11½	8½	11	+ ½	+ 4.8
TCA Cb	.12	10645	26	15¼	11	14	+ 1⅜	+ 10.9
TacViv		6712	16	9⅞	7	8	— 1¼	— 13.5
Tandem		997956	19	40¼	13	19½	— 15⅝	— 44.5
Tandon		1346541	10	20⅜	4⅝	6	— 14	— 70
TcCom		10763	9	19¼	5⅞	6	— 12½	— 67.6
Telco		38736	79	19	9¼	18¼	....	....
TlcmA	t	226182	57	24¾	15½	23¼	+ 3	+ 14.8
TelPlus		231851	....	11⅝	6¾	9⅞	....	....
Telcrft		17152	......	6	2¼	5	+ 1¾	+ 53.9
Telecrd	.28	65162	20	25½	15¾	21	— 1¼	— 5.6
Telepict		55334	14	17⅝	11½	16⅝	+ 2⅛	+ 14.7
Telvid		255070	30	16¾	2½	3¼	— 12⅝	— 79.5
Telabs		130041	14	28	13	15¼	— 9½	— 38.4
Telxon	.01e	42388	15	17½	8	15	+ 4¼	+ 39.5
Temco		16103	15	8⅛	4	4	— ¾	— 15.8
TndrLv		4270	......	8	3¾	4	— 3¾	— 48.4
TermD s		11204	14	14¼	9¾	10½	— 2¾	— 20.8
Tesdata		10161	......	9¼	2	2⅛	— 7	— 76.7
TexFdl		21220	8	43¾	16½	43¾	+ 26⅞	+ 159.3
Texon		37504	......	6½	1	1⅜	— 3⅝	— 72.5
Textne	.25e	13096	8	19¾	9¾	12	— 7⅛	— 37.3
TherPr		29941	24	15⅜	7⅞	13⅝	+ 2¾	+ 25.3
Thrmdc		11719	......	13	7½	10¾	+ 1	+ 10.3
Thetfd		7334	5	15	6¾	7¼	— 6⅜	— 46.8
ThdN s	1.08	15161	8	33½	21⅛	33⅛	+ 8⅜	+ 33.8
Thorln		14183	7	12	7½	10¼	....	....
Thortec		26657	......	10⅜	3½	8	+ 3	+ 60
ThouT s		218312	9	29½	12⅞	15	— ¼	— 1.6
3 Com		78833	25	10⅛	5½	7	....	....
TimeE s		28659	18	18½	10	11¼	— 3½	— 23.7
TmeFib		47228	......	13⅜	6½	10¾	— 2	— 15.7
Tiprary	t	42100	131	6⅞	1 3-16	1 5-16	—3 15-16	— 75
Tofu s		55570	80	18	3¾	13⅝	+ 9⅞	+ 263.3
TotlSy s		6113	25	14¼	9⅝	13¼	+ 2⅞	+ 27.7
TrakAu		30928	17	19¾	10	11¼	— 8¼	— 42.3
TriadSy		62301	15	16½	8¼	10	— 5¼	— 34.4
TribCm		16546	......	5¾	2⅛	2½	....	....
TrusJo	.36	7566	15	34	20	26¼	— 5	— 16
TBkGa s	1	34202	9	33¼	22¾	31⅝	+ ½	+ 1.6
TuckDr		17510	......	9⅞	4⅞	5½	— 4	— 42.1
TwnCty		22626	......	8	1	1¼	— 6½	— 83.9
TysonF	.08	24726	15	36	14¾	36	+ 19½	+ 118.2
— U—U—U —								
USLICO	1.20	10990	......	29¾	23	28⅜	+ 5⅜	+ 23.4
UTL		45154	21	21¾	12¾	18	— ½	— 2.7
Ultrsy	.06e	191105	11	21½	8⅞	10	— 7	— 41.2
Ungmn		164630	49	16¾	10¼	15¾	+ 2¾	+ 21.2
Unifi		78885	12	19	7¾	8⅜	— 8⅞	— 51.4
vjUnioil		136292	4	11⅛	⅝	15-16	—9 3-16	— 90.7
UnPlntr	.45j	40042	......	26½	14¼	18	— ¼	— 1.4
UnTrBc	2.40	5587	7	50¼	34½	49¾	+ 10½	+ 26.8
UACom	.12	60766	18	28½	17	27⅝	+ 6⅛	+ 28.5
UBAlsk	.10e	9954	16	11⅛	7	10¼	+ 1½	+ 17.1
UBCol	1.08	46384	8	23½	16⅞	22⅞	+ 5¼	+ 29.8
UnEdS		7685	13	11½	1¾	2⅜	— 7⅝	— 76.3
UFnGrp		39540	53	10	5⅜	10	+ 2¾	+ 37.9
UFstFd		89681	15	24	11⅝	12⅜	— 3½	— 22
UGrdn	t	21812	......	15¼	6¼	15¼	+ 6¼	+ 69.4
UPresd		18151	20	14	7¼	9¾	— 1⅜	— 12.4
US Ant		30924	......	7⅜	2¾	2⅞	— 2⅝	— 47.7
US Bcp	1	87957	8	25⅜	15½	25⅛	+ 4⅜	+ 21.1
US Cap		20269	4	12¼	2⅛	2½	— 8¾	— 77.8
US Dsgn		27800	......	7⅝	4¼	5⅜	— ⅝	— 10.4
US Ht s		184452	31	35½	11⅛	33	+ 19¼	+ 140
US Sh n	.06e	17669	18	6	3½	3⅝	— 2⅛	— 37
US Sur		112273	147	17½	10⅜	16⅛	+ 1	+ 6.6
USTrk	1.20	28902	26	12½	10	11¼	— ¾	— 6.3
US Tr	1.60	39278	9	47¼	36¾	45	+ 7¾	+ 20.8
UStatn s	.20	55331	25	28¾	13½	24¾	+ 11¼	+ 83.3
UnTelev		51308	230	18⅛	11¾	16⅛	+ 2⅜	+ 17.3
UVaBs	1.44	24073	8	34⅞	24⅞	34¾	+ 3⅝	+ 11.7
UnvFrn		27747	9	19½	11¼	14¼	— 3¼	— 18.6
UnvHlt		134374	13	15¼	9	10	— 1½	— 13
UnvHld		11778	......	6⅛	2¾	4¼	— 1½	— 26.1
UFSBk		10493	......	11¼	5½	8½	— 2¼	— 20.9
UrgeCr		44978	......	10¾	4⅛	5⅛	— 5⅛	— 50
Uscafe	.07e	17061	9	5	2¾	3½	— ⅞	— 20
— V—V—V —								
VLI		122332	....	20½	4½	6	— 12¾	— 68
VLSI		93418	28	17¼	8¼	8¼	— 4¾	— 36.5
VMX		82181	23	12⅝	6¾	9⅛	+ ⅛	+ 1.4
VSE	.15e	6270	6	11	6½	7¾	— 1¼	— 13.9
ValidLg		173434	33	17⅝	9⅞	12	— ⅝	— 5
ValFSL		30630	......	17⅝	7¼	8¾	— 7⅝	— 46.6
ValNtl	1.20	150014	9	29½	20½	29	+ 4⅛	+ 16.6
ValLn	.40e	66337	19	40	23⅛	24¼	— 10	— 29.2
VanDus	.40	32422	12	17	11¼	13¼	— 1½	— 10.2
Vanzeti		16117	44	15½	8	9¼	— 2¼	— 19.6
VectrG		56277	......	2½	⅛	3-16	—1 13-16	— 90.6
Ventrex		93764	......	11¾	3¼	3¾	— 4¾	— 55.9
Veta		99550	......	3⅛	¼	5-16	—2 9-16	— 89.1
ViconF		6624	......	6¼	2⅞	3	— 3¼	— 52
Vicorp	.12e	71313	12	21¾	13¼	15⅞	— 4⅞	— 23.5
VictraS		81618	......	8¼	2⅛	2⅝	— 5	— 65.6
VideoCp		24705	9	20⅛	10¼	19⅝	+ 9¼	+ 89.2
Vie deFr	.22e	32095	20	15¼	10½	12	....	....
Viking		29006	18	16¾	9¾	11	— 3¼	— 22.8
Viratek		14106	......	19¾	7¾	17¾	+ 7¼	+ 69.1
VisTech		63667	7	21	2¼	2⅝	— 14⅝	— 84.8
Vodavi		45255	......	13⅝	6¾	7⅛	— 3	— 29.6
Voltlnf		52613	9	27¾	15¼	17¼	— 5¼	— 23.3
Volvo		1031	......	26¼	23½	23½	....	....
— W—W—W —								
WD 40	.88	29194	16	24½	18½	21¼	+ 2½	+ 13.3
WalbrC	.48	6678	8	24	13¾	21	+ 7	+ 50
WlkrTel		37920	25	9	4⅝	8⅞	+ 1	+ 12.7
WshE	1.68	59774	9	20¼	13½	19½	+ 4	+ 25.8
WFSL s	.70t	42109	6	29¾	14½	29¾	+ 9½	+ 46.9
WMSB		46819	......	14⅛	7¾	11⅝	— 1⅝	— 12.3
Wavetk		89099	45	16¼	5⅝	6¾	— 6¾	— 50
Webb s	.36	21121	13	13⅜	8⅝	12¾	+ 2½	+ 24.4
WestFn		23615	4	9½	6	9½	....	....
WnCasS	2.84	31281	......	50¾	36½	46	— ¼	— .5
WstFSL		44468	8	11	5¼	6¼	....	....
WMicTc		25285	8	14¾	7¾	8⅞	— 2⅝	— 22.8
WMicr		11524	35	7¼	3¾	6	— 1¼	— 17.2
WtTIA s		19447	......	14	5½	12¾	....	....
WmorC	.40	41260	8	27½	16¼	17¾	— 6¼	— 26
WstwdO		20694	23	21	13¾	18¾	....	....
WstwdC		21189	30	14¼	9	14¼	....	....
Wettra	.88	93899	11	26	16⅛	25	+ 6⅛	+ 32.5
Wicat		93102	......	5	1⅞	3⅝	— 1⅜	— 27.5
Widcom		55032	......	13¾	4⅜	7¾	— 3¼	— 29.5
Willmt	1.50	61572	11	39¼	23¼	35	— 1¾	— 4.8
WillAL		70338	......	14	7¾	8⅝	— 3⅞	— 31
WmsSn		16875	175	14¾	8¾	10½	— 3¼	— 23.6
WilsnF		100934	....	12¼	6⅝	9¼	+ ½	+ 5.7
WilsnH	.20	33182	14	19	10⅜	12	— 6¾	— 36
Windmr	.07	104737	7	10⅜	4⅞	5⅛	— 3⅝	— 41.4
WinnEn		16829	......	7⅝	2½	2¾	— 3⅜	— 55.1
WiserO	.88	22364	15	26	17	19½	— 3¼	— 14.3
WoodD	.60	22995	13	21¾	12½	18¼	+ 4⅜	+ 31.5
Worthg	.56	57465	12	28⅜	18	23	— 5⅜	— 18.9
Writer	.15e	19024	8	12¼	6⅝	7½	— 4¼	— 36.2
Wyman	.80	50816	11	32½	24	24¼	— 6	— 19.8
— X—Y—Z —								
Xebec		167470	5	20⅛	3½	4¼	— 13½	— 76.1
Xicor		142533	....	19¾	8⅛	9¼	— 6½	— 41.3
Xidex		276470	11	21½	10¾	12½	— 9	— 41.9
YlowFt	1	184142	10	45⅝	23¼	32	— 11	— 25.6
ZenLbB		46936	35	20	12	19½	+ 6½	+ 50
Zentec		28233	......	9½	2¼	2¾	— 6¼	— 69.4
Ziegler	.48a	10990	9	15	9½	11¾	— 2	— 14.5
ZionUt	1.24	11284	8	34¾	27¾	31¼	— 3¼	— 9.4
Zitel		22659	16	11	4¼	4¾	— 5½	— 53.7
Ziyad		23896	12	12¾	6¼	6⅞	— 5⅛	— 42.7
Zondvn	.34	39723	11	18½	6½	9¼	— 7⅞	— 46
Zymos		51284	......	6¾	¾	1 7-16	—5 1-16	— 77.9
Zytrex		102317	....	7¾	1½	1 15-16	—3 3-16	— 62.2

OVER-THE-COUNTER QUOTATIONS NASDAQ

NATIONAL LIST DECEMBER 31, 1984

NEW YORK (AP) Over the Counter trading for 1984. The net change and percentage change is from the previous year on issues listed prior to Jan. 1, 1984.

		Sales (hds)	High	Low	Last	Net Chg.	Pct. Chg.
— A—A—A —							
A M Fd		12582	9¼	3⅜	3¾	— 3½	— 48.3
AA Imp		4536	6	2¼	2¾	— 2½	— 47.6
ABS h	.40	3517	6¾	4½	6½	+ 2	+ 44.4
AEC s	.24i	5094	14¾	10⅛	12	+ 1⅞	+ 18.5
AFP		18994	6⅛	2⅜	2⅞	— 2	— 41
AMCbl		15277	5⅜	1⅞	2⅝	— 2⅜	— 47.5
AST		15202	9⅛	7	9⅛	......	......
AT&E		12410	11	2½	6	— 3	— 33.3
AVM Cp		4425	8	6	7⅝	+ ⅜	+ 5.2
Abrams	.32b	951	10	8½	10	+ ½	+ 5.3
AcapRs		9805	6⅛	3½	3⅞	— 1⅞	— 32.6
Aceto	t	2445	24	17¾	24	+ 4¼	+ 21.5
ACMAT		2302	13	6½	6¾	— 6	— 47.1
AcmeG	.20a	2158	13⅝	9¼	12	+ 1	+ 9.1
AcroEn		7054	9	2¼	2¼	— 6¾	— 75
Acro un		2938	10¾	2¼	2¼	— 8½	— 79.1
Actvsn		121788	4¾	⅞	1	— 3⅛	— 75.8
Actmed		18720	24¼	14½	20¼	+ 2¾	+ 15.7
AdisnW	.70	5950	33	21¼	32	+ 8½	+ 36.2
Adia	.03e	16938	15¼	12½	15¼	......	......
AdvRos		13102	6¾	4½	6	— ⅝	— 9.4
AdCpt		4163	4½	2	2¼	— 1¼	— 35.7
AdvGen		13054	11½	2¼	4¼	— 7¼	— 63
AdvSem		29761	38	14¾	17	— 17½	— 50.7
AdvTel		10604	8¼	2¾	4¾	— 3½	— 42.4
AdvtLds		1888	3¼	1⅞	2½	+ ½	+ 25
AerSvc		12805	3⅞	1⅝	1¾	— ¾	— 30
AerSys		45415	4⅜	1¾	1⅞	— 1⅞	— 50
AflBcp	1	1598	26½	18½	19	— 3	— 13.6
Agnico g	.15	39587	16	7¾	9	— 4¾	— 34.5
AidAut		1673	4½	2	3¾	+ 1⅛	+ 42.9
Aigueb		2239	7½	4	4¾	— 2½	— 34.5
AlamoS	.60	8883	24½	7	11	— 3	— 21.4
Alanco		46918	1	¼	5-16	— 9-16	— 64.3
AlskAp		36594	2 3-16	⅝	⅝	— 9-16	— 47.4
AlskBc		4035	6⅜	4	5⅞	+ ⅞	+ 17.5
AlskNt		9374	15½	9½	14¾	......	......
Alaten	2.20	10441	43¼	27	41	+ 13	+ 46.4
Alcan wt		71	10⅛	6¼	6½	......	......
AlexEn		12238	4¼	2½	3	......	......
Alicoln	.30a	1237	58½	50	51	......	......
AllSea s		23054	16¾	4⅛	8¼	......	......
AlenOrg	.48a	691	48½	43½	48½	+ 2⅝	+ 5.7
AlldCap	1a	3988	23½	17¼	19	— 4½	— 19.1
AlldRsh		8722	4½	1¾	2½	......	......
AllyGar		10940	13¼	6¼	9	— 1¾	— 16.3
AloSchr		1412	16½	10	10	— 6½	— 39.4
Altair		1466	7¾	7	7¼	+ ¼	+ 3.6
Altrncr		28924	6⅞	4	4⅞	......	......
Altron		11475	13	9¼	9¼	......	......
Amrfrd	.07e	1110	9¼	4½	4½	— 1½	— 25
Amribc	1.32	1240	25¾	18¾	23	— 2¾	— 10.7
AmBusph		203	6½	6	6¼	......	......
AmAggr	1	1034	25	22½	24½	+ 2	+ 8.9
ABkCt s	.60a	371	15½	9¼	15½	+ 6¼	+ 67.6
ACellTp		12004	6½	3	3½	......	......
ACont pf	3.44	798	25½	21	21	......	......
AmEcol		28713	8¼	2¾	7	......	......
AExpl s		6442	5¾	3½	3⅝	— 1¼	— 25.6
AFiltrn	1.32	1737	25	17¾	25	+ 4½	+ 22
AFn pfD	1	136	9 5-16	8⅜	8½	— ¼	— 2.9
AFn pfE	1	59	9⅛	8¼	8½	— ⅛	— 1.4
AFn pfF	1.80	129	13⅜	11⅝	12⅝	— ⅛	— 1
AFurn	.28	6968	11¾	7¾	9	— 1⅝	— 15.3
AlndmF	1.12	2826	25⅛	15¼	15¾	— 6⅞	— 30.4
AIntegr		25469	13⅝	6¾	13	......	......
AInvLf	.20b	5383	9¼	6¼	6⅝	— ⅜	— 5.4
ALand		1749	8¼	4⅜	6¼	......	......
ALnd un		6840	9¾	4¾	6¾	......	......
ALeis un		7818	3 3-16	2 1-16	2 7-16	+ 5-16	+ 14.7
AmList		930	5¾	3¾	5	......	......
AMdSv	.15b	7790	13½	7¼	13	+ 2¾	+ 26.8
AMidl		152667	2	½	9-16	— ½	— 47.1
AMidl wt		70712	⅛	1-16	1-16	......	......
AMonit		36024	9	2⅞	3⅞	— 2⅞	— 42.6
ANtHld	1.16	2235	20½	15¾	19¼	— ¼	— 1.3
ANatPt		51961	1 5-16	⅝	21-32	—13-32	— 38.2
AmPac		1934	5⅛	2¾	2¾	— 1⅞	— 40.5
ARecr	.16b	7015	9¾	7⅞	9½	— ⅝	— 6.2
AmRest		10723	6⅛	2⅜	2⅞	......	......
AmShrd		13609	7¾	5	6	......	......
ATrust		2649	6	4½	5¼	+ ¼	+ 5
AWstCp	t	2326	5½	4	4	— ½	— 11.1
Amhrst		7938	19½	13¼	16½	— 2	— 10.8
Amistar		14481	8	5½	6¾	......	......
Amosk	..20a	1607	39½	33	38½	+ ½	+ 1.3
Ampal pf	.32	1372	9	5	5⅝	— 1⅞	— 25
Amstr pf	.68	1468	6	5¼	5⅞	......	......
AndrGr		6786	19½	9	10¼	— 9¼	— 47.4
Andrsn		12473	7¾	1⅞	2⅛	— 4⅞	— 69.6
Andrsln	.22i	1599	5¾	2¾	2⅞	— 2⅜	— 45.2
Andovr		6038	12¾	5¼	6½	— 6¾	— 50.9
AngSA	.66e	57030	20⅛	10½	11⅝	— 4⅝	— 28.5
AngAG s	.20i	51352	13¼	8	8⅛	— 2¾	— 25.3
ApldDt		8690	11	2¾	3	— 7¾	— 72.1
ArabSh		1189	12	4¾	6¼	— 4¾	— 43.2
Arden		9861	17	7½	13¾	+ 5⅜	+ 64.2
Arivaca		10433	4 7-16	1⅛	1½	— 1⅜	— 47.8
Armel		2830	14½	11	11¼	— 2¾	— 19.6
Arnold	.60	2549	29½	23	29	— ½	— 1.7
ArowB	2.04	659	42	38	42	+ 4	+ 10.5
Ashton		60161	14	5¾	6½	— 5¾	— 46.9
AspR un		11981	7⅛	4	4	......	......
AsdBcp	.76b	3387	27	15¾	26¼	+ 9	+ 52.2
AssdCo		1307	5	4	5	+ ⅞	+ 21.2
AstrMd		3969	10¼	5¾	6¾	+ ¼	+ 3.9
Astrcm		18993	5½	1⅝	3⅞	+ 2⅜	+ 158.3
Astron	.10	2610	9⅛	6⅛	8¼	+ 1⅛	+ 15.8
AstrSy un		54	19	12	12	— 3¾	— 23.8
AticoFn		3661	6	4½	5	— ½	— 9.1
AtlanTl		4625	9⅛	5½	6⅜	+ ⅜	+ 6.3
AtlGsLt	2.52	33507	29	19¼	28½	+ 8¾	+ 44.3
AtlPrm	.03e	2013	10¾	7½	8	......	......
AudVid		27864	16½	11	12¼	......	......
Ault		8466	13¼	2¼	2¼	— 11	— 83
Autoclv	.16	2858	14	8¾	9¾	— 3½	— 26.4
AutMed		14625	4¾	1⅞	3¼	— ¾	— 18.8
AutoSy		6740	10¼	8¾	9¼	......	......
Automtq		7120	3½	1¼	2¼	+ 1	+ 80
AutoCp		6089	9⅛	4⅛	4⅝	— 3⅞	— 45.6
Avalon		4722	5¾	4¾	5⅛	+ ⅜	+ 7.9
Avaln pf		2763	5¾	4¾	5⅛	+ ⅜	+ 7.9
— B—B—B —							
BGS		13631	18	5¼	6¼	— 11¾	— 65.3
Bacard s	1.02a	2334	32¼	18	20	— 12	— 37.5
BakrFn	.80a	10640	37	28½	34¼	+ ¼	+ .7
BaldLy	.80	627	44	36½	44	+ 6½	+ 17.3
Baltek		3869	14	4¼	14	+ 7¾	+ 124
BncO pf	5.50	1364	58½	53	54½	— 4	— 6.8
BnPonc	2.24	1390	36	26½	33½	+ 4½	+ 15.5
BancoP	2.20	3998	36	25¾	35½	+ 9	+ 34
BcOkl pf	2.50	479	25	22¾	22¾	......	......
BnTx cv	1.46	4060	17	11½	13¼	— 3½	— 20.9
BkDelw	2.88	2777	53	42	53	+ 11	+ 26.2
BkGran	.32	743	18	13¼	17½	......	......
BkLeu		249	15½	10	15½	+ 4½	+ 40.9
BkMonS	3.40	1031	38	30½	36½	+ 1	+ 2.8
BkNHm	1.12	612	29	23½	29	......	......
BkSou	.68b	7686	24¾	20¾	23	+ ⅛	+ .6
Bnkeast	1.20	3423	30	23	27¼	+ 1¾	+ 6.9
BnkFst		14733	10	6¾	10	......	......
BkrNte		7339	7¾	2⅛	2⅝	— 4¾	— 64.4
BTrSC s	1.40	17833	38¾	24	37	+ 12¾	+ 52.6
BknthG		224	14	12¾	13	......	......
Bklowa	1.56	2143	52¾	41½	42	— 5½	— 11.6
BkMAm pf	2.50	405	23	19	21	......	......
BarbGr		12333	12¾	3	3	— 8	— 72.7
Barden	1	1555	32½	21½	30¾	— 2¾	— 8.2
Barris		37269	9⅝	3⅝	9	+ 3⅞	+ 75.6

BsTnB	t	1237	15	7	9	— 1⅞	— 17.2
BasESc		49249	2¼	¾	1 5-16	—11-16	— 34.4
BsRInt	t	190605	1 9-32	½	½	— ¾	— 60
Bastn		5302	4	2⅛	2¾	+ ⅝	+ 29.4
BaukNo	.90	149	10½	8	10½	....	....
BayPac		11527	6½	4	4⅜	....	....
BayFdl	.12e	2423	8	2½	3½	....	....
Beamn s		1478	11½	9	11½	+ 1	+ 9.5
Beechm	.14e	82392	5	3⅝	4½	+ ⅛	+ 2.9
Begley	.68	720	16½	14½	15½	— 1	— 6.1
BellW	.10b	7977	12	7¼	8	— 3¾	— 31.9
BellPtr		2011	3¾	3	3	— ¾	— 20
Belwet	t	10100	3¾	2⅜	2⅜	— 1	— 29.6
Benhn un		2914	53½	10½	38½	+ 25½	+ 196.2
Berklne	.50	3728	12	8¼	9¾	— ¾	— 7.1
BerkGs	2	603	19½	17¾	19½	+ 1¾	+ 9.9
BerkHa		374	1360	1220	1275	— 35	— 2.7
Bibb s		6542	23⅝	13½	20¾	+ 6⅜	+ 44.4
BingKg		9219	7¾	3¼	3½	— 3¼	— 48.1
BioMed		11395	4½	2½	3	— 1¼	— 29.4
BiMed un		2523	6	3½	4½	— 1¼	— 21.7
Biomet		16054	12½	7½	11½	+ ½	+ 4.6
BioTcC		14288	4½	1⅜	1⅝	— 2⅝	— 61.8
Birdl pf	1.85	6043	16¼	9¾	13¼	— 2¼	— 14.5
Birdvw		93685	4 3-16	1½	3 11-16	— ⅛	— 3.3
Birtchr		11262	8	3⅞	5½	— ½	— 8.3
Bitco	.40	9486	19¾	5¾	11⅛	— 6⅞	— 38.2
Blasius		2872	7	3½	7	+ 3¼	+ 86.7
BlockD	1	1686	31¼	25	31¼	+ 4¼	+ 15.7
Blomfld		19115	13½	1½	2½	— 10¼	— 80.4
BlufdSp		5693	18	11⅞	17⅜	+ 4⅜	+ 33.7
BlRdg un		554	11¼	8⅝	11¼	+ 1¾	+ 18.4
Bluesky		2920	4	2¾	3¼	+ 5-16	+ 10.6
BlueOG g		8339	5⅝	2½	5⅝	+ ⅞	+ 18.4
Blyvoor	.85e	73775	16	7 3-16	7⅝	— 5¼	— 40.8
Bohema	.40b	21605	17½	7¾	10⅞	— 6⅝	— 37.9
BooleB		20108	11½	5¼	8	....	....
BoonEl	t	7691	8¼	5	6¾	....	....
Boothln		9075	3½	2¼	3	+ ½	+ 20
BoothF s	.30	6523	22	15¾	22	+ 5⅜	+ 32.3
Bowatr	.05e	158422	4 15-16	⅞	2 7-16	—1 13-32	— 36.6
BradyW	.10e	7223	30	20	30	....	....
Bralrn g	.05e	5815	5½	3¾	4	— ⅛	— 3
BrnchC	1.20	8471	28½	23½	27¾	— ¼	— .9
Branif		73754	10¾	1⅝	1⅞	....	....
Brenner		293	7	6	7	+ ½	+ 7.7
BrentB	.63	1109	14¼	11	11¾	— 2½	— 17.5
BroadF	.01e	15000	9	3⅝	4¼	— 3⅛	— 42.4
BrokHil	.56e	84263	12⅞	7 11-16	8¼	— 2¼	— 21.4
BrokrM		15285	9⅞	5⅝	8¼	....	....
BrwnRb		6143	11	6	8	— 3	— 27.3
BruceRb	.11e	5995	7⅝	5¾	6	....	....
BckeyF		7201	11½	8¾	10¼	— 1¼	— 10.9
Buffels	3.27e	29189	69½	32	34	— 23⅝	— 41
Burmh	.14e	39096	2⅞	2 1-32	2 17-32	+3-32	+ 3.9
BurnpS		47159	7⅞	5 5-16	6¾	+ 1¼	+ 22.7
Burrit		8529	11⅜	9⅛	10½	+ 1	+ 10.5
BurtH		27991	1⅞	17-32	9-16	—13-16	— 59.1
ButlrJ		11368	15¼	12½	15¼	....	....
ButlrMf	1.32	7750	26½	18½	25¾	+ ¾	+ 3
ButlrNt		11696	3¾	2 1-16	3	....	....
Butrfld		4676	6¼	1¼	1	— 4	— 69.6
ByerC s		7075	15	1	2⅛	— 8⅞	— 80.7

— C—C—C —

CCB s	.80	1649	24½	16⅝	24¼	+ 7⅝	+ 45.9
CCNB	.92a	710	23¼	20	23¼	+ 1¾	+ 8.1
CCX Nt		6064	15	12½	14½	+ 1½	+ 11.5
COMB		39790	13¾	7¾	13½	....	....
CTG		5031	4¼	1	1⅜	....	....
CVBFn	.67r	422	12	7½	7⅝	— 3⅞	— 33.7
CablTV		4595	4⅜	2¾	4⅜	+ ¼	+ 6.1
Cadmus	.28	5193	18¼	13¼	16¼	+ 2¾	+ 20.4
CalBio		8634	13¾	4¼	5¾	— 6¼	— 52.1
CalFBk	1.08	2323	18⅞	15¾	17¾	+ 1¼	+ 7.6
CalJky	.90e	1404	25	20½	25	+ 4	+ 19.1
CalWtr s	2.40	2627	31½	25	31	+ 5	+ 19.2
Calmar		22359	18½	13¾	15½	— 3	— 16.2
Caltn un		15830	4⅛	2¼	2⅜	— 1⅛	— 32.1
Calumt	.07e	1598	8½	6	7¼	— ¼	— 3.3
CanoG wt		7959	5	4	4	....	....
Canonl	.22e	66693	29¾	18⅛	26⅜	— 2⅝	— 9.1
Canrad		3222	8¼	5½	6¾	+ 1¼	+ 22.7
CapSwt	.16e	1606	16	13¾	16	+ 2	+ 14.3
CapBcp	1.28a	3523	28	21	28	+ 5½	+ 24.4
CapTrn	.25e	1677	6	2½	5¼	+ 2¾	+ 110
Carlsbg		3187	8	6½	7¾	+ ¼	+ 3.3
CaroCas		983	6¾	2¼	3½	— 3¼	— 48.1
Cargeln		13105	7⅜	3⅞	4¼	....	....
Cascade	1.40	1372	42½	34	42½	+ 5	+ 13.3
CentlSv	.30e	21	9½	9½	9½	....	....
Centbnc		3420	16¼	11¾	12½	— 2¼	— 15.3
CnBkSy	.40b	5738	23	15½	18¼	— 1¼	— 6.4
CnJerBk	1.10	5705	21¼	17	19¾	— ¼	— 1.3
CnJerSv		743	9½	9	9½	....	....
CnPacC	.04i	11595	9¾	4¾	5⅛	— 3¾	— 42.3
CPacMn		37615	1 1-32	17-32	23-32	+ 3-32	+ 15
CnPaSv	.30e	3299	9½	6¼	9½	....	....
CRsvLf	.12	9446	8	3	8	+ 4½	+ 128.6
CWisBn	.84b	960	24½	16	24½	+ 7½	+ 44.1
Centuri	3	67973	3 3-16	13-16	15-16	—1 11-16	— 64.3
CntyPa s	.09i	774	9¾	6⅝	9¾	+ 3⅛	+ 47.2
Cenvil	t	17495	18	11¼	17¼	— ¾	— 4.2
Cerdyn		24373	14¾	6¾	14¾	....	....
Certron		17285	3 5-16	1 3-16	1¼	— 1⅞	— 60
ChmpPt	.10	5212	6⅜	4⅝	5¾	— ⅜	— 6.1
Chapral		49457	3⅜	9-16	⅝	— 1	— 61.5
ChapE pf	1.20	16801	13¼	9½	10⅞	+ ⅜	+ 3.6
Chargit		20300	9	5	7⅝	+ 2⅝	+ 52.5
CharCh		4840	8¾	5¾	7	— 1½	— 17.6
ChartCp	1.02	6059	29⅛	16½	29	+ 8⅛	+ 38.9
ChrtFdl		5444	8	7	7¾	....	....
Charvoz		19682	10½	6	10	+ 2¼	+ 29
ChathM	.80a	4701	22½	18¾	19¼	— 3	— 13.5
Chattm	.48	10738	24¾	15½	17	— 6¼	— 26.9
CheezD	.10r	5099	6¾	3¼	3¾	— 1⅜	— 26.8
Cheflnt		47489	1¼	⅝	⅝	— ¼	— 28.6
Chemfx		18752	5⅜	2⅛	2¼	— 2½	— 52.6
Chmfx un		6137	11½	4⅞	4⅞	— 4⅞	— 50
ChmFab		5374	11¾	4¼	5	— 4	— 44.4
Cheroke		11203	8½	6	8¼	+ ¼	+ 3.1
ChesUt s	1.60	1558	24½	15	22	+ 6½	+ 41.9
Chessco		3487	8½	4¾	6	+ ¾	+ 14.3
ChfAut		19870	13⅝	9⅞	10½	....	....
Chilis		64683	24⅞	12¾	21¼	....	....
Chiron		11185	8¾	4¼	4⅝	— 3⅝	— 43.9
Chitend	1	3481	25	16¾	17½	— 7	— 28.6
CinnFin	2.20b	11723	76¼	55	75¾	+ 6¼	+ 9
CinMic	.01r	37092	13¼	8¼	10½	....	....
Circlnc	1.44	5451	13¾	11½	13½	+ ⅛	+ .9
CtzSou	1	10779	32¾	23¾	32¾	+ 5¾	+ 21.3
CtzFinl		6293	3¾	1⅞	2¾	+ ¼	+ 10
CzGtP	.48e	1040	17½	14¼	17¼	+ 3	+ 21.1
CtzSLn	.40i	1456	8¼	6	7	— ¾	— 9.7
CitzSF s	t	593	18½	15	17½	— 1	— 5.4
CtzTrst	1.36	213	42	19	42	+ 23	+ 121.1
CtyFd pf	2.20	21280	28	20	22	— 4½	— 17
CtFd pfB	2.10	17444	23	17¾	19	— 2¼	— 10.6
CityBcp	.96	4214	30	22	30	+ 6	+ 25
ClasicC		7718	12¾	5¼	6¼	— 6	— 49
ClasfdF		1371	9½	5¼	5½	— 3½	— 38.9
ClaySlv		9802	4¾	2⅝	2¾	— ⅜	— 12
ClowCp	.28	12036	11¾	7⅝	9	— 1¾	— 16.3
CoastM		3250	6	3	6	+ 2¾	+ 84.6
CoastRV		2863	4⅛	2⅞	2⅞	— ⅞	— 23.3
ccstllnt	.20e	6794	11½	7¼	7¾	— 1½	— 16.2
CstSav		9919	14¼	7	14¼	....	....
CobRsc		9145	5¼	3⅜	3½	— 1¼	— 26.3
ColFdl		24780	16	9¾	14⅝	....	....
ColABsh	.48b	2976	16½	11½	16	+ 4½	+ 39.1
CBcgp A	.60e	4182	12¼	10	12	....	....
ColnBcp	.80a	14661	31⅝	25	28¾	+ 1	+ 3.6
ColnGas	1.52	12880	15¾	10⅜	15¾	+ 4⅛	+ 35.5
ColGE pf	1.80	534	15	11½	15	+ 1½	+ 11.1
ColumFd		9239	8	5¼	5¾	....	....
ColSav		31111	10⅞	6½	7¼	....	....
ColuMil	1	1208	33	24½	32	— 1	— 3

Comar	.02	5376	14	8	9¼	— 2⅜	— 20.4
CmndAr		5860	8¼	3¾	4½	— 3	— 40
ComBcp	.45e	57	11¾	8	11½	....	....
ComBsh	2	3685	46¾	39¾	45	— ¼	— .6
ComClH	1.92	18782	70½	50	66½	+ 6½	+ 10.8
CmBCol	.24b	1550	18¾	13½	14¾	....	....
CmclBsh	2	4240	40¼	29	39¾	+ 6¾	+ 20.5
CmlDcl		679	5½	5¼	5¼	....	....
CmclFd		6474	8½	8⅜	8½	....	....
ComlNt	.80	1014	27	18	23¾	....	....
CwNtFn	.25e	5599	37½	28	37½	+ 9½	+ 33.9
CmwRt	.68e	1015	10	8¼	10	+ 1¾	+ 21.2
CmwSv		11215	16	9¾	14¾	+ 2½	+ 20.4
ComShr	.60	3895	10	6¾	8½	....	....
CmpU s		992	7	4	4¼	— 2⅜	— 35.8
CmpVid		35220	6¼	3⅛	3⅝	— ⅞	— 19.4
CmprsL		38892	10⅞	3¼	5	....	....
Cmptek		8166	11¾	7½	8¼	— ½	— 5.7
CmpSve		18091	95	4⅞	10	....	....
CmpDpt		11142	9¼	4¾	5½	....	....
CmHz un		1090	18	5¾	7¾	— 8¾	— 53
CmpNet		12336	9½	5	9⅛	+ 2½	+ 37.7
CmpSv s	.01e	829	33	14⅛	14½	— 14¼	— 49.6
CmSyn		14204	8½	4	4½	....	....
Cmptrc		5067	9	2¾	8	+ 4	+ 100
Comstk		13547	9½	7½	8½	....	....
ConcD s	t	43096	17¾	5¾	7½	— 4⅞	— 39.4
ConcCpt		2714	8	6¼	6½	....	....
Condctr		1895	5	2¾	3½	— 1½	— 30
ConStP		15	9½	9½	9½	....	....
Conna	.08	5438	12¼	4¾	7	— 3½	— 33.3
ConnWt	1.44	4168	14¾	11¾	14	+ 1⅝	+ 13.1
ConTom	.60e	412	36	32½	35	+ 2½	+ 7.7
ConWt s	1.40	2458	24½	16	19¼	— 2½	— 11.5
CtlFSL		8950	19¼	12½	12½	— 3	— 19.4
CtlHlt un		1885	14	8¼	12¾	+ 3¾	+ 41.7
ContStl		89662	2 7-16	½	9-16	—1 7-16	— 71.9
Contin s	.12	4684	34½	12	33½	+ 21½	+ 179.2
ConvFd	.36e	4487	8⅝	4¼	5	— 2¾	— 35.5
Conwed	.60	7487	21½	13¼	21¼	+ 6½	+ 44.1
CookDt		8535	6¼	2¾	3⅝	— 2⅜	— 39.6
CoreS pf	3.07	6607	24½	22	24⅛	+ ⅜	+ 1.6
CosCre		1608	3½	2⅜	2⅝	....	....
CosC un		7555	4	2½	2⅞	....	....
CotnSLf	.44e	4998	16½	8¾	15½	+ 5¾	+ 59
Courer	.60	5332	28¼	18	25¾	+ 7½	+ 41.1
CourDis		8491	7¾	3¾	4⅝	— 3⅛	— 40.3
CousnH		54928	18	2½	6½	— 8¾	— 57.4
CousP s	.32	22906	18½	10	18¼	+ 8¼	+ 82.5
Covngt		36005	2 15-16	⅞	1⅛	—15-16	— 45.5
CradTr	.56	5561	14¾	9½	12	— 2¼	— 15.8
CrftHou		2671	5¼	2⅜	2⅜	— 3	— 55.8
Cramer		3548	9⅛	6½	8⅞	+ 2¼	+ ½
CrwfdC	.66	6491	19½	13¼	19½	+ 6	+ 44.4
CrazEd		42772	11⅝	8¼	11⅛	....	....
CnAut s		2794	5½	3¼	3⅞	— 1⅝	— 29.5
CrwnA	.50	2076	9⅞	5⅜	5½	— 3¾	— 40.5
CueInd		1783	3½	1¾	2¼	....	....
Culp	.08	18304	15¾	5	6½	— 9¼	— 58.7
Cumo		115646	3¾	½	11-16	— 2¼	— 76.6
Cutco	.14	8690	10¾	2½	3⅜	— 6⅝	— 66.3
Cybertk		11189	8⅝	5⅛	5¼	....	....
CyprSv	.20e	4662	13¾	8½	11½	— 2¼	— 16.4
Cyprs wt		2780	6	2¼	3¼	— 2¾	— 45.8

— D—D—D —

DAB	t	3300	10⅞	4⅝	6¾	+ 1⅝	+ 31.7
DCNY	4.25e	11473	54½	31½	49	+ 9	+ 22.5
DH Tch		23166	7¼	2⅞	2⅞	....	....
DLites		37118	14¾	11⅜	12⅞	....	....
DMI		16812	12	3¾	10	— 2	— 16.7
DNA Pl		11232	5½	2½	3⅜	....	....
DNA P un		40191	6½	3⅜	3¾	....	....
DOC		10903	14⅜	6¾	6¾	— 6	— 47.1
DST	.20	15040	29	9¼	9¾	— 19¼	— 66.4
Dahlbrg		8084	6⅜	3¾	4⅝	— ⅝	— 11.9
Dai Ei	.05e	21	6⅜	4⅞	4⅞	— 9-16	— 10.3
DairMt	t	4014	13¾	9	10	— 3⅜	— 25.2
Daners	.20e	608	15½	7½	15½	+ 5	+ 47.6
DataPc		1389	9¼	5¼	7¼	+ 1	+ 16
Datcpy		24850	8¾	3¼	4⅜	— 3⅛	— 41.7
Datmar		1312	10¼	7½	7½	— 1¼	— 14.3
Dauphn	1.96	6377	33	25¼	33	+ 3¾	+ 12.8
DavisW	.19e	7128	12	7½	11	+ 3½	+ 46.7
Daxor		2407	11¾	6¾	8⅛	— 3⅜	— 29.3
DBeer	.23e	292522	9 3-32	4⅛	4⅛	—3 9-32	— 44.3
Decom		9621	5¾	2½	3	— 2¾	— 47.8
DeltNG	1.04	4985	11¾	8½	10⅛	+ ⅜	+ 3.9
Deltak		7394	7¾	5¼	5¾	— 1¾	— 23.3
DltaQn		1211	14¾	12¼	13½	— 1¼	— 8.5
DeniM A	1	8852	18½	10	11⅝	— 6⅝	— 36.3
DeniM B	1	5930	14⅝	9⅛	10⅞	....	....
DepGty	2.14	2746	43	35½	37¼	— 2¼	— 5.7
Desgnh		11102	15½	6½	6½	— 5¾	— 46.9
DetrxC s	1.20	1436	30½	21¾	28	+ 6	+ 27.3
DetCan	.90	794	13¾	12¼	12¾	— 1	— 7.3
Develcn		23311	20	5⅞	5⅞	....	....
Devry		12201	11⅞	6½	7¼	— 3¾	— 34.1
Dewey		3389	12¾	4¼	5	— 5⅝	— 52.9
DiaCry s	.80	3476	28⅝	23⅛	25⅜	— 1⅞	— 6.9
Dibrel	1	5547	28	18¼	25⅝	+ 7⅛	+ 38.5
DickenA		9484	5⅝	2⅞	3¾	—1 3-16	— 24.1
DickenB		1420	5½	2 13-16	3⅜	— 1½	— 30.8
Dickey		3343	16	9¾	10¼	— 3¼	— 24.1
DtrcRs		3899	3¾	1¾	1⅞	— 1⅞	— 50
DinnrBl	.40	3250	11½	8	9¾	+ ½	+ 5.4
DiplElc		19600	6¾	3¼	3¾	....	....
Distrib		1393	5⅞	4¼	4¾	— ¼	— 5
DixnTi		2834	7½	4½	6¾	+ 1¼	+ 22.7
DomMt		3738	5	3½	4⅞	+ ⅜	+ 8.3
Donovn	1.36	2529	17¼	11½	16½	+ 5	+ 43.5
Doskocl		136442	2 15-16	1 3-16	1⅜	—1 3-16	— 46.3
DblEg s		8939	5 5-16	1⅛	1¼	—4 1-16	— 76.5
DglLom	.40	6299	11½	8½	10	+ ½	+ 5.3
DresBk	1.65e	145	68½	49	60½	— 2½	— 4
Dreshr	.05e	5011	11¼	8½	9½	— 1	— 9.5
DressBr		11219	22	12½	21	— ½	— 2.3
DrewNt		108491	2 15-16	1	1⅛	—1 3-16	— 51.4
DriefCn	1.38e	89309	40⅞	22⅜	24⅛	— 8	— 24.9
DrugS s		9743	7⅝	3¼	3¾	— 3⅛	— 45.5
DualLte		14165	8½	2¾	3⅝	— 3	— 45.3
Dumag		444	4¾	3 1-16	3 1-16	....	....
DuqSys		7183	15	9¾	13	....	....
Durakn		20627	14¾	8½	11¼	....	....
Durlth		4715	15½	8	13½	+ ¾	+ 5.9
Durhm s	1.16	7605	35¾	25¼	33½	+ 8¼	+ 32.7
Dwight		7100	6	2	3⅝	— 1⅞	— 34.1
Dycom		770	9¾	8¼	9¾	....	....
DynRs		3300	10	5	5½	— 4	— 42.1

— E—E—E —

EB Mar		7919	19¾	6⅞	7⅛	— 12⅜	— 63.5
EIL Inst		3313	7	4	4⅝	— ⅞	— 15.9
EMC Ins	.48b	612	6½	5¾	6¼	+ ½	+ 8.7
EMF		16646	4¼	2⅞	3¼	— ½	— 13.3
EMPI		4755	9½	5¾	6	— 1½	— 20
EZEM		11848	14½	8½	11¾	— 1¾	— 13
Eastmt		58706	10¾	4¼	4¼	— 5¼	— 55.3
Eastovr	.40b	1153	33½	22	22¾	— 3¼	— 12.5
EatnF		4899	9	6¾	8	+ ½	+ 6.7
EatVan	.40	1743	24	15½	17½	— 3	— 14.6
EdgStl	t	4766	32	8¼	31	....	....
EdSault	1.36b	315	13½	11¾	13	+ 1¼	+ 10.6
Elco s	.72	3646	20⅝	13	15	— 3¼	— 17.8
ElderB	.22b	2068	14¼	11⅛	12	+ ⅞	+ 7.9
EldorB		3109	7⅛	4⅝	4¾	— 1⅝	— 25.5
ElcSci		18637	23	11	19	+ 1¼	+ 7
Elctmg		15349	21¼	13¾	18¼	+ ¼	+ 1.4
ElizWW	2.60	2526	29¾	25¼	28	+ 1½	+ 5.7
Elmans		5042	18	10	13¾	+ ⅜	+ 2.8
E&C Co		1086	12⅝	8¾	11	— ⅞	— 7.4
EmpCas	1.20	4681	36½	29	34½	+ 3	+ 9.5
Enrgas	1.60	16469	20	15¼	19¾	+ 3	+ 17.9
Engnth	1.08	2054	16½	8½	15¾	+ 6¼	+ 65.8
EnRsv		503904	6 3-32	3¼	6 1-16	+2 9-16	+ 73.2
EnrVnt		12424	15	6	8¾	+ 2¾	+ 45.8

EnginSy	.20e	9864	12	8¼	10½	....	....
EnexRs		38723	3⅝	1⅜	1 13-16	— 1⅛	— 38.3
EngMea		7905	5⅝	2¾	3¼	— 2⅜	— 42.2
EntrCpt		36172	19½	9½	13½	— 1½	— 10
Envrdn		15479	3⅜	2	2 15-16	+13-16	+ 38.2
EnvSys		5277	18	7¼	10	— 6¼	— 38.5
EnvrT s		3099	13½	2⅝	10½	+ 7⅞	+ 300
EnvrnP		594	4⅛	3¼	4	....	....
Epsiln		25952	17	9¾	16½	....	....
Epsco		6415	7⅝	5⅝	7	+ 1⅛	+ 19.2
EqtBcp	.72b	5792	19¼	16½	18¾	— ¼	— 1.3
EqtBcB		28	9⅜	9¼	9⅜	....	....
EqtlwaB	1.28	9322	24	17¼	18¼	— 4	— 18
EqtloA	1.28	1569	24½	17½	18½	— 4¾	— 20.4
ErbLm		899	25¼	17	18½	— 1½	— 7.5
ErckGd		11451	8¼	2¾	2⅞	— 3⅞	— 57.4
ErieLac		1954	88	68	87	+ 13½	+ 18.4
Essex		4783	5½	3¾	4¼	— ¾	— 15
EsexCt	2.32	331	21¾	19¼	21¾	+ 2½	+ 13
EvlR un86		920	11	4	5	— 3¼	— 39.4
Evrgd		6413	7¾	2	4½	— 2½	— 35.7
Exchlnt		2416	12⅞	10¼	11⅜	— 1⅛	— 9
Expdln		1617	8¾	7¼	7⅜	....	....
Expdl un		10997	10½	8⅝	8⅞	....	....

— F—F—F —

FM Nat	.54r	1296	24½	16	21	+ 5	+ 31.3
FMI wt		49465	2 15-16	¾	¾	— 1⅛	— 60
FabWhl	.20	4843	11¼	6	11	+ ½	+ 4.8
FairLn s	.16	6608	6¼	4½	4½	— 1⅜	— 23.4
FairFin		12222	8¼	5	6¼	+ ½	+ 8.7
FalcLt g		2846	66	41½	59½	+ 3½	+ 6.3
Falstaff		17131	5⅛	3⅞	5⅛	+ ⅛	+ 2.5
Fardy		3868	8¾	4¾	5	— 3¾	— 42.9
FrmHm		67968	26⅛	12¼	25⅝	+ 12⅛	+ 89.8
FrmHo	t	33293	6⅛	2⅝	3⅜	— 2⅝	— 43.8
FarmBr	.80	2827	35½	28	34	+ 2	+ 6.3
FarrCo	.20	3706	9¼	6¾	8½	+ ½	+ 6.3
FdScrw	.20e	5602	11	7	8¼	— ½	— 5.7
FdGrty s	.38	3599	11½	6⅜	9½	+ 3⅛	+ 49
FedNtl		4964	4½	2⅜	2⅜	— 1⅝	— 40.6
Fidclr pf	3.25	1108	41	31	40½	+ 6½	+ 19.1
FidFdl		939	9½	8½	9½	....	....
Figg pf	.40	636	11¼	9¼	9⅜	— 1⅝	— 14.8
Finllnd		409	3½	3	3⅛	— ⅛	— 3.8
Fininst	.20e	9808	10	5¾	6¾	— 2⅞	— 29.9
FnclSec		2769	19	7	7½	— 7¼	— 49.2
FineA un		8196	7¾	4	5¼	+ ¼	+ 5
Firstr	1.20	1122	24½	13½	24½	+ 4½	+ 22.5
FtAmar	.90	1463	26½	15¼	15½	— 6¾	— 30.3
FstAm s	1.20	15586	27	17½	26⅞	+ 8¾	+ 48.3
Ft ofA pf	.99	1675	14¾	10½	14¾	+ 4	+ 37.2
FABkPB A	.20	23172	10½	6⅞	7⅞	— 1⅝	— 17.1
FABkPB B	.20	471	12½	10	10	— 2	— 16.7
FtAFed		759	9	8	8¾	....	....
FBnLa s	.40	5756	20½	14⅝	16½	+ 1⅝	+ 10.9
FBncTx	.40	1890	6¾	5¼	5½	— 1¼	— 18.5
FtCapt s		918	26	21	26	+ 5	+ 23.8
FtCarln	.50	1003	19⅜	16	19⅜	+ 3⅜	+ 21.1
FtColBs	.10e	2683	9	8½	9	....	....
FtComB		2877	6¾	4¾	4¾	— 1¾	— 26.9
FtCmcl	1.44	4930	41	32	33¾	— 3¼	— 8.8
FConn s	1.20	2115	33	27¾	32¾	+ 3½	+ 12
FDtMgt		3983	14	8	14	....	....
FEstC s	1.90	2135	45¾	29½	44	+ 12⅞	+ 41.4
FtEmp	1.20	8140	46½	31¼	45¾	+ 8	+ 21.2
FExec pf	.95e	23326	25	22	22¾	....	....
FFwst		3048	14¾	11¾	13¼	— ½	— 3.6
FFdNH	.10e	2051	13¼	8	13	....	....
FFdAust		14928	27	13¾	15¾	+ 2	+ 14.6
FFdBrk		266	8½	8¼	8½	....	....
FFChar		3196	14¾	11¾	14¾	+ 3	+ 25.5
FtFdlVa	.10e	3520	16¾	12¼	13¾	— 3	— 17.9
FtFdSC		23877	7¾	4⅜	6¼	— ¼	— 3.8
FtFidSL		3886	10½	6	8	— 2¼	— 22
FFSvMon		2468	10	7	10	....	....
FtFncl	1.76b	723	34	29	34	+ 5	+ 17.2
FHawa s		3690	25⅛	20¼	24¾	+ 4½	+ 22.2
FtIllCp s	1	2550	18½	13½	18	+ 4¼	+ 30.9
FtIndBc	1.08	199	36	29½	36	....	....
FtIndi		7838	14½	8¼	10	— 3	— 23.1
FInstBk	t	2229	11⅛	8⅜	10¾	+ 1¾	+ 19.4
FInstCp	.92	1023	22	16½	19½	+ 2½	+ 14.7
FtJer pf	3	1508	46	32½	43¼	+ 4¾	+ 12.3
FJer pfB	2.88	3929	33	27	31¼	....	....
FtKyNt	1.44	10081	34¾	26½	33¾	+ 7¼	+ 27.4
FtMich	.56b	7974	11	8	10¾	+ 1½	+ 16.2
FtMidB	1.20	4416	17¼	12½	16½	+ 2½	+ 17.9
FMdwC		1215	6¼	4¼	4¾	— 1¼	— 20.8
FtMtlSv		24382	37½	22	24½	— 8¼	— 25.2
FNtShr s	.96	2731	29½	18⅜	25½	+ 7⅛	+ 38.8
FNtCal		2271	9⅜	6⅝	6¾	— 2⅝	— 28
FtNtLa	.75e	1162	22	9½	21	+ 11½	+ 121.1
FNtSt pf	4	909	45½	38¾	45	....	....
FtNatn		10882	22½	11½	13¾	— 4¾	— 25.7
FNHB	.60b	3696	22	18	20	— 2	— 9.1
FNthSL	.40	5290	12	9¼	12	+ 2	+ 20
FtOhBn	1.80	1403	35½	30½	35½	+ 5	+ 16.4
FtOklB		25967	15⅛	8⅛	9⅞	— 4⅜	— 30.7
FtPeoNJ		640	17	6½	8½	— 7⅝	— 47.3
FPeo pf	1.99	1545	18½	10¾	12	— 5¼	— 30.4
FSecKy	.76b	1107	26	21	21	— 1	— 4.5
1stSrce	.43e	6136	14¼	8½	14¼	+ 5¾	+ 67.7
FtSthn		19441	12	8	9	+ ⅜	+ 4.4
FtUtd	.50e	36	55	50	53	....	....
FtValy s	.80	3162	27	18¾	27	+ 5½	+ 25.6
FtVtFn	1.28a	1114	24¾	20	23½	— ¾	— 3.1
FtWnFn	.20b	38493	9	5	5	— 1⅝	— 24.5
Ftbnklll	1.20	138	19½	17	17½	....	....
Fstgulf	1.12	3265	42½	23	42½	+ 14	+ 49.1
Fststh		4302	38½	19	37	+ 17½	+ 89.7
Firster	2.20	4861	48½	38	44	+ 2½	+ 6
Fisons	.23e	18473	14⅜	9	13¾	+ 3⅛	+ 29.4
Flagler	.22e	2010	11¾	9¾	11	....	....
Flghtln		7911	8⅝	4	4⅜	....	....
Flockln		1099	5½	2¾	3½	— 1¼	— 26.3
Florfx s		66198	9¼	3	4⅝	— 3⅛	— 40.3
FlaCom	.56b	2101	28½	19¾	24¼	+ 2¾	+ 12.8
FlaCypr	.20e	6882	4⅜	2⅞	3⅜	— 1	— 22.9
FlaGulf	.40i	17562	18¼	13½	16⅝	+ 1⅞	+ 12.7
FlyTigr		2329	11	4	9	....	....
ForBetr	.10	214	5⅛	4	5⅛	+ 1	+ 24.2
Formst		23204	10¼	1¼	1¾	— 8½	— 82.9
Forsch		7177	10¼	4¾	5	— 5¼	— 51.2
FtWyne		162	38	34	38	....	....
Forum wt		7879	10¾	5½	9¼	+ 2¼	+ 32.1
FndrFn		8812	3¼	2¼	2½	— ¾	— 23.1
FrthFn	1.08b	2560	26	20½	23¾	+ ¼	+ 1.1
FourStr		2025	7½	3	3½	— 3¾	— 51.7
Frnkfd s	2	189	35	30½	34¾	....	....
FrnkBc	.80a	8069	15	12	15	+ 1	+ 7.1
FrnkCp	1.35e	754	15¾	12¼	13½	— 1	— 6.9
FrnkEl	.56	5990	19½	13¾	14	— 4¾	— 25.3
FrnkR s	.24	3708	24¾	13⅝	24½	+ 10½	+ 75
FreeSG	1.93e	39400	47¼	21¼	22	— 15	— 40.5
FreeFdl		9492	7¼	6⅝	6⅝	....	....
FreeSL		29783	19	9	10¾	— 6½	— 37.7
FreqCt		17417	7½	2¾	3⅛	— 1⅞	— 37.5
FrtFSL h		504	7	6½	6½	....	....
FrostS	.10e	6576	4¼	2⅛	3	— ⅝	— 17.2
FrznFd	.28	3541	17¾	11¼	12¾	— 5	— 28.2
FujiPh	.07e	305710	19⅝	11¾	12⅜	— 4½	— 26.7
Fdsnet		25911	5	1⅞	4	— ⅝	— 13.5
Funtme	.05r	3784	6½	4½	5	— 1¼	— 20

— G—G—G —

GK Sv s	.28	2283	14⅝	10¼	14	+ 3½	+ 33.3
GAC Lq	1e	6206	4⅜	3	3⅜	— ⅛	— 3.6
GalghrA		19272	29¾	13¾	29¾	....	....
Galoob		25269	12¼	10	10¼	....	....
Gambr s		22658	30¼	8⅞	9	— 15¼	— 62.9
GnBind	.36	12806	13¾	7½	10½	+ 2	+ 23.5
GenCer	.10e	1066	16	10½	15½	+ 2½	+ 19.2
GnMag	.05e	1569	10	8	9½	— ½	— 5
GnPhys		3504	8¼	5½	7½	— ½	— 6.3
GnShal	.75r	6632	17	10½	14¼	— 2½	— 14.9

GTel 56pf	.90	996	7¼	6¾	7		....		....
GTel 5pf	1	2083	8¼	6¾	7¾	—	¼	—	3.1
GenesB	1a	2157	40½	30½	37	+	¾	+	2.1
Geneve	.10	651	40½	34½	40½	+	3	+	8
GeoWsh		2591	3¾	2	2⅛	—	1¼	—	37
GaBnd	.05e	2325	7¼	4¾	5	—	½	—	9.1
GermF	.20e	5367	13	9¼	11½	+	1½	+	15
Gibson	.28	1066	12¼	8	10¼	—	1¾	—	14.6
GibHom	.30	7074	17⅜	11	17⅜	+	4⅞	+	39
GilbrtA	1.70	7174	27	19¾	24½	+	¼	+	1
Glamis	.10e	5145	5¼	2½	4⅛	—	¾	—	15.4
GlaxH	.18e	666205	13⅛	9⅞	12⅝	+	2⅝	+	26.3
Godfry s	.52	11135	15¾	7⅝	15	+	7⅜	+	96.7
GldFld	.53e	35847	27⅞	12⅝	12¾	—	8½	—	40
GoldRs	t	6430	4⅛	2⅛	2¼	—	1¾	—	43.8
GldCycl		3047	6¾	2½	2⅝	—	3⅞	—	59.6
GoldE s		6476	17	11¼	16¼	+	2⅜	+	17.1
GoldSt		514	12	7	12		....		....
Goody	.30	7641	13	7¾	9¾	—	2¾	—	22
Gradco		19766	14½	7¾	8½	—	5½	—	39.3
GrphMd		7414	4¼	2¾	3 1-16	—	7-16	—	12.5
GrayCo		8327	9¾	6	9¾		....		....
GtAmC	.71	965	21¾	15	21¾	+	6¾	+	45
GAmPrt	.60e	1679	8¼	3	3½		....		....
GtAMg		15711	16¾	11	13¼	—	3½	—	20.9
GtAmRs		6425	3½	1	1⅜	—	1⅜	—	50
GtLkFd		24904	9⅜	5½	7⅞	—	1⅛	—	12.5
GtSoFd		21819	9½	6½	8¼		....		....
GtWash	.50e	5431	7½	5¼	6	—	1	—	14.3
GrifTch		2209	9	3⅝	3⅝	—	3⅞	—	51.7
Groman		1600	10⅞	7¼	8	—	¾	—	8.6
GwthFd		11922	6⅛	4	4¼	—	1¾	—	29.2
GuarFn		642	8½	4¾	6¼	—	¼	—	3.8
GuarC	.60	936	21½	15¼	21½	+	6¼	+	41
GuarNt		18564	3⅞	1⅞	3⅛		....		....
GuardP	.44	4962	14⅝	9½	12	+	½	+	4.4
GuestS		11932	11½	8	11	+	2	+	22.2
GlfApld	.20	3556	10¾	6	7	—	3¾	—	34.9

– H–H–H –

HHOilT		8359	6½	3⅞	4¼	—	1	—	19
HEI Tx		13651	11	5½	9½	+	2	+	26.7
HEI Mn		4215	9½	3¼	3¾	—	4¼	—	53.1
HGIC		2113	4½	3½	4¼		....		....
HPSC		7656	8¾	4½	5¼	—	1	—	16
Hach Co	.24	650	17½	15	17½	+	1½	+	9.4
Halifax	.02e	4653	6¾	3⅝	4¼	—	2½	—	37
Halmi un		5671	4	2⅜	3	—	⅝	—	17.2
HamO pf	1.95	3637	16¾	13	16	+	2	+	14.3
Hamnd		2623	10½	4	4¾	—	5½	—	53.7
Hanvl s	.56	16428	30½	18½	27¼	—	½	—	1.8
HarknO		22850	5½	1⅝	1⅞	—	2⅞	—	6015
HrtfStm	3	5813	59½	49	58½		4½	+	8.3
Harvln		6653	36¼	17¼	36¼	+	16½	+	83.5
Hauser	.25e	2918	18	11	16	+	5	+	45.5
Havrty	.48	5643	16¾	12	13	—	3⅜	—	20.6
HawkC	t	964	5¾	3	3	—	2¼	—	42.9
HawthF	1.35e	597	22½	18½	22½	+	1¼	+	5.9
HltA wt		4736	9¾	5½	7¼		....		....
HlthRs		13481	17¾	9⅝	10⅞		....		....
HeistC		2058	8	7¼	7⅞	+	⅝	+	8.6
HeritFd		26723	14¾	10	12¾	+	1½	+	13.3
Hetra		2033	4⅜	2⅞	3	—	⅝	—	17.2
Highvld	.08e	30607	5 3-16	1⅝	1 21-32	—	2 17-32	—	60.4
HinesL	1	3165	44½	32½	40½	+	4¾	+	13.3
Hollyln	.20	66	16¼	10	15¼		....		....
HlwdPk	1.60	7306	30½	18½	20	—	10	—	33.3
HolmD	1	9343	21¾	15½	21¼	+	½	+	2.4
HmBn s	.84	5252	26½	18	26½	+	7	+	35.9
HFdAtl	t	1509	15	9	15	+	2½	+	20
HFdFl		30933	10	7⅛	8⅝		....		....
HFdMs		1007	6¼	4	4		....		....
HmFRk	.50r	3652	14¾	10	10	—	4	—	28.6
HmoSL		12839	16	9½	15¾		....		....
Hooper	.08e	1284	9¾	9	9½		....		....
HrznAir		18786	7¼	3⅞	4⅝		....		....
HstnOF		20849	5¼	1¾	1⅞	—	2⅞	—	60.5
HstnO pf		1795	10½	8¼	8¾		....		....
HwrdB	1.12a	1286	25½	19½	23	—	½	—	2.1
HydrO h		3089	5½	1¾	2¾	—	1½	—	35.3
Hytek un		3997	14	3¾	4	—	4¼	—	51.5

– I–I–I –

IBI		9492	4½	2½	3¼		....		....
IDB s		201	36	25	36	+	10	+	38.5
IIS		11463	5	4⅜	4⅞		....		....
IPC		8777	9¾	5¾	6¼		....		....
IRE Fn		16982	5⅛	2	2	—	2½	—	55.6
IVB Fn	2.20	7755	28¼	22	28	+	4½	+	19.2
IdleWld	.80	2023	29½	20½	24¾	—	¼	—	1
Imark	.25	1507	4½	3¾	3⅞	—	⅛	—	3.1
Imatrn		33759	3⅞	2½	3½		....		....
Imtrn un		7237	9¾	5¾	8⅝	—	⅛	—	1.4
ImprBc	t	9492	9¼	5⅞	7¼	—	1⅜	—	15.9
Impln un		971	17¼	10	11½		....		....
Imreg		21119	10¾	4¼	6½		....		....
IncaRs g		22274	5⅝	2⅛	2 3-16	—	1 7-16	—	39.7
IndBcp	1.92	3554	35¼	27¾	35¼	+	566	-	19.5
IndpBk	1.40	1880	30	17½	30	+	12	+	66.7
IndSqS	1.86a	3691	17	13¼	15¼	—	¾	—	4.7
IndBnc	.30r	1756	11	7½	7¾	—	2¼	—	22.5
IndInsr	1.32	13043	31	19¾	30½	+	6	+	24.5
IndnaF		2610	4⅜	3½	4¼	+	⅛	+	3
IndiN pf		1874	25⅞	24¾	25⅞		....		....
IdplWat	2.66	2783	28¼	23¾	27¾	+	1¼	+	4.7
IndnHB	1	1967	34	25	33½	+	5½	+	19.6
InAcous	.25e	1015	12½	4½	5½	—	7	—	56
IndEl		17071	6⅛	3¼	3⅝	—	2½	—	40.8
IndRes		35130	5 1-16	2½	3 7-16	—	⅜	—	9.8
InertD s		8287	9⅝	4¾	5⅛		....		....
InfoIntl	.20	15004	14	10	12½		....		....
InfoSc		11749	14	3¾	3¾	—	10¼	—	73.2
Initio		4264	6¼	1¾	2¼	—	3¼	—	59.1
InmedC		11005	10	7¾	10		....		....
InsituE		12895	11½	4	4¼	—	7½	—	63.8
InstCl		4204	8¼	8	8		....		....
InstCp s		14323	9¾	3⅞	3⅞	—	3⅝	—	48.3
Intech	t	4440	4⅝	2½	2⅝	—	⅞	—	25
ItgCirc		3614	10¼	5¾	5¾	—	1¾	—	23.3
IntegFn	.12e	5252	7½	4	4¼	—	1¾	—	29.2
Intelli		16662	8¾	3½	7¾	+	1½	+	24
IntrSBk	.60r	707	21½	17	19½	+	2½	+	14.7
IntrcDy		1386	9	3	4½	—	2	—	30.8
IntLfe	.18	15739	13⅜	9⅜	12⅞	+	2¼	+	21.2
Intlke g		5110	4⅜	½	⅞	—	2¾	—	75.9
IntLab		11712	5⅛	1¾	1¾	—	1⅛	—	39.1
InBWsh	.25	1493	11⅛	7½	8½		....		....
IBkWsA	.25	16459	9⅞	5⅝	7⅛	—	1¼	—	14.9
InCrna		16259	10½	3¾	4⅝	—	3¼	—	41.3
InDairy		2731	41	32½	40½	+	5	+	14.1
IntFlm		1703	4⅛	2⅝	2⅞		....		....
InFlm wt		555	⅞	½	⅞		....		....
InFlm un		7082	9½	6	6⅝		....		....
Int HRS		19579	3¼	1¾	2⅝	—	⅜	—	12.5
IntResh	.36	10063	10½	6¼	6¾	—	1¾	—	20.6
IntlSL		3684	10¾	7½	7¾	—	2¾	—	26.2
IntShip		1571	15	11¾	13¾	+	¼	+	1.9
IntThor		120620	5 13-16	4¼	5⅝	+	1⅛	+	25
InThr un		35489	6¾	4½	6⅝	+	1⅜	+	26.2
Intphse		6170	8	3	3¼		....		....
IntPip g	1.60s	1139	26¾	19¼	26	+	3⅛	+	13.7
Inthrm	.20	11076	10¾	6	8	—	1¾	—	17.9
Intrtrn		4515	7¾	5	5¾		....		....
Intrwst	.60e	19078	19	13¼	14½	—	1¼	—	7.9
InvtD s		3067	11	5¼	8½	+	2¼	+	36
InGNMA	2.74e	5431	22½	21	21	—	1	—	4.5
InvstSL		5501	4⅝	2¾	4⅝	+	1⅜	+	42.3
IwaSoU	3.28	5145	41⅜	32¼	41⅜	+	5⅜	+	14.9
Irwin g	.26	3427	6⅜	3 3-16	3⅝	—	2⅛	—	37
Irwin nv	.26	2741	5½	3 1-16	3 1-16	—	1 3-16	—	27.9
Isomet		1041	6½	1	3	—	2¼	—	42.9
IsrlInv	5.28e	603	29	22½	22½	—	1½	—	6.3
ItoYokd	.27r	11372	42¼	29¼	40⅝	+	10½	+	34.9

– J–J–J –

JLG		8280	10¼	4	4⅛	—	3⅝	—	46.8

JMB s	1.64	4902	19	15	19	+ 4	+ 26.7
JP Ind		7914	13¼	10¾	11½	— 1¼	— 9.8
Jacbsn s	.40	5116	16	11½	15¼	— ½	— 3.2
JeffrGp		30990	15½	9¾	14½	2⅝	+ 22.1
JeffBcp	t	707	17¾	14	14½	— 1	— 6.5
JeffBsh	1.60	3619	32¾	24	32¾	+ 2½	+ 8.3
JeffNL s	.44	5519	23¼	16¼	20½	— 2¾	— 11.8
JemRec		6270	3¾	2 9-32	3¼	....	....
JetA un		1493	10⅛	3¼	3⅜	— 5⅛	— 60.3
JhnsnE		9765	9	4¾	5¼	— ¼	— 4.5
JoneV s	.10e	4722	5⅛	2½	3½	— ⅝	— 15.2
Joslyn	1.28	15964	29½	20½	26½	+ 4	+ 17.8
Judys	.12	1137	5¾	4	4¾	— ½	— 9.5

– K–K–K –

KMW Sy		4550	14¾	8½	9	— 3¾	— 29.4
KTRON		7460	7½	3	3½	— 2¼	— 39.1
Kamnst		22070	10⅜	4½	4¾	....	....
KnCtyL	2.60	4204	72	56½	72	+ 14½	+ 25.2
Kappa		2913	6⅝	4	6¼	....	....
Kaypro		85073	8⅜	1⅞	2	— 5	— 71.4
Keane	.20	1173	12	7	9¾	+ 2¼	+ 30
KellyS A	.64	11347	27	19	27	+ 4¾	+ 21.4
KellyS B	.52	951	26½	19	26½	....	....
Kencop		12750	6	2¾	3½	+ ⅛	+ 3.7
Kengtn		7923	11⅞	8½	11⅞	+ 2⅛	+ 21.8
KyInvst	.28	271	11	10¾	11	+ ¼	+ 2.3
Kevlin		9202	6¼	3½	4	— ½	— 11.1
KewnS s	.16	3485	17⅝	14	17⅝	+ 3½	+ 24.8
Keycon		3733	11½	7½	9¼	....	....
KeyPort		2463	25	15½	23	+ 7½	+ 48.4
KingInt		13989	9	3¾	8¾	+ 5	+ 133.3
KngWld		16180	15¼	10¼	14	....	....
Kinney	.10e	4993	11¼	7¾	7¾	— 3¼	— 29.5
Kiney pf	1.37	2248	13½	10¼	10¼	— 2¾	— 21.2
Kiney un		520	25	17	17	— 8	— 32
Kleinrt		2226	8¼	4¼	6½	+ 2¼	+ 52.9
KloofG	1.74e	45575	57⅜	33⅝	36¼	— 9⅞	— 21.4
KlosVd		3705	8¼	2¾	3⅜	— 3⅝	— 51.8
KnapeV	1.30	3224	30½	24¼	30½	+ 5	+ 19.6
Kreislr	t	1405	9⅛	7¼	7¾	+ ¼	+ 3.3
KustEl		3485	5¼	3	4⅞	+ ⅜	+ 8.3
KyleTc		6185	4⅜	2⅛	2½	— ¼	— 9.1

– L–L–L –

LCS s		3329	5	2	3¾	— ¼	— 6.3
Lacan g	.15e	18187	10¾	7	7½	— 2⅛	— 22.1
LacldSt		3010	17½	12½	15¼	— 1¾	— 10.3
Ladlw pf	2.03	3946	28	22	25¼	+ ¼	+ 1
LdlwT A	.20	1694	14¾	9⅜	14¾	+ 3⅜	+ 29.7
LdlwT B	.20	46042	13⅞	8⅞	13⅞	+ 3½	+ 33.7
LamRs		40389	11⅞	7⅜	8¼	....	....
Lance	1. 0	30924	31	24	30¼	+ 3¼	+ 12
LdLnSL	.30	14477	13	7⅜	8½	— 2	— 19
LaneTl		11538	8½	1¼	1¾	— 6¾	— 79.4
Larsen	.56	5050	25	16	24½	+ 7½	+ 44.1
LaserCp		8728	6¾	3¾	5¾	....	....
LeadDv	.04e	4259	3¾	1¾	1¾	— 1¾	— 50
Lesco		5802	12¾	11¼	12	....	....
LbtFGa		9260	14	9½	14	+ 3¼	+ 30.2
LbtFPhi	.20e	7050	11⅝	7½	10	....	....
LibtyHo	.20	13745	16	9½	11¼	— 3½	— 23.7
LibUBc	1.42	2138	39¼	32¼	38¾	+ 6¼	+ 19.2
Liebrm		13459	15	13⅜	15	....	....
Lfelne		13046	9½	3½	4	— 5¼	— 56.8
LilChp	.24	481	22	16½	18½	— 3⅛	— 14.5
Lily A s	.34b	7528	14¼	9½	10¾	— 3⅜	— 23.9
LincFin	1.60	980	38	26½	38	+ 8	+ 26.7
LincLfe	.68	2641	18	14½	17¼	+ 2¼	+ 15
LinerCp		8843	1¼	5⅝	5⅝	— 5	— 47.1
LiqBox	.72	2332	30	23	26¾	+ 1¼	+ 4.9
LiqdAir	1.60	3330	23¼	18½	20¾	— 1¼	— 5.7
LittlArt	.70	1262	24½	22	23½	— 1	— 4.1
LondnH		10169	11	6	7¾	....	....
LouG 5pf	1.25	957	11	9½	10¾	....	....
LouG pf	1.86	852	16	13½	15½	....	....
LyonMt		17641	23¼	10¾	16½	+ ½	+ 3.1

– M–M–M –

MCI wt		328674	4	13-16	13-16	—2 13-16	— 77.6
MCM Cp	.24	1645	10¾	8	8¼	— 1	— 10.8
MMI		8209	8⅜	3⅜	3⅜	....	....
MPS Bc	1	748	27	21½	26	+ 3½	+ 15.6
MDmd s	.52	3865	30½	22	24	+ ⅜	+ 1.6
MagelPt		10120	5¾	1½	3⅜	+ ¾	+ 28.6
MagicC		35382	3½	⅜	½	— 2⅛	— 81
MagmP		30786	9⅜	6⅞	7	— ⅞	— 11.1
Magnal	.48	35382	14¾	11¼	13¾	....	....
MagBk		3392	11	6¾	10¼	+ ¾	+ 7.9
MagGp	.68	2484	14¾	10¼	11¼	— 3	— 21.1
Magnet	.02r	1400	9¾	6½	6¾	— 1¼	— 15.6
MaineN	1.20a	1486	31½	24	31½	+ 7½	+ 31.3
Makita	.32r	1923	28¼	17¾	20¼	— 5⅝	— 21.7
ManfH s		7930	9	3½	8⅜	+ 3⅜	+ 67.5
MarnC s	1.30	6084	24¾	18¼	24½	+ 4¾	+ 24.1
MarPet	2.35e	971	18¼	14	15	— 2	— 11.8
MarinT		15591	11⅝	5⅝	6	— 2¾	— 31.4
MarkIV		3040	8¾	5½	7¾	+ ½	+ 6.9
MTwan	.80	3256	21¾	17	19¾	+ 1¾	+ 9.7
MktFct	.60	1442	16½	11	13½	+ 2½	+ 22.7
Marline		811	6½	3½	3½	....	....
MarsSt		10463	8¾	3¾	7¼	— ½	— 6.5
MarshS	.48	7089	18⅝	13½	14¼	— 2⅞	— 16.8
Marshll	2.12	7093	52½	39¼	51¾	+ 2½	+ 5.1
Mascmp		56084	16⅞	7½	9¼	....	....
MathAp		2108	11½	5½	6½	— 4	— 38.1
MauiLP		217	49	39	40	+ 1	+ 2.6
Mavrck		11334	7⅛	2¼	2¾	— 3	— 52.2
Maxco		12973	3⅞	1¾	3⅛	+ ¾	+ 31.6
Maxxus	.10e	676	5⅜	4	5⅜	+ 1⅛	+ 26.5
MaySu A	.10a	2709	10⅝	5⅛	9	+ 1⅜	+ 18
MaysJ		168	9½	8¼	8¾	....	....
McGill	1.80	955	38½	31¾	32	+ ¼	+ .8
McGrth		3063	6½	5½	5¾	....	....
McGreg		784	22	15½	22	....	....
MechTc		2913	6	3¼	3⅞	— 1⅜	— 26.2
Mechtr s		5806	14⅞	3¼	13¼	+ 9⅛	+ 221.2
MedcoC		25820	30¼	14	23	....	....
MedShp		20069	19	12¾	19	+ 4	+ 26.7
MediGl		7564	9¾	3½	4	— 4¼	— 51.5
Medplx		24064	27¼	10½	26¾	+ 16	+ 148.8
MerBPa	1.50	3654	36¾	30¼	36½	+ 3½	+ 10.6
MerNY	1b	389	70	61¾	70	+ 5	+ 7.7
MerchN	1	6408	42	26	41	+ 13	+ 46.4
Merimc		7250	11¼	7	10½	+ ½	+ 5
MeryLd	t	1204	10¾	7¾	8	— 2½	— 23.8
MesbAv		7253	4	2⅝	3	— ¼	— 7.7
MethdA	.12	13229	9¾	6	9½	+ 1¾	+ 22.6
MethdB	.10	863	10¼	6¾	9¼	+ 1½	+ 19.4
Metrbnc		6875	10⅜	6½	9⅞	....	....
MetrTl	.03b	3588	7½	3	3¼	— 1¾	— 35
Metrml		34107	16⅛	8⅝	16⅛	....	....
MeyrP s		517	13	5¼	13	+ 4⅞	+ 60
MichJ	.24	960	7	6⅛	6¾	— ¼	— 3.6
MichStr		44686	4⅞	2 7-16	3⅞	....	....
MichNtl		34330	20½	10¾	17½	+ ¾	+ 4.5
Micrbio		4563	12½	4¾	5	— 7½	— 60
Micrpro		83705	10¼	2⅛	2¾	....	....
Micros		16831	4⅜	1⅞	2¼	— 2	— 47.1
MdAB s	.56	870	17½	14	17	+ 1	+ 6.3
MdANtl	1.20e	184	18½	17	17	....	....
MdStBc	1.81e	789	29½	23¼	27	+ ½	+ 1.9
MidsxW	3	1025	34¾	27¼	33¾	+ 5¾	+ 20.5
MdldCa		1570	20	13	20	+ 6⅜	+ 46.8
MdwCm	1	883	25¾	17	25¾	....	....
MdwFn	1.20	3085	16¼	13½	13½	— 2¼	— 14.3
Minden		14404	2⅜	⅝	⅝	— 1½	— 70.6
MineSaf	.88	1580	57	41	51	+ 7	+ 15.9
MnrRs	.20e	206344	11½	6 1-16	6¼	— 3½	— 35.9
MinnF	.16	18946	11	7⅝	10¾	+ 1	+ 10.3
Minetnk		111355	5¼	3¼	4⅜	+ ⅜	+ 9.4
Minst wt		59305	6⅜	2½	6⅜	....	....
MisVIA		8450	10	3	3¼	— 5¼	— 61.8
ModCtl	.05e	12605	6⅜	3	6	+ 2½	+ 71.4
MonAvl	.15	3846	8	3¼	3¼	— 3¾	— 53.6
Mongr		14721	4	1	1⅛	— 1⅝	— 59.1

MooreF	1.20b	16793	25	18	24⅛	— ⅝	— 2.5
MooreP	.88	3046	29¾	24½	25¾	— 2	— 7.2
Morlan		211	2¼	1¾	2¼	....	....
MCSB		15413	14½	10¾	14½	+ 3¾	+ 34.9
Mosinee	.34b	10873	16⅜	11⅜	12	— 3	— 20
Mueller	1.70	2314	32½	16¾	21½	— 9	— 29.5
Multbk s	.92	9718	35	25½	32	+ 6⅜	+ 24.9
Musto		227	2⅜	2⅛	2⅛	....	....
MutREI		1907	10⅜	8	8½	— 1½	— 15
MutOil		26743	6¼	2⅛	3¾	+ ⅛	+ 3.5
MutSvL	1	177	42	34	42	+ 8	+ 23.5

— N–N–N —

NBSC	.76	324	16	12	13	— 3	— 18.8
NCB	2.60	817	47½	40¼	47½	....	....
NEC	.07r	78463	32⅞	20⅞	24¼	— 7	— 22.4
Nanomt		10385	9⅛	7¾	9	....	....
Napcol	.30e	4825	14¼	10¼	13	....	....
NarrgC	3.20a	3560	49	38½	47	+ 4	+ 9.3
NashFn	.96a	3292	18½	13½	18½	+ 2	+ 12.1
NshCtBk	.64b	509	29½	17¾	29½	+ 11¾	+ 66.2
NB Als s	.50i	2895	30	24½	29¾	+ 1½	+ 5.3
NtBusSy		1055	8⅜	8	8⅛	....	....
NtCapit	.45e	6594	5¼	4	5	+ ½	+ 11.1
NCtyBn	†	6593	17¼	11¾	12⅜	— 3⅝	— 22.7
NtCty pf	3.70	4238	44	39	42¾	....	....
NtCity	1	1009	20⅜	13½	20⅜	+ 6⅜	+ 45.5
NCmBc	.68	1921	18¾	13⅝	18¾	+ 5⅛	+ 37.6
NCmNJ	2.40a	2838	47½	41	47½	+ 5½	+ 13.1
NHard s		3063	5⅝	3	3⅞	+ ⅛	+ 3.3
NParag		12667	5⅝	1⅛	1½	— 2⅝	— 63.6
NtlPenn	.96b	384	26½	20½	26	+ 3½	+ 15.6
NtlPza		8462	9⅞	7½	7¾	....	....
NtProp		687	7¼	4⅞	7¼	+ 2⅜	+ 48.7
NSecIns	.50	1189	16	13	13¼	— 2¾	— 17.2
NtShoe		4265	11½	7¼	11⅜	+ 2⅜	+ 26.4
NBkEliz	1.52	4041	29½	19¾	28	+ 6½	+ 30.2
NtWnLf		19974	13⅜	6⅝	10¼	— 1⅛	— 9.9
NtnwdP		28458	11	1⅛	3	— 5¼	— 63.6
NtrSun s		3086	8½	2⅝	3⅜	— 5⅛	— 60.3
Nautils	.83e	2580	39¼	23	24	— 13½	— 36
Nwk wt87		4283	4⅛	1¾	3¾	+ ¾	+ 25
NevNBc		3617	7¾	3¼	3½	— 4	— 53.3
NwAF s		1465	34	19¼	28¼	+ 7⅛	+ 33.7
NwFrPt		46212	2¼	½	½	— 1¼	— 71.4
NY Mar		10670	21¾	11	21	....	....
NYrkr	.60a	1809	172	127	172	+ 33	+ 23.7
Nwcntry	1.10	5157	19	13½	17¾	— ½	— 2.7
NwldB un		49641	13	1	11	....	....
Nwpk wt		3065	2	3-16	¼	— 1¼	— 83.3
Nico		12849	11	7¼	8¾	....	....
Nissan	.09r	132889	6½	4½	4⅞	— 1½	— 23.5
Nobel g	.31r	2889	7	4¾	7	+ 1½	+ 27.3
Nodway		2509	5	3	5	....	....
Noland	.56	2695	19¾	17¼	19¾	+ ¾	+ 4
NorisO	†	52902	7	2¾	2 13-16	—15-16	— 25
NoANat	.01r	6748	14¼	6¼	7	+ ½	+ 7.7
NCarGs	1.84	5865	22¾	15	22⅛	+ 7⅛	+ 47.5
NoFrkB	1e	3518	29½	24	28½	+ 1	+ 3.6
NthHill		6863	7½	3¼	3⅞	— 2⅞	— 42.6
NWstTl	1.44	854	23½	18½	22	— 1½	— 6.4
NestBc	2.40	3465	54	40	49	+ 3	+ 6.5
NestF un	2.07e	1377	48½	47¾	47¾	....	....
NestBn s	1.28a	3186	44¼	21½	30	+ 7¼	+ 31.9
NoAir		11024	7¼	2½	3⅝	— 3⅜	— 48.2
NthDta		7345	10	7½	8¾	....	....
NoTrust	2.72	16590	63¾	56	59	— 1	— 1.7
Nthvew s		4723	24¼	15	15¾	— 3¾	— 19.2
NwNG pf	2.37	3035	26½	21	26½	+ 4½	+ 20.5
NwTelp	.20e	1249	6½	3¾	6½	+ 2½	+ 62.5
Norws s	.14	2832	5⅛	3¾	4	+ ¼	+ 6.7
Novar	.01	14021	12¾	6¼	12	+ 2½	+ 26.3
NovoCp		24825	3⅝	2¼	2½	— ½	— 16.7
Novo un		3533	3¾	2½	2⅝	....	....
Nowsc g	.30	4591	17¼	13	14	+ ½	+ 3.7
NuHrz un		5978	9	5¼	6	....	....
NucMet		13187	25¼	10½	11¾	— 10¾	— 47.8
NuclSpt	.12	5937	7¾	8¼	14¼	— ¼	— 1.7

— O–O–O —

OKC un	.33e	5827	12¼	7⅞	9	— 1	— 10
OMI Cp		170452	5	1¾	3	— 2	— 40
Oce-van		10746	16⅜	15¼	16⅛	....	....
OceltB g		1582	4⅞	2⅜	2¾	— 2	— 42.1
OfLog pf	1.56j	8079	19¾	3¼	4	— 15½	— 79.5
OffLog pf	1.22j	8138	19¼	4	4	— 15⅛	— 79.1
Oglbay	2.16	6793	29	25	27¼	+ ¼	+ .9
OilDri s		1101	16½	9¾	16	+ 5⅞	+ 58
Oilgear	1.20a	1356	26¼	20¼	26¼	+ 5¾	+ 28.1
OldDom	.84	3328	11¾	9¼	10¼	+ ¼	+ 2.5
OldFsh		3436	7¼	4⅝	4¾	— 1¾	— 26.9
OlKnt pf	1.82	4406	24½	16¾	23½	+ 4¾	+ 25.3
OldNB s	2	440	44½	33	44½	....	....
OldNtB		5956	19¾	11¾	16	— 3¾	— 19
OldStne	2.08	4930	28¼	21½	28¼	+ 1	+ 3.7
OldS pfB	2.40	3488	19⅝	16¼	19	— ⅜	— 1.9
OlsonF	.25e	4242	18½	7	9¾	— 3	— 23.5
OneLbt	1.68e	5860	15	12½	14¼	+ 1¾	+ 14
Opto		15874	6½	4¾	6½	+ ¼	+ 4
OptelCp		970	29	23	26½	....	....
OpticSp		4227	7⅞	7	7⅝	....	....
Optim		2801	5½	¼	¼	— 4⅝	— 94.9
Optrtch		12909	15½	11	15	....	....
OregMt	.40e	21749	12	8¼	9¾	— ½	— 4.9
OrionR		12886	17¼	8¾	16½	+ 5	+ 43.5
Osmonc		5347	15⅛	10	14⅞	+ 3⅜	+ 29.4
OuachN	.72	393	40	30	35	+ 4	+ 12.9
Ovrsln g		926	2⅞	2⅛	2¾	+ ⅝	+ 29.4
Oxoco pf	3	5159	23¾	18	18¾	— 4	— 1816

— P–Q —

PCA Int	.48i	23222	9¼	5¼	6¼	— 1¾	— 21.9
PNC pf	1.60	501	18½	16	18	....	....
PcGaR	1.40b	9348	26	17¾	20	— 2¾	— 12.1
PacInld		350	11¼	8	9	....	....
PacIn wt		235	⅜	¼	¼	....	....
PacWB	.05e	2407	7½	4¾	7½	+ 1¼	+ 20
PackSy		3139	10	7¼	7¾	— 1¾	— 18.4
Pacwst		6616	13¼	10	12	— ¾	— 5.9
Par Ph		26134	17	8¾	13	+ 3¼	+ 33.3
ParTch		7227	18	11	12¼	— 1¾	— 12.5
ParkCm		6813	29	18¼	26¾	+ 5½	+ 25.9
Parkwy		2937	21½	17¼	18½	— ¼	— 1.3
Parlex		4232	14¼	12	13	....	....
PasF B s		958	18¾	6⅝	10½	+ 2½	+ 31.3
PasF A s		894	12¼	6	10	+ 2¾	+ 37.9
PatTc un		134	37	23	23	— 4	— 14.8
Patlex		12119	7	4¼	4¾	— 1¼	— 20.8
Patrk un		749	14	6¼	7⅝	— 3⅝	— 32.2
Patriot	1	2604	28	21	24¾	+ 2¼	+ 10
PawlSv		6253	17⅞	11¼	17½	....	....
Paxton	.48	4570	19¼	14½	17	+ 1½	+ 9.7
Payco s		3520	14⅛	7½	11½	— ¼	— 2.1
PeerCh	1	1071	20	15½	18½	+ 3	+ 19.4
PeerMf	.72	2549	17	9½	11½	....	....
PeninFd		6093	14⅝	8½	9½	— 2¼	— 19.1
PennVa	1.60a	5607	48½	38	38½	— 6½	— 14.4
Penbcp s	2	2890	40	32¼	40	+ 5⅝	+ 16.4
Penta		9889	10¼	1½	3	— 5	— 62.5
Penwst		5151	11¼	4	7¾	....	....
PeoE pf	2.64	11743	19⅛	14¾	17½	....	....
PeoBnC	1	7687	26¾	20	26¾	+ 3½	+ 15.1
PeopBc s	.48	2528	18	10⅛	16½	+ 6⅜	+ 63
PfctFit		3141	9	6	7⅛	....	....
PerpAm		36801	11⅞	7⅜	11⅞	....	....
PetInd		10119	6⅛	3	3¼	— 1¾	— 35
PetDv		17010	1¾	7-16	½	—1 1-16	— 68
PETCO		42060	7⅜	3⅛	3⅜	— 2½	— 42.6
PtHel vtg	.14	1950	7¾	5½	5¾	— 1½	— 20.7
PtHel nv	.14	12926	7⅞	5	6⅛	— 1¼	— 16.9
Petrmn		5313	3	1⅞	2⅝	....	....
Petibon		9678	9½	3	3½	— 4¾	— 57.6
Phrmcia		156135	23⅜	14¼	15½	— 3⅞	— 20
Phrmkt		31342	9½	5	8¾	+ 3¾	+ 75
Phrm wt		9268	8⅛	3⅞	7½	+ 3⅝	+ 93.6
Phrm un		2173	37	18½	34½	+ 15¾	+ 84

PhnxMd		4833	7	5⅞	7	....	....
PhnAG		8139	5¾	3⅝	5⅝	+ ⅝	+ 12.5
PhotoCt		2183	7½	6	6¾	− ½	− 6.9
Photron		10607	10¼	2	2¾	− 7½	− 73.2
PhyInMi		1114	3¼	⅞	1½	....	....
PhysIn	.26	6771	10½	6	6	− 4	− 40
PhysTc		4283	6½	2½	4¼	− 2¼	− 34.6
PiedBc	.68	507	25	14	24½	+ 9¾	+ 66.1
PiedMg	.36	13911	13⅜	8¾	9	− 3⅜	− 27.3
Pierce		688	36	27½	36	....	....
Piezo		446081	1 3-16	3-16	¼	−13-16	− 76.5
PionFdl		4772	9	6	9	....	....
PionG s	.30	8491	17¼	13¼	16¼	+ ¼	+ 1.6
PittBr	t	5690	14	8½	10½	− 2¾	− 20.8
PlainsR		26803	3¼	1⅝	1¾	− 7-16	− 20
PlantrC	.84	2083	25¼	18½	22	+ 3	+ 15.8
Plasmn		905	8	4¼	4¼	− 3¾	− 46.9
PlazCBc	.10e	2284	5⅞	4	4¾	− ½	− 9.5
Plenm s	.88	2987	26⅝	20½	22	− 4⅝	− 17.4
Plycast		4461	9¼	7	8¾	− ¼	− 2.8
PonceF	.25r	18228	8⅝	5⅞	6⅞	....	....
PoplBsh		9524	3 1-16	2⅛	2¼	−13-16	− 26.5
Possis	t	4732	10½	4	7	− 3	− 30
PrabRbt		3990	13	4¼	5½	− 7	− 56
PfdFncl		10845	5⅜	4⅛	4¼	− ¾	− 15
PfdRsk	.74	2505	27¾	19¾	27¼	+ 7½	+ 38
PfdSav		2124	10⅛	7¾	8½	....	....
PrsGM	1.85e	38956	50¼	23¾	25¾	− 10½	− 29
PresSty	2.42e	39496	60½	24¾	29	− 16¾	− 36.6
PresLf s	.12	1984	42½	15	37¾	+ 22¾	+ 151.7
PrstnCp	.50	23718	21¼	13	17¼	− 4	− 18.8
Primo		19385	7	2¼	2¾	....	....
PrinvD		2720	4⅞	4¼	4¾	....	....
ProMed	.41e	3343	5	3¼	3¾	− ⅝	− 14.3
ProfInvt		4695	4⅛	1⅞	3⅞	+ 2	+ 106.7
ProfitS	.40	5022	19¾	8¾	9¼	− 10½	− 53.2
ProgSys		6530	5⅞	3⅞	4⅛	− 1	− 19.5
Progrp		14347	8	4⅝	4¾	− 2¾	− 36.7
ProtCp	1.24	13266	38	28	38	+ 8¾	+ 29.9
ProvBc	.10e	368	49½	41½	41½	− 4	− 8.8
ProvLfA	2.88	11869	83	65	77	+ 11½	+ 17.6
PrvBost		15996	13	3½	5	− 7¾	− 60.8
PrudFn		7797	13¼	7½	13¼	+ 5½	+ 71
PrudBk		3004	10½	5½	6¾	− 2¼	− 25
PubcoC		53516	1⅝	9-16	1⅜	+11-16	+ 100
PbSvNC	1.72	5934	22⅜	16⅛	21⅞	+ 5⅛	+ 30.6
PublEq		13850	7	2⅞	3½	− 2⅛	− 37.8
PgSdBc	1.12	5930	27¾	20	27	+ 2¾	+ 11.3
PulasF	.60	5601	25	18½	24¼	+ 5½	+ 29.3
PutnTr	1.08	855	29½	24½	28½	+ 1½	+ 5.6
PyrmO		9265	9¾	6¾	9	+ 1½	+ 20
QualMil		603	6¾	4½	4½	....	....
Quantc		12119	7	2⅛	2½	− 3¼	− 56.5
Qntrnx s		6419	13	6⅝	11¼	+ 3	+ 36.4
Quarex		4613	9	4	5¾	− 1¼	− 17.9
QuebcSt		3212	7¼	2¾	2⅞	− 3¼	− 53.1
Questch		1510	8¼	6½	6¾	....	....
Quintel		7117	7¾	4⅛	7¾	+ 2¾	+ 55

— R—R—R —

RIHT	2.32	3837	54	44½	49½	− 2¼	− 4.3
RJ Fin	.0e	5158	10½	6¼	6¼	− 3	− 32.4
RLI Cp	.56	3318	13¾	10⅛	13¾	+ 3⅝	+ 35.8
RSI Cp		2745	4	2¼	2¼	− 1	− 30.8
RamFin	1.05	925	23¼	18	23¼	+ 2	+ 9.4
Rangair	.24	9905	8¾	5⅝	7⅝	+ ¾	+ 10.9
RankO	.15e	104511	3⅞	2 9-16	3 5-16	+21-32	+ 24.7
Rauch	t	2578	5¾	3¾	4	− 1⅛	− 22
Raymd s	.70	7136	20¾	13¾	19½	− ⅜	− 1.9
Rayrk g		5643	9⅛	5¾	6 5-16	− 9-16	− 8.2
REIT Ca	2.42e	3768	26¼	23½	26¼	....	....
RealAm		1892	5¼	3	3½	− ¼	− 6.7
RefacTD	t	13752	13¼	8½	9¾	....	....
Reflctn	t	8422	23	15¼	20	+ 2½	+ 14.3
ReidAsh		9612	8¾	4¾	8¾	+ 3¾	+ 75
ReidLb	.03e	11574	4¾	2⅝	3	− ½	− 14.3
RelbLfe	1.80a	544	39½	28½	37	+ 2½	+ 7.3
Reltron		2909	6¼	3⅝	4⅛	+ ⅛	+ 3.1
Repco		4951	6¾	3½	5⅝	+ ⅞	+ 18.4
RntCntr		14165	16¾	9½	16¾	+ 2¾	+ 19.6
RscPsn	2.32e	5010	27½	22	22	− 4¾	− 17.8
RscPn2	1.27e	5844	20¼	18	18	− 2	− 10
ReshInc	.32a	4015	11½	7	8¼	− 2	− 19.5
RshInd		41369	12¼	5	7	− 2	− 22.2
ResOM		4544	4	2⅛	2⅝	+ ¼	+ 10.5
ResExp		19878	4	2	2⅜	− ⅛	− 5
RestMg	.03e	2790	10½	9	10	....	....
ReverA	1.44	7239	15	10¼	11½	− 3	− 20.7
RiggsN	1.80	4569	34¾	27	33¼	− ¾	− 2.2
RivrFor	.50	388	26½	19½	26½	+ 6½	+ 32.5
RoanEl	.80	3002	17	10	10½	− 4½	− 30
RobMey		4569	14	10	10½	− 1¾	− 14.3
RckwHd	.54e	3483	19	10½	12	− 6	− 33.3
RckwdN		9385	2¼	1¾	2	+ 3-16	+ 10.3
RMUnd		14495	7	4⅛	6¾	....	....
RckMtG	.68	8560	11⅛	8⅜	9⅞	− ¼	− V¼.⅝
Rodime		55855	23¼	5½	7	− 13¾	− 66.3
RgrCbB		48341	10⅞	4⅛	5¼	− 3¾	− 41.7
Ropak		556	5½	3¾	4	− 1½	− 27.3
RossInd		801	9¾	8½	9¾	....	....
Rospath	.60	16337	21	13½	21	+ 6	+ 40
RossCs		2084	6¾	2½	3⅝	....	....
RoweFr	.12a	9020	8	5¾	6¾	− ⅛	− 1.8
RyApex		11970	4 11-16	1¾	1¾	−2 7-16	− 58.2
RoyGrp		64087	1 13-16	5-16	17-32	−1 5-32	− 68.5
RuleInd		6017	4	2¾	3½	+ ½	+ 16.7

— S—S—S —

S K		7469	11⅛	6	6⅜	− 4	− 38.6
SABHa s		2646	6⅞	5¾	6	+ 1⅜	+ 29.7
SAL Cm		4041	2¾	1⅛	1⅜	− ¾	− 35.3
SPI Ph	.10e	3764	12	8	12	+ 2	+ 20
STV		4998	11½	5	6½	− 3	− 31.6
Saatchi	.25e	20303	32¾	21½	31⅝	+ 9¾	+ 44.6
SageAl	.32a	3220	18¼	8	17½	+ 7½	+ 75
SageDrl		2809	7	2¼	3½	− 1¾	− 33.3
StHlGd	1.54e	27638	41¼	14½	16	− V⅛⅞	− 51.5
SalmNt		1447	8½	6½	8	− ⅛	− 1.5
StMonB	.60b	924	24	20	24	+ 3⅝	+ 17.8
Santos	.43e	50377	7 5-16	4 7-16	4½	− 2½	− 35.7
Sasol	.08e	11732	4 13-32	2 17-32	2⅝	−1 1-16	− 28.8
SavBcp	.15e	19742	16⅛	10½	15⅛	....	....
SavrFd	.60e	11488	24	15	23¼	+ 8¼	+ 55
SaxtnIn		9031	4⅛	1¼	3 7-16	+2 3-16	+ 175
ScanO wt		6523	7⅞	2⅝	2¾	− 3⅛	− 53.2
ScanO un		143	31½	15	16¾	− 7¼	− 30.2
SchakE		13508	9	4⅝	6⅛	− 1⅛	− 15.5
SchSky		4009	6½	2¾	3⅝	....	....
Scholas	.22i	12384	24	10	12¾	− 6¾	− 34.6
SciCom		10284	9	7	8¾	....	....
SciDyn		9913	12⅛	7	7¼	− 1¾	− 19.4
ScotCb		2885	6¼	3⅜	5	− ½	− 9.1
ScripH	.80	5750	32½	24¾	32½	+ 5	+ 18.2
SeaBnk	.36	11423	11¾	8¼	10¼	....	....
Seahwk	t	9159	3⅛	1½	1½	− 1¼	− 45.5
SeaIInc		5054	5½	2¾	5	+ 1½	+ 42.9
SeatleT	t	2175	26	17	23	− 1¾	− 7.1
SeawFd	.68	2688	14½	11	13½	+ ½	+ 3.9
ScNtBld	1	4962	16½	11	13½	− 3	− 18.2
SecNtl	1	2812	27	16⅝	27	+ 10⅜	+ 62.4
SecAFn	.10b	988	10½	6¼	9½	− ¼	− 2.6
SecBcp	1.12	3819	19¾	13¾	19	+ 2	+ 11.8
SecLfGa	1.05	2753	28¼	18	28¼	+ 8¼	+ 41.3
Select		6484	18	8	9½	− 8½	− 47.2
Srvmat		75948	3¾	1 13-16	1 15-16	−1⅜	− 41.5
Shanley		46941	1¾	¾	31-32	− 9-32	− 22.5
Shiseid	.08e	5....7	26⅞	20	22	+ ¼	+ 1.2
ShopG s	.20	15880	14¾	7⅛	14¾	+ 5¼	+ 55.3
ShpWld		1325	3¼	2⅛	2⅞	....	....
ShoreSv	.52	11425	15⅛	9¾	11¾	− ¼	− 2.1
Shorewd	.24	933	26½	16¾	26½	+ 8½	+ 47.2
SieraS		12544	9⅞	5⅜	9⅞	....	....
SigmaA	.60	8553	51½	43	51½	+ 2	+ 4
SigmC s		8277	9¼	6⅝	6¾	− 2½	− 27
SigmaR		5777	7¾	3⅜	3½	− 2⅝	− 42.9
SilvLis		38791	6¼	2⅞	3⅝	....	....

SlvKing		45761	5⅞	2¾	2 15-16	− ⅞	− 23
SlvStMn		204765	1¾	11-16	23-32	− 9-32	− 28.1
SimKar	.10r	648	18	12	15¼	+ 3⅝	+ 31.2
SimAir		9381	10¼	5½	8½	....	....
SkyExp		9115	4⅛	2¼	4⅛	....	....
SnelSnl	.28e	1046	9½	6½	7¼	− 2¼	− 23.7
SftwPb		19828	10⅛	7⅛	10⅛	....	....
Sonesta	.40	506	19½	17½	19½	+ 2	+ 11.4
SorgPrt		12437	24½	6½	8⅞	− 15⅝	− 63.8
SCarNt	1.76	8313	59	38¾	59	+ 18	+ 43.9
SoMicG	1.52b	1986	15¾	12¾	15¾	+ 1½	+ 10.5
SoBcpSC	.88b	8296	22	15½	22	+ 4½	+ 25.7
SCalWt	1.70	4893	17⅝	14⅜	17½	+ 1¾	+ 11.1
SoMinrl	.05e	565	11½	5¾	8	....	....
SthnNt	1.32	2842	35¾	29¾	35½	+ 2¾	+ 8.4
SoPcPt		88178	15-32	5-32	¼	....	....
SwtBcp		5944	4½	2⅛	2½	− 2	− 44.4
SwLsg		2255	9½	6	7½	+ 1½	+ 25
SwstRlt	1.32	16329	15½	11¼	11¾	....	....
SwElSv	1.80	1009	24½	17¾	24½	+ 3¼	+ 15.3
SprtM un		2481	5½	4	5	....	....
SpecCm		2392	5	3	4¾	+ 1	+ 26.7
Spctrm		7138	8¼	5½	8¼	+ 1⅛	+ 15.8
Spendth		3235	11½	6½	7	− 4½	− 39.1
Squarel	t	1403	8¾	4½	5¾	− 2⅞	− 33.3
StanWst		11478	5	2	2¼	− 2¾	− 55
StCTob	.50	1628	20	16	17	− 3	− 15
StanfdT		10393	17½	8½	10½	− 7	− 40
StarGlo		1125	4¾	2¾	3¾	+ 1	+ 36.4
StarTc		19642	9¼	9	9	....	....
Startel		18071	5¼	2½	3	− 1⅜	− 31.4
StwBcp	1.20	4652	27½	19	24	+ 3	+ 14.3
StwB wt		4776	6½	2	3¾	....	....
StwB pf	2.20	4651	29¼	21¾	26¾	....	....
StwB un	2.20	4747	35¼	24½	30	....	....
StearMf	.20e	1203	7¼	5½	7	+ ¾	+ 12
StereoV		6862	9¼	4⅞	8¾	....	....
StewSn	.15	3810	4¾	3⅜	3½	− 1	− 22.2
StckYle	.16	2626	13¼	9½	12¾	+ 1½	+ 13.3
Strata		5041	7½	3½	4⅜	− 2⅝	− 37.5
StrikPt		222348	11-16	⅛	5-16	+ 5-32	+ 100
StuDS		27856	16¾	7½	15⅝	....	....
StrmRg	1	1614	32½	22	23	− 8½	− 27
SubAirl	.05	2360	4	2¾	3½	+ ½	+ 16.7
Sudbry		3803	7½	4¼	7¼	....	....
SuffSB		7241	9½	6¾	8½	....	....
Sumito	1.16	5695	15	11½	13	− 1¾	− 11.9
SumitB	1.44	4581	29½	20¾	29	+ 4½	+ 18.4
SumBnA	2.20	690	44½	30¾	44	+ 7	+ 18.9
SunEqt		2357	4	2	2½	− ¼	− 9.1
Sunlite		6937	4½	3¼	3½	− ¾	− 17.6
SunstFd		6296	6⅝	3⅝	3⅝	− 2⅜	− 39.6
Sunwst	1.40	4815	34	28½	34	+ 2¼	+ 7.1
SuperEl	t	5459	16½	9	12⅞	+ 2⅛	+ 19.8
SurgAf		16041	14½	7½	8	....	....
SurvTc		2360	15¾	5½	5¾	− 8	− 58.2
SusqBc	1.76	640	34	31	34	....	....
SvenCel	.29e	1330	23⅜	13	13	....	....
Swedlw	.28	2740	13¾	9¼	11¾	+ 2¼	+ 23.7
SymTk		3861	16¾	9½	13¾	− 2	− 12.7
Symbin		30074	5⅜	2⅛	4	− ½	− 11.1
Symblic		30436	7⅜	6	7	....	....
Syngex		26142	17⅞	9	17⅞	+ 4⅛	+ 30
Syntc pf	2.75	5620	26¾	16¾	19¼	− 3½	− 15.4
SyrSup	.20	1542	18¼	14¾	16	....	....
Systnet		1231	3¾	1½	1¾	....	....

– T–T–T –

TEL Off	2.23e	32205	12⅜	8⅜	10⅛	+ ⅝	+ 6.6
TL		6020	7½	5	5	− 2¼	− 31
TRV g		18506	2¼	⅝	13-16	− 5-16	− 27.8
TSC Cp	.75e	866	2¾	¾	1½	− 1	− 40
TSC Inc		5352	8¼	4¼	6¾	− 1½	− 18.2
TSI	.08	6693	18¼	7¼	8¾	− 8½	− 49.3
TSR		13979	19¾	4¾	18¼	+ 12¾	+ 231.8
TacVila		4269	7½	4¾	7¼	+ ¼	+ 3.6
TaroVt		4556	3¼	1⅜	1⅜	− ¾	− 35.3
Tchnal	.20e	2166	14	7	10	− 3	− 23.1
TchCom		2919	13	3	3¾	− 9	− 70.6
TchEqC		218	21	21	21	....	....
Tchlnd s	.03	4006	6½	3½	5¾	+ 1⅛	+ 24.3
Tecum	3.20a	4364	97	78½	86½	− 4	− 4.4
TecoPr	.40e	1668	2	1 7-16	1½	− ⅜	− 20
TlCm wt		17527	8½	4½	8½	+ 1	+ 13.3
TlcmB	t	5038	23¾	17	23	+ 4¼	+ 22.7
TelMex	.02r	909163	31-32	11-32	11-32	− 19-32	− 63.3
Telemt		605	6¾	5¼	5¾	− 1	− 14.8
Telep wt		1431	11½	6¾	9¾	+ ¾	+ 8.3
Telram		20438	4½	5-16	⅝	− 3⅞	− 86.1
TmplE		45947	4⅛	1⅜	1⅝	− 2⅛	− 5.....8
Temtx s		3361	8¼	5½	6¼	− ½	− 7.4
Tennant	.88	6916	21½	16¾	20	− 1½	− 7
TennRs	1	5139	16⅜	11⅛	16⅜	+ 4⅝	+ 39.4
TenVEn	.60	1440	9	7	7¼	− ¾	− 9.4
TeraCp		43014	9¼	3½	5¼	− 4	− 43.2
TeraM g	t	21646	4⅝	1⅜	1 7-16	− 2⅜	− 62.3
Teva	.19e	6037	3	1	1 7-16	− 11-16	− 32.4
TexEng		7687	4⅛	2¼	2¾	− ⅛	− 4.3
TCBYg s		12918	13	3	13	....	....
ThrnAV		2294	8¾	4½	5¼	− 2¾	− 34.4
Thundr	.05e	14995	8¾	4½	5⅛	− 3⅛	− 37.9
TideR h	.53e	2125	8¼	5¾	6½	+ ½	+ 8.3
Tierco		2583	8	4⅝	8	+ 2¾	+ 52.4
Timbrld	t	6839	5⅝	3¼	5⅛	+ 1¾	+ 51.9
Tinsly		1218	8¾	6¾	6¾	− 1¾	− 20.6
TokioF	1.04e	7709	157½	104	146	+ 25¾	+ 21.4
ToledTr	1.90	5478	42½	33½	4½	+ 4	+ 10.7
TolTr pf	2.90	1659	32	27	31	....	....
TpBras		31767	10⅛	4¼	4½	....	....
TopsyA		3369	4½	2⅝	3¾	+ ¼	+ 7.1
TorRoy		11729	4¼	1¾	3	....	....
Toyota	.08r	31435	12⅞	9¾	9¾	− 3	− 23.5
TranInd	t	1226	7	3¼	3½	− 1¼	− 26.3
TranLa	1.24	4801	18¼	14½	18¼	+ ¼	+ 1.4
TrnNLs	t	477	5¼	4¼	4½	....	....
Trnsdcr	.02r	3820	11¼	5¼	5¼	− 4	− 43.2
Trnsnt		31652	4⅛	2⅜	2½	− ½	− 16.7
Trnstct		15956	8½	4¼	4⅝	....	....
TrwlBc	t	1323	6¾	4¼	5	− 1¼	− 20
TravRE	.39e	10588	9¾	8¼	9⅝	....	....
Treco		17448	3 5-16	2 9-16	2 9-16	− 11-16	− 21.2
TriChm	.52	2483	9¾	7⅛	8¾	+ 1⅛	+ 14.8
TriMic		11328	8¼	3¾	4¼	− 3½	− 45.2
TrbC un		5179	21	16½	17¾	....	....
TricoPd	1e	2576	45	34	43	+ 5	+ 13.2
Trilogy		139701	9¾	¾	1 1-16	− 8 5-16	− 88.7
TrinRs g		1512	7¾	3	3¼	− 4⅜	− 57.4
TrioTch		3525	6⅝	6	6⅝	....	....
Trion	.09	9023	9¾	5¼	7	− 2¼	− 24.3
TritonG		266113	2 7-16	1¼	1⅝	....	....
TrstNJ	1.20e	4124	32	23½	32	+ 8½	+ 36.2
TrsNY s	1.12b	1293	25½	19¾	25	+ 3	+ 13.6
TurfPar		21897	8½	4⅜	5⅜	+ 1	+ 22.9
TurnrB		13376	27	15	17½	− 6¼	− 26.3
202 Dta		10469	8	2¼	2½	− 4¼	− 63
II Morw		13306	13¼	7¾	9¼	....	....
Tylan		6899	25	14	15	− 9¾	− 39.4

– U–U–U –

UCI		2257	4⅝	3⅛	3½	....	....
UCI un		7935	10	7¼	8½	....	....
UMC El	.06	1119	6	1⅜	1½	− 3⅜	− 69.2
USP Rl	.91e	5899	12	8¾	12	+ 3¼	+ 37.1
UST	.94	3445	26½	17¼	26½	+ 3½	+ 15.2
UltrBcp	1.28	2585	26¾	19½	26¾	+ 5¾	+ 27.4
Unibcp		2304	16¾	10	12	− 3	− 20
Unibc pf	1.53	5477	19	12¼	14½	....	....
Unifi wt		5945	15¼	2½	2½	− 11¾	− 82.5
Unifrc s		18409	15¼	4⅝	15¼	....	....
Unimed		21780	19½	3	4⅞	− 8⅛	− 62.5
Unimet	.05e	7120	11	3	5	− 4	− 44.4
UnBcp s	1	2630	37	25⅛	37	+ 11⅜	+ 44.4
UnNatl	1.84	4099	38	25½	38	+ 10	+ 35.7
UnSplC	.22i	7154	16¼	9¾	9¾	− 6	− 38.1
UnWarn		20640	11¼	6	9⅜	....	....
UBArz s	.80	21669	28¾	19½	28¾	+ 7¾	+ 36.9

UBkSF		4024	11	6	6½	— 2¼	— 25.7
UBkSB		4942	12¾	7¾	10⅝	+ ⅞	+ 9
UnBkrs	.20b	7047	13	8¾	12¼	....	....
UCarBc	1	5420	24¼	20	24¼	+ 1½	+ 6.6
UCnBsh	.25i	68546	5 9-16	2¼	2⅝	— 1	— 27.6
UCtyGs	1.40	4174	15⅜	12¼	15¼	+ 2½	+ 19.6
UCount	1.60	856	29½	23	28¼	+ 3¼	+ 13
UFdBk	.52e	22760	14¾	7¾	14	6¼	+ 80.7
UFireCs	.80	460	32	14	16½	— 15½	— 48.4
UHltCr		13656	4⅞	3¾	3¾	....	....
UnHrn g		31828	3 9-16	1 11-16	1¾	— ⅜	— 17.6
UnMich	1.68a	3780	53⅜	30	53⅜	+ 18⅞	+ 54.7
UMoBn	1b	2237	33¼	27¾	32¼	+ 4½	+ 16.2
UnBkNJ	1.20b	326	42	37½	42	+ 4	+ 10.5
UnNMex	.25e	8172	12¼	7¾	9½	+ 1¾	+ 22.6
UnOkla	.24	2895	10	7	7½	— 2	— 21.1
UnSvMo	.28	18	12½	12	12	....	....
US Enr		18315	7¾	2⅛	5⅜	+ 1½	+ 38.7
US Hlthl		2391	12½	9	9½	— 2	— 17.4
USMed		13329	10	4¾	4¾	....	....
US Mutl	.30r	10347	7¼	2¾	3	— 3½	— 53.8
US Play		5010	16¾	12¾	14	— ½	— 3.4
US Pl wt		661	5½	5	5¼	....	....
US Sugr		226	57	44	49	— 8	— 14
US Vac		6310	8½	3¼	3¼	— 4⅜	— 57.4
UTelct		12216	9¾	4¾	5¾	— 2	— 25.8
UnTote		10197	12½	9¾	10½	....	....
UnVtBn	.76	328	15½	13	15½	....	....
UVaBk pf	2.75	160	34	29	33½	+ 1¼	+ 3.9
UnvDev	.10e	12042	13½	7½	12½	+ ¾	+ 6.4
UMoney		39478	7	⅞	1½	— 5⅜	— 78.2
UnvTIA		714	9⅝	6⅝	9	+ ⅝	+ 7.5
UpRight		8396	7	3¼	3¾	— 2½	— 40
UpPenP	2	2649	18	14½	17¼	....	....
UtahBc	1.08	6123	23¾	18	23¾	+ 3¾	+ 18.8

— V—V—V —

V Band		23291	10¾	4½	9⅜	....	....
VaalR s	7.42e	119649	14⅛	7 15-16	8 3-16	—2 13-16	— 25.6
VacDry		6250	7⅞	3¾	6	+ ¾	+ 14.3
VailAsc		2061	28	19¾	26¼	+ 3¾	+ 16.7
Vallen		1626	18¾	13¾	18¾	+ 3½ '	23
ValyBcp	1.08	1750	27	17	26	....	....
ValFrg	.10	2536	6¾	4¾	5½	— ¼	— 4.3
VlNBcp	3a	1921	59½	53½	59½	+ 6	+ 11.2
Valmnt	.60	5693	23½	16¼	19½	— 4	— 17
Valtek	.06e	11446	7⅛	5⅜	6⅜	— ⅛	— 1.9
VanShk	.15e	3894	11	5¾	8¾	— 2¼	— 20.5
VariCr	.04	2540	8	5¼	6⅜	+ ⅝	+ 10.9
Varlen	.60	4828	20½	12½	13	— 6	— 31.6
gawtp un		10336	7¼	⅞	1¼	....	....
VectAut		2643	3½	¾	1	....	....
Velcro	.92	8808	44½	26	39¼	+ 7½	+ 23.6
VeloBd		5886	15½	8½	14½	+ 6	+ 70.6
VtFedl		5954	13	7½	10½	....	....
VtFncl	1.20a	1092	27½	23	26	+ ¾	+ 3
Vicom		5242	3⅛	1¾	3	....	....
VictBn	1	3490	26½	20	22¾	— 3	— 11.7
VictMkt	.40b	4990	17⅛	11⅞	14¾	— 1½	— 9.2
ViewMs		10897	14¼	10	12¾	+ 1	+ 8.5
VaBech	.04e	13243	8¼	4¾	6	— 1½	— 20
VaFst		1593	5¼	3	5	+ 1⅛	+ 29
VistaRs	.20e	986	30	28	28	— 1¾	— 5.9
Vitram	t	6289	13½	4¾	6½	— 4¾	— 42.2
Vyqust s		5970	7	4¾	5⅛	— 1⅛	— 18

— W—W—W —

Wacoal	.23e	10	16⅝	14⅜	14½	....	....
Waldb	t	13661	18¼	14½	18¼	+ 3¼	+ 21.7
WlkrT un		2146	13¼	5½	12½	+ ½	+ 4.2
WarnEl	.80	10447	29⅝	18½	29⅝	+ 5⅝	+ 23.4
WshSc s	.12	8241	15½	7½	14¼	+ 5¾	+ 67.7
Watrslst	.10e	3836	8¼	4½	6½	....	....
WausPp	.40	6243	14¾	8¼	8¾	— 6	— 40.7
Waver	.44	2219	15¼	10¾	13¼	— 2	— 13.1
Waxmn	.06	6862	10⅝	4⅛	10⅝	+ 6⅜	+ 150
gwedgtn	1.20	5652	9½	6½	7⅜	— 1⅞	— 20.3
WeigTr	.30	2408	17½	10¼	13¼	— 4½	— 25.4
Weisfd s	.50	1241	13¾	10¾	11	— 2¾	— 20
Welblt s		3511	23¾	11⅛	20	+ 7⅝	+ 61.6
WelkG	.75e	32366	14⅞	6 13-16	7⅛	— 4⅝	— 39.4
Wespac	1.08	12207	12⅜	9½	9¾	— ¾	— 7.1
Wespc 2	.80	5537	10¼	8	8½	— 1½	— 15
WstChm		3749	9¾	5½	7	....	....
WAmBc	.70	4649	17	14¼	16	+ 1	+ 6.7
WnCmcl		1873	4½	3½	3½	....	....
WDeep	2.44e	43317	67	33¾	34½	— 17¾	— 34
WHold	3.03e	25679	56½	26⅛	28¼	— 14	— 33.1
WnWste		10980	14¾	6¾	7½	— 7¼	— 49.2
WMarE	.10e	3665	7¾	3¾	4⅝	— 2⅜	— 33.9
WStLf s	.34	2307	17	10½	13	— ½	— 3.7
WstSteer	.20	5505	12	9	9	— 2¾	— 23.4
WstBcp		775	17	.5½	17	....	....
WstsBc		9588	14	3½	3¾	— 6¾	— 64.3
WstwdGp		62	10	9½	10	....	....
Weynbrg	1.28	520	52	43	48	+ 3	+ 6.7
Wharf		22287	4⅛	2⅛	2¾	+ ⅛	+ 4.8
WheelC		5930	5¾	1⅜	2	— 2½	— 55.6
Wiener	.40	7113	9⅜	7	8½	— ¼	— 2.9
Wiland		7897	6⅜	5⅛	5⅞	....	....
WilyJ A	1.10	5823	36	27	30½	— 3½	— 10.3
WilyJ B	.98	828	36	28	31	— 4	— 11.4
WillWW	.56	914	11	6¾	10	+ 3¼	+ 48.2
Willml	t	5423	7⅝	4½	7½	+ 1¼	+ 20
WlmgTr	2	7819	44	31	44	+ 12½	+ 39.7
Wilton		13216	10	3¼	4	....	....
WiscRE		2126	5⅝	4⅝	5⅛	+ ½	+ 10.8
WisSGs	1.44b	817	31¾	19	29	+ 9	+ 45
Wolohn	.16	18181	6⅞	4	5⅛	— ⅝	— 10.9
WolvT s	.20	5631	11¾	8⅜	9	— 2¾	— 23.4
WrightW	.38	7907	10¾	8½	9¾	— 1	— 9.3
Wyse		23801	7½	5¾	7	....	....

— X—Y—Z —

XidMag		15805	15½	11⅜	14¾	....	....
YBear g	.12	4525	8¾	6¾	8½	— ¼	— 2.9
YorkFd	.10e	3172	11¼	9	10½	....	....
ZenNtl	.68	14685	15¼	9¾	14¼	— ¼	— 1.7
Zycad		59357	17¾	7¾	10¾	....	....
Zygo		5272	14	7	7	— 7	— 50

HOW TO READ THE BOND AND TREASURY BOND TABLES

The following yearly tables of bond trading on the New York Stock Exchange, and of over-the-counter trading of U.S. government bonds, are similar to the daily, weekly and annual bond tables that appear in newspapers and specialized financial publications.

The New York Stock Exchange bond table shows, reading from left to right, the name of the issuer; each bond's nominal or "coupon" interest rate and, after an "s," the last two digits of the year in which the bond is scheduled to mature; the number of bonds traded during the year; the highest, lowest and last prices of the bond for the year, and the net change the last price represents from the close of business in the preceding year.

The table for over-the-counter trading of government securities shows, reading from left to right, each bond's nominal or "coupon" interest rate per year; the month and year in which the bond is scheduled to reach maturity; the highest, lowest and last prices of the bond for the year, and the net change the last price represents from the close of business in the preceding year.

Bond price listings can be confusing to the unpracticed eye. The standard redemption value of each individual bond is $1,000, but prices are quoted on a basis of 100 rather than 1,000. Thus, a bond that trades at 98 actually changes hands for $980.

Corporate bonds are quoted, like stocks, in whole numbers and eighths. Thus a price of 98⅝, for example, is 98.625, or $986.25. But U.S. government and government agency securities are usually quoted in whole numbers and thirty-seconds. Thus a government bond quoted at 98.24 should be read as 98 24/32, or 98¾. In dollars, that amounts to $987.50.

NEW YORK STOCK EXCHANGE BONDS

DECEMBER 31, 1984

NEW YORK (AP) — New York Stock Exchange trading for 1984. The net change is from the previous year on issues listed prior to January 1, 1984.

CORPORATION BONDS

	Sales $1000	High	Low	Last	Chg
AMF 10s85	971	100	95⅝	99¾	+ 3⅛
ANR Pipe 8⅝93	167	84⅛	72⅝	82⅜	+ 2⅜
ANR Pipe 9⅝94	36	88⅛	76⅜	88⅛	+ 7⅛
ANR Pipe 10⅝95	96	92	81⅛	92	+ 4⅜
ANR Pipe 13¼97	20	99	85⅛	89	—12
ANR Pipe 11¾97	90	90¼	88	90	....
APL 10¾97	825	80	68⅛	72⅝	— 3⅜
AVX Cp 13½00	331	97	86⅛	93	— 1⅛
AbbtLab 6¼s93	28	81	76	80⅜	+ 3⅜
AbbtLab 7⅝s96	68	84⅛	82⅛	83¼	+ ⅝
AbbtLab 9.2s99	313	83	69	83	+ 3¼
AbbtLab 11s93	301	97	84⅜	97	+ ¼
Advest cv9s08	3204	101	68¾	70	—24¼
AetnaLf 8⅛07	2822	73	57	70⅝	+ 1½
AirPrdC 11⅝10	5	91	91	91	— 1¼
AirPrdC 14⅝87	119	106½	101	103½	— 4½
AirPrd 12¾94	348	97¾	93½	94¼	....
AlaBn 11.70s99t	755	100½	97⅜	100	+ ⅜
AlaPw 9s2000	2786	76¾	65	74¼	+ 3¾
AlaPw 8½2001	2198	72¼	59⅞	70¼	+ 2⅜
AlaPw 7⅞2002	868	68	56¼	65⅝	+ 3
AlaPw 7¾2002	1614	67¾	55⅜	65⅞	+ 4
AlaPw 8⅞s2003	4720	74¼	60⅞	71⅝	+ 2¾
AlaPw 8¼2003	1538	69¼	57½	66⅞	+ 2⅝
AlaPw 9¾s04	2971	80	67	79	+ 4⅝
AlaPw 10⅞s05	796	87½	72⅝	87½	+ 4⅜
AlaPw 10½s05	1540	85⅝	69⅞	82	+ 2⅝
AlaPw 8⅞s06	1235	73	60⅜	71¼	+ ½
AlaPw 8¾07	2315	73	58⅞	70¾	+ 3⅞
AlaPw 8⅝87	1483	94¼	85½	93⅞	+ 5⅜
AlaPw 9¼07	1867	75½	62⅝	72½	+ 2½
AlaPw 9½08	2470	77½	64⅝	75	+ 3¼
AlaPw 9⅝08	3353	79	65½	77½	+ 4⅞
AlaPw 12⅝10	2333	100	83	96⅝	+ 2⅜
AlaPw 15¼10	6896	111	99¼	104¼	— 5½
AlaPw 14¾91	316	109⅝	100	108¼	+ ¼
AlaPw 17⅜11	6408	114⅞	104¾	112¾	+ 2⅜
AlaPw 18¼89	8014	115¼	108	111¾	+ 1¼
AlskaAr cv9s03	3090	108	87½	102	....
AlskaHou 16¼94	1828	112	101⅞	112	+ 1⅛
AlskaHo 16¼99	1496	116½	102	112¼	+ 1¼
AlskaHou 17¾91	1931	116⅜	109	116	+ 2
AlskaHou 18⅜01	17168	114	105	112	— ¾
AlskaHou 15¼92	535	107⅜	102¼	105¾	+ ½
AlskaHou 15s92	847	107	101	103¾	— 1½
AlskaHou 11¾92	101	97¼	89	92⅞	....
AlskaHou 11½93	214	97½	90	96¾	— 2¼
AlskaHou 11⅜93	102	95⅞	87⅛	87⅛	— 7⅜
AlskaHou 10¾93	319	96	87½	96	+ 5⅛
AlskaHou 11½93l	150	96	84	93¾	— 1½
AlskHou 12⅞93	31	103	95	103	....
Alexnd cv5½96	3685	94	66	75	+ 9
AlleghWn 4s98	96	45	37	41½	+ 1¼
Allglnt 10¾99	546	78¾	66	73½	— 6
Allglnt 10.40s02	2037	73½	63⅜	69¾	....
Allglnt 9s89	645	84	78	84	+ 4
AlldCp 5.20s91	245	74½	59⅛	68¼	+ 4⅛
AlldCp 6.60s93	485	70⅞	61	69⅝	+ 3⅜
AlldCp 7⅞s96	330	73	60¼	71¾	+ 2⅝
AlldCp 9s2000	185	75¾	68	73⅝	+ 1½
AlldCp zr87s	4125	76¼	64	76	+11¾
AlldCp zr92s	5485	41½	32	41¼	+ 5¾
AlldCp zr96s	2434	28	22	27	+ 1⅛
AlldCp zr98s	7792	21	15⅞	20½	+ 2⅜
AlldCp zr2000s	13888	18	13¾	17¼	+ ¾
AlldCp d6s88	4734	83	72	81⅝	+ 5⅛
AlldCp d6s90	3223	77	63½	74⅞	+ 4⅛
AlldCp zr87s	10	68⅝	68⅝	68⅝	....
AlldCp zr95s	40	26⅛	26⅛	26⅛	....
AlldCp zr99s	135	20	14⅞	20	....
AlldCp zr05s	275	9⅜	6½	9⅛	....
AlldSt cv4½s92	12	233	230	231⅛	— 9⅞
AlldSt 10⅜90	1063	95⅜	84¾	95⅛	+ 2⅜
AlldSt cv9½07	6254	138	107	129½	+ 3½
AlldSt cv8¾09	2055	110½	105½	106½	....
AlsChal 10.35s99	466	78½	65⅝	66	— 8⅞
AlsChal 12s90	1756	93½	76⅞	80	— 9¾
AlsChal 16s91	4143	107	86¾	94⅞	—10⅝
AllstFn 8⅛87	419	95	86	93⅞	+ 3⅝
AllstFn 7⅞87	1036	94¼	85	94⅛	+ 5
AllstFn 9⅝86	652	99	93	99	+ 3¼
Alcoa 6s92	1007	71	62¾	69¼	+ 1⅝
Alcoa 9s95	1790	83½	72	82½	+ 2¾
Alcoa 7.45s96	1078	72	60	69⅝	+ ⅝
Alcoa 9.45s2000	909	83⅛	68⅜	81⅜	+ 1⅞
Alcoa 13⅞11	151	105¾	99	103	— 2
AluCan 9½s95	539	84½	72	83⅛	+ 3⅝
AluCan 14¼92	266	107½	96⅛	106	— 2
AMAX 8s86	2981	98	90½	95¾	+ 4⅜
AMAX 8½s96	212	73	54	64¼	— 3¾
AMAX 9⅜2000	354	74	65	66⅛	— 3⅞
Amax 8⅝s01	60	68	60	60½	+ ½
Amax 14¼90	2205	103⅞	96⅛	99⅞	— 2½
AmrHes 7⅛96	810	87⅞	80¾	85¼	+ 3⅝
AmForP 4.8s87	589	88½	79¼	86	+ 6⅛
AmForP 4.8s87r	40	84⅞	80	84⅞	....
AmForP 5s2030	2266	41	35¼	40	+ 3¼
AForP 5s30r	285	40	35	39½	....
AmAirl 4¼92	1255	60	51¼	59⅜	+ 5¼
AmAirl 5¼98	477	53	46¾	48¼	— ½
ABrand 4⅝s90	121	71	65⅝	71	+ 2
ABrand 5⅞s92	771	72	61	72	+ 3⅞
ABrand 8⅛s85	2903	100	96½	99 11-16	+2 7-16
ABrand 11⅛89	4349	100½	89½	100	+ 2¾
ABrand 9¾87	400	97	89⅞	96¼	+ 1¼
ABdcst 9.35s00	195	85	74	85	+ 8⅞
AmCan 3¾s88	139	78	71⅛	77⅝	+ 5⅝
AmCan 3¾88r	19	75¾	70	75¾	....
AmCan 4¾s90	173	75¾	63	69¾	+ 2½
AmCan 6s97	384	59¾	48⅛	58	+ 3⅝
AmCan 7¾2001	350	66½	57⅛	65½	+ 2
AmCan 11⅜10	1085	89	75	88½	+ 4
AmCan 13¼93	2054	105⅝	92	105⅝	+ 5⅜
ACenM cv6¾91	2017	93½	62½	66	—27½
AmCyan 7⅜01	603	66	57⅛	66	+ 3¼
AmCyan 8⅜s06	1093	71¼	60	71	+ 2
AExpCr 7.8s92	203	84	77¼	83⅝	+ 3⅝
AExpCr 8½s85	987	97½	93½	97½	+ 1¼
AExpCr 8½s86	1444	97¾	91¼	97¾	+ 3⅞
AExpCr 7.7s87	1892	94	87	93½	+ 4
AExpCr 10.1s90	2738	96⅛	82¾	95½	+ 3⅞
AExpCr 11¼00	697	94	81	91	+ 2¼
AmExpCr 12⅞91	3706	105	93½	105	+ 2
AmExpCr 14¾92	1056	112	100¼	112	+ 2
AmExpCr 11⅝92	1837	102⅜	87⅝	102	+ 2¾
AmExpCr 11¾12	193	94	84½	86⅝	— 6½
AmExpCr 10⅞13	50	71	71	71	....
AGenCp 8s94	18	72½	64	72½	+ 2⅜
AGenCp 9⅜08	202	76¾	66	67½	— 8½
AGenCp cv11s07	4545	146	119½	145	+12
AGenCp cv11s08	5526	146½	119½	144	+10¾
AHoist cv4¾92	17	75½	65	65	—30½
AHoist cv5½93	740	79	58	58	—16½
AHosp 7⅞07	201	68	54½	66	+ 1⅝
AmInvt 8¾s89	300	85	77¼	85	+ 9
AmMed cv9½01	8687	121	101	102	— 8¾
AmMed cv8¼08	8157	92¾	80½	83	— 2⅝
AmMed 11s98	289	89⅞	74	85½	+ 4⅞
AmMed 11¾99	204	91⅛	77⅛	86	— 1½
AmMot cv6s88	2677	102	74½	81	—10
ASmelt 4⅝s88	194	76	72½	73⅛	— 1⅞
AmStrs 9⅞s90	307	100⅛	90⅜	99⅜	+ 4⅞
AmStrs 12s90	10	100½	97	100½	— ½
ATT 4⅜85	13567	100	93½	98 13-16	+5 5-16
ATT 4⅜85r	536	98½	90 1-16	98½	....
ATT 2⅝86	9012	91½	84¾	91	+ 6¼
ATT 2⅞87	10098	87¼	80¼	85	+ 4⅞
ATT 3⅞90	20978	74⅞	67¾	73¼	+ 5
ATT 3⅞90r	495	73⅞	68	73⅞	....
ATT 8¾00	74015	78⅜	65⅛	76⅞	+ 2⅛
ATT 7s2001	53942	65⅝	53¾	64¼	+ 2¼
ATT 7⅛03	39570	64⅞	53¼	63⅞	+ 1⅞

ATT 8.8s05	60127	76⅝	63⅝	75¼	+ 2¾
ATT 8⅝07	35151	75	62	73¼	+ 2⅛
ATT 10⅜90	52934	97⅞	84⅞	97⅛	+ 2⅞
ATT 13¼91	82784	105½	95½	105⅛	+ ¼
AmesDSt 10s95	32	82⅝	78	82⅝	+ 2⅝
AmesDSt cv8½09	1751	104½	99½	103	....
Amfac cv5¼94	1117	79½	66	66½	—13
AMPInc 8⅝85	385	99 19-32	96 11-16	99 19-32	+2 27-32
Ancp cv13⅞02f	21234	75	32⅞	55	—16½
Anadarko 14¾91	124	108¼	98	102½	— 3¾
Andarko 14.70s94	161	107⅞	98¼	107⅞	— 2⅛
AnchHck 8⅝06	95	74½	60½	74½	+ 8⅝
Anheu 11⅞12	111	94	83½	89	— 5
Anheu 5.45s91	21	72¼	71	71	— 1
Anheu 6s92	233	75¼	72	75	+ ¾
Anheu 7.95s99	100	72	65	71¾	— 1¼
Anheu 9.20s05	741	80	66⅝	80	+ 4
Anheu 8.55s08	225	70⅝	59½	70⅝	— 2⅜
Anheu 9.9s86	2571	100½	92½	100	+ 3
Anixtr cv8¼03	2471	106½	80	84	—18½
AppalP 11s87	553	100⅞	91¼	100⅞	+ 2⅛
ArchDan 13s14	12	96½	95½	96½	....
ArcoPip 7¾86	2701	96¼	88	95¾	+ 3¼
Aristar 9½s89	221	94⅞	82⅝	91⅛	+ 6⅝
Aristar 14½99	2	95⅛	95⅛	95⅛	—12⅞
ArizPS 7.45s02	1545	63⅛	51⅛	62½	+ 4¾
ArizPS 10⅝s00	900	85	70¼	84	+ 5
ArizPS 12⅛09	2962	95¼	78	95	+ 1
ArlenRl cv5s86	64	78⅝	63	63	—15½
Armco 14.65s86	1228	105⅝	99¼	101	— 1¾
Armco 4½s86	9	89	84	89	+ 4
Armco 5.90s92	163	75	64⅜	71¼	+ 6¼
Armco 8.70s95	1131	75½	66	73⅝	+ 1¼
Armco 9.20s00	262	73½	65⅞	69	+ 1
Armco 8½01	692	68½	55⅜	63¼	— 3⅝
ArmCk 8s96	212	76	65¼	74	+ 3
ArmR 8⅝96	207	76¾	70	74⅛	+ 1⅞
Asarco 9¾2000	12	68⅞	65	68⅞	— 8⅛
AshO 6.15s92	213	68¼	62¾	68¼	+ 1⅜
AshO cv4¾93	403	85½	75½	81¼	— 1¾
AshO 8.8s00	243	73	60	70¾	+ ⅝
AshO 8.2s02	268	68	56	65	+ ⅞
AshO 11.1s04	776	86	75½	84	— ½
AssoCp 9¼s90	754	92	81	90⅝	— ¾
AssoCp 8.2s87	1116	94½	87⅛	94½	+ 4
AssoCp 8¾87	130	93¾	89⅛	93¾	+ 2¼
AssoCp 12⅛00	11	97½	95	97½	+ 3¾
AssoCp 13⅛00	49	100	99½	99½	— ½
AssoCp 11s87	881	99½	90⅜	99½	+ 1½
AssoCp 13⅞90	430	105⅞	100¾	105¾	+ 2¾
AssoCp d6s01	18	58	57⅞	57⅞	+ 2⅝
AssoCp 14½90	861	108	99¾	107⅝	+ 3½
AssoCo 13¼85	180	103½	98⅜	101 11-16	+3-16
AssoCp 12⅜89	272	100¾	95¼	100½	— ¾
AssoCp 11¼86	555	100¾	96¾	100¾	+ 1¼
AssoCp 11.85s89	85	94	92¾	92¾	....
AssoCp 11¾88	118	101	94	101	....
AssoCp 12.55s88	5	100	100	100	....
AssoInv 4⅝85	621	97⅛	93	97⅛	+ 5⅞
AssoInv 7⅜88	477	87¼	77	87⅛	+ 5
Atchison 4s95st	347	52	44⅝	50⅜	— 1⅝
Atchison 4s95st r	65	50⅝	44⅝	49⅞	....
Atchison 4s95	1061	55	44⅛	52⅜	+ 1½
Atchison 4s95r	389	55⅞	45½	55⅞	....
Athlone 11s93	234	84⅝	72¼	73¾	—10
Athlone 15½91	7	101¾	98⅝	98⅝	....
AtlCstL 4.95s88	286	80⅜	73½	80¼	+ 4¼
AtlCstL 4.95s88r	2	74½	74½	74½	....
AtlCstL 4¾s88	101	76⅝	70	76	+ 1⅜
AtlCstl 4¾88r	2	76	76	76	....
AtlRch 5⅝97	775	70½	55⅜	61½	+ 3⅞
AtlRch 8⅝00	1640	80⅜	62⅝	77	+ 3
AtlRch 7.7s2000	1587	69½	59⅛	68	+ ½
AtlRch 7¾03	1509	69½	58	68½	+ 1½
AtlRch 11⅜10	1417	96	80	94½	+ 3¼
AtlRch 13⅝11	2281	108⅛	94¼	102¾	— 3¾
AtlRch d7s91	4708	80	68	78⅛	+ 2⅝
AtlRch 12½12	779	101	87⅛	101	+ 3¾
AtlRch 11s13	272	90½	75⅜	87⅝	— 2⅜
AvcoCp cv5½93	11115	90½	63⅛	87¾	+15¼
AvcoCp 7½93	2502	72	60⅛	70¾	+ 3¾
AvcoCp 12s90	682	100	85⅛	98½	+ 4⅜
AvcoFin 6⅛s87	19	88½	86⅝	87⅝	— 2¼
AvcoFin 7⅞s89	424	91¾	78⅝	91¾	+ 9⅛
AvcoFin 9¼s90	145	95	84	89⅛	+ 3⅜
AvcoFin 9¼s89	457	93	83⅝	91⅜	+ 1⅜
AvcoFin 11s90	570	99	81½	95⅝	— 1⅝
AvcoFin 7⅞s92	266	82⅞	70	80⅜	+ 2¾
AvcoFin 7⅝s97	247	69⅛	60⅞	69⅛	+ 2⅞
AvcoFin 8.35s98	609	74½	61⅝	74½	+ ⅜
AvcoFin 8.2s86	1301	95⅜	87¾	95⅜	+ 5⅛
AvcoFin 8⅞91	238	83⅞	78½	80⅞	+ ¾
AvcoFin 9⅜93	141	82	76	82	+ ½
AvcoFin 9⅛98	363	79½	66	78	....
AvcoFin 9⅜98	230	81	70⅛	81	+ 7
AvcoFin 9⅞87	1406	97⅞	90⅛	97⅜	+ 3¼
AvcoFin 9¾99	503	95¼	86	94¼	+ 4¼
AvcoFin 14⅛85	233	105	100	100	— 3¾
Avnet cv8s13	4325	114	83	92½	—18¼
AvonCap 11¾90	383	100¾	89⅞	100¾	+ 1¾
— B—B —					
BPNoA 10s00	267	84¼	70½	84⅛	+ 1⅛
BPNoA 9¼01	500	79⅞	67½	77¼	+ ½
Bache 14s00	4818	106½	95	101¾	— 2⅞
BakerInt 7.55s87	205	91	83	91	+ 3
BakerInt 10.20s90	706	95	85⅝	91¼	....
BakerOil 7.8s97	35	68	60	65	+ 8¾
BaldwUn 10s09f	7020	39¾	14½	17½	—21⅝
Bally cv6s98	8350	89	59¼	59½	—21½
Bally cv10s06	19374	97	74⅛	75¼	—17¾
BallyPP 13⅞03	5	99	99	99	....
B O 4¼95	192	61½	50	61⅜	+ 9⅜
B O 4¼95r	6	60⅜	52¼	60⅜	....
B O 4½10A	1413	200	135⅛	151	—52
BaltGE 3s89	983	74	65¾	73¾	+ 5¾
BaltGE 3s89r	16	74	65	74	....
BaltGE 3¼s90	227	69¾	61⅞	69¾	+ 5¾
BaltGE 3¼90r	10	65	59	64½	....
BaltGE 4s93	171	61	50⅝	60¼	+ 5⅝
BaltGE 9⅞s05	958	82¾	69¾	81	+ 4
BaltGE 8⅜06	1538	74⅞	59	69¼	....
BaltGE 8¼07	838	72½	58¼	68⅝	+ 1⅞
BaltGE 9⅜08	1540	80	65¼	77⅞	+ 2⅞
BaltGE 12⅛90	1669	103¼	91½	103¼	+ 2¾
BaltGE 16¾91	1590	118½	108	113	— 1
BaltGE 14¾92	481	110	101	108	— 4
BkBos 8.3s85	1715	99¼	92½	99¼	+ 2½
BkBos 10.65s87	1060	99⅞	89	99	+ 1¾
BankNE 8.8599	228	77	67	72½	+ 1¾
BkNY cv6¼94	381	184	140	184	+18
BkNY cv12s06	6280	144	114	141¾	+ 9¾
Bankam 7⅞s03	2136	67¾	54⅝	67⅛	+ 4⅛
Bankam 8⅞s05	6217	74½	60⅛	74⅜	+ 3⅜
Bankam 8¾s01	2881	75	61¾	71	+ ⅜
Bankam 8.35s07	2377	70¼	58⅝	68	+ 3¼
Bankam zr87A	11347	76	63⅛	73⅞	+ 7⅛
Bankam zr90s	6784	53	40	52⅞	+ 7¼
Bankam zr92s	24566	41½	31⅜	40¾	+ 4¾
Bankam zr87D	8968	73⅜	60½	72⅝	+ 8⅛
Bankam zr91s	3642	51½	38	49¼	+ 6⅞
Bankam zr93s	14837	37¾	28⅞	37⅝	+ 4
Bankam 13¼88	769	105½	97¼	104	+ 1½
BankAm 11⅜86	491	101	95¼	101	+ 1¾
BankAm 11½95	13	100	97	97	— 3
BankAm 11⅜96	140	100	97	100	....
BkAm 12⅛94	38	101⅛	96½	101⅛	....
Bkamrty cv9½00	16	143	134	143	— 4
BkamRty cv9½08	3003	102	88½	101¼	+ 2¼
BankTr 8⅛s99	1521	74	58¼	72¼	+ 5
BankTr 8⅝02	1173	74	60	73½	+ 5⅝
BarcAm 8⅝85	651	99¾	97¼	99¾	+ 2½
BarcAm 8⅞86	792	97	91¼	96¼	+ 2½
BarcAm 7.95s92	210	80¼	69	80¼	+ 3⅜
BarcAm 8¾97	184	77	69½	76	+ 3¼
BarcAm 9¾86	584	98⅛	93⅛	98⅛	+ 2⅞
BarcAm 14¾88	696	105	101	104½	— ½
BarcAm zr90s	6540	53½	40⅛	51⅞	+ 7¼
BarcNA 14⅝91	675	108¾	100	106⅛	— ⅞

BarcNA 11⅝03	35	85½	80	85½	....
BarBks cv12¼06	9887	141	121½	139	+ 1½
BASIX d11⅝03	77	81⅝	75¼	75½	— 6
BaxLb cv4⅜91	106	187	132	132	—186
BaxLb cv4¾01	576	201	102½	111½	—108½
Bearng cv8½09	1463	102	86	102	....
BeatCo 7⅞94	144	87¼	74⅝	78	— 8¾
BeatCo 8½08	630	75	62	72	+ 3¾
BeatCo 10⅞10	628	88	76½	87⅛	— 2⅞
Becton cv4⅛88	917	92	86½	91	+ 1½
Becton cv5s89	2373	83	71⅛	80	+ 1¾
Bekerlnd 15⅞03	1828	105½	93	98⅞	— ⅜
BellCnda 8¾06	2340	75⅛	63	75	+ 4
BellCnda 9s08	1637	76¼	64⅜	74¼	+ 2¼
BellCnda 13⅜10	374	103½	95½	103½	— 1
BellCnda 14½91	1020	109½	101	107⅝	— ⅝
BellTPa 8⅝s06	5395	74⅞	62	73⅞	+ 4
BellTPa 7⅛s12	2767	62⅛	50½	60¾	+ 2⅝
BellTPa 7½s13	2829	64½	53⅛	64½	+ 3⅜
BellTPa 9⅝s14	7089	82	65⅝	79¼	+ 3¼
BellTPa 8¾s15	1332	74	60¾	72	+ 2
BellTPa 8⅛17	1423	69½	56⅛	67⅝	+ 2¼
BellTPa 9¼19	1945	78	65	76	+ 2⅜
BellTPa 11⅞20	4729	98⅞	80	96¾	+ 3¾
Bemis 6⅜s92	19	80	70½	70⅝	—13⅛
Bendix 6⅝s92	598	73⅝	65	73⅜	+ 4⅜
Bendix 11.20s05	108	89	78⅞	89	+ 1⅜
BenefCp 7½s96	711	71	58⅛	69⅜	+ 2⅜
BenefCp 7.45s00	375	66⅞	54⅛	66⅞	+ 4⅛
BenefCp 7½s02	309	65	54	63¼	+ 2⅛
BenefCp 7½s98	473	68	58⅛	66⅝	— ⅜
BenefCp 8s01	627	99¼	94¼	98½	— ¼
BenefCp 8.3s03	206	70	60½	69¼	+ 2⅜
BenefCp 8.4s07	804	69⅜	55	67	+ 2
BenefCp 8.35s88	2061	92⅛	82	92	+ 4¼
BenefCp 8.4s08	1054	94½	88	94½	+ 3½
BenefCp 9.4s85					
	1953	99 23-32	95⅜	99 23-32	+2 31-32
BenefCp 11.55s87t	3370	99¼	96½	98¾	+ 1⅜
BenefCp 9s05	512	75	57⅞	72½	— ⅝
BenefCp 13⅜91	955	104½	96⅜	103¼	+ 1⅛
BenefCp 12⅞13	5	97¾	97¾	97¾	+ 1
BenefCp 12¾13	108	100⅜	93	98⅜	+ 1⅜
BenefCp 12½93	23	97	95	95	....
BenefCp 12.45s94	448	102½	89⅝	101½	......
BenefCp 12.60s94	15	92	92	92	....
BenefCp 12⅜88	50	102¼	102¼	102¼	....
Berkey cv5¾86	333	86	79	85½	+ 5½
BestProd 9s94	17	56⅜	54¼	56⅜	+ 1⅜
BethStl 4½s90	2310	69	62	63¼	— 6
BethStl 5.4s92	513	65	58	58	— 2⅝
BethStl 6⅞s99	1110	61⅜	51⅛	53	— 4
BethStl 9s2000	3061	73⅛	60⅛	63	— 7
BethStl 8.45s05	5772	67	55⅝	57	— 6¾
BethStl 8⅜s01	1294	69	56½	56½	— 7⅝
Beverly 15s02	2214	106	93½	102½	— ½
Beverly cv7⅝03	4968	98	76	92	+10½
BigThr 8.55s01	31	75⅝	73½	73½	+ 1½
BigThr 9.85s09	127	79¾	79	79¾	— ¼
BigThr cv8½06	5903	84	74	77	— 3½
BlackD cv4s92	5	218	218	218	+ 2
BlackD 8.45s85					
	488	99 15-16	97 17-32	99 15-16	+2 11-16
BlairJhn 13⅝98	30	101	97½	97½	— 8½
BlairJhn 10¾90	20	85	84⅝	84⅝	....
Boeing cv8⅞06	29468	145½	106	136¼	+13¼
BoiseC 9.9s86	2386	98⅛	92⅜	97⅜	+ 2⅜
BoiseC 10.45s90	909	95¼	84½	94⅞	+ 2⅞
BoiseC 13⅛94	125	101⅝	94¼	101⅝	....
Borden 4⅜s91	68	72⅞	64	64	—10¾
Borden 5¾s97	92	65¾	59½	62	+ 1½
Borden 8½s04	1153	74⅞	62	72½	+ 2½
Borden 9⅜09	854	79	69	77⅛	— 1¼
BorgWAc 7⅞91	207	83½	73½	79½	+ ¼
BorgWAc 7½93	223	77⅝	70	77	+ 3¼
BorgWAc 8⅜86	590	97½	90⅜	96¾	+ 3⅛
BorgWar 6s01	121	56	46	56	+ 3
BorgWar 5½92	57	70	62	62	— 4
BosEd 9¼07	453	76⅞	64	74½	+ 5⅞
Bowatr cv9s09	223	101	98½	100¼	....
BrckwyG 8¾85					
	598	99½	95¾	99 11-32	+1 31-32
BrkUnG 4⅜s88	17	76⅞	74⅝	75	— ⅛
BrkUnG 4⅝s90	50	66	66	66	— 3
BrkUnG 6¼s92	244	71½	61	71	+ 1¼
BrkUnG 9⅛s95	1187	84⅜	70	82⅞	+ 4¾
BrkUnG 7⅞s97	180	71¼	60	70	....
BrkUnG 8¾s99	371	77	64⅛	75⅞	+ 3⅜
BrkUnG 9¾s85	1169	100¼	96	100¼	+ 3⅛
BrkUnG 9⅝s96	361	85½	71½	84¾	+ 4⅝
BrkUnG 17⅜91	493	117	109	116⅛	+ 1⅛
BwnShp cv9¼05	1618	82½	65	75	— 4¾
BrwnGp 7⅜s98	44	71	63½	63½	— 3¾
BrwnGp 9⅞00	24	84	78	84	+ 3½
BrwnF 10¼96	85	92	81¼	86	— 6
BrwnF 12⅞87	117	102½	95½	99	— 1⅜
BucyErie 9s99	82	71	68½	69	— 3
Bulova cv6s90	492	73	70¾	72¾	+ 1¾
Burllnd cv5s91	1299	92½	72¼	76	—21
Burllnd 9s95	176	80¼	70	80¼	+ 1¼
Burllnd 11¼90	424	98	87½	95⅛	— ⅝
Burlln cv8¾08	4374	96	72½	74½	—20¾
BurlNor 8½s96	1212	80¾	66	80¾	+ 7¼
BurlNor 8.6s99	612	78	66	75	+ 1¾
BurlNo 12⅞05	278	101⅝	88½	101⅝	+ 1⅞
Burrough 10¾87	1861	100¼	92½	99½	+ 1⅜
Burrough 13½91	611	105⅞	96¾	104¾	— ⅝
Burrough 11½10	583	93¼	79¼	93⅛	+ 2⅝
Buttes 10¼97	8754	69	36	51¼	—14⅜

— C-C —

CBS 7.85s2001	28	66½	60⅛	66½	— 3½
CIGNA cv8s07	9257	105½	84	86½	—10
CITFin 9½s95	1072	86	69½	86	+ 4¾
CITFin 7⅞86	1220	96⅞	89⅛	96⅛	+ 3⅝
CITFin 8⅜01	267	73	61	70⅛	+ ¼
CITFin 9s91	785	90	73⅝	86⅜	+ 4⅜
CITFin 8.8s93	752	85¼	67	82½	+ 1⅜
CITFin 8¾08	268	72⅛	60½	69¼	— 1
CITFin 9.85s04	170	80⅛	65	80⅛	+ 2⅝
CITFin 9⅝09	94	79¼	74	79¼	+ 4⅜
CITFin 11½05	1027	94¾	78⅛	92½	+ 3½
CITFin 15½87	1074	111⅜	103	111	— 1
CNAFinl 8½95	731	76¾	65⅛	73⅜	+ 1⅝
CTI 15s87	500	103	96⅜	99¼	— 1
CTI 18¼89	69	113⅝	107⅛	111⅝	— 6⅞
CaesrW 12½90	808	98	83	95	— 1⅝
CaesrW 11¼97	542	84½	74¾	81	— 3⅛
CaesrW 12s94	312	92¼	84	86½	— 3½
CaesrW 12½00	225	92	80	90	+ ⅞
Camerlrn 10¾86	69	98	94	94¼	— 2¾
CampbSoup 9⅞90	2296	97	84⅝	97	+ 5
CampblTag 15⅜91					
	80	105¼	105¼	105¼	+ 5⅜
CanPac 4sperp	3856	39¼	33	36½	+ ¾
CPac4pperp reg	242	37½	32¾	34½	....
CapitHld 12¾06	2182	101	86	98¼	— ⅜
CaroPwLt 7¾s	1680	66½	55	66⅛	+ 3⅛
CarTT cv5¾88	134	100½	83¾	94½	— 9
CarTT 9⅛s2000	840	79	66⅜	76¼	+ ⅝
CarTT 7¾s2001	260	66	56⅛	66	+ 1¾
CarTT 8.10s03	498	70	59	69⅜	+ 2¾
CaroTT 9s08	279	76	62¼	76	+ 4⅛
CaroTT 12.7s10	221	104	85	100½	+ 1
Carrier cv5⅛89	12	117	104	104	— 6
Carrier 8⅛s96	277	76	65½	72⅝	— ⅝
Carrier 7¾s98	134	72	63½	72	+ 6
CartH 9¼96	317	80	65	71⅞	— 2⅛
CartH 9.45s00	15	72½	70	72½	— 2½
CartH 9⅛08	386	71⅜	61⅜	69¼	+ 1
CartH 11⅞10	126	88½	79	79	— 8
CascNG 10½92	356	95⅞	90⅝	91½	— 1⅛
Case 5½s90	80	69⅝	62¾	69⅝	+ 2
CastCk cv5⅜94	3163	114½	67¼	79¼	—25¼
CastCk 8⅛85	624	95½	87 5-32	94½	+ ⅞
CastCk 8½97	5	71	71	71	— 1
CaterT 5.30s92	199	71⅛	62	66	....
CaterT 5⅛s86	101	90⅝	86	90⅝	+ 6⅛
CaterT 6⅞s92	296	87	73¾	83½	+ 9½
CaterT 8.60s99	919	77½	65½	76¼	+ 2⅝
CaterT 8¾s99	208	79	68⅛	76½	+ 3½
CaterT cv5½00	7558	110	72	73½	—27
CaterT 8s01	375	71	60	67½	+ ½

CaterT 14¾88	440	108⅜	100⅞	104⅞	− 2⅛
CaterT 12½90	1996	104	92¾	104	+ 4½
CaterT 13⅜07	341	102½	92	100½	− 8½
Cave 11½00O	4199	83	71	71⅝	− 8⅜
Cave 11½00N	2520	83	70¼	71	− 8½
Ceco cv4.75s88	315	100⅛	86⅞	88	− 8
Celanes cv4s90	2804	88	76⅝	88	+ 8
Celanese 10⅞87	1042	99⅞	92⅛	99⅝	+ 3⅜
Celanese 11⅞05	240	92½	80	88⅝	− 3⅜
Celanse cv9¾06	5992	119½	99½	119	+11
Cenco cv5s96	385	69⅜	63½	66	− 2
Cenco cv4¾97	145	48	45½	46⅝	....
CenSoya 6⅜s93	58	70	68⅞	70	+ 1⅝
CenSoya 7½97	1	64⅞	64⅞	64⅞	− 2⅞
Centel 8.1s96	257	75	64⅜	72¾	+ 1
CentrlTel 8s96	811	75½	62⅛	72½	+ 2
Centrn 7.85s97	353	67⅝	58⅝	67⅝	+ 4⅜
Cessna cv8s08	4163	102	76	82	−13¼
CATS zr88	5315	67⅜	59	67	+ 4
CATS zr91	11415	49	40¼	47½	+ 6¾
CATS zr92	4821	45	39⅛	45	+ 5¼
CATS zr94	5972	42	29½	41⅞	+11⅜
CATS zr95	2847	37¼	28⅝	34½	+ 4⅝
CATS zr96	3576	32	23	29¾	+ 1¾
CATS zr97	10524	27½	21¼	27	+ 4¾
CATS zr98	4077	26	20	24⅛	+ ¾
CATS zr99	10356	24⅝	15½	24	+ 1
CATS zr01	5963	21⅞	13½	19⅝	+ 1⅛
CATS zr02	2548	20½	13⅛	20½	+ 3¾
CATS zr03	8562	18	12½	17½	+ ⅞
CATS zr06-11	25810	10	6⅝	9⅛	+ 1
ChampS 5⅞s92	14	69⅞	67⅛	67⅛	− 2⅞
COUG zr93	....	29⅝	29½	29⅝	....
COUG zr95	10	22⅞	22¼	22⅞	....
COUG zr98	10	15⅞	15¼		....
COUG zr00	....	12⅝	12⅜	12⅝	....
vjChrtCo 10⅝98f	13429	71⅞	20¼	23⅜	−44½
vjChtCo d14¾02f	14523	92½	21	25⅞	−64
ChasBk cv4⅞93	370	92	66½	83½	+ 3½
ChasBk 8¾86	5475	97⅜	88	96¾	+ 3¼
ChasCp 6½96	5976	91½	66	83½	+ 4
ChaseCp 10.20s99t	1221	100¾	95¼	98¼	− 1
ChaseCp 11.3s09t	6163	93½	84⅝	92¾	+ 3⅜
Chelse cv5¼93	567	85	74	84¼	+ 5⅝
Chemetrn 9s94	1127	82⅞	71⅞	76	− 1¼
ChmNY cv5s93	324	107½	79½	103	+ 9
ChmNY cv5½96	829	108½	76	108½	+15½
ChmNY 8.40s99	904	74⅝	61⅛	74⅝	+ 6¼
ChmNY 8¼02	1022	70¾	59⅛	70	+ 3
ChemNY 11¾04t	2917	98½	90	97¾	+ 2⅞
COhRA 1st4s89	95	73½	65	73½	+ 5½
ChesOh 4½s92	456	67½	57½	66¼	+ 3¾
ChesOh 4½92r	143	67½	59¼	66½	....
ChePoMd 7¼12	1242	61½	50	61	+ 3⅜
ChePoMd 8⅞09	1588	74	62⅛	73¼	+ 3
ChePoMd 9s18	724	73⅞	61⅛	73	+ 3⅛
ChePoMd 12⅜17	641	100	84⅞	97⅝	+ 3¾
ChPotVa 7¼12	1047	63⅝	50¾	59¾	+ ¾
ChPotVa 8⅝09	3069	74	61⅝	72⅝	+ 4
ChPotVa 9¼15	1914	77¾	64⅛	75	+ 2
ChPotVa 9½19	1309	79¼	64⅝	79¼	+ 5¾
ChPoWas 7¾13	703	66¾	53⅛	63⅝	+ 2¾
ChPotWash 13s17	317	103	85	99¾	− ¼
ChPWVa 7¼13	772	60⅞	50½	60½	+ 3⅜
ChPWVa 9s15	897	73⅝	61½	70½	+ ½
ChPWVa 9¼19	754	75	61½	74¼	+ 1⅞
ChesbrPd 10⅝90	1170	97⅛	86½	97⅛	+ 2⅛
ChevrnCa 12¾87	2868	104¾	100⅛	104	....
ChevrnCa 11¾88	703	102½	100¾	101⅜	.. ..
ChevrnCa 12s94	1581	101⅞	99⅞	101¼	....
Chevron 5¾92	1685	71⅞	63	71½	+ 2
Chevron 7s96	4332	72	60⅝	71¼	+ 2½
Chevron 8¾05	5105	77	63	75	+ ⅛
Chi&NW 3s89	143	67¾	63	67¾	+ 3¾
ChiNW 3s89r	13	67	63	67	....
ChiNWTr 14¼04	51	92¼	92¼	92¼	....
ChiNwTr 15¾04	2	103	102½	103	....
ChiGW 4s88	87	77¼	70	77⅛	+ 5⅜
ChiGW 4½s38f	93	43	37	38	− 2⅛
ChrsCft 13s99	247	96⅞	85½	92⅛	− 1⅜
ChrsCft 15s99t	683	105	98½	102	+ ¼
Chrysler 8⅞95	5477	80	68⅛	79⅝	+ 6⅝
Chrysler 8s98	14936	70	59½	69⅜	+ 6⅜
ChryF 7⅜86	6143	95⅜	88	95	+ 6⅝
ChryF 8.35s91	1054	82	71⅛	78½	+ ¾
ChryF 7.70s92	815	78¾	66¼	74⅛	+ ⅞
ChryF 9s86	7480	96¼	89	95⅞	+ 5⅝
ChryF 8⅞84	1169	99 31-32	98 5-32	99 17-32	+1⅜
ChryF 9⅜87	2950	96	87	94⅞	+ 3¾
ChryF 13¼88	7634	104½	95¼	104	....
ChryF 13½91	3922	104⅜	93	104	....
ChryOv cv5s88	10	77	76¼	77	− 1⅛
CinGE 4⅛87	321	80	70¼	79¾	+ 5¼
CinGE 4⅛87r	20	77¼	76¼	76¼	....
CirclK cv8¾04	2576	105¼	95	103	....
Citicp 10s89t	7549	101⅛	90	100	+ ¼
Citicp cv5¾s00	5173	97	84	95	+ 4
Citicp 8.45s07	10614	72	57⅜	70	+ 2¾
Citicp 8⅛07	4510	69	55¾	69	+ 4¾
Citicorp 12.15s98t	8134	97⅜	87½	96⅜	+ ¾
Citicp 11¾04t	6304	96¾	88	96⅜	+ 2⅞
Citicp 14⅜86	1762	102⅛	100	100⅜	− ⅞
Citicorp 16s87	14523	106½	100	101⅞	− 4
Citicp 11¼87t	3442	101¼	92⅝	100⅜	+ 2⅛
Citicp 87t	31	98⅞	98	98	− 1½
Citicp 92t ap	200	99¾	99¾	99¾	....
Citicp 95t M	59	100	98	98	− ½
Citicp 10.86s98t	13	99⅞	98	98	− ¾
Citicp flt98t A	4	97¼	97¼	97¼	− ¾
Citicp 12¼93	7451	101	89	100½	+ 1½
Citicp 12s90	18816	101⅞	89	100⅝	+ 1⅞
Citicp 11⅞88	9502	101¼	92	100¾	+ 1¼
Citicp 12½93	10672	102	89	101¾	+ 1⅜
Citicp 13.60s99	244	104	100	103⅝	....
Citicp 12⅞89	21	103⅝	102	103⅝	....
CitiPP cv12½96	5	99¾	99¾	99¾	....
CitSvc 6⅛97	744	57	47⅝	53¼	− 1¾
CitSvc 6⅝99xw	1455	59½	49	55⅛	− ⅜
CitSvc 7.65s01	883	63⅞	53⅝	61½	− 1½
CitSvc 9¾00	471	79¾	65	76¼	+ ¾
CitSvc 13⅞11	2363	103	90	99½	− 2
CitSvc zr85	6896	90⅞	78⅞	90⅝	+10⅞
CitSvc zr86	5393	80⅞	70	80¼	+10⅛
CitSvc zr87	8144	72	60⅝	71	+10⅛
CitSvc zr88	10353	62⅞	53	62¼	+ 8¾
CitSvc zr89	24671	55½	46⅞	54⅝	+ 7⅜
CitSvcG 13s05	435	95¾	79	95¾	+ ¾
CityInv cv7½90	300	254½	203	225	− 9
CityInvst 8s91	4663	96⅛	66	94⅞	+21⅞
CityInv 8⅞s97	395	95½	65	95½	+21⅜
CityInv 8⅛s91	4040	95⅝	65⅞	95	+21
CityInv 9s96	11235	96¼	61	95¼	+26
CityInv 9⅛97	10200	96¼	62	95½	+24½
CityInv 14½92	1038	105	98⅜	104	+ 1⅞
CityInv 12¾87	6677	101⅞	92½	100½	+ ½
CityInv 13s90	473	104¼	96⅝	100½	+ 2¾
CityInv 13½03	223	103⅝	86	98½	+ ½
CityInv 12½03	6872	100	75½	100	+11⅛
ClarkEq 9⅝s99	49	76	66½	73	− 3
ClrkECr 7.85s91	865	79¼	70	78	+ 3¼
ClrkECr 8s87	1110	93½	86¼	92⅝	+ 5⅛
ClevEl 2¾85	290	95⅜	87¾	95	+ 8
ClevEl 7⅛90	2198	82	70½	81⅛	+ 5½
ClevEl 3⅜86	180	91¼	84⅛	89⅛	+ 7⅛
ClevEl 3s89	117	70	62½	68	+ 8
ClevEl 3⅞93	247	56½	50⅛	56½	+ 2¾
ClevEl 3⅞93r	35	54⅛	50½	53½	....
ClevEl 4⅜94	390	56	48⅝	55¼	+ 1½
ClevEl 4⅜94r	13	54	50	50	....
ClevEl 8⅜91	1584	81⅞	67	81½	+ 5
ClevEl 8¾05	2694	71⅜	56½	68⅛	+ 1
ClevEl 9¼s09	3589	74	57¼	71	+ ½
ClevEl 9.85s10	3223	78¼	62½	77	+ 2⅛
ClevEl 8⅜11	2317	67⅝	52¼	64⅛	+ ⅞
ClevEl 8⅜12	1347	67⅛	54⅜	64¼	+ 1½
ClevEl 11½85	632	100⅝	97½	100 11-32	+1 3-32
CocaCola 9⅞85	969	100½	97½	100 3-16	+1 7-16
Coleco 14⅜02	18448	91	75	88¼	+ 1¾
ColinFood 12s08	25	86	82¼	82¼	....

ColonStr	8s96	46	60	55	60	— 1⅜
ColoIntr	8½s91	81	86	79	79	— 2¾
ColuGas	5⅛s85	265	96½	89½	96½	+ 6½
ColuGas	5⅛85r	10	96	90¼	96	....
ColuGas	9s94	1086	85⅛	74⅝	85⅛	+ 5
ColuGas	8¾s95	1188	82	68	79½	+ 2⅝
ColuGas	9⅛s95	1107	83¾	69¼	82⅝	+ 4½
ColuGas	8⅜s96	645	77¾	63¼	77	+ 3⅞
ColuGas	8¼s96	579	76⅝	65	76⅝	+ 3¼
ColuGas	7½97M	510	71⅝	63	71½	+ 5⅜
ColuGas	7½97J	538	73	56½	72	+ 3
ColuGas	7½97O	380	70⅜	58⅝	70⅜	+ 3⅛
ColuGas	7½s98	510	69	59½	69	+ 3
ColuGas	9⅞s99	352	84¾	74½	83⅞	+ 5⅜
ColuGas	9⅝s89	740	94	84¾	92⅞	+ 2⅞
ColuGas	10⅛95	225	91⅛	80⅜	91⅛	+ 4
ColuGas	9⅛96	508	84¼	70	82⅞	+ 4⅝
ColuGas	10¼99	217	95	79½	95	+11
ColuGas	11¾99	408	99½	84	93⅝	+ 2⅜
ColuGas	12¾00	139	100	95	100	....
ColuGas	15⅜97	26	116⅞	102	102⅝	—11⅜
ColPict	11¾90	161	105	92	101	+ 2
ColuSOE	3¾86	86	87½	80⅝	87½	+ 6¾
ColuSOE	3¾86	2	83½	83½	83½	....
ColuSOE	4½87	374	85	75¼	85	+ 8½
ColuSOE	4½87r	5	86	86	86	....
ColuSOE	7⅝85	1041	98¼	92⅝	97 13-16	+6 3-16
ColuSOE	13⅝90	287	104	96	104	+ 2½
ColuSOE	16⅝91	356	112¾	103¼	108	+ 5
ColuSoE	13¾93	116	99	95	95¾	....
CombE	7.45s96	41	69⅜	64	67⅛	— 5⅜
Comdis	cv8s03	29686	77	55	63½	—10½
ComICr	8¾s91	1562	83½	72⅜	83½	+ 5½
ComICr	7¾s92	1242	77	67	76¼	+ 1⅛
ComICr	7¾s93	972	75⅞	62⅛	74	+ 2
ComICr	8⅞s86	2224	97	91⅜	96½	+ 2½
ComICr	8.8s86	776	95¼	88½	94⅛	+ 3⅛
ComICr	8.35s86	2711	95¼	87⅛	95	+ 4⅛
ComICr	8¾88	1187	91½	82⅛	91	+ 2¼
ComICr	9s88	1928	91½	82	89¾	+ 5½
ComICr	14⅛85	746	104⅝	99¾	102⅜	— 1⅛
ComSo	cv4½91	89	64	62	63½	— ⅛
ComwEd	2¾99	45	60½	47¼	60½	+12⅜
ComwEd	3s99	9	52½	48¾	48¾	+ 4
ComwEd	2⅞01	5	54	54	54	— 4
ComwEd	7⅝03F	1388	65½	52⅞	64	+ 4⅝
ComwEd	7⅝03J	1158	65⅞	53⅛	65⅞	+ 5¼
ComwEd	8s03	5506	69	54⅝	66⅝	+ 3¼
ComwEd	8¾05	4130	73	59	71⅛	+ 3⅝
ComwEd	9⅜04	4050	78	62	76¼	+ 4¼
ComwEd	8⅛07J	3116	67¾	54⅝	66½	+ 3½
ComwEd	8⅛07D	2239	68	54⅛	65⅛	+ 1⅞
ComwEd	8¼07	5043	68⅜	55	67½	+ 3½
ComwEd	9⅛08	4114	75⅝	60¼	74	+ 4⅜
ComwEd	9¼84	1349	101	98⅝	101	+1 21-32
ComwEd	12½86	7715	102⅜	96	102	....
ComwEd	14⅞87	3304	108½	100	107⅜	+ ⅛
ComwEd	15⅜00	1560	115	100	110½	+ 2
ComwEd	11⅛10	799	89	69½	87	+ 3⅜
ComwEd	14s91	2157	107¼	97½	104½	— 2½
ComwEd	16¼89	2611	112	103	108	— 3¼
ComwEd	17½88	1695	120	109	118	+ ¼
ComwEd	16s90	3925	112½	103	108¼	— 2⅜
ComwEd	14s89	40	109	104	109	....
ComwEd	14⅜94	89	105⅜	104⅞	105⅜	......
ComwEd	16¾11	2369	117½	101¼	114½	+ 1
ComwEd	14¼92	1413	107¼	97	106	....
ComwEd	15⅜12	1632	112⅝	97	110	+ ½
ComwEd	13s12	1123	100	83	99⅛	+ 1⅞
ComwEd	12⅛13	772	95⅞	79	94	+ 2½
ComwEd	12¼91	595	100¾	89½	100½	....
ComwEd	13⅜13	442	102½	88	102	+ 2½
CompSci	cv6s94	1414	89	68	73	—13
Cmptvsn	8scv09	822	104½	98¾	104	....
ConnM	11½90	45	97½	92	92	— 7½
Conoco	9⅜09	651	79⅜	66	79⅜	+ 2⅜
Conoco	13¼11	93	104¾	91	104¾	+ 1¼
ConEdis	3⅜s85	1147	95¼	86½	94⅞	+ 4⅞
ConEdis	3⅜85r	121	94⅝	88	94⅝	....
ConEdis	3⅝s86	557	91	85¼	90⅜	+ 6⅛
ConEdis	3⅝86r	35	89¾	86¼	89¾	....
ConEdis	4¼s86	1614	90½	84⅜	90½	+ 6⅞
ConEdis	4¼86r	22	86½	85	86	....
ConEdis	5s87	1785	87½	80¼	87½	+ 6¾
ConEdis	5s87r	99	86	80	85½	....
ConEdis	4s88	1094	81	72⅝	80⅜	+ 6⅛
ConEdis	4s88r	88	79½	74	79	....
ConEdis	4¾s90	610	73¾	65	73¾	+ 6¼
ConEdis	4¾90r	29	69¼	66⅛	68¼	....
ConEdis	5s90	1171	73½	64	73½	+ 6½
ConEdis	5s90r	116	73½	68	73½	....
ConEdis	4¾s91	454	71¾	57	69½	+ 4
ConEdis	4¾91r	58	69½	62	68	....
ConEdis	4⅝s91	777	70	59⅝	69½	+ 6⅞
ConEdis	4⅝91r	29	67⅝	65⅜	67⅝	....
ConEdis	4⅜92V	624	66⅜	55⅛	65⅜	+ 4⅝
ConEdis	4⅜92Vr	61	63	58	63	....
ConEdis	4⅜92W	638	65½	56⅛	65½	+ 7
ConEdis	4⅝s93	1169	63½	53⅝	63¼	+ 5⅝
ConEdis	9⅜00	6129	82	66⅞	78¾	+ 1¾
ConEdis	7.9s01	4953	71⅛	58⅛	69¾	+ 3⅝
ConEdis	7.9s02	3291	71	57⅜	69⅜	+ 2¾
ConEdis	7¾s03	3059	69½	56⅛	68	+ 3⅝
ConEdis	8.4s03	4377	74	59	71	+ 2½
ConEdis	9⅛s04	6188	79	64¾	76	+ 2½
ConFd	7⅜s96	91	73½	66	73½	+ 4⅛
ConFrg	7.95s96	43	75	71	73	+ 7
CGEBal	2¾s86	425	92⅞	85⅜	92⅝	+ 7¼
ConNG	5s85	176	98 15-16	94 15-16	98 15-16	+3 7-16
ConNG	5s85r	27	95	95	95	+ 4
ConNG	4⅜s86	67	93¼	87	93¼	+ 6⅝
ConNG	4¾s86	288	92½	85⅝	92½	+ 6⅛
ConNG	4¾86r	4	88	88	88	....
ConNG	4½s87	30	85⅛	83	85	+ 3¼
ConNG	4⅜s88	71	81⅛	74⅛	80⅜	+ 6
ConNG	4¾s90	230	73½	64	73½	+ 8
ConNG	6⅛s92	338	77	64½	72½	+ 4⅛
ConNG	7¾s94	355	78½	66½	78	+ 2¾
ConNG	8¼s94	700	82	68½	80⅜	+ 5½
ConNG	9s95	1060	85¼	72⅛	83⅞	+ 3⅝
ConNG	7⅞s95	557	77⅛	65⅛	77⅛	+ 4⅝
ConNG M	8⅜96	535	80¾	65⅛	79⅛	+ 1⅝
ConNG	7¾s96	205	75	60⅜	75	+ 3
ConNG	7⅝s97	143	73½	61⅝	73½	+ 2⅞
ConNG	7¾s98	121	72⅝	63¼	72⅜	+ 4
ConNG	8⅝s99	410	79⅞	65½	79	+ 6¾
ConNG	9¼s95	818	87	73¼	85⅝	+ 1⅛
ConNG S	8⅜96	289	83⅞	72¾	83⅞	+ 8⅞
ConNG	8⅛97	366	78	64	77	+ 5½
ConNG	12⅞00	204	105	90⅜	102	+ 2¾
ConNG	11⅛08	2	78	78	78	....
ConPw	4½s88	1711	73	59½	68⅛	+ ⅜
ConPw	4½88r	5	68⅛	68⅛	68⅛	....
ConPw	4⅝s89	1715	66½	52½	64½	+ 3½
ConPw	4⅝89r	63	62⅞	60	62	....
ConPw	4⅝s90	977	61	50	57⅛	+ 2⅛
ConPw	4⅝s91	2310	58	44½	54	— 2
ConPw	4⅝91r	7	56	46	49	....
ConPw	5⅞s96	3469	51½	38	46¼	— 1¼
ConPw	6⅞s98	3119	55⅜	42½	49½	— ⅛
ConPw	6⅝s98	5523	53	40⅜	46½	— 1¾
ConPw	7⅝s99	6696	59½	43½	51	— 2
ConPw	8⅝s00	5512	63¼	48	53¼	— 4⅛
ConPw	8⅛s01	5181	60	44	52¼	— 2⅛
ConPw	7½s01	3033	56	40⅞	48⅝	— 2⅞
ConPw	7½02J	2847	55⅛	41⅛	49⅝	— 1⅜
ConPw	7½02O	3917	56	41½	49⅞	— 1½
ConPw	8⅝s03	4632	62¼	46⅞	54	— 2⅝
ConPw	11⅜s94	3794	89	62¼	76	— 6⅛
ConPw	11½s00	2566	82	63	72½	— 3¾
ConPw	9¾06	7131	68	51¼	61¼	— 2⅜
ConPw	9s06	4739	64	48½	57	— 2⅝
ConPw	8⅞07	4511	63¼	47	55½	— 3⅜
ConPw	8⅝07	3985	60½	47	53½	— 2⅝
ConPw	9s08	8466	63⅞	48½	56	— 3
CntllCp	10.4s89	3774	100⅜	85	96⅝	— 3⅛
CntllCp	8½85	26290	97	70⅝	96½	+ 1
CntlllCp	11.30s87t	6541	98⅝	62	93⅞	— 3
CntllllCp	13⅝85	10999	103½	81¾	100	— 1½

```
CntlllCp zr89      9014 55     36⅝   55  + 6⅝
ContOil 4½s91       366 67½    61⅛   65⅜+  ⅞
ContOil 7½s99       483 70     60½   70  + 3½
ContOil 9⅛s99       490 80     70    79  + 1⅝
ContOil 8⅞s01       887 77¼    62    76  +  ¾
ContDat 5½s87       271 83     74    82½+ 1⅝
CoopL 10½s92        283 94½    81    94½+ 6½
Coppwld 7⅞s01       118 64     56    63¼—  3¾
CornPd 5¾s92        507 70⅛    63    70⅛+ 2⅞
CorngGl 7¾s98       289 70⅛    58    68¼—  ⅜
CorngGl 8¼s07      6176 111    83    97  — 7¾
CraneCo 6½s92       279 74½    62¼   74½+ 2½
CraneCo cv5s93        6 289    232   263 — 9
CraneCo 7s93        528 70⅛    63⅛   70⅛+ 4⅜
CraneCo 7s94       3297 64     55⅜   60¼—  ¾
CraneCo 8s85        834 97¾    92    97 9-32+5 9-32
Crane 10½s94        785 86     74½   83⅛— 1
CreditF 8s92        283 82     76    81½+ 1
CreditF 9s86        518 96⅜    88⅛   96⅜+ 5⅞
CreditF 8.2s87      836 91⅞    82⅞   91½+ 3¾
CreditF 8¾s88       431 90¾    81    90¾+ 3¾
CreditF 9⅜s92        37 77¾    73    77¾—  1¼
CreditF 10¼s89      293 95     84¼   94⅞+ 4¾
CreditF 10½s94       37 85⅛    83¼   85⅛+17⅝
CreditF 15½s91      299 110    101   107 — 3
CreditF zr90s       522 50⅜    39    49  + 7
CreditF 13⅞s92       85 105¾   101¾  101¾— 3¼
CreditF 12¼s95      175 100    94    95  ..........
CritAcc 12.30s13    232 102    89¼   96½—  2⅜
CritAcc 12s13       406 101    85    100 + 4½
CritAcc 12.15s13    206 100½   87    100½..........
CritAcc 11⅞s14      140 97     84    96½..........
CritAcc 12¼s14       55 99     87½   99  ..........
CritAcc 12.35s14     39 100    91⅛   100 ..........
CritAcc 13.30s14    211 103    93    100½..........
CritAc 13.10s14      34 100    96⅛   99½..........
CritAc 13⅛s14        39 100    99¼   99¼..........
CrocN cv5¾s96      1413 73     60½   64  — 3
CrocN 10s94t        195 100    88⅛   90  — 8¼
CrocN 8.60s02       728 69⅜    56¼   66  +  ⅛
CrwnCk 4⅜s88         26 76¾    75    75  +  ⅜
CrwnZel 8⅞s00       559 75     63    74  + 2
CrwnZel 9¼s05       554 78     65    74¼+ 1¾
CrwnZel cv9¼s09    3113 102    90¾   99¾..........
Crucible 6⅞s92       51 85     73    85  +13
Culbro 11½s05       211 88½    75    82⅛—  1⅞
CummEn 8⅞s95         68 78     73½   78  + 1⅞
CyprusM 8¾s85
                   1093 99 13-16 97½ 99 13-16+1 7-16
CyprusM 8½s01        68 75⅛    64⅛   71⅜—  4⅝
              – D–D –
DCS Cap 12.20s94     31 99¾    99¼   99¼..........
DanaCp 6s91         179 96¾    88½   91¾+ 3½
DanaCp 7.3s96       173 72     60⅛   69⅛+ 6½
DanaCp 9s2000       234 76⅛    65    76⅛+ 1⅞
DanaCp 8⅞s08         55 73     64⅜   64⅜—  9⅜
Dana cv d5⅞s06     9332 75¼    56½   63¾—7⅜
Dartln 7½s96         81 72⅛    62½   70⅝+  ⅛
DataGen 8⅜s02       329 75     57    68¾+  ¾
DataGen 13s05       125 100    89⅜   96  — 2⅛
Datpnt cv8⅞s06    10162 75     63    65⅝—6⅞
Dayco cv5¾s94       905 84¾    72    77  ..........
Dayco cv6s94       4228 93½    69    85  + 2
DayHud 7¾s94        165 78     63½   78  + 3½
DayHud 9¾s95        252 90½    75    90½+ 2¼
DayHud 10⅞s05        93 89⅞    78    89⅞+ 2⅞
DayHud 15¼s91       466 110    102⅜  108½+  ⅝
DayHud 14¾s12         7 124    104   104 —20
DayHud 11⅞s12       144 96¾    84½   84½—12½
DayHud 10¾s13        12 81     81    81  ..........
DaytnPL 8⅛s01       597 66¼    53    63⅜+ 5¼
DaytnPL 8s03       1567 64½    51¼   64½+8½
DaytnPL 10.7s05     208 81⅞    66⅛   79⅛+ 1⅛
DaytnPL 8¾s06       596 70¼    56¾   68¼+ 8¼
DaytnPL 8½s07      1432 67⅞    54    67¾+ 9½
DaytnPL 12⅛s09      972 90⅜    76    87⅜+ 5¾
DaytnPL 14⅜s88      201 103½   95½   101 — 1⅝
DaytnPL 17s91      1622 112    100½  109½+ 1¼
DaytnPL 16¾s12      876 113    98⅛   111 + 3⅜
DeereCo 7.9s87     1621 93⅝    86    93⅜+ 4⅝
DeereCo 8.45s00     325 74½    67    73¼+ 1¾

DeereCo cv5½01      726 120    82    96  —23½
DeereCo 8s02         45 69     69    69  ..........
DeereCo 10½285     1793 100½   97    100¼+ 1
DeereCo 11½289     2530 101⅜   90¾   99⅜+ 1⅜
DeereCo 9s08      13711 117    85½   99  —14
DeereCr 9.35s03     203 76¼    65    76¼+ 3¼
DeereCr 85t          75 100½   99    99¾—  ¼
DelmPw 3½285         40 90½    89    90½..........
DelmPw 3½285r        20 88     87½   88  ..........
DelaPL 3⅞s88        114 83     72¾   83  + 9½
DelmPL 6⅜s97        397 65⅜    52⅛   61¾+ 3¾
DelmPL 6⅜s97r        64 60     55    59  ..........
DelmPL 4⅜s94        139 57     49    57  + 3½
DelmPL 4⅜s94r         1 54⅛    54⅛   54⅛..........
Dennison 8¼s96       74 76¾    68    68  — 4½
Dennys cv9½207     2518 118½   107   114 — 6
DetEd 2¾s85         163 96¼    90    96¼+ 5¼
DetEd 6s96         2639 60¼    50    57⅛+ 5
DetEd 6.40s98      2257 60⅜    49⅛   58  + 3⅜
DetEd 9s99         2288 75¾    60⅛   71½+ 3⅜
DetEd 9.15s00      3798 76     61⅛   73½+ 4¾
DetEd 8.15s00      2391 69     56    66⅞+ 3
DetEd 8⅛s01        3743 69     55¼   67⅜+ 4⅞
DetEd 7¾s01        2539 63½    50    61⅝+ 2⅜
DetEd 7½s03        2170 64½    51    62¾+ 4¼
DetEd 9⅞s04AA      3730 79     64½   76¾+ 4¼
DetEd 11⅞s00       1093 94⅛    78¼   93  + 5
DetEd 10⅜s06       1594 83¾    67½   81  + 4¾
DiGior cv5¾s93      941 86¼    80    85  + 2
DiamSha 9⅛s00        74 76¾    65¼   76¾+  ¾
DiamSha 8½208       147 69¾    64½   64½—  2¼
DiamSha 7.7s01       81 66½    56¾   66  + 2⅜
DiaStTel 7s08       131 58½    50⅛   58½+  ½
DigitE 9⅜2000       409 82⅜    72    81  — 1
DigitE cv8s09      6140 118    99¾   117½..........
Diverln 10½291      319 86½    80    86½+ 6½
DomBks 7¾s96        255 69⅜    62¾   69⅛+ 2⅜
DowCh 4.35s88       144 81½    73⅛   81½+ 4¼
DowCh 6.70s98       910 65     55    64  + 1⅞
DowCh 7.75s99      1354 73⅛    59¾   73⅛+ 6⅛
DowCh 8⅞s00        2123 77¾    64⅜   76⅛+ 1½
DowCh 8.9s00       1917 78     64¾   76⅞+ 3¾
DowCh 7.40s02       459 65⅜    55¼   64⅝+ 1¼
DowCh 7⅝s03         275 68¾    57⅛   66½+ 1¾
DowCh 8½s05        2244 72⅝    61⅛   71¼+  ⅞
DowCh 8½s06        1891 72⅞    60¼   70¼+ 2¼
DowCh 7⅞s07        1351 67⅛    56⅛   66¼+ 2
DowCh 8⅜s08        1825 72¼    61⅛   72  + 2½
DowCh 11¼s10       3241 91¾    78    90½+ 2⅜
DowCorn 9⅜s05        93 78½    70    70¾—13¼
Dresser 9⅜s95       443 84⅜    71⅛   81  + 1⅜
Dresser 9⅜s00       293 85     74½   83½+ 5½
Dresser 8.65s85     439 99⅜    96    99⅜+ 2⅞
Dresser 11⅜407       70 92¼    85⅛   85⅛— 4⅝
Drey cv7⅜s08       6458 113    81    111 +29¼
duPont 8.45s04     6551 75¾    61¾   74½+ 3½
duPont 8s86        4171 97¾    90⅛   97  + 3⅛
duPont 8½s06       4844 76     62    74⅞+ 3
duPont 14s91      14107 109⅞   99⅝   108½+  ⅝
duPont d6s01      35703 58¼    47¼   57¼+ 2⅜
duPont 12⅛s85      1877 103    98⅜   101⅜—  ¼
duPont 12⅞s92      9236 106¼   93¾   105⅜+ 2⅜
DukePw 7⅜s01       1772 67     54½   65½+ 4¾
DukePw 7¾s02       1794 69½    56⅜   68⅜+ 3⅜
DukePw 7⅞s02       1834 66¼    53½   63⅛+  ⅞
DukePw 7¾s03       1486 68⅛    54¾   66  +  ¼
DukePw 8⅛s03       3737 71     58⅛   68½+ 3⅛
DukePw 9¾s04       3034 81¾    69    80⅛+ 2⅛
DukePw 9½s05       1101 79¾    67    78⅛+ 2⅛
DukePw 8¾s06       1959 70⅝    59⅜   69⅜+ 2⅛
DukePw 8⅛s07       1157 70     58⅜   67⅜+  ⅞
DukePw 9⅜s08        743 78     65½   77⅞+ 3⅞
DukePw 10⅛s09      1491 84     70    82⅝+ 3⅜
DukePw 10⅞s09      1790 92     75    89  + 4½
DukePw 14⅞s10       406 118    98    112½+ 4½
DukePw 14⅜s87      4947 106½   100   102½— 3¼
DukePw 13⅛s10       310 105½   88⅛   103⅜+  ⅜
DukePw 12s90       1209 103    92    101¼—  ⅝
DuqsnLt 3½286       227 90½    83¾   89½+ 7
DuqsnLt 3¾s88       161 76½    71½   76  + 5⅞
DuqsnLt 4¼s89        93 72⅝    64½   72½+ 8⅜
```

DuqsnLt 5s10	31	47	38	38¼	− 3¼
DuqsnLt 5s2010r	14	43	42	42	....
DuqsnLt 8¾00	1604	71⅞	58⅝	70¾	+ 2⅞
DuqsnLt 9s06	1709	71	58½	68⅛	+ ⅛
DuqsnLt 8⅜07	1184	66½	55	64⅜	+ ⅜
DuqsnLt 10⅛09	1129	80	64⅜	76	+ ½
DuqsnLt 12¼10	1072	93⅞	75	91½	− ¼
DuqsneLt 14¼10	365	103⅝	91	99	− 1¼
DuqsneLt 16s11	478	110	99⅛	105¾	− 1¾
DuqsneLt 12⅛13	202	92½	84¼	90	− 2
DuqsneLt 13s13	344	99	82	95	....
DycoPet 13s88	285	101¾	93⅞	98¾	− 1⅛

— E—E —

EGG cv3½87	3	295	294	294	+ 6
EstAir cv5s92	3379	49⅜	41	44½	− 1½
EstAir cv4¾93	1451	48	39	42½	− 1¼
EstAir cv11½99	28061	77	58	62¼	− 5½
EstAir cv11¾05	6524	84	63	67	− 6
EstAir 17½97	8587	105⅞	95⅛	101¼	− ¾
EstAir 17½98	5338	106	94	101	− 1
EstAir 16⅛02	12711	103⅞	91	98	− ⅞
EasKodk cv8¼07	35111	101	85	94	− 6½
EKodl cv4½88	228	94	83⅝	88	− 8
Eaton 7.60s96	206	72	59	68¾	+ 3¼
Eaton 6s92	43	69¼	60½	69¼	+ 3¼
Eaton 7⅞s03	124	67	58	65⅝	+ 5⅝
Eaton 8¾01	46	74	60½	74	+ 3
Eaton d7s11	71	58	52¼	58	− ¼
EatonCr 8½84	248	99⅝	98 9-16	99⅝	+1 1-16
EatonCp cv8½08	2918	103½	86	101	....
EdisElIll 5s95	55	56¾	49⅛	56¾	+ 4⅝
ElPaso 12.45s97	602	99⅝	83⅝	98½	+ 4
ElPaso 15s00	847	108	99	106¾	+ ⅞
ElPaso 15¾92	185	110½	99½	107½	− 5
ElPaso 16.7s02	293	116	106	114	+ ⅞
ElPaso 12⅞02	16	97¾	90	93	− 1
Emhart 11.70s90	250	99⅜	91	95	− 5⅞
Englhd 11¾05	497	94½	82	88	− 2
Ensrch 9¾95	700	88	71½	85⅞	+ 7⅛
Ensrch 7.65s98	279	69½	58⅜	68⅜	+ ⅞
Ensrch 8.95s99	138	77	69	77	+ 1¾
Ensrch 10⅝00	395	88	74⅜	86⅛	− 1¾
Ensrch 8¾01	55	72½	65½	72½	− 3
Ensrch 8½02	55	71¼	64	66¼	− 6
Ensrch 10⅞05	91	90⅞	79	90⅞	+ 6¾
Ensrch cv10s01	9347	99¾	86	94	− 4
Ensrch 16⅜07	1	117	117	117	+ 2¾
Enstar 12¾99	902	94	78⅛	92⅝	− 1⅜
Entex 8⅞01	104	74	64⅞	70	+ ⅛
Entex 12¾08	163	97⅜	86⅛	93	− ¼
EquitRes 9⅝95	222	84	76	82⅝	+ 5⅝
EquitRes 9s96	378	82	73⅞	79¾	+ ⅝
EqtRs cv9½06	2657	151	121½	144	+22
Equitc cv10s04	457	91	84	84	....
Esmark 9¼00	148	74	70	73	− 1
EssexCh 11⅜98	250	87	75	84	+ 1
Esterl 12½95	79	91⅛	85⅜	89⅛	− 1
Exxon 6s97	17584	65	55½	63⅛	+ 2⅞
Exxon 6½s98	12670	67¾	56¾	66	+ 2⅞
ExxonFin 11s87	952	102	93¼	102	+ 2⅜
ExxonFin 10½89	2047	99½	89	99	+ 1¼
ExxonP 9s04	5569	80½	66¾	78¼	+ ⅜
ExxonP 8⅞s00	1937	82⅛	68	80	+ 3⅛
ExxonP 8¼01	1667	77⅝	63½	75	+ 2⅜
ExxonP 5⅝97	117	61	51⅛	61	+ 3½
ExxonP 6⅝98	128	65	53	64⅜	+ 2

— F—F —

FMC cv4¼s92	1101	149	100¾	136½	+24
FMC 7½s2001	80	65⅞	61⅛	65⅞	− ¼
FMC 9½s2000	132	80	67½	73	− 5
Fairch cv4⅜92	2	181	181	181	− 3
Fairch 9¾98	266	79	69⅜	75	+ 2⅞
FalcnM 8.85s96	258	74⅞	56	59¼	−14¾
FamFin 4¾s90	54	65⅜	60	60	− 5
Farah cv5s94	1233	87½	62	62¼	−21⅞
Fedders cv5s96	1383	44	39⅛	42	+ 3
Fedders 8⅞s94	190	67	59¼	65	+ 4⅞
FedHmLn zr92	458	39	35½	39	+ 3⅜
FdMogul 7½98	25	64½	64½	64½	− ¾
FdMogul 12½90	78	99	93½	93½	− 7½
FdMogul 13s05	10	100	100	100	+ 1
FdNMt cv4⅜96	1917	96	68½	94	−21
FdNMt zr14s	336	4½	3⅝	4½	....
FedDSt 8⅜95	275	82½	77⅞	82½	+ 2½
FedDSt 10¼10	304	86½	74¼	86½	+ 1
FedDSt 10⅝13	13	89⅝	87¼	89½	+ 2⅛
FerroCp 5⅞s92	8	91½	89⅝	89⅝	− 1⅜
Finan 10¼s90	499	90¼	82⅛	87⅞	− 2¼
FinCpA 6s88	1096	77	63	72	− 2⅝
FinCpA 11⅞98	6871	89	60½	82⅜	− 4½
FinCpA 6s10	945	51¾	30	43	− 4
FinCp cv d11½02	24086	155	50	81	−58
Firestn 9¼04	292	76	61½	76	+ 3⅞
FstAtlan 11¾93	70	96	71	96	....
FstBkSy 10.70st	1336	99	94½	98⅛	+ ⅜
FstBost cv9¼09	481	106½	101	106	....
FstChiCp 7¾86	4079	95	86¾	93¾	+ 2⅞
FIntrsB cv7¼04	1054	118	85½	115	+ ½
FstMdB 13¾92	85	101½	99	101	− 4¾
FstNStB 8⅞88	586	91¼	84¼	91¼	+ ⅞
FstNStB 11½93	15	90¼	90¼	90¼	....
FstPenn cv5½93	3747	65	53½	61½	+ 5½
FstSecur 10.90s99t	1002	101	98⅝	100	− ½
FstUnRE cv10s06	120	152	122	152	+34
FstUnRE cv10¼09	1528	103	101⅛	102	......
FstWisc 8½96	1628	74½	65	73	+ 2
Fischb cv4¾97	384	96	66	66	−24
Fischb cv8½05	71	151	127	150	+23½
FishFd cv6½94	954	67	60¼	62	....
FleetFncl 9¼96	550	81	67¼	80¾	+ 4⅝
FleetFncl 12½90	10	96	96	96	− 3¾
FleetFn 10½07	1970	147½	115	147½	+19⅜
FleetFn 11¼93	29	95	91	95	+ ⅝
Flemg cv8s08	2802	120	93	118	+11
FlexiV cv4¾97	196	123¼	100	119	+ 3½
FlexiV 12s00	10	90⅛	90	90	+ 3⅞
FlaECst 5s01	81	52	45½	46½	− 8½
FlowGen 14.30s04	637	80	74	79	....
FlyTiger 9s91	472	80⅝	65	73⅛	− 1⅞
FordMt 8⅛s90	1277	89	76¼	84	− 1½
FordMt 7.85s94	681	79⅜	66	79⅜	+ 8⅞
FordMt 9¼s94	3199	87⅜	71	84	+ 5
FordMt 14¾85	12105	104⅞	100½	101 1-16	−2 5-16
FordMt 14¼90	5363	108	99⅞	106½	+ 1
FordCr 8⅞90A	800	89½	76⅜	87⅜	+ 2¼
FordCr 8⅞90N	898	88	76¼	87	+ 3¾
FordCr 8½91	2692	86	73⅜	85⅝	+ 5
FordCr 7½91	1547	80⅞	68⅞	78⅛	+ 4⅞
FordCr cv4½96	4323	120½	82	107¾	+ 4¾
FordCr cv4⅞98	1964	136	91¾	121	+ 2½
FordCr 7½92	1056	78	66⅝	77¾	+ 4⅝
FordCr 8.7s99	2560	78½	63¼	77⅝	+ 7½
FordCr 7½93	977	77⅛	66	76⅞	+ 4½
FordCr 7⅞93	1700	80	67½	80	+ 6⅝
FordCr 10½94	2542	94½	78⅛	92⅞	+ 4
FordCr 9½95	1572	89	72	87	+ 6
FordCr 8.85s85	3806	99 13-16	95½	99¾	+ 3¼
FordCr 9.7s00	4294	85	67⅞	82	+ 4½
FordCr 8⅞86	3185	99	92⅛	98⅝	+ 3⅜
FordCr 9¾01	2205	84¾	68½	82⅝	+ 5
FordCr 8⅝86	3599	99	90	97½	+ 4⅜
FordCr 9⅛01	2998	79⅞	63	79¼	+ 6
FordCr 8¼88	4323	90	78½	88⅞	+ 5⅛
FordCr 8⅜01	4035	72	59	69⅞	+ 1⅞
FordCr 7⅞89	5024	87½	77	87	+ 6
FordCr 7.85s88	2669	91¼	80⅛	91¼	+ 5½
FordCr 8⅜02	1765	71¾	57	71	+ 2¾
FordCr 8½02	1629	74	61	73	+ 3¾
FordCr 8½88	3428	93	82⅝	92⅛	+ 4¾
FordCr 8⅞90	3939	88¾	76	87½	+ 4⅜
FordCr 9½85	8137	100	97 31-32	99 29-32	+1 21-32
FordCr 9.55s89	4418	95⅜	82⅜	94⅛	+ 5⅛
FordCr 12.60s87	7673	102⅞	95	101⅞	+ ⅞
FreptM cv10½14	851	85½	84	85	....
FremntGnl 12⅞90	269	97⅝	82⅛	93	− 4⅝
Fruehf 6s87	213	86⅞	80¾	86¾	+ 5
FruehF cv5½94	3055	109¾	79	86	−14¼
Fruehf 9.70s96	166	80⅛	73⅛	78⅝	+ 2⅝
FruehFn 8s87	2299	93½	83½	92⅜	+ 4⅝

FruehF 12½93 35 97⅝ 88 97⅝— 1⅞
Fuqua 7s88 1568 93½ 85⅜ 93½+ 4
Fuqua 9½s98 5712 74¾ 64¼ 72 + 3
Fuqua 9⅞97 1525 78¾ 65⅛ 74½— 1⅜

— G—G —

GATX 16⅜92 155 108⅛ 102½ 108⅛— 3⅛
GNAC 11¾94 812 97⅜ 80⅝ 90 — 4½
GNAC 14¾95 50 98 93⅝ 96 —10
GTE cv10½07 11976 114¾ 97 105½— 8¼
GTE 12¼94 26 102 91 102 ....
GTES 10s2000 102 81½ 77⅛ 81 — 5½
GardDen 9¼05 90 76 70¾ 72 — 8
GelcoCp 14⅝99 4312 105 87 97⅞— 2⅛
GelcoCp 14s01 1596 105 90 98⅜— 3⅝
GelcoCp 14¼87 506 104 97½ 101½+ 1⅜
GenCorp 11⅞93 20 93½ 93⅜ 93½............
GAccept 4⅞s85 11 96⅛ 92 96⅛— ⅜
GnATr cv5¾99 3878 73½ 61 68 — ½
GenCig 5½s87 61 96⅞ 83⅛ 93 + 9⅜
GnCinema 10s08 10157 125 102 125 +13⅝
GnCinema 10s09 5017 110¼ 93¾ 109½ ....
GenElec 5.3s92 2530 71⅞ 63¼ 70⅜+ 3⅞
GenElec 7½s96 4428 75½ 64⅛ 75½+ 3⅜
GenElec 8½s04 9669 77⅝ 64½ 77⅛+ 2⅝
GenElCr 8.6s85 5152 99⅞ 96¾ 99⅞+ 1⅝
GenElCr 8¼86 4432 98¼ 92 98 + 3⅝
GenElCr 7⅝88 4088 92½ 82⅜ 91¼+ 4¼
GenElCr 8¼97 1055 80½ 65 77 + 4⅛
GenElCr 9¾87 7956 98⅝ 90 97⅞+ 2⅞
GenElCr 11¾88 6668 102⅝ 94⅞ 101½+ ¾
GenElCr 11½90 7744 102¾ 90½ 101⅜+ 1⅜
GenElCr 11¾05 10309 99⅞ 83⅞ 99⅞+ 5¼
GenElec 14s90 4470 108¼ 100 106½............
GenElec 13⅝91 5491 107½ 97¾ 107½+ ½
GenFds 8⅞s90 1837 98¾ 90⅛ 91 — 1
GenFds 14⅜89 2987 108¾ 102 108 — 1⅜
GnHost 6s90f 119 68⅞ 62⅛ 62⅛— 2¼
GnHost 7s94 773 69 59½ 65⅜— 2⅛
GnHost 11¼92 116 83 77 77 ....
GenIn cv5s92 172 154 88 89 —61
GenMills 8⅞95 925 83½ 71 83½+ 3¼
GenMills 8s99 452 73½ 60½ 72¼+ 2¼
GenMills 9⅜09 449 79⅜ 69 79⅜+ ⅜
GenMills zr88s 4782 71½ 62 71 + 9
GenMills 12⅝85 47 101½ 97½ 100 — 3
GMotAc 4½s85
4770 97 90 96 19-32+6 19-32
GMotAc 4½85r 169 95 25-32 90½ 95 25-32
GMotAc 4⅝s86 6530 92⅞ 85⅜ 92¾+ 5½
GMotAc 4⅝86r 111 92 86⅝ 92 ....
GMotAc 4⅞s87 5318 86¾ 79⅜ 85⅝+ 6¼
GMotAc 6¼s88 6898 86⅞ 77⅞ 85⅞+ 5
GMotAc 7⅛90 4918 83 72⅛ 81½+ 4
GMotAc 8s93 6821 82 69¼ 80⅝+ 4
GMotAc 7¾s94 4138 78½ 65⅜ 77 + 4
GMotAc 7¼s95 2535 73⅜ 61⅜ 73 + 3⅛
GMotAc 7⅛s92 2934 78¼ 67 78¼+ 4¾
GMotAc 7.85s98 4631 73¾ 60¼ 72⅜+ 2½
GMotAc 8⅞s99 4561 79 64⅞ 77⅝+ 2⅞
GMotAc 8⅝s85
4315 99 7-32 94 99 3-32+3 19-32
GMotAc 8¾s00 3809 77¼ 65½ 77¼+ 3¼
GMotAc 8⅛86A 4403 97⅜ 90¼ 96⅜+ 2⅞
GMotAc 8⅛86J 4373 97½ 87⅝ 96⅞+ 4⅛
GMotAc 8¾01 1571 76¾ 63 75⅝+ 4⅝
GMotAc 8.15s86 4789 96⅝ 89¾ 95⅞+ 3⅛
GMotAc 8⅛96 2817 77½ 64⅜ 76¾+ 3⅜
GMotAc 7.35s87 5251 94 86 93¾+ 4
GMotAc 8s02 2406 71⅜ 59¾ 71⅜+ 2⅝
GMotAc 7.3s85
2377 99 3-32 93⅝ 99 3-32+4 31-32
GMotAc 8s07 3267 69 56⅛ 67⅛+ 3
GMotAc 8¼06 2415 71⅞ 58¾ 70¾+ 3
GMotAc 8.2s88 3175 93¼ 82⅜ 92⅞+ 6
GMotAc 8.65s08 770 75 61½ 73 + 2⅞
GMotAc 8⅝88 6148 93½ 83½ 92⅛+ 3⅝
GMotAc 8⅞85
6479 99⅞ 95½ 99 11-16+2 13-16
GMotAc 9⅝89 4360 95⅜ 84¼ 94 + 2¼
GMotAc 9¾03 1606 83½ 70 83¼+ 4⅛
GMotAc 9¼89 5378 93½ 81½ 92⅝+ 3¼

GMotAc 9.4s04 1516 82⅜ 65¾ 81 + 5⅞
GMotAc 11.9s87 5557 102⅜ 95½ 101 — ¼
GMotAc 12s05fb 3905 100⅜ 82¼ 98 + 1¼
GMotAc 11⅝90 9266 103⅜ 89½ 100⅝+ 2
GMotrAc 12s05 10269 100 82⅛ 98 + 3
GMotAc 10⅞87 7414 100½ 93⅛ 100⅛+ 1¾
GMotrAc 11¾00 4472 98⅜ 84 98⅜+ 4⅝
GMotrAc 12.90s90t 2908 105 99¾ 103⅜ .. ..
GMotrAc 14⅜91 7370 109¼ 100¼ 107⅝+ ⅛
GMotrAc d6s11 23549 54 44¾ 52⅜+ 1⅜
GMotr 14⅝89 11660 109⅞ 101 108⅜+ ⅜
GMotAc 10.10s92t
2385 101⅜ 96⅜ 101 + 1¾
GMotr 14.40s85
3012 108¼ 97⅛ 102 25-32—2 7-32
GMotAc 12⅝85
3826 103½ 99⅛ 101 25-32—7-32
GMotr 12s86 4408 104⅛ 97 102¼+ 1½
GMotAc 11¾89 12789 102¼ 91⅞ 101½+ 1½
GMotAc 10s85 1323 100¼ 97 9-32 100¼+1
GMotAc zr12 1693 80 61½ 64⅜— 5⅝
GMotrAc zr15 2844 80 48¼ 49⅝—11⅜
GMotrAc 13⅛87 1588 104¾ 100¼ 104¾ ......
GMotrAc 12⅝88 2869 104 98¼ 104 ....
GMotrAc 11⅞86 138 102 100¾ 102 ....
GMotCp 8.05s85
4774 99 21-32 95¾ 99 21-32+2 1-32
GMotCp 8⅝s05 4139 75⅝ 63 74¾+ 2⅜
GSignal 8⅞s99 96 76⅝ 75 75 — 3½
GTE cv4s90 536 96 81⅛ 88¼— 7⅞
GTE cv4s90r 23 89 81 89 ....
GTE 6⅝91 1502 83⅞ 64⅜ 80 +10⅞
GTE cv5s92 1634 99½ 81 91⅞— 8⅛
GTE 10⅛95 1117 93 76 91½+ 6½
GTE cv6¼96 683 127½ 104½ 116½—10½
GTE 9⅜99 1388 86⅛ 68 85⅞+10½
GTelCal 8⅞96 400 78 67¼ 77¾+ 2⅛
GWatwk 8¾s96 408 74¾ 64 74 + 1¾
Genesco 14¼94 36 96 90⅛ 93¼— 6¼
Genesco 15¼94 100 103 95 95 — 9
Genesc d9¾93 350 72⅛ 68⅛ 72 ....
GaPac cv5¼96 4192 93½ 72 85⅝— 7
GaPac 7¼85
1847 99 23-32 96⅛ 99 23-32+3 31-32
GaPac 10.35s87t 1961 100⅜ 98 98 — 2
GaPac 10.10s90 2020 94¾ 83⅛ 94¾+ 3⅝
GaPac 12¼13 199 94½ 86 89 ....
GaPow 8⅞2000 3811 74⅝ 61⅝ 72⅝+ 2⅝
GaPow 7⅜2001 1424 64⅛ 52¾ 62⅞+ 2⅝
GaPow 8⅛2001 3394 69½ 54¼ 67¼+ 3¼
GaPow 7⅝2001 1437 65½ 54 64⅞+ 4½
GaPow 7½02J 2164 64 52¾ 62⅛+ 2⅞
GaPow 7½02D 1626 65⅞ 52½ 61⅞+ 1⅞
GaPow 7⅞2003 1259 66⅛ 54¼ 64½+ 3⅛
GaPow 8⅝s04 3741 71⅜ 59 69⅛+ 1⅝
GaPow 11⅝s00 3285 93 81⅛ 92 + 4
GaPow 11¾s05 4261 91½ 77½ 90⅛+ 2⅛
GaPow 9⅞06 504 80¾ 66¾ 76 + 1
GaPow 9⅝08 1264 76 65 75¼+ ⅞
GaPow 9¾08 1028 77½ 65½ 76⅛+ 2⅝
GaPow 10½09 3109 82¾ 70 81 + 2¾
GaPow 11s09 3378 85½ 72⅛ 84⅛+ 2⅛
GaPow 14½10 3308 106 92 103¾+ 2⅝
GaPow 16⅛11 2692 110 99¾ 106½+ ¾
GaPow 16¼11 8650 111 100⅛ 107⅞+ 1½
GaPow 17½91 11000 114 105 113½+ 2½
GaPow 16¼12 4940 109⅞ 100⅛ 107⅞+ 2⅛
GaPow 13⅛12 2234 100 84½ 96¼— ⅛
GaPow 13¼13 1480 100¾ 85¼ 100¾+ 3¾
GaPow 16s14 252 110 105¾ 107⅝............
GettyO 10s87 8740 98¾ 90⅞ 98⅛+ 2⅞
GettyO 13⅞85 1050 105 100 13-32 102⅝—1⅜
GibralFn cv9¼08 7297 108½ 75 97½— 2
GlobMar 12⅜98 4716 86⅝ 65⅛ 76 — 4
GlobMar d16s01 9500 103 79⅞ 89⅞—10
GlobMar 16⅛02 32909 102⅝ 77⅞ 87¼—13
GlobMar cvd13s03
19828 92 64½ 70¾—18¾
GlobeUn 8s97 3 70 70 70 — 3¼
GoldNgt d13½96 1192 99 88½ 96⅞— 2⅝
GldNgF d8⅜93 1366 76¼ 66¼ 69⅛— 3⅞

Goodrch 4⅝s85	431	95½	88⅝	94 17-32	+7 1-32
Goodrch 4⅝85r	2	88¼	88¼	88¼	....
Goodrch 8¼s94	514	76	62	74	+ 4½
Goodrch 7s97	205	64½	56¼	60⅜	— 2⅝
Goodyr 8.60s95	1211	80½	70	78	+ 1
Goodyr 7.35s97	823	70½	57⅜	70	+ 1½
Gould 9¼s95	297	83⅞	68⅝	83¼	+ 4¼
Grace cv4¼s90	1409	87	80⅛	80½	— ⅝
Grace cv6½s96	208	157	123	144¼	— 4¾
Grace 12⅝90	633	102	91¼	101	+ ¾
Grace 12¾90	643	102¾	93¾	102½	+ 1½
Granit cv4⅝94	737	64½	57½	64⅛	+ 6⅝
Granit cv4⅝94r	54	60¾	58	60⅛	....
GtNNek cv4¼91	4	260	260	260	+37
GtNNek 7⅞98	1	68⅛	68⅛	68⅛	+ ⅝
GtNNek 8.7s08	77	71¾	65⅞	65⅞	— 5⅛
GtNoRy 3⅛00	429	41⅞	32	39¾	+ 3⅝
GtNoRy 3⅛00r	40	39	37¾	37¾	....
GtNoRy 2⅝10	394	30½	24⅝	30	+ 2¾
GtNoRy 2⅝10r	282	29	24	27	....
GtNoRy 3⅛90N	112	69	61	67	+ 4⅞
GtNoRy 3⅛90r	31	69	58	69	+16½
GtWstFin cv8⅞07	6001	101	77½	101	+ 3¼
GtWstUnit 6s87	61	99	75	75	—15½
GwstH 8¼03	2082	109	72	86	+ 8⅝
GGiant cv4¼92	30	165	139	165	+25
Greyh cv6½90	1390	139	109	128	— 8½
Greyh 9⅜01	1480	78	66	76½	+ 1⅝
Greyh 9⅞00	337	84¼	71¼	79⅛	— 4
GreyF 9¼92	397	86⅞	80¾	80¾	— ½
GreyF 12½00	277	96⅜	89½	96	+ 3⅞
GreyF 14⅞91	440	106½	100⅝	105	— ½
GreyF 16⅛92	587	112	104	111	+ ⅜
GreyF ar94	6593	31½	23¼	30¾	....
GreyF 13⅝94	212	101⅝	95⅝	101⅝	....
Grolier 13s02	3370	89	76	81	— 5½
Grolier 13⅝03	1280	91⅛	78½	83⅝	— 8⅜
Grumman cv9¼09	913	101¾	94	94½	......
GulfWn 6s87	72	89½	80½	89½	+ 9½
GulfWn 6s88	1022	83¾	76¾	83⅝	+ 6
GulfWn 7s03A	12380	59⅝	49	58⅝	+ 1⅝
GulfWn7s03 B	7108	59⅝	49	58¼	+ ¼
GulfMO 5s15Af	204	70	45½	70	+13
GulfMO 5s15Arf	14	52	46	52	....
GulfMO 4s44Bf	719	66	41⅝	62⅛	+15⅛
GulfMO 4s44Brf	254	66	42	61⅝	....
GulfMo 5s56f	448	43	37½	38⅛	— 1⅜
GulfMO 5s56rf	171	42½	38	39	....
GulfOil 8½s95	3212	81⅜	69½	80¼	+ 2½
GulfOil 12.05s09t	5256	102⅝	99½	102	+ 2¼
GlfResCh 10⅞97	510	80⅞	69½	75⅛	— 2⅜
GlfResCh 12½04	729	91½	74⅛	82⅜	— 3
GlfStUt cv7¼92	71	85	80	81¾	—32¼

— H—H —

Hallibrt 7.95s95	598	76¾	65	76⅛	+ 2⅝
Hallibrt 9¼00	739	81⅛	72	80¾	+ 1¾
Hallibrt 10.20s05	372	87¼	73¼	87¼	— 8½
Hallibrt 16s88	2099	111	105	110⅛	— 2⅝
HamPa cv5s94	507	135	104⅝	116	— 2
Harnisch 15s94	445	102⅛	94¼	101½	....
Harnsch d12s04	305	83	73	79½	....
Harra 9½96	310	80¼	72	77⅝	— 1
Harris 7¾01	95	68	61⅝	68	+ 3
Harris 11½10	34	90	87	90	+ 1¼
Harsco 5½s92	174	64⅛	62½	63	— ⅛
Harsco 12¼10	5	93	93	93	— ¾
HartfdN 8½s96	423	73¾	61¾	72¼	....
Hartmarx 8½96	37	80⅛	68¼	71¾	—10¼
Hartmarx 8½08	1604	121	101¼	106	— 8
HawaEl 9s00	661	76⅛	65	74⅛	+ 2½
HawaEl 8.2s01	372	69	56¼	68¼	+ 3⅛
HawaEl 7⅝02	125	64	53⅜	64	....
HawaEl 8.35s03	329	70	61¾	68½	+ 3¼
HawaEl 11¼04	394	90⅞	76	90⅞	+ ⅞
Heilman 11⅝05	212	90	77	87	— 2
HeinzHJ 7¼s97	113	86¼	83⅝	83⅝	+ 2
HellerW 9½s89	1699	92⅝	77⅝	91½	+ 4¼
HellerW 9⅛s91	411	86⅛	76¼	84¼	+ 4⅜
HellerW 7¾s92	612	79	68¾	78	+ 3⅝
HellerW 8s93	130	75⅞	68	70½	— 3½
HellerW 7¾s93	511	77⅞	68	77⅞	+ 4⅝
HellerW 10½86	615	100	95⅝	99¾	+ 3¾
HellerW 10⅛91	236	89⅝	81⅜	86⅛	— ⅛
HellerW 8.1s87	1803	95	85¾	94⅜	+ 6¼
HellerW 8¾02	58	69⅜	56½	69¼	— ¾
Hercul cv6½99	3688	110	91	100	— 4
Hercul 10½89	90	97⅛	97⅛	97⅛	....
Hercul na cv08	25	99¾	98	99¾	....
HershFd 9½09	145	78½	73½	78	— 1
Hertz 8⅞s01	97	73⅛	64¼	72	— 1
Heubln cv4½97	415	101	85	100½	+13½
Heubln 8⅜85	1880	99 13-16	96¾	99 13-16	+3 1-16
HiltNJ 11⅜92	153	98	91¾	91¾	— 5⅛
HiltNJ 10⅝94	112	92¾	82	92¾	+ 1⅛
HockVal 4½s99	150	50	37¾	44¾	— 6⅜
HockVal 4½99r	46	46	42	45¼	....
HolInn 9½95xw	363	90⅛	70½	86⅛	+ 4½
Holilnn 14⅛92	38	105	103⅛	103⅛	+ 2⅞
Holilnn 13¼.&&	65	102⅛	102⅛	102⅛	.. ..
HmeDepot cv8½09	6045	108	78	88¼	.. ..
HonyFn 8.2s98	349	72½	60	70	....
HonyFn 8.7s86	1559	98¾	91¾	98¼	+ 3½
Honeywl 6.1s92	215	75	64	71	+ 1⅞
Honeywl 9⅜09	523	77¾	67⅛	74½	— 9½
Honeywl 14⅛11	531	109	95¼	108½	+ ½
HookCh 4⅞s91	112	65	58	63⅝	+ ¾
HoovUnv 8⅜96	30	66	63½	63½	— 5½
HospAffil 10s99	337	80	70½	78⅞	— ⅛
HospAffil 10s91	533	93¼	86	86¾	— 3⅞
HospCp 10¾s90	164	101	82⅛	95½	+ 4½
HospCp 16½07	60	114½	110	110½	— 1½
HospCp 15⅝07	20	110¼	108¾	108¾	— 2⅜
HospCp cv8½08	15927	112	97½	99	— 1
HospCp cv9s98	6079	100	90	98½	+ ½
HousFin 4⅜s87	624	86½	78⅞	86½	+ 7½
HousFin 7½s95	288	74¼	61⅞	74¼	+ 2¼
HousFin 7¾s99	913	69¼	56	67½	+ 2⅛
HousFin 8½s01	217	71	61	71	+ 2⅜
HousFin 10½94	58	92⅛	83⅛	90	— 3
HousFin 8.3s86	1362	98½	93	98	+ 3⅝
HousFin 9s00	274	76¼	66	74	— 1½
HousFin 7.85s86	1020	96½	88⅜	96	+ 5
HousFin 8⅜03	101	71	58½	71	+ 5⅜
HousFin 8.45s97	855	78	62½	75¾	+ 2
HousFin 8.2s07	659	69¼	59	69¼	+ 4⅝
HousLt cv5½85	1481	99⅛	95½	99⅛	+ 2⅜
HouNG 9.75s95	121	85½	73⅜	85	+ 3¼
HouNG 8.2s01	135	69	65¾	68	— 8½
HughesTl 9s00	215	77¼	69	76¾	— 1¾
HughesTl 9s08	95	73	64	73	+ 1⅜
HughesTl 14¼88	571	106⅝	100⅛	105½	— ⅜
HughesTl cv9½06	11611	88	69	79¾	— 5¾
Human 11.7s98	6545	95	81	94⅛	+ 2
Human cv5s97	99	94¾	92	92	—16
Human 9½98	268	79¼	74⅝	79¼	+ 3¼
Human d13½02	324	101	86¼	101	+ ⅞
Human 14½02	19	101½	97⅝	101½	— 6½
Human 13¾13	85	104⅝	99⅜	100⅝	— 2⅝
Human cv8½09	4010	95	88	89	....
HuntIR 9⅞04	6456	76	18	22⅝	—49⅜
Hutton 12s05	3012	95	82	91⅛	+ ⅛

— I—I —

ICPrd 10¼s95	115	85½	77	85½	+ ½
ICINA 9.05s95	144	85⅛	67⅞	85⅛	+ 9¾
ICI NA 8⅞03	892	74	63	73	+ 2
ITTBkg 9¾s95	307	84¾	75⅛	83¾	+ 4¼
ITTFin 8.1s92	177	80¼	74	80¼	+ 1⅞
ITTFin 10½95	405	90¼	81	90¼	+ 4⅜
ITTFin 11¼85	1417	101¾	97	100 13-32	+13-32
ITTFin 9⅝96	163	86¾	75⅛	84¼	+ 3½
ITTFin 8½02	170	72	64	72	— 7
ITTFin 8⅞03	817	95	86⅛	94¾	+ 4
ITTFin 11.85s99	203	96	83½	90	— 6
ITTFin 11s88	1326	100	90⅜	99½	+ 3½
ITTFin 14¾91	811	110	101	108¾	+ 3⅝
ITTFin 11¼90	121	98½	92	98	— ¼
ITTRay 8s96	10	68⅝	67½	68⅝	— 2⅜
ITTWor 8½s96	365	75¾	64⅛	75⅜	+ ⅞
IdealB 9¼2000	470	74	61	71⅝	+ 4½

IllBell 7⅝s2006	4296	67¼	55¼	66⅝	+ 3⅝
IllBell 8s04	4145	71⅝	58⅛	69⅞	+ 2⅝
IllBell 8¼16	1816	70⅝	56	69⅞	+ 4¼
IllBel 12¼17	7384	102	83½	99	+ 2
IllCenG 11¼99	275	89	81	84⅝	— 1⅜
IllCenG 15½94	34	103	99	102¾	....
IllCen 3⅜s89H	100	65⅛	60¼	62½	— 1½
IllPow 7.60s01	701	66¼	53½	65	+ 3½
IllPow 7⅝s03	579	66	53⅛	66	+ 5½
IllPow 10½s04	914	84⅛	70⅛	82	+ ¼
IllPow 8⅝06	1099	73	57⅛	70½	+ 4½
IllPow 8¼07	919	68	56	65½	— ⅛
IllPow 8⅞08	680	72½	59½	72¼	+ 3¼
IllPow 11⅜87	859	100	91⅞	99½	— ½
IllPow 12⅝10	756	100	81	96¼	+ 3⅛
IllPow 14½90	10	102	102	102	—13
IllPow 12s12	310	94⅞	82	92¾	+ 3¾
IncoLtd 6.85s93	801	66¾	55⅞	60⅜	— 1⅝
IncoLtd 12⅜10	578	90⅜	77	83	— 7⅜
IndMich 10¼87	935	98¾	89⅛	97¾	+ 3⅞
IndMich 13⅞87	273	105	97⅛	101¾	— 1⅞
IndMich 11⅜90	109	96	85⅛	96	+ 2
IndMich 14¾89	2233	106¼	98½	106¼	+ 1
IndMich 15⅝91	127	107½	98¾	104	— 3⅛
IndBellT 8⅛11	2018	69⅛	57¼	68⅜	+ 2⅝
IndBellT 10s14	1288	83⅞	70¼	81½	+ 3½
IndBellT 8⅛17	1221	70	56⅛	68	+ 2⅝
IndBellT 8s14	785	68⅞	56¼	68	+ 3⅞
Inexco cv 8½00	10675	85	57⅛	58¼	—13¼
IngRd 8.05s04	224	67½	56½	66	+ ½
IngRd 8¾s85	1399	99 19-32	95 13-16	99 15-32	+2 31-32
IngRd 12⅜90	1584	101½	92½	100¾	+ 1¼
IngRd 12⅞10	44	99	90	97	— 3
InlandSt 4⅜s87	228	83½	78¾	83½	+ 6½
InlandSt 4⅜87r	9	83⅛	83⅛	83⅛	....
InlandSt 4½s89	230	73⅝	70	73½	+ 4½
InlandSt 6½s92	373	66¾	60⅝	66½	+ 2⅜
InlandSt 8¾s95	886	76	62	71⅜	— ¾
InlandSt 8⅞99	497	72½	62	72½	+ 2⅝
InlandSt 9½00	369	75⅜	67	72¼	— ⅞
InlandSt 7.9s07	853	64	51	58¼	— 5¾
InlandSt 11¼90	548	94	86	93	+ 2
Insilco cv9s10	1288	102½	100⅝	102	....
IntgRes d8⅝97	195	72	58⅝	60¼	— 8⅜
Interco 14¼91	200	106	101	106	+11½
Intrfst 9¾99	377	80	68	75	+ 1
Intfst 11.60s87t	310	98½	87	95	— ½
Intrfst 7¾05	10732	84¾	58	70½	—10¾
Intrlak 8.80s96	258	77⅛	67	76⅛	+ 3⅛
IBM 9½86	46111	99	93	98⅜	+ 1⅞
IBM 9⅜04	101660	86¼	73	84½	+ 2
IBM cv7⅞04	30352	101½	98¼	100¼	....
IntHarv 4⅝88	194	80½	68½	73½	— 1¼
IntHarv 4⅝88r	7	78	73	78	+10
IntHarv 4.8s91	926	81⅝	64⅞	65⅞	+ 1
IntHarv 6¼98	3052	50	41	47¼	— 2⅝
IntHarv 8⅝95	5789	64⅞	50	63¾	+ 2½
IntHarv 9s04	11297	65⅜	50	60¼	— 2⅜
IntHarv 18s02	14923	110⅞	94¼	106⅛	— 1⅜
IntHarCr 8⅝91	2841	75¼	64	70⅛	— 1
IntHarCr 7⅝93	1088	67½	55⅞	65⅞	+ ¼
IntHarCr 7½94	1343	65	53⅝	61⅛	— 1⅞
IntHarCr 8.35s86	10391	90½	81	89⅝	+ 4⅝
IntHarCr 13½88	8546	97½	87⅛	95½	....
IntMin cv4s91	23	157	134	140½	—36½
IntMin 9.35s00	70	75	70	75	— 4
IntMin 11⅞05	215	93½	85	93½	+ 2⅜
IntMulti 9⅛s96	111	83	73⅝	77¼	— 1⅛
IntPap 8.85s95	1882	84¼	71	83	+ 3¾
IntPap cv4¼96	642	142	84	88	—43½
IntPap 8.85s00	437	77½	72½	76½	+ 2⅛
IntPap d5⅛12	1036	47½	41½	44½	— ½
IntSilv cv5s93	235	98	72¼	88	—12
IntTT 4.90s87	330	87¼	80⅛	87¼	+ 6
IntT 4.90s87r	6	80⅞	80½	80⅞	....
IntTT 8.90s95	576	84⅜	70½	81⅜	— ¾
IntTT cv8⅝s00	354	179	95	118¼	—56¼
IntTT 10s2000	282	86	69	82½	— 3½
InTT 12⅝05	441	101¼	89	100	....
InTT 14¾91	713	110	101	107	+ 1
Intnth 10¾90	1226	98	86½	98	+ 3⅝
Intnth 17½91	1240	115	108	111⅜	— 3⅝
Intnth 12¼02	10	96	96	96	— ⅛
Intnth cv10½08	18127	102¾	87	93½	— 6⅞
IntrBak 5½87	1099	84¼	73¼	84¼	+11
Ipco cv5¼89	178	88½	78½	87	+ 8½
IrvgBk 8½02	209	71½	58½	67⅞	— 1⅛
IrvgBk 9¾04t	1691	97⅞	90½	97⅞	+ 3⅛
— J—J —					
JerCPL 10¼s85	1645	99⅜	95	99 5-32	+3 5-32
JerCPL 9⅝s06	537	71½	57	71	+ 3
JerCPL 9¾06	648	72¼	61⅛	71⅛	+ 2⅝
JerCPL 8¾07	145	64⅞	59¾	64⅞	+ 2¼
JerCPL 9s08	29	66	60	65⅞	+ ⅞
JohnsM 7.85s04f	9684	75	59½	59½	— 4
JohnsM 9.7s85f	15147	90 11-32	75¾	77 15-32	—17-32
JoneLInd 6¾94	4891	62½	53⅞	55	— 4¾
JoneLInd 6½88	266	79	70⅛	74⅜	— 4⅝
JonesLau 6¾94	1059	67⅞	52½	54¾	— 3⅜
JonesLau 9⅞95	714	77	66½	67½	— 8⅛
JonesLau 8s98	76	63¾	51¼	57¼	— 4⅞
JonesLau 9¾96	178	76⅛	62⅛	66½	— 8¾
— K—K —					
K mart cv6s99	15527	109½	86	103¾	+ 3¾
K Mart 9⅞85	2509	100⅛	96⅞	100⅛	+ 2⅝
Kaisr cv9s05	897	99⅞	74¾	77	—15½
KanCSo 3¼s84	41	98	94	98	+ 4⅛
KanCSo 3¼84r	6	97	97	97	....
KaufBrd 12¼99	783	92¾	80	90	+ ¾
Kellogg 8⅝s85	1866	99⅝	93¼	99⅝	+ 3¼
Kennect 7⅞s01	831	69⅜	62	68¾	+ 1¾
KentyCen 4s87	44	82	76⅝	82	+ 5
KerrMcG 8½06	151	70¼	64	69⅝	— ⅛
KeyBks 7¾02	593	67	54¾	63¼	+ 2
Keystn cv8½05	944	110	92½	93¼	—11¾
Kidde 8¾02	45	67⅜	61⅛	61⅛	— 5½
Kidde 9¾03	43	77⅞	73	73	— 1
KimbCl 4⅝s86	17	87½	85¼	87½	+ ½
KimbCl 5⅞s91	199	72	68	71½	+ 1
KimbCl 5⅞s92	326	70	67⅛	70	+ 1
KimbCl 11⅛90	327	99¾	89⅛	99	+ 3
KimbCl 11½13	76	89½	86½	86½	—13½
KingsCEI 6s97	44	57	50⅛	57	+ 2⅞
Koger 2000s	896	125	113⅞	123⅛	+ 8⅜
KogerPr cv9¼03	1159	95	77	88½	— 1½
Kolmrgn 8¾09	2202	104	79	81	....
Kraftco 6⅞s96	216	81	60⅝	69⅝	— ⅝
Kraftco 8⅜s04	818	84	62½	74½	+ 2¼
KraftCo 7.6s07	250	67½	59¾	66⅝	+ 2⅛
Kroger 9s95	313	85	73	81¼	+ ¾
Kroger 8.7s98	458	77	64	75¾	+ 2¼
Kroger 8½01	25	71½	61	71	+ 1⅞
Kroger 12⅜05	95	94	85	90	— 6
Kroger 14⅜91	328	109	99	103⅝	— 4⅞
Kroger 9½95	19	99¾	94¾	99¾	....
— L—L —					
LFE 10s92	66	77⅛	65	76	— 1
LTVCp 5s88	12857	77⅝	73⅝	77	+ 2
LTVCp 9¼97	5271	74	62⅛	64½	— 3½
LTVCp 11s07	10775	82	67	71	— 5½
LTVCp 13⅞02	2867	100	86	86⅜	—11¾
LTV Int cv5s88	11	91⅞	70	70	....
LaQuint cv10s02	2973	108	86	87	—20
LearSieg 10s04	863	80½	70	80¼	+ ⅞
LearSieg 11½98	728	89¼	76⅜	86⅞	+ 1¾
LearSieg 11¼98	515	86½	74½	85	+ 4⅜
LegPlat cv8⅛01	1375	113	90	102	—10
Leucadia 13¾99	328	98½	88⅜	96	— ¼
LiggtGp 6s92	303	75½	69¾	75½	+ 3¾
LiggtGp 7.6s97	184	70½	55	69⅜	+ 1⅜
LiggtGp 8⅝01	304	73	60	70¼	+ 4¼
LincFtBk 8½96	497	77	64⅛	72	+ 2
LincNtl 13⅞92	188	103¾	95¾	103½	— 1⅞
Litton cv3½s87	4	145½	138	138	+ 3
Loews 6⅞s93	16464	74¼	64	73	+ 3⅛
LomN cv5½91	8	310	230	310	+63
LomN cv9¾08	5105	135½	98¾	135½	+20¾
LoneSln 4⅞s90	130	65	60¼	64¼	— ⅛
LoneSln cv5⅛93	75	107½	77	91	—15

LoneSln 8s97	198	69	64	68	+ 1⅞
LoneSln 11¾90	139	96¾	81⅛	85⅝	— 6⅛
LongIsLt 12⅝92	1721	94	70	90	— 2
LongIsLt 13½13	10514	94⅞	68¼	85½	— 5⅛
LongIsLt 17½89	1730	107½	101	106¾	....
Loral 10¾97	330	86¼	77	84	+ ⅜
Lorillrd 4⅞s86	59	90½	86	90½	+ 4
Lorillrd 6⅝s93	362	75⅞	70	75	+ 1⅜
LouNsh 4⅞s87	54	82⅜	77⅝	79⅝	+ 2
LouNsh 2⅞03	168	33	28	33	+ 2⅜
LouNsh 2⅞03r	21	33	29	33	....
LouNsh 3⅜03F	65	36⅞	29	32½	+ 2½
LouNsh 3⅜023Fr	4	31⅛	29½	31⅛	....
LouNsh 3⅜03I	15	85½	78	85½	+ 12¼
LouNsh 3⅜03r	1	82	82	82	....
LouNsh 3¾03	35	78	70⅛	72	+ 3⅞
LouNsh 7⅜s93	551	81	60	72⅝	+ 7½
LouNsh 11s85	605	102	98	100	+ ⅜
LouGE 4⅞s87	164	86¼	79⅞	85½	+ 4¾
LouGE 4⅞s90	136	73	65	73	+ 6½
LouGE 4⅞90r	90	71⅞	70	71⅞	....
LouGE 9¼2000	642	79⅛	67¼	79⅛	+ 4⅛
LouGE 8¼s01	420	71½	61	70⅞	+ 5⅜
LouGE 7½s02	273	66	53¾	66	+ 5⅛
Lowenst 8½s96	105	74⅛	60	70⅝	— 3½
LuckySt 8½96	50	80½	72	74	— 5½
LuckySt cv6¾00	14	134	121½	121½	— 34½
LuckySt 11⅛87	188	98¾	94¾	98½	— ¼
LuckySt 11¾05	37	93	80½	88⅛	— 3⅞
Lykes 7½94new	2009	65½	56½	57⅝	— 4⅝
Lykes 7½94old	10527	65	57	58	— 4¼
Lykes 11s2000	1915	81⅞	69	72	— 5
— M—M —					
MACOM cv9¼06	10049	99	80½	90	— 1¼
MCI Com 15s00	3478	109½	95	102	— 1⅛
MCI d14⅛01	1702	102⅞	88⅜	98	— 3¾
MCI Com 12⅞02	1548	97⅞	79½	89	— 6½
MCorp 10s99t	35	98	95	95	— 3
MGIC cv5s93	98	85¼	75	85	+ 10
MGIC 8⅜s88	2527	90	78⅜	86⅛	+ 4⅛
MGM 9s92	238	82	75⅛	76⅝	— 3
MGM 10s93	202	85	70⅝	80	— 2
MGM 10s94	1106	80⅛	72⅛	78⅝	+ 1½
MGM 10½s96	557	83⅞	70⅝	79	— ½
MGM 9¾s86	738	99¼	93⅛	98⅛	+ 2⅞
MGM cv9½00	6790	92	77	84	— 5
MGM d12s96	749	89⅜	75¾	84	— 6¼
MGMUA 10s90	1974	83⅞	72½	79¼	+ 2
MackF 9⅝s90	562	89	76½	87⅛	+ 7¼
MackF 9¾s91	144	83⅜	77	83⅜	+ 4⅜
MackT 7⅞s97	100	66⅜	58⅛	66¼	+ 6¼
MackT 10¾s85	414	98 25-32	91	98 17-32	+ 2 5-32
Macmill cv4s92	59	180	118	180	+ 41
MacMill cv8¾08	1879	145½	98	145	+ 39
MacyCr 5⅜85	63	93½	92¾	92¾	....
MacyCr 13⅞91	302	106	99⅛	106	+ 1¾
MacyCr 13¾88	75	105	100	100	— 4
MeYnkP 9.1s02	872	77	59⅝	76⅛	+ 5⅜
MeYnkP 8½02	505	74¾	55⅝	74¾	+ 7
MeYnkP 7⅝02	139	66¼	58½	66¼	+ 4½
MfrHan 8⅛04	1865	67¾	55⅝	66⅛	+ ¾
MfrHan 8⅛07	1043	70	54¾	65	+ 1
MfrH 11¼87t	4619	99½	90	99½	+ 1¾
MfrsHTr 8½85	1335	99¼	93⅛	98 13-32	+ 2 1-32
Mapco 10¾99	220	84	79	79¾	— 2¼
Mapco cv10s05	13114	95	81½	87	— ¼
MaraOil 4⅜s87	123	86	78⅝	86	+ 10¼
MaraOil 4⅜87r	12	82¼	77⅝	82¼	....
MaraOil 8½00	1191	70½	58⅞	70½	+ 2⅞
MaraOil 8.5s06	942	69	56	67⅛	— ⅜
MaraOil 10¼87	3905	98¼	89	98	+ 3¼
MaraOil 12½94	114498	98⅝	85¼	96½	+ 1
Marcor 6½s88	9154	82¼	76⅛	81½	+ 3⅛
Marcor cv5s96	40	92	89¾	89¾	— 10¼
MarMid 7⅝s03	615	65	52½	65	+ 3
MarMAl 9⅜s96	171	95⅝	70½	95⅝	+ 21⅜
MartMar d7s11	232	58	53½	56	+ 1
MartM 15.55s87	700	105¾	101½	105½	+ ½
MdNtlCp 8s86	523	94¼	86	94¼	+ 5
MdNtlCp 15½87	205	107½	102	104⅜	— 2½
Masco 8⅞01	20	61½	61½	61½	— 3½
MassM cv6¾90	160	88½	83	83	— 5
MassM cv6¼91	419	73	65	71	+ 2¾
MassM cv7s00	368	87¾	78	87¾	+ 4¾
Mattel 11⅝03	13448	84	62⅛	81	+ 17
MayDSt 7.95s02	104	68	58½	66	— ⅛
MayDStCr 9s89	733	94¾	80⅛	93⅞	+ 4⅞
MayrOs 7.85s96	127	74½	66⅛	74¼	+ 2⅛
MayrOs 11⅝10	67	90¾	81¾	82	— 10⅝
McCror cv6½92	95	63⅜	60	61	— 2⅜
McCror 7½s94	646	64¾	54⅛	58⅛	— 2⅜
McCror 10½85	181	99	94¼	99	....
McCror 7½94n	116	65	56⅜	59⅛	— 3½
McCror 7⅝s97	252	62¼	53	57½	— 1¼
McCror 7¾s95	908	64⅞	55¼	58⅛	— 5
McDerm 10.20s99	211	83⅜	79	83	+ 2
McDerm 9⅝04	92	83	75⅛	83	+ 6
McDerm 10s03	6037	84	75½	82⅛	+ 2
McDnld 9s85	1351	99¾	96 17-32	99¾	+ 1¾
McDnld 8⅝88	472	93⅛	83¾	93⅛	+ 2¾
McDnld 10¼89	830	97½	85¾	97½	+ 3
McDnld zr88s	2402	69	58	69	+ 8
McDnld zr94s	7407	37	28½	35½	+ 4¼
McDD cv4¾91	223	235	175⅛	224	+ 34
McGrEd 7½96	417	70	61	69	+ 4⅞
McGHI cv3⅞92	20	137	115¼	130	— 8
McKeson 6s94	89	141	104½	127¼	— 4¾
McKeson 9¾06	5161	109½	91	100⅜	— 3⅝
McLean 12s03	3157	90¾	72⅜	81	— 6
MeadCp 8½s95	465	77	66¼	77	+ 3½
MeadCp 9⅞s00	268	80½	69⅜	78	+ ⅞
MeadCp 15⅞92	68	112⅝	107	112⅝	+ ⅛
Mellon 11.05s89t	963	100½	97⅞	100	....
Melln cv9½89t	3180	97⅞	92½	96¾	+ 1⅛
Melvill cv4⅞96	11	250	244	250	+ 9
Memx 5¼90	2516	76	68¼	75	+ 6½
MercStr 8.7s95	116	80	75½	78⅝	— 2
Merck 7⅞s85	2274	99 13-32	95⅛	99 13-32	+ 2 29-32
MLCPS 15¾06	1547	110½	97⅛	107½	+ 2
MerLyn 11⅝87	627	104	94¼	101½	+ 1
MerLyn 9¾86	913	99	94⅛	99	+ 1½
MerilL cv8⅞07	39088	124	94½	106½	— 9
MesaPt cv8½00	52	89¼	85	89¼	+ 1¾
MichBT 3⅛88	662	77	72	76	+ 3¾
MichBT 3⅛88r	22	72½	71¾	72	....
MichBT 4⅜91	235	65	61⅛	65	+ 3¼
MichBT 4⅜91r	10	65	65	65	....
MichBT 7¾s11	5722	66⅜	54⅛	64¼	+ 2½
MichBT 7s2012	2755	60¼	48¾	60	+ 3½
MichBT 9.6s08	6779	81	66½	79¼	+ 3⅝
MichBT 8⅛15	3774	68¼	55¾	66⅝	+ 2⅛
MichBT 9⅛18	2797	75⅞	63	75¼	+ 4¼
MichBT 15¾21	5847	117½	103⅝	115	....
MichCG 8⅛98	507	68½	59⅜	67⅜	+ 2⅞
MichCG 10⅞95	61	87½	82¾	86½	— 2⅞
MichCG 15⅝91	181	107¼	101⅛	107	— ¼
MichCG 13½03	58	103¼	103⅛	103⅛	+ ⅛
Midcon cv10¼09	3217	111	97½	110½	....
MidIndAm 12¾03	60	93½	93½	93½	....
MidlRoss 5¾92	3	60¼	60¼	60¼	+ 3¼
MidlRoss 10¾87	550	98⅛	92	98⅛	+ 2⅝
MidlnBk 11.35s93	160	95⅛	87	87	— 8
MilesLb 6½92	267	69	62¼	68	+ 3
MilesLb 8.7s96	35	73	71⅛	71⅛	+ 1⅝
MplsStL 6s85	28	100	91¾	93⅜	+ 1⅞
MplsStL 6s85r	9	96	93⅝	94 11-32	....
MStPSS 4s91f	258	66	58	66	+ 6
MinMM 8.20s85	4024	100	96	99¾	+ 3
MinMM 8.85s05	1276	78½	66¾	77	+ 2
MissnIns 11⅞93	10	81⅝	81⅝	81⅝	....
MisRivTr 9¾90	127	93½	88⅞	92⅝	+ ⅛
MoKnTx 4s90	870	65½	57	65½	+ 6½
MoKnTx 5½33f	1510	41⅜	25¾	27½	— 10½
MoKnTx 5½33fr	91	39½	26	28¼	....
MoPacRy 4¼90	1017	75½	66⅛	75½	+ 5⅛
MoPacRy 4¼90r	14	73⅜	68½	73⅜	....
MoPacRy 4¼05	2586	43½	35	41¾	+ 2⅝
MoPacRy 4¼05r	195	42	36	41	....
MoPacRy 4¾20f	1699	41½	33¼	38⅝	— ¾

MoPacRy 4¾30f	1581	41½	32	38¼	+ ¾
MoPacRy 5s45f	7232	43	34	40	— ⅜
MoPrtC 10s97	360	72⅛	65½	71¾	+ ¾
MobilAl 8.45s05	816	75	62¾	73	+ 4¼
Mobil 8½s01	25685	76½	63⅜	75	+ 2¼
Mobil 14.40s04	126831	108	96½	106½	....
MobilOil 7⅜s01	1769	68⅜	56	68	+ 3
MobilOil 10⅞92	9213	98½	83⅞	96¾	+ 2⅛
MobilCp 13.76s04	47460	105⅜	98⅞	104¾	.. ..
MohkD cv5½94	592	59	54	54¼	— 3¼
Mongrm 10s99	646	74	63	67¾	— 3¼
Mongrm 11s04	379	78¼	68	76¼	— 1¼
Monon 6s2007f	87	49¾	45½	49¾	+ 3¼
Monon 6s07fr	18	47½	45½	46	....
Monsant 9⅛00	1305	80	68¼	79½	+ 4
Monsant 8s85	1924	99 9-16	94⅝	99½	+ 3¾
Monsant 8½00	279	76	64	73½	+ 2
Monsant 8¾08	628	74⅜	62	72¾	+ 1⅝
MontWd 4⅞s90	1128	69⅝	60½	69½	+ 6¼
MontWd 9⅜s00	866	74¾	64	73	+ 2½
MtWdCr 6½s87	893	88½	79⅛	88¼	+ 8⅞
MtWdCr 7⅜s88	1880	86⅛	77¼	84¼	+ 6⅜
MtWdCr 9s89	2746	88⅛	76¾	84⅜	+ 1⅜
MtWdCr 9¼s90	2027	86	75⅞	85½	+ 3½
MtWdCr 9.6s95	354	79⅛	72	77¼	+ 1⅛
MtWdCr 8⅝86	1005	95	88	95	+ 8⅝
MtWdCr 8¼02	387	66	57	63⅜	+ 3¼
MtWdCr 8⅜02	580	66¼	56¾	63⅞	+ 1⅛
MtWdCr 8⅞03	652	69⅞	59⅛	64⅜	— 2
MtWdCr 13⅝87	3072	103½	98⅛	102	+ ⅜
MtWdCr 16s86	2345	107⅝	102⅛	104½	— 1¾
MtWdCr 13½89	121	99½	98	98½	....
MonyM cv7s90	308	90	76	79	+ ⅞
MoranE cv8¾08	2849	98	71¼	72	—15
MorgJP cv4¾98	3917	100½	70	96¼	+10¾
MorgJP 8s86	3391	97¼	91⅛	97¼	+ 4¼
MorNor 8⅞s95	98	80¾	70	79	+ 1⅝
MorNor 9⅝s00	25	80	80	80	— 2¾
Motorola 8s07	20	64¼	56	64¼	— 3¾
MtStTT 2⅝s86	223	91	84½	90⅛	+ 6⅜
MtStTT 7⅜s11	2620	63⅞	51⅜	62⅝	+ 3⅞
MtStTT 7¾s13	3377	65⅞	53⅜	64⅞	+ 3⅞
MtStTT 9¾s12	3502	80¾	67	79½	+ 3¾
MtStTT 9⅝s15	2899	79¼	65⅝	78⅝	+ 3⅝
MtStTT 7⅞16	2062	66½	54	65¾	+ 3¼
MtStTT 8s17	4238	68⅞	55	66½	+ 3¾
MtStTT 8⅝18	4759	73	59⅛	70	+ 2⅛
MtStTT 9¼14	2507	77⅛	63	76⅛	+ 3¾
MtStTT 11¼19	5038	92¼	76¼	92¼	+ 5¾
MurphyG 7⅜97	60	71⅜	61	66¾	+ 6⅝

— N—N —

NAFCO 9s03	1135	104½	84	85	—18¼
NBI cv8¼07	5984	89½	66⅜	69½	—14¾
NCNB 14½92	186	108½	99½	99¾	— 9¼
NCNB 9.40s95	983	83⅝	69	83	+ 5⅝
NCNB 8⅝97	462	76¼	66	74¼	+ 1⅝
NCNB 8⅜s99	553	72	63	72	+ 4
NCNB 12.65s96	7	94⅝	94⅝	94⅝	....
NCR 9s85	1628	99 13-16	96 13-32	99 13-16	+2 9-16
NLInd 7½s95	193	71⅝	65	71⅝	+ 2¾
NLInd 9⅜2000	123	79⅛	65	75	....
Nabisco 7¾s01	254	71	61½	71	+ 4⅝
Nabisco 7¾s03	151	68¼	59	68¼	+ 1½
NashCSL 3s86	25	92	84⅝	92	+10
NatBisc 4¾87	351	87½	81	87½	+ 4¾
NatBisc 4¾87r	156	84½	80	84½	....
NatCan cv5s93	105	125	90	118	+30
NatCan 8⅜s96	93	75	65¼	68⅛	— 5½
NatCash 4¾s85	129	94	92⅛	93 5-32	+1 9-32
NatCash 4⅜s87	170	85⅛	79½	85⅛	+ 6
NatCash 5.6s91	524	72½	62¾	70⅝	+ 1⅝
NatCash 7.7s94	601	76¼	64⅞	74⅝	+ 1⅝
NConv cv9s08	3559	104	86½	98¾	— ¼
NatDairy 4⅜92	76	65	60	64	+ 2⅛
NDist cv4½92	213	110	92	99	— 1⅝
NHom cv4¾96	985	50¾	36¼	42	— 8⅛
NatInd 10s99	322	74	65⅝	71¼	— 2½
NatLead 4⅜88	175	81	74	80	+ 6
NatLead 4⅜88r	5	73⅞	71	71	....
NatMed 12¾00	210	98	84	96	+ 3⅞
NatMed cv9s06	15282	112	97⅝	109½	+ 3½
NatMed cv d12⅝01	24172	114	88⅛	110⅛	+ 3⅞
NatMed 8s08	18378	94	76½	90⅛	+ 4⅜
NRurUt 8.95s85	1238	99 11-16	97⅝	99 11-16	+1 9-16
NRurUt 9⅛s85	955	99½	94¼	99½	+ 2¾
NRurUt 12⅝90	354	102¼	93½	102¼	+ ¾
NRurUt 7.40s07	10	60⅛	60⅛	60⅛	—10⅞
NRurUt A9¾09	158	77⅛	69	77⅛	— 1½
NRurUt S9¾09	91	81⅞	73½	80⅝	+ 3⅝
NRurUt 14¾11	318	108	97¼	108	— ½
NRurUt 14⅞91	260	111	102	110	— 1⅜
NRurUt 15¾91	47	112	105½	110	— 2
NRurUt 14⅝88	690	107¼	101	105⅛	— 1⅞
NatSteel 3⅞s86	120	84½	79¼	84	+ 4¼
NatSteel 4⅝s89	260	71⅞	68	71½	+ 3⅜
NatSteel 8s95	724	71	59	65½	— 2½
NatSteel 8⅜06	1077	66	52½	59½	— 5½
NatrlGas 9¼95	52	81⅝	77¼	81⅝	....
NatrlGas 8.2s86	445	96⅝	90⅛	96⅝	+ 4½
NEnMLf 7⅜97	220	69	54	66⅞	+ 1⅛
NEngTT 8⅝09	5355	73¾	60½	72½	+ 4
NEngTT 8.2s04	5784	72	59⅛	69⅞	+ 2¼
NEngTT 7⅜07	3792	64	52⅛	62⅝	+ 1¾
NEngTT 8s03	2102	70⅝	58¼	69¾	+ 3½
NEngTT 9½10	3714	80	66⅝	79	+ 3⅞
NEngTT 12.2s17	5472	99½	82	98	+ 4½
NEngTT 15¼18	1754	117	100⅜	114½	+ 1¼
NJBell 3⅛s88	949	79½	73	77¼	+ 3¾
NJBell 7¼s11	3143	62½	52⅛	61¾	+ 2⅞
NJBell 7⅜s12	1623	64	52¾	64	+ 4
NJBell 7¾s13	2688	66½	54⅝	65¼	+ 2¾
NJBell 8¼s16	1297	70	58⅝	69⅛	+ 3½
NJBell 8s16	1648	69	56¼	67½	+ 2½
NJBell 8¾18	2695	74	61⅛	72½	+ 2⅞
NJBell 14⅝21	4648	114¼	98	112⅝	+ 4⅛
NYChStL 3s86	16	84⅜	82½	83⅝	+ 1⅛
NYCHStl 3s86r	6	82⅞	82	82⅞	....
NYSEG 7⅝s01	825	64	52½	63	+ 5
NYSEG 9⅜s05	1022	75	63⅝	71½	+ 1⅛
NYSEG 9⅜s06	937	76	62½	72¼	— ⅜
NYSEG 8⅝07	275	68⅞	58	67	+ 1
NYTel 3s89	1348	73	67⅞	71⅛	+ 3¼
NYTel 4½s91	1295	71⅝	62	71⅝	+ 7⅛
NYTel 4½91r	98	70	64½	70	....
NYTel 4⅛s93	1349	61½	53	59⅛	+ 2⅛
NYTel 4⅛93r	49	58	57¼	57½	....
NYTel 3⅜s96	537	51¾	44⅛	51½	+ 3⅞
NYTel 3⅜96r	34	49	45½	45½	....
NYTel 7¾s2006	3304	67½	55⅛	66⅜	+ 2½
NYTel 8s2008	4713	68⅞	56⅛	68¾	+ 3⅞
NYTel 7⅜s2011	3125	63⅛	51¾	62⅜	+ 2¾
NYTel 8.30s12	4509	70⅜	57	68⅜	+ 1⅞
NYTel 9s14	9018	76	62⅜	73	+ 1⅛
NYTel 8⅞s2015	3103	74⅞	62	73½	+ 3⅝
NYTel 8⅝s16	1441	73⅜	59¾	70¼	+ 1⅞
NYTel 8¼15	2263	69⅞	56⅜	67¾	+ 2½
NYTel 7⅞17	840	67	55⅛	65¾	+ 2½
NYTel 8⅞18	2312	74¾	61⅛	72⅝	+ 2½
NYTel 11⅝19	5173	96½	79¼	93⅝	+ 3⅛
NYTel 14⅝91	3159	109½	101⅝	106¼	— ⅜
Newell cv8¾03	4125	93	82	88	+ 3⅞
NiagMP 4⅞s87	719	83⅞	76	83⅜	+ 4⅞
NiagMP 4⅞87r	46	83¼	76	82½	....
NiagMP 10.2s05	879	82	66	78½	+ 1⅝
NiagMP 10⅝85	1259	100⅝	95	100½	+ 2
NiagMP 8.35s07	690	67¼	57⅛	66⅜	+ 1⅜
NobleAfil 11½90	40	95	94⅞	95	....
NorfWn 4s96	542	51⅞	42	50⅝	— ⅝
NorfWn 4s96r	175	50½	46½	49	....
NorfWn 4.85s15	335	45	35	42	....
Norlin 9s89	13	74	72¼	72¼	— 6¾
Nortek 12½99	1663	91	80	90	+ 3½
Nortek d15s02	656	103⅞	94½	100⅛	— 2¾
vjNoACar 8.1s92f	48	74	70	70⅝	+ 6⅝
NorAPh cv4s92	79	70	57⅛	60	....
NorAPh 9¾s00	468	83½	69⅞	81⅛	+ 1½
NorAPh 11s87	856	100¼	93½	99¼	+ ⅞
NorIllG 8¾01	123	75½	67⅛	75½	+ 1⅞

NorNG 4⅞s85	90	96	90¼	96	+ 7¼
NorNG 9½s90	997	99¼	92	93	— 3
NorNG 8s91	686	89	77⅛	84	+ ⅞
NorNG 7⅜s92	279	84	71½	76¾	— 1⅛
NorNG 9s85	1079	99 27-32	96⅜	99¾	+ 1¼
NorNG 9s95	246	86¼	77¾	81⅜	+ 3⅝
NorPac 4s97	917	53	45	50⅜	+ 1⅞
NorPac 4s97r	314	51½	45⅜	50½	....
NorPac 3s2047	1555	44½	34⅝	36⅛	— 7⅞
NorPac 3s47r	301	46	35	38	....
NorStaP 4¼s86	202	91⅛	84½	91⅛	+ 6⅝
NorStaP 4¼86r	5	84	84	84	....
NorStaP 4s88	339	79⅜	73⅛	79⅜	+ 5⅜
NorStaP 5s90	410	74	64¾	74	+ 4⅜
NorStaP 5s90r	8	72	66½	72	....
NorStaP 4⅞s91	256	72	62	68	+ 2
NorStaP 4⅞91r	10	64½	64½	64½	....
NorStaP 4⅜s92	88	62	55¾	59¼	— ¾
NorStaP 4⅜s93	275	60½	51⅜	60½	+ 3¾
NSPWis 4⅝87	43	84⅞	80⅛	84⅞	+ 4⅜
NSPWis 4½94	143	57⅝	49½	57⅝	+ 4⅜
NSPWis 4½94r	2	54	53	54	....
NthTel 12¼90	372	100	94	99½	— ½
NwstAir cv7½07	1738	110	90	98	— 7½
Norwst 7⅞86	1606	94½	88¼	94½	+ 3¼
Norwst cv6¾03	992	104	77	79	—42
Norwst 11¼t	1130	99	96	97¾	....
NwstInd 7½s94	678	72	53⅜	66⅜	— 2⅝
NwstInd d7s11	151	55⅛	50	55⅛	+ 1⅛
NwstPipl 10¼91	125	91	78½	84¾	— 3½
NwtPip 9½98	146	80	65½	80	+ 2¾
NwtPip 16¾01	295	112	100	106	— 5¾
NwnBell 3¼s96	865	53⅛	45¼	49½	+ 4½
NwnBell 3¼96r	2	48⅛	48⅛	48⅛	....
NwnBell 7⅞11	3178	67⅞	55⅜	66¼	+ 2
NwnBell 7½05	2278	66½	54¼	65⅛	+ 2⅞
NwnBell 10s14	1944	83	70⅛	81½	+ 3½
NwnBell 8⅝s12	1829	73	60⅛	71¾	+ 2¼
NwnBell 8⅛17	1144	69¼	57⅞	67½	+ 2
NwnBell 9½16	2020	81⅜	65	80¼	+ 6¼
Norton 9s95	135	85¾	68¼	80	— 1½
Norton 9⅞2000	35	78½	77⅛	77⅛	— 3⅜
Norton cv9½05	2853	95½	84½	92	— 2
NortSim 6s98	847	60⅜	47¼	56⅞	+ 4½
NortSim 7.7s96	280	70	61½	68⅝	+ 2⅝
NortSim 9½s99	56	77¾	73½	73½	— 1¾
NorwstFin 8¼89	241	85¼	80⅜	83½	+ ½
— O—O —					
OakInd 11⅞98	1567	82⅞	57¼	62	—17¼
OakInd d13.65s01	1687	92⅝	69	69	—17⅞
OakInd cv10½02	9535	71¾	42	54½	—10¼
OcciPet 16s89	4346	112	104	108¼	....
OccPt 11.69s88t	15	100	100	100	....
OcciP 9.65s94	10	78	76½	78	....
OcciP d8.95s94	1744	75½	68¼	72⅛	....
Ogden cv5s93	852	92	77	88	— 2
OhBellT 7½s11	2732	66	52¼	63	+ 3⅛
OhBellT 7⅞s13	4097	67	54¾	65½	+ 2⅝
OhBellT 9s18	1288	75½	61¼	73⅛	+ 2½
OhBellT 12⅝20	2664	102	84	100⅝	+ 3½
OhioEd 9½06	2028	73	55⅛	70¼	+ ⅜
OhioEd 8½06	1279	65	53	63	— 1½
OhioEd 8⅜07	2493	65	51½	62	+ ¾
OhioEd 9½08	3386	74	59	70	+ 1¼
OhioEd 15¼87	4130	105½	100	104¼	— 1¼
OhioEd 15½10	1611	107	93½	105	— 1
OhioEd 11⅞10	2906	89¾	72⅛	86⅛	+ 1⅛
OhPw 15¼88	120	107⅛	104½	107⅛	+ 1⅜
OhPw 17⅝88	261	117	101½	112¾	— 5⅛
OklaGE 3¼85	30	95 7-16	94⅝	95 7-16	+3 7-16
OklaGE 4½87	251	88½	82	88½	+ 6½
OklaGE 4½87r	10	83½	83½	83½	....
OklaGE 3⅞88	61	79	71⅝	79	+ 2½
OklaGE 4¼93	199	59½	54¼	58	+ 2
OklaGE 4¼93r	16	59	52¾	52¾	....
OklaGE 4½95	130	55⅛	51	55⅛	+ 1⅛
Olin cv8¾08	6325	102	88¾	97⅞	— 3⅜
OrionCap 12½97	820	93⅞	85	88⅝	— 2⅞
Orion 11s98	2134	80⅞	69⅛	73½	— 5¾
Orion 10s99	664	73	62	68⅛	— 2
Orion d10s94	278	76	69¼	73¼	....
OutbM 7¾s96	204	69¾	59⅞	69¾	+ 5⅛
OwenCg 6⅞s94	129	71	62	69	+ 4
OwenCG 9½00	99	77½	68	77	....
OwenCg 12s10	707	95	80	90⅛	— ¾
OwenIll 3¾s88	18	90⅜	83	83	+ 5¼
OwenIll cv6s92	169	147	113⅛	135	+ 9
OwenIll 7⅝s01	338	76¼	56¼	67½	+ 3⅞
OwenIll 9.35s99	473	79½	69⅛	75⅛	— 4⅞
OwenIll 10⅜90	513	95	84½	95	+ 3⅛
— P—Q —					
PPGInd 9s95	770	84⅜	72½	83⅛	+ 3⅛
PPGInd 8s85	791	99 9-32	96¾	99 9-32	+2 21-32
PPGInd 8½00	26	75	71⅝	75	+ 2¾
PPGInd 9⅜89	1308	93¼	83½	93	+ 3⅜
PSA cv11⅛04	1827	108	86	93	— 8
PacGE 3⅜s85	229	93 25-32	87¼	93 25-32	+6 17-32
PacGE 4½s86	1158	90	83	90	+ 6½
PacGE 4½86r	134	89	82⅛	88	....
PacGE 3⅜s87	53	80	74⅜	80	+ 7
PacGE 3⅜87r	10	77	73½	77	....
PacGE 3⅜s88	153	76½	69⅝	76½	+ 6¼
PacGE 5s89	1546	80	70¼	78	+ 6
PacGE 5s89r	89	79¾	71	78	....
PacGE 4½s90	742	74⅛	62½	71¼	+ 5¼
PacGE 4½90r	11	66½	64	64	....
PacGE 5s91	2050	71⅝	58¾	70⅛	+ 5⅛
PacGE 5s91r	186	69	34⅜	69	....
PacGE 4⅝s92	632	64⅝	56½	63⅝	+ 4⅜
PacGE 4⅝92r	39	62½	58¼	58¼	....
PacGE 4½s93	500	62¾	50⅛	62	+ 6¼
PacGE 4½93r	14	57¼	54⅝	55½	....
PacGE 4⅜s94	401	60¾	49¾	60¾	+ 8¼
PacGE 4⅜94r	2	54	54	54	....
PacGE 4¼s95	401	55½	45	53⅛	+ 3⅛
PacGE 4¼95r	20	52	50	51⅛	....
PacGE 4½96J	400	53½	46	52⅝	+ 4⅝
PacGE 4½96JJr	22	50	48	50	....
PacGE 4½96K	250	52	44½	51⅜	+ 1⅞
PacGE 8⅞s02	4194	75½	61½	73⅝	+ 3⅛
PacGE 8s03	5362	69	55¾	67¾	+ 3¼
PacGE 7½s03	3902	65	52⅜	63⅞	+ 3¼
PacGE 7½s04	3099	65	52⅝	63⅜	+ 2⅝
PacGE 7¾05Z	1971	66⅝	53⅝	65¼	+ 2½
PacGE 7¾05A	1079	66½	55	65	+ 3¼
PacGE 9⅛s06	5889	76	62⅛	73¾	+ 1⅛
PacGE 9⅝s06	6097	79½	65½	78⅛	+ 3⅛
PacGE 9½s85	4938	100¼	95 1-32	99 27-32	+1 27-32
PacGE 8¼08	6772	68½	56⅞	67⅞	+ 2⅜
PacGE 8½09	5333	70½	58⅛	68¼	+ 2⅞
PacGE 9⅜11	4674	76¾	63¾	74⅝	+ 1⅝
PacGE 10⅛12	5832	82	67⅝	79½	+ 2¼
PacGE 12¾13	8182	101	82	98¾	+ 2½
PacGE 12⅞13	8587	101	83⅜	99⅞	+ 2⅛
PacGE 16¼14	7604	117	104¾	114⅝	+ ¾
PacGE 15⅜92	1429	113	101	109½	— 1¼
PacGTran 8s90	439	88	80⅛	84¼	+ ¼
PacLtSv 7⅝s91	92	80⅛	68⅞	80⅛	+ 2¼
PacLtSv 8⅜s93	345	81	70½	79⅝	+ 4⅜
PacLtSv 9s85	898	99 25-32	97 3-16	99 25-32	+2 13-32
PacLtSv 9.3s85	1053	99 7-16	93¾	99 7-16	+2 13-16
PacNwTel 8⅝10	3840	73	59⅛	71¾	+ 3¾
PacNwTel 8¾08	3946	75	61	73	+ 3¾
PacNwTel 9s12	2178	75¾	62¼	74⅝	+ 3⅞
PacNwTel 8¾18	1148	74	59¾	73¼	+ 5⅛
PacNwTel 10⅛19	2593	83⅝	69	82⅜	+ 3⅞
PacNwTel 11s20	1778	92	75¼	88⅞	+ 3⅛
PacSci cv7¾03	6376	76	58	64½	— 9½
PacSwA 6s87	728	82¾	79⅝	81½	+ 2⅜
PacTT 2¾85	1250	94	86⅜	94	+ 7⅜
PacTT 2¾85r	75	89¼	87	89¼	....
PacTT 2⅞86	875	88⅝	82	88⅝	+ 5¾
PacTT 2⅞86r	5	83	83	83	....
PacTT 3⅛87	1304	84⅜	78⅝	83¼	+ 6¾
PacTT 3⅛87r	107	82⅞	79	82⅞	....
PacTT 4⅜88	1503	80¾	74	80¾	+ 6¾

PacTT	4⅜88r	42	77¾	73⅜	77¾	....
PacTT	3⅝91	793	65	59⅝	65	+ 3¾
PacTT	3⅝91r	24	64	62	64	....
PacTT	8.65s05	9534	73¾	60½	72½	+ 3⅜
PacTT	8¾06	9533	73¾	60¼	72⅝	+ 2⅞
PacTT	7.8s07	6300	67	55⅛	66¼	+ 4
PacTT	7¼08	8235	63	51	62¼	+ 3⅝
PacTT	7⅝09	4936	64¾	53¼	64	+ 3⅝
PacTT	9½11	13034	79	64⅛	77⅝	+ 3¾
PacTT	8⅞15	5042	74¾	61¾	72¾	+ 1¾
PacTT	8⅜17	5189	69⅜	57¼	69⅜	+ 4½
PacTT	9⅝14	3921	79½	66	78½	+ 3
PacTT	9s18	5993	75⅞	61½	72⅝	+ 2⅛
PacTT	9⅝18	5596	79⅞	65¼	78¼	+ 3¾
PacTT	9⅞16	4073	81½	67⅛	79½	+ 2⅞
PacTT	9¾19	5405	80¼	66	79⅛	+ 4
PacTT	12.7s19	13146	101½	84½	100	+ 2⅝
PacTT	15⅛88	23293	107¼	101⅞	103	— 4
PacTT	15½20	1820	116	103½	113½	+ 3
PacTT	12.35s20	5167	99½	82	98	+ 4
PacTT	11.35s90	5175	100¾	88½	99½	+ 2⅞
PacTT	15s20	4427	114	99¼	111½	— 1⅜
PacTT	15s91	4864	109	102¼	106	— 1
PacTT	16⅛21	3124	119	106½	116	+ 1
PacTT	13⅝90	1853	105½	97½	103⅞	— ¼
PaineW	11½99	3770	87¾	77	86¼	+ 1
PaineWb	cv8¼08	9781	94¾	74½	74½	—11½
PaineWb	13⅜94	312	102¼	88⅛	102¼	....
PalmBch	16⅛02	2241	109	98¼	103	— 4⅝
PAA	cv4½86	6168	84⅞	76¾	84⅞	+ 4⅞
PAA	cv5¼89	4958	76½	60	63¼	— 8
PAA	11¼s86	2222	100	96¼	99	+ 2⅜
PAA	11⅛s86	2417	99½	95⅛	99	+ 3⅞
PAA	11½94A	799	86	78⅛	81⅛	— 2⅝
PAA	11½94B	879	85	78⅛	84	+ 2⅞
PAA	d13½03	6768	94½	75⅛	76	—12½
PAA	15s04	1174	92	80⅞	90	....
PAA	cv15s98	37235	161	100	105¼	—38¾
PanhdlEP	15⅛95	313	107	99	107	+ 2
PanhdleEP	15¼97	70	109¼	107	107	— ½
PantPr	cv8¾98	1264	115½	92	92	—13
Paprct	cv5¼94	5	138½	138½	138½	—55½
ParkH	cv4s92	11	150	137⅛	146¼	+ 7¼
Pembrke	14s91	166	106	103	105	+ ½
PenncpF	10¼97	588	79⅞	68¼	75⅛	— ⅜
PennCp	13¾00	77	102⅞	85⅝	102⅞	+ 2¾
PennyF	5⅜s87	517	90	83	90	+ 6⅞
PennyF	7⅞s91	1185	83¾	72	82½	+ 5⅛
PennyF	10.2s94	238	92	77	92	+ 4⅞
Penney	8⅞s95	1516	84	70⅝	82⅜	+ 4⅝
Penney	9s99	943	80½	67⅛	80½	+ 4⅜
Penney	10¾90	2855	98¾	86⅛	97	+ 2¾
Penney	11½10	256	94	82¼	93⅛	....
Penney	12s10	567	97½	82½	97½	+ 2½
Pennwlt	9⅛s95	420	82	74	80½	+ ½
Pennwlt	9s85	490	99	96½	98 29-32	+2 17-32
Pennzoil	7½s88	684	89¾	80¼	88	+ 4⅞
Pennzoil	7⅜s88	671	88¾	80¼	88⅝	+ 4⅛
Pennzoil	cv5¼96	21	170	119	170	+40
Pennzoil	8⅜s96	1044	79⅛	64½	78⅜	+ 5¾
Pennzoil	8¾01	156	74½	63	73¼	— ¾
Pennzoil	14s91	1114	106½	97¾	102	— 2
Pennzoil	15s92	707	109⅞	99	105	— 3⅝
Pennzoil	12⅛07	280	95⅜	86	93	+ ½
PepsiCa	10⅛86	2255	99⅞	94	99⅞	+ 1⅞
Pepsi	cv4¾96	9	204	177	204	+34
Pepsi	8¼85	1281	99 19-32	97 5-16	99 19-32	+2 11-32
Petroln	14⅞91	10	108	108	108	+ 3
Pfizer	cv4s97	88	164	123½	164	+10½
Pfizer	8½s99	475	77¼	65⅝	77¼	+ 1¼
Pfizer	8⅞s85	2128	99 13-16	95¼	99 23-32	+3 3-32
Pfizer	9¼s00	216	81½	71½	81	+ 1
Pfizer	cv8¾06	8275	148	117	147	+17
PhelpsD	8.1s96	639	67¼	53⅜	58	— 7⅛
PhelpsD	8½s85	1914	98⅜	92⅛	98	+ 2⅞
PhilaEl	3⅛s85	421	98	90⅛	97½	+ 7⅝
PhilaEl	3⅛85r	45	93¼	91	91½	....
PhilaEl	4⅜s86	1509	88¼	79¼	86¼	+ 5⅛
PhilaEl	4⅜86r	98	87	80¼	86	....

PhilaEl	4⅝s87	854	85	72¼	83	+ 6½
PhilaEl	4⅝87r	48	81	75	81	....
PhilaEl	3¾s88	382	77¼	68	77¼	+ 7
PhilaEl	3¾88r	5	69	69	69	....
PhilaEl	5s89	1000	73	62¼	71¾	+ 4¾
PhilaEl	5s89r	30	72	64	72	....
PhilaEl	6½s93	1363	68	55	67⅞	+ 6¾
PhilaEl	4½s94	601	54½	43	54	+ 3⅝
PhilaEl	6⅛s97	3131	57	46	54½	+ 1½
PhilaEl	9s95	5111	76¾	59¼	73¾	+ 2⅝
PhilaEl	7¾00	1926	65	50	64⅜	+ 5⅞
PhilaEl	8¼s96	2565	70⅛	55	67⅞	+ 2⅞
PhilaEl	7⅜01	3998	60¼	48	58⅝	+ 4
PhilaEl	7½s98	2708	63¾	50⅝	61⅞	+ 1⅞
PhilaEl	7½s99	1699	63¾	51	63¾	+ 6
PhilaEl	8½s04	5695	66¾	53⅜	66¾	+ 5½
PhilaEl	11⅝00	2769	87⅜	71	85½	+ 4¼
PhilaEl	11s00	1748	88¼	71¼	81¼	+ 1¼
PhilaEl	9⅛s06	3985	70⅞	57	67	+ 2¼
PhilaEl	9⅝s02	1752	74⅛	60	71½	+ 2½
PhilaEl	8⅝07	1518	68½	54	65	+ 3¼
PhilaEl	8⅝03	1099	67¾	55⅛	65¾	+ 3⅝
PhilaEl	9⅛08	3382	69¾	56	67	+ 1¾
PhilaEl	12½05	5408	91¼	74¾	90¾	+ 5¼
PhilaEl	14⅛90	2228	105	92	103¼	+ ⅜
PhilaEl	14¾05	10411	103⅞	87	99⅜	+ ⅜
PhilaEl	13¾92	1426	102⅞	90	101½	+ ½
PhilaEl	17⅝11	11900	116⅛	96½	113¾	+ ⅞
PhilaEl	18¾09	12600	121	102	118⅝	+ 3⅝
PhilEl	18s12	8540	118	103	116¾	+ 5⅝
PhilEl	15⅜10	4558	107¼	91½	104⅛	+ 1½
PhilEl	13⅜13	2892	97½	79⅛	95	+ 4⅛
PhilEl	14½09	1879	101	85½	98½	....
PhilMor	6⅝s93	289	75	63	71¾	+ 3⅛
PhilMor	8⅞s04	360	76½	65	76	+ 3¾
PhilMor	8½s85	1714	99 13-16	96¾	99 13-16	+3 3-16
PhilMor	9⅛03	748	78½	65	76¾	— 1¼
PhilMor	9.55s86	2378	98⅞	93⅛	98⅞	+ 2½
PhilMor	14s91	934	107⅛	100	105⅞	— ⅛
PhilMor	15¼91	674	112¼	103½	110	— 2½
PhilMor	14⅛88	859	107⅞	100½	105½	....
PhillP	7⅝s2001	1552	69¾	58⅛	66¼	+ ¼
PhillP	8⅞s00	881	77⅛	67	75	....
PhillP	12⅞92	4495	104⅞	93⅜	102	....
PhillP	12¼12	952	98½	85	95⅜	— ⅛
PhillP	11¼13	407	92⅜	87½	89½	+ 1½
PiedAv	cv11s07	1584	145½	113	134	— 3½
PiedAv	6s07	801	113½	90	106	+ 2
PiedNG	8⅝97	67	74	64	73⅜	+ ⅜
PierOne	d11½03	171	84	77⅞	82	+ 1⅞
Pillsby	5¾s86	63	92	89	92	+21⅞
Pillsby	8¾s95	165	85	69⅛	80	+ 2
Pillsby	14s91	285	108	99½	106¼	+ ½
PionCp	12¼90	30	99½	93¼	93¼	— 5⅜
Pittston	cv4s97	736	50⅞	38	40	— 4
Pittston	cv9.2s04	2785	79¾	62½	64	—12½
Pneumo	9⅝98	293	77¼	68⅛	74¾	— 1⅝
Pneumo	11⅝94	92	90	89½	89¾	— 8⅜
PogoPrd	cv8s05	4020	77½	60	62½	—10½
Polard	11⅞90	763	101	90⅞	100⅝	+ 2¼
PortGE	9⅞s85	935	99¾	93½	99⅝	+ 3
PortGE	11⅝05	1372	89	74⅛	86⅝	+ 3⅝
PortGE	9½s06	641	74⅞	63	72	+ 6¼
PortGE	8¾07	557	69½	57⅛	68¾	+ 7½
PortGe	13⅞10	1903	105	90	101⅜	+ 4⅜
PortGE	13½12	848	102	89½	99	+ ¾
PotEPw	9½05	3450	80	66½	77¼	+ 1⅛
PotEPw	7¾07	769	66	55	65¼	+ 2¾
PotEPw	8⅜09	2116	70½	59¼	69⅝	+ 3⅜
PotEPw	10¾04	362	92	76½	87⅝	— 6⅜
PotEPw	14½91	806	109½	100	105⅞	— 1⅛
PotEPw	14¼92	420	110⅞	101½	104	— 7
PotEPw	11⅞89	379	102½	91½	100½	— ⅜
ProctG	7s2002	1167	68¾	55⅛	68¾	+ 5½
ProctG	8¼s05	7009	76	63	73	+ ¼
PrudRlty	zr86s	37	86½	77	86½	+ 9¾
PrudRlty	zr87s	66	76½	69⅞	76½	+ 8½
PrudRlty	zr88s	1	61¼	61¼	61¼	....
PrudRlty	zr89s	47	59½	54	59½	+ 5½
PrudRlty	zr90s	41	50¼	46¼	50¼	+ 2¼

PrudRlty zr91s	180	49	33	49	+ 6¼
PrudRlty zr92s	10	42	42	42	+ 1¼
PrudRlty zr93s	77	38¼	28⅛	35½	+ 1¾
PrudRlty zr94s	63	34	28⅛	32	....
PrudRlty zr95s	110	30	25½	30	+ ¾
PrudRlty zr96s	7	24¼	23	24¼	+ 1¼
PrudRlty zr97s	6	20¾	19¾	20¾	— 5½
PubSvCol 8¾00	1543	75	63	74	+ 3
PubSvCol 7¼01	502	64⅛	53	63¼	+ 3¼
PubSvCol 7½02	703	66	54⅜	64½	+ 3¼
PubSvIn 7⅝s01	1869	59½	48	55¼	+ ¾
PubSvIn 7s02	1952	55	44	53⅛	+ 2⅛
PubSvIn 8s04	1893	60⅜	49⅝	56½	+ 1¼
PubSvIn 9.6s05	4872	72	56¼	65	— ¼
PubSvIn 7⅝07	1962	58⅞	45⅛	54½	....
PubSvIn 8⅛07	2743	61⅛	50	57⅛	+ ⅜
PubSvIn 8⅞08	2579	65⅜	53⅞	62¾	+ 2¾
PubSvIn 9½85	4309	98	91⅝	98	+ 2½
PubSvIn 14s87	9050	102⅜	90⅝	99¼	— ¾
PubSvIn 12⅛90	4109	97	81⅝	93	+ 3⅜
PubSvIn 14¾11	7299	102½	83½	96	— ¾
PubSvIn 15¾11	3451	105⅞	82	101	+ 1
PubSvIn 12⅞12	1059	90	75⅛	85	— 3
PubSvNH 12s99	19513	80	52	71	— 3½
PubSvNH 14½00	13082	94⅝	56½	77⅝	—12⅜
PubSvNH 18s89	30322	108	59½	94⅞	—10⅝
PubSvNH 15¾88	36018	101½	57	86½	—11¼
PubSvNH 14⅜91	27442	95½	52⅝	77¾	—12
PubSvNH 15s03	24416	95⅛	56	76	—14
PubSvNH 17½04	808	85	83	83	....
PubSEG 8s2037	159	64	60	63	+ 2
PubSEG 8s37r	12	62	59	62	....
PubSEG 5s2037	313	41½	36½	37	— 1⅝
PubSEG 5s37r	7	37	37	37	....
PubSEG 9s95	2003	82⅝	70¾	80⅝	+ 1⅞
PubSEG 8½s04	1735	72⅞	60	71	+ 3
PubSEG 12s04	735	96½	80¼	95⅞	+ 4⅞
PubSEG 8¾s06	869	72½	60	70⅞	+ 2⅜
PubSEG 8.45s06	985	70⅛	59	68¾	+ 1¼
PubSEG 8¼07	2210	70	58	69½	+ 3⅛
PubSEG 9⅜08	689	76¾	64¼	76¾	+ 4¾
PubSEG 9¾09J	538	80	63¼	78	+ 1⅝
PubSEG 12s09	1611	96	80	94	— 1½
PubSEg 12⅛10	902	96½	81⅜	95¾	+ 3½
PubSEG 15⅞91	1619	112½	104¾	110	— 2½
PubSEG 14⅜12	481	108⅝	95⅛	108⅝	+ 4⅛
PubSEG 12⅛12	662	95½	82¾	94⅝	+ 1⅝
PubSEG 12⅝93	637	104	91⅞	104	+ 4
PugetS 10.45s85	1453	99 25-32	95⅝	99 25-32	+1 1-32
PullmL 10s85	492	100¼	96⅛	99⅞	+ 1⅞
PullmL 8¾s85	216	100	92⅛	96	— 1⅞
PullmL 7¾s92	38	74½	74⅛	74½	— ½
QuakOat 7.7s01	615	70½	58	68¼	+ 5⅞
QuakStOil 9s95	443	85⅝	68	80	+ 1½
QuakStO cv8⅞08	3672	103	92½	101	+ 1¼
Quanex 14¾99	11	100	95	99	....

— R—R —

RCA 9¼s90	739	91½	85	90	+ 2
RCA cv4½92	8278	81	68	76	— 1
RCA 10.20s92	663	91⅞	82	89⅛	+ ¾
RCA 11½90	664	101	90¼	100½	+ 2½
RCA 12¼05	1323	99½	84	97¾	+ 2¾
RCA 12¾92	448	102¾	94	102	+ ½
RCA 12½08	96	99½	95	99½	+ 1½
RainBnc 9½s85	916	99 11-16	95⅛	99⅝	+ 3¼
RalstP 7.7s96	189	75½	62⅛	75½	+ 2¾
RalstP cv5¾00	332	225	170¼	225	+34
RalstP 12⅞14	10	103½	103½	103½	....
Ramad cv5s96	1451	75	55	56¼	—18¾
Ramad 10s93	5017	81¼	70¼	78⅜	+ ⅜
RapAm72 7s94	2707	63½	54	57¾	— 6
RapAm69 7s94	2461	63¾	54¾	57¾	— 6
RapAm 7½s85	489	98	93¼	98	+ 4½
RapAm 6s88	2169	79	71⅝	77¾	+ ¾
RapAm 10¾03	4435	78½	67	73⅞	— 1⅛
RapAm 12s99	1177	86⅛	79	83¾	— ¼
RapAm 10¾04	384	77	68	70⅝	— 1⅝
RapA 11s05	608	77	67⅛	74	— 1
RtyRef 12s98	415	84¼	79⅛	83⅛	— ⅝
RtyRef 11⅜98	288	85⅞	73	83	+ 1
RecogE cv11s06	2123	111½	93½	107	+ 5½
ReichChm 8s94	243	77½	64¾	74⅞	+ 5¼
RelianEl 7¼96	67	70½	63	69⅛	— 1⅞
RelianEl 9⅝94	69	85	85	85	— 3⅞
RepAir cv10⅛07	18788	75	56	72½	+14¾
RepNY 9s01	779	76½	62¼	76½	+ 5
RepNY 8¾02	312	75	60	74	+ 1½
RepNY 13¾05	16	103	97	98	— 5
RepNY 15¾91	74	116	101¼	109	— 7
RepNY 16s07	67	115	105¼	112	— 2
RepStl 4⅜s85	625	96	86½	94 11-16	+7 5-16
RepStl 4⅜85r	7	91⅝	87	91⅝	....
RepStl 8.90s95	678	73½	63⅛	65⅝	— 6
RepStl 12⅛03	960	86	72	77¼	— 6¾
RepBncp 9⅜01	386	76½	65	76½	+ 5⅛
RepBnc 11¾04t	2280	97¾	90¾	97¾	+ 2⅞
ReshCtl cv10½06	2368	117	102	110	+ 4¾
Revere cv5½92f	2573	78½	61¾	78½	+13⅜
Revlon 8.45s85	1061	99⅜	96 5-16	99	+ 2¾
Revlon 10⅞10	101	87½	80½	86¼	+ 1¼
Rexnd 8.95s95	242	77½	72½	75	— 1
Rexnd cv5⅞01	42	118	113	118	+11½
Rexnd 10½85	461	99½	97 11-32	99	....
Rexnd cv9¼05	2447	107	85	88	—12
Reynlnd 7⅜01	796	67⅞	57¼	67	+ 2
Reynlnd 8s07	257	69⅝	58	68⅛	+ ⅛
Reyln 10.45s90	4761	98½	85⅛	98⅛	+ 4
Reyln 9⅝85	96	99¾	98 1-16	99¾	+ 1¼
Reyln 9¾86	123	98⅞	96⅛	98⅞	+ 2⅛
ReynM cv4½91	4605	80	61	69½	— 8
ReynTob 7s89	288	91	79	83¼	— 2¼
ReynTob 7⅞94	521	78½	70⅝	78	+ 1¼
Richs 7.35s97	22	70¼	65	65⅝	— 2¾
RiegelT cv5s93	300	118	80	80	—15
RochGE 9¼06	766	74⅞	61¼	74⅞	+ 3¾
RochGE 8⅜07	498	69¾	56⅛	67½	+ 1½
RochGE 16¾91	431	117⅞	105	112⅜	+ 1¼
RochT cv4¾94	28	141	121	141	+12
RockInt cv4¼91	93	270⅝	210½	256	—34
RockInt 5¾91	27	71	64	71	+ 5
RockInt 8.3s96	235	77	66¼	77	+ 5⅝
RockInt 8½95	103	76⅜	68⅝	75	+ 1½
RockInt cv4⅞87	430	86¼	80¾	86	+ 3
RockInt 8.90s86	1019	98⅛	91	97⅜	+ 3½
RockInt 9⅜96	328	83¾	73½	81⅞	+ ⅞
RohmH 9⅞2000	333	82¼	71½	80½	....
RohmH 9s85	539	99⅝	96⅜	99⅝	+ 1⅞
Rohr cv9s03	1468	160	113	155	+17
RyderS 11½s90	381	101½	89⅛	99	....
RyderS 8⅛s92	44	85	80¾	80¾	— 1
RyderS 10s94	107	88⅝	81½	87⅛	— 4¾
RyderS 9¼98	88	80⅞	71	80⅞	+ 1
RyderS 12¼86	175	101	94	101	....
RyderS 11⅝93	65	98	90	97½	— 1⅝
RyderS 14s94	40	105	105	105	....
RyderS 13⅜94	5	101	101	101	....

— S—S —

SCM 5¾87	49	85	84	84⅜	+ 1¼
SCM cv5½88	2403	99	88⅛	97	+ 8¼
SCM 7¼88	50	85	81⅛	83¾	— ⅜
SCM 9¼90	270	88⅜	80⅞	87⅞	+ 1⅞
SCM 10s96	159	83⅝	80½	83⅜	+ 1⅞
SCM cv10s09	737	111	105	109½	....
SFN 15⅜94	461	105½	97½	103	....
Safeco 7.6s86	794	94½	87	93½	+ 4
SafgdSci d12s96	1114	91	78	83	— 4⅛
SafewyS 7.4s97	102	82⅝	78	80¾	+ ½
StLouSF 4s97	398	50½	42⅛	49¾	+ 1¾
StLouSF 4s97r	32	46½	43¼	45⅛	....
StLouSF 5s06f	1199	45¾	34½	45	+ 3½
StLouSwt 4s89X	136	72½	66	72½	+ 1
StLouSwt 4s89Y	15	68	63	63	+ 1½
StReg cv4⅞97	108	188½	113	187½	+70½
StReg 10s90	1368	94⅛	82⅜	93	+ 2¾
StReg 10⅝10	692	84⅛	72	80	— 3¾
SallieM zr22	5	3	3	3	....
SallieM cv7¾09	177	97	95	95	....
SanDGE 10s06	1471	81	67⅞	81	+ 4¼
SanDGE 8¾07	1488	74¼	60	70¼	+ 2⅝

SanDGE 9¾08	1002	79¾	65	78	+ 3
SFeNRs 8.35s02	20	68½	65	68½	+ 3
SavEPw 9.8s86	1162	100	91⅛	96⅛	+ 3½
SavinCp 11⅜98	2017	79¾	62¾	68⅜	— 6⅝
SavinCp 14s00	1751	91	76	83	— 4
SciotoV 4s89	42	72½	64½	72½	+ 8¼
Scoa cv10s07	3592	121	100	116	— 1½
ScottFetz 9¼85	504	99¾	96⅜	99¾	+ 2¾
ScottP 8⅞s2000	1083	79	65½	79	+ 4¾
ScottP 8¾s2000	307	78⅜	66⅛	78⅜	+ 3⅞
ScottP 8.15s85	639	99 11-16	97 1-32	99 11-16	+2 15-16
SbdCsL 8.35s96	171	78	65	77¾	+ 3¼
SbdCsL 7¾98	53	71¾	60½	65⅜	— 3
Seaco 10¼98	495	76⅜	66	71⅛	— 2½
Seafirst 9¼01	928	74¼	59½	71⅞	+ 2¼
Seafirst 10½90	380	89	80⅛	87	+ ½
SegrmJ cv8¼08	16361	115	96	115	+ 8½
Searle 8.70s95	92	81½	77	80½	+ 1⅜
SearsR 6⅜s93	1520	73⅝	63	72⅛	— 1
SearsR 8⅝s95	3344	84⅞	71⅜	82¾	+ 3¼
SearsR 7¾s85	5341	99⅝	96¼	99⅝	+ 2¼
SearsR 8s06	4160	72⅞	58⅜	71⅛	+ 4⅜
SearsR 7⅞07	3977	71	57½	69¼	+ 3
SearsR 14⅛89	9202	111⅜	100¼	110	+ 1¼
Sears 13¼92	5631	108	95⅝	108	+ 2⅛
SearsR 10¼88	7811	100	90⅜	99	+ 2
Sears 10¾13	1637	90	76¾	84	— 4⅛
Sears 12s94	11112	103⅝	88¼	102¼	....
Sears 12s87	70	103	97⅝	103	....
SearAcc 8⅜86	3262	96⅜	89	96	+ 4½
SecuPac 8.8s85	2040	99	93¼	98¾	+ 2⅞
SecuPac 11¾93	1278	100⅛	85	99	+ ¼
SedcoM 7.15s92	163	78½	70	78	+ ⅜
ShearL 10¾03	1153	88	74⅜	84½	— 1½
SheraL 15¼90	702	109½	101	107	— 2
ShellOil 4⅝86	881	90⅝	85⅛	90⅝	+ 5⅛
ShellOil 4⅝86r	10	86½	85½	85½	....
ShellOil 5.3s92	842	71½	62	70¼	+ 3
ShellOil 8½00	2619	76¾	64	75¾	+ 2¾
ShellOil 7¼02	1228	68¼	53¾	66¼	+ 3½
ShellOil 8¾05	2121	77⅝	62¼	76½	+ 3⅝
ShellOil 8s07	3292	71¼	58⅝	70¼	+ 3⅜
ShellOil 13⅞91	3156	108¼	99½	108	+ 2⅞
ShellOil 14¼11	1480	112	97	111½	+ 2½
ShellPip 7½99	528	69⅞	57⅛	69⅞	+ 4⅝
ShelrGlb cv7⅞08	1510	98½	70½	93	— 2
SherW 5.45s92	354	66⅜	60¼	63¼	+ 1⅛
SherW cv6¼95	64	272	193	249½	+36½
SherW 9.45s99	64	76	69	73	— 2½
Showbt d13s04	126	85	84¼	85	....
Signal 8.85s94	2129	91	81⅛	81¼	— 3½
Signal cv5½94	2824	102	82½	94	— 2
Signal 5⅞97	117	56⅛	48	56⅛	+ 3⅝
Signal 11¾05	1485	97	79⅜	94	+ 4
Signal cv8s09	3978	97	82	93	....
Sinclair 4.6s88	834	81½	72⅝	80	+ 4
Singer 8s99	1661	67¼	56¼	66	+ 2½
Singer cv9s08	7264	110½	88	102	....
SkilCp cv5s92	81	153	130	153	+ 3
Socony 4¼s93	750	62	54⅛	60⅞	+ 3⅜
Socony 4¼93r	24	59¾	52½	59¾	....
SohioBP 9¾s99	450	84⅝	74⅜	83½	+ ½
SohioPL 8¾01	1460	76½	65⅛	75⅞	+ 3¼
SoCenBl 8¼s04	4283	72¾	59⅝	70⅞	+ 3⅜
SoCenBl 7⅜s07	2187	64⅝	53⅛	63⅝	+ 3⅜
SoCenBl 7⅜s12	1628	63½	52	62¾	+ 3¼
SoCenBl 8¼s13	4963	70¼	57¼	68½	+ 2⅜
SoCenBl 10s14	3163	83¾	70	82	+ 3¼
SoCenBl 9.2s10	4157	79	63⅛	76⅜	+ 3
SoCenBl 8¼17	2924	69¼	57	67⅝	+ 2¼
SoCenBl 8¼15	2521	69⅞	57¼	68¼	+ 2¼
SoCenBl 9⅝19	10658	81⅛	66¼	80¼	+ 4
SoCenBl 9⅞18	2976	82	67	81	+ 3⅜
SoCenBl 12⅞20	11223	103¾	87	102⅜	+ 2⅞
SoestBk cv4¾97	1135	77	67½	71½	+ 1½
SoestPSv 11⅞98	68	81⅞	72½	81⅞	— 6⅜
SoBellT 2¾s85	736	96 19-32	89¼	96 19-32	+8 3-32
SoBellT 2⅞s87	816	84	78¼	83⅜	+ 3⅜
SoBellT 7.60s08	3165	65½	54	64½	+ 2½
SoBellT 7⅜s10	3616	63¼	51⅝	62¾	+ 2⅜
SoBellT 7⅝s13	5011	65	53½	64⅛	+ 2¾
SoBellT 8s14	8391	67¾	55½	67	+ 3
SoBellT 8¼s16	7821	69⅝	57¼	69	+ 3⅝
SoBellT 8⅛17	3747	68⅛	56½	68	+ 3⅝
SoBellT 12⅞20	10749	103½	87	102⅝	+ 2¼
SoBellT 8⅝18	1953	73¾	59⅝	71⅞	+ 4
SoBellT 10.9s19	8629	90¾	74	89⅛	+ 4
SoCalGs 8.85s95	976	82	68	80⅞	+ 3⅞
SoCalGs 7⅝s97	256	67½	60¼	67½	+ 1¾
SoCalGs 8¾s96	212	83	72	80⅝	+ 2⅝
SoCalGs 8½97	209	80⅞	64⅝	80¼	+ 6
SoCalGs 12¾99	634	100	90	99¼	+ ¼
SoCalGs 15s01	178	110	101⅛	105	— 4½
SoCalGs 17⅜01	1151	119	108⅛	118⅞	+ 5¾
SoCalGs 15¾92	148	110½	104	105	— 7¼
SoCalGs 12¼93	36	100¼	100	100	— ¼
SoCntGs 9½s95	424	86	72	84½	+ 4⅝
SoNGas 7.70s91	434	88⅝	79¼	86⅛	+ 1⅛
SoNGas 8¼s86	1504	97⅝	90	96¾	+ 3½
SoNGas 15s91	87	109	104⅛	108	+ 1⅝
SoNEngT 8⅛08	5457	70	57¾	67⅞	+ 2½
SoNEngT 9⅝10	1545	80⅜	67⅛	79½	+ 2½
SoNEngT 14⅛20	457	110	96⅛	108⅝	+ 4
SoPac 10.35s94	2185	91	76¼	88¾	+ 3¼
SoPac 2⅞s86	205	92¾	84⅛	89½	+ 4
SoPac 2⅞86r	24	87	85	87	....
SoPac 2¾s96	386	45	39⅜	44½	+ 4½
SoPac 2¾96r	98	43¾	38½	43	....
SPacTr 8.2s01	68	69	60⅞	65¼	— 3¼
SouRy 4⅝88	96	78	75⅛	75⅝	+ ⅜
SouRy 4⅝88r	5	76½	76½	76½	....
SouRy 4½88r	10	77	77	77	....
SouRy 5s94	763	64	53	62	+ 3¾
SouRy 5s94r	124	62⅛	52⅛	61¾	....
SouRy 8½01	368	76	63¼	76	+ 2½
SoRyMem 5s96	91	58⅛	49	56¼	+ 4¼
SoRyMem 5s96r	1	51	51	51	....
Sothlnd 8⅜02	93	70	63⅛	70	....
Sothlnd 9⅜03	226	79⅜	68	79⅜	+ 5⅜
Sothlnd 9½04	59	77⅛	70½	73⅝	— 3⅜
SouthF 10⅛s86	245	101⅛	92⅞	96⅛	— 3⅞
Soumark 16.16s87t	6	98	96⅞	98	— ¾
Soumark 15¼91	10	100	100	100	....
SwAir cv10s07	1311	157	105	128	—21
SwBcsh 9⅜01	331	75¼	63	75¼	+ 6⅛
SwBellT 2¾s85	1370	95¾	88	95½	+ 7½
SwBellT 8¾07	11606	75	61½	72½	+ 2⅞
SwBellT 6⅞11	8576	59⅝	49	58⅛	+ 2⅛
SwBellT 7¾09	4587	67	53⅞	66	+ 3⅝
SwBellT 7⅜s12	6085	63¼	51⅜	62	+ 2½
SwBellT 7⅝s13	6181	64¾	53	63¾	+ 2¾
SwBellT 8¼s14	6756	69¾	57⅛	67⅝	+ 1⅞
SwBellT 9¼15	7663	76⅞	63¾	75⅛	+ 2½
SwBellT 8½16	4606	71⅜	58½	69½	+ 2⅜
SwBellT 8¼17	4591	69⅛	56⅛	68	+ 2⅞
SwBellT 8¾18	3515	72½	60	70⅞	+ 1⅜
SwBellT 9⅝19	19840	79⅞	65¼	78½	+ 2⅝
SwBellT 11⅜20	21123	92¾	76⅛	91⅛	+ 3⅝
SwBellT 14¼20	25257	111⅜	94	109⅜	+ 1⅞
SwtnPS 9⅝86	409	100	92⅞	100	+ 3¼
Sovran 8⅞86	722	97¼	91	97⅛	+ 3⅝
Sperry 8.2s96	299	75	67½	73¼	+ 4⅝
Sperry 10½87	2618	99¼	91	99¼	+ 3⅞
Sperry 13⅞92	217	108⅝	98	108	....
SperryFn 7⅞85	1742	99¾	96 13-32	99¾	+2⅞
Spiegel 5s87	267	84¼	77¾	84¼	+ 7⅝
Spiegel cv4½90	19	59¼	55⅛	59¼	+ ⅝
SquibbCp 8s85	1048	99½	9½	99 5-16	+2 15-16
StaleyM 8⅛s95	120	78¼	70	70½	— 5½
StaleyM 8⅞s01	295	77½	65	74	+ ½
StBrand 6¾s93	290	75	65½	72½	+ 1½
StBrand 7¾s01	160	68⅝	61½	68⅝	+ 5⅛
StBrand 9½04	185	79½	71½	73½	— 5½
StOilInd 6s91	3298	75¾	67½	75¾	+ 4
StOilInd 6s98	3489	64¼	53½	62⅞	+ 3¾
StOilInd 9.2s04	8437	81⅜	68⅛	80⅜	+ 1⅜
StOilIn 11¼89t	5623	102¾	98⅛	100⅛	+ ⅛
StOilInd 8⅜s05	3063	75⅞	60	73½	+ 2⅛
StOilInd 7⅞07	2575	71⅝	58⅛	68⅝	+ 1¾

StOilInd 14s91	8755	108¾	99¾	108	— ⅛
StOilOh 7.60s99	1389	71¼	59⅝	71⅛	+ 5⅛
StOilOh 8½00	2650	76⅝	63⅜	75¼	+ 3⅛
StOilOh 7½86	5992	95¼	87⅝	94⅞	+ 4⅝
StOilOh 8⅜07	1373	73	60	72⅛	+ 3⅛
StOilOh 13⅜92	2487	106¾	96	105¾	+ ⅜
StdOilOh 10⅞13	98	89¾	85⅞	89¾	....
StdPac 12¾99	253	95	80	85½	+ 1⅜
StanlyW 9¼s00	20	74	67	74	....
StaufCh 8⅛s96	381	76½	66	70	— 3
StaufCh 8⅛s86	934	97⅜	92	97	+ 2½
StaufCh 8.85s01	350	76	64½	75⅜	+ ⅞
SterlBcp cv6½90	1701	86¼	76	78½	— ½
StrlBcp cv na92	270	125	103	104	—24
StrlBcp na94s	142	106	103	104	....
Steven cv4s90	175	95⅛	90	93	+ 4½
Steven cv9s08	2137	93	74½	76	—11
Stokely 8s98	182	74½	68	68	—28
Stokely 10¼00	34	87	78¾	84	+ 1¾
StopShp cv8¾07	1029	167½	119½	150	—20¾
Stor cv9s01f	30306	73½	24	26	—45
Stor 11⅝93f	2078	90	47	49½	....
Storer cv8½05	9177	125	100½	122½	+15
Storer 10s03	8048	78½	68½	74	— ¾
SuavSh cv5s97	859	65¼	54	54	—10
SunCh 11½96	16	86⅝	79⅛	83	— 3⅝
SunCh 11¼96	295	87	75	83⅛	— 9⅞
SunCo 7⅛s2002	280	66½	55⅝	64¼	+ ¼
SunCo 9.15s86	1224	98¼	92⅛	97⅞	+ 2⅝
SunCo 10¾06	20763	100	85	97¾	+ 1½
SunCo 13.4s07	148	104	90½	103¾	+ 1¾
SunOil 4⅝s90	95	76	70¼	75	+ 4
SunOil 8½s2000	1206	76	64	74	+ 3⅞
Sunbm 5½s92	176	65⅞	64⅝	65	+ 1
Sunray 4¼s87	25	82⅞	81½	82⅞	— ⅜
SunsM 8½95	4112	112½	97	97½	— 9½
SunMSlv 8½95	4218	112	94¼	96⅞	— 9¼
SunmSlv 8s95	9653	104¼	88	92¼	— 8¾
SupOil 9⅝89	1800	94¼	85	94¼	+ 3
SupOil 9⅝99	412	84	72	84	+ 2⅝
SupOil 14⅜91	1192	111⅜	101	107⅝	— 2⅜
Sybron cv4½87	191	82	77	82	+ 2½
Sybron 7½s94	217	70	62⅞	68¾	+ ¼
Sybron 9⅛s85	677	100	95⅝	99 1-32	+3 21-32

— T-T —

TRE cv9¾02	20	330	193	193	—138
TRW 5½92	128	67½	62	66¾	+ ¾
TRW 8⅛04	284	70⅛	57⅝	69½	— ½
TRW 9⅞00	202	81½	77	81½	+ ½
TRW 9s85	898	99⅞	96 13-16	99 13-16	+2 7-16
Talley 8⅛s97	61	67½	61¾	67½	+ 2⅛
Tandy 10s94	1131	89	75⅛	88	+ 4½
Tandy 10s91	2716	91¼	78⅛	90¼	+ 3⅝
Tektrnix 11s90	69	97½	90	97½	+ 2⅛
Telecom 13⅜99f	312	85¼	57⅛	85¼	+32¼
Teledy 6½s92	136	72⅛	63¾	72⅛	+ 2¼
Teledy 7⅞s94	235	75⅝	66	73⅜	+ 1⅝
Teledy 7s99	1711	63	52	60¼	+ ¼
Teledy 10s04A	11090	81⅜	67⅝	78	— ½
Teledy 10s04C	15716	81	67⅝	78½	— 1
TelexCp 9s96	1243	87⅛	66¼	72⅜	—12⅞
TelexCp 11¾96	691	91⅞	80	90	+ 1
Tennco 7s93	3870	75¾	65	72⅝	+ 3⅜
Tennco 6¾87	88	93	88	91½	....
Tennco 7s88	95	88¾	83	87	....
TenncInc 8¼91	928	86	75⅛	85¼	+ 4⅛
TenncInc 9s94	1062	86	73⅛	84⅞	+ 3⅛
TenncInc 9⅞00	499	83¼	72⅛	81¾	+ ¾
TenncInc 8⅜02	398	74¼	60⅞	72½	+ 5
TenncInc 8⅞03	762	75	64	74	+ 3
TenncInc 9½04	567	79	66⅜	79	+ 5
TenncInc 12⅛05	2411	99	81¾	96	+ 1⅛
Tenncl 13⅜91	4460	105¾	95⅝	104½	+ 1⅛
TenncInc 14½06	244	110	98	107⅛	— 1½
TenncInc 15s06	103	115½	98	102	— 5
TenncInc 14½91	1976	108½	100	107½	+ 1¼
Tennco d6s11	16617	51⅞	42	50¾	+ 2
TenncInc 13.70s92	929	109¼	96⅞	108⅞	+ 1
TenncInc 13⅝07	884	104½	90	104½	+ ¾
Tennco 11⅛13	139	88¾	78½	88¾	+ 1½
TenncInc 12⅝88	451	104⅛	102½	104	....
TVA 7s97	3082	70	58⅝	68⅛	+ 2½
TVA 7s97r	1230	70	58⅞	68¼	....
TVA 7.35s97B	2663	72	60⅜	71⅛	+ 3½
TVA 7.35s97Br	1286	71⅜	60¼	69⅞	....
TVA 7.35s97C	2476	72¼	60⅜	72¼	+ 5
TVA 7.35s97Cr	1491	71¼	59⅝	69⅞	....
TVA 7.40s97D	2181	71⅜	60½	69¾	+ 1⅞
TVA 7.40s97Dr	957	71	60⅜	69¾	....
TVA 7.35s98A	1777	72	60	70	+ 2⅛
TVA 7.35s98Ar	590	71	59⅛	71	....
TVA 7.35s98B	1986	71⅜	59¼	69⅜	+ 2⅜
TVA 7.35s98Br	1239	70⅜	59¼	70	....
TVA 7¾s98C	2569	73¼	61½	71½	+ 2¼
TVA 7¾98Cr	1780	73⅛	61⅞	71½	....
TVA 7.70s98	1722	72⅜	60⅞	70½	+ 2¼
TVA 7.7s98r	964	72⅜	61½	70⅞	....
TVA 8.05s99	2563	75	63	73	+ 2⅛
TVA 8.05s99r	1560	75	63½	73	....
TerASL 2⅞s85	194	93⅝	87½	93⅝	+ 7⅝
TerASL 2⅞85r	12	90½	90½	90½	....
TerASL 4s2019	101	37	34½	34½	— 2½
Tesoro cv5¼89	966	120	79¼	80½	—10¼
Tesoro d12¾01	2263	95⅝	78⅛	82	— 6
TexacCap 13¼99	708	104¾	99⅜	104¾	......
TexacCap 13⅝94	681	108¼	101	108	....
TexacCap 13s91	2788	105¾	98¾	105¾	....
Texaco 5¾s97	2337	61	51	59⅝	+ 1
Texaco 7¾2001	2995	70¼	58½	68¼	+ 1
Texaco 8⅞s05	3230	76½	64	74½	+ ¾
Texaco 8½s06	3768	73¼	61⅛	72¼	+ 1
TexNO 3⅜s90	129	70	57¼	70	+ 9
TexNO 3⅜90r	15	64⅛	62¾	64⅛	....
TexPac 5s2000	139	51½	45	50	+ 3
TexPac 5s2000r	2	50	45½	50	....
TexAmBnc 15½92	217	113	102	109	— 3½
TexAOil 12s99	211	86	75	75⅛	— 4⅞
TexCBn 8⅞s85	1208	99⅝	94½	99⅝	+ 3⅛
TexEstn cv12s09	1773	103¾	100	100½	....
TexGsTr 7⅞86	245	95½	91⅜	94	+ 1⅝
TexInd 7¾s92	232	76¾	72	75	— ⅜
TxInd cv9s08	3431	106	86½	89¼	— 8¾
TexInst 4.80s90	146	68	64	65½	— 1¼
TexInst 12.7s05	1916	101½	85	101	+ 2½
TxInt 11½old	1285	76	46	49	—25
TxInt 11½new	373	77⅜	49	50⅜	—24⅝
TxInt d13⅛93	114	90	79	79	—11
TxInt 9s95	5	70	70	70	—30
TexO&G 7½s92	27	76⅝	73	73	— 6⅛
TexO&G 7⅜s92	88	77	71⅞	77	— ⅜
TexO&G 8¼s94	61	78½	73	78¼	+ ¼
TexO&G 10¼95	26	86	78	84	— 6
TexO G 8¼97	93	75	69	75	+ 3
TexO&G 9s98	35	81	73⅛	81	+ 1
TexO&G 16⅝91	736	116¾	109	115½	+ 2½
Texfi cv4¾96	1707	52¾	29¼	30½	—20
Textron 5⅞s92	369	70½	62⅜	68⅜	+ ⅝
Textron 7½97	149	66½	60⅜	64	....
Textrn cv7¾05	4545	104	88	96¼	— 5¾
Thackeray 9s90f	41	107½	90	107½	+23¼
ThermoEl cv8½05	3946	96	78½	87	— 6
ThoRW 5¼s86	66	90	87⅛	90	+ 4⅝
Ticor 9½08	149	73¾	60⅞	63⅜	— 7¾
Tidewtr cv7¾05	3928	75⅞	55⅛	57	—15¾
TideOil 3½s86	365	90⅞	85	90⅞	+ 5⅞
TigerInt 11½95	2042	80	65	73	+ 3
TigerI cv8⅝05	978	68¾	55	60	— 1
TimeInc 8¼86	566	98⅜	92	98⅜	+ 4⅞
TimeInc 9⅞09	56	82	77	81	+ 2¼
Timeplx cv7¾08	966	103	79	97	— 5
TimeM 9⅝86	578	99¼	93	99¼	+ 3½
TimeM 10¼85	815	100¼	97	100¼	+ 1½
ToledEd 9s00	1713	70	58	66	— 2
ToledEd 7½02	695	59½	48¼	58½	+ 2⅜
ToledEd 8s03	528	62¼	50	62	+ 1⅛
ToledEd 9.35s85	1560	99½	94	98¼	+ 4
ToledEd 9.65s06	1155	72	60⅛	70¾	— ⅛
ToledEd 9⅝08	439	74½	59⅛	68½	— 2½
ToledEd 11s09	1026	82	68⅜	79¾	+ 2¼

TowleM cv9½00	4166	106¼	73	74	—28
Tracor cv9s07	8428	106½	86½	103½	— 4
TrailFin 8½96	5	61½	61½	61½	— 2½
TrailFin 8.2s87	764	92½	83¼	92½	+ 4
TWA 4s92	6651	54	43⅜	49½	+ 2
TWA 5s94	1752	58	46¼	50⅛	— ¾
TWA 10s85	267	99⅞	97⅜	99 1-16	+1 11-16
TWA 11s86	1260	99¾	96	99	+ 2⅞
TW Cp 10s99	23300	91¾	73	74⅞	— 9⅞
Transa 8⅝01	45	72	67	69¾	— ¼
Transa 10⅝04	483	85⅞	73	82½	— 1⅞
TransA 11⅞05	279	93½	81	93½	+ 2½
TranFin 7⅞s91	648	82⅛	70½	81½	+ 2⅛
TranFin 8½01	884	99½	95	99	+ ½
TranFin 9¼87	1216	95⅝	88½	95½	+ 3
TranFin 9⅞99	110	84	70	83¾	+ 2¼
TranFin 10¼85	1501	100¼	96	100¼	+ 1½
TrnGPL 6¼87	61	89⅞	82⅛	89⅞	+ 3⅞
TrnGPL 8⅜89	394	89⅛	77⅜	87¼	+ 1⅝
TrnGPL 8⅞90	610	91⅝	80⅜	85⅝	....
TrnGPL 9½90	802	95	80½	89¼	+ ½
TrnGPL 8⅞91	241	87¾	75⅝	87¼	+ 4
TrnGPL 9¾86	504	98	92⅞	98	+ 2¼
TrnGPL 17¼91	162	120	105	115	+ 2
TrnGPl 15⅝92	45	106	104⅜	104⅜	—10¾
Traveler 8.7s95	2481	83¼	71⅜	80⅛	+ ¾
TriSoMt cv7s92f	162	67¾	60	61½	— 3
TrinInLs cv10s06	3411	106⅞	84	88¼	—14¾
TritonEn 13½94	59	90½	89	90½	....
TucsnEP 8⅛01	1059	70½	60	68½	+ 1⅞
TucsnEP 7.55s02	532	66	55½	66	+ 3⅛
TucsnEP 7.65s03	725	66	56	66	+ 3
TucsnEP 10½05	1172	87	74⅛	83¾	+ 1¼
TCFox 10¼98	2926	79	70	77½	— ¼
TCFox 13¼00	1899	98	83½	88	— 6⅛
Tyler 10½98	75	82	76⅛	78⅛	— 6
Tyler 12⅞94	93	106	90¼	92	—14
— U—U —					
UCCEL cv7¼95	367	62⅝	53¾	59	— 2⅞
UGICp 11s90	95	98⅜	87	92¾	+ ⅞
UNC Res 12s98	1952	85½	60	82⅞	+ 2
URS cv8¾08	1445	99	79¾	95	— 5
UT Cred 8⅝86	616	97⅝	90	97⅝	+ 5¼
UT Cred 8¼02	10	66	66	66	— 3
UT Cred 8.85s03	155	73¼	61	73¼	+ 1¾
UT Cred 9s03	10	72	72	72	— 2½
UT Cred 11¼93	52	93⅞	88¼	93	— 1⅛
Unidyn 9½99	13	69½	62	69½	— 8½
UnBk 7.35s01	754	61¾	50	61¼	+ 2⅞
UnCamp 7½96	163	72⅜	66	68	+ ¼
UnCamp 10⅞10	60	86⅞	82½	82½	— 6⅛
UnCamp 11s13	30	89½	89½	89½	— ½
UnCarb 5.30s97	2282	65	53	64⅝	+ 3½
UnCarb 8½s05	7672	72⅞	61	64⅞	— 4⅝
UnCarb 7½06	931	67	54	60	— 2½
UnCarb 9⅛86	4277	97½	91½	94⅞	— ⅜
UnCarb 14½91	6875	110½	99⅛	103⅛	— 5⅛
UnCarb 9.35s09	3477	78	65½	69	— 6
UnCarb cv10s06	26766	117	77	81½	—33½
UnCorp cv6s88	231	90½	81½	90	+ 8½
UnCorp cv7s89	637	108	92⅞	94	— 1
UnCorp d14½01	75	100½	93⅝	96⅞	— ¼
UnElec 10½s05	1302	82⅝	68⅛	79⅝	+ 2⅝
UnElec 8⅞s06	797	69½	58	69⅜	+ 4⅝
UnElec 8⅝07	687	68⅞	56⅝	67¼	+ 3⅝
UnElec 15⅜91	1091	108½	99½	108⅛	+ 1⅜
UnElec 15s92	1821	108	99	106	+ ⅜
UnElec 13s13	1106	99½	80¼	97½	+ ½
UnOCal 4⅞s86	348	91⅜	85	91⅜	+ 4⅜
UnOCal 4⅞86r	21	89½	86	89½	....
UnOCal 6⅝s98	1010	65⅝	54	65⅜	+ 2⅛
UnOCal 8⅜s85					
	2458	99 21-32	95½	99 21-32	+2 29-32
UnOCal 8⅝s06	629	75¾	63½	75¾	+ 5¼
UPacCp cv4¾99	145	361	255	282½	—65½
UPacCp 8.4s01	662	74	63¼	74	+ 3½
UPacCp 11⅞10	566	97¼	84	97¼	+ 3¼
Uniroy cv5½96	5584	81	63⅛	70¼	— 9¾
UnAirL 5s91	1542	68	56	66¼	+ 8⅞
UnAirL 4¼92	1490	62	44½	62	+ 7½
UBkCpNY 7¾87	351	93¾	84	93¾	+ 5¼
UBrand 7¼88	545	87⅞	76⅛	84	+ 4⅝
UBran cv5½94	7685	62	50¾	56¾	— ¼
UBran 9⅛98	2075	71	60⅛	68	+ 4⅞
UBrand 14¾99	74	101	94	94⅞	....
UtEnrRs 17s91	206	110	104⅝	107	— 3
UtEnrRs 13⅜94	20	96	96	96	....
UtEnrRs 13s93	136	99	97	97	....
UtdFin 8⅛87	720	92¼	83¾	92¼	+ 6½
UnGasP 8⅜s89	660	90⅛	80¼	87¾	+ 6¼
UnGasP 10⅛90	196	93¾	84¼	93¾	+ 4
UnGasP 9¾s90	63	87	83¼	87	+ ½
UnGasP 10½89	161	94	88⅝	94	+ 1½
UnGasP 15½91	323	110	97⅜	110	+ 3⅜
UJerBk 7¾s97	519	70	61	68⅛	+ 2½
USAir cv9¼07	5090	131	99¼	127½	+ 4
USAirG cv8¾09	862	114	97¾	113½	....
USGyp 4⅞s91	145	71	62⅛	66¾	+ 2¼
USGyp 7⅞s04	40	66½	63½	63½	— 1¾
USHom cv5½96	757	103	65	67	—36
USHom 10s87	1318	94	86	87	— 2¾
USHom 12¾89	40	99½	98	98	— 4
USInd 8¼97	50	68½	63½	63½	— ⅛
USLsg 15¾87	54	109	103¾	109	— 2
USLsgl cv9s07	1468	103	89	99	— 4
USNBOr 7¾02	394	65¼	54⅜	62⅞	— ½
USPlywd 8s96	467	73⅞	65⅞	67	— 3⅝
USSteel 4½s86	840	94¼	89⅝	92¾	+ 3⅛
USSteel 4½86r	51	91½	88⅝	91	....
USSteel 4⅝s96	16320	54	47¼	52¾	+ 5⅜
USSteel 7¾s01	2416	65	56¼	63	+ 1⅛
USSteel cv5¾01	26495	68	53½	57¼	— 6½
USTrNY 8½01	462	74⅜	65¼	74¼	+ 9
UnTech 4½s88	19	78	72⅞	76¼	— 1¼
UnTech 5⅜91	264	69	61⅜	69	+ 4⅛
UnTech 4½92	195	63	57½	63	+ 3¼
UnTech 9s85					
	1222	99 15-16	96 29-32	99 15-16	+1 13-16
UnTech 9⅞00	225	83	69	82	— ⅝
UnTech 9.45s89	1078	94¾	85	94¾	+ 4
UnTech 9⅜04	569	80½	68	79½	+ 2¾
UnTech 11¼12	10	90¼	89¼	90¼	— 3⅝
UTelecm 9.4s99	234	78½	70¼	78½	+ 4½
UTelecm 11s00	105	86½	74⅛	86½	+ ½
UTelecm 10¾88	80	97⅛	91	91⅜	— 4⅛
UnTelOh 7.6s02	314	67	53¾	67	+ 3½
UnTelOh 9s08	116	73½	65	73½	+ 2½
UnUtils cv5s93	557	78	66¼	78	+ 1
UnVaBksh 7¾97	265	68⅛	58⅜	68⅛	+ 2⅛
Univar 9¾s99	97	84⅜	79	82⅛	— 1⅝
Upjohn 8⅛s85					
	2198	99 11-16	96⅜	99 11-16	+2 15-16
Upjohn 10.65s90	2983	98	87	98	+ 2¾
USLIFE 9½s85	1162	100	96⅛	99⅞	+ 2⅝
USLIFE 12½90	776	102½	92⅛	102½	+ 1¾
UtahPL 10¼05	1139	87	72¾	82½	— 1½
UtahPL 9s06	385	74⅞	63¾	74⅞	+ 4¾
UtahPL 8¾06	317	72⅞	62	72¼	+ 2¾
UtahPL 8⅜06	731	69⅞	59	68⅜	— ½
UtahPL 8½07	425	71	60	69⅜	+ 2⅜
UtahPL 8¼07	964	70	58¼	66¾	+ ¼
UtahPL 9⅛08	916	75⅝	64	74	....
UtahPL 10⅛09	940	82⅞	71⅛	80¼	+ 2¾
UtahPL 10¼09	578	83½	73	81⅝	— 3⅜
UtahPL 14¾10	170	111½	101	107	— 1½
UtahPL 16⅜11	491	120	104⅞	112	— 3
UtahPL 13s12	325	102½	93	102½	+ 2½
— V—V —					
Valero 7¾91	766	76⅞	62	65½	— 9½
Valero d16¼01	23231	112½	65	76⅝	—33⅜
ValeroNG 16¾02					
	2149	115½	86½	101⅞	—13⅝
ValeroNG 13½03	177	100	80	90	— 8¼
VerYNuc 9⅝98	1209	81¼	66½	80⅜	+ 3½
VerYNuc 8½98	125	76⅛	58¾	76⅛	+13
Viacom cv9¼07	3678	116	100	112	— ½
VaSw 5s2003	56	50	37¼	40	— 2
VaEPw cv3⅝86	1222	93	84⅞	92¾	+ 7⅞
VirgRy 3s95	201	84⅜	78⅛	84	+ 2
VirgRy 3s95r	27	82½	82	82⅙	— 1⅞
VirgRy 6s08	338	55⅛	45⅛	51⅝	+ ⅝
VaRwy 6s08r	120	52	45	49	....

Vought 6¾s88	183	83⅛	75⅛	80	− 1¼
VulcM 10¼2000	396	84⅛	72	84⅛	+ 4

— W—W —

Wabash 4¼s91	81	64⅞	60¼	64⅞	+ 3⅜
Wabash 4¼91r	47	67	60⅛	67	....
Wachov cv8¾09	697	107	103	107	....
WagEl 6⅞s86	173	92	81⅛	90	− 7
WaltrJ cv5¾91	2343	97	80	96¾	− 2¾
WaltrJ 7⅞97	65	65⅜	60	60	− 2⅛
WaltrJ 8s98	274	66¼	51⅝	63⅝	+ 1½
WaltrJ 9½96	247	77	67	75	+ ⅜
WaltrJ cv9s07	3367	113	92	113	+ 3
WaltrJ 13¾03	120	101⅞	89½	95	− 5¾
WaltrJ 10⅞08	90	83⅞	81	83⅞	+ 2⅞
WarnC 8⅛86	2184	92½	84	91⅞	+ 3⅞
WarnC 9⅛96	844	75¼	59½	68⅝	− 2⅞
WarnC 10⅞95	127	85	76	80	....
WarnL 8.30s85	1417	99¾	96 21-32	99 11-16	+3 1-16
WarnL 8⅞2000	329	78½	64⅝	77	+ 1
WeanU 5½93N	825	53½	49	50½	+ ½
WeanU cv5½93	1288	52½	49	49	+ ½
WellsFar 7⅞97	682	70	58	69½	+ 2
WellsFar 8.6s02	280	73	63¼	69	+ 2
WellsFar 9.55s85	1768	99 15-16	95	99⅞	+ 1⅞
WellsFar 10⅝85	1205	100¼	95½	100¼	+ ⅝
WellsFar 14½91	1733	108½	98⅛	108	+ 1⅜
WellsFar 12.3s90	140	101½	93	100	....
WellsFar 11.40s87	246	99⅛	95⅛	99⅛	....
WlFrM cv12s05	2710	116	100½	103	− 9
WtPtP cv7¾00	6	223	223	223	−22
WAirL cv5¼93	1502	74	50½	63	+ 1
WAirl 10¾98	3922	75½	57	63⅜	− 7½
WAirl 14s98	14300	120¾	78	89	....
WnAuto 7.85s96	214	68	57	63⅝	− 3
WnCoNA 10⅞97	2120	80	62⅝	71⅜	− 6⅛
WCoNA 10.7s98	913	80¼	65	70⅛	− 9⅞
WnElec 8⅜s95	2557	80½	68⅜	78¾	+ 1⅝
WnElec 7½s96	611	73⅝	64¾	73⅛	+ 1⅝
WPI 10s01	1259	80⅞	61½	74½	− 1½
WPI 15s06	272	104	97	99½	− 4½
WUCp cv5¼97	11903	70	35	37	−28¼
WUCp 10¾s97	4230	85	58	62¼	−19
WnUnT 5¼87	255	87	73	75	−10⅛
WnUnT 5¼87r	20	84	79⅜	79⅜	....
WnUnT 6½89	876	80⅞	60⅜	63	−11⅝
WnUnT 5s92	667	62⅛	50	53	− 8
WnUnT 8.45s96	1156	77¼	52	57¾	−12¼
WnUnT 7.90s97	996	69	51⅝	55½	− 9⅛
WnUnT 8.10s98	565	66¾	49½	56½	− 6⅝
WnUnT 10s86	2104	97⅝	83⅜	88⅛	− 6½
WnUnT 9¼97	368	75¼	58½	62	−11
WnUnT 16s91	2524	113	85¾	88⅞	−24¾
WnUnT 13¼08	377	100	74	81	−17
WnUnT 13⅝94	30	99	99	99	....
WestgCr 8½s91	313	85	80¼	84⅛	+ 2½
WestgCr 7.6s97	333	70	60	68	− ¼
WestgCr 10⅞90	1270	98⅛	85⅝	98	+ 3
WestgCr 14¾91	1034	109¼	100½	108¾	+ 2¼
WestgCr 11⅞96	50	96⅞	96⅞	96⅞	....
WestgEl 5⅜s92	571	70⅛	62	70⅛	+ 3⅝
WestgEl 8⅝s95	4699	82½	70⅝	80⅜	+ 2⅜
WestgEl cv9s09	4029	108	100⅝	105½	....
WestgEl 10¾89	185	97½	88¼	88½	− 7
Wstvaco 9¾00	250	83⅝	72	82½	+ 4¼
Wstvaco 8⅛07	70	68⅞	60	66⅛	+ 3⅞
Westvaco 12⅛12	35	95	82	82	−11¼
Weyerh 5.20s91	530	87	75⅛	87	+ 6⅝
Weyerh 7.65s94	924	78⅞	67	77	+ 3
Weyerh 8⅝s00	758	77½	65⅛	77	+ 1¼
Weyerh 8.9s04	941	77⅞	64¾	77⅞	+ 2⅜
Weyerh 8s85	5237	99 29-32	97 1-32	99⅞	+2⅜
Weyerh 7.95s06	569	70½	58⅛	70½	+ 5⅛
Whirl 5¾s86	294	91	86	88¼	+ ⅛
Whirl 9⅝s00	5	74	74	74	− 7
WhitCn cv5½92	85	165	100	102	−76
Whitkr cv4½88	348	84	74⅜	80½	+ 6½
Whitkr 10s88	409	91½	84⅛	90	+ 4⅜
Whitkr 9⅝93	53	81½	76½	78	− 3
Whitkr 10s96	1026	80	69	75⅝	− 1¼
WillRs cv5¼89	639	140	96	140	+38½
WillRs cv4½92	371	130	92½	130	+25
WmsCos 9.4s96	188	78	73	77¾	+ 4⅛
WilmEl cv12¾96	4155	93	64¼	68	−23½
WilsFd 7⅞97f	65	72	68½	71⅛	+ 3½
WilsFd 8⅜97f	165	78½	69¾	77½	+ 7¾
WisCen 4s2004	118	40	38	39½	+ ¾
WisCen 4s2004r	11	38	37½	37½	....
WisCen 4½s29f	167	39⅞	36	38	− ½
WisCen 4½29fr	12	37	37	37	....
WiscGs 10⅝s95	247	95	90⅛	94¼	+ 2¼
WiscPL 13⅜91	319	104⅜	99½	104⅜	+ 1⅜
WiscTel 7¼07	1370	63⅝	52¼	61⅜	+ 1⅜
WiscTel 8s14	2465	68⅞	56⅜	68	+ 3
WiscTel 8¼16	1517	69¾	58⅛	69	+ 3¾
WiscTel 11⅜17	428	93¾	81⅛	93⅜	+ 3⅞
Witco cv4½93	59	174	140	148	−15
Witco 9½09	27	73⅛	71⅜	71⅜	− 3⅜
Woolwrth 7⅜96	1162	71½	59	70⅜	+ 6⅛
Woolwrth 9s99	3633	76¾	64	75⅜	+ 3½
WorldAwy 10s93	740	77	66⅛	69⅝	− 4⅜
WrldAir 11¼94	1247	81⅞	72	74½	− 3
WyleL cv5¼88	531	167½	90½	94	−71

—X—Y—Z-

XeroxCrd 15¼91	370	112½	104½	110½	+ ⅜
XeroxCrd 16s91	1225	115¾	105⅛	113	− 1
XeroxCrd 14¼88	1947	107	101⅛	104	− 1⅜
XeroxCr 12⅞88	506	103½	100⅜	103½	....
Xerox cv6s95	13777	76½	63¼	69	− 5
Xerox 8⅝s99	1200	77¾	64½	76⅝	+ 2⅞
Xerox 10½88	1451	99⅞	90⅛	99⅞	+ 3⅞
Xerox 10⅝93	1296	95½	83¼	94⅜	+ 1⅜
YngsST 4½90	321	65	60	62⅞	− 1⅞
YngsST 10½00	1191	77⅝	69	69⅜	− 2¾
YngsST 9⅞91	717	82½	76½	82	+ 1⅜
Zapata 10⅞01	1701	81	71	76½	+ 2¾
Zapata 10¼97	3220	78⅞	68¼	74	+ ⅛
ZapatOff 7⅞85	167	99⅞	95	98 9-16	−1 5-16
ZapatOff 8⅝96	258	80½	71	77⅞	− 1⅝
Zayre 8s96	121	72⅜	69	72⅜	+ 3¾
Zayre 12⅝05	32	98½	93	98½	+ 4½
Zurn cv5¾94	1426	104	81	93	− 2½

U.S. GOVERNMENT TREASURY BONDS
DECEMBER 31, 1984

NEW YORK (AP) — Over the Counter U.S. Government Treasury bonds 1984 price range.

Prices in dollars and 32nds.

Subject to Federal taxes but not State income taxes.

Issue		High	Low	Last	Chg
9.25 Jan 1985	n	100.3	98.11	100.2	+ 1.2
8.00 Feb 1985	n	100	97.13	99.31+	2.3
9.63 Feb 1985	n	100.28	98.10	100.7	+ .31
14.63Feb 1985	n	104.21	100.10	100.23—	3.23
9.63 Mar 1985	n	100.10	98	100.7	+ 1.3
13.38Mar 1985	n	103.20	100.28	101.5	— 2.5
9.50 Apr 1985	n	100.13	97.25	100.10+	1.14
3.25 May 1985		98.9	92.16	98.8	+ 5.29
4.25 May 1975-85		98.18	92.31	98.18+	5.24
9.88 May 1985	n	100.23	97.25	100.16+	1.10
10.38May 1985	n	100.24	98.18	100.24+	.28
14.13May 1985	n	104.23	101.13	102.1	— 2.14
14.38May 1985	n	105.2	101.19	102.6	— 2.18
14.00Jun 1985	n	104.29	101.17	102.21—	1.30
10.00Jun 1985	n	100.24	97.19	100.20+	1.12
10.63Jul 1985	n	101.3	97.31	101	+ 1.1
8.25 Aug 1985	n	99.24	95.30	99.23+	2.26
9.63 Aug 1985	n	100.15	96.28	100.13+	1.27
10.63Aug 1985	n	101	97.23	100.28+	1
13.13Aug 1985	n	103.27	100.14	102.13—	1.4
10.88Sep 1985	n	101.12	97.29	101.8	+ 1.1
15.88Sep 1985	n	108.4	103.19	104.25—	3.3
10.50Oct 1985	n	101.3	97.10	101	+ 1.12
9.75 Nov 1985	n	100.16	96.8	100.12+	2.1
10.50Nov 1985	n	102.5	97.3	100.31+	1.14
11.75Nov 1985	n	102.6	99	102	+ .13
10.88Dec 1985	n	101.18	97.10	101.14+	1.12
14.13Dec 1985	n	106.6	101.20	104.16—	1.9
10.63Jan 1986	n	101.11	96.27	101.7	....
10.88Feb 1986	n	101.20		101.15	....
13.50Feb 1986	n	105.10	100.21	104.3	— .21
9.88 Feb 1986	n	100.16	95.13	100.12+	2.8
14.00Mar 1986	n	106.14	101.13	105.2	— .25
11.50Mar 1986	n	102.12	97.17	102.6	....
11.75May 1986	n	102.22	97.24	102.18	....
7.88 May 1986	n	97.27	91.16	97.22+	3.30
9.38 May 1986	n	99.22	93.28	99.20+	2.27
12.63May 1986	n	103.26	99.1	103.21	....
13.75May 1986	n	106.9	100.31	105	— .19
13.00Jun 1986		104.20	99.22	104.12	....
14.88Jun 1986	n	108.25	102.28	107	— 1.8
12.63Jul 1986	p	104.5	99.30	103.28	....
8.00 Aug 1986	n	97.12	90.17	97.8	+ 3.30
11.38Aug 1986	n	102.9	96.23	102.1	+ 1.7
12.38Aug 1986	p	103.25	99.18	103.12	....
11.88Sep 1986	p	103.5	99.18	102.24	....
12.25Sep 1986	n	103.22	98.6	103.12+	.21
11.63Oct 1986	p	102.26	100.12	102.13	....
6.13 Nov 1986		94.16	88.21	94.2	+ 4.22
10.38Nov 1986	p	100.31	99.25	100.16	....
11.00Nov 1986	n	101.25	95.20	101.13+	1.19
13.88Nov 1986	n	107.6	101.7	106.8	— .13
16.13Nov 1986	n	112.17	105.21	110	— 2.1
9.88 Dec 1986	p	99.28	99.24	99.24	....
10.00Dec 1986	n	100.6	93.4	100	+ 2.18
9.00 Feb 1987	n	98.3	90.17	97.28+	3.16
10.88Feb 1987	n	101.20	94.18	101.9	....
12.75Feb 1987	n	105.3	98.25	104.24+	.26
10.25Mar 1987	n	100.12	92.28	100.4	+ 2.23
12.00May 1987	n	103.29	97.1	103.18+	1.20
12.50May 1987	n	104.28	97.26	104.12	....
14.00May 1987	n	108.3	101.10	107.11+	.2
10.50Jun 1987	n	100.24	92.24	100.11+	2.19
12.38Aug 1987	p	104.24	99.7	104.7	....
13.75Aug 1987	n	107.26	100.21	107.9	+ .16
11.13Sep 1987	n	102.2	93.29	101.15+	2.3
7.63 Nov 1987	n	94.1	85	93.15+	4.13
11.00Nov 1987	p	102	99.20	101.10	....
12.63Nov 1987	n	105.20	97.23	104.31+	1.11
11.25Dec 1987	n	102.10	93.24	101.22+	2.4
12.38Jan 1988	n	105.4	96.26	104.16+	1.19
10.13Feb 1988	n	99.10	90.1	98.31+	3.7
12.00Mar 1988	n	104.1	95.8	103.17	....
13.25Apr 1988	n	107.15	99.1	106.25+	1
8.25 May 1988	n	93.22	84.3	93.2	+ 3.21
9.88 May 1988	n	98.5	88.23	97.18+	3.1
13.63Jun 1988	n	108.20	99.30	107.28	....
14.00Jul 1988	n	109.23	101.5	108.28+	.14
10.50Aug 1988	n	99.25	89.30	99.2	+ 2.23
15.38Oct 1988	n	114.14	105.16	113.14—	.8
11.38Sep 1988	p	102.12	99.1	101.15	....
8.75 Nov 1988	n	94.14	84.6	93.27+	3.24
11.75Nov 1988	n	103.6	93.16	102.15+	1.28
10.63Dec 1987	p	99.13	99.10	99.10	....
14.63Jan 1989	n	112.7	102.19	111.12+	.3
11.38Feb 1989	n	101.28	91.25	101.4	+ 1.29
14.38Apr 1989	n	111.17	101.26	110.23+	.8
9.25 May 1989	n	95	84.16	94.11+	3.6
11.75May 1989	n	103.3	92.25	102.1	....
14.50Jul 1989	n	112.11	102.10	111.14+	.5
13.88Aug 1989	n	110.7	100.10	109.9	....
11.88Oct 1989	n	103.16	92.25	102.18+	1.21
10.75Nov 1989	n	99.28	88.12	99.12+	2.29
12.75Nov 1989	p	106.19	99.7	105.22	....
10.50Jan 1990	n	98.10	87	97.18+	2.26
3.50 Feb 1990		91.8	87.24	90.2	+ .4
11.00Feb 1990	p	100.15	98.21	99.17	....
10.50Apr 1990	n	98.6	86.20	97.7	+ 2.14
8.25 May 1990		90.24	78.8	89.23+	3.20
10.75Jul 1990	n	98.28	87.5	97.29+	2.12
10.75Aug 1990	n	98.28	87.4	97.30+	2.12
11.50Oct 1990	n	101.30	90.3	100.22+	1.25
13.00Nov 1990	n	108.2	96.12	106.22+	1.6
11.75Jan 1991	n	102.25	90.22	101.17+	1.19
12.38Apr 1991	n	105.17	93.7	103.27	....
14.50May 1991	n	114.21	102.21	113.9	+ .17
13.75Jul 1991	n	111.16	100.2	109.25	....
14.88Aug 1991	n	116.18	104.8	114.27+	.3
12.25Oct 1991	p	105.8	100.27	103.14	....
14.25Nov 1991	n	114.6	101.12	112.11+	.17
14.63Feb 1992	n	116.5	102.31	114.13+	.20
13.75May 1992	n	112.8	98.29	110.11+	.24
4.25 May 1987-92		91.8	87.26	89.15—	.8
7.25 Aug 1992		81.29	68.11	79.12+	2.11
10.50Nov 1992	n	96.10	83.4	94.30+	1.29
4.00 Feb 1988-93		91.10	87.26	89.16—	.8
6.75 Feb 1993		79.2	65.24	76.22+	2.29
7.88 Feb 1993		83.17	69.24	81.14+	2.15
10.88Feb 1993	n	98.2	84.20	96.15+	1.18
10.13May 1993	n	94.4	80.23	92.15+	1.19
7.50 Aug 1988-93		80.28	67.4	79.1	+ 2.20
8.63 Aug 1993		86.6	72.26	84.18+	2.4
11.88Aug 1993	n	103.2	89.10	101.16+	1.11
8.63 Nov 1993		86	72.16	84.16+	2.11
11.75Nov 1993	n	102.16	88.16	100.25+	1.3
9.00 Feb 1994		87.26	73.31	85.27+	1.25
4.13 May 1989-94		91.22	87.23	89.11—	1.12
13.13May 1994		110.16	95.16	108.15	....
8.75 Aug 1994		86.2	72.4	84.5	+ 2
12.63Aug 1994	p	107.30	98.12	105.28	....
10.13Nov 1994		94.3	79.10	92.13+	1.29
11.63Nov 1994	p	102.9	98.29	100.13	....
3.00 Feb 1995		91.6	87.26	89.12—	.30
10.50Feb 1995		96.2	81.1	94.6	+ 1.31
10.38May 1995		95.7	80.6	93.7	+ 1.30
12.63May 1995		108.16	92.17	106.17+	1.15
11.50Nov 1995		102.4	86.7	100.13+	2.7
7.00 May 1993-98		72.8	59.4	70.21+	2.3
3.50 Nov 1998		91.19	87.26	89.8	— 1.8
8.50 May 1994-99		81.4	66.4	78.26+	2.4
7.88 Feb 1995-00		75.19	61.25	73.22+	2.2
8.38 Aug 1995-00		78.28	64.24	76.21+	1.25
11.75Feb 2001		102.8	85.24	100.20+	2.1
13.13May 2001		112.3	95.1	110.13+	1.24
8.00 Aug 1996-01		75.24	61.12	73.11+	1.7
13.38Aug 2001		113.26	96.20	111.28+	1.15
15.75Nov 2001		131.19	114.24	130.1	+ 1.26
14.25Feb 2002		120.28	102.8	118.14+	1.4
11.63Nov 2002		101.8	84.26	99.9	+ 2
10.75Feb 2003		94.19	78.24	92.30+	2.5
10.75Aug 2003		94.20	78.24	92.28+	2.2
11.13Aug 2003		97.17	81.3	95.19+	2.7
11.88Nov 2003		103.3	86.14	101.5	+ 2.3
12.38May 2004		106.31	89.21	105.2	....
13.75Aug 2004		118.4	101.18	115.19	....
11.63Nov 2004	k	101.21	98	99.14	....
8.25 May 2000-05		77.4	61.18	75.6	+ 1.24
7.63 Feb 2002-07		71.7	58	69.9	+ 1.5
7.88 Nov 2002-07		73	59.11	71	+ 1.7
8.38 Aug 2003-08		76.15	62.8	74.17+	1.11
8.75 Nov 2003-08		79	64.12	77.6	+ 1.11
9.13 May 2004-09		81.30	66.27	80.2	+ 1.14
10.38Nov 2004-09		91.24	75.9	89.30+	1.26
11.75Feb 2005-10		102.19	84.31	100.25+	1.23
10.00May 2005-10		88.21	72.21	87.5	+ 1.31
12.75Nov 2005-10		110.17	91.23	108.15+	1.27
13.88May 2006-11		119.19	99.21	117.16+	1.30
14.00Nov 2006-11		120.20	100.20	118.24+	1.30
10.38Nov 2007-12		91.23	75.7	89.29+	1.15
12.00Aug 2008-13		104.20	86.12	102.23+	1.22
13.25May 2009-14		115.12	95.3	112.30	....

12.50Aug	2009-14k	109.12	99.5	107.2	....
11.75Nov	2009-14k	103.22	99.24	101.23	....

k—Non U. S. citizen exempt from withholding taxes. n—Treasury note. p—Treasury note and non U.S. citizen exempt from withholding taxes.

NEW YORK (AP) — New York Stock Exchange trading for 1984. The net change is from the previous year on issues listed prior to January 1, 1984.

TREASURY BONDS

	Sales $1000	High	Low	Last	Chg
US 7¼s92	1	71.18	71.18	71.18	....

INT-AM DEV BANK

	Sales $1000	High	Low	Last	Chg
IAm 5.20s92	43	80	79	79.16	+ .12
IAm 6½92N	120	82	69.8	82	+ 8.31
IAm 6⅝s93	35	89	73.6	89	+ 16
IAm 8⅝s95	779	93	83.2	93	+ 6.7
IAm 8¼s85	399	99.12	97.8	99.12	+ 2
IAm 8s85	1077	99.20	96.14	99.20	+ 3.14
IAm 8⅜86	323	97	91	96.16	+ 2
IAm 9s01	154	77.16	63.4	77.8	— .8
IAM 8¾s01	375	75.20	69	71.16	— 1.16
IAm 8⅜02	101	72.16	66	71.1	+ 1.25
IAm 9⅝04	75	75.24	74	75.24	— 6.8
IAm 10¾87	257	98.16	94.17	98	+ 1
IAm 14s86	231	106.8	101.8	101.16	— 5.8
IAm 15s89	119	110	108 3-16	110	+ 1
IAm 14⅝92	92	107	102.26	104	— 8.28
IAm 12⅛93	78	100.1	99.28	99.28	— .13

WORLD BANK

	Sales $1000	High	Low	Last	Chg
IntBk 5s85	797	99.12	94.24	99.12	+ 6.8
IntBk 4½s90	1058	76.16	66.16	76.16	+ 6.12
IntBk 5⅜s91	125	75.3	67.10	75.3	+ 8.19
IntBk 5⅜s92	367	71	70 25-32	+70 21-32	
IntBk 5⅞s93	138	69.28	60	69.28	+ 4.28
IntBk 6½s94	359	72	61	72	+ 4.2
IntBk 6⅜s94	373	70.9	60	70.9	+ 3.13
IntBk 8⅝s95	950	81.24	70	81	+ 2.15
IntBk 8⅛s96	1751	79.24	67	79.5	+ 4.24
InBk 8.15s85	1713	99.22	96.18	99.6	+ 2.6
IntBk 8.6s85	1436	99.16	94.21	99.16	+ 2.16
InBk 8.85s85	1041	100	93.18	99.8	+ 3.3
InBk 9.35s00	662	82.9	69.16	82	+ 2
IntBk 8⅜86	1716	97.1	91	96.30	+ 3.7
IntBk 8.85s01	401	77.4	67	75.8	+ .3
IntBk 7.8s86	1660	95.16	86.20	94.1	+ 3.5
IntBk 8⅜01	887	74.23	63	71.17	+ .17
IntBk 7.65s87	1013	93	83	93	+ 5.16
IntBk 8¼02	2572	75	62.5	73	+ 3.16
IntBk 7¾87	744	92.16	85.4	91.9	+ 2.9
IntBk 8.35s02	524	75	60	74.8	+ 4.20
IntBk 14⅝86	937	109.2	100	105.16	— 2.23
IntBk 16⅜86	461	112	103	107.14	— 3.18
IntBk 16⅝91	77	121.16	116	120.17	+ 1.1
IntBk 15s88	451	111.12	103.16	111.2	+ .2
IntBk 15⅛91	252	115	102	114	+ .8
IntBk 14¾92	34	112.16	105	107	— 5
IntBk 14⅝87	364	109.28	101	108.16	+ 1.16
IntBk 13.45s87	278	106	100	105	— 2.16
IntBk 13⅝92	195	107.16	97.17	107.16	....
IntBk 12⅜02	310	103	95.8	100.17	— .7
IntBk 11s89	979	99	87	99	+ 1.6
IntBk 10⅜88	802	97.1	94	95.10	— .6
IntBk 10.9s93	401	94	82.2	93.1	— 1.7
IntBk 10s88	152	95.12	88.17	94.13	+ .13
IntBk 10⅜93	179	95	82	95	+ 3.16

FOREIGN BONDS

	Sales $1000	High	Low	Last	Chg
AsianDv 8⅝86	203	95¼	90	94¼	+ ¼
AsianDv zr92s	3279	42½	34	42½	+ 5½
Austral 5¾s85	35	98½	92	98½	+ 8½
Austral 8¾86	160	99½	90½	93⅝	— 1⅜
Austral 9⅛96	326	85¾	76	80	— 3
Austral 9s96	191	83	73½	82	— 2
Austral 8⅞97	186	81	75	78¾	— 1⅞
Austral 9⅛93	230	89	81¾	89	+ 4
Austral 12¾92	251	103½	97½	103½	— 1¾
Austral 13s07	487	105½	96	104¼	+ 1¼
Austral 11⅜93	306	98½	90½	96	— 1
Austral 12⅛08	128	99¼	91	91	— 6⅜
Austria 8⅝92	3	81	81	81	— 2
Austria 11¼90	266	98¾	90¾	95	— 2⅞
Brazil 8¼s87	19	78	78	78	+ 2½
CaisseAut 9⅛97	153	82	65	82	+ 3
CaisseN 9.3s96	148	81	66⅛	80	— 1
CaisseN 11⅛90	248	97½	88	97½	— 1½
CaisseNtl 12s89	17	99½	94½	94½	— 5½
Cuba 4½77mf	387	17⅝	10	11⅝	— 2½
CzechSt 6s60mf	23	64	40	63	— 2
Denmrk 6s85	16	98¾	91	98¾	+ 9½
Denmrk 14s88	893	106	98	103½	— 3½
Denmrk 14⅝88	325	107¾	100¼	105	— 1⅜
EleFran 8.9s86	545	97½	91½	97½	+ 5½
EleFran 8½87	237	93⅞	89	92½	+ 2
Estonia 7s67mf	67	20	20	20	— 8
EurpCS 9s96	154	84	75½	82	+ 2⅞
EurpCS 8⅞96	458	80¾	70	79	+ ½
EurpCS 9⅛97	168	81⅞	75¾	79	+ 2
EurpCS 9¾99	386	86	76	79	— 3¼
EEC 11.6s99	18	92	90	92	— 3
EurpInv 6s85	4	88½	88½	88½	— 1½
EurpInv 8⅞96	462	81½	71	81½	+ 3½
EurpInv 9s97	210	81⅞	71½	79	+ 3
EurpInv 8⅜92	84	82⅝	74½	80⅝	— ⅞
EurpInv 8⅝85	168	99 15-32	95	99 15-32	+2 19-32
EurpInv 9¼98	203	82	69	82	+ 3½
EurpInv 8⅞86	416	96	91½	96	+ 1
EurpInv 9⅛98	210	81½	69	81½	+ 3½
EurpInv 9⅝86	353	98⅜	95	98⅜	+ 2¼
EurpInv 9⅞99	15	86	81⅝	81⅝	— 5⅜
EurpInv 9⅞87	282	98⅞	90¼	98⅞	+ 3⅛
EurpInv 10s99	60	84⅞	78	80½	— 2
EurInv 10⅛87	325	99¼	91	98⅛	+ 1⅞
EurInv 10.15s99	107	86⅞	83	83	— 6⅜
EurInv 11⅝87	535	102	96	100½	+ ¼
EurInv 11⅞00	249	97	87	92	— 5⅝
EurInv 12¾88	148	104½	98	102½	— ⅝
EurInv 13½00	384	107	100½	106	....
EurInv 14⅝91	429	113½	101½	113	+ ⅞
EurInv 13⅜12	343	107¾	97	107¾	+ 2¼
Eksprtf 13⅜92	40	101¾	97	97	....
Finland 8¾92	130	86	70	86	+ 5
Finland 9s88	287	92½	82	91	+ 3½
Finland 9⅝89	97	91¾	82	91¾	— 1¼
Finland 14¾86	35	106	102	102	— 4¼
Finland 13⅝87	195	105	99½	103	— ¼
Finland 11¾93	10	95¾	95¾	95¾	— 1
HydroQue 10s08	774	83	69	81¾	+ 5⅝
Mexico 8½s87	71	95	87	95	+ 9¼
Mexico 8½87r	34	95	95	95	....
Mexico 8⅛s97	670	70	63⅝	67	+ 4⅝
Mexico 10s90	94	90	75⅛	85	+13
Mexico 15s88	393	102	97¼	99½	+ 3
Mexico 15½86	491	103	98	101	+ ½
NZeal 5¾s85	21	98	90	98	+ 8
NZeal 6½s86	17	90½	90	90½	+ ½
Nippon 8⅛87	149	91¾	89	91¼	— ½
NorgesKb 9⅛98	79	79¾	77½	79⅛	+ ⅛
NorgesKb 9⅞99	5	81¾	81¾	81¾	— 1¾
Oslo 5¾s85	6	98	92	96	+ 4¼
Oslo 9s85	4	98	98	98	....
Oslo 8¾97	159	77¾	69¾	76	+ ½
OesterrchBk 1988	250	61¾	57¼	61¾	+ 3¾
SocNCF 9s92	77	83	80	81	— 1⅛
Stckhlm 8⅞92	73	84	80	80⅞	— 3⅛
Stckhlm 9¾94	58	93⅛	85	93⅛	+ 2⅛
Sweden 8½87	162	90⅛	86	89	— 1
Sweden 9s97	248	81¾	65	81¾	+ 4⅛
Sweden 9¼98	179	81⅛	70	81	+ 2½
Sweden 9½86	384	98	93	95⅛	— 2⅜
Sweden 11⅝99	229	96⅝	88	94	— ½
Sweden 10⅝90	225	97½	86	97½	+ 4½
Sweden 11⅜00	128	96	84	96	+ 2
Sweden 13.65s85	151	104½	101	103	— 1½
Sweden 14⅝88	614	110	100	109⅞	+ 1⅝
Sweden 12¼89	458	99¾	95	98⅛	— 2⅜
Sweden 12¾97	42	101	93⅝	97½	— 3½
SwedExpt 15½90	60	112	107	108	— 3¾
UK 8½85	59	98⅜	96 31-32	98⅜	+ 1⅜
UK 8⅞93	92	85	78¾	84	....
Venezla 8¾92	178	78	72½	76	+ 4
Venezla 15⅝86	61	102⅜	102	102⅜	+ 3⅜

HOW TO READ THE MUTUAL FUND TABLES

The "price" mutual fund investors can receive for their shares at any given time is the prevailing net asset value per share. This net asset value is normally calculated daily, and reported to the National Association of Securities Dealers for distribution to the public.

The annual mutual fund table in this book is similar in format to the daily, weekly and annual tables that appear in newspapers and financial publications. It shows, reading from left to right, the funds' names; the highest and lowest asset values per share they reached during the year; the asset value as of the close of business on the last day of the year; and the net change, in dollars and cents, from the end of the previous year.

In the case of "load" funds, which impose sales charges when you buy shares, the cost of purchasing a share may be as much as 8.5 percent more than the current net asset value. "No-load" funds, which can be bought at the net asset value without a sales charge, are designated in the table by an "n" after the name of the fund.

MUTUAL FUNDS
DECEMBER 31, 1984

ANNUAL INVESTING COMPANIES
NEW YORK (AP) -The following table compiled from quotations supplied by the National Association of Securities Dealers Inc., gives the high, low and last from the closing bid in 1984 with the net change from the previous year or from inception of trading if less than a year.

	High	Low	Last	Chg.
ABT Family:				
Emerg	11.63	9.55	10.86—	.12
grwthInc	12.86	11.02	12.48+	.01
SecInc	11.75	10.01	11.02—	.53
UtilIncm	15.82	12.58	15.80+	2.33
AcornFd n	32.54	26.70	30.89—	.93
ADV Fund n	21.57	17.26	19.32—	1.52
AfutureFd n	16.54	10.43	11.08—	4.81
AIM Funds:				
ConvYld	13.58	10.94	11.28—	2.12
Greenway	9.55	7.17	7.70—	4.63
HiYield	10.46	9.47	9.61—	.72
Sumit	5.53	4.54	5.03—	.39
Alliance Cap:				
Intl	11.00	9.02	10.53—	1.24
Mortg	9.56	8.83	9.54+	.04
Tech	22.42	14.78	16.52—	4.92
AlphaFnd	26.99	18.69	19.79—	6.05
Amer Capital:				
CorpBd	6.97	6.17	6.53—	.24
Comstk	15.00	12.05	12.96—	1.72
Enterp	12.84	9.83	11.17—	4.34
ExchFd n	47.59	40.30	44.18—	1.81
FundAm	12.19	10.76	10.99—	3.92
GovtSec	11.95	11.48	11.90+	.24
Growth n	30.18	20.79	23.11—	6.27
Harbor	16.91	11.29	12.10—	4.32
HiYldInv	10.14	8.96	9.50—	.48
MuniBond	17.60	16.53	17.39+	.16
OTC	10.35	8.24	8.64—	1.43
Pace Fnd	21.14	17.99	18.78—	1.68
Providnt	5.93	4.43	4.59—	1.24
Venture	15.64	12.91	13.39—	1.72
American Funds:				
AmBalan	11.06	8.96	10.06—	.85
AmcapFd	8.86	7.22	8.27—	.47
AmMutl	15.04	12.97	14.94—	.47
BondFd	12.72	11.44	12.34—	.07
Eupac	14.22	12.57	13.83+	.10
FundmInvs	12.52	9.96	11.94—	.23
GrowthFd	13.97	11.14	12.41—	1.17
IncomeFd	10.70	9.53	10.70+	.21
InvCoA	11.49	9.50	11.00—	.26
NewEcon	14.33	12.08	14.10+	.30
NewPerspFd	8.63	7.15	7.56—	.91
TaxExpt	9.67	8.93	9.50+	.04
WshMut	10.31	8.15	9.40—	.67
AmGwth	9.19	7.18	7.43—	1.33
AmHeritge n	3.73	2.65	2.73—	.91
Am Invest n	9.34	6.54	6.83—	1.97
Am InvInc n	10.90	8.48	8.54—	2.09
Am medAsc n	30.28	26.49	29.62+	.23
Am NatGrth	4.85	3.42	3.58—	1.11
Am NatInco	19.74	16.92	17.31—	1.83
Amway Mutl	6.24	5.07	5.55—	.49
Analytic n	144.02	129.64	143.13+	4.52
Armstng n	8.75	6.52	6.62—	1.86
Axe Houghton:				
Fund B	9.89	8.50	9.60—	.15
IncomFd	4.66	3.90	4.63+	.13
StockFd	7.29	5.77	6.85—	7.17
Babson Group:				
Bond n	1.54	1.40	1.50+	.01
Enterp	9.20	9.11	9.20—	.72
Gwth n	13.96	10.43	11.89—	1.81
UMB Stock n	11.58	9.79	11.20—	.14
UMB Bd n	10.39	9.07	10.37+	.78
BLC GthFd	19.05	13.60	15.55—	2.94
BLC Inco	16.44	12.79	14.26—	1.79
BeaconGth n	14.67	12.71	14.19—	.28
BeaconHill n	17.51	14.90	17.42+	.64
Benham Capital:				
CalTFI n	9.95	8.97	9.60—	.38
CalTFIn n	9.73	9.13	9.50—	.22
Cap TNT n	10.41	9.76	10.40+	.21
Berger Group:				
100 Fund n	18.21	13.06	13.81—	3.89
101 Fund n	13.87	12.70	13.07—	.61

	High	Low	Last	Chg.
Boston Co:				
CapApr n	28.31	22.13	25.91—	2.01
MgdIn n	10.72	9.88	10.60	....
SpGth n	18.74	14.78	15.87—	2.18
BostFound	13.68	12.02	13.60+	.78
Bowser n	2.95	2.53	2.55—	.45
BruceFd n	107.47	62.40	103.79—	105.97
Bull & Bear Gp:				
CapGth n	16.22	11.53	12.80—	3.07
Equitl n	11.33	9.97	10.93—	.20
Golconda n	14.12	9.33	9.43—	3.31
HiYield n	14.37	13.23	13.76—	.91
Calvert Group:				
Equity n	18.64	15.21	16.30—	1.66
Inco n	15.18	13.20	15.13+	.41
Social n	17.29	15.74	17.21+	.23
TxFlt n	10.44	10.16	10.33+	.05
TxFLng n	15.31	13.55	14.70—	.24
Calvin Bullock:				
AggresGth	10.81	6.69	7.03—	3.40
BullockFd	18.79	15.10	15.86—	1.67
Canadian	8.92	7.27	7.80—	1.08
DividSh	3.32	2.83	2.97—	.23
HilncoShr	11.83	10.36	10.78—	.92
MonthlyIncm	11.09	9.68	11.08+	.24
NatnWde	10.96	9.90	10.91+	.48
TaxFree	9.79	8.86	9.50—	.04
Cappiello	13.67	9.79	11.03+	1.03
Cardinal	12.06	10.59	11.04—	.67
CentryShr n	14.21	10.80	14.02+	.40
CharterFd n	6.73	5.44	6.18—	.38
ChpsdeDollr n	11.21	9.01	9.96—	.85
ChestnutSt n	48.18	41.79	46.40—	1.13
CIGNA Funds:				
Growth	15.64	11.61	12.82—	2.51
HiYld	9.95	8.98	9.43—	.41
Income	6.91	6.36	6.74—	.04
MuniBd	7.17	6.51	6.89—	.11
Colonial Funds:				
CapApr	16.50	11.93	13.58—	2.54
CorpCsh	47.80	44.04	47.02+	.20
Fund	14.27	12.82	14.11+	.16
GvtSec	11.84	10.85	11.79—	.87
Grwth Shrs	10.80	8.57	9.61—	.80
High Yield	7.51	6.73	7.07—	.26
Income	6.97	6.16	6.68—	.11
OptInc	9.33	7.62	8.04—	1.06
OptInII	11.56	11.21	11.47+	.03
TaxExpt	13.71	11.49	11.82—	.51
Columbia Funds:				
Fixed n	12.39	11.23	12.14—	.07
Grth n	26.00	18.26	21.52—	3.92
Muni unavail				
Comwlth A&B	1.40	1.25	1.40—	.01
Comwlth C&D	1.94	1.71	1.92—	.05
Composite Group:				
B&S n	10.45	8.81	9.28—	.94
Fund n	11.14	9.32	9.56—	1.34
Tax n	6.62	5.86	6.37—	.07
ConcordFd n	26.59	24.76	25.00+	.19
ConstellGth n	22.60	14.70	16.95—	4.55
ContMutInv n	7.29	5.67	5.83—	1.27
Copley n	7.51	5.99	7.51+	1.45
CorpCsh	49.94	45.04	45.81—	2.87
CountryCapGr	17.10	12.91	15.15—	1.47
Criterion Funds:				
ComrceInc	9.49	8.27	9.38+	.01
InvQual	9.84	8.47	9.73+	.10
PilotFund	8.55	7.17	8.20—	4.78
QualTx	9.81	8.73	9.57—	.02
Sunblt	14.88	12.74	14.35—	.14
DFA SmI n	171.26	144.32	149.46—	17.77
DFA Inf	102.33	99.64	101.10+	.36
Dean Witter:				
CalTaxFr	10.31	9.93	10.31+	.31
DvGth n r	9.46	7.25	7.55—	1.59
DivGth n	13.02	11.52	12.93+	.43
HiYld	14.03	12.47	12.75—	1.09
IndVal r n	11.55	8.93	10.06—	2.50
NtlRsc n	8.19	6.36	6.70—	1.16
SearsTE n	10.20	9.48	10.14+	.03
TaxEx	10.21	9.15	9.80—	.05
USGvt n	10.49	10.00	10.47+	.47
WrldW n	10.60	9.04	9.89—	.41
Delaware Group:				
DMC Tx	9.58	8.89	9.58+	.03
DecaturInc	15.89	13.99	14.74—	.53

Delawre	20.06	16.54	18.07— 1.40
Delchstr	7.92	6.90	7.37— .40
TaxFree Pa	6.95	6.47	6.83+ .07
Delta Trend	11.61	10.51	10.87— 2.89
DepstCap n	11.07	9.22	10.72— .07
DepstTr n	16.89	14.14	15.77— .43
DepstCurInc	9.86	8.94	9.76+ .05
DirectCap n	1.11	.71	.75— .32
DG Div n	25.03	21.00	25.03+ 1.65
DodgCox n	27.68	23.49	25.91— 1.42
DodgCoxStk n	26.56	21.37	24.45+ .04
DrexlBurnh n	17.73	15.80	17.57+ .19
Dreyfus Grp:			
A Bonds n	13.32	11.81	13.16— .01
CalTx n	13.83	12.52	13.00— .16
Dreyfus	15.94	10.73	12.45 2.95
Interm n	12.61	11.84	12.28— .14
Leverage	17.81	14.74	16.04— .21
GwthO n	12.32	9.04	9.38— 2.37
NY Tax n	13.55	12.05	13.14— .14
SpclInc n	7.91	6.90	7.42— .38
TaxExmpt n	11.29	10.37	10.95— .12
ThirdCntry n	7.35	5.58	6.39— .71
EagleGth Shs	7.96	6.27	6.87— .83
Eaton Vance:			
EH Balancd	7.77	6.83	7.73— .98
EH Stock	12.23	10.43	12.14— 1.36
GvtOblg	12.50	12.19	12.22+ .56
Growth	6.99	5.82	6.10— .72
HiYield	4.85	4.23	4.84+ .08
IncBos	8.97	7.90	8.77+ .20
Invest	8.50	7.03	7.99— .39
SpecEqty	19.81	15.61	18.89— 4.61
TaxMgd	15.29	12.42	15.29+ 2.09
VS Specl	15.27	10.20	11.00— 3.82
Eberstadt Group:			
Chemical	11.72	8.39	9.18— 2.30
EngyRes	12.99	9.89	10.39— 1.10
Surveyor	15.48	11.41	12.02— 2.82
EmpBld	15.47	14.81	15.36+ 1.07
EngvUtil n	22.47	18.64	22.42+ 1.93
Evergrn n r	45.58	35.06	39.74— 5.38
EvrgTtl n	16.14	13.27	15.52— .38
FPA Funds:			
Capit	11.98	8.10	9.17— 2.57
NewInc n	8.53	7.47	8.50+ .34
Parmnt	13.87	12.08	13.07+ .03
Perenn	16.26	13.71	16.09+ 2.36
FarmBuroGt n	14.44	12.09	12.96— 1.16
Federated Funds:			
Am Leaders	11.45	9.47	10.88— .42
CorpCash	10.37	10.26	10.27.........
ExchFd n	35.09	30.68	33.94+ .27
FdIntr n	9.70	9.07	9.65— .35
GNMA n	10.71	9.55	10.66+ .17
Hi IncmSe	12.11	10.92	11.56— .37
Inco n	10.41	9.35	10.38+ .13
Short n	10.17	9.29	10.15+ .04
ShIntGvt	10.31	10.22	10.28.........
StockTr n	16.27	13.72	16.04+ 1.35
TaxFree	9.39	8.21	8.83+ 1.84
USGvtSec	8.58	7.70	8.44+ .01
Fidelity Invest:			
CorpBd n	6.77	6.04	6.58— .07
Congress n	55.41	47.19	53.57— .74
Contrafnd n	13.16	8.62	9.77— 2.96
Destiny n	13.70	9.88	11.45— 1.73
Discover n	21.05	16.33	18.17— 2.26
EqutIncm	27.18	20.88	23.95— 2.58
ExchFd n	44.36	38.29	43.21+ .09
Fidelity n	20.46	13.15	14.82— 5.07
Fredm n	13.03	10.61	12.52— .05
GovtSec n	9.37	8.57	9.24— .04
HilncoFd n	9.12	8.06	8.59— .31
HighYield n	11.54	10.14	11.18— .03
Ltd Muni n	8.38	7.65	8.15+ .12
Magellan	38.93	28.26	33.69— 3.64
MuniBond n	6.91	6.16	6.70— .02
MassTx	10.15	8.86	9.78— .17
Mercury	13.42	10.39	12.10— 1.01
Puritan n	12.26	10.79	11.57— .67
SelDefAer	11.85	10.76	11.41+ 1.41
SelErgy	10.64	9.08	9.83+ .10
SelFncl	19.96	15.51	19.96+ 2.91
SelHlth	18.33	14.94	17.06— .34
SelMetl	16.12	9.43	9.85— 3.74
SelTech	26.29	17.60	20.87— 4.33
SelUtil	17.33	13.75	17.33+ 2.76
SpecSit	11.59	9.55	10.89+ .88
Thrift n	9.86	8.74	9.82+ .10
Trend n	39.51	32.42	36.86— 1.69
FiduCap n	18.34	15.17	16.68— 1.24
Financial Prog:			
Bond n	6.84	5.83	6.22— .43
Dynamics n	9.93	6.04	6.71— 2.81
FnclTx n	14.79	12.76	13.95— .14
Industrl n	4.53	3.66	4.16— .26
Income n	9.20	7.17	8.16— .82
WrldTc	8.93	6.37	7.13— 1.51
Fst Investors:			
Bond Apprc	14.13	11.87	12.16— 1.87
Discovery	18.95	10.12	10.46— 7.13
Govt	11.68	11.12	11.58+ .45
Growth	11.16	6.13	6.38— 4.25
Income	6.55	5.69	5.76— .75
IntlSec	16.84	12.21	12.50— 2.46
NatResc	7.49	4.19	4.31— 2.34
90-10	14.44	12.77	12.93— 1.33
Option	5.92	4.88	4.96— .88
Tax Exmpt	8.89	8.22	8.70— .06
FlexFd n	12.24	10.12	10.48— 1.67
44 Wall Eq	6.83	3.48	4.02— 2.51
44 Wall St n	13.24	4.35	4.62— 1.91
Fndatn Grwth	5.28	4.37	4.50— .68
Founders Group:			
Grwth n	7.64	5.93	6.45— .15
Incom n	14.53	13.48	14.14— .02
Mutual n	10.93	9.03	9.38— 1.34
Specl n	28.05	22.09	23.40— 3.89
Franklin Group:			
AGE Fund	3.85	3.36	3.56— .21
DNTC	10.97	9.25	9.72— 1.79
FedTaxFr	10.09	9.73	10.09+ .06
Gold	13.51	8.03	8.33— 3.27
Growth	11.86	9.95	11.65— .24
NY Tax	10.14	9.29	9.80— .12
OptionFd	6.93	5.80	6.17— .72
Utilities	6.24	5.14	6.24+ .60
Income Stk	2.04	1.78	2.02+ .03
USGovt Sec	7.23	6.41	7.10— .07
RshEquit	4.78	4.25	4.69— 1.42
CalTFr	6.48	6.02	6.31— .01
FreedGoldG	14.86	14.27	14.77+ .51
Fd ofSW	13.00	9.49	9.84— 2.95
GIT HYld n	10.39	9.55	10.09— .12
GT Pacific n	19.55	14.15	16.98— .91
GatwyOptn n	15.19	13.04	14.22— .69
Gen Elec Inv:			
ElfunInco	10.78	9.57	10.71+ .71
ElfunTr n	23.31	20.01	23.31— .60
ElfunTxEx n	11.01	9.52	9.89— 1.29
S&S n	34.46	29.26	34.25— 1.49
S&S Long n	9.04	9.64	10.94+ .56
GenSecurit n	12.05	9.88	10.46— 1.50
GintelEris n	38.73	31.92	34.66— 2.91
GintelFd n	91.09	67.70	74.94—12.36
GrdsnEm	8.93	7.54	8.60— .29
GrdsnEs	10.92	9.41	10.91+ .20
Growthlnd n	11.92	9.49	10.29— 1.40
GrdnPkAv	19.82	15.31	18.17— 1.03
Ham HDA	5.87	4.85	5.40— .56
HartwellGth n	15.10	9.14	9.91— 4.53
HartwllLevr n	16.53	9.56	10.66— 4.93
Homelnvst n	10.25	9.07	10.24+ .20
Horac Man n	24.78	20.26	23.06— 1.36
Hutton Group:			
Bond n r	10.92	9.33	10.88+ .02
Calif	9.79	8.80	9.57+ .01
Emrg n r	11.30	9.17	9.94— 1.88
Gwth n r	13.57	11.71	13.05— 2.02
OptnInc n	10.16	8.57	9.26— .83
GovSec n	10.05	9.32	10.01+ .01
Natl	10.11	9.01	10.10+ .30
NY Mun	9.91	8.97	9.81+ .19
IRI Stk	16.05	12.32	14.41— 1.14
IDS Mutual:			
IDS Ag r	5.95	5.17	5.43+ .43
IDS Eqt r	5.59	5.22	5.59+ .59
IDS Inc r	5.92	5.10	5.33+ .33
IDS Bond	4.85	4.35	4.58— .18
IDS Disc	8.23	5.79	6.01— 1.87
IDS Ex	5.09	4.60	4.75— .25
IDS Gth	18.33	13.68	14.30— 3.34
IDS HiYield	4.01	3.71	3.93+ .01

```
IDS NewDim      9.30   7.23   7.46—  1.51
IDS Progr       7.16   5.94   6.08—   .81
Mutual         11.18  10.07  11.00+   .02
IDS TaxEx       3.51   3.21   3.43..........
Stock          16.78  14.31  15.71—   .57
Select          8.01   7.19   7.66—   .24
Variabl         8.45   6.92   7.46—   .69
ISI Group:
  Growth        6.53   6.06   6.21—   .13
  Income        3.80   3.38   3.71+   .09
  Trst Shr     10.65   9.88  10.50+   .23
IndustFd n      7.84   6.15   6.33—  1.50
Int Investors  16.32   9.99  10.25—  3.70
Invst Portfolio:
  Equit n       9.48   8.27   8.85+   .35
  GovtPl        8.53   8.52   8.52+   .02
  HiYld n       8.77   8.20   8.66+   .16
  Option        8.57   8.57   8.57+   .07
ITB Group:
  InvTrBos     11.58   8.36   9.55—  1.70
  HiIncPlus    13.76  12.95  13.60—   .31
  MassTxFr     14.49  13.35  14.34+   .05
InvRsh          5.34   4.41   4.57—   .66
IstelFd n      15.90  12.42  13.58—  2.11
IvyGth n       15.89  11.87  13.88—  1.61
IvyInstInv n  111.24  93.09 110.73+10.73
JP Growth      15.38  12.27  13.79—  1.16
JP Income       8.32   7.02   8.24+   .17
JanusFund n    13.63  11.07  11.61—  1.73
John Hancock:
  Bond         14.43  12.75  14.36+   .37
  Growth       13.87  10.71  12.13—  1.36
  US Govt       8.66   7.85   8.61+   .21
  TaxExmp       9.41   8.55   9.32+   .06
Kaufmann n       .14    .10    .14—  9.86
Kemper Funds:
  Calif        12.37  11.36  11.90—   .17
  Income        8.36   7.72   8.14—   .12
  Growth       13.86  10.90  11.22—  2.41
  HighYield    10.51   9.55   9.97—   .34
  IntlFund     16.11  12.37  12.48—  2.50
  MunicpBnd     8.13   7.48   7.99+   .05
  Option       12.50  10.79  11.02—  1.31
  Summit       25.02  20.52  22.19—  2.37
  Technology   12.86  10.05  10.44—  2.16
  TotReturn    14.05  11.80  12.78—   .94
  US Gvt        8.92   8.26   8.73—   .08
Keystone Mass:
  InvBd1 n r   15.94  13.80  15.59—   .15
  MdBdB2 n r   18.67  16.39  17.82—   .95
  DisBB4 n r    8.41   7.40   7.58—   .64
  IncoK1 n r    9.20   7.65   8.08—   .87
  GwthK2 n r    7.60   5.49   6.18—  1.19
  HGCmS1 n r   21.02  17.22  18.48—  2.24
  GthS3 n r     9.74   7.35   7.56—  1.88
  LopCS4 n r    7.44   4.53   5.00—  2.12
  Intl n r      5.41   4.32   4.54—   .71
  KPM r        22.36  12.32  12.67—  6.30
  TaxFr n r     7.88   7.13   7.57—   .09
KidrPea r      15.44  14.73  14.96—   .04
LeggMason n    21.30  17.62  21.30+  1.72
LehmnCap n     21.48  14.84  16.52—  4.27
LehmnInv n     21.97  15.59  17.61—  3.84
Leverage n      8.63   5.84   6.70—  1.59
Lexington Grp:
  CorpLead fr  12.68  10.43  11.43—  1.35
  Goldfund n    4.61   3.00   3.05—  1.09
  GNMA Inc n    7.94   6.84   7.74+   .02
  Growth n     10.41   6.91   7.98—  2.26
  Research n   20.25  13.78  15.37—  4.65
LindDv         22.59  21.04  22.52+   .90
Lindner n      19.41  17.40  18.34—   .26
Loomis Sayles:
  Capital n    18.71  14.82  17.27—  7.94
  Mutual n     19.43  14.42  17.01—  1.81
Lord Abbett:
  Affiliated    9.66   8.19   8.98—   .43
  Bond Deb     10.92   9.13   9.84—   .84
  Devel Gth     9.65   6.74   7.15—  2.32
  Income        3.08   2.77   2.99+   .01
  TaxFr         9.41   9.12   9.41—   .12
  TaxNY         9.53   9.18   9.47—   .06
  ValuAppr      9.71   7.35   9.04—   .34
Lowry           9.42   8.11   8.51—   .68
Lutheran Bro:
  Fund         14.93  12.83  14.75+   .41
  Income        8.62   7.80   8.59+   .07

Municipal       7.20   6.38   6.83—   .16
Mass Financl:
  MFI          10.27   9.18   9.36—   .58
  MFG          10.06   9.67  10.02+   .02
  MIT          11.92  10.08  11.02—   .59
  MIG          12.29   9.94  10.32—  1.71
  MID           8.99   7.89   8.53—   .29
  MCD          12.85   9.36  10.11—  2.34
  MEG          14.65  11.82  12.99—  1.25
  MFD          12.69  10.04  10.47—  1.83
  MFB          13.01  11.57  12.74+   .07
  MMB           9.39   8.63   9.30+   .11
  MFH           7.91   6.46   6.70—   .98
  MMH          10.09   9.06   9.64—   .36
  MSF           8.15   6.17   6.70—  1.22
Mathers n      24.69  16.97  19.97—  4.10
Meschrt n      22.17  21.01  22.17+  1.14
Merrill Lynch:
  Basic Value  14.77  12.53  13.38—   .93
  Capital      22.61  16.61  19.33—  1.30
  Equi Bond    11.33   9.84  11.00+   .13
  FedSecTr      9.69   9.38   9.64+   .26
  FdTomr n     10.98   9.73  10.98+   .98
  Hilncom       8.24   7.42   7.72—   .38
  Hi Qualty    10.49   9.30  10.44+   .20
  IntHld        9.78   9.15   9.32—   .08
  IntTerm      10.53   9.58  10.52+   .15
  LtdMat        9.80   9.68   9.74—   .02
  MunHiYld      9.22   8.47   8.96—   .05
  Muni Insr     7.16   6.44   6.88—   .09
  Pacific      16.62  12.75  15.48—   .54
  Phoenix      12.42  10.41  10.65—  1.04
  SciTech       9.90   8.27   8.83—   .73
  Sp Val       12.89  10.50  11.10—  1.35
Mid Amer        6.79   5.66   6.02—   .58
MidAmHiGr       5.20   4.16   4.40—   .61
MidwBBVal n    10.68   9.37  10.53+   .25
MSB Fund n     21.67  17.12  19.00—  2.12
MdwIGvt n      10.13   9.60  10.09+   .06
Mutual Benefit 14.37   9.86  11.07—  2.86
Mutual of Omaha:
  America n    10.15   9.00   9.77+   .03
  Growth        5.88   4.95   5.41—   .32
  Income        8.51   7.61   8.28+   .05
  Tax Free      9.99   8.96   9.70—   .01
MutlQual n     18.01  15.91  16.75+   .84
Mutl Shrs n    55.51  49.51  50.32+   .83
NatAviaTec n   10.52   7.81   9.21—   .92
NtlInd n       12.49  10.81  11.94—  1.89
Nat Securities:
  Balanced     14.05  12.41  13.82+   .61
  Bond          3.44   3.01   3.20—   .16
  CalTxE       11.56  10.49  11.01—   .33
  FedSecTr     11.70  11.59  11.59—   .07
  Growth        9.64   7.57   7.99—  1.39
  Preferred     7.28   6.68   7.13+   .01
  Income        7.19   6.15   6.88—   .20
  Stock         9.53   7.72   8.84—   .49
  Tax Exmpt     8.49   7.66   8.29+   .01
  TotRet        6.40   5.37   5.95—   .35
  Fairfld       9.50   6.91   7.53—  1.56
NatTele        14.49  11.02  11.89—  2.21
Nationwide Fds:
  NatnFd       10.28   8.98   9.99+   .05
  NtGwth        8.84   7.06   7.65—   .25
  NtBond        9.33   8.35   9.27+   .15
NELife Fund:
  Equity       22.93  16.03  18.68—  3.76
  Growth       24.58  17.03  19.73—  3.91
  Income       10.54   9.67  10.45+   .08
  Retire Eqt   23.30  15.74  18.31—  4.39
  TaxExmt       6.76   6.21   6.67+   .05
Neuberger Berm:
  Energy n     19.07  16.93  17.26—   .65
  Guardian n   39.59  33.53  38.44+   .16
  Liberty n     4.12   3.65   3.89—   .17
  Manhat n      6.62   5.56   6.56+   .24
  Partners n   15.18  12.94  14.85+   .09
NY Muni n       1.09   1.02   1.07..........
NY Ventur       8.12   6.83   7.33—   .53
NewtonGth n    28.73  22.96  24.32—  2.74
NewtonIncm n    8.41   7.81   8.23+   .11
Nicholas Group:
  Nichols      26.43  21.62  25.84..........
  Nich II n    11.79  10.63  11.79+  1.46
  NichInc n     3.70   3.36   3.65—   .02
NrestInTr n    11.97  10.33  11.39—   .10
```

```
NrestInGt n      11.56  9.60 11.35—  .02       HighYld          16.74 14.42 15.16— 1.11
NovaFund n       17.44 11.39 12.38— 4.57        Income            6.85  6.10  6.81+  .10
NuvenMun n        7.41  6.92  7.31+  .03        Invest           11.69  8.55  9.84— 1.57
OmegaFd n        13.26  9.10 10.78— 1.91        NY TaxEx         14.64 13.58 14.38+  .04
Oppenheimer Fd:                                 Option           12.51  9.85 10.89— 1.41
 Aim             20.11 14.24 14.33— 5.17        TaxExmpt         22.59 20.35 20.98—  .98
 Direct          22.83 16.17 17.83— 4.07        US Gtd           14.26 13.13 14.23—  .06
 EqInc            7.84  6.17  6.87—  .85        Vista            21.04 12.28 14.60— 5.34
 Oppenhm fd       9.98  7.54  8.20— 1.55        Voyage           17.38 13.60 14.70— 2.16
 Gold            10.39  6.40  6.63— 2.66        Quasar n         49.95 38.43 42.00— 5.90
 High Yield      18.93 16.47 16.81— 1.83        Rainbow n         4.15  3.64  3.87—  .20
 Premium         24.57 20.52 21.00— 3.08        ReaGra           13.47 10.80 12.96—  .33
 Rgncy           13.72 10.94 11.39— 4.42        RochTax          10.13  9.15  9.77— 4.43
 Special         23.89 16.90 19.04— 3.98        RoyceFd n         7.35  6.32  6.97—  .17
 Target          19.86 14.43 15.16— 3.90        SFT Eqt          10.10  8.64  9.59—  .25
 TaxFree          7.95  7.36  7.87+  .10        Safeco Secur:
 Time            14.39 11.17 11.89— 2.04         Equity n        10.32  8.85  9.22—  .93
OverCount Sc     17.21 13.88 14.88— 1.88         Growth n        19.85 15.28 16.07— 3.08
PacHrzCal        11.99 11.84 11.99—  .51         Incom n         12.92 11.42 11.76—  .89
Paine Webber:                                    Munic n         11.74 10.45 11.46+  .01
 Atlas            9.33  7.75  8.47—  .69        StPaul Invest:
 Amer            13.39 12.02 13.21+  .69         Capital         11.09  8.58  9.59— 3.97
 GNMA             9.88  9.55  9.74+  .17         Growth          15.82  9.81 10.82— 4.35
 HiYld            9.99  9.62  9.80+  .23         Income           9.87  8.73  9.41—  .23
 InvGrd           9.80  9.77  9.77+  .20         Special n       19.86 12.23 15.90— 7.62
PaxWorld n       11.92  9.90 11.47—  .50        Scudder Funds:
PennSqre n        9.66  7.58  8.50— 1.10         CalTx n          9.81  8.71  9.42—  .18
PennMutual n      6.67  5.48  6.10—  .45         Develop n       64.12 51.18 54.07— 8.17
PermPrt n        11.99 10.32 10.34— 1.54         CapGth n        14.29 12.34 13.14—  .75
Phila Fund        9.33  7.66  7.87— 1.16         GrwthInc n      14.98 10.37 11.90+  .16
Phoenix Series:                                  Income n        11.85 10.52 11.70+  .06
 BalanFd         11.09  9.63 10.95+  .50         Internatl n     24.37 19.41 21.32—  .83
 CvFdSer         20.60 14.96 16.36— 4.13         MangdMun n       7.88  6.95  7.69+  .02
 Growth          13.21 11.51 13.21+  .78         NY Tx n         10.21  9.19  9.96+  .04
 HiYield          9.49  8.54  8.79—  .50        Security Funds:
 StockFund       11.54  9.65 11.53+  .54         Action n         7.69  6.52  7.04—  .38
 PC Capit        11.00  9.59 10.08— 3.05         Bond             7.97  7.13  7.80—  .01
Pilgrim Grp:                                     Equity           5.63  4.75  5.06— 1.80
 MagnaCap         6.86  5.85  6.86+  .56         Invest           9.36  7.98  7.99— 1.20
 MagnaInc         8.21  7.25  7.96—  .07         Ultra            7.85  6.99  7.44—  .20
 PAR             23.70 21.16 21.84— 1.25        Selected Funds:
 Pilgrim Fd      13.33 11.59 13.32+  .43         AmerShrs n      10.57  8.99 10.54— 1.16
Pioneer Fund:                                    SpeclShrs n     23.80 15.86 17.68+ 8.00
 Pionr Bd         9.09  8.27  8.85—  .03        Seligman Group:
 Pionr Fund      23.49 17.53 20.08— 2.00         CapitFd         13.34  8.73  9.80— 3.16
 Pionr II Inc    16.63 13.25 14.82— 1.45         ComStk          14.54 10.38 11.97— 2.33
 Pionr III Inc   13.19 11.91 12.79+  .12         Comun            8.73  6.54  7.57—  .97
Plitrend n       14.00 10.89 11.43— 2.18         GrowthFd         7.80  4.99  5.59— 1.97
Price Funds:                                     Income          11.80 10.34 11.56—  .10
 Growth n        15.54 12.11 14.20— 1.01         MassTx           7.04  6.68  6.99—  .15
 GwthInc n       13.45 11.02 12.41—  .64         MichTx           7.15  6.96  7.15..........
 Income n         8.33  8.05  8.26—  .01         MinnTx           6.97  6.53  6.91—  .23
 Intl n          14.99 11.84 13.19— 1.12         NatlTx           7.11  6.61  7.11—  .03
 NewEra n        18.94 15.14 17.13— 1.31         NYTax            7.11  6.58  7.05—  .09
 NewHorizn n     18.56 11.81 12.78— 5.12         OhioTx           7.00  6.58  6.96—  .18
 S+T Bond n       5.03  4.89  5.02+  .02        Sentinel Group:
 Tax Free n       8.61  8.17  8.37—  .08         Balanced         9.84  8.33  9.60+  .43
 TxFrSl n         4.99  4.90  4.98—  .02         Bond             6.28  5.72  6.17+  .01
PrinPresrv        9.66  9.00  9.15—  .44         Common Stk      18.27 15.47 17.01+  .08
Pro Services:                                    Growth          14.47 11.12 12.47— 1.62
 MedTec n        10.39  7.70  8.52— 1.30        Sequoia n        39.30 32.31 39.26+ 2.15
 Fund n           9.83  8.63  9.76+  .16        Sentry Fund      10.57  8.78 10.07—  .27
 Income n         8.73  7.88  8.39—  .21        Shearson Funds:
Prudential Bache:                                ATIGth n         71.74 60.32 71.43..........
 AdiPfd n        25.54 22.90 22.91..........     AggrGr           11.94  9.06  9.91— 1.53
 Equity          14.89 12.38 14.41+  .01        Appreciatn       18.57 15.54 17.79—  .29
 Globl nr        10.73 10.06 10.42..........     CalMun           13.72 13.21 13.71—  .46
 GvtSc           10.08  9.33 10.06+  .29         FundVal          6.69  5.90  6.32+  .07
 HiYield         10.26  9.27  9.76—  .35         Global          20.04 19.14 19.45+  .45
 HYMuni          13.98 12.86 13.86+  .23         HiYield         19.34 17.09 18.14—  .72
 MuniNY          10.14  9.94 10.14..........     MngdGvt         12.88 12.43 12.77+  .42
 NwDec           13.62 10.60 11.70— 1.48         MgMun           13.88 12.36 13.25—  .03
 Option          15.53 12.64 14.29—  .77         NY Muni         14.06 13.00 13.90—  .33
 Qualty          15.05 13.83 14.99+  .24        ShrmnDean n       8.07  4.77  4.96— 2.23
 Rsch n r         9.24  7.98  8.36—  .73        SierraGrth n     12.89  9.78 10.29— 2.18
 Utility         11.24 10.32 11.24+ 1.16        Sigma Funds:
Putnam Funds:                                    Capital         13.26 11.18 12.70—  .27
 Convert         15.24 11.85 13.01— 1.89         Incom            7.68  6.71  7.61+  .11
 CalTax          13.79 12.74 13.21—  .32         Invest           7.91  6.75  7.76+  .04
 Capital         13.20  5.87  6.82—15.47         Specl n          7.42  6.04  6.68—  .58
 CCsArp          49.88 45.08 45.41— 3.34         Trust Sh        11.18  9.86 11.18+  .32
 CCsDsp          48.67 45.73 46.49— 2.26         Venture Shr     10.65  8.10  8.75— 1.47
 InfoSc          13.08  9.88 10.91— 1.78        SmthBarEqt n     16.36 11.68 12.79— 3.21
 Intl Equ        20.10 13.70 15.76— 3.95        SmthBarI G        9.98  7.90  8.69— 1.15
 George          15.20  9.94 10.95— 3.67        SoGen            16.75 12.64 14.01— 2.47
 Gro&Inc         13.32  9.73 10.91— 2.19        SwstnInvInc n     4.74  4.27  4.64..........
 Health          16.87 13.52 14.85— 1.26        Sovereign Inv    19.49 16.98 18.90+  .46
```

State Bond Grp:

Commn Stk	5.90	4.52	5.09— .69
Diversifd	6.46	5.47	6.12— .15
Progress	9.50	7.06	7.45— 1.63
StatFarmGth n	10.15	8.33	9.17— .73
StatFarmBal n	13.64	11.49	12.82— .52

StStreet Inv:

ExchFd n	84.28	71.10	80.19— 2.22
Grwth n r	53.88	46.76	50.74— 2.31
Invst	72.06	62.51	62.51— 7.22

Steadman Funds:

Amerlnd n	3.60	2.67	2.68— .81
Associated n	.96	.82	.82— .12
Invest n	1.64	1.25	1.39— .19
Oceanogra n	6.92	5.56	5.89— .72

Stein Roe Fds:

Bond n	8.60	7.70	8.41— .05
CapOppor n	27.49	18.18	19.37— 7.06
Discovr n	9.14	6.87	7.75— 1.11
Specl n	18.08	12.66	14.88— 2.85
Stock n	17.74	12.74	14.04— 7.32
TaxExempt n	7.93	7.23	7.89+ .18
TotalRet n	23.82	19.21	21.37— 2.03
Univrse n	19.07	14.19	14.71— 3.73
StrategCap	7.79	6.57	6.70— .94
StrategInv	11.24	5.65	5.87— 3.47
StratInGth n	18.80	14.70	16.45— 1.76
Strngln n	17.66	15.82	17.62+ .14
StrngTot n	16.67	14.55	16.35— .13
Tel IncSh	13.97	11.79	13.97+ 1.04

Templeton Group:

Foregn	11.98	9.86	10.70— .48
Global I	34.81	30.65	31.60— 2.55
Global II	10.42	9.08	10.10— .14
Growth	10.10	8.43	9.53— .31
World	12.84	11.12	11.51— .81

Thomson McKinnon:

Grwth n	11.11	9.81	10.76+ .76
Inco n	10.06	9.20	9.72.........
Opor n	11.72	9.65	10.82+ .82
TudorFd n	21.85	15.61	17.67— 3.25

20th Century:

Gift r	4.97	3.64	4.14— .69
Growth n	16.20	10.77	12.25— 3.40
Select n	25.74	19.79	22.53— 2.74
Ultra r	8.59	5.71	6.42— 1.79
USGv n	98.50	92.60	98.17+ .91
Vista r	5.18	3.82	4.27— .83

USAA Group:

Grwth n	14.71	11.59	13.03— 1.30
Income n	11.14	9.77	11.12+ .33
Snblt n	17.01	11.96	13.56— 3.10
TxEHY n	11.99	10.71	11.73+ .04
TxEIT n	11.36	10.50	11.00— .06
TxESh n	10.36	10.12	10.24+ .03

Unified Mgmnt:

Accum n	8.84	7.63	8.84+ .66
Gwth n	17.25	14.67	17.25+ .65
Inco n	12.69	10.77	11.21— 1.21
Mutl n	12.73	10.88	12.73+ .38

United Funds:

Accumultiv	7.81	5.25	7.64— 2.49
Bond	5.60	4.91	5.43— .05
GvtSec	5.22	4.94	5.20+ .20
IntlGth	6.61	5.10	5.34— 1.14
Cont Income	14.43	12.50	14.43+ .79

High Income	13.94	12.07	12.78— .88
Income	13.95	11.20	13.11— .42
Municpl	6.40	5.84	6.27+ .02
NwCcpt	5.22	4.48	4.60— .49
Retire	6.00	5.19	5.50— .38
SciEngy	11.45	8.88	9.23— 2.08
Vanguard	5.97	5.09	5.30— .49

Utd Services:

GldShr	9.42	5.03	5.23— 2.63
GBT n	12.90	11.23	12.65— .01
Growth n	9.31	6.42	6.64— 2.38
Prospctr n	.97	.52	.55— .32
ValFgre n	10.71	10.16	10.71— .82

Value Line Fd:

Bond n	12.10	10.47	12.06+ .21
Fund n	13.42	9.57	10.77— 2.10
Income n	6.98	5.53	6.16— .61
Levrge Gth n	20.63	14.25	16.56— 3.10
MunBd	9.82	9.43	9.82— .18
Specl Sit n	17.09	11.20	11.91— 4.20
VKmpMr	14.47	14.36	14.47+ .18
VKmpUS	15.23	14.24	15.07+ .78

Vance Exchange:

CapExch f n	62.13	52.95	60.88+ .14
DeposBst f n	40.03	33.76	38.12— 1.47
Divers f n	68.01	57.40	66.85— .16
ExchFd f n	105.26	87.77	99.35— 3.46
ExchBst f n	85.56	71.96	84.03— .31
FiducEx f n	56.05	46.10	53.34— 1.85
SecFidu f n	61.28	51.86	58.54— 1.42

Vanguard Group:

Explorer n	37.94	27.89	28.98— 7.73
Gold n	8.30	6.50	6.74— 3.26
IvestFund n	17.35	14.34	15.08— 1.09
Morgan n	14.16	10.04	11.45— 2.39
NaesThm n	49.48	33.80	35.86—12.03
QualDivl n	17.33	14.06	16.51+ 1.17
QualDvll n	7.78	6.71	7.20— .22
QulDvlll n	25.00	22.05	22.67— 1.84
TCEF Int n	28.10	23.32	24.58— 1.28
TCEF USA n	36.77	29.76	30.56— 5.16
GNMA n	9.32	8.24	9.23+ .10
HiY Bond n	9.13	7.91	8.33— .61
IG Bond n	8.08	7.05	7.86+ .01
ShrtTrm n	10.14	9.50	10.12+ .25
IndexTrust n	20.59	17.77	19.52— .18
MunHiYd n	9.29	8.24	8.99— .05
Munilnt n	10.88	9.90	10.54+ .04
MuniLong n	9.62	8.47	9.24— .12
MulnsLng n	9.99	9.90	9.99— .01
MuniShrt n	15.23	14.99	15.14+ .02
Wellesley n	13.76	11.81	13.28+ .62
Wellington n	13.22	11.43	12.32— .13
Windsor n	13.14	11.02	12.65+ .95
VenturInco	11.28	9.86	10.21— .80
WallStFd	8.73	7.10	7.96— .57
WeingrtnEq n	16.01	11.60	13.45— 5.89
Westgrd	11.81	9.19	9.79— 1.66

Wood Struthers:

deVeghM n	44.15	33.34	36.85— 6.07
Neuwirth n	19.80	14.51	16.46— 2.38
PineStr n	14.19	10.56	12.25— 1.49
YesFd	9.04	7.80	8.49— .51

n—No load fund. f—Previous day's quote.

HOW TO READ THE STOCK AND BOND MARKET AVERAGES

Many statistical measures have been devised over the years to track overall trends in securities prices. In the case of stocks, the oldest, best known—and probably most controversial—yardstick is the Dow Jones industrial average. The "Dow," as it is often called in the short-hand of Wall Street, can be calculated at any time by adding up the going prices of the 30 stocks that make up the average and dividing by a divisor that is changed periodically to reflect such things as stock splits and stock dividends. This divisor is reported regularly in the Wall Street Journal.

Dow Jones & Co., publisher of the Wall Street Journal and other financial-information services, also maintains averages of 20 transportation stocks, 15 utility stocks, and a 65-stock composite of the industrials, transportations and utilities. The industrial average is the one most commonly used, however, when investors seek a short answer to the question, "How did the stock market do today?"

Detractors of the Dow say its relatively narrow sample of stocks, all of them old-line established "blue chip" companies, often gives a misleading picture of what is happening in the general market. Professional money managers usually prefer to use Standard & Poor's composite index of 500 stocks as a standard thermometer of "the market." Investors whose primary interest lies in newer, smaller companies may watch the market value index at the American Stock Exchange, or the indexes of the over-the-counter market compiled by the National Association of Securities Dealers (NASD).

Indexes like those of Standard & Poor's or the NASD differ fundamentally from the Dow Jones averages. Rather than using actual stock prices as a base, they are set at an arbitrary starting point with, say, 1982 closing prices equal to an index reading of 100.

Indexes and averages of bond prices are also common, but are generally less familiar to the public. Dow Jones maintains an average of 20 bonds, which is calculated simply by adding up the prevailing prices of the bonds in the sample and dividing by 20.

No one average or index serves all purposes well for all investors. Nevertheless, the popular indicators quickly become part of the working vocabulary of most investors as they learn the ins and outs of the securities markets. The 30 stocks that make up the Dow Jones industrial average, as of late 1984, are:

Allied Corp.
Aluminum Co. of America
American Brands
American Can
American Express
American Telephone & Telegraph
Bethlehem Steel
Chevron
DuPont
Eastman Kodak
Exxon
General Electric
General Foods
General Motors
Goodyear
Inco
International Business Machines
International Harvester
International Paper
Merck
Minnesota Mining & Manufacturing
Owens-Illinois
Procter & Gamble
Sears Roebuck
Texaco
Union Carbide
United Technologies
U.S. Steel
Westinghouse Electric
F.W. Woolworth

DOW JONES STOCK AND BOND AVERAGES
DECEMBER 31, 1984

NEW YORK (AP) — The following gives the range of Dow Jones closing averages for the year 1984.

STOCK AVERAGES

	Open	High	Low	Close	Chg.
Ind	1252.74	1286.64	1086.57	1211.57	—47.07
Trn	593.94	612.63	444.03	558.13	—40.46
Utl	131.26	149.93	122.25	149.52	+17.68
65Stk	500.14	514.02	421.36	489.86	—13.08

BOND AVERAGES

	Open	High	Low	Close	Chg.
20 Bnds	69.62	72.92	64.81	72.45	+ 2.98
Utils	66.07	70.31	59.43	68.83	+ 2.90
Indus	73.17	76.22	69.61	76.07	+ 3.05

STANDARD & POOR'S STOCK AVERAGES
DECEMBER 31, 1984

NEW YORK (AP) — Standard and Poors Annual Stock Index:

		High	Low	Close	Chg.
400	Indust	191.48	167.75	186.36	+ 0.12
20	Transpt x	161.46	117.21	143.91	—14.90
40	Utilities	76.47	62.90	75.89	—+9.72
40	Financl	18.88	14.09	18.80	+ 0.67
500	Stocks	170.41	147.82	167.24	+ 2.31

x—Transportation index revised by S&P Jan 26, 1984. 100 equals average of entire year 1982.

NASDAQ AND NMS INDICES
DECEMBER 31, 1984

Annual NASDAQ Indices:

	High	Low	Last	Chg.
Compos	288.41	223.91	247.35—	31.25
Indust	337.08	248.14	260.73—	62.95
Banks	230.23	192.37	229.77+	26.02
Insur	284.08	226.13	283.11+	25.48
Financl	298.63	251.67	298.62+	21.09
Transpt	292.54	192.86	239.29—	41.51
Utils	283.86	192.68	238.66—	30.73

Annual NMS Indices:

	High	Low	Last	Chg.
Compos	110.06	93.15	104.72+	4.72
Indust	111.02	91.56	98.03—	1.97

NMS indicies from inception. July 10, 1984 equals 100.

INDEX

DATE DUE			

REFERENCE